EMPIRE
OF THE AIR

EMPIRE OF THE AIR

THE MEN WHO MADE RADIO

TOM LEWIS

Edward Burlingame Books
An Imprint of HarperCollinsPublishers

Grateful acknowledgment is made to the following for permission to quote from copyrighted material:

"Anything Goes" by Cole Porter. © 1934 Warner Bros. Inc. (Renewed). All rights reserved. Used by permission.

David Sarnoff Library, Princeton, N.J., for the song lyrics on page 353.

FIRST EDITION

Designed by Irving Perkins Associates

Library of Congress Cataloging-in-Publication Data
Lewis, Thomas S. W.
  Empire of the air:the men who made radio/Thomas S. W. Lewis.—1st ed.
     p.   cm.
  Includes bibliographical references and index.
  ISBN 0-06-018215-6
  1. Radio—United States—History.   2. Radio—United States—Biography.   3. De Forest, Lee, 1873–1961.   4. Armstrong, Edwin H. (Edwin Howard), 1890–1954.   5. Sarnoff, David, 1891–1971.   I.   Title.
TK6548.L48   1991
621.384'0973—dc20   90-56385

---

91 92 93 94 95 AC/HC 10 9 8 7 6 5 4 3 2 1

For
Jill, as always,
and
to
the memory of
Jack Unterecker,
teacher, poet, friend

Contents

Illustrations follow page 421.

EMPIRE
OF THE AIR

Prologue:

A NEW EMPIRE
FOR A NEW CENTURY

I discovered an Invisible Empire of the Air, intangible, yet
solid as granite.   —LEE DE FOREST

Most people believe Guglielmo Marconi invented the radio; he did not. His
contribution—however great—was actually the wireless telegraph, which
permitted the transmission of coded messages through the air. Radio made a
huge leap beyond the coded confines of the telegraph. It brought to the
human ear the sounds of the human voice and music, sounds it seemed to
pluck magically from the air. The telegraph and telephone were instruments
for private communication between two individuals. The radio was democratic; it directed its message to the masses and allowed one person to communicate with many.

The new medium of radio was to the printing press what the telephone had
been to the letter: it allowed immediacy. It enabled listeners to experience an
event as it happened. Rather than read about Lindbergh meeting President
Coolidge after his flight to Paris, people witnessed it with their ears and
imaginations; rather than learn of the *Hindenburg* explosion the next day,
people felt the power of the inferno the moment it occurred. Soon the
human ear and imagination became insatiable: people wanted more of
everything—music, talk, advice, drama. They wanted bigger and more powerful sets, and they wanted greater sound fidelity. Radio became a "godlike

presence," as one essayist described it, which had taken over American lives and homes.

Radio as we know it was created by three men of genius, vision, determination, and fascinating complexity: Lee de Forest, the self-styled "father of radio," whose invention of the audion made long-range reception possible and provided the foundation for the modern electronics industry; Edwin Howard Armstrong, the resourceful inventor who created the unique system of FM broadcasting and whose discoveries form the framework for virtually all radio transmission and reception today; and David Sarnoff, the immigrant from Russia who rose from delivering telegrams for the Marconi Company to head the Radio Corporation of America (RCA). We never turn on a television, tune a radio, or listen to a voice from space without being touched by one of Armstrong's or de Forest's inventions, inventions that Sarnoff was responsible for manufacturing and selling.

In this world of high-definition television bringing satellite-transmitted pictures from around the globe, we tend to think of radio as merely a quaint prologue to the present age. Radio was in fact the *first* modern mass medium. Radio made America into a land of listeners, entertaining and educating, angering and delighting, and joining every age and class into a common culture. The various entertainers in the thirties and forties—the "golden age" of broadcasting—captured the imaginations of millions. People talked then as much about the schemes of Amos and the Kingfish or the visitors to Fibber McGee and Molly as they talk today about the latest guest on "Donahue" or Vanna White's dresses. Radio created national crazes across America, taught Americans new ways to talk and think, and sold them products they never knew they needed. Radio was the first national medium Americans knew, and it brought them the world.

In 1899, the year that wireless telegraph came to America, talk of electricity was everywhere. An advertisement in the *New York Times* proclaimed:

> ELECTRICITY lights our city.
> ELECTRICITY runs our street cars.
> ELECTRICITY causes wagons without horses to go.
> ELECTRICITY permits us to talk great distances.
> ELECTRICITY will do our cooking and heating.
> ELECTRICITY will soon do everything.

Many people possessed an unbounded hope that science would redeem the world, and many felt secure that the future greatness of the United States—

and therefore human destiny—lay in discovering new ways to harness the electron.

People were beginning to see just what electricity could do. In American homes, people were emerging from the shadows of the evening and changing the natural rhythms of the body by staying up at night: "Electricity makes it so very natural and convenient to light the room all at once," wrote the author of an article on equipping the modern city house in *Harper's Magazine*, that people would choose to "live by night in a medium which facilitates their movements by day."

From his office at 826 Broadway in New York City, Dr. Alfred Sanden was selling his electric belt that cured "impotency, lame back, nervousness, varicocele," among other maladies. "It gives you strength because Electricity is Strength," the doctor confidently declared. Electricity was lighting cigars, running automobiles, and raising people in elevators higher than ever before. Many people believed in an alchemy of the electron. Not unlike the scientist and student of natural philosophy Dr. Frankenstein, they hoped that the electron would enable them to create an ideal servant to do the work of the world. The electron would bring humanity to a new golden age.

In September 1899, Guglielmo Marconi, a twenty-five-year-old from Italy, arrived in New York with his recent invention—a wireless telegraph that, he promised, would report the international yacht races off Sandy Hook, New Jersey. Two steamships outfitted with his equipment would follow the yachts and send messages on the yachts' progress to a nearby shore station. The previous April, Marconi had prepared the United States for his visit by explaining the origin and development of his telegraph system in the *North American Review*. "The possibilities of [wireless] radiations," Marconi concluded, "are enormous." He was proving this almost daily. That very month he had successfully transmitted a message from France to England. American newspapers reported that the London *Times* had printed a brief dispatch from France. That the message had come by wireless was news. The next month, at an electrical show in New York's Madison Square Garden, engineers gave small-scale demonstrations of Marconi's wireless telegraphy apparatus to enthusiastic and awed onlookers.

Wireless, Marconi and others realized, promised a revolution in communication. Using electromagnetic waves, Marconi had been able to send messages over great distances at the speed of light. The telephone and telegraph could do the same thing, of course, but they were tethered to places wires could reach. The new technology suggested that a person in a remote corner of Kansas—or on a ship at sea—might someday be able to send an instantaneous message to a person across a continent or across the water. Wireless messages would shrink the globe and change the pace of the people who lived on it.

Communication before wireless had been limited by mechanics and costs. In 1899, it cost 2 cents and took six days for a one-ounce letter to travel from New York to San Francisco; a ten-word telegram sent and delivered by Western Union moved a great deal faster but cost $1. Rates to foreign countries were even higher. A half-ounce letter sent from New York to London cost 5 cents and, under the most favorable conditions, took nine days; a telegram cost 25 cents a word. Marconi hoped someday to bring those costs down, but he never saw the possibilities of sending voices through the air.

Though few wished to acknowledge it in 1899, America's position in the world was changing from a parochial, isolated nation into a significant world power. The nation had just won a victory over Spain in what Secretary of State John Hay once called a "splendid little war." That victory set the tone for much of the close of the century. Of short duration (about 111 days), the Spanish-American War cost little (about $250 million), produced new territories (the Philippines, Puerto Rico, and Guam), and claimed but a few battle casualties for the United States (gross mismanagement of sanitation in the army—and consequent dysentery and fever—stood as the primary cause of suffering). Most important, the war created two authentic heroes: Theodore Roosevelt, who with his Rough Riders "liberated" Cuba; and Commodore George Dewey, who swiftly destroyed the feckless Spanish fleet at Manila Bay without the loss of a single American life. With new vistas opened to it in the Caribbean and Western Pacific, the United States was now an imperial power secure in its sense of self and its future, and possessed of imperialist thoughts of greatness and expansion.

Despite its ever-widening sphere of influence, the United States of 1899 presents a picture of singular insularity. A total of 21,173 newspapers were published in the United States, but only 2,200 came out daily. The rest appeared weekly, monthly, and semimonthly. More important than the number was the coverage. In Illinois, for example, 1,732 newspapers served an estimated 5.8 million people; almost every paper had a regional circulation confined to a particular city, town, or village. Only a few newspapers in the United States reached across state lines. For four successive days in June 1899 during the commencement week of important eastern colleges, the *New York Times* chose to run as its lead story on page 1 the results of the Ivy League boat races at New London, Connecticut, including Yale's ignominious defeat by the men of Harvard.

When newspapers looked to Europe for political news that spring, it was usually to report on the fortunes of Captain Alfred Dreyfus. The trial of

Dreyfus, an Alsatian Jew, for treason in 1895 had been controversial from the beginning. In June 1899, the conviction was set aside by the French courts, and Dreyfus was returned from his prison cell on Devil's Island off the coast of French Guiana for his second trial. Daily, the papers told of the progress of the cruiser *Sfax*, which was carrying the prisoner to France, or of the trial and conviction of Emile Zola, whose open letter about the affair, *J'accuse*, had earned the novelist a year's imprisonment.

Mostly, however, people were interested in Europe not for its political events but for its culture. In France and England that spring, a woman was playing the lead role in *Hamlet*. "It is strange that after all these centuries which divide us from the poet's lifetime it should be a woman who reveals Hamlet to us," a reporter wrote. "But so it is. Sarah Bernhardt, with that amazing intuition and subtlety of performance which are her leading intellectual and artistic qualities, takes our hand in hers and places it right over Shakespeare's heart."

Even news of direct interest to Americans came slowly and incompletely. In 1898, it had taken three days for Americans to learn that George Dewey had defeated the Spanish fleet at Manila Bay in the Philippines. Americans read the reports of the war carefully, but they read them late, without the immediacy that the new medium offered. Radio would bind Americans together, enabling them to partake of a national event as it was happening.

The work of Lee de Forest, Edwin Howard Armstrong, and David Sarnoff spanned a half century—from a time when the country possessed unbounded confidence in the power of science and technology, through two devastating world wars, a staggering economic collapse, the New Deal, and the Korean War. In the course of their careers, the role of the inventor changed. No longer would an individual—a Thomas Edison or a Charles Goodyear—work alone or with a few assistants to make great discoveries. Now groups of anonymous technicians would labor for giant corporations.

Those who created radio experienced stunning defeats as well as extraordinary victories. De Forest made and lost three fortunes, was married four times, saw most of his companies go bankrupt, and nearly went to jail for fraud. Sarnoff's aggressive nature earned him the enmity of many in the broadcasting and electronics industries. Armstrong, once the largest shareholder in RCA, lost almost his entire fortune suing the company and promoting his FM inventions, including radio, stereo, and multiplexing.

Each of these men acted as a protagonist in a drama with Olympian overtones, replete with the elements of classic tragedy: anger and distrust; hubris and blindness; destruction and death. Distrust led to numerous bitter patent suits. De Forest successfully sued Armstrong for patent infringement in a long and acrimonious case that lasted nearly twenty years, yet the radio industry has generally believed that Armstrong was in the right. Litigation with RCA and other companies over patent rights left Armstrong in debt, ruined his marriage, and destroyed his health. Declaring he had "made a mess of his life," the inventor committed suicide in 1954. Though saddened by Armstrong's death, Sarnoff believed deeply in the power of the corporation over the individual inventor. He devoted much of his later life to creating a legend about himself and his own business abilities.

The world de Forest, Armstrong, and Sarnoff helped to make was altogether new, but they were driven to create it by ancient qualities: idealism and imagination, greed and envy, ambition and determination—and genius.

1

THE FAITH IN THE FUTURE

"Finis to Yale" wrote Lee de Forest in his journal on the last Wednesday of June 1899, his last day at the university. The twenty-six-year-old Yale graduate was a man with unusually great ambitions, even for a doctoral student. Earlier that day he had sat in the university's Battell Memorial Chapel with 615 candidates for degrees, listening to President Timothy Dwight tell the graduates they were at the threshold of a new century. "Let us take to ourselves," Dwight said, "the hopes which it opens for us—the energy which it asks of us—the grand thought and purpose which it inspires—the faith in the future which may fitly find its abiding place in the soul of every man who has known the spirit and life of Yale."

The spirit of Yale. Some called it "grit," likening it to the sand put beneath train wheels to give them traction. Yale's spirit and the future of the nation fused into one. Yale, and the country it served, stood poised together at the start of what they imagined would be the "American century." They shared a faith in an American future defined by advances in science and technology, victory in war, and triumphant nationalism. Yale graduates took for granted that with their determination and training—and their connections—they would be a part of the dominant class in America and the world.

Lee de Forest shared the sentiments of the occasion and many of the experiences of his fellow graduates. Less wealthy than most of the other Yale students, he had come north from Alabama for his education. Like others, though, he had rowed on Lake Whitney, debated the merits of evolutionary theory, walked down Chapel Street with a pipe in his hand looking for girls,

7

cheered when Yale took on Harvard or Princeton in football or baseball, jeered when William Jennings Bryan came to speak about the gold standard, and wholeheartedly supported America's role in the recent Spanish-American War and the subscription to arm the *Yale*, the American gunboat named after the university. Most of all, he shared with others President Dwight's unbridled faith in the future and of the part he would play in it.

Spending his years at Yale studying mechanics and electricity, de Forest had tinkered and invented, all the while recording his thoughts in a voluminous journal. He had invented a steam condenser for an engine and a novel trolley system, a pants creaser and an ear cleaner; he had designed improvements for the draftsman's compass and the typewriter, and he had devised puzzles. Though manufacturers rejected all his proposals, he was undaunted. Assured of his own genius, he knew that with his grit and determination he would prevail in the coming century.

Even de Forest's dissertation focused on the future. He had studied and extended the experiments concerning the length and velocity of electromagnetic waves that the German physicist Heinrich Hertz had recently conducted. He had studied as well the writings and patents of the great electrical engineers of the day—Edison, Westinghouse, Tesla, and Marconi—and he vowed to be counted among them by inventing in the new and largely unexplored field of wireless. "I must be brilliant, win fame, show the greatness of genius and to no small degree," he recorded in his diary. And he believed wireless—the invention that made possible the transmission of sound through the air—would carry him to his greatness.

Lee de Forest's family roots ran deep in the soil of America. His mother, Anna Margaret Robbins, could trace her lineage to Richard Robbins, thought to be a passenger on the *Mayflower*, and to John Alden, as well. His father, Henry Swift De Forest, was descended from one Isaac De Forest, a French Huguenot who in 1636 established a tobacco plantation in Harlem on Manhattan Island. Though only in his early teens, Henry's grandfather, Gideon, fought for two years and two months in the Revolutionary War under General Light Horse Harry Lee, and received a pension of $80 annually for his service. Later he settled in Otsego County, New York, married, and named his second son after his former commander. Lee De Forest (the elder) also farmed in Otsego County, married, and raised two daughters and four sons, of whom Henry Swift De Forest was the third.

Henry De Forest was different from his brothers and sisters, for he wanted more education than the local school could provide. A combination of industriousness, frugality, and a De Forest Scholarship (long before established by a member of another branch of the family to assist those who held the name) enabled him to join the class of 1857 at Yale College.

While an undergraduate, Henry De Forest determined to enter the ministry, bringing to his Christian mission the fervor of an Old Testament prophet. As a soldier fighting in the ranks of Christ, De Forest sought to be good and valiant in God's war, which at that time was being waged between the states on American soil. Ordained as a Congregational minister in August 1863, he was commissioned a chaplain with the 11th Connecticut Volunteers. After the Civil War, he served the Plymouth Congregational Church in Des Moines, Iowa. A few years later, he was called to pastorates in Muscatine, Waterloo, and Council Bluffs. In Muscatine, he met Anna Robbins. The daughter of the Congregationalist pastor and fourteen years his junior, Anna at first wished "Mr. De Forest would desist from his attentions." But Mr. De Forest would not. They were married in August 1869. Their first child, Mary, was born in 1871 in the parsonage of the Congregational Church in Council Bluffs; Lee followed two years later, on August 26, 1873; and a second boy, Charles Mills, five years after that.

Lee de Forest spent the first six years of his life in Congregationalist parsonages in the stern presence of his father and what he remembered as the "sainted presence" of his mother. At his father's knee he listened to stories of the Civil War: while in the Wilderness, Henry had filled all the canteens he could find and delivered them through heavy Rebel fire to his thirsty comrades. He was greeted with shouts of "Bully for the chaplain." He was in Richmond on April 4, 1865, to see President Lincoln ride into the city surrounded by a mob of newly liberated blacks. On quiet afternoons, De Forest and his sons would set up targets in a vacant lot and fire the Colt revolver the chaplain had removed from a Rebel prisoner.

Henry Swift De Forest had lived the words of the "Battle Hymn of the Republic"—he had "read a fiery gospel, writ in burnished rows of steel." His duty was to crush the serpent of the Confederacy with his heel. As Christ had died to make men holy, so *he* would die to make them free. When he saw Lincoln in Richmond, he declared "Nemesis is satisfied. Even handed justice is finding the scale-beam horizontal." When the call came in 1879 to assume the presidency of Talladega, an institution founded to educate freedmen, about forty miles southeast of Birmingham, Alabama, he accepted purposefully and without hesitation. His work would be part of a larger struggle to bring justice to the former slaves by educating them. "I shall never see our Appomattox," he told a friend, "but some one will." And Henry De Forest was proud to count himself among those preparing the way for the conquerors to follow.

The year he came to Talladega, the American Missionary Association, a group devoted to educating the freedmen, had decided to elevate it from a school to a college. But it was a college in name only. Begun in 1867 by former slaves, with only nominal backing by the association, Talladega possessed but two buildings: Swayne Hall, a handsome three-story Greek revival structure built for a Baptist college by slave laborers in 1850, and Foster Hall, a dormitory for women. Located about a mile from the town, Talladega's grounds suggested more a barnyard than a campus, with chickens, pigs, and cattle ranging freely across the land. Students plowed the college's farm fields with sharpened sticks. The curriculum of the institution resembled that of a grade school. After learning the alphabet, freedmen were taught reading and writing, grammar and spelling, geography and arithmetic. Those who had mastered these elements were given classes in teaching, science, moral philosophy, theology, agriculture, and industrial arts.

The town of Talladega, a stop on the East Tennessee, Virginia, and Georgia Railroad, was just as primitive. In a memorable battle, Andrew Jackson had defeated the Creek Confederacy there in 1813. A small battle of the rebellion had been fought there on April 22, 1865, *after* Lee's surrender. Of its 1,933 inhabitants, 1,013 were "colored"; the rest were whites, whom Lee de Forest called "Rebs." They were unfriendly to all northerners and hostile even to the thought of educating the freedmen.

Undaunted by his task, Henry De Forest set out to make Talladega into a college modeled on his alma mater, with a heavy emphasis on classical study. His object was to show "that the colored race *were capable of receiving not only an English but a classical education.*" He built new buildings, including a house for the president (before then the family of five endured two rooms in Foster Hall); created courses in the natural sciences, including botany, zoology, physiology, chemistry, and physics; began a model grade school, in which his children were educated; and raised the educational standards. Students who had graduated from the college preparatory department before his arrival voluntarily returned for a year's additional study.

Because of Henry De Forest's commitment to educating the blacks, the family was excluded from the daily life of the whites in the town. The wounds of the Civil War still festered in Talladega. It was the custom of the head of the theology department to keep a loaded pistol at his side in the pulpit just in case hostile whites should try to disrupt his sermon. "I don't wish to be spoken to, suh, by a damned Yankee!" exclaimed a Confederate colonel when the elder De Forest bade him good day.

Life was harder still for the children. The blacks shunned them and the "Rebs" hated them. At times things seemed unbearable for young Lee. Acutely aware of his small size (his father called him "puny") and his homely appearance (big ears, broad nose, and thick lips), he felt himself alienated from the rest. From the blacks, Lee quickly earned the sobriquet "Lego" for protesting "Le' go of me; le' go of me" when they shoved him about. To sneak into town past the white boys, he had to muster all the ingenuity of a scout in war. "May no Rebs get me today," he would pray at the start of the journey. And if successful, he would proclaim, "No Rebs got me!" on his return. Sometimes, however, the Rebs came to him. A trio of children—the Lewis boys—frequently rode over from their farm in a pony cart filled with rocks. Before the president's house, Rebs and the Yank fought their pitched battles. "Doggone the Rebs and Nigs anyhow" Lee de Forest exclaimed at the close of a particularly trying day.

Even Lee's brother, Charles, tormented him in quarrels that seemed both continual and physical. He recorded them in his journal. "We pounded each other. . . . He hit me on the jaw with a rock & I caught him & slapped his head good." One day, he reported, he hurled a hammer at Charles, barely missing him.

In the grammar school Lee de Forest surpassed everyone easily. Soon he progressed to the higher levels of arithmetic and mathematics, and when he was sixteen, "hateful Greek" and Latin were "inflicted upon" him by his father.

The opportunity for informal learning, however, offered de Forest the best chance to excel. When the college opened a carpentry shop complete with lathes, drill presses, and saws, he was there to study the workings of the machinery as much as to make things. A company from the North began an ill-fated venture of mining a nearby hill for ore and smelting it into pig iron. De Forest followed with fascination the erection of the blast furnace for smelting and the building of the narrow-gauge tracks to carry the ore from the mountain to the furnace. Later, when the smelter was operating, he studied "the details of how pig iron is made, the relative quantities of ore, limestone, and coke that are dumped into the furnaces." Still later, when the company closed, he and Charles delighted in careening down the incline in the ore cars. "It was then," de Forest once said, "that the real value of the blast furnace became apparent to us boys!"

The most important element of de Forest's informal education, however, came through his own reading. His appetite was insatiable, his range eclectic. He read his Bible carefully, considering the Book of Daniel his favorite. By his early teens he had secured a key to the college library in Swayne Hall. There he spent hours poring over the *Patent Office Gazette*. He read voraciously in other areas as well. In fiction, his tastes ran from pulp novels and George Wilbur Peck's *Bad Boy* series, to morally uplifting works, including *Tom Brown's Schooldays*, Lamb's *Tales from Shakespeare*, Dickens's *Tale of*

Two Cities, "every word" of Cooper's *Leatherstocking Tales,* romances about King Arthur, and the two volumes of Prescott's *Conquest of Peru.* In poetry his tastes ranged from Henry Wadsworth Longfellow to John Milton, from Anne Bradstreet to William Shakespeare.

The illustrated *Youth's Companion,* published by the Perry Mason Company of Boston, arrived at the De Forest household every week. "A fine paper—couldn't be without it," Lee declared. "I don't believe my offspring will have better reading matter than I have." The tabloid-sized magazine possessed everything a boy or girl living in the late nineteenth century could possibly want to inspire the imagination: heart-stirring patriotism (an editor of the magazine first published the Pledge of Allegiance there in 1892), uplifting adventure stories ("Their Perilous Journey," "Kathy's Conscience—An Incident in a Girl's School," and "Life in a State Prison— *With Illustrations*"), and fact-filled articles about exotic places and practical science ("Kensington Palace, Its Remarkable History" and "How to Build an Induction Coil to Deliver Electricity to the Body"). While de Forest read the adventure stories in the *Youth's Companion* faithfully, and even attempted to place a story of his own in its pages (it was rejected), he paid more attention to the scientific reports, especially those concerning mechanics and electricity. He carefully preserved articles that described how an electric motor works, how to create an induction coil, how to make an electric bell, how to make magnets, and other experiments in electricity.

Best of all, the YC, as de Forest called it, contained advertisements that inspired his enterprising and creative imagination. In addition to Bakers Cocoa, Cuticura soap, and Allcock's Porous Plasters (to prevent "La Grippe" and pneumonia), were illustrations of bicycles costing from $20 to $100, a "complete" printing outfit for 15 cents, and a typewriter capable of "the same quality of work as a Remington" for $1. There were money-making offers to become an agent selling items from ink to patent medicine. From the YC's pages he learned about electroplating and was able to purchase "a small silver plating outfit." With it he renewed the utensils of his neighbors. "Got Mrs. Andrews' 1/2 doz. forks & plated them for 75c" he recorded in his journal, "making money." With the profits from his plating business, he purchased an electric lamp ("very good"), a Weeden upright steam engine with a small alcohol spirit lamp, and a small electric motor. Wrapping some copper wire about a steel core, probably a nail, he also built his first electrical device. Attaching it to a battery, he could create an electromagnet capable of lifting iron filings or small tacks.

Lee de Forest, relying on his imagination, powers of close observation, and ingenuity, was beginning to build and invent. With wood gathered from the cellar of his house, he created scale replicas of a locomotive engine, a blast furnace (which destroyed the family's fire bellows), and a medieval fortress complete with moat and operating drawbridge and portcullis. The locomotive was of special import. After studying diagrams in the *Mechanical Encyclopedia* and an engine in a nearby railyard, de Forest used "an elaborate assortment of large, square packing cases, sugar barrels, paint kegs, barrel heads (for locomotive driver wheels), wooden strips (for driving rods), and a tin can (for a whistle)." The impressive engine attracted the attention of all in the neighborhood and even the gentry of Talladega, who brought their children out from town to see the Yankee boy's creation. More than six decades later, Miss Kate Savery, the daughter of one of the slaves who had worked as a carpenter building Swayne Hall, wrote de Forest of the vivid memories she and her sister had of their childhood in Talladega, "especially your train on the lawn."

From the *Patent Office Gazette* and the *Mechanical Encyclopedia*, de Forest studied carefully for hours the pictures of inventions. Soon he had filled a flat pasteboard box with intricate copies of drawings that particularly interested him. When a neighbor asked, "Does Lee know what he is doing?" his mother replied simply, "Oh yes, he must understand those subjects very thoroughly, for he is always inventing and drawing."

As he grew older, de Forest increasingly turned from mechanical imitation to invention. For the double bed he shared with Charles, he invented a "bedstick," a thickly padded piece of black walnut with which he kept his brother from sleeping on the diagonal. Successful with this, he turned his attention to a perpetual motion machine. In this there was no thought of failure. To the completed plans, de Forest appended a note:

> I am actually amazed that I, a mere youth of 13 years, by my inventive genius and concentrated thought and study, have succeeded where illustrious philosophers in times past have failed. I have at last furnished to humanity a machine which, without cost, can supply forever any and all demands of the human race for power.

Not all his inventions were quite so successful. "I had yet to learn that invention is itself a process of constant disillusionment, of tearing down and building anew, and that many an invention has been destroyed in a single blast by the sudden emergence of new facts," de Forest reflected many years—and many disappointments—later. That lesson came early on, however. Attaching the family hairbrushes and combs to a machine of his own creation, he tried to improve on the cotton gin, but with unfortunate results. Undaunted, he drew up plans for a farm gate that could be opened without dismounting from a horse or carriage.

Set apart from the others by his size and his homeliness, Lee de Forest tended to follow a "usual routine," as he called it—of doing chores and schoolwork; tending to his nearly blind roan mare, Jenny Lind; playing tennis or football; chopping wood; swimming in the creek; shooting sparrows; practicing his cornet; making models; playing with electrical and mechanical gadgets; "inventing"; praying; and reading the Bible.

Working for, with, and against his father, whom he viewed with respect mingled with dread and trepidation, was also a part of Lee's daily life. Henry De Forest brought the same uncompromising and dour resolution to his family affairs that he did to his college and his religion. To the students he was "Old Man Dee"; to Lee, he was an Old Testament patriarch of puritanical sternness. "Walk straight, throw your shoulders back," he commanded his children, and he set the example himself as his six-foot-two-inch frame strode with determination across the campus. Citing the saying of his grandfather, Gideon, the elder De Forest solemnly adjured his children to "never leave your wedge in the rail." He stirred them to act like "Gideonites," the sons of the renowned judge and warrior of the Israelites, to spread God's word.

When Lee de Forest failed to toe the line, he was "whaled into good behavior and to a wholesome reverence for the law." Henry De Forest believed strongly in corporal punishment and "erred on the side of severity" by taking his elder son to the cellar or the woodshed and strapping him into submission. The stubborn boy resisted as long as he possibly could before bellowing in pain.

With his emphasis on order, religion, and physical and mental discipline, the Reverend De Forest could appear cold and without compassion. Once when Charles was carried home unconscious and near death after a fall from a horse, Henry De Forest went on writing in his study while the rest of his anxious family awaited the doctor and ministered to the boy. "I was never able to understand this calm indifference," Lee reflected many years later. Bearded, looming over his children and his slight wife, at times aloof and emotionally detached, and always fervent in his knowledge that *he* was God's soldier, Henry Swift De Forest could be fearful to behold.

Yet there were gentler moments. After his weekly bath on Saturday nights in the winter, Lee would go to his father's study. There he would sit on Henry's knee, warming his toes by the fire, and listen to him speak "lovingly, almost caressingly, about the events of the week past." In the summer of 1888, when Lee was fifteen, father and son went on a trip to Colorado and climbed Pikes Peak. On the iron balcony under the portico of Swayne Hall, Lee and Henry De Forest studied Latin, quietly reading together Virgil's pastoral *Eclogues*.

From the beginning, the Reverend De Forest had great aspirations for his eldest son; life as an inventor did not square with his plans. "How I cherish, that if God so will, Anna, the daughter and wife of a minister, may also be the mother of a minister," he had written to his mother the day his first son was born. Henry knew he would have to send his son away to school to prepare him for the rigors of a classical education at Yale College and, later, at the divinity school. But Lee wanted another course, that given at Yale's Sheffield Scientific School. A contest of wills ensued.

Henry possessed an intense interest in science himself, particularly in astronomy and geology, which he had learned to appreciate as an undergraduate at Yale. Nevertheless, like many students and alumni of the classical course, which was called the "college," he considered the education at Sheffield *infra dig*, indeed, unworthy of a Yale degree. The course lasted but three years. It did not require any Greek, nor did it demand the training that the college did in the humanities. The faculty and men of the college had taken to calling it "darkest Sheff," after Stanley's "darkest Africa," and the rivalry was at times intense. It is likely Henry was also aware that Sheffield had no chapel for morning prayers, and perhaps he had heard from his friends on the faculty at Yale that the scientific school was known about the campus as a "hotbed of agnosticism."

The battle ranged over several years. As the date for Lee's departure grew closer, the arguments became more intense. On October 4, 1890, Lee composed a letter to his parents:

Dear Sir: Will you favor me with your ears for a few moments? . . . I intend to be a machinist and inventor, because I have great talents in that direction. . . . If this be so, why not allow me to so study as to best prepare myself . . . and take the Sheffield Scientific course . . . besides I could prepare for it in one more year and the cost would be much less. . . . I think that you will agree with me about this on reflection, and earnestly hope you will act accordingly and educate me for my profession. I write this with no ill will in the least, but thinking that it is time to decide and choose my studies accordingly.

Your obedient son,
Lee de Forest

On the reverse of the page, Lee quoted Longfellow in a note to his mother:

Lives of great men all remind us
We can make our lives sublime,
And departing leave behind us
Footprints on the sands of time.

And he added: "Dear Mama: The only footprints I will leave will be my inventions. I had better take the scientific course. Don't you think so?" The reply from both parents was a firm refusal.

The young de Forest continued to persist, however, and in late January and February 1891, he even resorted to forgery. With the hope that Thomas Edison might be able to sway his father, he sent a letter, what he called an "advice asker," to the inventor, asking counsel about a son who wished to pursue a career in science. He signed it by "forging Pa's name." The wizard of Menlo Park stood as an idol to the boy, the man who combined hard work and inventive genius to master the environment and win great fame. Surely he would help. Edison never replied.

Though Henry De Forest could win a grudging submission from this stubborn son in the woodshed, he could not prevail in the matter of the boy's education, and by March 1891, he had reluctantly consented. In the fall, Lee would enter Mount Hermon Academy in Massachusetts to begin two years of preparation for the Sheffield Scientific School. Once Henry De Forest had given his permission, the tensions between him and his son faded.

Lee de Forest recorded much of his argument with his father about education in a journal, which he began keeping on New Year's Day, 1891. At first, he resolved to write in it for a year, thinking it would be "a pleasure at college and all my life to read it." And, he added, "it is said to be good discipline for the mind." He kept it faithfully that year, and, though sometimes sporadically, for the next fifty years. Throughout his life, he delighted in rereading it, sometimes commenting in the margins on events he had recorded, and sometimes trying to blot out embarrassing words or passages. Later, when he came to write his autobiography, the journal served as its foundation.

Journal entries did not constitute de Forest's only form of literary expression at this time. For years he had written poetry, his earliest effort being a commemoration of his first pair of long breeches ("Short clothes, farewell, farewell!"). The trip to Colorado and Pikes Peak provided an occasion for a variety of verses: about popcorn; about the writer and crusader for the rights of Indians, Helen Hunt Jackson ("She, whose pen the world *inspired,*/Like all mortals has *expired*"); and about the view from the top of the mountain. In the spring of 1891, he began a novel—mercifully unfinished—entitled *Talzec, the Cliff King.*

During his final spring in Talladega, as he prepared to leave for Yale, Lee de Forest also experienced the first glimmering of his sexual awakening.

Mingled as it was with both biblical and racial guilt, it was not entirely pleasant. It began innocently enough with Annie Williams, a black servant to the De Forest household who was given a room over the kitchen in exchange for doing chores about the house. When the family was away at prayer meetings or college events, Lee often would stay behind to dine alone with her "in solitary splendor." For an April Fool's joke, he tried to pour water on her head. Affection manifested itself when the berries ripened in June. Together, the two spent afternoons picking berries, sometimes accompanied by Charles and the daughter of the college treasurer. Lee and Annie would easily shake their companions and slip away alone.

"I was in the fire of temptation the strongest I will ever be in likely & I withstood it," de Forest recorded in his journal after picking berries one afternoon. Three nights later, he "had a scene with Annie in her night dress." Then, he said, he would have liked "to yield," but he did not. Two nights later, however, he "yielded a little." Considerably more yielding followed on the last Saturday of the month, causing de Forest to record with shame: "Sinned with nigger Annie—sorry."

Though the "sin," as he called it, was probably nothing more than heavy petting, it brought de Forest to a crisis of conscience and spirit. Both religion and Annie's color combined to burden his conscience. After recording the "night dress" scene in his journal, he wrote tersely, "Read Bible." Before this time, Annie had simply been a companion to him, never identified pejoratively by her race. After this encounter, increasingly, and probably to excuse his behavior, he took to calling her by degrading terms. "A nigger hasn't any virtue" he declared one evening. When she went away briefly on the last day of June, de Forest conceded, "I'm lonely without her." But he added, "I have no girl company & so go to excesses towards her—nigger tho' she be." This riot of conflicting emotions over sex and Annie would continue for many years.

De Forest never really wished to acknowledge his affection for this girl whose color, especially in the interior of Alabama in 1891, was such a stigma for him as well as for her. For a while, they corresponded. From Mount Hermon the next year, he mailed her "a soft, almost vulgar" letter. But in August 1892, after receiving a "soft letter from Annie," he remarked, "How silly Niggers are." Such sarcastic and crude language masked a deeper and more genuine affection. In the summer of 1892, de Forest had his photograph taken in Brattleboro, Vermont. The trip to the studio came as a prize for placing first in a walking race at Mount Hermon. He was especially proud of the photograph that showed the eighteen-year-old dressed in a suit with a vest and wide striped tie. Two copies went to Talladega: one to Henry and Anna De Forest and one to Annie Williams.

After 1891, Lee de Forest returned to his boyhood home but two times: in 1918, to dedicate a chapel named in Henry De Forest's memory; and again in 1951, to receive an honorary degree from Talladega and deliver the commencement address. In his talk to the graduates, he remembered only the pleasures of his boyhood, especially his reading and schooling. Memory had softened the edges of his zealous father's sternness. No trace of the pain, humiliation, or conflict remained.

No matter where he went, whether he was selling shoes or saving souls in New York or London, Chicago or Glasgow, Dwight Lyman Moody always regarded the town of Northfield in northern Massachusetts as a haven from the cares of his missionary work. Located in the Connecticut River Valley near the Vermont and New Hampshire borders, it provided a quiet place for Moody to meditate after the rigors of his crusades in Scotland, Ireland, England, and the major cities of the United States, and to gather strength for more sermons and crusades. Frivolous recreation, dancing, tobacco, and card playing had no place in Northfield—the town that Moody regarded as the most beautiful in the world. Naturally, when Moody conceived a plan to educate girls who had been born to "the unstimulating routine of farm life" and boys who needed "a training in elementary English branches and also the Bible," he located the schools in the environs of Northfield. He built his "seminary" for women in the town in 1879 and his "school for young men" four miles away across the Connecticut river at Mount Hermon two years later.

A Congregationalist minister who possessed an extraordinary talent for speaking and persuading, Moody appealed to Henry De Forest. Each man believed he was on a crusade for God to save young souls. While Henry Swift De Forest did his work at a black college, Dwight Lyman Moody did his on the sawdust trail. He attracted young souls to God first as a general missionary for the Young Men's Christian Association and later at lavish crusades in Europe and the United States. Everywhere he went, he drew immense crowds who flocked to hear his message. President Grant heard him in 1869, as did many thousands of others. A fellow evangelist remembered, "He was a master in moving men," as, "with tears rolling down his face," he pleaded with them to turn to Christ. No doubt Henry De Forest thought his children would be safe at Northfield and Mount Hermon, schools that would educate them and keep them on the path of Christianity. He enrolled Mary in 1889, Lee in 1891, and Charles in 1893.

Henry De Forest, who made only $1,250 a year as president of Talladega, was aware of some other advantages, too. The tuition, room, and board was fixed at $100 a year, making Moody's institutions far less expensive than better-known private schools like Exeter or Andover. That fee covered half the costs; Moody canvassed wealthy patrons for additional funds. Each school had a large farm and bakery and was generally self-sustaining. Students kept the costs down by doing all the house and farm work. In the summers, A. J. Moody, nephew of the evangelist, often secured the boys jobs canvassing books in the country towns of Vermont and New Hampshire. And De Forest knew his children could stay at the school during vacations if they worked for their board on the farm. This would save him the cost of having them travel to and from Alabama.

Within a month of his arrival, Lee de Forest knew Mount Hermon was not the place for him. It was a far cry from the life he had read about in Thomas Hughes's *Tom Brown's School Days*, an immensely popular book among boys in America at the end of the nineteenth century. Tom Brown inhabited the peculiar world of straightforward muscular Christianity that distinguished the English public school run by Thomas Arnold. In learning to read and think, resist temptation, and be manly—especially on the playing field—Tom becomes mature and responsible, a thorough Christian gentleman. Pupils at Tom Brown's school, said the author, "lose nothing of the boy that is worth keeping, but build up the man upon it."

The muscular Christianity at Mount Hermon was more often found in the fields, barns, laundry, and kitchen, where the boys performed their daily chores, than in the soul. To de Forest, the combination of work and study was nothing more than a "foolish scheme," a "diabolical system" to make "intelligent minds go to waste," he wrote in his journal. "Studies suffer for work here I'm sure," he complained after just a month. Compounding his difficulties was the fact that, much as favorite students in *Tom Brown* held positions of power, the farm work at Mount Hermon was supervised by the older students. De Forest ran afoul of his supervisor in his final year, a cause for significant distress. Though he considered the man a "brute," and his treatment scandalous, he concluded stoically, "I *will* keep alive."

Perhaps more serious than the regimen of farm work was the lack of friendship. Life in Talladega had been no preparation for the northerners at Mount Hermon. "Such a lot of men—most of them big and grown, I'll never get acquainted," he said when he arrived. Some of his classmates took to calling him "monkey face," alluding no doubt to his broad nose. But de Forest himself kept apart, finding the other students to be "hayseeds, farmers, ignorant, uncouth, rough fellows." Though he changed roommates twice in the fall, he was compatible with none of them. In his journal, he failed to record the development of a single friendship with a Mount Hermon boy.

Life was no better with the girls four miles away. From the start, Lee spent much of his leisure time visiting his sister, Mary. He went there for chapel often, and to see her in her dormitory. Through Mary, he met Miss Julia Winter, a blond-haired "Jewel" for whom he developed a deep and unrequited love. De Forest courted his Jewel as though they both were participants in an Arthurian romance, supplicating himself to her beauty, praying always that she would be his someday, but never voicing his feelings. "I felt a certainty & conviction as I shook hands with her & stood up by her that her form I should sometime press, her glorious mat of hair I should sometime smooth, her fair cheeks I should yet kiss and Oh! what a prize! what a happy what a lucky mortal I shall then be. Oh may it be, may it be. O *Lord give her to me!*" he wrote fervently in his journal. Too bashful and uncouth to know the ways of courtship with the young ladies of Northfield, he never hinted to Julia of his feelings and never received even a kiss. In de Forest's eyes, she possessed a purity that he could not bring himself to touch. It was a pattern of love that would persist for many years.

Lee de Forest did not entirely refrain from touching, however. During summer vacation between his junior and senior years, he met Gladys, the daughter of a rooming house proprietor. She regarded the Mount Hermon student as "half hero," and her charms were "too much" for him to resist. Three days later they were kissing. They continued to see each other for several years. "Ah Gladys is a 'duckie,' " he concluded. "She enjoys kissing." But her character and education would not enable him to see her as anything more than an agent of pleasure. Nor did the touching end with Gladys. Often, however, a Christian lesson followed the squeezes. On meeting a "loose girl" who was "glad" to have him touch her, de Forest recorded that he "didn't fear my duty but talked to her" about becoming a Christian.

"I begin to think that as I am different & more sensible than most of the boys here so I will find it in the world. People don't think for themselves & are poor fools," Lee wrote in the fall of his senior year. While he disliked the work regimen at the school and failed to make friends or to make his mark with the girls, he did distinguish himself in the classroom, especially in mathematics and the sciences.

"NOTICE: Love of Physics Class," de Forest wrote at the end of his first term. The class he was responding to was taught by Professor Charles E. Dickerson, who gave the boy encouragement, inspiration, and the incentive to study, and whom he grew to love as "an elder brother." The physics book Lee used, Dr. Elroy Avery's *Elements of Natural Philosophy*, was a standard introduction with chapters on dynamics, simple mechanics, liquids, sounds, heat, and light. The longest chapter by far, taking a full third of the book, concerned electricity and magnetism, which the class took up in February 1892. De Forest received the highest mark in the class.

Abundantly illustrated, Avery's chapter defined electricity as a form of energy that produced "peculiar phenomena," which may be "converted into other forms of energy, and . . . all other forms of energy may be converted into it." This was probably the first definition of electricity de Forest encountered. At the same time he read Avery's words encouraging students to experiment with this phenomena, saying "the ability to invent is often very valuable and may be acquired early in life. Most of the great inventors began making experiments when mere children." While Avery made no mention of atoms, he did speak of the ways in which electricity "reveals" itself as a current flowing through a substance. He talked of conductors; condensers that could store electricity, such as the Leyden jar; current; amperes; different sorts of batteries and how to arrange them; and types of magnetism. Though he did not identify them as such, Avery also spoke in abundant detail about direct and alternating currents and how to create them. Direct current, which flows in one direction, could be created when "a strip of copper and one of zinc are placed into dilute sulphuric acid" and connected by a wire conductor. Alternating current, so important to de Forest's later experiments with wireless, could be created with a magnet and a coil. "When the magnet is thrust into the interior of the coil, an induced current will flow while the motion of the magnet continues. . . . When the magnet is withdrawn, an induced current flows in the opposite direction." From this point, Avery described the electric telegraph, which was merely an electromagnet and a key placed in the circuit of a battery, electric coils, and dynamos.

Toward the end of the chapter, Avery explained two uses of electricity that would become central to de Forest's interests in later years—the incandescent lamp and the telephone. "When a conductor of high resistance is heated to incandescence by the passage of current," Avery wrote, "we have . . . the fundamental principle of incandescent electric lighting." He then described the use of carbon filaments (which Edison was employing) to prevent fusion of the conductors and the use of a vacuum or inert gas within the globe of the lamp to prevent the carbon from burning up. With regard to the electric action of the telephone, Avery described how electromagnetic vibrations could be duplicated across a distance through a telephone wire and therefore produce sound. Just what de Forest made of these explanations can be seen in the problems he solved, which concerned lamps, batteries, wires, and resistance. For receiving the highest grades in the class, he was awarded still more "honorary" problems to complete. And he did so enthusiastically.

Still very much a Christian, de Forest earnestly believed in the power of prayer to bring him rewards. Continually, it seemed, he was left to mourn his expectations. "I felt *sure* I had that Bible prize [a cash award Mount Hermon gave for the best essay on a biblical subject] not from conceit or sizing up me & the others but I had prayed to God so much & *earnestly* that I really had *Faith.* I know I did & I knew I had it & trembled as though my name were on the program & I had got to get up. My faith sustained a blow for Chas Snow got the prize. I'd rather see him get it than T. Hazen. Farewell to a bicycle. I got my diploma anyway."

An intimate relationship grew up between Lee de Forest's endeavors—be they spiritual or secular—and financial rewards. If prayer did not yield the results he wanted, talent would. As early as 1891, Lee was dreaming of becoming a "rich and famous inventor." With the money he earned, he would do great good. When he began his journal, his father urged him to choose a Latin motto that he could live by. The boy had selected "Esse Benedictus," which he mistranslated as "to be a blessing"; it actually means "to be blessed." In truth, some of each desire was within him, and he hoped for both.

With such thoughts as these in mind, Lee set forth his goals in a letter marking his father's sixtieth birthday: "You have the great satisfaction of looking . . . on three children, earnestly endeavoring . . . to be forces for good in this needy world." Though he had not been "called to be a minister or a teacher, I know that . . . the Lord will put in my way great opportunities for doing good. May I not miss them." And then he revealed his hopes:

> I feel and pray that the Lord will make me rich sometime, and I will be of great use to humanity by my money. I have always prayed to be the means of endowing and building up the College for which my father has given his strength and life.

To be a blessing through good deeds was his wish; to be blessed with fame and riches was his want. Each of these twin desires would war for preeminence throughout Lee de Forest's life.

"The long looked forward to and talked of era in my life has come at last!" Lee de Forest wrote on his arrival at the Sheffield Scientific School in September 1893. Created in 1858 with funds given by Yale's first great benefactor, Joseph Earl Sheffield, the school was, like the schools of law, medicine, theology, and art, one of the largely autonomous branches of the university, having for the most part separate funding, buildings, and instructors. There were nearly 550 students, including 228 in the freshman class. The tuition was $260 a year, plus books; for those lucky enough to get a place in the university dining hall, board was $4 a week. Sheffield's course lasted three years rather than the usual four, which is perhaps why many in the college regarded it with suspicion. However, it offered one of the more progressive and practical educations in the country. While college students at Yale watched laboratory experiments in biology, chemistry, and physics—as was the custom then in higher education—the men at Sheffield performed those experiments. In addition, some of Yale's most illustrious professors of English, biology, and physics were members of the Sheffield faculty.

Although Sheffield did not demand a knowledge of Greek for entrance, as did the college, the requirements were formidable nonetheless. In addition to being at least fifteen years of age and presenting "satisfactory testimonials of moral character" applicants had to submit to an exhaustive set of examinations given in New Haven every June, which tested their knowledge of English grammar; the history of the United States; Virgil, including an ability to scan Latin hexameters; and arithmetic, algebra, geometry, and trigonometry. De Forest passed them all.

Lee arrived at Yale armed with letters of introduction: one Henry De Forest had written to his friend Timothy Dwight, and the other Professor Dickerson at Mount Hermon had written to George Jarvis Brush, a mineralogist and dean of Sheffield (who had decided on his field of study because "minerals would not talk back"). Though he did not realize it that September, Lee would stay six years, study both mechanical and electrical engineering, and earn his doctorate as well as a bachelor's degree.

Lee de Forest also arrived at New Haven with a considerable ego, which he reinforced continually through his journal. "All these years I never doubt for a moment my genius, that faith which became a part of myself at 13 yrs. of age," he wrote in the spring of his senior year, adding, "Should that hope fail me or prove false it would be the most momentous disaster *possible*, blasting my *whole* existence worse even than my own death."

The Sheffield senior book for the class of 1893 reveals much about de Forest's classmates and what they thought of him. Many were from New York or New England—including fifty-two from Connecticut; de Forest came from the farthest point south. Many said their fathers were bankers, merchants, company presidents, or real estate men; only one—not de Forest—revealed his father to be a minister. Many said they had attended the leading preparatory schools—St. Paul's, Andover, Lawrenceville; de Forest was the only graduate who had attended Mount Hermon.

The book also reveals another more subtle difference between de Forest and his classmates: The average student spent $1,123 a year, including $6.58 a week on board. The De Forest Scholarship, which Lee shared with others of the same name, did not go very far. De Forest spent but $2.75 a week on board. To get by, he waited tables in the restaurant where he ate ("wrestling with the *roaches* & indigestion"), tutored, and tabulated figures for psychology experiments at 10 cents an hour. Even this was not enough, for Lee was often in debt to classmates, girls, his boardinghouse (Sheff men could not room in Yale dormitories), even his professors. But he always repaid his loans. "I get my $100. & pay my debts, returning to my nominal condition of 'broke,' " he wrote after receiving an installment of his De Forest Scholarship.

Continually short of cash, de Forest turned as early as the fall of his freshman year to entrepreneurial dreaming, seeking an invention or a prize that would make him lots of money—quickly. In the fall of his freshman year, he created the improved type bar for the "De Forest Ideal Typewriter"; an improved draftsman's compass, a puzzle, even an ear cleaner soon followed. Still other inventions issued from his active brain: a kerosene lamp, a chainless bicycle with hydraulic gears, a micrometer, a pants creaser, a chronograph, a momentum brake, a pipe filter, and several mysterious ones: an "atmospheric electric generator," a "double mirror illusion," a "telephote" and a "photoscope." Eagerly he sent each new design away to manufacturers. All were rejected.

The scheme on which he pinned his greatest hope was a contest to design an underground trolley for a $50,000 prize. Because de Forest's idea came in a moment of epiphany while he was attending church, he vowed to give the Lord a tithe of $5,000 when he won. With the fervor of one addicted to the lottery, he mentally spent the winnings for the next several months: "What good I dream of doing with it." He would pay for his education, hire a nurse for his ill grandfather, and send his parents on a vacation. But in June, his entry was returned, for the contest had been canceled. "Now Papa & Mama cant take a trip to Colorado as I hoped," he wrote in his journal. But then, his optimism returning, he added, "I must look about for something else."

Several times he turned his attention to writing for prizes. One attempt was a prescient essay on aerial navigation, submitted to a contest at Yale. He speculated—eight years before Kitty Hawk—on designs for a heavier-than-air flying machine, concluding, "We are on the verge of a new and intricate science." Perhaps because of the novelty of the subject, it did not win. To the *Youth's Companion*, he sent a story that he again hoped would win him money. When it was returned, he reflected on the latest setback in his plans: "the last of a long series of zealous trials for prizes which all failed—

inventions, puzzles, compasses . . . ear cleaners, pants creasers, Bible prize, Trolley . . . prize essays—all N.G. [No Good]. Yet I am not discouraged!"

Through all these adversities, de Forest's dreams never dimmed. He would equip Sheffield with a proper library and ensure that its instructors' "salaries are big"; he would pay for his brother's tuition at Yale; he would endow Talladega; he would free his father from the oppressive shackles of financial worry. He would make millions.

De Forest did not always meet his penury with frugality, however. Indeed, his spending habits were often prodigal in the extreme. When living at Talladega, he had gone on an "order spree," succumbing to the enticements at the back of the *Youth's Companion*, and at Mount Hermon he suffered from a "money spending craze"; now with more freedom and more temptations, he became truly wasteful and imprudent with his—or his friends'—money. Though he didn't play the game, he bought himself a golf outfit for "comfort & good looks." Though his shoes fit so poorly that he was hobbled with pain, he purchased a pipe with which to impress the women on Chapel Street. Though his food was so substandard that he became run down and seriously ill as a consequence, he purchased a Yale banner for his wall. Then there were tickets and trips to football and baseball games—at home and away—to regattas and to the theater.

Nor was Lee's lack of self-control limited to his wallet. It was custom at the time for the men of Yale to walk down Chapel Street in the evening, "squeezing" the young women—"chippies"—who had come for that very purpose. Lee joined in the parade. At night he would walk along Chapel Street or wait at the stage door of the Hyperion Theatre looking for "chippies," squeezing them, sometimes kissing and letting them go. At times he adopted an alias, "Franklin M. Stires," and as he became more familiar with some of the women, corresponded with them through general delivery at the post office. "I am a giddy fool! but I enjoy it once a week. I must watch & not go too far."

The encounters also brought back guilt: "Am crazy after girls—lack strength, sense, manliness, don't improve all my opportunities, always resolve better but often repeat follies. Don't know my own opinions—lack the individuality of character my life's work demands—am a fool!" When he proved unable to control himself, his remorse deepened:

> let me not be ill fitted for the task, or unqualified to think on certain lines because my younger leisure was squandered—because when I should have read Electricity & Physics, or pondered on Philosophy et al I daddled away evenings on the street. . . . Life is too short—too short . . . God's truth is too immense.

The thought of Julia Winter only heightened his remorse. Though he had received not so much as a squeeze or a kiss from her, he fervently desired her to be his wife. With the earnings from his trolley prize he would "dazzle" his Jewel and even pay for her brother to study at Yale.

De Forest's love for Julia was really part of a much larger romantic impulse, a desire he came to harbor for a "golden girl." She must possess charm, nobility of character, and, above all, blond hair. "I am anxious to find the *blonde* ideal I am looking for & get in love!" he pleaded in his journal. "I long for a blonde to love!; Give me a pretty blonde!" Yet at the same time, he would settle for girls with somewhat different attributes walking Chapel Street. They could lack character and nobility, and perhaps even be brunette.

There were other indulgences, which filled de Forest with shame. Had he known, Henry De Forest would have called them certain evidence of his son's moral decline, his failure to act as one of the tribe of Gideon. Counter to a pledge Lee had made to himself and rationalizing that he could indulge in "one or two" without violating its spirit, Lee began smoking cigarettes. Though he stayed away from "Freshman's Drunk" ("Deliver me O Lord"), later that year he drank hard cider with his landlady in violation of his promise—"I wish I hadn't pledged, for just such occasions."

At other times, however, when de Forest's silly acts indicated arrested development, he showed no remorse. From the top box of the theater one evening, he started a "snow stunt," tearing up his program and letting it rain down into the orchestra. At another performance, he tossed a banana onto the stage. At the hazing for the academics, his arms grew numb as he whacked the freshmen. At rallies for sports events, he incited mobs of Yalies to near riot, taking pride that he was the chief instigator. It was all good sport to him, part of being at Yale. "Truly," he said, "this is the divine university."

Despite his foolishness, Lee de Forest applied himself assiduously to his study. The curriculum in his freshman year was rigorous: German, plane and analytical geometry, chemistry, physics, elementary drawing, and history of the English language. German proved his toughest subject, but with the help of a "well cribbed up" book, he placed in the first division. (So fine was the interlinear translation from which de Forest read that the instructor once had to warn him, "This is not an elocution class!") Although he did not do well enough to receive the general excellency prize for which he had fervently hoped (to impress Julia), he did receive an honorable mention for his work in chemistry.

In his second and third years at Sheffield, de Forest chose to concentrate on mechanical engineering, taking such subjects as solid analytics, mechanics, and drafting, as well as French and German. On his own he studied in the Chittenden Library, reading in both mechanics and electricity, and thinking up various inventions. In the interests of making the engine more efficient, he designed a "condenser" to collect the steam from an engine and return it to the boiler in place of cold water. With the thought of impressing one of his professors, he showed him the scheme. The man showed no interest but instead proceeded to "condense my exhaust steam with the ice water of his learned contempt." To de Forest, the professor didn't "know enough practically to be aware that engineers seek to get as hot feed water as possible. . . . Blind." His independent study of the subject paid off in other ways, however. "I rushed the pants off the exam in the steam engine & feel good over it," he exulted in the spring of his second year. In his senior year he wrote a thesis on the Laval steam engine.

◄▬

As at Talladega and at Mount Hermon, de Forest read voraciously. At the end of his freshman year, his reading became more focused. Inspired during graduation week by a talk given by Nikola Tesla, the Serbian inventor of the alternating current motor and the Tesla coil, or transformer, he began studying various electrical subjects including telegraphy. Electricity, he realized, would be part of the golden age that was dawning. In the fall of his senior year, he audited lectures in electricity. "I must learn all electricity possible . . . lectures 3hrs per week . . . check my calculus & learn how to apply it to electricity." A lecture on cathode ray photography sealed his intentions to pursue electricity as a career, which he hoped would someday include a place in Tesla's laboratory. It was widely acknowledged that Professor Michael Pupin at Columbia University offered the best electrical engineering course in the country, but the De Forest Scholarship at Yale forced Lee to stay in New Haven.

◄▬

When not reading or attending lectures in electricity, Lee de Forest was busy taking in all manner of new ideas that were sweeping the country. In his freshman year, he resolved to "read Darwin & learn facts & be able to make and defend sensible views on such subjects," reasoning that seeking truth with an "*open, unbiased* mind . . . can not offend the Deity or harm the soul, for God is truth." Heavy doses of metaphysics and Herbert Spencer's *Principles of Ethics* soon followed. Then Lee turned to Emerson, especially "Self Reliance," with its statement "I would shun father and mother, and wife and brother, when my genius calls me." As his thinking gradually increased in its independence, Lee allowed his religious beliefs to slip away so that by the fall of 1894, he emerged an agnostic believing in materialism. By the fall of his senior year, his mother cautioned him about his " 'liberal' tendencies."

"I know myself to be different from what I was once," de Forest wrote that fall, "more developed, more independent, more of a man." Through a synthesis of his understanding of science and with unbounded confidence in its power, he adopted a belief in progress and ultimately in the perfectibility of human beings. In his journal, he eagerly outlined his vision of a moral and political utopia:

> No war . . . private dwellings, easy & rapid & cheap transit. . . . Small cities, small farms & establishments, Cheap & universal *power*, universal education & lots of *common sense*. Over populating prevented by law. . . . Few very rich *men* but richly endowed colleges etc. Little manual labor, much mental work, little sickness, no contagion, no drink, lust, or tobacco. Scientific Research *the great* pursuit & ultimate end. Air ships et al. No smokers, Christian like gov't control of all great universe affairs. Climate changed & moderated & regulated. Thousands of comfort giving devices. . . . *Fools have died out.* People live long. Doctors understand every secret of disease & body. . . . Common sense & golden rule run everything. All voters, male & female, are educated. Why *don't* women devote themselves to quiet scientific research like Biology, chemistry or medicine? It is lady like, not boisterous requires *brains* & when not married will make a *decent aim in life* which most old maids lack.

Material progress became the foundation of Sheffield Scientific School's new religion, progress that was the logical outcome of a natural and organic evolution. It would regulate climate, kill off fools, and eliminate war, lust, and old maids, and finally achieve a new harmonic order. But evolution involves dissolution and struggle, what Spencer termed the "survival of the fittest." Just how humans would evolve without conflict, de Forest failed to contemplate.

When human conflict did come in 1894 in the form of the strike of railway workers against the Pullman Palace Car Company, led by Eugene Debs, de Forest stood four-square against the change. He was glad when President Cleveland sent federal troops to Chicago to crush the strikers and even seemed pleased at the violence that ensued. They were "toughs & foreigners," he reasoned, who were destroying property. "Better for the country to kill them."

Another experience in Lee de Forest's senior year served, with his Sheffield education and political events, to destroy the vestiges of his belief in the God of his family's religion. On the last Saturday of January 1896, Mary telegraphed him from Talladega: Henry De Forest had been hurt in a fall. In fact, he had suffered a stroke and tumbled down a flight of stairs. He would live but one more day. "Are the long years of peace & happiness of unbroken love & good fortune to end?" Lee asked.

Can't they continue as I have prayed to God for 10 years that they should, till I have a home for my dear ones, & that they may live to see me make the College independent. Oh, it *must* be. . . . If God is the God *of love* as well infinite wisdom he must interfere in nature's processes in such cases. I *want to* believe he does. Can I, intelligently?

Later, he returned to the passage and wrote at the margin, pressing hard on the thick nib of his pen, "NO."

Often in the past, Lee had prayed to God, but always it seemed in vain: that he not yield with Annie; that he win the Bible prize at Mount Hermon; that Julia love him; that his design for the underground trolley receive the $50,000; that companies buy his inventions; that his parents enjoy wealth and health; and now that his father's life be spared. Though he would say, "A Man of God has gone to God," he would also say he no longer believed in a faith that would keep him alive. From now on, he would rely upon nothing save "prudence, common sense, & good luck." He would pray no more.

Henry De Forest's death forced both wife and daughter to vacate the president's house in Talladega almost immediately. Lee urged his mother to move to New Haven and open a rooming house on Temple Street. There she could rent rooms to freshmen while her sons attended Yale. Though he would have to engage in "hypocrisy" and "keep silent" his views about God and faith, de Forest knew this to be the best course for all. By the end of the spring, the shattered family was reunited in New Haven.

Returning to New Haven after burying his father in Otsego County, New York, Lee de Forest plunged into the final weeks of his senior year. By March, when he was busy writing his thesis and the history of the senior year for the Sheffield class book, he joined other students in spinning tops, which was the current rage on campus. There were disappointments at Yale, too. Though he was to graduate among the top 20 of the 157 in his class, he was passed over in elections to the honor society, which included, in de Forest's opinion, "almost every pimp & jerk in all Sheff's notorious crew of half-shot instructors." That June, his classmates elected him "nerviest" and "homeliest." Others named him "most conceited" and "windiest," while one, probably Lee himself, chose him "most likely to succeed." He received but one vote for being the "brightest"; however, sixteen voted "thinks he is."

"I am beginning Tesla's book again & from *now on* will begin my lifelong study of electricity," wrote Lee de Forest shortly after graduation, and with only one hiatus in the next three years, he read and studied steadily. From his first reading of Nikola Tesla in the summer of 1896, de Forest had been inspired by this mystical man, who at times credited his inventions to the "appearance of images often accompanied by strong flashes of light," committed huge portions of Goethe's *Faust* to memory, and visualized his creations so clearly that he rarely kept a scientific notebook, conducted an experiment, or made a model.

Much of the world at this time was inspired by Tesla, too. In Europe and the United States in 1891–92, he had delivered a series of lectures that made him at once a celebrity. At the Royal Society in London, he was escorted to Michael Faraday's chair and given a generous portion of the great scientist's own whiskey to drink. In New York City, he was lionized by the cultural and social luminaries, who enjoyed his modest yet urbane manner and his refined English, which he spoke with a sophisticated European accent. Tesla's laboratory in Manhattan became a gathering place for these men and women as well as some sometimes skeptical scientists. Before his guests, the impeccably dressed (often in white tie and tails), six-and-a-half-foot-tall, long-limbed, thin man demonstrated his latest creations: harmless balls of red, electrically generated flame that Tesla passed over his hands into the laps of his guests; brilliant illumination with no apparent source; and, the most famous feat of all, a platform charged with several hundred thousand volts on which Tesla stood like a wizard of fantasy, silhouetted by a halo of electrical sparks and energy. The pianist Paderewski visited, as did the conductor Gericke; Robert Underwood Johnson, editor of *Century Magazine*, and Mark Twain came often.

A mixture of philosophy, poetry, mysticism, pure science, and prophecy, Tesla's lectures and writings conveyed the fascination and the intriguing potential of electricity. "Unique among the forces of nature," it functioned, he said, in its own "infinitesimal world" of molecules and atoms "spinning and moving in orbits" as celestial bodies, and "carrying with them static charges." It was Tesla's predictions, not his poetry, that earned him the skepticism of some scientists. By controlling these electrons, the inventor predicted, it would soon be possible for lamps and even motors to operate without wires. Perhaps most preposterous of all, Tesla foretold of the day a small tube charged with these seemingly magic electrons would enable messages and sounds to be sent across great distances without wires.

In the fall of 1896, when he was beginning the first year of his electrical study, de Forest sent Tesla a copy of his senior thesis, with the hope that he might take a job in New York the following year with the master, even if it meant low wages. More letters and a "cordial" interview followed in April, but Tesla had no positions open.

Tesla's influence on de Forest should not be underestimated, however. Indeed, Tesla and a professor at Yale inspired de Forest's work. "To read those chapters on the higher vibratory forms," he wrote with elation while perusing Tesla's book, "the intimate connection between light & energy & electricity, the delicate experiments made (and to be made), & the weird, almost frightful results . . . *fires* me with ambition to emulate, to myself enter into that tenuous realm that is the connecting link between God and mind and lower matter." And Tesla served to reinforce his own sense of genius. After reading him, he vowed not to attempt imitating Tesla; trusting in Emerson, he would "believe" in himself and bring about the truth he considered his to find.

The professor de Forest most revered was Josiah Willard Gibbs. In the fall of 1896, he was fortunate to be able to take courses with Gibbs, one of the most important mathematicians and physicists in the history of science, a person who contravenes Alexis de Tocqueville's contention that democratic America could not produce a great mind in abstract science. Gibbs was a modest, self-effacing man whose career and eminence in science was largely ignored in the United States, especially by his colleagues at Yale, until he was elected a fellow of the Royal Society. With Gibbs, de Forest studied mathematics and astronomy. De Forest recognized immediately that he was in the presence of a great mind, and that without this training he would never be able to master electromagnetic wave theory, so necessary for his "future greatness."

Through his reading of Tesla and his study with Gibbs, de Forest came to believe that the future of electricity lay in these unexplored and unexploited waves. To "deal intelligently with light and wave phenomena," he knew he would need more training. "*I aim at Tesla*," he said, adding, "if I reach that I am a long way ahead." This was a bold decision, and in it his prescience was exceptional. While his companions were learning about dynamo construction, de Forest devoted himself to studying the essentials of this new branch of electrical engineering, especially the work of Michael Faraday, James Clerk Maxwell, and Heinrich Hertz. He decided to stay at Yale for two more years.

In teaching de Forest, Gibbs was simply extending the chain of understanding of magnetism and electricity, the first link of which had been forged in the reign of Queen Elizabeth. In 1600, the queen's own physician, William Gilbert, published a treatise with the portentous title *De Magnete Magneticisque Corporibus et de Magno Magnete Tellure* ("Of the Magnet and Magnetic Bodies and of the Great Magnet, the Earth"). Gilbert demonstrated with a compass needle the magnetic fields of the Earth, showing that in the space around a magnet, which he called the "orb of influence," the needle would turn but not be attracted. And through his experiments with amber, he speculated that there must be an underlying principle between static electricity and magnetism. Two centuries later, a Danish physicist, Hans Christian Oersted, found that an electric current could deflect a magnetic needle, and the French physicist André Marie Ampère formulated the law behind Oersted's discovery: an electric current flowing through a conductor (like a wire) produces a magnetic field that interacts with any magnet in the vicinity. The importance of these findings was simple yet profound: electricity and magnetism are inextricably bound.

The most important links were still to be forged. In 1831, the English physicist Michael Faraday discovered "electromagnetic induction": if a magnet was moving it would produce electricity. His theory lies at the base of all electric generators. Through further experiments, Faraday also completed the theory of "lines of force" so tentatively and sketchily postulated by Gilbert. In 1864, a young Scottish physicist from Edinburgh, James Clerk Maxwell, built on the findings of Faraday and others to produce a series of mathematical equations that for the first time accounted for the action of all electromagnetic waves. "Maxwell's equations," as they came to be known, showed that electricity and magnetism travel in waves at the speed of light, 186,000 miles—about seven times around the world—a second. Light, therefore, is a type of electromagnetic wave that is visible; not, as the conventional wisdom had it, minute material particles. Believing that these waves had to have a medium through which they traveled, Maxwell theorized the existence of "ether." Although his speculations about ether were incorrect, Maxwell was right about everything else. Every appliance we have today, from an electric generator to the microwave oven in the kitchen—and, of course, the radio— operate according to his fundamental equations. As Newton revolutionized mechanical science in the seventeenth century, so Maxwell revolutionized electrical science in the nineteenth. His discoveries stand as nothing less than the scientific equivalent of Columbus's voyage. They led to a new world for physical science, one that people like de Forest would seek to conquer.

Gibbs, whom Maxwell held in high esteem, tutored de Forest in this essential knowledge, showing him the various connections in the chain of understanding and giving him an excellent mathematical foundation with which he could use the yet unknown potential of these relatively new equations. His work caused him to dream of the new powers given him through an understanding of that "revealer of deity," mathematics: "At a step we merge from our physics into the vague, vast, and tenuous land of spirit," Lee wrote. "At a stroke we merge from the earth to heaven, from the temporal to the infinite." And, he asked, who might be capable of ascending to these heights but a "materialist"? Placing himself apart from the rest of his fellow students, no doubt with Emerson in mind, he concluded, "I am not like the rest." "From the very first," bolder thoughts had taken hold in his brain. They would guide him to his destiny.

There was one last link in the chain of electromagnetic theory, forged within the decade, that de Forest still had to learn: the discoveries of Heinrich Hertz, a young German scientist working at a technical college in Karlsruhe. In September 1897, de Forest reported he was "beginning on Hertz," reading his *Electric Waves* in German. Soon he was working through Hertz's experiments in the laboratory and writing to Tesla for advice in conducting them.

In 1887, when he was barely thirty, Hertz had assembled the apparatus to prove Maxwell's theory that electricity travels through the "ether" in waves. To create the waves, he released a sudden discharge of electricity in the form of a spark across a gap between two wires. As the electricity crossed the gap, it sent out electromagnetic waves. Across his laboratory, he assembled a loop of wire, itself broken by a tiny gap. The loop, which was really the first aerial, received the waves, and the electricity crossed the gap in the form of a faint spark. At once elegant and simple, the apparatus Hertz created was the first transmitter and receiver of electromagnetic waves. Hertz did not stop with this. Among other things, he experimented with the resonance of his transmitter and receiver, created a crude coaxial transmission line, discovered the photoelectric effect, studied the relations between light and electricity, and attempted to measure the strength and distribution of electromagnetic fields.

By the spring of 1898, de Forest had decided to write his doctoral thesis on Hertz, concerning the reflection of ultrahigh frequency waves from parallel wires. It was a topic that put Maxwell's equations to work and gave de Forest a thorough understanding of Hertz's discoveries. But the intensity of his study was broken by the outbreak of that "holy struggle," the Spanish-American War.

"The whole country is excited over the dastardly, fiendish, blowing up of our warship *Maine*. . . . War is not far away." Calling for action, de Forest boiled over the "cringing, temporizing, pusillaminous policy" of the McKinley administration, wrote senators and congressmen demanding "instant action for American honor," and took up a subscription to buy a flag ("a big Old Glory") for his dormitory. When war was declared, however, Lee did not rush to the enlistment office. Initially, he stayed in New Haven to prepare for his "destiny." Only after he had decided that the war would not last more than six months did he sign up. "I will get the benefits—*and the glory* (!) of the campaign without the danger. I do not risk my destiny." He could be a bugler, he thought, "a fat cinch," get a horse to ride, and be free of guard duty. Perhaps his lovelife would improve there, too: "If I could win the girl of all the world meant for me," he mused, "I should amply profit for any losses."

Though the girl was not to be won, de Forest predicted the rest of his army service correctly. He had to stand guard, but he did eventually get to be a bugler. His hunch about the war's duration was correct, too. After a desultory summer spent at an army camp in Niantic, Connecticut, with "coarse" and hostile farmers who were "jealous of [his] snap," de Forest was mustered out at the end of October in time to return to Yale and his dissertation.

Acutely aware that this was to be his last year for study, de Forest determined at the outset to exchange his past follies for a new wisdom, his past indulgence for self-denial. Quickly he reviewed the notes he had made the previous spring on Hertz's experiments, as well as his work with Gibbs on electromagnetic theory. At the beginning of the new year, he took an examination on Maxwell that he had postponed from the previous May because of his enlistment. All the while, he worked intensely in the basement of Sloane Laboratory on his thesis, carefully calculating the angles of reflection of Hertzian waves. By May, after "dreary hours" in the cold, dark basement laboratory, he finished it, just in time to cram for his final examinations, especially Professor Gibbs's in "Electromagnetic Theory of Light" and "Orbits." By mid-June, he was finished. At last he could enjoy a "brief respite" to rest and plan for his future. Triumphantly he recorded in his journal: "*Dr. Lee De Forest. Ph.D.!!!*"

2

THE WILL TO SUCCEED

While Lee de Forest was in his second year in New Haven, studying mechanical engineering, another man, eight months younger and several thousand miles away, was experimenting with electromagnetism in the gardens of his parents' estate outside Bologna, Italy. Guglielmo Marconi was the son of a wealthy Italian businessman, who lived the life of a country gentleman, and of an Anglo-Irish mother, whose family was the Jameson distillers of Belfast. Marconi possessed soft, aquiline features. He was a mama's boy and a loner; he never got along well with his father. He was tutored at home, keeping to himself, and always encouraged by his mother. Annie Jameson taught her son English, supported his early tinkering with mechanical contrivances, and persuaded a professor at the University of Bologna to allow her boy to attend his physics lectures. There Marconi learned about Faraday's theories, Maxwell's equations, and Hertz's experiments.

Though only an novice, Marconi realized with remarkable prescience the potential of what he was learning; indeed, his dreams about the practical applications of these new discoveries far surpassed those of the most knowledgeable scientists. Certain that others must have similar ideas, Marconi worked without respite on an idea he had to send telegraph messages through the ether.

First, he improved Hertz's spark transmitter and loop aerial receiver. For a transmitter, he adapted his professor's more powerful spark gap design, which produced waves of higher frequency that could travel a greater distance. He attached to it a Morse telegraph key with which an operator could send out signals of dots and dashes. For his receiver, he adapted what was called a "coherer," a detector of electronic impulses first invented by the French scientist, Edouard Branly, and improved by the English scientist Oliver Lodge. About the size of a small thermometer, the coherer was a glass tube with a metal rod inserted at each end. A thin wire connected each rod to the aerial. Lying between the rods inside the tube was a small quantity of metal filings. When the aerial received a current from an electromagnetic wave, the filings inside the tube would cling (or cohere) to the rods and complete the circuit of electricity. The small electrical impulse then traveled through a wire to a "Morse inker," a machine telegraphers used to record the dots and dashes of code onto a paper tape. When the waves stopped (that is, when the telegraph key wasn't pressed), a small hammer outside the coherer tapped the glass tube to loosen the filings, thereby preparing it for the next signal.

The most remarkable change Marconi made in Hertz's apparatus came from a chance discovery rather than an adaptation or improvement of existing equipment. While experimenting in his parents' garden one day, Marconi absently placed one part of his aerial on the ground while holding the other part in the air. The accident resulted in a dramatic improvement in reception. When he grounded both the transmitter and the aerial, he was able to send signals across the estate and several miles over the hills.

Marconi was no pure scientist, nor did he discover secrets of the physical laws that control the planet. But he possessed the vision to harness the discoveries of others. Scientists experimenting with Hertzian apparatus before him certainly had the ability and might easily have adapted electromagnetic waves for wireless; however, Marconi alone did it.

Marconi refined his system for two years until he felt it was ready for demonstrations. Here his mother stepped in. When the Italian government evinced no interest in his invention, Annie Jameson took her son and two trunks of his equipment to England, where, drawing on the strength of her family's name, she secured a hearing before Sir William Preece, the person in charge of technological improvements for the Post Office, which then (as now) controlled telegraph and telephone communication in Britain. Preece saw immediately the importance of Marconi's creation. Wireless telegraphy could cross great distances, connecting points separated by water and mountains. In June 1896, the month de Forest earned his bachelor's degree from Yale, Marconi took out patents in England on his system of "wireless telegraphy." Then, with the help of the Jameson family fortune and connections, he began the Wireless Signal Telegraph Company (soon changed to the Marconi Wireless Telegraph Company). In just three years, the inventor had taken scientific experiments from the laboratory into the marketplace. Faraday, Maxwell, Hertz, and electromagnetism remained but names and concepts for scientists; for the first decade of the twentieth century, Marconi and wireless would replace them, and for much of the public the two words would be synonymous.

Although he left the administration of his company to others, Marconi promoted his new invention with the skill of a P. T. Barnum. In January 1898, he connected Madeira House at Bournemouth with the Needles Hotel on the Isle of Wight. When a snowstorm knocked out the telegraph lines between Bournemouth and London that winter, Marconi's wireless telegraph relayed reporters' stories about the imminent death of Gladstone to Fleet Street. Extolling the virtues of the new system almost daily, the press rewarded the young inventor with abundant publicity. He conducted a demonstration for members of Parliament. A wireless link between France and England soon followed. That summer, he reported the results of Ireland's Kingstown Regatta to the Dublin *Daily Express*. He linked Queen Victoria, in her mansion on the Isle of Wight, to Prince Edward, convalescing from a recent appendectomy aboard the royal yacht. Newspapers reported on each of the 150 medical bulletins and messages exchanged, making much of their unique method of transmission. In late September 1899, he reported the results of the International Yacht Races off Sandy Hook, New Jersey. While in the United States, he opened the Marconi Wireless Telegraph Company of America. With the help of his friends among the press, Marconi demonstrated the practicality of his new technology to all.

Marconi was, it turned out, the first entrant—and thereby the first leader—in what had become a race—a race to control wireless communications. But he knew that the field would not remain his alone for long. Soon others would compete to create even more effective wireless systems. Marconi did two things to protect his lead: he took out patents on every device he or his company had improved and marketed, regardless of who had been the actual inventor; and from the laboratory of the Edison Electric Company in England, he hired John Ambrose Fleming, a fifty-year-old Englishman, to be his scientific adviser. A professor of electrical engineering at the University of London and a former employee of Thomas Edison, Fleming, who had studied under Maxwell, would concentrate on improving Marconi's wireless apparatus, particularly his crude detector, the coherer, which many believed a weakness of the system.

Among the first to join in the race was Oliver Lodge, the man whose improved detector had figured in Marconi's first experiments. Heretofore Lodge had been a pure scientist, who considered his findings public property. But after Marconi adapted another of the Englishman's inventions, a tuning device that enabled an operator to select the proper wavelength of a wireless set by turning a dial, Lodge abandoned the high moral ground. In 1901, he formed a syndicate to push some of his claims against his Italian rival and develop his own radio apparatus. Germany also claimed rights to wireless when Adolph K. H. Slaby and Count George von Arco took out patents and developed a system that, they held, modified and improved upon Marconi's.

There would be competitors in the United States as well. In Pittsburgh, a thirty-three-year-old university professor from Canada with the august name Reginald Aubrey Fessenden, had been studying and lecturing on Hertzian waves, wireless telegraphy, and X-rays for several years. August was his demeanor, too, for Fessenden had a reputation for arrogant remarks ("Don't try to think. You haven't the brain for it"), condescending airs, and pride. Having served as chief chemist to Thomas Edison, he also had practical experience in the day-to-day competition of a company. In Fessenden's opinion, the Marconi system was inherently flawed in its spark gap transmitter (which sent out waves intermittently) and its coherer. His chance to change these parts of the system came in 1900, when he was asked by the weather bureau to develop a wireless system so that it might better predict the coming of floods and hurricanes.

Such was the world of wireless when Lee de Forest graduated from Yale in 1899. His route into that world was somewhat circuitous. The job in Tesla's laboratory never came about. The Serbian inventor's fortunes had begun to founder as scientists and the public began to scrutinize him and his work with increasing skepticism. That summer, in an experiment transmitting huge amounts of energy by wireless, he had destroyed much of the electrical system of Colorado Springs and plunged the town into darkness; soon he would declare he had received messages from another planet, possibly Venus or Mars, and that certain pigeons telepathically gave him an understanding of the world of electrons.

In 1899, de Forest took a job in the dynamo department of Chicago's Western Electric Company. The work had nothing to do with wireless ("chasing parts and mopping up grease"); the pay was low ($8 a week); and the day was long (ten and a quarter hours). When the great inventor of the wireless arrived to report on the yacht races and demonstrate his system to the United States government, de Forest wrote "Senior Marconi," in his most formal prose, "begging to be allowed to work under" him. Telling of his graduate work at Yale and using Josiah Willard Gibbs as a reference, he continued his appeal: "As a young man, you will, I know, fully appreciate the desire I feel, in just starting out, to get a start in the lines of that fascinating field, so vast in extent, in which you have done so much." Marconi never replied.

Still, de Forest wanted work that would use his training. He spent his free evenings in the private John Crerar Library reading technical journals, which carried reports of the latest developments in the study of Hertzian waves, and especially in ways of improving the receiver. Promoted to a place in Western Electric's laboratory in October, he declared, "Now, at last can I be fascinated in my work." For de Forest, however, work did not include the telephone. To his foreman's distress, Lee spent his time devising a new type of wireless receiver to replace Marconi's coherer, something he called a "responder."

Unhappy with his telephone work, de Forest took a job in April 1900, conducting experiments for the American Wireless Telegraph Company in Milwaukee for $15 a week. He lasted just five months. "On the lake first," he dreamed, "then with the navy, then navies, foreign travel, scientific investigations, success!" The reality was different. Finding the company's crude system utterly impractical, de Forest surreptitiously employed his own responder to receive the signals. When this was divulged by a jealous employee, and the company president demanded he share his system, de Forest refused. Sure of his accomplishment, he declared, "I will not let it go into the hands of any company until that company is my own. . . . If I fail it will not at least be for grit, nor because I was afraid to try."

Returning to Chicago, de Forest worked briefly as an editor of an electrical publication and taught part-time. Most evenings he spent in his room developing his responder. De Forest was even more impoverished than he had been before. To help defray the costs of his research, Ed Smythe, an engineer, friend, and former colleague at Western Electric, gave him $5 a week. Smythe and Clarence Freeman, a professor at the Armour Institute who had designed a crude transmitter, helped with research and necessarily became his collaborators.

Though de Forest enjoyed immersing himself in the laboratory, research was not the lure. The laboratory would bring him fame and affluence: "I am risking mediocrity & weak contentment for a chance of *great success*. Now it is up to me & lies with *me*, I think—& it *shall be success!*" The diarist was not entirely candid about the source of his achievement. In truth, he had derived his responder from discoveries reported in a German scientific periodical. A simple device, the responder consisted of two pieces of metal separated by a space about as thin as the slice of a razor. Between the metal, he put a solution through which flowed the current received by the aerial. For a workable solution, de Forest tried everything in his kitchen and medicine cabinets and the toolshed—water, benzine, alcohol, glycerin, olive oil, gasoline, blotting paper saturated with india ink, wet silk. Finally, he settled on a paste of glycerin and lead peroxide, to which he gave the scientific term "goo." Derivative or not, the responder worked more efficiently than Marconi's coherer, and it allowed a person to use sensitive earphones rather than a crude Morse inker to receive weak signals. Because there was no delay while a tapper dislodged filings, messages could be transmitted more quickly. While a Morse inker attached to a coherer could mark its tape with about twelve words a minute, a good operator using de Forest's system could hear and copy about thirty-five. In August 1900, de Forest and Smythe, acting as partners, took out their first patent.

The next task before him, de Forest realized, was to put his wireless system through a series of transmission tests. First, he sent messages between the Armour Institute and a nearby hotel, and then, with considerable publicity, to a yacht on Lake Michigan.

Now de Forest felt ready to "make my name at least rank with that of Marconi," and win some of the fame and success he so coveted and so earnestly believed he deserved. He saw his chance in September 1901. Marconi again had the contract to report the International Yacht Races for the New York *Herald* and the Associated Press. Over the objections of Smythe, de Forest decided that "*my fame,* my independence of management, my whole future possibilities" demanded he challenge Marconi. With funding from Manning Stires, his friend from Mount Hermon and Yale, and Henry Siedler, the former mayor of Jersey City, de Forest decided he and his associates, Smythe and Freeman, would report the races for the Publisher's Press Association. The trio soon found their equipment no match for Marconi's, and they probably would not have been able to install it in time had not President McKinley's death by an assassin's bullet on September 14 forced a postponement of the races until the end of the month. When the contest did begin, the rivals found that their transmitters jammed each other. The results had to be reported by flags and crude hand signals. "We gave Marconi a blacker eye than we ourselves received," de Forest said in self-consolation. Perhaps. But his first wireless venture had ended in complete failure.

That fall, after visiting his mother; his sister, Mary; and classmates and professors in New Haven, and resting at a friend's house on Rockaway Beach, de Forest returned to the city to sell his wireless system again. Siedler in Jersey City refused him, as did twenty-five others on Wall Street. Five-dollar bills from Smythe in Chicago came sporadically. With the help of one minor financier, de Forest and his Chicago colleagues formed the Wireless Telegraph Company. But it was a company in name only; there were no assets.

As unsettling as his financial distress was, de Forest had even more cause for anxiety in the success of his archrival. With an eye toward publicity, Marconi went to Newfoundland attempting to receive a wireless signal from a station of his in England. On December 15, newspapers across the country proclaimed his achievement: the inventor had received the · · · of the Morse letter S through the ether. "Signor Marconi has played a shrewd *coup d'etat* . . . the *fame* is his, & will probably always remain so."

But again, he closed with a note of optimism: "I shall yet succeed. It is not too late."

With the public's imagination fired by these spectacular and seemingly magical wireless feats, it was only a matter of time before some speculator stepped forward to take advantage of a naive public through a giant stock promotion and fraud. He was Abraham White. Distinguished by his flaming red hair and mustache and his china-blue eyes, and always looking urbane and elegantly dressed in silk hat, chesterfield coat, and a broad gold watch chain across his robust chest, White played the part of a turn-of-the-century merchant prince. In truth, however, he possessed the avarice and slick acumen of a modern-day Wall Street arbitrager. When he met de Forest, White realized he had found a dupe. Lee de Forest offered him a fast passage to an easy fortune.

Born Abraham Schwartz about 1863, White grew up in Corsicana, Texas. About 1896, he decided to move east, change the color of his name, and get rich. In his first big deal, White bought $1.5 million in treasury bonds on money borrowed from the financier Russell Sage, and sold them the same day at a $100,000 profit. Similar transactions followed, never illegal, but never quite honest, either. In January 1902, he incorporated the De Forest Wireless Telegraph Company in New Jersey with a $1 million stock offering. White would be president; de Forest, vice president and "scientific director."

White's simple plan involved conjuring an illusion: create a company with de Forest's name in the title, circulate elaborate stock brochures, generate publicity through press releases, build wireless stations, make elaborate claims, and sell stock to anyone gullible enough to buy. Before he had run away from school at age thirteen, White had won a gold medal in oratory; one person who met him in 1907 likened him to Mark Twain's Colonel Sellers. His abilities as a honey-tonsiled salesman would be the company's greatest asset. Through it all, de Forest willingly assisted, regarding White as "all & more than a Brother," and the person who could bring him fortune. Indeed, de Forest enlisted the help of his brother, Charles, to sell stock in the new company. Soon he too would become a director.

De Forest's backers in Chicago were less than wildly enthusiastic. To the inventor they were the "Chicago leeches . . . who thirst to batten also off my *fame*," but they did hold legitimate claims to the company and apparatus he was handing over to White. Smythe was particularly exercised that his name had not been included in the company's. The dispute rekindled de Forest's contention that he had labored harder than the rest. "Not for Smythe did I toil six years at Yale . . . not for him did I leave a good salary in

Milwaukee; . . . not for him have I worked thru days, studied nights, *for my bare living*," de Forest had complained a year earlier. Now he made a clean break. "I have myself performed more than nine tenths of the work . . . the worry has been mine, the gnawing care, the sleepless nights of anxiety." He alone had dared to take the risks, and now he was taking the ultimate risk of allowing his name to be used, "which failing, will well nigh compel me to change my name, if I should *live* through such a disaster." Nevertheless, when the new stationery was printed, White took a cautious approach: "De Forest-Smythe System" appeared beneath the company name.

"Executive offices" were opened at 100 Broadway, an "Operating Department" at 17 State Street, and a "Manufacturing Department" in Jersey City. On the roof of 17 State Street, a glass-walled, glass-roofed "laboratory" was constructed. In it, prospective purchasers could see the inventor busy sending and receiving messages, though the signals were coming from a station on Staten Island just several miles away. Before the Stock Exchange on Wall Street, the De Forest Wireless Telegraph Company parked "Wireless Auto No. 1." Inside was an operator who transmitted stock quotations to a broker's office nearby.

"Soon, we believe, the suckers will begin to bite!" de Forest confided to his journal in early February. "Fine fishing weather, now that the *oil fields* have played out. 'Wireless' is the bait to use at present. May we stock our string before the wind veers, & the sucker shoals are swept out to sea!"

From the Naval Academy in Annapolis, de Forest sent President Theodore Roosevelt "the first greeting by an American wireless telegraph system" and, no doubt thinking of the time it took word of Dewey's victory in the Spanish-American War to reach the United States, he boasted "within eighteen months" the company would be able to send a message "from Manila, via Hawaii, to California." White reprinted the telegram and a reply from the president's secretary in a stock brochure. Press releases, often with false information, were sent to newspapers, which published them without question. In these, White promised a string of stations from New York to San Francisco. When the stories appeared, White cited them as factual accounts of the company's progress. Not content to wait for the releases, White began publishing the *Wireless News* in 1903, which carried the stories along with glowing testimonials from users.

The suckers bit so well that White offered more bait. In February 1903, the De Forest Wireless Telegraph Company was incorporated in Maine, absorbing the New Jersey company of the same name and offering $3 million in stock. Nine months later, White created the American De Forest Wireless Telegraph Company, this time with a $5 million stock offering. In 1904, he increased the capitalization to $15 million. Shares sold for $7.50. It was,

White told prospective buyers, "the greatest investment of the age," all the while reminding them of the way Bell Telephone stock had soared. A small investment now would make a person independent for life, and he warned "there is not enough stock to go around." The clever ones would grasp it at the flood tide, "and ride on to the shore of plenty."

De Forest took his place among the suckers, too, for White never allowed his scientific director very much money. Most of the capital generated by the various schemes flowed only into the president's pockets, while de Forest made do with a comparatively modest salary of $30 a week. The research budget was almost nonexistent; it was even difficult to get the money necessary to file a patent. White ordered stations built not to be links in the wireless chain he had promised would ring the country, but to sell stock. In Atlanta, the De Forest Company established a station, complete with impressive transmitting tower and aerials, for $3,000, sold $50,000 of stock to credulous buyers who flocked to the construction site, and then abandoned it without sending a single telegram.

Yet de Forest served his new backer faithfully; White was after all the only financier who had taken an interest—albeit one motivated by greed—in his wireless system. "Without *him*," he recognized, "the patient labor of years would have come to little or naught. At best I could hope only for a position with some other wireless company." White gave him an opportunity to realize—if only in a Potemkin way—his dreams for fame and success. At last his work could absorb him and he could stay apart from the financial dealings. "*Wireless Telegraphy* the choice of all callings!" he exulted in a letter to a friend. "I have been called by the all knowing to explore this greatest of wonders, summon up & hearken to those silent etheric voices, which seem often less of *nature* than of the *spirit* realm!" He alone realized the "many knotty & intimate problems" he had to solve to make the system perform well. His joy lay in seeking those solutions, and knowing the certain fame that would follow.

There was at least the simulacrum of success, as well. Within months of its creation, the De Forest Wireless Telegraph Company had installed stations that operated in New York City, Cape Hatteras, Coney Island, Atlantic City, Buffalo, Cleveland, and Chicago. It opened radio stations on the Great Lakes and the Atlantic seaboard. Steamboats were fitted with De Forest equipment; Sir Thomas Lipton installed a system on his yacht, *Erin*; and orders came in from the army and navy. In July 1904, after impressing officials of the navy with the accuracy, speed, and distance of his system, he secured a contract to erect long-distance stations at Panama, Cuba, Puerto Rico, Pensacola, and Key West.

De Forest Wireless enjoyed some spectacular triumphs, too: on the return passage from England in 1904 (where he had attempted without success to interest the British in his system), de Forest met the war correspondent for the London *Times*, who was on his way to the Orient to cover the imminent Russian-Japanese war. De Forest sold him on the efficacies of wireless. When the Japanese attacked Port Arthur a month later, the reporter signaled the word to an operator on the mainland, who immediately relayed it to London. Almost as quickly, White published the story in his latest stock offering.

At the World's Fair in St. Louis in 1904—a rich and gaudy celebration of the centennial of the Louisiana Purchase—the De Forest Company reached its zenith. De Forest supervised the construction of an imposing 300-foot-high steel tower, the tallest structure there, with his name in large letters attached to the side. Dozens of light bulbs surrounding each letter created a glow that could be seen from any place on the grounds. "A bright day has at last broken," de Forest exulted when seeing his tower one night, "and the tall monument has not *this* time vanished like a dream." For de Forest, the tower became a symbol of his accomplishment. That summer, he ordered a cot to be placed at its top. From his vantage point in the cool night air, he would survey the "magical scene beneath" and fall asleep secure that the company bearing his name was swiftly outdistancing all its competitors.

In a building beside the tower, an elaborate exhibit featured a map of the theater of "The War in the Far East" and Wireless Auto No. 1, the car White had parked on Wall Street. From a station at the exhibit, wireless messages were sent to Kansas City, Missouri; Springfield, Illinois; and even Chicago, some 300 miles distant. On "Electricity Day," the De Forest exhibit took the grand prize medal for "general excellence in wireless telegraphy."

On March 28, 1906, the De Forest station on Coney Island sent a 1,000-word message to the inventor, who was in Glengariff Harbour, Ireland, 3,360 miles away; 572 of the words were received. The first such transmission since Marconi's three dots in 1901, it represented a triumph for De Forest equipment. It also marked the high-water point for the De Forest Wireless Telegraph Company. By the end of the year, he had been dismissed, and the company bearing his name was liquidated.

All the time that he had been running about the country creating companies and establishing stations for his wireless system, de Forest had also been searching for his "golden girl" to share the new golden age of electricity and the fame that would accrue to him. The ideal he had formulated in his Yale days, when he sought a woman of charm, nobility of character, and blond hair, gradually became more refined to suit his aesthetic tastes. "Oh I love Music, & certain Poetry, real poetry, music in words, and *Romance*," he wrote in a stream of emotion the summer of the St. Louis World's Fair. "*She* must be a musician, to sing to me, play for me . . . and *She* must be artistic in all she is and does; and tender, sympathetic to my moods, bringing to my life all things good and beautiful which I so love and lack." Together he and the golden girl would travel to the "fair lands of Poesy and Romance" to drink of the great beauty of nature. At the same time, he insisted that his golden girl not be encumbered by narrow religious beliefs. Since he had been schooled by the "High-priests" of nature, Emerson, Spencer, and Huxley, his values were broad. If she possessed all these qualities, he concluded, "She will fit into my nature, and fill its vacancies, and I shall be *happy*, at last!"

The essential prerequisites for his ideal woman had not developed by chance, either. In the summer of 1899, immediately after his graduation, de Forest left for a month's visit to the Wallaces, old family friends who lived in the town of his birth, Council Bluffs, Iowa. Deacon Wallace was now the minister in Henry De Forest's old parish. It was not family ties that brought de Forest to Council Bluffs, however; he fondly remembered the deacon's two handsome daughters, Nettie and Jessie, whom he considered "the rarest of God's Girls." After just a few days in Council Bluffs, he confided to his diary "*I think I am beginning to love again!*"—this time, Jessie Wallace.

It was a delirium he had never known before—not with Julia Winter of his Mount Hermon days, not with Helen Wyatt, a second cousin who had turned his fancy when he was a graduate student, not with the scores of "chippies" on Chapel Street. He read her poetry and prose of Tennyson, Ruskin, Pater, and Poe; she sang him songs of "trust & love." Together they went rowing on a nearby lake; on the shore they lay "heart to heart" and "marked the lapse of time by the beating of their pulse."

When he left for his job in Chicago with the Western Electric Company, de Forest was sure of Jessie's deep commitment: "*Steal away* to me, my love . . . *steal away* and you shall steal away the cares and loneliness of a weary heart . . . *steal away* and you shall drive anxiety and misgivings from a brow grown dear to you . . ."

But within a fortnight, Jessie wrote of her "complete reversal of affection." In shock, de Forest returned immediately to Council Bluffs, but there could be no mistaking her intentions. In the letters from Chicago that followed, he gradually grew angry that she had dropped him, counting it as an insult not only to him, but to the good name of his university, which, he emphatically assured her, stood for loyal and true hearts. "Is this your thought of the true & constant, and is it *thus* you interpret *Yale*?" he asked in one letter. Other letters he filled with the vain hope she would resume her affection. Yet the harder he tried to win her, the more confirmed became Jessie's resolution to resist, until her letters ceased.

Though devastated by this rejection, de Forest realized Jessica Wallace had shown him what a golden girl might be. She had been inspired by his reading of poetry; he had been inflamed by her singing. Surely these empathetic qualities were exactly what the ideal one should possess.

Early in 1950, when he was anticipating the publication of his autobiography, *Father of Radio*, in which he devoted part of a chapter to Jessie Wallace, de Forest sent his former love a letter. This time, after a lapse of forty-eight years, she replied. Now she was Jessie Wallace Millar, living in Corona, California, east of Los Angeles. De Forest was married to his fourth wife and living in Hollywood. As the correspondence developed, he addressed Jessie as "Dear Heart." The two couples met for lunch occasionally, and Jessie and Lee exchanged letters and postcards. Jessie preserved de Forest's correspondence carefully until her death in 1954. The last she received, a postcard from de Forest, who was traveling with his wife in Europe, shows St. Mark's Square and the Grand Canal in Venice. A gondola floats in the foreground. De Forest's note was brief: "Had you not turned me down in '99 *you* would be in this gondola with me under the full Venetian moon! But it's futile to regret!"

◄

De Forest did not waste all his time pining for Jessie Wallace, however. In New York, he sported with a woman named Nanet in Battery and Riverside parks, and sailed with her off the New Jersey coast. With another he embarked on a moonlit excursion down the Hudson. To a barmaid, Kathleen, he wrote a poem. He had a golden girl whom he used to see in Kansas City, and another named Helen in New York. For a while in late 1904, he was engaged to a woman named Marie, and in early 1905, he tried to persuade the daughter of a Louisiana senator to elope, even though she was engaged to another man.

Lonely and in need of companionship, he took a large apartment, which he named the "Yale Eyrie," high above the Hudson at 97th Street and Riverside Drive in New York City. He found its rooms "delightfully cozy, miserably lonely." His plight was to be "forever chasing phantoms." It was, de Forest concluded, maudlinly remembering Jessie, "a curse" put on him by the Gods, "because I worshipped once too earnestly, too madly, an earthly personage, and made of her a Deity."

De Forest would later come to think of his first marriage as a curse put upon him by immortals. In October 1905, he was invited to the home of Mrs. M. T. Sheardown on West End Avenue, near his apartment. She was giving a dance in honor of her pretty daughter, Lucille. Proficient in languages, purportedly educated in Switzerland and France, though a brunette, Lucille immediately caught the fancy of de Forest, who thought her a person of culture. At last, here was one who would fulfill his desires. Within a few days of their first meeting, so the story went, he installed a wireless set in her home and taught her the Morse code. From his Yale Eyrie, he courted her with dots and dashes. Early the following year, just before he was to leave on a trip to sell De Forest equipment in England, he tapped out on his key: "Won't you marry me at once and come with me?" On February 17, at a small private ceremony in the Louis XVI Room at the St. Regis Hotel, de Forest and Lucille were married. Among the few guests attending were his brother, Charles, and Mr. and Mrs. Abraham White.

The voyage to England and the weeks that followed were no honeymoon, however. The trip went off in high style. The evening of their wedding, de Forest and his bride sailed for Liverpool on the Cunard liner *Lucania*. In London they stayed at the Savoy. But Lucille refused to consummate their union, a rejection that left de Forest "baffled and maddened." To add to his "black hopelessness," with each day his wife became increasingly surly, disagreeable, and sour, repulsing his advances and criticizing his every fault.

The purpose of his trip to England was to inspect some De Forest Company equipment that had been installed there and to attempt signaling from Glengariff Harbour, Ireland. Lucille accompanied him for a while, but to de Forest's dismay, she neither thrilled to the natural beauty of the countryside nor responded to "the charm of historical associations." Worse still, she hated poetry. After a "vigorous spanking," he sent his bride back to London.

De Forest took solace in the countryside, which he believed subsumed human desires and deeds in its "immortality." He filled his journals with elaborate descriptions of rocks, trees, mountains, and seas, and some of his most purple prose. Speaking of legend and the way it animates nature, he wrote, "Waters! ye are drenched with the ghost light evermore. Rocks and trees, like faint and tenuous vapors, the memories of her romance cling to you forever." Nature was not his only solace, however. Returning to England and the cold torments of his wife, he turned to another woman, Anne, "a human soul of sweetness and lovableness," one who assuaged for a time his frustrations.

Just what was the cause of the couple's difficulties? Perhaps, as de Forest speculated once, Lucille's frigidity came as a consequence of her overbearing mother and manifested itself in hatred for her husband. But evidence also suggests that Abraham White had a hand in the liaison, and perhaps he conjured up the entire marriage as a crude publicity gimmick in which de Forest played the ultimate sucker. Certainly he had encouraged de Forest to marry Miss Sheardown, and he had made sure the press knew the details of the match. Though newspapers were filled with news of another famous wedding that took place on February 17—that of Nicholas Longworth, congressman from Ohio, to President Roosevelt's daughter, Alice—they still found space for the nuptial story, placed by White's and the De Forest Company's clever press agent, of the bride who was "Wooed and Won by Wireless."

De Forest came to believe in a third reason for his marital torment: Lucille had refused him lest he learn she had another lover and was not a virgin. In divorce court that October, he cited as co-respondent DeWitt Clinton Flanagan, a brewer, real-estate owner, and former congressman, and sued him for $50,000. He had engaged a detective to follow his wife while he was out of town. Flanagan had visited her several times, taken her to the theater, and stayed at the house "until long after midnight." The couple visited Flanagan's camp in the Adirondacks and registered under false names at hotels in New York and Trenton. "After all these years," he grieved, "I find a harlot where I sought a wife." The divorce was granted in December, but the damages were denied.

In poor imitation of Tennyson, de Forest filled his journal with sentimental verses:

> She kissed me upon my eyes
> My wearied eyes, which ached from looking longingly
> Upon the world for sympathy. . . .

"Drown and die, my soul," he wailed in his journal. From this point on the entries were "but the bubbles which rise to the surface from one who drowns." "I have damned my own soul!" But in truth he was glad to be free of "unnatural cohabitation" with this "vampire."

De Forest tried to obliterate the entire painful episode from his memory and the memory of others, too. In a scrapbook he kept for these years, he removed three pages of wedding notices. Later he declined to mention the marriage either in a biography he commissioned in 1932 or in his autobiography. When two friends who were also thinking of writing his biography asked him about the marriage, he first reacted with surprise that they knew it had occurred. After they produced newspaper clippings and a photograph of the affair, de Forest told them sternly, "Forget that one. That never amounted to anything." It was a secret known only by a few. Indeed, the inventor had been married to his fourth wife for twenty years before she learned of Lucille.

Lee de Forest had been responsible for all the technical accomplishments of the American De Forest Wireless Telegraph Company, for he had devised the system, worked tirelessly to make it operate correctly, demonstrated it to prospective clients, supervised its installation in places as far distant as Key West, Cape Hatteras, Kansas City, and Cleveland, and hired and trained a staff of wireless operators to run it. Indeed, de Forest had done everything in the company that bore his name but hawk stock certificates, a job left to Abraham White and his salesmen.

Personally, de Forest had come a long distance from his first skirmish with Marconi at the yacht races in September 1901. To go as far and as fast as he did, however, he had created a wireless system with components adapted— some would contend, stolen—from others. In the case of his responder, this was especially true. Early on, he found that the "goo" paste he and Smythe had developed was subject to clogging and failure. On a visit to Reginald Fessenden's laboratory at Fortress Monroe in Virginia, early in 1903, de Forest found his Canadian rival was using an "electrolytic detector," consisting of two thin wires immersed in acid. In his own lab, de Forest and Clifford Babcock, a former employee of Fessenden's, developed what they called the "spade detector," two flat platinum wires sealed in a glass tube with only their extreme end surfaces dipped in a small cup of sulphuric acid. It became the basic wireless detector for the De Forest system. Later, in competition with the Fessenden system for lucrative naval contracts, the De Forest Company sold its spade detector at prices well below those of its rival.

Feeling that the invention had been stolen right from his laboratory bench, Fessenden sued. The De Forest Company had faced other suits, most notably from Marconi, but this one, what de Forest called "the hateful patent suit by my arch enemy," was a different matter, if only because Fessenden was clearly in the right. In 1906, after three years of litigation, a federal judge in Vermont denied the De Forest Company use of the spade detector and assessed damages for infringement. Fessenden had been vindicated completely. When he returned from his trip to England in late April, de Forest was greeted by his brother and the company's attorney, who hustled him off to Canada, so he might avoid arrest for failure to pay Fessenden the money he had been awarded. There he waited idly for about a month until White came up with the cash.

Probably Abraham White was just as happy to leave de Forest foundering in Canada, for it gave him time to complete the reorganization of his business schemes. Interested only in personal gain from selling as much stock as possible to hapless speculators, and wanting nothing to do with spending money on patents or litigation, he held his scientific director responsible for the adverse judgment. To protect his interest, White created yet another company, United Wireless Telegraph, and had all the assets—but none of the liabilities—of American De Forest transferred to it. In this way, Fessenden was frozen out of collecting more than a fraction of the damages he had been awarded.

Also frozen out of the new venture was Lee de Forest. When he finally did return to the United States, he found the company president, whom he had loved like a brother, basking on a huge estate (White Park) at Long Branch, New Jersey. Inside his mansion could be seen silver doorknobs and crystal chandeliers.

"I am daily more disgusted with the man and this newly-revealed side of his character," wrote a disillusioned de Forest on the last day of September. "I will never be intimately connected with the meta-morphosed 'Schwartz' again." His distrust proved in the end well placed. White now enlisted in the aid of a former Confederate "colonel" and fellow Texan with another unlikely name: Christopher Columbus Wilson. The colonel's flamboyance and ability to sell fraudulent paper rivaled even White's. United Wireless Telegraph would go on with a new carborundum detector created by General H. H. C. Dunwoody, company vice president and manager of its "Washington Department." Carborundum, which has much the same property as the quartz later used in crystal sets, worked well. Stock sales were brisk.

At its apex in 1910, United Wireless boasted seventy stations in communication with 400 ships sailing on the Atlantic Ocean and Great Lakes, far more than its competitors. The reason for its success may not be attributed to superiority of the system, however; United Wireless rarely charged for equipment or the messages it sent. Instead it depended on ever-expanding stock sales to keep it afloat. Soon the colonel forced out his fellow Texan. By 1910, Wilson's unslakable avarice had lofted him to the presidency, borne on a ponderous bubble of worthless wireless stock.

On June 15, 1910, the bubble finally burst. Inspectors from the Post Office raided United Wireless's opulent offices on suspicion of mail fraud. Though it had recently listed in its assets about $6.5 million in cash on hand, the company was in fact insolvent. On May 29 of the following year, Wilson and four other officers were convicted. The colonel was returned to the South, this time to the federal penitentiary at Atlanta.

On November 28, 1906, de Forest sent a terse, one-sentence letter of resignation as vice president and director of American De Forest Wireless Telegraph Company, "to take effect immediately." On his copy, he appended a note to himself:

This is the funeral of my first-born child! This the *finis* to the hopes and efforts which have made up my strenuous life for the past five years. That which I had wrought with pain and ceaseless endeavor to make grand and lasting & triumphant is prostituted, sandbagged, throttled & disabled by the Robber who has fattened off my brain. *But my work goes on*, while I live.

Abraham White and his shifty associates believed they had cleaned de Forest out entirely. They kept rights to all the patents the inventor had used in his wireless system, though most were counted useless after Fessenden's successful suits. They had given de Forest just $1,000 in a severance settlement and had seen to it that an unscrupulous attorney took half the amount in legal fees. De Forest had been hurt by his association with White, but he had not been ruined. Acting the way he always did when faced with defeat, he reaffirmed his belief in his abilities and genius (if only in his journal), gathered his few remaining resources, and with typical grit and determination, plunged resolutely onward.

De Forest's most valuable resource lay in a small invention that Abraham White and his lawyer had deemed worthless, a new method of detecting wireless waves with a small incandescent electric lamp or tube which he called the "audion." As was the case with the spade detector—that device de Forest copied from Fessenden—his audion did not spring entirely from his brain. But when pressed to tell its genesis, the inventor became murky in his explanations. He was unwilling to admit the debt he owed to others, including Thomas Edison and John Ambrose Fleming.

By 1880, Edison had created a lamp that glowed brightly when direct current passed through its carbon filament in a vacuum. But he found that over time particles of the carbon were transferred to the glass. In experiments to correct the fault, the inventor learned that electric current could flow from the filament through the vacuum surrounding it to a positively charged metal plate, a process later dubbed the "Edison effect"—meaning that no one could explain precisely how the process worked. Furthermore, the amount of current that flowed from the filament to the plate stood in direct proportion to the incandescence of the lamp. He noted his findings in a patent that showed how such a modified lamp might measure the flow of electrical current. But the date was 1883, half a decade before Hertz's experiments, and fourteen years before an English physicist named Joseph John Thomson discovered the existence of the electron. Besides, the untheoretical Edison believed inventive genius to be "one percent inspiration and ninety-nine percent perspiration." Decidedly uninspired at this point, he saw little commercial value for his discovery. Without further speculation, Edison proceeded with his quest to perfect the electric lamp.

John Ambrose Fleming, then an employee of the Edison Company in London, knew of the inventor's patent. His studies of the same carbon deposits led him to publish four papers on the subject to the Royal Society between 1883 and 1896. But then, diverted by other work, Fleming suspended his inquiry for nearly eight years. In 1904, when he had become scientific adviser for the Marconi Company, he was charged with the job of creating a new detector of wireless waves.

"Why not try the lamps?" Fleming remembered thinking years later. This time, working with the alternating current of wireless waves, he made a remarkable discovery: while the current flowing into the filament alternated between a positive and negative charge, the current leaving the lamp from the metal plate was direct. Fleming's bulb was acting as a valve that allowed only the negative electrons to pass. Indeed, he entitled his patent an "instrument for converting alternating electric currents into continuous currents," and he called his bulb an "oscillation valve." Fleming's valve stands as a dramatic achievement. The electrons liberated by Marconi's spark gap transformer imperceptibly traveled through the air at the speed of light. Now they could be captured and converted into direct current through the agency of a small filament and plate in a little glass bulb. From there the current could flow into an earphone and become a perceptible sound once again. Fleming had created a new detector of wireless waves, one that worked with a modified Edison-effect lamp.

In the spring of 1905, Fleming published his discovery for the Royal Society, but the tube was a crude apparatus and needed more study to be practical. If he had had more encouragement, Fleming might possibly have developed the potential of his tube, but in this he was thwarted by his employer. The Marconi Company, which held all rights to his patent, was more interested in developing galena crystal as a detector. Instead, two years later, Lee de Forest took the fame and some of the fortune for Fleming's work.

De Forest always avoided acknowledging Edison's and Fleming's obvious antecedents to his own work. Though he read voraciously in scientific periodicals—at Talladega, at the Chittenden Library at Yale, at the John Crerar Library in Chicago, among others—and though he subscribed to technical periodicals, he steadfastly claimed ignorance of their discoveries.

Since 1900, de Forest had occasionally experimented with the possibility that heat from a gas burner created electrical vibrations. Early in 1905, after Fessenden had launched his suit and de Forest realized he might be forced to abandon his spade detector, he intensified his tests and took out patents on several "oscillation responsive" devices, which used a gas flame. No evidence suggests these inventions ever worked, but patent them he did. In the late summer of 1905, he read Fleming's article on his valve in the *Proceedings of the Royal Society.*

Late that fall, an assistant of de Forest's brought a bulb about the size and shape of a small pear to Henry W. McCandless at 67 Park Place in New York City and asked him to duplicate it. A manufacturer whose principal trade was making automobile lamps for Westinghouse and General Electric's Mazda, McCandless had no difficulty meeting this special order. With a brass candelabra screw base and a carbon filament, the lamp resembled others available at the time. But there was one significant difference: beside the filament inside the bulb was a nickel plate. To that was attached a short wire that protruded through the top of the glass. The assistant explained that it was a Fleming valve. On December 9 that year, de Forest took out a patent on a "static valve for wireless telegraph systems." Five weeks later, he made another application for a similar tube and circuit; this time he ran wires from a small battery to both the filament and plate. This he called the "audion," and he claimed in a talk to a gathering of the American Institute of Electrical Engineers in New York on October 26, 1906, that his tube was "a new receiver for wireless telegraphy."

All that de Forest had developed thus far bore a remarkable resemblance to the valve Fleming had described to the Royal Society in 1905. He had introduced the use of a battery on the plate as well as the filament circuit, but that was all. Nor was de Forest's change necessarily an improvement, for the small positive charge of electrons flowing from the filament to the plate was no match for the positive charge of electrons flowing to the plate from the battery. What came next, however, was de Forest's idea alone, and without question will endure as the inventor's greatest insight.

On November 25, 1906, after further experiments and several false starts, de Forest ordered another tube from McCandless. The specifications called for *three* elements: a filament; a plate; and, interposed between the two, as close to the filament as possible, another nickel wire. As was the case with the other wires, it too was drawn out through the side of the lamp. When this wire was positively charged, de Forest found it would attract the stream of positive electrons flowing from the filament, accelerate them, and send them toward the plate, and the more positive the charge, the greater the charge on the plate circuit. On the suggestion of John Grogan, one of McCandless's assistants, de Forest decided to bend the wire zigzag fashion in order to create a greater surface to attract the electrons flowing from the filament. To this de Forest gave the name "grid." Now he could regulate the flow of electrons from the filament to the plate and amplify them. Precisely how the filament, grid, and plate worked, he was not sure. The theories he did propose about their action were in fact incorrect. But the sounds coming from his earphones showed that his audion *did* work. With the simple addition of the grid to Fleming's tube, modern electronics was born.

Throughout the thirties, forties, and fifties, when subsequent inventions failed to earn him fame, de Forest proudly embossed his stationery with the electrical engineers' symbol of his invention:

the inverted T at the top representing the plate; the zig-zag, the grid; and the looped line at the bottom, the filament. Without question, the symbol signifies one of the most profound advances, not only in the radio art but in all electronics.

Just as de Forest was creating his tube, Abraham White was forcing him out of the company that bore his name. De Forest realized this invention would be his salvation, the very thing that would enable him to start anew. Giving in to his most romantic impulses, he addressed his creation directly in his journal:

> You, little Audion, have been a supporting companion to me in all the troubles of the months that are past; thru all their dark hours *your* light has alone gleamed dazzlingly bright to my eyes; my ears have hearkened to your fluttering whisper amid the discordant noises of these crashing times . . . you rest on the table before me excelling all devices which man has achieved in sensitiveness to the infinitesimal forces I have built you to detect.

Three days after he ordered his grid audion from McCandless, de Forest resigned from White's company with his two-element audion patent in hand. Mired in litigation as he was, he did not have time to test his invention of the three-element tube until the last day of December. Compared with any wave detector he could use, the results showed a marked improvement. Signals could be heard more clearly and reliably through earphones, over distances never crossed by wireless before.

Any account of the often serendipitous process of discovery inevitably leads to speculation on what might have been: if Edison had worked with alternate rather than direct current, which he mistakenly championed as the safest and best way to deliver electricity to homes; if he had been more inclined to theory; if the Marconi Company had supported rather than thwarted Fleming's research; if Fessenden had not instituted the infringement suit that caused de Forest to search for an alternative to the spade detector.

But such conjecture about the way the beginning of radio might have been different is fatuous. De Forest *did* add the grid to the vacuum tube, something no one else had done before. Though his discovery was unwitting, and though he scarcely understood how his tube worked, it was his invention. No detractor can take from him the fact that he made the discovery that so significantly shaped the twentieth century. The audion was, as he put it nearly a half century later, his *"greatest* invention."

3

"WHAT WIRELESS
IS YET TO BE"

Some time during the summer of 1904, the same year that Lee de Forest was enjoying his triumph at the World's Fair in St. Louis, a thirteen-year-old boy named Edwin Howard Armstrong sat in the bedroom of his family's solid Victorian house overlooking the Hudson at Yonkers, New York, reading *The Boy's Book of Inventions: Stories of the Wonders of Modern Science*. A present his father had brought him from London, the book had a powerful and immediate effect: then and there Howard Armstrong decided to become an inventor. Of what, or in what field, he was not sure, but an inventor he would be.

Profusely illustrated with nearly 150 diagrams and photographs, *The Boy's Book of Inventions* was filled with the wonder of new technologies being discovered at the opening of the century. It had been written in 1899 by Ray Stannard Baker, then a young reporter for *McClure's Magazine*, who was later to compile a five-volume biography of Woodrow Wilson. Baker described inventions ranging from the bizarre to the useful. He told of Simon Lake's submarine that rolled across the sea floor on motorcycle wheels; and the "flying man" Otto Lilienthal's bat-winged gliding contraption that, when strapped to the inventor's arms, enabled him to leap from tall cliffs, and glide all the way to the ground. But Baker also wrote of Thomas Edison's phonograph, Roentgen's X-ray machine, and Duryea's motor vehicles. In some cases, the author personally visited and interviewed the inventor, taking a trip to the ocean floor with Lake, for example, or stopping by the great Edison's laboratory in Orange, New Jersey.

The chapter that had the greatest effect on Armstrong, "Telegraphing Without Wires: How Marconi Sends Messages Through Space," repeated the oft-told story of the inventor's feat. He was "a mere boy" when he began to dream, and a "shy, modest, beardless youth" when he journeyed to London "to tell the world of one of the greatest inventions of this century." Baker's narrative had romance, practical explanation, and heroism. Marconi dealt with the "mysterious, all pervading . . . ether," the name then given to the element that scientists supposed filled space and through which electrical waves traveled. Baker explained, imperfectly, the action of the coherer, telegraph key, spark gap transmitter, and Morse inker. Use of the wireless, he told his readers, had saved the crew of the Goodwin Sands lightship off the coast of Dover. When the ship was struck by another vessel, the crew telegraphed to shore some twelve miles away for help. "We have seen clearly what [wireless] already is," Baker concluded, "and with a half discernment of what it is yet to be."

The next year, Howard Armstrong received another book from his parents that reinforced the effect of the earlier gift: Russell Doubleday's Stories of Inventors: The Adventures of Inventors and Engineers, True Incidents and Personal Experiences. Doubleday emphasized "the trials, the disappointments, the obstacles overcome, and the final triumph of the successful inventor." His first chapter, "How Guglielmo Marconi Telegraphs Without Wires," repeated much of the romance of Baker's book, dwelling on the details of the first signals the inventor sent over his father's estate in Italy, and added an account of his transmitting the letter S across the Atlantic.

The inventor in Baker's and Doubleday's books always conducted his life as a gentleman at work for the betterment of "mankind." He faced his trials and disappointments as momentary frustrations, challenges to be met and conquered in a manly fashion. Usually the inventor operated on a simple paradigm: he had an idea (sometimes called a "dream") and then worked to realize it. More often than not, he followed the Edison model of trial and error, until he enjoyed success. If he should borrow an idea from another, he always gave credit. Thus Baker wrote of Marconi's paying tribute to Edouard Branly when he adapted the Frenchman's coherer. The authors sometimes concluded their chapters with an account of how the world welcomed the accomplishments of these gentlemen, rewarding them with great esteem and even financial success. The implications were clear: with the creations of the inventor, America would realize its true greatness in the new century. This was the life Armstrong—and many other boys of the time—wished to lead.

Baker's and Doubleday's inventor worked alone or with a small cadre of assistants whom he supervised. None worked in a corporation as part of a team of technicians. The vision was his and his alone. It never belonged to a company. Often, as was the case with Marconi, the inventor himself began a company to manufacture and deliver his product to the world.

Since invention was the province of gentlemen, neither Baker nor Doubleday broached the idea of stealing another's creation. Nor did they mention patent litigation, which occupied so much time of men like Edison and Marconi, and which would so dominate the career of Armstrong.

◄

Howard Armstrong passed his childhood and youth in the calm and comfort that middle-class families were able to maintain during the last decade of the nineteenth century and the first decade of the twentieth, no less an ideal and secure setting than that of his books. This was the twilight of innocence before the First World War, a time when people like the Armstrongs believed in the certainties of rock-solid Republican nationalism, financial mobility and stability, and the assurance of unlimited opportunity. As the product of an old New York family, Howard Armstrong enjoyed these comforts as well as the spiritual haven—and occasional dourness—of parents who were strict Presbyterians.

John Armstrong and his wife, Emily Smith, had married in New York's Old North Presbyterian Church in 1888, and settled in a comfortable brownstone house at 247 West 29th Street. At first a salesman for the Oxford University Press in New York, John Armstrong eventually rose to be vice president of its American branch. Each year he traveled to London for a conference with his superiors, returning with the latest books and the aura of European culture and sophistication. (It was there, according to family tradition, that he acquired The Boy's Book of Inventions for his son.) For many years before and after she married, Emily had been a teacher in the New York City schools, and retired only when she became pregnant with their first child, Edwin Howard, who was born on December 18, 1890. Two daughters, Ethel and Edith, soon followed, and the family was complete.

Nearby lived Emily's extended family—uncles, aunts, cousins, many of them teachers and principals in the public school system. Pedagogy was in the air always, along with the irenic air of Presbyterianism. Grandfather Smith had been an elder of the church, and his son would follow. He and his wife had taken a trip to the Holy Land. Many of the Smith women taught Sunday school and one played the organ, while the men served as deacons or sang in the choir.

When the Presbyterian elders decided to relocate their church to the Upper West Side of Manhattan in 1895, the Smiths and Armstrongs moved to a brownstone on 97th Street just off Central Park West. From there it was an easy walk for Howard to the local public grade school on 89th Street. In the summers, fear of disease drove the family to extended vacations upstate to a farm in Richfield Springs, a camp on Lake George, or to Lake Bomaseen near Fairhaven, Vermont.

In his ninth year, Howard was struck down with a severe case of Saint Vitus's dance. A type of chorea—a term derived from the Greek word for dance—the disorder causes involuntary contortions and contractions of muscles, especially in the face, neck, and shoulders. Doctors of the period sometimes described it as an "insanity of the muscles." Typically, Saint Vitus's dance struck children between five and fifteen years of age, and twice as many girls as boys. We know now that in 70 percent of the cases the child has had rheumatic fever, an inflammation of the heart caused by a streptococcus bacteria. But in 1900, doctors attributed it to a sudden fright or a gradual deterioration of general health. They prescribed quiet and rest, a nutritious diet, an absence of excitement, and occasionally a tonic of zinc and arsenic. After the patient recovered, doctors cautioned against excitement, excessive study, and exhaustion.

Following their physician's advice, John and Emily Armstrong kept their boy at home for two years, where he was ministered to by his maternal great aunt and others in the family. They tutored him in his schoolwork and made him rest. Only when the symptoms of his affliction had abated did the Armstrongs allow their boy to return to school and resume his activities. The disease left its legacy, however. For the rest of his life, Howard Armstrong suffered from a twitch in his neck, mouth, and right shoulder. Whenever he was under stress, the spasms became more pronounced, frequent, and difficult to mask.

Because of Howard's illness, the dirt of the city, and concerns about the ever-rising tide of immigrants, the Armstrong and Smith families decided in 1900 to move once again, this time retreating about fifteen miles farther up the Hudson to a new house in Yonkers. A small city in the throes of changing into a large suburb of New York, Yonkers had become one of the first havens for urban middle-class families in Westchester County. Between the last decade of the nineteenth century and the first decade of the twentieth, the population of Yonkers jumped nearly 150 percent, from 32,000 to nearly 80,000 people. The fire department grew from a group of volunteers with just three pieces of equipment to a paid force housed in seven companies about the city. Speculators divided former estates and farms into building lots as small as twenty-five by sixty feet—most a short walk from stations on the New York Central and Hudson River Railroad that hugged the shore. To better accommodate the new settlers, the railroad added more stations and faster trains. New York City was just forty-five minutes away.

The Armstrong and Smith families chose two imposing houses next door to each other on a hill overlooking the river at the north end of the city.

Everything about the houses and properties was large. Number 1032 Warburton Avenue, which was to be the Armstrong address for the next half century, stood in the center of a lot 150 feet wide and 130 feet deep. Of mixed pink granite, brick, and wood construction in the popular Queen Anne style, the three-story house featured a polygonal turret at its front that was capped with three pediment windows on the top floor under an imposing curving cupola. Anticipating the future, the builders had wired the house for electricity (it was then illuminated by gas) and installed a burglar alarm "at every entry."

Though he would later live in New York City, "1032," as it came to be known, always served as Howard Armstrong's anchorage. There the Armstrongs and Smiths would gather for holidays and reunions; there Howard Armstrong could always return. Across the front and down the south side of the house ran a wide verandah. From there the family could see the expanse of the river for twenty miles, including the place near the opposite shore where, tradition has it, Henry Hudson first anchored the *Half Moon* in August 1609. The Hudson of 1900 was filled with traffic: cargo and passenger ships plying their way to and from the port at Albany; small pleasure craft that were berthed at a nearby yacht club; and ferries that crossed from Yonkers to Alpine, New Jersey. Directly opposite the house rose the steep dark brown rocks of the Palisades and the still unspoiled land of New Jersey, whose colors changed with each season.

In such secure surroundings, Howard Armstrong passed a youth marked by solid comfort and affluence, if not great luxury and elegance. Always described as a "serious" child by his family, he seemed preoccupied and reserved, taking his measure of the world about him with a quiet intensity, a word family members and friends often used when remembering his engagement with all his activities. Tennis he took up with a vengeance, practicing his serve at the Hudson River Country Club until it possessed withering speed and force. He was fascinated by all machinery, especially by the trains that ran along the Hudson. Among the children of the neighborhood, Howard earned a reputation for being able to fix almost any broken toy. When he grew older, he would take his tools to a nearby road leading to New York. There he would wait for automobiles—still a novelty—to break down so that he might fix them. On the Palisades and the steep escarpments around Yonkers, he developed a fearless enthusiasm for climbing to high places, a passion that never left him.

Sober and resolute Presbyterianism provided a structure for his daily life. Before dinner each evening, grace was said at length and with conviction. Sundays were spent in activities centered on the church. Emily gave her son a scroll illuminated with part of the fifteenth verse from Psalm 50: "Call upon me in the day of trouble: I will deliver thee." Howard hung it in his room over his work table.

Emily might have done better to include the rest of the verse, "and thou shalt glorify me," for the religious fervor of the family never took hold in her son. Rather than a crisis in faith such as de Forest experienced, Armstrong seems to have maintained his belief in God, but only in an oblique way. After high school, he rarely went to church. As one family member reflected, he was too fervently preoccupied with his own experiments and ideas to sit still and listen to someone speak about the Deity. Never authoritarian and always tolerant of their son's decisions—even about a matter so central to their own lives—John and Emily Armstrong appear to have masked whatever disappointment they might have felt about their son's lack of interest in religious matters.

Clearly the overriding passion in Howard's mind by the time he entered Yonkers High School in 1905 was the idea of invention and his own intention to make discoveries. "Somehow, for reasons I cannot recollect," he wrote many years later, "the decision favored wireless." Stirred by another article Ray Stannard Baker published in *McClure's Magazine* celebrating Marconi's achievement of telegraphing across the ocean without wires, Armstrong sought to emulate the acknowledged master. The Italian inventor stood forth in Armstrong's mind as the trailblazer, the one who pointed the way for the rest to follow. Armstrong would never waver in his admiration. "To me the astounding thing is undoubtedly how Marconi's prophecies turned out to be uncannily correct" he wrote to a friend in England half a century later, while preparing a speech about the inventor for the American Institute of Electrical Engineers.

From the three windows of his room underneath the cupola on the top floor of his house, Howard had a commanding view of the Hudson and the Palisades; the space and relative distance from the rest of the family offered an excellent place for him to construct radio equipment. By this time the house had electric light, and Howard suspended two lamps from the ceiling over his work table so that he might work through the night. His was the highest point in the house, the place where he could best send and receive wireless signals. His parents helped him to acquire the necessary wireless paraphernalia—including induction coils, coherers, a telegrapher's key and earphones, Leyden jars, and condensers—and he busied himself constructing and experimenting with electrical circuits.

Soon Armstrong was receiving and sending wireless messages to other boys and young men who also were taken with Marconi's invention. They became his circle of companions. Two, Tom Styles, who lived down the hill from his house, and Randy Runyon, who lived about a mile away closer to the center of Yonkers, became lifelong and unfailing friends, and valued assistants in his experiments.

Through one of his uncles, Frank Smith, Armstrong met another more influential wireless enthusiast and inventor. Charles Underhill lived on the grounds of Pinecrest, a large estate farther up the hill from Warburton Avenue. Underhill had invented an early version of the teletype, the printing system that transforms the dots and dashes of the Morse code into letters and words, and had written books on electromagnetism. He became the boy's first mentor. For nearly two years, from 1907 to 1909, Howard would bicycle up the hill to Pinecrest after school to probe Underhill's knowledge of electricity. "Leaning back in his chair with his head against the wall," Underhill remembered, Howard would ask him a carefully considered question. When the answer came, the boy would "meditate for a while and then follow up with another question. This often went on for hours at a time." Patiently, he explained to Howard the principles of Faraday, Maxwell, Hertz, and electromagnetic waves, and he supplemented Armstrong's instruction with copies of his own books. As valuable as Underhill's training were the pieces of wireless equipment he occasionally gave Armstrong, including the first vacuum tube—a two-element de Forest audion—Armstrong ever saw. Clifford Babcock, de Forest's engineer, had given it to the inventor to experiment with in his teletype printer. After he had tried it, Underhill passed the tube on.

"Who of us in the old days at Pinecrest, could have realized the value of the instruction that I was receiving in the fundamentals of 'wireless' and what made it go?" Armstrong asked Underhill many years later. More important than either the information or equipment was a simple word of encouragement he gave to the boy one afternoon. Armstrong remarked he had been puzzled to find that a spark transmitter performed better when he connected it contrary to the way one of his wireless books specified. "What do you care about what's in the book," asked Underhill. "You're an original thinker." As Armstrong later recognized, "the lesson that the things that are not in the books are the most important of all was the most valuable lesson ever given to me."

Of all the young wireless enthusiasts in the area, Armstrong stood out as the most advanced. Stories began to circulate around Yonkers of the youth with powers of extraordinary concentration, who was experimenting with and designing remarkable wireless equipment. In 1907, he built a powerful receiver set with a piece of crystal he also had acquired from Underhill. He talked of little else but wireless and tennis. In matters of electronics, none of his friends could keep up with his thinking. At his first meeting with Runyon, arranged over the airwaves, Armstrong carefully explained his design for a transformer, complete with formulas, mathematical calculations, and intricate diagrams.

"The only trouble with it," he remarked at the end of a discourse far too complex for Runyon to fathom, "it's too big to get out of the house."

In 1910, he set out to build his own antenna from long sections of wood that would be taller and better than any other. For the base, he anchored two eight-by-eight wooden posts in the ground with concrete. Next he stood a tall piece of eight-by-eight between these larger posts. Hoisting himself on a bosun's chair up his mast, he successively attached more lengths of wood, each time securing them with guy wires. As he proceeded upward in this fashion, the dimensions of his lumber got smaller until a slim length of two-by-four holding his antenna wire projected at the top. His completed mast stood 125 feet from the ground, nearly 300 feet above the Hudson. Howard's first experience of creating a tower of great height clearly had exhilarated him. Often on spring and summer afternoons, he liked nothing better than to hoist himself in his chair to the top of what was one of the tallest structures in Yonkers and survey the scene about him.

All this activity had its rewards for Howard Armstrong. The combination of his equipment and tower enabled him to receive messages from a far greater distance than any other amateur in the neighborhood. Even in 1908, when he was a senior in high school and before he had built his tall antenna, he awakened his family in the middle of the night to hear the sounds of a naval telegraph key as it tapped out a message at Key West, Florida, 2,000 miles from Yonkers. It was a feat few others had equaled. As he and his equipment grew more sophisticated, Armstrong was able to pick up the Marconi station in Newfoundland regularly.

Consumed with his study of wireless, Armstrong never excelled in his schoolwork. He had above-average grades, especially in those subjects he enjoyed—algebra, geometry, advanced drawing, and American history. Curiously, he achieved only average grades in physics, though he designed and built a wireless receiver for the school.

On June 24, 1909, Howard Armstrong sat with ninety other seniors on the stage at Yonkers High School auditorium under two large American flags and a sign emblazoned with the school's motto PERFERRE EST SUCCEDERE—"to persevere is to succeed." He had managed to graduate with an overall average of 89.8. Thirty-seven of the graduates were headed for college—places like Yale, Princeton, Cornell, Lehigh, and Columbia. Determined to continue his study of electricity, Armstrong enrolled in Columbia University's engineering school. To continue his wireless experiments, he decided to live at home and commute on the graduation present his parents had given him—a new Indian motorcycle, painted bright red.

When Armstrong entered Columbia in September 1909, the university was in the midst of an extraordinary expansion that had begun twelve years before when the campus was moved from Madison Avenue downtown to its present location uptown on Morningside Heights. President Nicholas Murray Butler had recently added schools of journalism, medicine, and business, and a university extension for adults. A new engineering facility on Broadway between 116th and 117th streets had been opened in 1907, and across the campus on Amsterdam Avenue, Philosophy Hall, one of the main buildings on the campus, was nearing completion. By 1911, Columbia's endowment of $31 million would rank as the largest of any university in the country.

At the time of Armstrong's entrance, Columbia's School of Mines, Engineering and Chemistry, as it was formally known, was separate from the college. Entrance was gained only after a rigorous admissions process. In addition to presenting a certificate of good moral character, a candidate had to pass examinations in chemistry, drawing, English, mathematics, physics, French or German, as well as three other examinations from a group of subjects that included Latin, Spanish, ancient history, zoology, and physiography. Once admitted, students could expect to pay $250 for tuition, $30 for books, and $65 for "Camp Columbia"—a five-week surveying program given between the first and second years on a large tract of land near Litchfield, Connecticut. A typical course load numbered thirty-three hours of instruction each week—seventeen in class and sixteen in the laboratory.

After the first year, students in the engineering school chose to major in civil engineering, mechanics, or electricity. The electrical department of the school had been started in 1889—just a year after Hertz's experiments and eight years before Thomson's discovery of the electron—under the leadership of the physicist Michael Pupin. As was the case with other such programs of the day, Columbia's emphasized electric machinery and power production, with courses like "Metallurgy of Iron and Steel," "Dynamo and Motor Practice" and "Steam Power Machinery." Courses in telegraph and telephone did not come until the senior year. Nevertheless, someone with the inclinations of Howard Armstrong would find the work in mathematics, physics, and alternating and direct currents relevant to his interests.

The attrition rate of the majors suggests the department was especially rigorous. Twenty-eight students declared electrical engineering their major in their second year; twenty-one remained in the third year; fifteen graduated with Armstrong in June 1913.

In many ways, Armstrong was typical of the students of the time. Like everyone else, in the first year he took the standard curriculum of inorganic chemistry, drafting, descriptive and analytical geometry, elementary mechanics, the theory of surveying, spherical trigonometry, and Physics 4, "Light,

Sound, Electricity and Magnetism." Wearing his pale blue beanie, he entered the activities of other freshmen, the tug-of-war and flag rush, a spirited competition with the sophomore students for control of their class banner. Friendly with his classmates, he was given the nickname "Army." Early on he established himself as a formidable opponent on the university's tennis courts.

In a picture taken of Armstrong standing on the edge of the cliffs of the New Jersey Palisades, he seems like a typical college student. He had reached his full height of six feet. A white shirt open at the collar covers his broad shoulders; he gazes into the camera with a full smile. Above his high forehead is a thick shock of sandy hair; there is no sign he would be bald in less than a decade.

In other ways, however, Armstrong was very different from his peers. Others pledged fraternities, followed the fortunes of the football and baseball teams, and traveled up the Hudson each spring to attend the annual regatta at Poughkeepsie. Armstrong did not. Instead he filled his days and nights with the study of wireless and directed his unswerving vision toward his career as an inventor. His sister Edith often brought friends home from Vassar where she was attending college, but Armstrong stuck to his third-floor bedroom and rarely socialized. He asserted an air of mystery. When asked what he was doing, he would reply cryptically, aware of the vast chasm of ignorance about wireless that separated him from the rest. Sometimes he would give an intrepid visitor a ride to the top of his antenna mast in his bosun's chair, but requests of this sort did not come often.

Not only did Armstrong eschew all such socializing as might be expected of college students, in his freshman year he even declined an invitation to join the new junior wireless club that a group of youths in the New York area had begun, with Lee de Forest's old antagonist, Reginald Aubrey Fessenden, as their adviser. It wasn't until 1912, when the group had changed its name to the Radio Club of America, that he took out a membership.

Being a person of remarkable self-assurance and possessing a clear understanding what was to be his life's work, Armstrong appeared unusually detached, often inquisitive, sometimes engaging, and occasionally arrogant as a student. It was not unusual for him to shun textbook explanations of physical phenomena, preferring to devise his own reasons. He completed his coursework in a perfunctory fashion, with a studied aloofness from the professor and his subject unless it had a bearing on electromagnetic waves. Professors who perceived his indifference to their subjects found him an intractable annoyance. Others complained that he flaunted the established rules of conduct in their laboratories, especially when he disregarded the steps of their assignments, failed to keep accurate records in his notebook, and stayed long after hours to work in private on experiments of his own.

In one instance, a professor found his self-assurance and arrogance positively painful. For weeks, Armstrong had chafed as the visitor from Cornell's engineering school, supposedly a distinguished authority on electromagnetism, stood at the front of the lecture theater presenting misinformation about his subject to the assembled students and faculty. At one point, he had even disparaged the discoveries of Nikola Tesla, saying there was "very little originality" about them. One day, when demonstrating spark discharges from a grounded coil, the professor declared authoritatively that it was impossible to touch the coil without receiving a severe shock. Armstrong had observed that first grasping the end of the coil emitting the sparks and *then* the grounded end created a safe circuit that one could hold all day. After class, he decided to prove the man a fool by doing just that in front of the others. "Everyone gave him the laugh," Armstrong wrote to Charles Underhill:

> Then he wanted to try it, but . . . . he took hold of the ground-wire first. . . . Before he got within six-inches of the terminal the spark jumped to his hand. . . . he pulled most of the apparatus off the table before they turned the current off.

The incident instructs us in Armstrong's methods of investigation. The end of the coil emitting the sparks appeared to be more dangerous, and one naturally touched the grounded end. He ruefully admitted having once done so himself: "If he got as much juice as I have taken in the same way from my own coil, I don't blame him for the way he acted." But Armstrong had not been content to let the matter rest. "Two years ago I noticed how the current could be by-passed through the body by first touching the coil and then the ground-wire." Conventional wisdom like the professor's stopped with the observation of the shock; Armstrong's unorthodox reasoning and his discontent with blindly accepted rules never allowed him to rest.

At Columbia, Armstrong developed another trait that displeased some of the staff and would annoy others later in his life: his distrust of mathematical explanations to account for phenomena of the physical world. All too often, he found his professors taking refuge in such abstractions when faced with a difficult and seemingly intractable conundrum. Close observation of nature and a refusal to accept the findings of experts, even when they were backed up by mathematical "proofs," became hallmarks of his approach to such problems and to his investigations as an inventor. This is not to say Armstrong was a poor mathematician or that he refused to use mathematics when they were called for; rather, he refused the security of a glib mathematical reason to explain why something could not be done. Such thinking, he always contended, could verify false theories and serve to choke off the speculative desire to approach a problem from a different perspective. "It ain't ignorance that causes all the trouble in this world," drawled Armstrong frequently, in his deep Bronx accent, "it's the things that people know that ain't so."

While the narrow and routine professors regarded him with suspicion, the ones whom Armstrong respected—usually younger instructors who were teaching the courses he liked—found him to possess a remarkable mind capable of bringing fresh insight to problems that absorbed him. Fortunately, Columbia had a good number of these professors as well. Three in particular became his champions, saving him from himself as well as from those faculty members who would have liked to see him depart without a degree. Later, they became his friends and colleagues.

Morton Arendt first encountered Armstrong in his telegraph and telephone course, which covered a historical review of Morse's and Bell's work, wireless telegraphy, and the elements of modern telegraphic and telephone systems. An inventor himself and an authority on storage batteries, Arendt specialized in motors, electricity distribution, and design of direct current machinery. His knowledge of telegraphy and telephone was limited. Almost immediately, he recognized in his student "something . . . the others did not have," and realized Armstrong knew more about the subject than he. Not only did Armstrong distinguish himself with the speed he had acquired on a telegraph key, but he knew everything about the latest changes in technology and the state of current investigations. Rather than regard Armstrong as a threat, Arendt encouraged him to make his own way with his research.

Arendt's colleague John H. Morecroft, an instructor in the alternating current laboratory, immediately earned Armstrong's respect. Just nine years his senior, Morecroft had studied at Syracuse and at Columbia under Pupin. Before he took his alternating current course with Morecroft in his senior year, Armstrong began to frequent the laboratory. With the older man's experience to guide him and Columbia's sensitive equipment to give him accurate measurements, Armstrong began a series of experiments with the currents leaving the vacuum tube at the plate circuit, which would have far-reaching consequences.

The faculty member who influenced Armstrong most profoundly was the leading researcher of the electrical engineering department, Michael Pupin. A Serbian immigrant, Pupin stood as an example to all in the early twentieth century of what one might do with one's talents in the United States. Born of intelligent though illiterate peasants in the village of Idvor on the frontier of Austria-Hungary, Pupin lived as a sheepherder before he emigrated to the United States at the age of fifteen. Arriving at Castle Garden in New York Harbor with just five pennies in his pocket and knowing no one save "Franklin, Lincoln, and Harriet Beecher Stowe" (words that purportedly impressed the immigration officer who questioned him), he set out to make his way in the New World. Through assiduous study and extraordinary industry, he passed the entrance examinations and received a full scholarship to study at Columbia College. There Pupin's physical strength, athletic prowess, and intelligence enabled him to advance among the socially prominent undergraduates. After study with the finest minds in physics at Cambridge and Berlin, including Hertz's mentor Hermann von Helmholtz, he returned to Columbia as a teacher of mathematical physics in its new electrical engineering department. Success also came to Pupin as an inventor. His creation of the Pupin coil in the late nineties stepped up the force of electricity in a telephone circuit and improved the clarity and distance of conversations. That and other telephone, wireless, and X-ray inventions had made him a millionaire. He built a large estate, patterned on a medieval Serbian landlord's home, in Norfolk, Connecticut, maintained an apartment on Park Avenue in New York, and enjoyed substantial influence with Andrew Carnegie and other men of great wealth. Students were used to seeing Pupin's Rolls Royce, tended by a chauffeur, parked on 116th Street in front of Low Library.

Yet to his students, it was not the trappings of success that made Pupin popular; it was his intelligence, his energy, and the force of his personality. He worked at the edge of the infant science of electromagnetic waves, studying and evaluating new discoveries as they appeared in the literature and making several important ones himself. Pupin was often at the center of intense controversy and himself responsible for many of the developments his students were then learning. Late in the previous century, he had enjoined the bitter dispute between the forces of Edison and Westinghouse over electric power distribution by direct or alternating current. While Edison and powerful interests in New York favored the first, Pupin courageously advocated alternating current because of its superiority. After Roentgen discovered the X-ray late in 1895, Pupin succeeded in taking the first X-ray photograph in America two weeks later. Then he made the invention a practical tool of medicine by reducing a patient's exposure time for a photograph from almost an hour to a few seconds.

Most of all, students and colleagues respected Pupin's reverence for the study of pure science. Like Milton, whom it was his habit to quote, he regarded science as "divine philosophy," a moral philosophy on the order of Plato. Yet at the same time, sailing against the currents of pedagogy then in vogue, he stressed laboratory work over study of abstract theory as the best way for his students to learn of the forces in the world. To all he imparted two precepts. First, the science of electricity is "one of the most exact of all physical sciences, one that follows precise physical laws, not just 'rules of thumb.' " And, second, on its abstract side, science is "poetry . . . a food which nourishes not only the material but the spiritual body of man."

In his junior year, Armstrong took Pupin's course in electrical theory. In class, he distinguished himself with ready answers to all Pupin's questions about the history of electrical discoveries. Pupin began to take notice of this curious and obviously talented youth.

Columbia had just made Pupin head of its new research laboratory in the basement of Philosophy Hall. Named in honor of its donor, Marcellus Hartley, the laboratory contained the latest electrical equipment and an elegant, walnut-paneled office decorated with pictures of Pupin's masters, Faraday, Maxwell, and Ampere. Here Pupin carried out his current investigations of wireless. In crucial ways, his inquiries began to parallel those of his quiet and intense student.

Being a full-time student at Columbia enabled Armstrong to engage his investigations of wireless with even more fervor. John Morecroft's laboratory had an oscillograph with which to chart the flow of electrons through a de Forest audion tube, while his Yonkers workroom possessed all the components necessary for conducting experiments with new electric circuits.

Though Lee de Forest had invented the three-element tube late in 1906, his public statements clearly indicated that he did not understand how it worked. The very name he gave it, "audion"—an amalgam of "audio" and "ionized"—suggested his essential mistake. De Forest believed that the flow of current depended not on a high vacuum of gas from the bulb, but on the ionization of gases within it. In the passage of electrons from the filament through the grid to the plate, he supposed, the gas atoms lost their negative electric charge. Thinking the tube's "sensitiveness" to diminish "if the exhausting process were carried too far," de Forest actually experimented with introducing a number of different gasses into the bulb to determine if one might not increase its strength as a detector. None worked. He was forced to conclude in a later patent application that he was "unable to explain this action of the audion." As late as 1915, he stated "the behavior of different bulbs varies in many particulars, and to an astonishing degree. . . . What may appear to be a fixed law for one bulb may not hold for another."

Because no one knew how the tubes functioned, no standards existed for their manufacture. Lacking specifications to follow, Henry McCandless changed the design from time to time to save manufacturing costs. If a tube worked well, it was marked "grade X," and de Forest charged more for it; all others were marked "grade S." To a customer who complained that his order for the better tube had not been filled, de Forest wrote: "X grade Audion bulbs cannot be willfully made, but simply occur in the testing process and so their supply is beyond our control." Because the tubes cost $5, their quality was erratic, and their life short, few used them except for experiments. More often than not, serious experimenters chose the two-element Fleming tube over the de Forest audion because the Fleming tube did not require the critical adjustments of the grid to give off a proper plate voltage. The average wireless operator employed a solid-state crystal as the detector rather than a tube, as the crystal was unquestionably more dependable, usually gave better results, never wore out, and was cheaper.

Even in 1911, five years after its invention, no one understood precisely how de Forest's audion worked. Armstrong set out with the help of John Morecroft—and Columbia's sophisticated testing equipment—to investigate its operation.

Early in 1912, the results of his investigations led Armstrong to some dramatic conclusions. The audion was essentially a device that relayed electrons. Careful measurements of the current emanating from the plate element of the tube to the earphones revealed that it oscillated in a steady, uninterrupted rhythm. Acting on his discovery, Armstrong then thought of feeding the oscillating current flowing from the plate back into the grid circuit to have it amplified over again. He reasoned that as electrons move at the speed of light, he might feed the current through the grid many thousands of times a second, each time increasing the signal that had been received by the antenna. No longer would the audion be a simple detector of electromagnetic waves; with this process the tube would be an amplifier of signals.

Armstrong's challenge in the spring and summer of 1912 was to make a circuit capable of achieving such a result. That summer, he went with his family to Lake Bomaseen in Vermont, climbed mountains, swam, and played tennis, all the while meditating on his problem. While climbing a mountain that August, he had an idea, and he returned to his bedroom in Yonkers as soon as possible to try it out. On the night of September 22, he awakened his sister Ethel, shouting, "I've done it! I've done it!" She got up to hear the loud noise of dots and dashes coming through the earphones. As he had expected, the proof of his theory was astounding.

"Great amplification obtained at once," Armstrong noted in an account of his elegant invention some years later. The circuit Armstrong devised used electrical currents in the antenna as well as those in the vacuum tube. Marconi had discovered long before that the tiny current picked up by an antenna could be increased if the antenna were grounded. Later, researchers found that the addition of a coil to the antenna and a secondary tuning coil leading to the vacuum tube created a still stronger current flowing into the tube. Armstrong placed a coil in the wing circuit, that is, in the path of the current flowing from the plate to the earphones, and located it near the secondary coil of the tuner. As the electrons flowed through the wing circuit, they set up an electromagnetic field of alternating current that joined with the field of electrons flowing through the secondary coil of the tuner.

"Energy from the wing circuit is transferred freely to the grid circuit and the oscillations build up therein and are rectified in the usual way," Armstrong laconically wrote several years after he had made his invention. From the start, the results astounded all who heard them. Weak signals never detected before now came in with remarkable clarity. Dots and dashes from the Marconi station at Clifden, Ireland—always a test for wireless receivers on the Atlantic coast—were heard plainly, as were those from Honolulu. Armstrong soon found that his circuit freed listeners from the tyranny of earphones, too. Designed to grip the head so tightly as to exclude other sounds—and circulation to the brain—they could be positively painful to wear. With the addition of a small telephone speaker, stations heretofore received weakly or not at all could be heard across his work room and even on the second floor of the house.

"Feedback" or "regeneration," as the principle of Armstrong's circuit came to be known, unshackled the potential of the vacuum tube. Now de Forest's invention would have a place in almost every piece of electronic equipment, from the simple wireless sets and telephone systems of the day to the complex radar, television, and early computers of the future. Even today, when the vacuum tube has given way to the transistor, and the transistor to the integrated circuit, Armstrong's principle of regeneration has remained basic to electronics.

Armstrong's inquiries about the potential of regeneration did not stop with his discovery of its application to the amplification abilities of the vacuum tube. In the same account about his finding of regeneration on September 22, he wrote: "Noticed peculiar change in tone just as maximum amplification was obtained. Signals changed from clear to hissing . . ." The hissing was part of his second major finding of the circuit's capabilities: under proper circumstances, regeneration could make the vacuum tube into a transmitter of wireless signals.

For many years, researchers had realized the limitations of a Marconi spark gap transmitter; it was adequate only for sending the intermittent signals of the Morse code. The undulations of voices and musical notes required a continuous electromagnetic wave to carry them through the air. Furthermore, the machinery was so noisy that it usually had to be kept apart from the telegraph operator in another room.

Early in the century, two people developed machines to generate continuous waves: Valdemar Poulsen and Reginald Aubrey Fessenden. Poulsen, a scientist from Denmark, had noticed that the flame created by two carbon rod electrodes in an arc lamp pulsated as a continuous wave. From this observation, he developed transmitters able to carry voices. But the waves were unstable and the machines, though widely used, were never wholly satisfactory.

Fessenden enjoyed greater success. As early as 1900 he had turned his thoughts to the alternating current generator, the same type of generator Nikola Tesla had installed at Niagara Falls, to create current for electric lighting and machinery. If the alternator speed could be increased to generate waves of 100,000 cycles per second, Fessenden reasoned, the resulting high frequency electromagnetic waves could carry sounds of voices and music. He turned to Charles Steinmetz of the General Electric Company to create the generator.

One of the foremost experts in electrical engineering, Steinmetz had formulated the law of hysteresis, the Greek word for "deficiency," that engineers used to account for the loss of efficiency in the magnetic circuit of electric motors. This law, along with Steinmetz's calculation of the properties of alternating current, made the electrification of the nation practical. The American writer John Dos Passos suggested that Steinmetz was the most valuable piece of apparatus General Electric had. The company realized it too, tolerating his regimen of about 500 cigars a month, despite strict rules forbidding tobacco. But Steinmetz could not produce the alternator Fessenden had asked for. Its speed was limited to 4,000 revolutions per minute—beyond that the armature began to fly apart—and the electromagnetic waves of 10,000 cycles per second it generated were incapable of carrying sounds properly.

Fessenden did not give up. "With very much reluctance," and with the assurance that Fessenden would pay for the costs of development, General Electric accepted another order for an alternator in 1904; this time it would create waves of 100,000 cycles per second. Steinmetz enlisted Ernst Alexanderson, a recently hired immigrant from Sweden, to help him. "The alternator," Alexanderson was fond of saying later, "was one of the inventions I had to make in order to hold my job."

That job demanded Alexanderson employ all his skills and ingenuity as a designer in cooperation with all the resources of General Electric. The new alternator he designed had a stationary armature on which rotated a tapered disc. Resembling a gargantuan discus, the disc created an alternating current as it revolved in the strong magnetic field of the armature. At its operating speed of 20,000 revolutions per minute, producing a current of 100,000 cycles per second, the speed at the disc's periphery was an incredible 700 miles an hour. Yet because of its ingenious design, it wobbled no more than three-hundredths of an inch. Alexanderson had succeeded in realizing Fessenden's revolutionary concept. Soon there would be huge 200-kilowatt alternators capable of hurling the sound of a human voice across a continent or an ocean.

In the early fall of 1906, Alexanderson's alternator arrived at Fessenden's station at Brant Rock, Massachusetts. Soon he was transmitting voices in tests, and by Christmas Eve, he was ready to give his first broadcast. That night, ship operators and amateurs around Brant Rock heard the results: "someone speaking! . . . a woman's voice rose in song. . . . Next someone was heard reading a poem." Fessenden himself played "O Holy Night" on his violin. Though the fidelity was not all that it might be, listeners were captivated by the voices and notes they heard. No more would sounds be restricted to mere dots and dashes of the Morse code.

Fessenden was in the forefront of the entirely new concept of "broadcasting," the agricultural term for spreading seed across a field. For the most part, a wireless transmission had been a coded telegraph message directed to a single person. Because it traveled on waves through the air and could be heard by anyone with a receiver tuned to the proper frequency, the message could never be private. This was viewed as the chief drawback of wireless systems. Now Fessenden was exploiting the public character of the medium by sending words of a general nature to a broad audience. To accommodate this new concept, the word "wireless" soon gave way to "radio," suggesting the rays of electromagnetic waves radiating from a transmitter.

Soon others, including Lee de Forest, were sending voices rather than code. Amateurs, too, were creating continuous waves for such transmissions, but only with limited success. While Fessenden's and Alexanderson's mechanical generator worked acceptably, its cost to manufacture and maintain—as well as its gargantuan size—limited its use to stations with large resources. A more compact generator was still needed.

The "peculiar" hissing or whistling Armstrong had noticed just at the point he was obtaining the maximum amplification from his vacuum tube augured an invention of far-reaching significance in the quest for a generator of continuous waves. In the fall of 1912, he turned to Frank L. Mason, a Columbia graduate of 1909 and an instructor in the instrument laboratory, for equipment with which he might measure the mysterious noises. His experiments led him to conclude that the tube was putting forth radio waves of its own, and if controlled properly, it could be a powerful transmitter as well as a receiver of continuous waves. In the early part of 1913, he modified the circuitry to make it generate continuous waves. What formerly required a machine the size of a squash court to produce now took a comparatively small vacuum tube. Armstrong's circuit had solved the problem of creating a continuous wave by substituting the power of the indiscernible electron for the force of the brute machine. We may trace modern radio reception and transmission as we know them today to Armstrong's invention.

During the fall and winter of 1912–13, as Armstrong worked hard exploring the potential of his new invention, he appeared driven by a peculiar demon, thinking of little else but his work. His classmates and professors found him remote, private, and uncommunicative, increasingly reluctant to discuss his ideas about wireless. Indeed, he rarely bothered to submit them even to the quiet secrecy of a laboratory notebook. When professors and those in a position to give him counsel did offer advice, Armstrong listened, but only diffidently. Such traits were ingrained and became even more so when he faced the vicissitudes of lawsuits that occupied so much of his career.

Rumination—obsessive rumination—was the only way Armstrong could solve a problem. He had to give it his complete attention and talk about it with no one else. He had to keep his thoughts to himself lest he make extravagant claims. This he had done that summer at Lake Bomaseen, Vermont, as he considered the regenerative receiver. Now his mind was occupied with thoughts of a continuous wave generator, but he told no one and wrote nothing until he was certain his new invention would work.

Beneath the intricacies of Armstrong's character lay a simplistic view of life that made him no match for the modern world of invention and business. Part of his view had been formed by his secure family life; part by the learned and generous Underhill; and part by Baker's and Doubleday's stories.

The differences between the character and inventive practice of de Forest and Armstrong are striking: de Forest was extroverted and gregarious; Armstrong was introverted and shy. De Forest read voraciously in the technical literature searching for new ideas; Armstrong read technical literature, but to learn rather than pillage. De Forest liberated ideas from others and adapted them for his own purposes; Armstrong generated ideas himself that often stunned the art. De Forest kept copious notes of his experiments; Armstrong kept almost none. Raised in comparative poverty, de Forest thought of radio as a way of achieving money, fame, and success; raised in relative comfort, Armstrong thought of it solely as his life's work.

For a while that fall, Armstrong said nothing of his invention to fellow students and professors at Columbia. On December 7, he confided in Herman Burgi, a close friend and classmate interested in electric motors and transformers, that "he had made a connection for intensifying sound," information Burgi thought important enough to record in his diary. Two days later, Armstrong told him he had heard Clifden. He then began to drop hints of what he was hearing to his professors, especially Morecroft, Mason, and Arendt. Arendt advised him to take out a patent immediately.

Had Armstrong made a patent application in September 1912, and had he made claim for all the regenerative circuit's potential applications, he might not have been plagued by litigation later in his life. Not having the $150 for the legal fees, he turned to his father for help. But John Armstrong refused. The patent could wait until his son had graduated; then his father would pay.

Why neither father nor son thought to seek advice from a lawyer is something of a mystery too. They would have had to look no further than to their neighbor, Thomas Ewing, whose property lay close to the Armstrongs'. Well known to all in Yonkers, he was an eminent patent attorney, whom President Wilson was about to appoint commissioner of the United States Patent Office. Ewing knew of Howard's interest in radio and quite possibly of his recent experiments, for that September he had given the inventor permission to anchor guy wires for his antenna on Ewing's property. Later Ewing would represent Armstrong's interests in his suit with de Forest over the discovery of regeneration. Characteristically, Armstrong said nothing of his invention to his neighbor at this time.

Desperate for money, Armstrong sold his motorcycle and asked his uncle, Frank Smith, to loan him the balance. Smith could not help him either. However, he sagely advised him to take a sketch of his circuit to a notary public. On January 31, 1913, four months after he had awakened his sister, he and Burgi stopped by a real estate office on Lenox Avenue at 123rd Street. With Burgi serving as witness, Edwin Howard Armstrong paid 25 cents to have the first diagram he had *ever* made of his regenerative circuit notarized.

After that act, word of Armstrong's powerful receiver soon got about the neighborhood. Friends climbed to his third-floor room at 1032 Warburton for a demonstration. Tom Styles came down from Hastings-on-Hudson, Randy Runyon stopped by, and Charles Underhill journeyed to Yonkers from his new home in New Haven. Soon the news spread to members of the Radio Club of America, which Armstrong had recently joined. Leo P. Lang, a wireless amateur in the Bronx, listened in February 1913 in the company of a Mr. Royce and a Mr. Wallace. The signals were "of much greater intensity" than he had ever heard before, especially those from Key West "in all parts of the room and after further adjustment of the apparatus . . . on other floors of the house." All the time Armstrong carefully kept his receiver out of sight. "During the operation of the apparatus, particularly during certain adjustment of the set," Lang later remembered, "a hiss appeared during the reception of signals and . . . the usual musical tone of the signals was lost and changed."

Growing curious as to what Armstrong was doing, his instructor Frank Mason visited his home on March 12, 1913, to witness a demonstration.

Armstrong "disclosed and explained" to his professor the various "electrical connections and details," Mason remembered. Signals came in from the various spark stations up and down the coast, and the continuous wave of telephone signals were "clear notes." Then Armstrong made the tube "oscillate . . . so that signals received came in with a hiss." Mason listened into the night as his student gave cryptic explanations of the theory involved and of what he was achieving.

Next to come was Professor Morton Arendt. Armstrong brought in San Francisco; Pensacola, Florida; and Arlington, Virginia. Enthusiastic about what he was hearing, Arendt suggested the oscillations of the tube might be used as a transmitter. Ever secretive, his student evaded the suggestion by answering he was only interested in receivers.

Arendt thought enough of what he heard that evening to direct Armstrong to William H. Davis. The appearance of the two suggested a mismatch. A short, stocky man whose most distinctive feature was his unruly dark hair, Davis looked decidedly different from Armstrong, who at six feet towered over his counsel, and was beginning to go bald. Arendt's advice proved excellent. Though just eleven years Armstrong's senior, Davis had extensive training in the specialized field of patent law. He had become interested in the field while working as a stenographer for his brother, A. G. Davis, who headed General Electric's patent department in Washington. Soon he decided to study at the Corcoran Scientific School and then worked for a year as an examiner in the U.S. Patent Office. After graduating from George Washington Law School, he joined the foremost patent law firm in New York, Betts, Betts, Sheffield, and Betts. Now a junior partner at another prestigious New York firm, Pennie and Goldsborough, Davis had filed patents for Arendt and Pupin and other members of the electrical engineering department, and also served as an adjunct member of the faculty at Columbia.

Before he could meet with Davis, however, Armstrong had to concentrate on graduating from Columbia. For the last eight months, almost all his thinking had been directed to his invention. That spring, he managed to pass all his courses, and though some faculty members still harbored resentments about his attitude toward their courses and his unorthodox and extracurricular experiments in the university laboratories, Army Armstrong was graduated on June 13, 1913. Pupin assured him an appointment as an assistant to teach a navy class in wireless for $600 a year. More important than the money was the access he would have to a well-equipped laboratory.

When Armstrong did get around to demonstrating his regeneration receiver to Davis that June, the lawyer told him to write up a description with claims and file for a patent as soon as possible. Though he received the advice in June, he did not make application until October 29, 1913. The delay was caused by his deliberateness and his commitment to spend some time with his family. Even then, Armstrong made a crucial mistake: he failed to disclose to his lawyer the transmitting abilities of his circuit. His patent described "new and useful improvements in wireless receiving systems"; each of the eighteen claims he made was for "an audion wireless receiving system."

Armstrong's omission was a foolish and costly error. It suggests a combination of youthful inexperience and his characteristic distrust of anyone he did not know intimately, even the lawyer he had engaged to represent his interests. Later in his career, he would develop close personal friendships with his attorneys and confide in them, but not yet. Within a few months, his mistake would redound upon him, and it would continue to do so for the rest of his life. Unwittingly, Armstrong had written the opening scene of a tragedy of many acts in which he would be the chief protagonist.

"You are certainly getting astounding results, and it seems to me that the invention ought to be worth a lot of money," Davis wrote Armstrong. "I feel great responsibility in connection with the patent end of the invention, and think you ought to keep your eyes wide open to see any indications that may point to the importance of features other than those covered in your application." On December 18, 1913, Armstrong made his second patent application, this time for a circuit that used the vacuum tube as a generator of continuously oscillating electromagnetic waves—the basic circuit of a radio transmitter. This was the circuit that changed forever the way radio waves are created and rendered the arc transmitters and huge Alexanderson alternators obsolete.

For a time, all went well with the young instructor. He earned the pride of his father, John Armstrong. "They call him a wizard," he wrote to his daughter Edith at Vassar. His supporters among his former professors now were his good colleagues. A proud Pupin showed him off to engineers from the Marconi Company and American Telephone and Telegraph. It was only a question of time before he would be able to sell his patent at a considerable profit. Best of all, he had the run of a laboratory in which he could continue his experiments. An unclouded future filled with great promise of research, invention, and even money lay before him.

On the night of November 4, 1913, Lee de Forest visited Morningside Heights to present a paper on "The Audion Amplifier" to the Institute of Radio Engineers—another new organization formed by professors, inventors, and impassioned amateurs to further understanding of the art. After his talk, he met Armstrong, word of whose receiver had reached him. It was a meeting born of distrust, which began a lifelong relationship of intense animosity and obsessive vindictiveness.

In the nearly seven years that had passed since his invention, de Forest's life had been filled with romance, a second marriage and parenthood, a bitter second divorce, a third marriage, the creation of six companies (five of which had gone bankrupt), a costly and time-consuming defense in federal court against charges of fraud, but little in the way of understanding his audion or creating other useful discoveries.

By the first day of 1907, de Forest's romantic life, which had reached its nadir with his disastrous liaison with Lucille Sheardown, rebounded gloriously. "Now Fate, mocking the wild plans of men has brought *Her* to my door!" he exulted in his diary on January 1. This time, Fate had contrived to bring him Nora Stanton Blatch, granddaughter of Elizabeth Cady Stanton, who lived with her mother in the apartment next door to his. "Propinquity had brought acquaintance," he remarked many years later. Possessed of a fine singing voice, good looks, and a "rare *soul quality*," Nora Blatch commingled "maidenly reserve with a whole-hearted frankness, mental gifts of a rare degree with all the glad enthusiasms of wholesome, beautiful, girlish nature." At last, de Forest thought, he had found his golden girl.

De Forest was right in his assessment, though some of the qualities in Nora that he now praised would come to bother him acutely in the coming months. A Cornell graduate, she was the first woman in the United States to hold a degree in civil engineering. At the time they met, she was working for the New York City water department, designing an aqueduct and leading a life modeled on the example of her grandmother. Though Nora had been named for the heroine of Ibsen's *Doll's House*, de Forest often called her "Eleonora" after the heroine of Poe's eponymous tale. "I am come of a race noted for vigor of fancy and ardor of passion," begins Poe's Eleonora. The role Nora played, however, was Ibsen's. She protested, marched, often flaunted convention, and campaigned for women's suffrage and equality with a spirit that he first admired but gradually came to loathe.

Shortly after they met, the inventor revealed for Nora the bright future of wireless communication, a world "framed by new & boundless horizons," and disclosed some of his plans to create a new company manufacturing a radio telephone. Enthralled by his vision, she left her job with the water department, enrolled in Michael Pupin's classes in electromagnetism at Columbia, and planned a new professional life with her husband-to-be. She would be his "complete companion" and as proficient in the art as he.

Nora and Lee's plan, developed in love letters each slipped under the door of the other's apartment every evening, was to work together in the new De Forest Radio Telephone Company, which he was organizing with about $400 gathered from his Yale classmates and additional capital from the father of a sixteen-year-old youth who wished to learn about radio, John V. L. Hogan. For the new company they planned "grand years of labor & achievement, of accomplishing the good & winning the beautiful in life & the world." But lack of capital from his small circle of backers limited the scope of his experiments and plans. De Forest resorted to stock sales once again, this time incorporating yet another venture, the Radio Telephone Company, and hiring James Dunlop Smith, one of Abraham White's outstanding salesmen, to be its president.

What de Forest called the "radio telephone" closely resembled radio as we know it today. Five years earlier, in May 1902, he had told Abraham White that "ultimately, wireless *telephony* will be possible through the medium of Hertzian waves" and urged that the De Forest Wireless Telegraph Company take out broad patents on the idea. White had never replied, but de Forest now had a chance to realize this new concept. While Fessenden had sent messages and music to wireless operators aboard ships on Christmas Eve, de Forest would make general broadcasts for all to hear. He acquired a Poulsen arc generator capable of creating waves of radio frequency, set it up in the company's new laboratory atop the Parker Building at Fourth Avenue and 19th Street, and began transmissions that anyone with a receiver tuned to the proper frequency might hear. It was "another bound into the radical future," he wrote to Nora on the last day of February 1907, and he felt his mind floating like a cockleshell in some unknown sea, "drawn by the possibilities, buffeted by the perplexities" of this new method of communication. In the future, he would play more music and opera over a phonograph, advertise audion tubes and other radio equipment he sold, present a suffragist speech by his mother-in-law Harriot Stanton Blatch, and broadcast live from the stage of the Metropolitan Opera the tenor Enrico Caruso singing in *I Pagliacci*.

De Forest placed his emphasis on broadcasting culture to the masses. He had been the outsider, the boy from rural Alabama, the penurious undergraduate voted the homeliest at Yale. Now he would be able to reach other outsiders, transmitting music and cultural entertainment to ordinary people. "I look forward to the day when opera may be brought into every home. Some day the news and even advertising will be sent out over the wireless telephone." Thirteen years before KDKA made its first broadcast, de Forest had conceived a radical idea and in his own unpolished way was realizing his dream by broadcasting his programs to the few listeners about the city who had the equipment to hear him.

However, de Forest's concept of the radio telephone was far ahead of the technological abilities of the equipment he sold. The same *New York Times* article that reported Caruso's singing also complained that the sound was "not clearly audible to the reporters who were summoned to hear it." De Forest was learning the same thing from people who wrote him about their reception. "I heard your music yesterday and also speech, but there was so much interference I could not get what was said," one listener complained. "The music seemed to have a whine which did not respond much to tuning."

De Forest's first customers were those who realized the possibilities of two-way radio communication rather than broadcasting. Equipment was installed in a ferryboat on the Hudson and its terminals at Hoboken and Manhattan. The U.S. Navy hastily installed twenty-six De Forest radio telephone sets on the ships of its "Great White Fleet" for its tour of goodwill and might around the world; the signal corps built two stations. In February 1908, de Forest and his wife played phonograph records before a microphone and transmitter atop the Eiffel Tower that were heard in Marseilles, 400 miles away. While in Europe, he installed sets in Italian and British warships. Beneath all the surface glitter and attendant publicity, these accomplishments were meager. Navy signalmen, who had little training with the new equipment, found that Fessenden's electrolyte detector worked just as well as the audion and didn't burn out. Halfway through their journey, after transmitting only the sounds of phonograph records and occasionally a ship's band, and after failing at many attempts to signal other ships, the seamen reverted to their old equipment. When the fleet returned to Brooklyn, the equipment was stored away at the navy yard.

Compounding de Forest's troubles was the lack of capital for his company. Serious investors had grown wary of any wireless stock offering, and for good reason. In June 1907, *Success Magazine*—a turn-of-the-century equivalent to *Money*—had published a series of articles on the "Wireless Telegraph Bubble." Pictures of White and de Forest appeared beneath a cartoon depicting powerful electromagnetic waves drawing cash from the pockets of naive investors. Nothing but a fraud, the author declared of the various wireless schemes, and though men like Marconi and de Forest were "honest, hardworking geniuses," they had fallen prey to "unscrupulous promoters." With such press, even the creative salesman James Dunlop Smith found it difficult to raise the necessary capital.

Lacking a commercial base for radio telephone sales, Smith, de Forest, and the directors of the company resorted to the methods that had worked so well for Abraham White and that *Success* had condemned: establish more companies, set up demonstration stations, generate publicity, and sell stock to the gullible. This time shareholders received modest dividends in the beginning, which encouraged more purchases. First came the Great Lakes Radio Telephone Company in 1908, capitalized at $1 million. In the next year, the directors created the Atlantic Radio Telephone Company and the Pacific

Radio Company, each capitalized at $2.5 million. They circulated a song to boost the spirits of the stock salesmen:

> Then "Hello! Hello!" on the wireless phone.
> The good old radio.
> It is working fine all along the line
> From Chicago to Buffalo.
> Oh! you cannot guess what a great success
> Is the wonderful radio wireless telephone.

An article in *Modern Electrics*, a new magazine devoted to the bright future of electricity, reported that "over 100 wireless men" attended a banquet in de Forest's honor at New York's "historic Fraunces' Tavern." Other stories described in optimistic terms the strings of stations the de Forest companies would erect from Portland to Pensacola; New Orleans to Galveston; Chicago to Sheboygan; Mackinaw to Buffalo. Despite the bold promises to erect scores of stations, only eleven operated fitfully on the Great Lakes, five on the Atlantic, and none on the West Coast.

Concurrent with the fluctuations in the fortunes of the various companies were the fluctuations in Lee de Forest's romantic life. By May 1907, Nora and her mother were entertaining second thoughts about the efficacy of the match, and it was not until mid-February 1908 that they "yielded at last." Some of the doubts were generated by Mrs. Blatch, who never seemed far from her daughter's side. Nora had even spent the first night of her marriage, February 24, 1907, in her mother's apartment, while de Forest languished next door. Not until the next evening was the couple able to slip away to a hotel. The following morning, they sailed to Europe on the *Carmania* to demonstrate de Forest equipment to the British, French, Germans, and Italians. For de Forest, it was the "beginning of a new life, united and one in heart, in mind, and soul in a happiness . . . that deepens thru each night of impassioned companionship." Company business called de Forest home in June, while Nora remained to visit her birthplace in Basingstoke, England, and to visit manufacturers of wireless apparatus in Germany. In September, he returned to be with his wife and accompany her home on the *Lusitania*. As the ship entered New York harbor late that October, the suffragist made headlines by unfurling from its bow a banner that boldly proclaimed in purple and green letters on a white background, "Votes for Women."

"I know I'd never tire of living with you, nay not for one thousand years," Nora had declared in a letter to her husband that summer while they were apart. Their conjugal state seemed even more assured when they learned in the fall that she was expecting a child. But early the next year, she left him.

Part of the couple's incompatibility arose from Nora's abilities as an engineer, her understanding of the fraud being perpetrated by the management of the De Forest Radio Telephone Company, and her insistence on work—and independence. Possessed of an insatiable appetite for learning and formidable mental powers, she presented something of a challenge to de Forest when she mastered so quickly and completely the latest theories of electricity, electronics, and radio. The tension between the two increased because she wanted to use the knowledge she had acquired from Pupin and in Germany to oversee the manufacture of equipment in the Radio Telephone Company's Newark factory.

De Forest wanted only that his wife raise their child and preside over their house. To keep her away from Newark he began construction of a large house, "Riverlure—where dreams come true," high above the Hudson at Spuyten Duyvil in the Bronx. De Forest conceived it as "a nest for the nestlings," but Nora saw it as Ibsen's doll's house in which her husband might isolate his wife and family from the world. She would have nothing to do with living there. Refusing to abandon her professional life and the electrical engineering laboratory for motherhood and the home, she left her husband to live with her mother in Milford, New Jersey. When their daughter, Harriot Stanton de Forest, was born on June 19, 1909, Mrs. Blatch informed her estranged son-in-law by telephone. In the coming months, she and her daughter would do their best to keep him from the child.

Nora was also troubled by the management of the radio telephone companies and especially by its president, James Dunlop Smith. While de Forest remained willfully ignorant of the fiscal operation, Nora saw clearly that it was based on gross deception. The fraud became manifest late in 1909, when Smith told a meeting of directors that the four companies had amassed $40,000 in debts and were bankrupt. It turned out that Smith, like Abraham White and Christopher Columbus Wilson, had diverted the money accrued from stock sales into his own pockets. Persuaded by Elmer E. Burlingame, a stock salesman and director, de Forest and the remaining directors decided to merge the companies into yet another venture—the North American Wireless Corporation, capitalized for $10 million. Burlingame became the new president.

De Forest spent much of the next year on the West Coast, as far from his failing marriage, his dominating mother-in-law, and his foundering North American Wireless Corporation as possible. For the most part, he did what he liked best, tinkering and experimenting with electrical equipment, writing poetry about the landscape, walking on the beaches, and climbing in the mountains. At Seattle and the port in San Francisco, he installed radio telephone equipment on navy transports. When he did return to the East, he spent most of his time making experimental broadcasts from a new studio atop the Metropolitan Building on lower Broadway.

The imminent dissolution of his marriage and North American Wireless forced de Forest once again to face the fact that money, success, fame, and secure home life were mere illusions. Early in 1911, he returned to New York to resign from his job with the corporation and begin divorce proceedings with Nora. Impressed by the potential of his audion and de Forest's ideas for long-distance communication, Cyril Elwell, president of the Federal Telegraph Company in San Francisco, had offered him a job. California, the state of "freedom and progressiveness," would be the perfect venue for him to exercise his genius and build his dreams once again.

Before he went west, de Forest decided to spend spring and summer with his daughter. Nora reluctantly consented to his visits. Each morning, he showed up at Nora's apartment on West 91st Street after she went to work at her new engineering job to spend the day with Harriot. As the summer progressed, he fell deeper into a self-flagellating depression about his plight. "I was *born to be robbed* . . . robbed of . . . the best of college associations . . . social influences . . . opportunities to invent . . . robbed of the fruits of my years of toil (twice robbed there)." Thinking of his estranged wife and family, he continued histrionically, "robbed of my wife . . . of a house and a home . . . and now . . . robbed of so much of my Baby's life, her daily growth in charm and love—her first companionship." To complete his despair, he turned blindly inward. "Surely something is wrong with my character, some vital lack there must be," he wrote in his diary. But ever fearful of examining himself directly, he returned to his refuge of self-pity: "I have permitted myself always to be thus defrauded and despoiled."

Though de Forest's tenure with the Federal Telegraph Company had been short, his work in Palo Alto had been full and enjoyable, and his life pleasant. He had established telegraph communication between San Francisco and Los Angeles, created a diplex system of telegraphy that enabled two telegraphers to transmit simultaneously over a single wire, and adapted the audion to amplify electrons as they flowed through long distance telephone lines. His mother, who had moved to Iowa after he and Charles were graduated from Yale, now joined him in Palo Alto, but the irresistible forces of a new love and the enticement of new riches lured de Forest back to the East Coast.

De Forest's next golden girl was another singer, whom he first heard in October 1912, when on a business trip to New York. With a friend, he attended a performance of the *Quaker Girl*, a musical comedy playing at the Grand Opera House in New York. Immediately he was captivated by one of the buxom chorus girls, Mary Mayo, especially the "very unusual quality . . . pitch . . . and birdlike purity" of her voice. Two days before Christmas, they married and headed for California. Hearing her "soft, rich, voice" sent de Forest into ecstasy. "My heart, happy at last, sings in tune," he exclaimed in his journal within a month of their union.

Mary Mayo's singing career, which de Forest wanted her to continue, required that she be near her voice trainer in New York. When the inventor received an offer from a group of businessmen to return and develop his audion for the purpose of adding sound to motion pictures in April 1913, he quickly accepted. He ordered builders to complete Riverlure, his new home at Spuyten Duyvil, and had it filled with furniture he bought on credit.

Almost as soon as de Forest arrived, the money from the businessmen for talking pictures evaporated. No matter. Since October 1912, he had been negotiating with the American Telephone and Telegraph Company to sell his audion, and the price mentioned was as much as $100,000. Perhaps the company would come through with an offer. By late July 1913, when he had heard nothing from AT&T for several months, he received an offer to buy the rights for $50,000 from a lawyer representing an anonymous client. Only after he had consummated the deal did he learn he had been "robbed." The purchaser was AT&T. Nevertheless, the money gave him enough capital to start a new venture, the Radio Telegraph and Telephone Company, in December 1913. Soon he acquired a factory at High Bridge in the Bronx. There he would create his next fortune.

Marriage, leaving the employ of the Federal Telegraph Company, returning to New York, and starting a new business venture were bold moves for de Forest, especially as he made all of them under the broad shadow of an impending trial in federal district court on four counts of fraud.

The inevitable outcome of the meteoric crash of the radio telephone companies, indictments against Smith, Burlingame, de Forest and his lawyer, Samuel Darby, came at the end of March 1912. Stockholders who had watched their dividends stop and the value of their paper dwindle into worthlessness filed complaints with the federal authorities, for the federal mails had been used to perpetrate the fraud. They had good cause. Of the $1,507,505 of stock sold, only $345,694 went into the companies, while the rest went to the defendants and their agents.

The ugly and embarrassing trial, which did not commence until November 26, 1913, examined much of de Forest's life, many of his inventions, and the potential of the radio telephone. Though he could say with assurance that he had not enjoyed any direct personal gain from the stock sales, in his natural exuberance he had left a trail of paper that misrepresented the achievements of the company. More than a hundred witnesses "from nearly every state in the Union" revealed they had been duped by misleading stock offerings, deceptive claims about accomplishments, and false prophecies about future achievements. De Forest had sent a letter to his laboratory assistant urging him to stay close to a prospective stock buyer and "get the $1500. if you have to live with him." And he had signed it "Yours for the rocks." The Chicago station of the Great Lakes Company was supposed to have received a message from Paris and relayed it to the editorial room of the Milwaukee *Journal*. With de Forest's knowledge, the message had actually come from a telegraph station just four blocks from the newspaper.

At 1 A.M. on the first day of 1914, the jury announced it had found Smith and Burlingame guilty while Darby and de Forest were innocent. At word of the decision, "de Forest collapsed" in his lawyer's arms; it had been a close call. That morning, the *New York Times* reported the verdict on page 1. On the same page, an article told of a New Year's greeting the navy had sent from its powerful radio transmitters in Arlington, Virginia, to the Eiffel Tower, the Panama Canal, and Honolulu.

Lee de Forest had a great many matters pressing on him when he spoke to the Institute of Radio Engineers in November 1913. Years later, after decades of bitter dispute over the audion and its circuits, de Forest remembered the occasion as one in which he aroused "great astonishment and applause" among the audience. Using the audion in a circuit he had developed while working for the Federal Telegraph Company, he amplified the "crashing sounds" of a handkerchief dropping.

De Forest remembered also the details of his meeting with Armstrong that evening, but what actually transpired is open to question. He recalled that Armstrong "wrapped in deepest mystery" gave him and his assistant, C. V. Logwood, a demonstration of his new receiver, but kept his box of circuits concealed from sight in another room. " 'C. V.' and I thought we had a pretty fair idea what the young inventor had concealed in his box of mystery."

Very likely Armstrong was among the audience of the Institute of Radio Engineers, but it is unclear whether he even met de Forest then, and it is most unlikely that he gave a demonstration of his receiver that evening. In some fragmentary notes probably made early in the 1920s, Armstrong remembered he had met Logwood in the winter of 1913 when university business brought him to de Forest's High Bridge factory. A fellow employee, Elman Myers, had spoken to Logwood of the remarkable receiver, and Logwood was interested in learning more. On a subsequent visit on Columbia business to the factory, Armstrong met de Forest, "who became very inquisitive concerning the receiver." But, Armstrong continued, "I told him nothing whatever in regard to its nature." Perhaps warned by Pupin, who never liked de Forest, perhaps because the reputation of de Forest's suit with Fessenden preceded him, Armstrong became even more careful and circumspect than usual.

Whether or not he ever listened to the sounds of Armstrong's regenerative receiver in the basement of Philosophy Hall, de Forest had heard enough talk among members of the Institute of Radio Engineers to be chagrined and exasperated. Here was a young man seventeen years his junior and fresh out of college who had accomplished more with the de Forest audion than he had since he had conceived it in late 1906. Better than anything he had produced, Armstrong's working receiver would be worth a fortune. Just three months earlier, desperate for funds and facing the uncertainties of his impending trial for fraud, de Forest had been robbed of his rights for the general use of the audion (except in wireless telegraphy and telephony) for a mere $50,000.

Just as maddening to de Forest as the loss of a lucrative invention, one he had been so close to discovering for so many years, was the idea of young Armstrong himself. De Forest had known other formidable rivals—Marconi, Fessenden, Fleming—but they were about his age or older. Armstrong was a mere child whose quiet understatement of facts and reticence seemed so different from his own methods of operation. Armstrong also had a university education; but *he* was the true pioneer, the man who had produced the first doctoral dissertation on Hertzian waves, the first audion. Armstrong came from privileged circumstances; de Forest had had to scrape continually for money. There had been a job and well-equipped research laboratories waiting for Armstrong after his graduation with a mere bachelor's degree; de Forest had to strike out with his Ph.D. alone. Armstrong had never faced adversity, much less the rough and tumble of inventors fighting over rights. De Forest had; he did so now; he would prevail.

As the months wore on, de Forest would learn something else about his new rival: always meticulous in his research and scrupulous in his statements, Armstrong neither employed salesmanlike tactics nor made the extravagant claims that so characterized other radio entrepreneurs. His technical presentations before the Radio Club of America and the Institute of Radio Engineers, delivered with a studied and laconic understatement, stood as models of clarity, intelligence, and scientific method.

De Forest learned of this side of Armstrong's character in March 1915, when his rival delivered a paper entitled "Some Recent Developments in the Audion Receiver" to the Institute of Radio Engineers. Through a careful presentation of oscillograph measurements, Armstrong demonstrated the ways the audion could be used as a receiver and as a generator of oscillating waves. His studies showed that the audion could operate simultaneously as a rectifier and repeater of radio frequencies—that is, the "oscillations in the grid circuit set up oscillations of similar character in the wing circuit." No one before Armstrong had made use of that repeating action; instead they had used the audion as a simple detector. "In conclusion," Armstrong said in his final paragraph, "I want to point out that none of the methods of producing amplification or oscillation depend on a critical gas action." It was a statement that betrayed Armstrong's scornful contempt for the inventor of the three-element audion.

Such a caustic attack could not go unanswered, and the editors of the *Proceedings* were quick to ask de Forest for a response. De Forest steadfastly maintained that no oscillations could be found at the plate and that the oscillating characteristic of the audion did not depend on regeneration. More ominously for Armstrong, de Forest wrote: "As I stated in an article in the *Electrical World*, February 20th, the *oscillating* quality of the audion was discovered by me several years ago." This was the first salvo of a battle that would last for the rest of each inventor's life.

During 1914 and early 1915, Armstrong had negotiated with prospective buyers for rights to his regenerative circuit, for which he had been issued Patent 1,113,149 on October 6, 1914. The demonstrations to officials of the Marconi Company and American Telephone and Telegraph did not bring an offer for a license, nor did one to de Forest's old employer, the Federal Telegraph Company. It took war in Europe to bring him his first royalties. When the British cut the telegraph cables linking Germany and the United States, the Germans had to depend on wireless. Armstrong licensed his circuit to the Telefunken Company for $100 a month, an arrangement that lasted until the United States entered the war in April 1917.

At the same time that Armstrong was seeking a buyer for his invention, de Forest was frantically trying to find a regenerative circuit of his own. In March 1914, he applied for a patent on an "ultra-audion," which he claimed would do the work of Armstrong's circuit without duplicating it. However, when the patent examiner analyzed the diagrams accompanying the application carefully, he found beneath their twisted knots of confusion a regenerative circuit.

In September 1915, de Forest shifted tactics in his next patent application, this one for an "oscillating audion." Acknowledging that the invention involved regeneration, he claimed to have discovered it by chance in 1912. In making such a declaration, de Forest obviously was taking a bold risk. But he had little to lose, and if his gamble worked, he would be counted the man who had created not only the audion tube, but the circuit that made it work as a receiver and a transmitter. It would take nineteen years, interminable depositions, rulings in thirteen different courts, millions in legal fees, and, most damaging of all, ceaseless anger, before his bold move paid off.

De Forest filed his patent for the oscillating audion at a time when Armstrong was preoccupied with a more personal matter that shattered his tranquil innocence. That August of 1915, while swimming off Beach Haven, New Jersey, his father had died suddenly of a massive stroke. To the surprise of many in the family, John Armstrong, head of the American branch of the Oxford University Press, had left only a small legacy. They turned to Howard for spiritual and financial support. He would have to shoulder the burden of his mother's care and his younger sister's education, as well as the maintenance of the house in Yonkers. Confronted with these financial exigencies, his Columbia salary and royalties from Telefunken seemed meager indeed.

The import of de Forest's dark challenge to his patent on regeneration seems to have come on Armstrong slowly, and it signaled a different sort of assault on his innocence. No doubt he had heard stories from his mentors, Pupin, Morecroft, and Arendt, about such matters as litigation, and no doubt those tales contributed to his natural inclination to privacy and reticence. Now he had to face the litigation squarely. It was preposterous to think he might lose to a person who claimed to have made an invention three years before he had applied for a patent, yet the legal expenses would be formidable and impossible to meet when coupled with his family obligations.

In the fall of 1915, Pupin helped first with a loan of money and then by securing him an assistantship in the Marcellus Hartley Laboratory. The following April, Armstrong licensed his patent to the American Marconi Company for royalties of $500 a month.

Overshadowing Armstrong's concern about his family and the security of his patent were the events of the spring of 1917, which destroyed for all time the country's innocence. On Good Friday, after four American ships were sunk without warning, the United States declared war on Germany. Edwin Howard Armstrong, assistant to Michael Pupin at Columbia University, litigant in a patent suit that was just beginning, holder of patent licenses yielding $500 a month in royalties, became Captain Armstrong in the United States Army Signal Corps, and was headed for Europe.

4

SARNOFF AND MARCONI: INVENTING A LEGEND

━◢

Except for its capital—which contained a small "grand hotel" catering to European visitors—the province of Minsk at the end of the nineteenth century offered nothing beyond the unrelieved bleakness of the Pale of Russia. Peasants constituted two-thirds of the population. Living in small villages or on solitary farms, most kept bees, raised cattle unsuccessfully, or struggled at farming. Many suffered from the uncontrollable epidemic of *plica polonica*, a disease of the scalp that caused the hairs to grow together like a cow's tail. The century's advances were still many years away; there was no telephone, no electricity, only primitive sanitation, no gas, no telegraph. Isolated as they were, they cared little for and often knew nothing of the political currents beginning to flow in Moscow and St. Petersburg.

The plight of the Jews in Minsk was especially dark. Since the reign of Catherine the Great, they had been confined to small shtetls, villages of at most a few hundred inhabitants, where the streets were mean, the houses squalid. The shtetl of Uzlian, where David Sarnoff was born on February 27, 1891, resembled an isolated, impoverished, and ingrown village. Though it was located close to the capital, no railroad stopped there; indeed, with the exception of minor officials like the tax collector, who was inevitably guarded by Cossacks, no one stopped there. Even the thunder of the pogrom, that wanton destruction of Jewish property and often Jewish lives, was unknown in Uzlian while Sarnoff lived there. The last census, taken nearly a century earlier in 1795 at the partition of Poland, found fifty-one Jews in the village, including seven tavern keepers, three innkeepers, one tailor, and one barber. No doubt Uzlian had grown since then, but only among the families who had lived there for generations.

No different from the rest, Leah and Abraham Sarnoff, David's parents, survived on Abraham's earnings as a house painter, hardly a thriving occupation in the Pale. A studio photograph of this period shows Abraham sitting in an ornately carved chair, facing the camera squarely. His dress of a heavy coat, vest, shirt, and tie, suggests he is in the clothes he wore to worship. His beard and mustache are cropped neatly. His eyes and soft features give him an almost ascetic expression. One would not suspect from the way he is sitting that he was tall and thin; his clothes mask his hollow frame. Standing at his left side, dressed in a blouse and skirt, Leah Sarnoff appears four-square and authoritative, her right hand on her husband's shoulder. Her round face and intense eyes suggest David Sarnoff's own appearance in his later years. Though short herself—again like her eldest son—her demeanor is one of complete control. So she seemed in life, too. Leah always stood forth as the dominant partner, ever in charge of the family destiny.

That destiny, Abraham and Leah Sarnoff decided, lay in the United States. In 1896, after his wife had given birth to two more sons, Lew and Morris, Abraham left home to join the great tide of Russian Jews flowing into New York. There he would earn enough money so that in due time his family might follow. David would not see his father for four years.

Nor would David see much of his mother for the next four years. An "American widow," Leah Sarnoff and her three sons moved in with her parents, brother, and seven sisters. Doted on by his maternal grandmother and aunts, as well as his mother, David had proven an intellectually precocious boy. They taught him to read from the Old Testament at an early age. To them he was destined to become a Talmudic scholar, surely the highest position any male in Uzlian could attain. By placing him with his grandmother's brother, Rabbi Schlomme Elkind, in the shtetl of Korme, 100 miles east of Uzlian in the region of Borisov, they would help his studies—and not incidentally relieve the house of one body to feed.

Life in Korme, Sarnoff learned, was even more isolated than life in Uzlian. For the next four years, he followed a simple and unrelieved routine of what might be best described as a Talmudic boot camp: from Sabbath to Sabbath, sunup to sundown, he learned and chanted the Talmud and the Psalms. He made no friends with other children, never played a game, rarely went outside except to and from temple, and, aside from his great uncle, saw few others. Instead, he was charged with memorizing 2,000 words of the Talmud and the Hebrew prophets a day. He literally had to sing for his supper. Should he fall short, he was not fed. "Four years of the prophets was enough,"

Sarnoff remarked half a century later, but at the same time he believed the rigorous mental training he received had served him well in business. He viewed his life as a series of tasks that must be managed with continual discipline.

It took Abraham Sarnoff four years to gather the $144 necessary to bring his family to America (a place in steerage cost $36). During that time, he endured a tenement room with three other men and destroyed what remained of his health in the untold hardships of menial jobs that only occasionally included painting and paperhanging. In 1900, when he was nine, David returned to Uzlian for a brief reunion with his grandparents, aunts, uncles, and cousins before embarking with his mother and brothers for the New World.

The passage the Sarnoff family took was not the one we typically associate with immigrants from Eastern Europe: sailing in a crowded vessel from some continental port across the Atlantic to the safe harbor of New York, passing beneath the blessed Statue of Liberty, and finally clearing through the authorities at Ellis Island. That journey usually lasted about two weeks. Leah Sarnoff chose an altogether different route for her sons and herself. Though longer and more difficult, it was cheaper and, immigrants thought, offered an easier way to get past the feared immigration officials. It began with a 300-mile train trip from Minsk to the port of Libau on the Baltic Sea. There they boarded a boat that plied its way past Denmark into the North Sea, through the English Channel, and around the southern tip of England to Liverpool. At the English port they changed to the steerage section of a larger steamship for the 3,000-mile passage across the Atlantic and up the St. Lawrence River to Montreal. Finally in North America, Leah and her sons boarded a train for Albany that crossed the border into the United States at the small immigration outpost of Rouses Point, New York. At Albany, they changed conveyances for the last time to a Hudson River steamboat bound for New York. Very likely David Sarnoff got *his* first glimpse of the Statue of Liberty not from a ship's deck, but from the promenade of the Brooklyn Bridge.

Years later, Sarnoff was fond of telling two stories of his rough passage to America, and though they were embellished over time—and might have been apocryphal—they contained essential truths about his character. The first concerned a political demonstration at Minsk: in the company of his mother and brothers, he saw Cossacks ride into a "wailing mob" of Jewish people. The sickened boy looked on in horror as he clung to his mother's skirt while the guards trampled "women and children under the hooves of their horses." The second concerned a hamper of kosher foods his mother had prepared for their journey: at Liverpool the precious package got mixed up with other luggage and was placed with the cargo. David jumped from the deck into the hold to retrieve it and was fortunate enough to land on a soft bundle. "I still remember one of the seamen telling me," Sarnoff later said, " 'Boy, you're going to do alright in America.' "

Sarnoff's first story took on greater meaning as he grew older. To him those Cossacks and the thug Soviets who followed were trampling essential human freedoms, which he always equated with his adopted land of liberty. In the forties and fifties, he became the ultimate hot and cold warrior, designing the communications operations for D-Day, regarding Eisenhower and other powerful generals with deep reverence, relishing his title of brigadier general, even proposing to parachute hundreds of thousands of small radios into Russia, each of them tuned to a station transmitting American propaganda. The second story, too, contained an essential truth of Sarnoff's indomitable will to survive in the New World. His character and his discipline augured well for his success.

From a pier on the Hudson River on July 2, 1900, Leah Sarnoff and her three boys stepped at last onto the soil of Manhattan. The air was clear and dry, and the temperature in the seventies. A dark cloud of smoke hung heavily over the western side of the Hudson River, as a fire in Hoboken the day before had destroyed several ships, piers, and warehouses, and killed 361 people.

But Leah Sarnoff and her children had wholly different concerns. First her husband had failed to meet them as they had arranged. Owing to a mix-up in communications, Abraham Sarnoff was waiting at the wrong dock, while his wife and children spent some frightening hours in the unknown city before the family was reunited that evening. Then there was the sheer overwhelming size of the city before them, and the living conditions they would have to endure. With a population of almost 3.5 million, New York was the largest city in the United States, boasting taller buildings than any other city in the land, made possible by the electric elevators the Otis brothers had perfected. David Sarnoff saw more people on a single block of Manhattan than he had seen in his lifetime. The travelers were shocked by the fourth-story flat on Monroe Street on the Lower East Side to which Abraham Sarnoff led them in the dark. That section had the dubious distinction of housing more people per square mile than any other place in New York. The railroad flat awaiting them, three narrow rooms of filth and darkness, rented for $10 a month. A single toilet in the hallway served all the inhabitants on the floor—about twenty people. As was the case with most buildings on the Lower East Side, a distance of four feet separated their tenement from the structure beside it. Through that narrow space passed all the light and air for the flat.

Neither the delayed family reunion, New York's size, nor even the squalor of their tenement equaled the shock Leah Sarnoff and her eldest son felt at seeing the physical state of Abraham Sarnoff. Thinner and more consumptive than they remembered him, he clearly had not fared well in the New World. His position as an occasional laborer, with only infrequent jobs as a painter and paperhanger, told of his own failure. He had been barely able to feed and clothe himself; how would he provide for a wife and three children?

Like so many of her neighbors, Leah Sarnoff would take in sewing to sustain her husband and children. But much of the responsibility of earning enough money for the family fell on her nine-year-old boy. "If I don't help my family," Sarnoff remembered asking himself, "who will? . . . It was like being tossed into a whirlpool—a slum whirlpool—and left to sink or swim."

Sarnoff did not sink. Before long, he took a job selling a Yiddish paper every afternoon, the conservative and Orthodox *Tageblatt*, at a penny each. For every fifty sold, he received a quarter. To be successful, he had to pick up the papers at the East Broadway station of the elevated railway line and race with them into the street before the other boys had covered the territory. Soon he added to his task by delivering Abraham Cahan's more liberal *Forverts* (*Jewish Daily Forward*) each morning to tenement doors. The bundle of papers was dropped from an elevated train at 4 A.M.: "I schooled myself to awaken at the first sound of the approaching train," he remembered, getting to the street "about the same time the bundle landed." From there he would run up and down the tenement stairways, often saving steps by running over the roofs of the buildings.

"They were uncomplaining, if not patient," the novelist William Dean Howells wrote after a visit to New York's Jewish ghetto in 1896, "in circumstances where I believe a single week's sojourn, with no more hope of a better lot than they could have, would make anarchists of the best people of the city." Howells was impressed by the Jews' ability to maintain an appearance of cleanliness and neatness, as well as by their "heroic superiority to their fate" in the face of squalor and deprivation. Many, of course, did not thrive in the capitalist manner. Some *did* become anarchists. Not every Jewish boy studied philosophy, literature, and politics at a settlement house, worked hard in a sweatshop or made clothes at home, attended the City University of New York, and eventually entered into a marriage brokered by a *shadkhan* on Hester Street. Many intellectuals emigrated to America, but others came too. Some roamed the streets as tough thugs searching for fights with Irish and Italian gangs. Some pitched pennies and played poker. Some held up, and extorted money from, boys like Sarnoff who were hustling at their legitimate jobs. These were destined to become the gunmen and bootleggers of the 1920s. And there were others like the Sarnoffs, not intellectuals, but people of intelligence who worked hard to succeed.

Each of these immigrants was experiencing the exhilaration of living in America. They were learning how to play marbles or stickball, and to drink soda water or buy a sweet at the true social center of the neighborhood, the candy store. As crowded and filthy as Monroe Street was, it still contained more spirit and energy than the dark rutted roads of Korme or Uzlian. Sarnoff's last encounter with state authority before coming to America occurred when he saw brutal Cossacks trample Jewish peasants; in his new land, the most visible symbol of state authority was the city policeman, who had not yet started brutally crushing labor unrest that would occur in that part of Manhattan. Sarnoff was free at last of his aged great uncle, and more or less free to roam the streets as he wished, to meet with other boys, and to make his way in the world.

Possibly his great uncle's training, or his family's situation, or a combination of the two led Sarnoff to establish quickly a rigorous daily routine that began and ended with newspaper deliveries. Sandwiched between these two activities seems to have been much study and reading. On Saturdays, he earned additional money by singing in his synagogue. Soon he enrolled in English-language classes and availed himself of much that the Educational Alliance at Jefferson Street and East Broadway had to offer.

Organized by German Jews who had made their way to America earlier in the nineteenth century and staffed largely by volunteers like the poet Emma Lazarus and the diplomat Oscar Straus, the Educational Alliance was the earliest settlement house on the Lower East Side. An amalgam of the Young Men's Hebrew Association, the Hebrew Free School Association, and the Hebrew Technical Institute, the alliance served as a community home, *the* center of acculturation for many East European immigrants. Under its aegis were a variety of educational, recreational, and social services, and these were not limited to Jews. Al Smith, the governor of New York and a Democratic presidential candidate, often remembered with pride his participation in its activities. English was the official language of the alliance, and it was stressed in most of the activities. Besides English classes, the alliance offered a night school, a fine library, a gymnasium, art studios, lessons in personal hygiene, and showers.

The Educational Alliance enjoyed great success. Evening lectures in the 700-seat auditorium were often filled to overflowing. Pictures of the library invariably show it to be packed with readers. Eddie Cantor sang at a summer camp the alliance sponsored in upstate New York; Sholom Aleichem wrote in its library; Arthur Murray first learned to dance in its recreation and physical culture classes; and Jo Davidson, William Auerbach-Levy, and Jacob Epstein were three of the better-known students of its art classes.

Avoiding the gymnasium, teams, and competitions, Sarnoff preferred to spend his time in the Educational Alliance's classes and library and attending evening lectures in its auditorium. Some of the first children's books he read in its library concerned the life of Abraham Lincoln, and he liked to remember later in life that he was inspired by the rail-splitting romance surrounding the sixteenth president's boyhood. By the end of 1900, after just five months in America and three months in grade school, he had developed enough ability in his newly acquired tongue to read English-language newspapers. By the time of his bar mitzvah in 1904, David Sarnoff had developed into a proficient speaker, honing his skills in the alliance's debating club. When he was fourteen, he participated in his first public debate, winning the affirmative position on the resolution, "The United States should grant independence to the Philippines."

Sarnoff was also busy developing his talents as an entrepreneur. At fourteen, he purchased a newsstand at 46th Street and Tenth Avenue in Hell's Kitchen where his father (now too ill to work as a painter or paperhanger) and younger brothers might work. Along with the stand came the rights to a delivery route. Family tradition holds that he received the $200 for the purchase from a wealthy anonymous benefactor. Almost entirely alone now, David supervised a family that had grown with the additions of a sister and brother, Ede and Irving, born in quick succession after Leah Sarnoff and her husband were reunited in New York. By 1906, when David was fifteen and had been graduated from elementary school, his father's death was imminent. High school, David realized, was out of the question; his education would stop at the eighth grade. His role was shifting from a paper boy—albeit one with his own newsstand—to the sole support of the family. It would demand a full-time job.

Until he purchased his newsstand in Hell's Kitchen, David Sarnoff had followed the pattern of many children in the rough triangle of the Lower East Side of Manhattan Island, an area bounded by Lafayette Street, the East River from the Brooklyn Bridge to the Manhattan Bridge; and, to the north, Delancey Street. He had emigrated from Russia like thousands of others, lived in a tenement, learned at the Educational Alliance, and worked hard to help support his family. It was possible—and many immigrants did so—to sustain one's life, spirit, and culture very comfortably without ever leaving the triangle.

David Sarnoff had chosen a different path from many on the Lower East Side, and now, in 1906, his life took an even more dramatic and unusual turn. In seeking a full-time job, he thought of the newspaper business. Perhaps he might become a reporter, but not for one of the papers he had hawked daily that were published from offices on East Broadway. Instead, he would work for an English-language paper. English had been his favorite subject in elementary school. He enjoyed speaking the language and had the energy necessary to travel about town in search of stories. He would try his luck with the newspaper he most admired, the New York *Herald*.

Largely because of the publicity efforts of its ambitious publisher, James Gordon Bennett, the *Herald* enjoyed wide circulation and a reputation for gathering news faster and better than any of its rivals. Capitalizing on the public's infatuation with exploration, speed, and technology, Bennett sponsored events that actually created their own headlines. In 1869, he sent the Anglo-American journalist Henry Morton Stanley into Africa on a three-year search for the Scottish missionary and explorer David Livingstone and published vivid accounts of his journey. A decade later, he outfitted George Washington De Long in his disastrous attempt to reach the North Pole, and reported graphically on the death of De Long and his party from cold and starvation. Interested in telegraphy, Bennett had formed the Commercial Cable Company in 1883 and constructed a cable to speed communications between America and Europe. An avid yachtsman, Bennett had paid $5,000 to bring Marconi and his wireless apparatus to New York in 1899 and again in 1901 to report the results of the International Yacht Races. At the same time the *Herald* presented detailed accounts of the races, it ran stories about Marconi's wondrous invention.

No doubt James Gordon Bennett appeared the very model of success to Sarnoff. The son of a Roman Catholic Scottish immigrant, the publisher had made his fortune in New York, and he now spent most of his time in Paris, indulging in his hobbies of yachting and ballooning. He showed what an immigrant (and one who was not a Protestant) might achieve. Though he would begin as a reporter, someday Sarnoff himself might become a publisher of his own paper.

To reach the *Herald* offices, Sarnoff had to go south from his newsstand to 34th Street and Broadway. The journey the fifteen-year-old made by foot one Saturday morning marked a dramatic turning point in the direction of his life. If successful in landing a job with the paper, he would be able to "rise above," as he put it nearly a half century later, his "ghetto background." However, when Sarnoff entered the building to ask for a job, he went not into the newspaper's offices, but into those of Bennett's other enterprise, the Commercial Cable Company. The error was a stroke of luck for his future career, a mistake Sarnoff never regretted.

"I don't know about the *Herald*, but we can use another messenger boy in our shop," the manager of the Commercial Cable Company replied when the short, thin youth dressed neatly in a suit and tie asked for a job with the newspaper. He would deliver cables to the *Herald*'s offices in the same building and around the city on a bicycle the company provided. The pay would be $5 a week, and Sarnoff could start on Monday. He accepted on the spot. On the margins of his day he still would deliver the Yiddish papers, while he would spend the rest of his working hours delivering telegrams.

But Sarnoff's first full-time job lasted only until September. The same office manager who had hired him several months earlier refused to consider granting a three-days' leave on Rosh Hashanah and Yom Kippur so that the boy might sing with his choir at the Vilno-Senya Synagogue. When Sarnoff protested the manager's decision, he was fired. This was his first experience with intolerance since he had crossed Delancey Street. It would not be his last.

It was in the Commercial Cable office that Sarnoff first saw telegraph operators tapping out the Morse code on telegraph keys. After work, he would hang about the office, watching the men and occasionally playing with the equipment. With $2 from one of his earliest pay envelopes, he purchased his own key. For many months thereafter, he stayed up late into the night mastering the code.

From 1906 until the day of his death, a telegraph key was never far from Sarnoff's side. Years later, when he became president of the Radio Corporation of America, he ordered one specially installed in the top drawer of his desk, frequently using it to "talk" with a fellow RCA executive in another building, and proudly demonstrating his never-forgotten skills to visitors. Proficiency with a telegraph key goes far beyond simple knowledge of the code to the speed and rhythm of the sender. Those accomplished with the key were said to possess good "fists." Indeed, in the early days of telegraphy and wireless, practiced listeners knew the sender by the particular rhythm of the key taps, what operators termed "swing," just as those with well-trained ears may tell the difference between a Horowitz and a Rubinstein at the piano. Through many hours of practice, Sarnoff developed one of the best fists in the business.

He was drawn irresistibly to the clicking sounds of the key and the receiver. In the Commercial Cable office, he had practiced assiduously during his off hours, striking up friendships on the line with other operators in the company's Broad Street office downtown whom he had never met. After he had been fired, he looked up one particular friend from the "circuit," Jack Irwin, who told him of an opening for a junior operator with a small new business, the American Marconi Wireless Telegraph Company. Sarnoff knew about Marconi and his inventions from the numerous newspaper accounts of his exploits and his visits to America, especially as they appeared in the *Herald*. This would be his opportunity to work for the man who had miraculously telegraphed the letter S through the ether from Europe to America. Perhaps someday he would have a chance to meet the inventor himself. At the William Street offices of the Marconi Company, where he went on September 30, 1906, Davey Sarnoff, as he was called, was offered work, not as an operator, but as an office boy sweeping floors and running errands. The pay of $5.50 a week represented a 10 percent raise over his salary with the Commercial Cable Company. Without hesitation he took the job.

Getting work at American Marconi marked the second stroke of good luck for David Sarnoff. He worked for that company and its successor, the Radio Corporation of America, for the next six decades. Of the twenty companies that had begun since Marconi made his wireless discoveries, this was the first and best. More important, the Marconi Company had a reputation (at least in 1906) for honesty. Unlike the unscrupulous directors of companies with which Lee de Forest was associated (one of which was being liquidated at that very time), Marconi executives went out of their way to tell prospective purchasers not to expect a dividend or even a profit for many years. At times the directors suggested *better* investments to those who wanted to buy company stock.

The directors had good reason to damp down speculators out for a quick profit, for the American Marconi Wireless Telegraph Company, as it was officially known, was little more than a money-losing American presence for the parent company in England. It had erected only four shore stations—Sea Gate on Coney Island; Sagaponack on Long Island; Siasconset on Nantucket; and South Wellfleet, Massachusetts—and had installed equipment on just four American ships—*New York, Philadelphia, St. Paul,* and *St. Louis.* Other ships with Marconi installations regularly sailed to America and of course used the service, and telegraph operators sent daily news dispatches to Cunard and White Star ocean liners traveling between New York and Liverpool. Still it appeared a somewhat neglected American cousin to its powerful relative in London.

With fewer than a dozen employees, the Marconi Company was small enough for even an office boy to make his presence felt among his superiors and for Sarnoff to gain an understanding of the business. He took advantage of every opportunity to learn. He soon discovered that the finances of American Marconi were precarious, a point often underscored when the manager sent his office boy on errands about the city to bring back loans he had arranged to enable the company to meet its payroll. As the filing clerk, Sarnoff logged in all the company's correspondence and memoranda, including letters from the great Marconi, which gave him a chance to observe its management firsthand. American Marconi maintained a small library of wireless publications; Sarnoff soon became its cataloguer and the chief user. And every moment he could spare from his duties as an office boy, he spent talking with the operators and practicing his own telegraphic skills.

Something other than his earnest industry separated Sarnoff from the rest of the Marconi employees, especially the telegraphers. Sarnoff could joke and play with the others, but only to a point. Deprived of amusement and even isolated from other children in Korme, he had difficulty making friends in New York. Independent and often hard-drinking, the average telegrapher was a very rough fellow; the ones who came into port after several months at sea, even rougher. As the Marconi manager complained, they seemed interested only in "careless living" and "women and wine." They were almost exclusively Protestants, too. More than once they remarked that Sarnoff was a Jew, and often they called him not "Davey" but "Jew Boy."

All of Sarnoff's characteristics, even his faith, which kept him apart from the others, worked to his advantage with his superiors. John Bottomly, the general manager, and George DeSousa, the commercial manager, soon gave him more responsibilities, including an occasional turn at the telegraph key at the Coney Island or Long Island stations when one of the regular telegraphers was sick, as they often were.

All the time David Sarnoff was learning the mechanics of the wireless business, he also was studying everything he could read about Guglielmo Marconi. He searched through the New York Public Library for old newspapers and magazines for stories of his accomplishments, questioned fellow workers, and paid special attention to the letters the Italian inventor regularly sent to the American branch of his company. Sarnoff fashioned him into a hero and surrogate father. Marconi alone, so the newspaper and magazine stories said, possessed the vision to boldly create instruments no one else thought possible. He was the immigrant from Italy who had succeeded in England; he was known about the world for his invention; he was the one whom Sarnoff sought to emulate.

One evening in December 1906, the great inventor entered the William Street office. When Marconi left to walk to a small experimental laboratory he maintained on Front Street, the office boy saw his chance and, unnoticed, slipped out behind him. At the appropriate moment, just as the inventor was unlocking the door at Front Street, David Sarnoff, fifteen years old, stepped forth to introduce himself as the Marconi Company's newest employee.

It was a story Sarnoff enjoyed telling later in life, for it spoke well of his own ability and enterprise. Unlike some others he frequently told, it was true. "We were on the same wavelength," Sarnoff always replied when asked about the boldness of his gambit. Of that there could be no doubt. Within moments of his unusual introduction, the boy was recounting his emigration from Russia, his life on Monroe Street, his newspaper delivery business, and his desire to become a telegraph operator; and Marconi was showing him his laboratory and giving him leave to peruse the extensive files of technical literature he maintained there. By the time Sarnoff left that evening, he had established himself as Marconi's personal messenger boy. In subsequent visits, the inventor came to rely on him to deliver flowers, gifts, and messages to his numerous female liaisons about the city.

Sarnoff's bold strategy, which he had been quietly pursuing since he began with the Marconi Company, now began to pay off handsomely. In the spring of 1907, shortly after Sarnoff celebrated his sixteenth birthday, Guglielmo Marconi approved his promotion to the rank of junior wireless operator with an increase in his salary to $7.50 a week. The new earnings enabled him to move his family from Hell's Kitchen to a fifth-story walk-up in the Brownsville section of Brooklyn. He sold his newsstand at a profit, relinquished his paper routes, and entered a world that he was confident would give him security and much more.

A photograph taken of Sarnoff at the time of his promotion to junior telegrapher at the Marconi Company frames him from the waist up as he sits in a high-backed wooden chair. He is dressed in a double-breasted suit jacket with a handkerchief rising from its breast pocket, a shirt with a collar that has ridden up his neck, and a jaunty bow tie. More important than his clothes is the fold of his arms, the cant of his neck and head, and the expression on his face. His arms cross his chest firmly; his head is thrust slightly forward to make the viewer almost feel the tension in his neck; his forceful stare, especially his eyes and lips, suggests a seriousness of purpose, a person who is intensely set on achieving a goal. By this time, Sarnoff's goal went far beyond assuring the well-being of his family. Blazing in his mind were the opportunities the new world of wireless offered him.

The death of Abraham Sarnoff when David was sixteen caused hardly a ripple of unhappiness. Little more than a shadow to the boy since he had left for America, the eldest Sarnoff seemed simply to fade from the family picture, yielding at last to consumption. Since Abraham's family already looked to Leah and her first son for support, his death left no void. Abraham Sarnoff's plight was the dark side of the American dream, the story of the man who through no fault of his own succumbs to forces beyond his control in the New World and is simply forgotten. His four sons tried their best to banish this picture from their thoughts. Industriousness, getting ahead, which was always in the minds of David Sarnoff and his three brothers, seemed the best way to avoid the trap of desperation into which circumstances had forced their father.

In reality, from the time he picked up his first bundle of papers on East Broadway, David Sarnoff had functioned much as the father in the household. He had organized his younger brothers Morris and Lew in the paper business. Both emerged as highly successful businessmen later in their lives. His American-born brother, Irving, became immensely successful in the best American way by establishing an RCA distributorship in New York that made him very wealthy. Eventually, each of Sarnoff's younger brothers amassed substantial fortunes, too.

In the twilight of his father's life and after his death, David Sarnoff became increasingly close to his mother. For Leah Sarnoff's welfare, he strove to succeed. His errands to the better places in the city for the Marconi Company and his reading of newspapers gave him his goals. He would raise his family from the dark tenements in Monroe Street and Hell's Kitchen, to the better circumstances of Brooklyn. His mother still took on the odd sewing job for extra cash, but her son alone brought home enough money to keep the family going. Later, he would move them all to a handsome new apartment house in the Bronx just two blocks from the benches and verdant paths of the then-elegant Bronx Park. No more a tenement, no more a walk-up, the apartment was a regular American home near trees and grass.

Sarnoff's rising fortunes allowed him to keep company with girls occasionally. His unfortunate choice for mentors in these matters of the heart were the wireless operators and, of course, Marconi. The operators were often crude in their talk as well as their actions with women, and boasted of their sexual conquests like triumphant heroes. Marconi himself acted like a Byronic hero transplanted to twentieth-century New York. Sarnoff grew well acquainted with the intimacies of the Italian inventor's private life: the boxes of candy, notes of devotion, and duplicitous love letters he sent to several ladies at once. Was not this the pattern of the successful inventor and businessman? Might not Sarnoff behave in a similar fashion someday? For the time being, however, his work schedule, family obligations, and general penuriousness left opportunity for little more than an occasional date.

Knowing that Sarnoff enjoyed the tacit backing of their employer, John Bottomly and George DeSousa made opportunities available for his advancement through a succession of jobs: operator on the SS *New York*; operator at the Siasconset station on Nantucket; chief operator of the Marconi station at Sea Gate on Coney Island; operator on the seal-hunting ship *Boethic* out of

Newfoundland; operator on the SS *Harvard*; and finally chief operator at the Wanamaker station in New York City. Each position offered a set of challenges that Sarnoff met well, and often in an unusual way.

The first, a fifteen-day round trip to Europe on the *New York* that came up suddenly in 1907 after the regular operator became ill, gave him the greatest satisfaction. At this time, the Marconi Company leased its equipment and operators to the steamship companies for substantial fees, a policy that raised charges of monopoly in some quarters, but ensured an enviable quality of signal over the primitive and often quirky transmitters and receivers. Though he looked young, Sarnoff was eager to wear the operator's uniform. He had the ability, and was hired. Seven years after embarking on a miserable three-week journey from Europe to America in steerage, Sarnoff returned in the comparative luxury and privacy of the ship's radio shack, all the while handling the wireless traffic between the *New York* and Marconi installations in Europe as well as other ships at sea. The comparison between this and his first journey was not lost on him. In the future, he would mark his rise in the world by the comfort and elegance of his accommodations on trans-Atlantic crossings.

Sarnoff volunteered eagerly for his next important assignment at desolate Siasconset because it offered him the prestige and responsibility of a vital position in the chain of communication for the Marconi Company, a chance to practice his skills as an operator, solitude for study, and more money. He stayed eighteen months. As much of the important telegraph traffic in the Marconi system passed through the Siasconset station, the company was careful to place only its best operators there. Already well known about the circuit for the speed and distinct swing of his messages, Sarnoff knew Siasconset would give him the opportunity to become even better. In his off hours, he studied the technical books in the station's extensive library; took correspondence courses in algebra, geometry, and trigonometry; and each week made the fourteen-mile round trip by bicycle to read books in the Nantucket village library. And the pay was good. Considering Siasconset a hardship post that few wanted, the managers set the salary at $60 a month to start ($10 more than the going rate at other stations) and soon raised it to $70. Sarnoff had more than enough to live on, even after sending $40 to his mother in Brooklyn.

Photographs have recorded some of Sarnoff's activities at Siasconset. In a sober pose of the four operators at the remote outpost, he is clearly the youngest. Other informal snapshots show the young operator in a more relaxed mood. He sits on his bicycle, perhaps about to make the journey to the library, with the waste of sand and scrub bushes behind him. He clowns in a mock battle with two operators, each combatant dressed neatly in a shirt and tie. He sits contemplatively at a desk beneath a window, earphones on his head and his right hand at a telegraph key. In still another picture, he and a fellow operator, both dressed with rounded collars, stand in front of the station, their arms about each other's shoulders.

His correspondence courses concluded and his reading in the technical library at Siasconset complete, Sarnoff applied for and received a promotion to manager at Sea Gate on Coney Island in 1909. (The company reduced his salary to $60 a month because it did not consider Sea Gate a hardship post. Sarnoff's protests over the diminished wage succeeded only in affronting the manager, John Bottomly.) Sea Gate gave Sarnoff his first experience with the alluring power of authority, and he found he enjoyed it. Now operators reported to *him*; he oversaw the general operation of the station and reported directly to Bottomly and DeSousa. Work at Sea Gate put him back in touch with his mentor Marconi, who visited the station whenever he came to New York. Sarnoff could give the inventor a tour of the operation while others worked busily under his direction. He could describe the 30 percent increase in wireless traffic that occurred while he was manager. And he could speak not as an eager office boy but as a competent manager. It was a role he took to immediately, and one that spelled his future. No longer "Jew Boy" or "Davey," he was now nineteen years old, "Dave" to his superiors, "Mr. Sarnoff" to those beneath him.

As Sarnoff was rising within the company, American Marconi was making a greater impact on the field of commercial wireless. No more a novelty, or simply a toy for enterprising youths, wireless was fast becoming a necessity to the increasing complexities of travel and communication. Steamship companies like the White Star Line offered telegraph facilities as a convenience for their wealthier passengers to send and receive business and personal messages from London and New York. And wireless ensured safety, too. On January 23, 1909, Jack Binns, the wireless operator on the White Star liner *Republic*, became a hero after his ship collided with the *Florida* in the Atlantic. When Binns signaled "the hurry call of the sea—CQD! CQD!" the *Baltic* picked up the call and sailed to the rescue. More than 1,200 passengers were saved from certain death. For four days, New York newspaper editors, who received the story by wireless, made the collision and Jack Binns their most important story. Wireless, so the editorials suggested, had robbed death itself, for now, as the article in *Harper's* said "an invisible network of ethereal communications unites ship to ship."

The prudence and perseverance of the Marconi managers was starting to pay off, too. Tainted neither by unfulfilled and extravagant claims nor by dishonest stock swindles, Marconi had emerged as the premier wireless company. The Italian inventor of course knew how to use the press to his advantage—something he proved when he transmitted the letter S—but he always used it carefully. For Sarnoff, the rise in American Marconi's fortunes meant a rise of his own. From the time he stepped up to introduce himself to the inventor, he had made a series of very careful moves calculated to give him increasingly responsible positions within the company. More clearly than ever, he saw the future that lay before him.

Just why Sarnoff volunteered for his next assignment—wireless operator on a seal-hunting expedition out of Newfoundland—is unclear, for the expedition on the *Boethic* hardly offered the natural next step after managing one of the most important stations in the company. Perhaps the lure of adventure and a new experience enticed him. That he volunteered for this distant assignment suggests his willingness to take risks and his confidence in his future role in the company. Perhaps he made his move with the knowledge and encouragement of his mentor.

At the behest of a girl he had been seeing in Brooklyn, Sarnoff kept a journal of his exploits. If one excludes the "biographies" he wrote or caused to have written about himself when he was president of the Radio Corporation of America, this represents the only autobiographical account he ever made. Remarkably devoid of personal insight or reflection, the journal contains simply a narrative of his adventures: the time he walked across the ice to take pictures of a brood of seals, only to be chased by the huge, irate male (Sarnoff was saved from the attack when a crew member shot the animal); his trip across the ice floes to repair broken wireless equipment on a sister ship; how he relayed medical instructions from a doctor on the *Boethic* to a ship a hundred miles away to save a seaman with an infected tooth.

Sarnoff was able to turn his service on the *Boethic* to good account. Of all the operators in the fleet of ships on the expedition, he alone turned in a report filled with accomplishments. Marconi equipment had proved its worth in extreme conditions, as the ships were able to maintain contact and catch more seals than ever—36,000—during the six-week hunting season. In the most impressive part of his report, Sarnoff noted that he negotiated a deal for permanent installation of the equipment. He had proved himself to be not only an operator but a salesman as well.

After Sarnoff served a brief stint as the radio man on the SS *Harvard*, Bottomly and DeSousa promoted him to manage (and serve as the sole operator of) a new Marconi station being opened atop the Wanamaker Building at Ninth and Broadway in New York. In communication with a wireless installation at the department store's main building in Philadelphia, the station served mostly as a publicity gimmick for the Wanamaker and Marconi managements to attract customers and introduce them to the new way of communication. For Bottomly and DeSousa and even Marconi, Sarnoff represented the perfect choice, a proficient operator who was not as

rough hewn as so many others in the company's employ. He had demonstrated his ability to manage a station and handle the traffic at Sea Gate, and
to sell the idea of wireless (along with the equipment) to the owners of the
Boethic. For Sarnoff, too, it was a perfect opportunity. Since the station
would keep the business hours of the store, he could live at home and take
an intensive night course in electrical engineering at Pratt Institute, three
years of lectures compressed into one.

The Wanamaker job was a comfortable one. There was little traffic between New York and Philadelphia, and Sarnoff spent much of the day explaining his apparatus to curious customers and talking with amateurs in the
city who did not have access to the other more remote Marconi stations. One
young boy, Earle Cadwell, took the elevator to the top of the Wanamaker
Building in March 1912 and chanced to meet Sarnoff at the door of the
station. Sarnoff was between his transmitting schedules and appeared eager
to show off the station to anyone who wished to see it. Perhaps seeing himself
as he had been just a few years before, he went out of his way to be friendly.
Seventy-five years later, Cadwell remembered being as impressed by the
manager's openness as by his first look at professional equipment. His talk
with Sarnoff helped him decide his career. He went on to become a ship
operator shortly after their meeting and later worked at the Marconi Sea
Gate station.

At 10:25 P.M. on Sunday, April 14, 1912, a single message brought wireless, Marconi, and eventually Sarnoff to prominence: the *Titanic*, fastest and
most luxurious ocean liner of its time, was sinking in the North Atlantic.
The catastrophe would serve to make radio communication indispensable to
safety at sea.

"The *Titanic* disaster brought radio to the front," Sarnoff was fond of
saying in later years, "and also me." He was right. The *Titanic*'s wireless
distress call was heard fifty-eight miles away by the Marconi operator on the
Carpathia, which enabled those in lifeboats to be rescued three and a half
hours later, saving them from certain death by exposure. But inadequate
wireless installations on two other ships in the vicinity (which were in fact
closer than the *Carpathia*) meant that the *Titanic*'s distress signal "CQD" and
the recently adopted "SOS" went unheeded. Conflicting messages about the
fate of the passengers caused confusion among their relatives waiting in New
York. Marconi, who was in the city at the time (and held a ticket for
return passage on the liner) wrote to his wife in Italy, "I've witnessed the
most harrowing scenes of frantic people coming here to me and to the
offices of the Company to implore and beg us to find out if there might not
be some hope for their relations." Because he had invented the one link
to survival for the fortunate few who managed to secure a place in the

lifeboats, he became a hero to all, mobbed everywhere he went, and lionized in newspaper editorials.

There are a number of questions about Marconi and the role wireless played in the disaster and the days following. From Monday morning, when the *Carpathia* picked up the survivors, until 8:35 P.M., Thursday night, when it docked at Pier 58 at the foot of 14th Street and the Hudson River, the wireless operator *and* the operator rescued from the *Titanic* gave out only a partial list of those saved and none of the tales of heroism and ignominy that went with the story. Why was the *Carpathia* so silent? The explanation, that the wireless apparatus aboard the ship had a range of only eighty-five miles, does not coincide with the facts. Disturbed that his longtime aide Archie Butt had been lost, President Taft ordered two navy vessels to sail within transmission range to learn about survivors. Their messages were acknowledged but not answered. Yet at the same time survivors such as Mrs. George D. Widener; Lord and Lady Duff Gordon; the Countess of Rothes; and the infamous Bruce Ismay, head of the White Star Line who took a woman's place in a lifeboat instead of going down with his company's ship, made reservations by wireless for accommodation at the Ritz-Carlton Hotel. Others of lesser means made reservations at the Belmont, Manhattan, Netherland, and Plaza.

Evidence suggests that Marconi himself colluded with some of his operators to limit news of the *Titanic*'s demise, even the list of survivors. The longer the public remained in suspense, the more his company would benefit, as the delay underscored the importance of making wireless mandatory on all ships. For a time, the stock of American Marconi rose to new heights. Ever adept at manipulating news, Marconi helped to spirit a *New York Times* reporter aboard the *Carpathia* when it docked. The next morning, the paper presented an exclusive story from the *Titanic*'s surviving radio operator, Harold Bride. Bride began his narration: "In the first place, the public should not blame anybody because more wireless messages about the disaster to the *Titanic* did not reach shore from the *Carpathia*."

Marconi was not the only one to manipulate the news. The story surrounding the *Titanic* catastrophe served as the basis of Sarnoff's legend. Later, when he became president of the Radio Corporation of America, his publicity department improved upon the fiction in a biography it sent to the United States Army:

On April 14, 1912, he was sitting at his instrument in the Wanamaker Store in New York. Leaning forward suddenly, he pressed the earphones more closely to his head. Through the sputtering and static . . . he was hearing a message: "S. S. Titanic ran into iceberg. Sinking fast." For the next seventy-two hours Sarnoff sat at his post, straining to catch every signal that might come through the air. That demanded a good operator in those days of undeveloped radio. By order of the President of the United States every other wireless station in the country was closed to stop interference. . . . Not until he had given the world the name of the last survivor, three days and three nights after that first message, did Sarnoff call his job done.

The *Titanic* episode illustrates Sarnoff's ability to turn history into fable. As the story receded in the memories of most people, he encouraged a fiction composed of carefully slanted and romantically presented facts. Since the Wanamaker store was closed Sunday evening, Sarnoff did not hear the message that evening and probably did not get to his equipment until the next morning. In any case, he would have heard only the information that the stronger ship transmitters and shore stations chose to relay. It is doubtful that he stayed at the telegraph key until all were accounted for, as that would have been about ninety hours from his arrival on Monday morning. There were some hysterical scenes at the Wanamaker store as people gathered to learn the fate of their relatives, but most went to the offices of the White Star Line or the Marconi Company's main office on William Street. By Wednesday, April 17, interference of wireless traffic was so intense that the Marconi Company closed down all its stations save four. The one atop the Wanamaker department store was not among the ones kept open.

Nevertheless, Sarnoff and the Wanamaker store did play a part in reporting the disaster. Picking up faint signals from other Marconi stations, he and two other operators labored to transcribe reports of survivors for William Randolph Hearst's *American*. Never undertelling a story, the *American* reported that "eager thousands," including Vincent Astor, descended on the store in search of news. This might have been the case, since in the hours after he learned of the ship's sinking, Astor was almost incoherent about the fate of his parents (his father perished) and seems to have visited every newspaper and telegraph office in the city between Monday and the arrival of the *Carpathia* Thursday evening.

Of all the wireless operators from Newfoundland to Cape Sable, Siasconset to New York, and on the *Titanic* and *Carpathia*, Sarnoff alone had the prescience to embellish his role as the sole wireless link between the *Titanic* and the mainland. In that single incident he saw better than anyone else the power of the new medium. Within a week of the disaster, the Senate's Committee on Commerce held hearings on the matter; soon the Congress imposed regulations demanding all ships install powerful wireless equipment and staff it with operators at all times. The *Titanic* disaster would enhance the prosperity of the Marconi Company.

While the *Titanic* disaster did assure the Marconi Company's success, it also brought more competitors into the race that the inventor himself had begun in 1899. The company faced new and more serious rivals than ever before, as well as a growing resentment in America of a "foreigner" owning the "ether." In San Francisco and Palo Alto, the Federal Telegraph Company, for which de Forest worked, was progressing with its development of the Poulsen arc transmitter; in Schenectady, Ernst Alexanderson was developing his alternating current generators for General Electric. But the American Marconi's chief rivals were the American Telephone and Telegraph Company and the United States Navy.

As AT&T steadily enlarged its network of telephone wires, it became increasingly interested in the possibilities of wireless. With de Forest's vacuum tube, the company achieved transcontinental telephone communication early in 1915. It seemed but a matter of time before transoceanic calls would be possible, but AT&T did not possess the requisite wireless technology. Realizing it would have to lease equipment from Marconi, it turned again to de Forest. In 1914, it had paid $50,000 for rights to the audion. (De Forest retained only the title to sell the tubes for "amateur and experimental use.") For the next three years, de Forest harassed the company with a series of patent infringement suits with the thought that it would purchase more rights.

The United States Navy proved an even more powerful rival to American Marconi. Its threat became imminent when, in response to the *Titanic* disaster, Congress passed an act ordering the navy to develop radio communications. The threat became a reality on March 4, 1913, when the newly inaugurated Woodrow Wilson appointed Josephus Daniels, the reform-minded newspaper editor from Raleigh, North Carolina, to be secretary of the navy. A landlubber, teetotaler, and devout Methodist who affected wide-brimmed hats, low collars, and bow or string ties, Daniels was ridiculed by many outside his native South. He held decided opinions that often got him into trouble with the press and public on just about everything—from prohibiting wine in the officers' mess and expounding the qualities of "beautiful Christian women," to the preparedness of the fleet and the navy's ownership of radio. The navy, Daniels firmly believed, should control the ether. Whenever the opportunity arose, at a cabinet meeting or before Congress, he pressed his case. Preparing for the navy's entry into the World War gave him the opportunity to effect an unprecedented measure of control.

Daniels found a ready ally in Admiral Stanford C. Hooper, graduate of the Naval Academy and wireless amateur, who as early as 1908 began to see how wireless could enhance communication among ships in battle. With Daniels's help, Hooper was able to capitalize on his enthusiasm for the new technology, which he realized advanced well beyond the primitive light and flag signal systems of the fleet.

AT&T and the navy began to cooperate in their employment of wireless. Working increasingly hand in hand, they made a potent challenger to American Marconi's interests. When the navy built a wireless station at Arlington, Virginia, AT&T engineers equipped it. By 1914, naval transmitters were sending signals around the world. In one demonstration in late September 1915, Theodore Vail, president of AT&T, spoke from the naval station at Arlington to receiving stations in San Francisco and Pearl Harbor, Hawaii. He made certain that newspaper reporters were present for the demonstration. Daniels proved to be a showman equal to de Forest, Vail, or even Marconi, when in May 1916, with AT&T officials gathered around his desk at the naval department in Washington, he spoke with the captain of the *New Hampshire* then cruising off Hampton Roads, Virginia. Later, the captain's wife spoke to her husband from their house. To Daniels, the event was "indisputable proof that whether American businessmen are acting as individuals or as corporations, their hearts respond readily and unreservedly to the call of their country." To which the chief engineer at AT&T replied, "There is no Navy in the world which has the power of the United States Navy to mobilize instantly its resources through such a system of communication." The yoking of American government and an American corporation to the exclusion of foreign competition was now complete.

Sarnoff was at a crucial juncture in his career. What course, he was asking himself, should his own work in wireless take? In addition to his enterprise, quick intelligence, skills, and contacts with Marconi, Sarnoff had demonstrated a flair for garnering at least some public recognition for his role in reporting the *Titanic*. He had tasted publicity, seen his name in newsprint, and he liked it. He had seen how the media might be used to his advantage. Hearst's *American* affirmed his success as well as that of his company and his mentor. Because of his good sense of "public relations"—a term coined close to a century before by Jefferson, and yet still to be understood by corporations—he had positioned himself at the age of twenty-one to rise in what many still counted the premier company in a growth industry. But to what height? Though he had no conventional schooling past the eighth grade, he had proven himself, and he jealously measured his progress. In his correspondence courses, he had done well. Of the fifty who enrolled in the formidable electrical engineering course at Pratt, he was one of just a dozen to finish, and the *only* person without a college degree. Yet his lack of formal training limited his chances to advance much higher in wireless engineering. Would he remain a telegrapher all his life, especially as his reading and close scrutiny of the changes in technology taking place told him the wireless art would advance far beyond mere dots and dashes? Although the Marconi Company did not seem especially interested in voice communication, the word "radio" was appearing with greater frequency in the literature. How much further could he rise without an engineering degree? How much more money could he make? Management clearly offered greater opportunities. When a position as inspector opened, Sarnoff took it.

Sarnoff advanced steadily. As inspector, he examined Marconi equipment on ships as they arrived in port. His skills with a telegraph key got him a job as an instructor at the Marconi Institute, a school organized to meet the growing demand for telegraphers. Soon he was made chief inspector in charge of equipment on all ships entering the harbor, and given an additional title of assistant chief engineer, with an office near the general manager's in the company's new headquarters on the eighteenth floor of the recently opened Woolworth Building.

To work in the Woolworth Building! On the evening of April 24, 1913, President Wilson had pressed a button in the White House turning on 80,000 lights in the Woolworth Building, which reminded the famous preacher Samuel Parkes Cadman of St. John's vision of paradise. Cadman proclaimed it the "Cathedral of Commerce—the chosen habitation of that spirit in man which, through means of change and barter, binds alien people into unity and peace, and reduces the hazards of war and bloodshed." Frank W. Woolworth had paid $13.5 million cash for his cathedral; in the lobby, at the top of a pillar supporting the principal Romanesque arch, the architect, Cass Gilbert, had placed a gargoyle of the great merchant prince himself counting his nickels and dimes.

Surely the observation deck of the nickel dime tower, the highest in the world, offered the most spectacular view in New York. From that eyrie, 792 feet above Broadway, Sarnoff could survey all of lower Manhattan, the Statue of Liberty, and Staten Island to the south; the Hudson River and New Jersey to the west; Central Park and Harlem to the north; and the magnificent Brooklyn Bridge to the east. From the Marconi offices he could look down on the Lower East Side and the poverty of Monroe Street, where he had begun his life in America. Frank Woolworth had been born to impoverished farmers in upstate New York; his building was called "an everlasting example to American youth." Now Sarnoff was following that example closely. His office was right down the hall from John Bottomly and George DeSousa; they consulted him daily, respected his opinions, and appreciated his knowledge of both the technological and commercial parts of the business. The life of a manager was the one he would follow. Who knew just how high in the American Marconi Company he would rise?

At this time, David Sarnoff disclosed his plans to a colleague, Robert Marriott. "He would quit trying to be an engineer," Marriott remembered:

> I don't believe I am as good . . . as you fellows and . . . even a good engineer has a small chance to make money. An engineer or scientific experimenter is at the place where money is going out. The place to make money is where money is coming in. . . . I . . . am going to solicit the sale of contracts and service that will bring money into the company.

Accordingly, he defined his various jobs in the broadest possible way, and used his positions to keep his superiors at Marconi abreast of the latest developments.

In a general reorganization of the Marconi Company's management that came in response to the expansion of wireless and the challenges of AT&T and the navy, Edward J. Nally, a man with experience in transoceanic telegraph cables, but with little understanding of wireless, was appointed its vice president and general manager, Frederick Sammis became the chief engineer, and George DeSousa, the man who had hired Sarnoff six years before, remained commercial manager. For Sarnoff, Nally represented a new challenge, a new superior to impress as he had all the rest.

At first glance, Nally and Sarnoff appeared to have little in common. Fifty-four years old, reserved to the point of dourness, cautious, and conservative, Nally must have been startled by his quick-talking assistant chief engineer more than three decades his junior, whose boldness and assurance seemed almost limitless. But the two soon realized they shared much in common. The son of a Roman Catholic immigrant, Nally had known extreme poverty as a boy. Because of his father's illness, he had been forced to quit school at an early age and provide for himself and his family. And he, too, had steadily worked his way up from messenger boy with the new Western Union Telegraph Company to head the Marconi Company in America.

Sarnoff was fortunate that Nally was a "cable" man, virtually ignorant of wireless. Sarnoff could instruct the general manager in the fundamentals of the new technology. The lessons he presented at the Marconi Institute in the afternoon he gave privately to Nally in the evening, embellishing them with his vision of the shape the new age might take. Sarnoff was a good tutor, for his variety of experience with the company meant he knew more than anyone else. His appetite for learning seemed insatiable. As assistant chief engineer, he visited not only the Marconi installations but also those belonging to other companies. He knew the engineering and could evaluate the merits of rival equipment. His experience as an operator meant other operators knew him, if not by face, at least by his distinctive swing with a telegraph key. All the knowledge he gathered he wrote up in carefully worded informative reports to Sammis, DeSousa, Nally, and, occasionally, Marconi, with whom he still enjoyed a warm relationship.

Quickly, Sarnoff proved to be indispensable. New government requirements for radio transmitters meant that much of the Marconi equipment aboard ships would have to be replaced, a matter that caused consternation in management. Sarnoff's task was to convince them. "I fully appreciate the seriousness of having to scrap so considerable an amount of apparatus as we now have on our ships," he wrote to Nally, "but . . . if we are to continue in the ship to shore business and be successful in its operation, we must be recognized as a company which supplies the best equipment for the money." The skills required in this conservative organization were those of an accomplished diplomat.

One evening just before Christmas 1913, the chief inspector, David Sarnoff, led a delegation of three Marconi engineers to Michael Pupin's cluttered laboratory in the basement of Philosophy Hall. There they witnessed a demonstration of the powerful new regeneration receiver created by Pupin's protégé and assistant, Edwin Howard Armstrong.

For some months, Pupin had been boasting in professional meetings as well as private clubs about the city that the recent Columbia graduate was a genius and his receiver the most effective in the world. To skeptical colleagues, he gave fantastic accounts, that few believed possible, of hearing stations from around the world. This was a time of extravagant claims—and not a little fraud—about new and powerful transmitters and receivers. At first, the visitors from Marconi were naturally suspicious. Then at 9 P.M., they heard what were purported to be telegraph signals from Marconi transmitters in Glace Bay, Labrador, and Clifden, Ireland—stations normally received with considerable difficulty in the United States. While there was no positive proof, the note of the sparks corresponded to the frequency of Marconi stations. At 9:30, they tuned in a small continuous wave station in San Francisco. That night, Armstrong and his remarkable receiver made a great impression on Sarnoff.

Sarnoff and Armstrong liked each other immediately. They got to know each other better at the end of the following month when they spent the last two days of January at the Marconi Company's high-power transmitting station at Belmar, on the New Jersey coast. The weather was bitterly cold, and the shack where they set up the receiver could not keep out the wind. But the messages they received through the air were most impressive: from 4 o'clock on the afternoon of January 30 to 5 o'clock the following morning, they listened to signals from around the world. When they connected Armstrong's receiver to a speaker, they could hear the dots and dashes of Clifden from an adjoining room. Strong signals of a transmission from San Francisco to Portland, Oregon, came in clearly, even through heavy static. The message they plucked from the air concerned a price quotation from the wire manufacturer John Roebling and Sons for galvanized steel cloth. They even heard scraps of a conversation between Honolulu and San Francisco: "Lightning bad. Shall ground aerial wires."

Something more than the mere reception of messages occurred that evening. "Well do I remember that memorable night at the Belmar station when, by means of your 'magic box,' I was able to copy the signals from Honolulu," Sarnoff wrote to Armstrong two decades later, "Whatever chills the air produced were more than extinguished by the warmth of the thrill which came to me at hearing for the first time signals from across the Atlantic and across the Pacific." That frigid night sealed a friendship that would be slow to dissolve.

The rapport between Armstrong and Sarnoff might appear unusual at first. Armstrong was tall, slow-speaking, cerebral, and gentle; Sarnoff was short, talkative, quick-thinking, and aggressive. Armstrong's background was middle-class, Presbyterian, and American; Sarnoff's ghetto slum, Jewish, and Russian. But they were bound by a fraternal pioneering spirit and mutual respect for each other's abilities. A little more than a year separated them in age: at the time of their first meeting, Armstrong was just twenty-three, while Sarnoff was not quite twenty-two. And David Sarnoff realized that Howard Armstrong had made a discovery that would revolutionize the entire art of radio transmission and reception.

Shortly after his visit, Sarnoff reported to Frederick Sammis, chief engineer, on his trips to Pupin's laboratory and Belmar, New Jersey. "Armstrong's receiver," Sarnoff wrote, "was compared with our standard navy type tuner." The differences were striking: "Signals from Clifden . . . could be read with ease with telephones on the table when signals on our receiver were barely readable with the telephones on the ears." After providing details about origin, number, and quality of messages received, he concluded:

I would state that the results obtained with Mr. Armstrong's receiver are sufficiently convincing to warrant our most careful investigation of his patents and circuits, etc., for I believe that his device had tremendous advantages and unless there be other systems of equal merits which are unknown to me, I am of the opinion that he has the most remarkable system in existence.

Sammis and Bottomly were sufficiently impressed by Sarnoff's reports to send them on to Marconi in England, with the thought that he would be "very much interested." The receiver, they thought, was "a wonderful piece of work."

While professing to be "much interested" in the reports, Marconi was actually indifferent. The tests took place during the afternoon and evening, the time when signals from Clifden "reach about their maximum strength in North America." The report sent by the Canadian engineer Weagant (who accompanied Armstrong and Sarnoff to New Jersey) was "very incomplete." After all, Marconi reasoned, his company had already conducted similar tests with the "so called Audion and other vacuum detectors."

In Marconi's response lay a real problem: though the company had more installations of wireless equipment than any other, though it enjoyed a reputation for quality, it was not in the forefront of technology or experimentation. The coherer had performed well enough, and now the various mineral detectors worked adequately. Though his employee John Ambrose Fleming had pioneered development of the vacuum tube, its application was limited, and it had proved unreliable. Most important, in light of future developments, Marconi and his company were cool to the idea of broadcasting music and voices over the radio. Machines for creating continuous waves were preferable to the old spark gap transmitters, but only because they were a more powerful means of sending dots and dashes through the air.

Part of the Marconi Company's failure to evolve its technology may be attributed to its management on both the American and British sides of the Atlantic. Other than Sarnoff, the managers seemed in stasis, slow to take advantage of the significant improvements being made by inventors and content with only the single purpose of wireless for telegraphic communications. To them it was still the American Marconi Wireless *Telegraph* Company, with little place for voice communication. Of all the managers, only Sarnoff, the lowest of them all, knew all parts of the business. He alone visited the ships, kept up with the developments of the German Telefunken Company and the United Fruit Company (which used wireless extensively to maintain communications between its boats and the various plantations in Central and South America), as well as the equipment used in Lee de Forest's latest enterprise. He could only urge his superiors, as he did Nally, "to look forward to the future and this can only be done by frankly discussing the viewpoints for all those who have suggestions to offer."

Then there was the matter of the lawsuit between Marconi and de Forest over rights to the three-element vacuum tube. Though engineers like Sarnoff, who remained close to the operators, understood the value of the third element in the tube, the company's managers appeared hostile to any circuits that used de Forest's invention. Armstrong's regeneration receiver was among them.

◄━

As an operator for Marconi, David Sarnoff demonstrated his skill with a telegraph key; as a manager of the Wanamaker station, he exhibited his skill in publicizing the advantages of wireless; as assistant chief engineer and de facto assistant to Edward J. Nally, he proved his skill as a procurer of technology from a variety of sources. Now, using all the information he had accumulated from his study of radio, he became a prophet.

Since December 1906, when Reginald Fessenden had given his Christmas Eve broadcast, people had been experimenting with the transmission of music and voices through the air. In 1914, Sarnoff had also experimented with a continuous wave transmitter (a small Poulsen arc generator) from the top of the Wanamaker Building. Using a phonograph, he transmitted music to the Wanamaker department store in Philadelphia.

In the fall of 1916, with just such experiments in mind, Sarnoff addressed to Nally a memo that possessed a prophetic quality and that, if followed, would take the Marconi Company's sales into an entirely new area. "I have in mind," Sarnoff wrote, "a plan of development which would make radio a 'household utility' in the same sense as the piano or phonograph." He would bring music into the homes by wireless. While such a scheme had been tried before using wires, it had never succeeded; now, however, using the recent developments in radio equipment, such a system would be "entirely feasible." For example, he continued, describing how such a system might work:

> a radio telephone transmitter having a range of, say, 25 to 50 miles can be installed at a fixed point where the instrumental or vocal music or both are produced. The problem of transmitting music has already been solved in principle, and therefore all the receivers attuned to the transmitting wavelength should be capable of receiving such music. The receiver can be designed in the form of a simple "Radio Music Box" and arranged for several different wavelengths, which should be changeable with the throwing of a single switch or pressing of a single button.

In addition to being able to receive several different stations, the Radio Music Box "can be supplied with amplifying tubes and a loudspeaking telephone, all of which can be neatly mounted in one box. The box can be placed on a table in the parlor or living room, the switch set accordingly, and the music received. There should be no difficulty in receiving the transmitted music perfectly . . ."

Sarnoff then embraced the concept of broadcasting, that "hundreds of thousands of families" could "simultaneously receive from a single transmitter." Transmitters would be strong enough to supply "extra loud signals in the home if desired. The use of head telephones would be obviated by this method." Recent developments of a loop antenna would enable the Radio Music Box to pull in a strong signal.

Going further, Sarnoff presented a wider vision of the future:

> The same principle can be extended to numerous other fields as, for example, receiving lectures at home which can be made perfectly audible; also, events of national importance can be simultaneously announced and received. Baseball scores can be transmitted in the air by the use of one set installed at the Polo Grounds. The same would be true of other cities. This proposition would be especially interesting to farmers and others living in outlying districts removed from cities. By the purchase of a "Radio Music Box" they could enjoy concerts, lectures, music, recitals, etc., which may be going on in the nearest city within their radius. While I have indicated a few of the most probable fields of usefulness for such a device, yet there are numerous other fields to which the principle can be extended . . .

Finally, he turned to the crucial area of finances: If manufactured in quantities of 100,000, the Radio Music Box could sell for "perhaps $75 per outfit," and would "yield a handsome profit" for the company. In addition, "Secondary sources of revenue would be from the sale of transmitters and from increased advertising and circulation of the *Wireless Age*," a magazine the Marconi Company published to promote its technology. The company would arrange "for music recitals, lectures, etc.," and, he implied, would bear the cost of their production. The Radio Music Box would become a way of advertising the Marconi Company.

> It is not possible to estimate the total amount of business obtainable with this plan until it has been developed and actually tried out; but there are about 15,000,000 families in the United States alone, and if only one million, or seven percent of the total amount of families, thought well of the idea it would, at the figure mentioned, mean a gross business of about $75,000,000 which should yield considerable revenue.

Prophecy aside, Sarnoff's memo provides a brilliant example of his mode of operation. His was an acquisitive mind, one that carefully gauged the developments in technology. When the moment was ripe, he would bring that technology to the public in an attractive package. By November 1916, he knew (perhaps from listening to de Forest's broadcasts) that technology had advanced far enough to make a radio as we know it today possible. Never mind that no one had used the word "broadcasting" yet, or that there was no demand. By transmitting programs, especially music, the company would create a need for the product where none had existed before.

Yet Sarnoff had not gauged the political moment correctly. In Europe, the British, French, and Germans were mired in mud and rain in Flanders, losing about a million soldiers in the process; in the United States, Woodrow Wilson had barely defeated Charles Evans Hughes for a second term as president, and was busy preparing for his country's entry into the war. Edward J. Nally was preoccupied with the challenges posed by the navy and AT&T, and with the numerous government contracts (including ones from the navy) for equipment. This was not the time for Sarnoff to present his vision. Nally left the memo unanswered.

Sarnoff also came to realize that the fall of 1915 was not the right political moment for him to suggest the creation of a Radio Music Box. In fact, he had stepped beyond the limits of his job as chief inspector. His memo called for a dramatic reorientation of a company that thought principally in terms of ship-to-shore communication. In addition, he was in no position to see his proposal to a successful completion. No matter. When the proper moment did come, he would be ready.

Lee de Forest, however, did not feel the constraints of a large company. Earlier in the decade, while experimenting with his "radio telephone," he had used a Poulsen generator to transmit Caruso's voice from the stage of the Metropolitan Opera House, as well as the voice of his mother-in-law Harriot Stanton Blatch. In the fall of 1916 at his High Bridge plant in the Bronx, he went further by using the audion as a small transmitter. This time he directed his messages not to a particular receiver, but to many. Without knowing it, de Forest was exploring new territory, the territory Sarnoff had outlined: regular broadcasting.

Soon amateurs and professional operators as far as 200 miles away were tuning in their crystal sets to hear "radio phone concerts" made possible by the Columbia Graphophone Company. De Forest's motivations were an alloy of his desire to spread good music and culture—enrichment he had never been able to enjoy at Talladega—to his listeners, and his need to sell his radio products. Between the music and occasional lectures, he would make a pitch for the superior quality of his equipment, especially the audion. On the evening of November 7, he broadcast the results of the presidential election. Signing off before the returns from California were in, he declared Hughes the winner over Wilson.

Others, too, began broadcasting, including C. V. Logwood, de Forest's colleague from the Federal Telegraph Company. In November 1916, he and a friend broadcast music from 9 to 10 P.M. weeknights from their amateur station 2ZK in New Rochelle, north of New York City. The broadcasts could be heard in Manhattan.

Sarnoff became too preoccupied with threats from the navy and with the political events that were moving the United States toward war with Germany to press his Radio Music Box proposal. Nally recognized that the skills of his chief inspector could be used in discussions with officials in Washington. In November 1916, Sarnoff had accompanied him to testify against one of the many proposals for governmental takeover of radio communications. Then he had spoken not for the Marconi Company, but for the Institute of Radio Engineers, for which he served as secretary. He had performed superbly.

"Government competition, or confiscation by the Government," Sarnoff asserted in his statement, "would effectively stifle inventive efforts." It was a theme he would emphasize again and again; the nation depended on its inventive resources, which the government should assist, not oppose. Without any trace of an accent, Sarnoff spoke in a quiet and reasoned manner, an approach that quickly earned him the respect of officials. He enjoyed his new role. Here he was, barely fifteen years in his adopted land, sitting among the powerful, walking the halls of the Capitol, and earning the respect of the senators and congressmen who ran the country. With his broad understanding of the state of the art, he could influence their decisions about its regulation. It was a heady feeling for a twenty-five-year-old.

More and more, Nally came to rely on the chief inspector. Here was a person with the knowledge of an engineer, the skills of an accomplished operator, the imagination of the best inventors, and the abilities of an able politician. Accordingly, on January 1, 1917, he appointed Sarnoff commercial manager of the Marconi Company to head a newly consolidated commercial department. In the reorganization, this would be the creative department, a new hub around which all commercial activities of the Marconi would revolve. Some 725 employees and 582 radio installations would fall under his supervision. Now on the eve of America's entry into the war, David Sarnoff had skillfully used his talents and loyalty to become second in command of the largest and best wireless company in the country.

De Forest at age 8.   De Forest at age 17.

"I must be brilliant, win fame, show the greatness of genius and to no small degree," Lee de Forest wrote when at Yale. His fellow students in the class of 1896 at the Sheffield Scientific School, voted him "nerviest" and "homeliest," while others named him "most conceited" and "windiest."

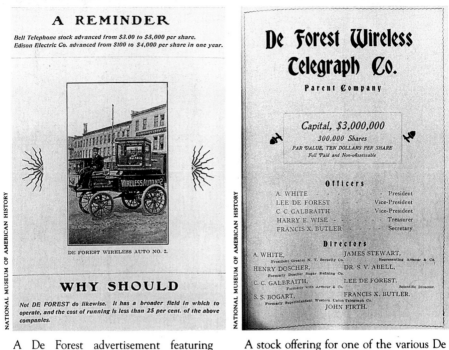

A De Forest advertisement featuring "Wireless auto #2." Salesmen parked the car on Wall Street and transmitted stock quotations to a broker's office nearby.

A stock offering for one of the various De Forest companies.

"Soon, we believe, the suckers will begin to bite!" wrote Lee de Forest as the company bearing his name began selling stock. Here he appears with an assistant before one of his wireless telegraph offices.

Abraham White, whom de Forest regarded as "all & more than a Brother" until White forced him out of the wireless company bearing his name. Here the two pose at the 1904 St. Louis World's Fair.

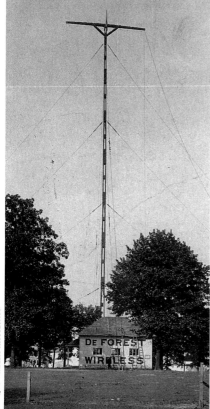

One of the De Forest Company wireless towers at the fair.

DE FOREST CRUEL, SAYS 'WIRELESS' BRIDE OF WIZARD.

Wife of Inventor Who Seeks Divorce from Her Declares She Could Not Tolerate His Conduct.

DETECTIVES TELL OF TRIP TO ADIRONDACKS.

Employed to Follow Wife, After Husband Received Hints from Servants.

With all the vehemence that voice and gesture could express, Mrs. Lucille De Forest denied last night the charges made against her by hr husband, the young and celebrated inventor of a wireless telegraphy system, who has brought suit for divorce. The two were married on Feb. 17 in the Hotel St. Regis, following a brief courtship in which the wireless telegraphy was Cupid's courier.

"Cruel treatment," and that alone, is responsible for our separation," Mrs. De Forest said. Protest was stamped in every line of her lithe, girlish figure, gowned in a close-fitting costume of champagne cloth. She is only twenty-one. Her wedding ring was guarded by a ruby circlet which flashed as she raised her hand in emphasis.

She Denies All Allegations.

"I deny in detail the accusations made against me, and against others named by my husband in his suit. Soon after our marriage, little more than six months ago, his conduct became well-nigh unbearable. This was during the time of our honeymoon in Europe. I submitted to this cruel treatment until it became intolerable, and then I left him to return to my mother. I will contest his action, and I am confident that the courts will vindicate me. I must not say any more at this time."

Mrs. DeForest and her mother, Mrs. M. T. Sherdowne, have moved into a cosy apartment in Fifty-sixth street, the address of which is confided to only a few personal friends.

Besides this action for divorce, Mr. De Forest has brought suit for $50,000 damages against De Witt C. Flanagan, the millionaire president of the Flanagan-Nay Brewing Company. Mr. Flanagan is named in the divorce proceedings brought by Mr. De Forest. Mr. Flanagan said last night:

Mr. Flanagan's Statement.

"I am not surprised by the stories

HE PROPOSED, SHE ACCEPTED, BY WIRELESS—DIVORCE SUIT.

MRS. LEE DE FOREST.   LEE DE FOREST.

"I long for a blonde to love!; Give me a pretty blonde!" de Forest had said while at Yale. His first three marriages (to brunettes) ended in divorce. His first marriage, to Lucille Sheardowne, was never consummated.

RHODA BARNEY JENKINS

De Forest's second wife, Nora Stanton Blatch, the granddaughter of Elizabeth Cady Stanton, wanted to work with him in wireless. He wished only for her to stay at home and raise a family. She left him.

Mary Mayo, an opera singer of "birdlike purity," de Forest's third wife, made Riverlure their home.

"Riverlure—where dreams come true." De Forest conceived it as "a nest for the nestlings," but Nora refused to live in it.

The "serious" child. Howard Armstrong before his family's New York brownstone.

Armstrong, about eleven.

Armstrong with his family in Yonkers.

"Great amplification obtained at once." Armstrong discovered regeneration in his third-floor tower room of his family's house in Yonkers.

Behind the house he had erected a 125-foot antenna.

Armstrong while he was at Columbia.

Sarnoff the junior telegrapher for the Marconi Company.

" 'Boy, you're going to do all right in America.' " Sarnoff with his mother in a photograph taken before they left for the United States.

At his key at the Marconi Company's Siasconset station.

The New York Times.

"The *Titanic* disaster brought radio to the front, and also me," said Sarnoff. The *New York Times* for April 15, 1912, the morning after the luxury liner struck an iceberg.

Years after the disaster, writers in RCA's publicity department maintained the fiction that Sarnoff had been the *only* person at the telegraph key to relay news of the survivors to anxious relatives and friends, and distributed this crudely air-brushed photograph of their boss at the key to prove it. The story was false.

DAVID SARNOFF LIBRARY

Major Armstrong. During World War I Armstrong invented the superheterodyne, the tuning circuit found in virtually every radio and television today. He also built, installed, and tested radio sets for the U.S. Air Corps, a job that enabled him to indulge his twin passions: speed and height.

Armstrong with other members of the French and United States armies posing at the base of the Eiffel Tower.

"My company prospers," Lee de Forest wrote of the orders for military equipment he received from the United States and foreign countries. He also developed receiving sets for the navy's new dirigibles, work he found "intensely interesting."

Anti-Semitism kept David Sarnoff from receiving a commission in the navy. Instead he filled orders for equipment for the Marconi company. He also took time to marry the French-born Lizette Hermant. "I could speak no French and Lizette could speak no English, so what else could we do?" When RCA was formed in 1919, Sarnoff became the commercial manager.

RCA's principal business in the early years was in radiograms, telegrams sent by wireless and delivered by teams of messenger boys.

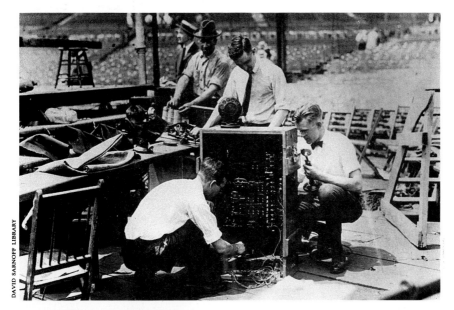

"I have in mind a plan of development which would make radio a 'household utility' " Sarnoff had proposed in 1916. He had been ignored. But in 1921 he arranged the broadcast of the Dempsey-Carpentier fight to more than 300,000 people, the largest radio audience ever assembled. (Here engineers prepare for the broadcast.) Radio soon became a craze.

"Edwin H. Armstrong found the radio telephone talking like a hare-lipped man and left it singing like a nightingale." Armstrong's invention of the superheterodyne made radio practical. Soon everyone was listening.

"Armstrong, why do you do these damnfool things?" In 1923 Armstrong's fondness for heights led him to pose for a series of day and night photographs at the top of the RCA broadcasting tower, 400 feet above 42nd Street. Sarnoff was not amused at the stunt and for a while banned him from the RCA offices.

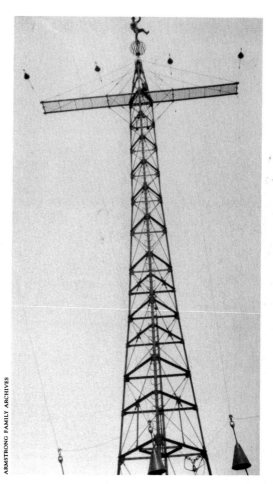

In 1923 Armstrong was the largest private stockholder in RCA and was considered a millionaire. He wooed and won the hand of Marion MacInnis, David Sarnoff's secretary. After they were married the couple went to Palm Beach in a new Hispano-Suiza. Armstrong's wedding present to his wife was the first portable radio.

5

WIRELESS GOES TO WAR

"I myself leave for Berlin tomorrow," a grave Kaiser Wilhelm II declared as he stepped ashore at Kiel late in the afternoon of the last Sunday in June 1914. Some of the finest ships of the British and German navies had sailed to the port on the Baltic Sea to take part in the yachting competition the kaiser held there each summer. By gentlemen's agreement, both countries had pledged to ban any "undue curiosity in technical matters." Instead, the British and Germans gave themselves up to a week of spirited races, festive banquets, and fulsome speeches. It was summer, the final brilliant hiatus before the dark fall, when, as one subaltern in the British Army, the poet Wilfred Owen, put it, "night crushed out the day." The weather that Sunday was fair with a faint breeze, excellent for the races that the kaiser was directing from the deck of his own yacht, *Hohenzollern*. However, Wilhelm received news that destroyed the tranquillity on the Baltic: at midday in Sarajevo, capital of Austro-Hungary's province Bosnia, an assassin had shot and killed the kaiser's friend Archduke Franz Ferdinand and his wife, Sophia.

How had the German kaiser learned of the murders? And how did Americans find out that the loose fabric of European alliances had been irreparably torn? Shortly after the murders, the archduke's private secretary, Baron Rumerskirch, sent a telegram from Sarajevo to Kiel, 800 miles to the northwest. It was the practice for the operator there to transmit all messages by wireless to the kaiser on his royal yacht. But his transmitter was broken that Sunday, so the dread news was given to Admiral Mueller, chief of the kaiser's naval secretariat, who embarked in a small motorboat to deliver it personally. The kaiser halted the race (a task made all the more painful because his own boat, *Meteor*, was holding a comfortable lead of fifteen minutes over its closest English rival), ordered all flags flown at half-staff, and headed for the port. From the *Hohenzollern*, whose wireless did work, he sent a message canceling the large dinner party he was to host that evening. Once ashore, he quit Kiel for Berlin in "considerable agitation."

Traveling by "Special Cable," from Sarajevo, the dispatch of the archduke's assassination was front-page news in the *New York Times* the next morning. The words tapped in Morse code on a key in Sarajevo went first to Vienna and thence to Emden on the North Sea. At Emden, the message entered a submarine cable owned by the German government, which passed southwest to the Azores, and then to Long Island. The six-hour time difference between Kiel and New York had made it relatively easy for newspapers to compose their stories for Monday morning's editions. The *Times* also gathered other special cables from Paris and London to complete its story. In each case the telegrapher's dots and dashes were converted into words by a machine in the United States similar to the one Armstrong's first mentor, Charles Underhill, had invented. A story of this length almost always came through the submarine cable. Though the *Times* had maintained a page headed "Cable and Wireless Messages from Europe" for a number of years, interference and weak transmitters made the wireless equipment unreliable. While shorter reports sometimes carried the by-line, "By Marconi Transatlantic Wireless Telegraph," longer ones invariably said "By Special Cable."

Reliance on telegraph wires was changing, however, and in ways that alarmed cable companies and governments. More and more governments and private companies were employing wireless to transmit their messages over great distances of land and sea. Five months before the shots at Sarajevo, Wilhelm had used the occasion of his own fifty-fifth birthday to send a telegraphic message through the ether to President Wilson, with the hope that "wireless communication will become a new link between our countries." The words had traveled 4,062.5 miles from a transmitter near Hannover, Germany, to a receiving station at Tuckerton, New Jersey. But even that message caused concern: representatives of the German company that manufactured and installed the equipment claimed it was more powerful than any available, and boasted it could send secret wireless messages by simultaneously altering the wavelength in its transmitters and receivers. As Europe's leaders prepared for war, statesmen began to wonder—and worry—about the darker possibilities of wireless: espionage and the transmission of coded messages and orders.

Since 1855, when the London *Times* received the first cabled dispatches from the Crimean War, telegraphy had been an important method of relaying the news. Increasingly, newspapers and diplomats relied on wireless as well as cable to convey messages. The news of Dewey's victory at Manila Bay in 1898 (without benefit of wireless, of course) had taken three days to reach the newspapers in New York; with the assistance of de Forest's weak system, word from the battlefront in the Russian-Japanese War had taken less than twelve hours to reach London. Coming over telegraph lines, the news from Sarajevo had taken just six hours. Two months after the assassination, and days after her declaration of war, Great Britain's admiralty cut the German submarine cables to the United States, thereby forcing the enemy to rely on its radio transmitters at Hannover and Nauen outside Berlin. The simple act of cutting the telegraph cables caused developments in radio to take place more quickly than ever before.

Less than four years after the assassination at Sarajevo, Woodrow Wilson delivered his Fourteen Points for world peace by wireless and cable across the Atlantic. Almost instantly, they were received in London, Paris, Berlin, and the other European capitals. By the beginning of June, the navy had installed a 200-kilowatt Alexanderson alternator at New Brunswick, New Jersey, unquestionably the most powerful transmitter in the world. On October 12, a new parliamentary government in Germany sent a wireless message to Washington, approaching President Wilson for the terms of an armistice based on his Fourteen Points. Many of those negotiations were carried out through wireless.

The Great War, as it came to be called, altered the nature of radio, just as radio began to alter the nature of war. In the United States, radio became an official interest of the government. Stations were commandeered; operators were trained by the thousands; patent suits that had hindered radio's development were put in abeyance; equipment was standardized; new equipment was developed; and orders for manufacture multiplied.

Shortly after 1 P.M. on Good Friday, April 6, 1917, the operator at station NAA, the huge naval wireless installation in Arlington, Virginia, tapped out a message to the world that President Wilson had signed the congressional resolution declaring war with Germany. The navy secretary, Josephus Daniels, saw the opportunity—at least temporarily—to get his wish: with the president's consent, the navy took over all amateur and commercial radio stations not belonging to those operated by the signal corps of the U.S. Army. Essentially, the secretary had commandeered all the wireless interests in the nation.

The order brought a halt to de Forest's nightly broadcasts from his amateur station in the Bronx; however, the navy was not interested in such small operations. It set its sights on the giant Marconi transmitters, which it quickly integrated into its communication system. These stations had equipment the government needed: acres of needlelike aerials, powerful generators for transmitting radio waves, and sensitive receivers. Already the government controlled Siasconset on Nantucket (which it had seized in a fit of neutrality for handling secret war messages); now it added Sea Gate on Coney Island; Sagaponack on Long Island; and South Wellfleet on Cape Cod. (Smaller Marconi stations, like the one at Belmar, also came under naval control.) Perhaps the biggest prize of all was the station at New Brunswick, where Marconi had been installing a fifty-kilowatt Alexanderson alternator (predecessor to the larger one installed in 1918), then the most powerful available. It had already transferred the German equipment it had confiscated at Tuckerton, New Jersey, to its station at Arlington; and it had also taken over another German station at Sayville, Long Island, which had been found to be relaying by code the positions of British ships to its lethal fleet of submarines cruising in the North Atlantic.

The government soon learned that other smaller stations caught in its web could serve the war effort with distinction. In 1916, Alessandro Fabbri, an impassioned and wealthy yachtsman and radio amateur, had offered the navy his station on Mount Desert Island, Maine. Though the navy first declined, after the declaration of war it commandeered the station and his yacht, made Fabbri an ensign, and placed him in command. Largely with his own money, he expanded his operation and moved it a few miles from Bar Harbor to the Otter Cliffs, a pink granite outcrop overlooking the Atlantic. Radio engineers came to regard the cliffs as the best location for transatlantic reception. Outfitted with improved equipment, the remote outpost received clearly all the frequencies used by transatlantic transmitters. Through Fabbri's station passed most of the official communications between the battlefronts in Europe, and later the Peace Conference in Paris and Washington. The traffic often amounted to 20,000 words a day, most of them in cipher.

Stations on naval ships, as well as installations on both sides of the Atlantic, demanded qualified operators. The government established training schools for operators at Harvard and Mare Island, California. Together, they could accommodate 5,000 operators for a four-month course. Amateur experimenters were the first to join. Soon the training school was graduating them at the rate of 100 a week. By 1918, the number had increased fourfold.

Some of these operators would not return from the war. From his office in New York, David Sarnoff, acting as secretary of the Institute of Radio Engineers, composed black-bordered pages for the quarterly issues of the *Proceedings*: "The Institute of Radio Engineers announces with regret the death of . . ." Some, like Jesse Edgar Baker, succumbed to illness: "He contracted scarlet fever and died"; others died in combat: "On August 8, 1918,

Lieutenant-Colonel Leibmann was killed in action while leading his men in a charge at the front in Flanders."

Shortly after the declaration of war, the federal government imposed a moratorium on radio patent litigation for the duration of the hostilities, a step made necessary because of the claims and counterclaims of the various inventors and the companies that represented them. These cases had retarded and at times blocked completely the development of radio. Typical was the suit over rights to manufacture the audion brought by the Marconi Wireless Telegraph Company of America against the De Forest Radio Telephone and Telegraph Company.

By 1916, de Forest had found his patents on the audion far from secure. In federal district court, the American Marconi Company claimed that his addition of the third element (the grid) to the tube constituted only minor modification to John Ambrose Fleming's invention. In his defense, de Forest contended that the audion's origins lay in his patents of the gas burner detector.

Judge Julius Mayer of the Southern District of New York decided that de Forest had built his defense on "an unsteady theoretical structure." The gas burner detector had nothing to do with the discovery of the audion. Instead, the judge determined, its true origin might be traced to de Forest's reading of Fleming's article on the vacuum tube in the *Proceedings* of the Royal Society. "Within a very short space of time," Mayer concluded, de Forest "changed his mind." It was then, so the judge reasoned, "he used the language of the incandescent lamp." Crushed, de Forest characterized the decision as "illegal and half-baked." Nevertheless, Mayer upheld Marconi and barred de Forest from manufacturing his audion without consent of the company.

To complicate the matter even further, de Forest had contended in a suit of his own that the Marconi Company was illegally using his invention of the grid in its tubes. In an out-of-court settlement, the Marconi Company allowed that it had manufactured tubes containing the third element without de Forest's consent. Combined with Mayer's decision, this admission produced a stalemate; neither de Forest nor Marconi could manufacture the audion without the other's consent.

As with the Fessenden case a decade earlier, this devastating litigation threatened de Forest's company. Though he was determined to appeal, and could continue to manufacture audions while doing so, he estimated the legal costs would set De Forest Radio Telephone and Telegraph back "$40,000, easily." The decision was also crushing personally. Mayer had appeared to ridicule the experiments that formed the foundation of his defense.

Taking the stand as an expert witness for Marconi had been none other than Edwin Howard Armstrong. De Forest's rival from Columbia had impressed the judge, who in his decision cited Armstrong's testimony as well as a paper he had published in 1914 on the "Operating Features of the Audion." Armstrong had presented the "most convincing" explanation of the tube's action. Even more painful to de Forest than the expense of an appeal or Armstrong's testimony against him had been the loss of his "greatest achievement" to a "wop outfit."

The moratorium the United States government imposed simply ignored the Marconi and de Forest suits and all other patent infringement cases. In effect, the government's action had created a well-stocked pool of radio inventions for the duration of the war. From that pool, manufacturers could choose whatever they liked. After years of contention and rivalry, they were free to develop radio technology without hindrance. In an effort to be even-handed, the government awarded contracts among the various companies so that no one could gain an advantage.

World war and government contracts forced manufacturers to think on a larger and more uniform scale than ever before. For the first time, they had to produce components in enormous numbers to particular specifications. Companies applied principles of mass production to the manufacture of components—especially vacuum tubes. Before the war, companies had made radio tubes of erratic quality by the hundreds in a process that was time-consuming, tedious, and expensive; during the war, they made them by the hundreds of thousands on assembly lines with government inspectors watching over them carefully. The Corning Glass Works in upstate New York supplied cylindrical tube blanks, while Leo Hendrik Baekeland, a Belgian-born chemist from Yonkers, New York, supplied bases composed of a new substance highly valued for its insulating qualities, Bakelite. From each Bakelite base on the tube projected four pins that fit into standard porcelain and metal sockets.

For radio inventors, manufacturers, and operators, the United States entry into the Great War simply hastened changes that had begun to take place nearly five years prior to April 1917. Beginning with the Wilson administration in March 1913, the navy had sought to control the ether and eliminate foreign competition. It had been using the enormous power of contract awards to equip its fleet and standardize radio components. While many contracts went to Marconi, others went to AT&T and lesser companies like De Forest Radio Telephone and Telegraph. The government already was the largest developer and customer for radio equipment; after April 6, it became the only customer for most manufacturers. The navy found that radio enabled its ships to remain in communication well beyond anything imagined with flags or lights. It ordered the installation of 10,000 sets. The army found radio communications could support the projected force of 2 million men it would need to win the war. It ordered the development of equipment that might be carried on the back of a horse. Both the navy and the army had developed standards for radio equipment to be used on vessels or in the trenches so that operators would not be forced to master a new system each time they were transferred to a new vessel or outfit.

The implications of the government's actions were wider reaching than anyone envisioned in 1917. Its orders brought about an institutionalization of radio development that signaled the end of the lone inventor—the Marconi, de Forest, or Armstrong—who had brought radio to life. Increasingly, individuals who possessed great talents would have to submit them to the whims of a large corporation like Marconi or American Telephone and Telegraph, or to the government. The war had transformed radio from a novelty into a necessity whose worth was greater and more important than any single inventor's reputation.

At forty-four years of age, Lee de Forest considered himself too old to join the 4.5 million men mobilized to crush the Hun, but even if he had been younger, it is doubtful he would have enlisted. He had regarded Wilson's reelection as "4 years of distortion and 'easy prosperity' " under his "craven and shameless" leadership. Before America's entry into the conflict, he became a trustee of the American Defense Society, debated military preparedness with Josephus Daniels, and proclaimed that "Defenseless virtue stands naked for the despoiler." Yet at the same time he believed:

> [The] stupid nation richly deserves the punishment she invites. I'm sure I would not be willing to fight & die for such a people as ours have shown themselves to be—a characterless, incohesive, goulash. It takes more than broad lands, freedom, & nature's benefice to make a race & a people.

While de Forest might have been reluctant to give his life for an incohesive goulash, he was ready to manufacture equipment that would help the Allies with their fight. Orders poured in from Australia, New Zealand, Russia, and Japan. In 1915, he received a contract from the navy to supply thousands of small radio tubes. By the fall of 1916, he could write, "My company prospers" (though poor business management meant it was only "slowly advancing"), and his laboratory work, where he was developing sets for the navy's new dirigibles, was "intensely interesting."

Nevertheless, these orders were not enough. Financial circumstances forced him to give up most of the rights to his patents to a large corporation. Over the autumn of 1916, he negotiated with American Telephone and Telegraph, and for the first time in his life he was driving a very hard bargain, "$250,000 for exclusive rights to all pats.—*but* my Co. must retain rights for all . . . foreign, & government fields." In addition, he stipulated that Western Electric "must agree not to license anyone whom we are suing for patent infringement." For the first time ever, the De Forest Radio Telephone Company would pay some handsome dividends over the next four months of $1.45 a share, $174,000 on de Forest's 120,000 shares. Early in April 1917, just at the time the United States was declaring war upon Germany, he completed the deal.

"So *at last*—after 17 years of hard & unrelenting struggle," de Forest recorded triumphantly in his journal, "with never a letup, never a *certainty* of success . . . I have at last reached a safe & secure resting place." No more would he feel "the dread uncertainty of the morrow." Counting himself a very wealthy man, de Forest spared no extravagance. "*Now* at last I can live a little . . . now beautify my home, now adorn my pretty wife . . ." He did all three, and more. He built a wide verandah with awnings on the western side of Riverlure, so that he and Mary might look out over the Hudson and the far palisades each evening at sunset. He bought Mary an elaborate wardrobe. He ordered a limousine top placed on his Hudson automobile. Each morning, a chauffeur would roar down from Riverlure to his factory on Sedgwick Avenue in a new Roamer Roadster. "And meantime," de Forest exulted, "the company thrives."

In later years, as inventors discovered more and more uses for his radio tube, and his own fortune dwindled, de Forest came to believe the sale of the audion to AT&T had been at a bargain price. Forgetting that the patent on the audion tube had just seven years before it expired, that the Marconi Company had successfully challenged his rights to the invention, and that Armstrong was successfully contending his right to the oscillating and regeneration patents, de Forest thought only of the money AT&T had made. Surely he had been robbed. Why had his lawyers settled so easily? Why hadn't he retained his rights to the audion and simply granted a nonexclusive license? Then he would have been able to license his patents to other radio manufacturers and he and the De Forest Company would be worth millions. At that moment though, secure in the rising tide of government and foreign orders, de Forest thought only of his great (and immediate) wealth.

Such riches as de Forest accrued came at a deeper and more spiritual expense. Giving up the rights to the audion meant not only the sale of his greatest invention, but the sale of a part of himself, a part he would later call "my child." He had already grown angry when he lost a certain cachet after selling the initial patent rights to AT&T. The company had then used his audion to create the first transcontinental telephone service. At the Panama-Pacific International Exposition in San Francisco in 1915, an exuberant celebration of that city's post-earthquake reconstruction and development, AT&T had arranged for Alexander Graham Bell to repeat his famous words of 1876 to his assistant, Thomas Watson; but this time the command, "Come here, Watson, I want you," spanned the continent between California and New York. Never did AT&T mention the tube that had made the feat possible. When it distributed a handsome brochure, "The Story of a Great Achievement: Telephone Communication from Coast to Coast," at its exhibition booth without mentioning his name or his invention, de Forest became incensed. In a white heat he wrote his own account of the long-distance telephone, and on the following day he distributed from his own booth at the exposition a brochure that matched AT&T's, even to the details of typeface and paper stock: "The Story of a Great Achievement: Which Made Telephone Communication from Coast to Coast Possible." True, other inventions beginning with the Bell telephone had contributed to the feat of transcontinental telephone conversations, but "the one last missing link—the genuine *sine qua non* is the AUDION AMPLIFIER OF DE FOREST."

In October 1915, de Forest learned that American Telephone and Telegraph intended to commence wireless transmission of voices between the Eiffel Tower and the U.S. naval station at Arlington. For years, he had been trying to fulfill his dream of "trans-Atlantic Radio Telephony." Now, someone other than he, a corporation other than his own, would attain it. He traveled to Paris, but was barred from the tower. The invention he had labored over since late 1906 had been consumed by a giant with resources his struggling company could never hope to match.

As a youth, Lee had revered Edison and Bell and sought to emulate them. As a young inventor, he had dreamed of making his name rank "at least . . . with that of Marconi." Their three names were secure with their eponymous companies; but "de Forest" would be forgotten. Even the word "audion" was fading from popular language. It would never take its place in the vocabulary as "Vaseline" or "Bakelite" had. Increasingly, people were calling it simply the "radio" or "vacuum" tube. A dozen years before, a tower in St. Louis proclaimed in blazing lights DE FOREST before the world. He had medals to prove his worth, stock certificates emblazoned with wireless towers and lightning bolts surrounding his name. But the fame he had sought—along with the money—was in eclipse.

A subtle change was taking place in America, one de Forest did not understand. More than ever the corporation was assuming control, and it was becoming harder and harder for an individual to make a mark outside its structure. Those individuals whose names survived history were from another era. Bell and Edison had preceded him by a quarter century; Henry Ford, creator of a car and a company after his name, by a decade, and even their companies were slowly being incorporated into larger corporations.

Nor did the emoluments of wealth—the wide verandah at Riverlure, the chauffeured automobiles, the expensive clothes—bring de Forest much happiness at home. In the years since their marriage in 1912, his third wife, Mary, had steadily become more dependent on alcohol. The voice lessons became fewer and eventually stopped; the grand piano in the living room at Riverlure was silent. By 1915, de Forest would often return home after a long day at his laboratory in Highbridge to find Mary in an alcoholic stupor. She attempted cures, which relied mostly on willpower, but she always failed. She began to suffer acutely from the effects of rheumatism. More and more she took to her bed and bottle.

On the verge of his major sale to AT&T, de Forest complained in his journal of being "more or less a dead man alive . . . due more than all else to the recurrent sadness & despair of soul which the lapses, ever recurrent, of my wife have caused me." Though Riverlure was supposed to be the place where dreams came true, he reflected in a maudlin mood, "month after month, year after year, one dream after another has atrophied & died."

Evidence of just how much the dream had died appeared in a letter he wrote to Mary, his "dear Desire," on stationery of the Hotel Edouard VII in Paris, where he was trying to sell his radio telephone sets to the French for use in the trenches. He told of learning French, attending the Opéra Comique and La Bohème. He alluded to some of his adventures on Armistice Day, though he left out an account of the "charming brown-eyed grisette" with whom he celebrated the evening, and the tale of stealing the American flag from a bank. But then he turned to his greater concerns of Mary's alcoholism and abandoned singing career. Certainly she had "suffered terribly," but he also had endured "mental agony" on account of her intemperance. He implored her to "stay on the wagon forever." With regard to her singing he wrote:

> O, dear girl, if you but only realized the value of your voice, & what you could, and ought to achieve with it—I would, as I wrote you before, devote my life to your success. But it means work, work, hard work, yet with the greatest joy you

have ever experienced withal, because you can so quickly achieve *great things* for us both.

Still, there were times at Riverlure and elsewhere "filled with happiness," when they were as happy as they had been on their first meeting. In 1915, on a trip to England aboard the Cunard liner *Cameronia* through the submarine-infested North Atlantic, Mary sang at a shipboard gala organized to aid the Red Cross, and de Forest demonstrated his audion. During those times when Mary remained sober, she and Lee spent pleasant hours together. Often Mary would play the piano and sing while her husband listened from the verandah. These were the moments he longed for, the times, he reflected in his journal, when Riverlure was truly the place where, in his romantic mind, dreams came true.

Part of another dream came true, too. De Forest had always wanted a son, a "Lee Junior," who, he imagined, might someday follow him to attain glory at Yale. For years his marriage had been barren, so it with some surprise that he learned in early 1919 that his wife was pregnant. The child, not a son but a daughter, arrived on the last day of September 1919. The new father quickly dispelled his disappointment. He named his new daughter Eleanor, after the heroine of Poe's tale. In the ensuing years he would devote numerous entries in his journal to minute discussion of Eleanor's every action. Though not a boy, Eleanor gave him great pleasure, and there was always the hope Mary would bear another child, a boy.

"It looks like a long war," Edwin Howard Armstrong wrote his mother after he arrived in France in the fall of 1917. Though wrong in his prediction, his tone suggests his commitment to the cause of the Allies. There had been no question about his signing up for service; he accepted his obligation with little comment and volunteered almost immediately. He realized, too, as did the army, that his knowledge of wireless would be valuable. After a hasty summer of officers' training, he embarked for France. He was to work in Paris at the division of research and inspection, a laboratory the signal corps had established on the Boulevard Montparnasse. There he was to keep his eyes open for the problems plaguing wireless communications among the Allies, and solve as many of them as possible.

World War I marked a period of expansion for Armstrong, a time when he made two significant additions to his small circle of friends, and, most important, his second great radio discovery, the superheterodyne, the circuit that makes possible the precise tuning of virtually every one of today's radios and televisions.

Enlisting meant interrupting a number of commitments. Armstrong had been teaching and working in the laboratory at Columbia University, developing and licensing his regeneration invention to interested companies, and, with his lawyer, systematically formulating a strategy to keep de Forest from taking his patents. In addition, he served as the titular head of his family, managed its finances (which had become precarious with the death of his father), and oversaw his younger sister's education at Vassar College as well as the maintenance of his mother's house in Yonkers.

The trip to France via Southampton was uneventful. As soon as the ship left New York harbor, he looked up the radio shack, which was equipped only with a primitive carborundum detector. "The ordinary ship receiver does not carry audions but the operator happened to have one of his own aboard," Armstrong wrote his mother in his first letter home at the end of September, "so I borrowed some wire from the electrician and rigged up a regenerative circuit that brought in signals from all over the map. We got press from both sides of the Atlantic which is unheard of in ordinary ship practice."

Armstrong filled his letters home with practical details, associated with trying to oversee family affairs from abroad: "What payments have been made by the Marconi C," he asked his mother, and then implored her to tell him "what you find your living expenses are running per month . . . Incidentally, have you all the coal you need?" To his sister, Ethel, he voiced even more concerns about their mother: "Have you had the rail put on the cellar steps yet? If not, do it immediately, regardless of what kind of argument you start. Second, is mother working too hard?"

Once he had established himself at the Boulevard Montparnasse, Armstrong made a hasty review of the communications on the French lines, where he found wireless conditions to be primitive. While manufacturers like de Forest in the United States produced tubes by the thousands, few of them seem to have made it to the American Expeditionary Forces, especially at the front. Back in Paris, he built two sophisticated transmitters and receivers with regenerative circuits. After completing these, he worked to create a communications system for the army air corps, personally installing radio sets in the planes and testing them in the air. Armstrong delighted in being able to indulge his twin passions of speed and height.

Gradually, Armstrong began to concentrate on a problem the American Expeditionary Forces regarded as most important: detecting radio communication at very high frequencies. He had learned of it in London from Henry Joseph Round. An engineer for the Marconi Company since 1902, Round was now one of the master's personal research assistants. He had been graduated from the Royal College of London and worked for a while at the

Marconi Company's school for operators in Babylon, Long Island, all the while actively engaged in creating his own inventions to improve wireless. In 1911, he had developed a crystal detector that enabled sharper tuning of receivers. He, too, had discovered a regeneration circuit similar to Armstrong's (but just a few weeks later, so there was no question of claiming interference), and was known as a pioneer in the development of voice transmission over microphones.

As part of his war work, Round was perfecting a system he had devised that employed radio waves to detect the movements of enemy ships and planes. The system had served the British well on May 30, 1916, when they used it to detect a seven-mile shift in the position of the German fleet at Wilhelm-shaven 300 miles away. The information allowed the Royal Navy to intercept the enemy at the Battle of Jutland off Norway. His achievement was all the more remarkable since the Royal Navy considered wireless undependable. "Nothing ought to be trusted . . . except direct visual signaling by searchlight flashes," the former first lord of the British admiralty, Winston Churchill, remarked in his account of Jutland. "To trust so cardinal a matter to the wireless reports of cruisers which are out of sight is to run needless risk." But wireless soon proved itself despite Churchill's doubts.

When adverse weather delayed his troop ship at Southampton for three days, Armstrong traveled to London and looked up Round, whom he found late in the evening at the Marconi House, hard at work on his own radio experiments. They had much in common. Each was an individualist with little regard for protocol, and each distrusted technical explanations when engineers used them to mask their ignorance. Like Armstrong, Round possessed boundless energy and an abundance of ideas about radio and its future uses.

Over a late dinner, Round told his new acquaintance of a difficult problem the British—and now the Allies—faced: they suspected the Germans had devised a way of sending messages over very high frequency waves in the range of 500,000 to 3 million cycles, higher than any frequency they had dealt with. With vacuum tubes and a series of transformers, Round and French physicist Marius Latour had created ingenious amplifying circuits capable of detecting signals up to 1 million cycles, but tuning their receiver proved to be extremely difficult. The problem was great, if only because radio waves that inventors like Round and Armstrong dealt with fell within the range of 10,000 to 100,000 cycles. No equipment in France, England, or America could match what the Germans were believed to possess. Round asked if it could be created.

Armstrong ruminated on the question in France. On his inspection of communications at the battlefront, he was asked again how weak high frequency signals might be detected. One night, during a German air raid over Paris, he wondered if it might be possible to detect the ultrahigh frequency (in the range of 10 million cycles, or higher) electrical waves emitted by the engines in the German planes. If it were, he reasoned, anti-aircraft guns might be able to track their fire accurately. But he did not have time to seek a solution until, in 1918, a young sergeant, Harry W. Houck, appeared at the division of research and inspection, announcing he was assigned to assist Captain Armstrong.

The captain was naturally surprised when the sergeant arrived, as just the day before he had received a message that Houck was dead. (The mix-up was not entirely the fault of bureaucracy. Ill and delirious, Houck had wandered from army doctors to the skillful care of a French hospital. When he recovered, he went directly to the Boulevard Montparnasse, bypassing all American posts.) Now that the sergeant appeared before him very much alive, Armstrong wondered what this boy from the farming country of New Cumberland, Pennsylvania, knew about radio. Plenty, he quickly learned. Armstrong had him sketch the circuit of a receiver with a carborundum detector. Houck did so quickly, but then went on to draw something "new," which he claimed to be far superior: a regenerative circuit. Armstrong was impressed by the young man's knowledge and taken with his unaffected and naive innocence: "Captain," Houck remarked, after discussing the virtues of the circuit, "the fellow who invented this has the same name as you."

From that moment, Harry Houck became Howard Armstrong's trusted associate. Always neat and economical in his design and construction of equipment, he possessed technical abilities that proved a good match with Armstrong's imaginative ones. Like his superior, he combined patience with a single-minded attention to technical questions. Though not a genius, he possessed the capacity for original thought. And, as Armstrong quickly learned, his new assistant was willing to work as hard and long as he did. Soon they were working together to solve the problem of detecting high frequency waves and converting them to a lower frequency range audible to the human ear.

The challenge for Houck and Armstrong was to devise a means of bringing these weak and elusive electromagnetic waves down to a level where they could be amplified. Ever since Hertz proved their existence in 1888, people have likened electromagnetic waves to their more tangible and visible counterparts in water. Indeed, electromagnetic waves have some qualities in common with those of the ocean: amplitude (their height and depth); frequency (how fast they move past a fixed point); and length (the distance between their crests). But there the similarities end. Electromagnetic waves travel at the speed of light (which is, of course, simply a part of the electromagnetic spectrum); their frequency is far greater; and their lengths can vary from a few inches to a few miles. The low frequency radio wave Armstrong and others had been working with had a length of about 6,600 feet (2,000 meters). The high frequency waves he had been called on to detect were as short as 330 feet (100 meters).

Armstrong began to connect his notions about high frequency wave detection (and the low power waves given off by airplane engines) with a discovery made early in the century by Reginald Aubrey Fessenden. Guided by an elementary knowledge of harmonics, Fessenden found that two incoming radio signals, each with a different frequency, could be mixed together to produce a *third* signal with a frequency equal to the difference between the two. The model for his thinking had been sound waves. The inventor knew that middle C on a piano produces sound with a frequency of 256 cycles, while B produces a sound with a frequency of 240. Yet when both piano keys are struck together, the chord produces a third sound of sixteen cycles per second. Fessenden applied this same principle to radio waves. If the incoming wave of, say, 51,000 cycles is mixed with a wave created by an oscillator within the receiver of 50,000 cycles, the result is a third, audible, wave of 1,000 cycles. To name this phenomenon, Fessenden turned to Greek: *hetero*, meaning "other" and *-dyne*, meaning "force." In the case of the heterodyne, two different waves were literally forced together to produce a third wave, which he called a "beat" note. Unfortunately, Fessenden's idea of heterodyning the incoming radio signal ran ahead of the available technology. Until Armstrong recognized the oscillating qualities of his regeneration circuit in 1913, there was no reliable method available to produce a radio wave at a correctly regulated frequency within a radio receiver. Armstrong had already used his regenerative circuit to the heterodyne principle, and had presented a paper on the subject to the Institute of Radio Engineers in 1916.

Now Armstrong's conversation with Round, the air raid over Paris, and his work on the heterodyne came together to produce a solution in a flash: "all three links of the chain joined up and I saw the way these signals could be handled." He would call it the "superheterodyne." The arrangement he visualized used his regeneration circuit both as a receiver and oscillator of radio waves and employed eight vacuum tubes in four different stages. First, his superheterodyne receiver would pick up a high frequency wave and heterodyne it with another wave produced by one of his vacuum tubes in oscillation, thereby creating a wave of intermediate frequency. Second, the intermediate frequency wave would travel through an amplifier to increase its power several thousand times. Third, his regeneration circuit would detect the wave and convert it to direct current. Finally, the current would pass through an audio amplifier to earphones or a speaker.

In lectures and papers about the superheterodyne that he delivered later, Armstrong illustrated his invention by receiving a high frequency wave of 3 million cycles per second and heterodyning it with a wave produced by his oscillating vacuum tube circuit of 2,900,000 cycles. This process created a "beat" wave of 100,000 cycles, which then traveled through an intermediate frequency amplifier, his regenerative circuit, and finally through an audio amplifier to a speaker. Sounds of this power from radio waves of this frequency had never been heard before.

Reduced to these basic four stages, the circuit appears relatively simple to us today, yet it was a heady discovery for Armstrong and Houck. No one had thought of such a complex circuit before, a circuit that changed a radio wave from its initial frequency to one that is heterodyned, amplified, changed into direct current, and finally transformed into sound vibrations. And no one had ever thought that such a new wave would preserve essential qualities of the old—its information, modulations of voice, tone of music, patterns of sound. It seemed sorcery or ethereal prestidigitation. Just as the vacuum tube and the regenerative circuit took radio into new territory, so would this novel method of reception and tuning, for it opened up an entire new area of the electromagnetic spectrum. While the principle was obvious to Armstrong at the time, putting it into practice was another matter. Each circuit required careful experimentation until just the correct wiring was found.

In light of the complex circuitry employed in most of today's televisions and stereos, Armstrong's superheterodyne circuit seems remarkably simple and essential. And the circuit has survived because of its economy. It does its job simply and elegantly. Today it forms the basis of the tuner found in virtually every radio and television, as well as in such other devices as radar detectors and police scanners.

Foreseeing the superheterodyne's potential, Armstrong became secretive. "I have been doing a lot of ground work during the bad weather and some of it looks pretty good," he wrote home with typical understatement at the end of February 1918. "I would very much like to get copies of the *Wireless Age* from the time I left the States to date and would appreciate it tres beaucoup." The "ground work" was really all he was able to complete during the war. Much more research awaited him when he returned home. But he had developed it enough to show Round when the English engineer visited Paris after the Armistice of November 11, 1918, and to take out patents in France and the United States. (There was no question in his mind about ownership, because army policy at this time allowed inventors to retain rights to discoveries made while in service.) He filed for a patent for his second great invention on December 30, 1918, in France, and on February 8, 1919, in the United States.

Protecting his invention meant spending vast sums of money, which was very scarce. "Draw positively everything you need from my account," he wrote home guardedly. "By all means be sure you do not go short on food because that is absolutely the poorest way to economize." But then he added, "Before drawing on my account if either Ethel or Rissie [his sister Edith] have anything left of what I gave them before leaving I think they ought to use it because I am going to have some very heavy lawyers' bills after the war and will need everything I can lay my hands on." Later, he returned to the subject of money: "Now in regard to finances I have considerable trouble in view and the situation is considerably complicated over here also."

De Forest also was on Armstrong's mind. Learning that his rival was in Paris, he wrote in a letter home, "You may be interested to know that de Forest is over here now and will report to me before a great while. Don't say anything about this outside Ethel and Rissie. If he had come over before the armistice was signed one or the other of us would have stayed in France but at present I guess he is fairly safe." De Forest also knew that *his* rival was stationed in Paris. The two managed to avoid each other.

Armstrong was too absorbed in the development of his new invention to visit with anyone. On Christmas night 1918, he stopped briefly to enjoy a turkey dinner and plum pudding. On another occasion, he "took time to watch some of the tennis at the Racing Club in the Bois de Boulogne" where he saw the French champion Gobert, and "the great Mlle Lenglen." But such interludes in his work were few.

Armstrong's contributions were recognized by honors he received from his colleagues home and from the French. Early in 1919, he was raised to the permanent rank of major. He was invited to lecture on radio at the University of Paris and the Sorbonne, and General Ferrie, the head of French military communications, pinned the chevalier de la légion d'honneur on his jacket. While in Paris, Armstrong received official word that he had been awarded what he always considered the single greatest honor of his career, the one he valued more than any other of the many he received: the Institute of Radio Engineers medal of honor. It was the first ever awarded by the institute, which recognized his invention of the regenerative circuit. Fifteen years later, in 1934, his conscience would demand that he return it.

So busy was Armstrong with his work in Paris after the war that he neglected his affairs at home. The De Forest Radio Telephone Company was using his regeneration invention without any acknowledgment, as were other companies. His chief rival was seeking to overturn his patent through an interference in the Patent Office, while Armstrong lingered in France with the remnants of the Allied forces. A simple telegram from William H. Davis brought him home: "De Forest pressing action. Your presence urgently needed." The summer of 1919 was fading; no longer could he afford to ignore his responsibilities.

At the end of September 1919, Edwin Howard Armstrong walked up the hill from the Harriman railroad station to his mother's house. She happened to be sitting on the porch at the time, and was shocked to see his head covered by a bloody bandage—the result of an anthrax infection he contracted at Cherbourg. He had returned home to recover. First he would spend two weeks in the hospital to take care of his infection; then he would reclaim his career in the laboratory at Columbia, where he would refine his superheterodyne; finally he would engage de Forest in their struggle over the right to regeneration. After his head had healed, he posed for one final photograph in his military uniform. The twenty-nine-year-old officer, dressed in a high-collar jacket with his arms folded, faces the camera slightly to his left side. On his collar appear the crossed flags of a signal corpsman; on each epaulet a single oak leaf. A leather Sam Browne belt crosses his chest. Chevrons given for his war wounds (even if the enemy was disease!) grace his left sleeve. A soft overseas cap with a single oak leaf denoting the rank of major covers his head. His face reveals determination and confidence. He appears supremely assured of his worth and of his future.

Proud of the part he played in the war, Armstrong henceforth was known by the title "major." Honoring his service as well as his inventions, the Radio Club of America gave a dinner in his honor at the Hotel Ansonia in New York City that fall. A picture taken to commemorate the occasion reveals that his large melon-shaped head, which had been prematurely balding before the war, had been made into a complete dome by the anthrax infection. Only the sandy trace of a friar's fringe remains. His firm mouth, long upper lip, and blue eyes, and, by all accounts, his modest and laconic speech, (tinged with a Bronx accent) and the occasional involuntary twitch of his neck and shoulders (a chronic reminder of his bout with Saint Vitus's dance) survive unchanged.

When the United States declared war on Germany, David Sarnoff held the position of commercial manager for the Marconi Company. In addition to managing the 725 employees reporting to him and the 582 wireless installations on ships that were under his control, he had many other duties. He negotiated all the wireless service contracts for Marconi in the United States; supervised the sales of millions of dollars of equipment to the U.S. government and other private concerns; maintained a voluminous correspondence as the person in charge of Marconi's "customer relations"; and, as the traffic manager, regulated the flow of messages to and from the various Marconi stations around the country. Sarnoff had been correct in his assessment of the possibilities for advancement as a manager: the office boy who had started at $5.50 a week in 1906, and who had advanced to $7.50 as a junior wireless telegraph operator, had grown into an executive whose annual salary approached five figures.

Sarnoff saw the entry into the war as a chance to prove himself a complete American. Almost from the day he had arrived at Monroe Street, he had ceased to consider himself a Russian. Recently he had been reminded of his origins when he was arranging the sale of Marconi equipment to the Russian Army. Too bad Sarnoff could not go back to his native land to install the apparatus, a czarist general had remarked jocularly. But then, he added darkly, Sarnoff would be arrested as a deserter. Returning to the shtetl of his memory was the farthest thought from Sarnoff's mind. Now that he had the chance, he wanted to serve his adopted country.

He did so, but not before he had encountered what he considered anti-Semitism in Washington. Like others with his abilities, he applied for a commission in the navy, only to have his request intolerably delayed without an answer. As he progressed steadily from the lowest level at the company to be the commercial manager, less and less was he referred to as a "Jew Boy." But the *idea* of his Semitic background remained in the minds of some. Could it be his faith, Sarnoff speculated, that kept him from the commission in the military he so prized?

He was probably right, for race consciousness and anti-Semitism were certainly in the air, especially in the experience of the Marconi Company. The parent company in England had endured one of the nastiest attacks of anti-Semitism in recent history, and some of those feelings had traveled across the Atlantic. In late 1911 and early 1912, Marconi's managing director, Godfrey Isaacs, arranged a contract with the postmaster general, Herbert Samuel, for a chain of wireless stations to ring the island. Isaacs's brother, Sir Rufus, was the attorney general in the British government at the time. Gossip circulated that the terms had been extremely favorable for Marconi, neglecting the fact that it was the only British company—and the only company in the world save Telefunken of Germany—capable of installing such equipment. Newspapers and some members of Parliament suggested that some in the government, especially Sir Rufus, had made enormous sums of money speculating in American Marconi stock, which increased in price dramatically in the aftermath of the *Titanic*. They were, so their accusers said, stock jobbing on inside information. And never far from the minds of journalists and the public was the fact that Samuel and Isaacs were Jews. Always, it seemed, commentators in the British press identified them contemptuously and disagreeably as "Hebrews."

Sarnoff himself had not been safe from such indignities, which would become more frequent in the future. At a meeting of the Institute of Radio Engineers, the anti-Semitism came close to being voiced openly. "Are you accusing me of stock jobbing?" an angry Sarnoff snapped in a heated exchange with a former Marconi employee. In the context of the time and of the Marconi Company's recent history, "stock jobbing" suggested "Hebrew." "If the shoe fits," came the answer to Sarnoff, "put it on." While listeners separated the men, the chairman of the meeting struggled to maintain order. Such scenes represented the last gasp by those whom Sarnoff surpassed in talent and business acumen to degrade him and put him at a disadvantage. When all else failed, when nothing else could stop Sarnoff's advancement before his Protestant colleagues, why not a sly reminder of his faith?

Not about to miss this chance to prove his patriotism, Sarnoff sought to be drafted as an army private. Fortunately for the Marconi Company and the war effort, Rear Admiral Robert S. Griffin, head of the Bureau of Steam Engineering, which oversaw the acquisition of radio equipment, interceded with an urgent telegram. "Exemption is considered absolutely necessary," Griffin wrote, "in order that the Fleet will not suffer delays due to unsatisfactory deliveries in existing contracts." The admiral might well have mentioned contracts to come, for in 1917, American Marconi enjoyed $5 million in sales, most to the United States government. As the commercial manager, Sarnoff oversaw all these orders, commuting regularly between Penn Station in New York and Union Station in Washington. Walking the corridors of the War Department and the Congress as well as the Marconi offices gave him experience he would find invaluable in the coming years.

Thus, staying with Marconi in 1917 enabled Sarnoff to render valuable service to *his* country and continue his upward progress through the ranks of the company's management. But always he would believe his faith had cost him the commission in the military he so deserved.

But it was not the nation's struggle to make the world safe for democracy or his place in that struggle that preoccupied Sarnoff's mind in the summer of 1917. He was getting married. His bride was to be Lizette Hermant, the handsome blond daughter of a French Jewish family that had recently emigrated to the Bronx. Their meeting had been arranged by their mothers, who themselves had met by chance in a synagogue. Son and daughter took to each other immediately, and soon turned their thoughts to matrimony. "I could speak no French and Lizette could speak no English, so what else could we do?" Sarnoff was fond of asking sardonically in later years. The modest ceremony took place on July 4, 1917.

July 4, 1917, Sarnoff always quipped, was the day "I lost my independence." Not exactly. His father had never really served as a model for a husband, nor had his parents' relationship served as a model for marriage. The person whose intimate life he most closely observed was Marconi, that arch philanderer, known to intimates as a sexual conquistador, the man whose amorous assignations in New York, Rome, and London were the stuff of legend. As Marconi's confidant and discreet messenger early in his career, Sarnoff had seen how the master operated. This was the way the successful businessman and entrepreneur behaved; surely, as he moved up through the ranks of Marconi and RCA, he was entitled—perhaps even obligated—to act in the same fashion.

In the coming years, Sarnoff would emulate his mentor with a result that often tried the patience of Lizette and the bonds of their marriage, but never to the breaking point. Her strength and forbearance, sometimes in the face of great provocation on her husband's part, prevented that from happening. For fifty-four years, Lizette Sarnoff watched and tolerated (though not without bitter argument) her husband's actions, forgave his infidelities, and remained loyal no matter his failings. She regarded him with fierce Gallic pride and spirit, and worked to make the marriage survive.

✦

"Do you not know the world is all now one single whispering gallery?" a tired President Woodrow Wilson shouted out to an audience of 10,000 gathered in the Des Moines, Iowa, Coliseum on Saturday evening, September 6, 1919. "Those antennae of the wireless telegraph are symbols of our age." Haggard, close to the massive stroke that overcame him nineteen days later, Wilson betrayed an uneasiness about the impact of the new technology that had developed so quickly during the war. The president recognized the nature of communication was changing, and the effect was not always salutary:

> All the impulses of mankind are thrown out upon the air and reach to the ends of the earth; quietly upon steamships, silently under the cover of the Postal Service, with the tongue of the wireless and the tongue of the telegraph, all the suggestions of disorder are spread through the world.

Now the tumultuous events taking place in Russia could be known across Europe and the rest of the world within hours. Wireless was spreading the "poison of revolt, the poison of chaos."

But wireless need not spread poison; it might have a mithadratic effect upon the world as well. Wilson himself had witnessed the salutary effects of bringing a world together through wireless, the ability of this new method of communication to spread news quickly. His Fourteen Points had been considered in the capitals of Europe almost immediately after he had delivered them. People in those capitals had resisted his Fourteen Points, but at 8:58 P.M. on October 6, 1918, wireless had brought him the message for which he had so fervently prayed:

> quote German government request President of United States of America to take his hand in restoration of peace comma to inform all belligerent states of this request and to invite them to send plenipotentiaries for the purpose of making negotiations stop It accepts programme presented by President of United States of America in message to Congress of Eight of January nineteen hundred eighteen and his later declarations comma especially address of twenty seventh of September as foundation for peace negotiations stop In order to prevent further bloodshed German government requests immediate conclusion of a general armistice on land water and in the air unquote stop

On December 4, when he sailed on the *George Washington* to oversee the peace negotiations in Europe, Wilson would find in wireless the power to keep him in touch with affairs in the United States; and the people of the United States would find in wireless the power to keep them in touch with him. Wireless had prepared Parisians for the arrival of the "Apostle of International Justice," as one banner proclaimed. The cheers he heard from his carriage on his arrival were "inhuman—or superhuman," wrote one reporter in his wireless dispatch to America. But other dispatches would reveal "Wilson the Just" mired in the minutiae of negotiations, clinging desperately to the shards of his Fourteen Points. Wireless brought home to the nation, especially those in Washington, his failures.

A new method of communication, wireless would prove no more benign or evil than those who used it. But in the larger sense, Wilson was right. The world had become a whispering gallery, and wireless had made it so.

6

RELEASING THE ART:
THE CREATION OF RCA

On the afternoon of May 12, 1919, Owen D. Young, vice-president of General Electric Company, and Edward J. Nally, vice-president of American Marconi, met for lunch at the Bankers Club in the General Electric Building, 120 Broadway, in New York City. Young had arranged the meeting to discuss an important matter of business between the two companies. He quietly told Nally that General Electric had decided not to sell Marconi $5 million worth of Alexanderson alternators and improved vacuum tubes, because the United States government did not want control of this equipment to pass into foreign hands.

On the face of it, Young's announcement appeared devastating to the Marconi interests in the United States and across the world. General Electric held all the patents to Alexanderson's invention, the most powerful generator of radio waves then known. Guglielmo Marconi himself had toured the Schenectady General Electric plant with Young in 1915 and agreed to purchase exclusive rights to the machine for close to $4 million. Under that contract General Electric had delivered the 50-kilowatt alternator to New Brunswick and was about to install a huge 200-kilowatt machine when the United States entered the war. Though the navy operated the alternators for the duration of the war, Marconi had been convinced that they provided the only way he could ring the world with wireless messages. And in an extensive evaluation of the machines written in March 1916, Nally's trusted associate David Sarnoff had declared Alexanderson's by far the best, and predicted it

141

alone would be in demand. When the war had ended, the company reopened negotiations for exclusive rights to its use.

Ever since he had taken charge of the business operations for American Marconi in 1913, Edward Nally had to defend the company against charges that it was in the hands of foreigners. Before the war, he and Sarnoff had to defend the company in Congress against the attempts of Josephus Daniels to have the navy control all wireless. Recently, Congressman Joshua Willis Alexander of Cincinnati had introduced a bill in the House to give the federal government in peace the same monopoly over radio communications it had enjoyed in war. Secretary Daniels had lent his support, suggesting "we would lose very much . . . by opening the use of radio communication to rival companies." True, Nally, Sarnoff, and a chorus of amateurs had managed to organize congressional opposition to the bill, introduced by William S. Green of Massachusetts. But Daniels and others would continue to claim that radio communications should be safe from foreign hands under government authority.

The issue of foreign control had motivated Owen D. Young to notify the navy at the end of March of General Electric's discussions with Marconi. British Marconi wanted ten of the huge machines, and its American counterpart wanted fourteen. Stanford C. Hooper urged that General Electric suspend negotiations. On Friday, April 4, the assistant naval secretary, Franklin Delano Roosevelt, requested the company "confer with representatives of the Department" before reaching a final agreement. When Young received Roosevelt's note on the following Monday, he immediately suspended discussions with Marconi until the end of the week.

The next day, representatives of the navy, including Admiral Bullard and Captain Hooper, met with General Electric managers in Young's office at 120 Broadway. Their case was compelling: since the first submarine cable had been laid successfully in 1866, the British had held a virtual monopoly on transoceanic telegraph communication. Not only did all important lines terminate in the British Isles, but the British also produced all the gutta-percha, the rubbery substance extracted from Malayan percha trees for insulating and waterproofing wires, and so they controlled the manufacture of all cable. The navy did not wish to see radio fall under British domain as had cable. An Italian might have invented the wireless telegraph, but with the Alexanderson alternator, Americans had the best radio system available. Surely it would not be in the national interest to allow technology developed in the United States to fall under the exclusive control of a company subsidized by the British government.

The representatives had an offer to make. Over the years, the navy had acquired licenses to some valuable radio patents; perhaps, as the naval takeover of radio seemed unlikely given the opposition to Alexander's bill in the Congress, an American company might be started with the navy's patents as well as those of General Electric.

Young and Charles Coffin, the chairman of the board at General Electric, listened carefully but still wavered. At a break in the discussion, Bullard took Young into another room to impart a private message with the import of "a state secret." He had just returned from Woodrow Wilson's side at Versailles, where Lloyd George and Clemenceau were steadily whittling away at the president's Fourteen Points. Bullard reported that Wilson wished to check- mate British domination of worldwide communications. Wouldn't Young help? Bullard asked—implying the request was the president's as well. Young understood immediately and without hesitation decided to follow the patri- otic course. As he said later, "for the first time radio made an indelible impression on my mind." American soldiers had been shipped across the Atlantic—over there—to usher the angel of peace onto the continental stage. The United States stood before all as the most powerful, richest, and surely the most self-righteous nation in the world. Now was the proper time for the premier company of the ever-expanding technology of electricity to create a new *American* communication corporation to protect and advance American interests in the world.

Owen Young's passage from an eighty-acre hops farm in central New York to the Bankers Club had been remarkable by any standard. Since pre- Revolutionary times, the Young family had made a modest living tilling the land near Van Hornesville, an isolated hamlet in the fertile Schoharie Valley south of the Mohawk River, and there was little reason for Jacob and Ida Young to think their only son, Owen, would do otherwise. But at the one-room schoolhouse in Van Hornesville and later at a small academy about seven miles away, Young showed himself, as his mother remembered, to care "more for books than he did for the farm." Recognizing the boy's abilities, his parents mortgaged their land so that he might attend St. Lawrence College, then a small but fervent Universalist school in Canton, New York. Gradu- ated at age twenty in 1894, he went to Boston University, where he com- pleted a three-year law degree (cum laude) in two years, all the while holding down a job. Life as a Boston lawyer had led him into utilities law, and then, in 1913, to be vice president and general counsel at General Electric.

The Universalist faith, with its irenic and serene doctrine of getting into "the right relationship with God," held a very real presence in Young's think- ing. "Believers ought to be careful to maintain order and practise good works; for these things are good and profitable unto man," Universalist doctrine stated. It was a perfect credo for Young, one that suited his personality and shaped his actions. All his professional life he enjoyed a reputation for a calm and reflective temperament, as well as for being a person conversant in the languages of business, law, labor relations, and diplomacy. He applied his talents to negotiation. During the war, he had settled a strike at the General Electric plant in Lynn, Massachusetts, the last labor strife while he was associated with the company. Later he instituted profit-sharing, pension, and insurance plans for the workers. At the same time, managers at General Electric developed a high regard for Owen Young's vision, what he called "good hunches," about the shape of the world then being created by electricity.

And by doing good, Owen Young had done well. By 1917, he had a house on Long Island Sound at Riverside, Connecticut; an opulent apartment at Park Avenue and 76th Street; and a herd of Holstein-Friesian cattle on his extensive farmlands in Van Hornesville. He had purchased a handsome Italianate Victorian house for his mother in the village, which he and his family visited as often as they could. In later years, he would increasingly indulge his passion for collecting rare books, including James Fenimore Cooper's copy of Shakespeare's First Folio.

Young exercised his natural skills as a negotiator at lunch with Edward Nally that May afternoon, quietly allowing the vice president of Marconi to come to the conclusion he himself had reached a month before. It would be foolish for General Electric to compete with Marconi by starting up an entirely new American enterprise that duplicated Marconi's expensive facilities. It would be far wiser for GE to take over Marconi's American interests—including its patent licenses—add them to the patents controlled by the navy, and place these holdings in a new American company. By the end of the meal, Nally was asking what Washington's attitude might be if General Electric were to form such a company. Young's answer was oblique: American Marconi interests were "greatly menaced because of English holdings in the company." While the government had a right to prevent GE from negotiating with Marconi, it did not have the right "to force us into competition with you." With those words, Nally and Young wove the first threads of the unique alliance. Each committed himself to the formation of a new radio enterprise.

For Young, the commitment meant meeting upon meeting in Washington and New York; with Hooper, with Daniels, with General Electric's top managers, lawyers, and full board of directors. In Washington on May 23, he sought Secretary Daniels's assent. Emphasizing that the suggestion to form a new company had come originally from Admiral Bullard and Commander Hooper, he made clear the advantages of the arrangement for the United

States. Holding to his own plans for naval management, however, the secretary refused to give up without a fight. General Electric's purchase of the Marconi interests would merely substitute a private, domestic radio monopoly for a foreign one. One last effort to convince Congress of the efficacy of government control was in order, Daniels thought. Should that fail, Daniels said, he would reluctantly assent to the creation of a new company. Realizing that this was only a face-saving gesture and that the secretary would most certainly fail once again, Young quietly directed General Electric's lawyers to draft a contract with the navy for a transfer of rights to important inventions.

At a conference on June 2, Young and Nally agreed the new company should "control as many patents as there is a possibility of our owning or using." Then Nally boldly turned to the most obvious but as yet unvoiced question that had been on his mind from the start: what his position would be in the new company. Answering with a speed that suggested he had considered the matter carefully, Young said: "I assume that if an arrangement is made for the Marconi Company to participate . . . their present organization would do the operating and the General Electric Company would do the manufacturing. . . . As far as the operating is concerned, we know nothing about it and we ought to take advantage of your experience." It was all Nally might hope for.

Given Young's assurance, no doubt, Nally was more willing than ever to effect the sale of the British interest in American Marconi. He certainly had much to gain from the venture. Though he functioned as the titular head of his company, he did not have as much control of its direction as he would like. Above him was a president, John William Griggs, former governor of New Jersey and attorney general of the United States under President McKinley, who served mostly to lend a conspicuous American presence to the board of directors. More important, Nally's actions as vice president were scrutinized carefully by Guglielmo Marconi and Godfrey Isaacs in England, who did not allow him to promote American Marconi's interests in the way he would like. Since 1914, his assistant Sarnoff had been keeping him apprised of new and promising advances Americans were making in the technology. Though he would have liked to employ them, the managers in England were indifferent.

Though Young had carefully avoided making a formal commitment, Nally saw he had a chance to lead the new American "radio corporation," as they were coming to call it. In just two meetings, he and Young had formed a strong relationship based on mutual respect for each other's talents, and Nally understood he would work well with this man. No longer would he have to look to London for approval and direction; that would come with a minimum of oversight from the General Electric headquarters in New York, and most likely from Young himself.

At the end of July 1919, after tentative agreements between General Electric and American Marconi had been signed, Nally and the head of GE's patent department sailed for London to meet with Godfrey Isaacs. From his office in New York, Young remained in touch through voluminous cables and radiograms. He had a hunch that Isaacs would realize he had to capitulate, for if he did not, British Marconi would not be able to acquire the Alexanderson alternators it needed. Worse, General Electric, with the government's blessing, would start a rival company to challenge Marconi's interests in America. Young's instinct was correct. Using the technology over which they were negotiating for control, Nally sent a message on September 6:

> Agreement has been made subject to approval of stockholders. Arrangements have been made covering practically entire world assuring new Radio Corporation world wide wireless connecting arrangements with equal opportunities for sale and exploitation. Marconi Wireless Telegraph Company Ltd., disposes to Marconi Wireless Telegraph Company of America all Marconi Wireless Telegraph Company Ltd. interests, but will be equal partners. South American field furnishing half capital stock Radio Corporation to operate and control. Am confident new deal will be enormous advantage new Radio Corporation.

On October 17, 1919, the Radio Corporation of America, with the patents of General Electric and Marconi, was incorporated in the state of Delaware. General Electric purchased all Marconi stock not in private hands. The new corporation would always remain under American control. No more than 20 percent of its stock could be owned by foreigners; its executives had to be United States citizens; a representative from the navy was invited to attend meetings of its board of directors.

For the most part, the old Marconi staff remained intact in the new Radio Corporation of America: Nally became president; Sarnoff, commercial manager; and George S. DeSousa, treasurer. By Christmas 1919, Owen D. Young was named chairman of the board of directors of the company he had envisioned in the previous May.

With the support of Nally, Young moved quickly to realize the rest of his vision: shortly after its formation, RCA drew up plans for a powerful new station on a desolate ten-acre site at Rocky Point on Long Island. The station resembled a giant wheel with dozens of needlelike transmission aerials radiating like spokes from two 200-kilowatt Alexanderson alternators at the hub. The property would be RCA's center of international radio communications. From there the corporation would be able to circle the globe with wireless messages. More powerful than any station in Germany, France, or England, Rocky Point would demonstrate to all the importance of pooling radio patents. Rocky Point would make radio telegraph reliable in any weather, revolutionize communication between nations, and not incidentally make the United States preeminent in the new technology.

As the negotiations between Marconi and General Electric progressed, Nally came to rely more heavily on his assistant David Sarnoff than at any time since they first met in 1913. Sarnoff had proven himself in mid-December 1918 when he had testified for five days against Congressman Alexander's bill to create a government monopoly over radio communications. The act would "stifle the development and growth of the radio art," Sarnoff declared, for it would destroy the vision of the various inventors who worked for commercial interests. Now, with Nally in England completing the sale of American Marconi, Sarnoff was busier than ever testifying in Washington against Josephus Daniels's last attempt to effect government control. By the end of August, as Nally was completing the sale, he could cable London: "My opinion Government ownership feature dead but think proposition Navy handling commercial business requires additional opposition. Confident our ultimate victory."

In mid-September 1919, Nally had asked Sarnoff to convene a technical group to consider the advantages and disadvantages of the agreement he had brought with him from England. As Marconi workers were uncertain of what their role would be in the new company, this could have been a difficult assignment for Sarnoff. But he handled it with unusual sensitivity and grace because he held the Marconi engineers in high esteem. Each felt free to speak about concerns. The Alexanderson alternator and the patent pool certainly were the chief advantages of forming a new company. But the engineers had worries, too, and Sarnoff did not hesitate to list them as "disadvantages." Chief among them was the "elimination of the Research Department and the Engineering Department and their transfer to the General Electric Company," for "radio work will constitute such an insignificant part of the work of the General Electric Company that it will give little attention to it and the results will be meager." To address this fear, Ernst Alexanderson was made head of engineering in the new company (though still retaining his position with General Electric), and the new corporation established a laboratory on Long Island to explore the nature of radio waves. Dr. Alfred Goldsmith of the City College of New York, an imaginative inventor and engineer who had served as director of research for American Marconi from his laboratory at the City University of New York, remained with the new corporation. Later, when RCA created a developmental laboratory near Van Cortlandt Park in the Bronx, he was made its head. From the start it was clear that development would be a high priority of the new corporation.

At the same time, Sarnoff was using his position of commercial manager to recapture the ship radio business that Marconi had ceded to the navy during the war. At every opportunity, he wrested control of ship communications away from the government, so that on the last day of September 1919, he could write: "It is safe to assume . . . that of the 330 ships which went out of our jurisdiction by the sale [during the war], we shall have back in our fold at least 225. . . . When we sign the contract with the Shipping Board for 400 additional ships, we shall be operating a total fleet of approximately 900 vessels and will go after the one thousand mark." No doubt the memo pleased Nally, for the business Sarnoff had been gathering would be an integral part of the Radio Corporation Young and Nally were then putting into place.

On Christmas Eve 1919, Edward J. Nally sent David Sarnoff a brief letter announcing that his salary would be raised to "$11,000 per annum as of January 1, 1920." As commercial manager for RCA, he could rest secure that his talents were just as valuable in the new company as they had been in the old.

However, for Sarnoff there still was the question of Owen D. Young. Sarnoff had long enjoyed special status, since all knew Guglielmo Marconi kept a watchful eye on the progress of his protégé. But his mentor had no interest in the new company. Sarnoff had met the new chairman just a few weeks before the Radio Corporation was formed, when, at Nally's request, he gave an accounting of the financial position of American Marconi. It soon became clear that Young would be forceful and energetic in his new position. How would the commercial manager prosper under him?

The answer came shortly after the beginning of the new year. Though not a technical man, Young recognized that the industry was undergoing dramatic changes. Thousands of radio amateurs had been drafted into the war effort; they had emerged radio professionals, committed to staying with the art, and requiring tubes and equipment from RCA. How much, Young wondered, would these sales develop? He asked his commercial manager to set forth his views of RCA's needs and requirements, along with estimates of probable business available in the future.

Sarnoff took the request from his chairman as a chance to review the entire field of radio communications, demonstrate the breadth of his understanding, and share a part of his vision. On the last day of January 1920, he sent a twenty-eight-page memo to Young. Containing nine sections, with headings like "Patent Situation," "Marine Business," "Sales to Amateurs," and "Sales and Merchandising Policies," it stood as a blueprint for making RCA into the dominant radio company in the world. Beginning on a sober note, Sarnoff acknowledged the dilemma RCA faced: "We must have suitable apparatus for sale, before we can sell it in large quantities." The apparatus must be accessible, reliable, and cheap to manufacture. But "rapid changes of the art" meant it was not feasible to order "large quantities of any one item" as it might be made obsolete. Nevertheless, the war had taught the governments of the world that they should be equipped with a high-power station capable of international communications. Undoubtedly this meant an increased demand for the Alexanderson alternator.

Thinking the political moment was better than it had been in 1916, Sarnoff turned in Section VI, "Sales of Radio Music Box for Entertainment Purposes," to his long cherished idea of broadcasting. It was, he said, a proposal he had made in detail to Nally, but "circumstances attending our business at that time" had not made "serious consideration" of the project practical. Word-for-word, he copied the proposal he had composed seven years earlier to make radio "a household utility."

Young was intrigued. This was not international communications or safety at sea, but an entirely new use for the radio. He asked the commercial manager to send the Radio Music Box proposal along to GE's president, E. W. Rice. Sarnoff did so, with an additional estimate that sales could number a million Radio Music Boxes "within a period of three years." At $75 a set, the gross receipts would quickly mount:

First Year	100,000 Radio Music Boxes	$ 7,500,000
Second Year	300,000 Radio Music Boxes	22,500,000
Third Year	600,000 Radio Music Boxes	45,000,000
Total		$75,000,000

Rice was also a visionary who took a personal interest in electronic research; he had hired the great Steinmetz. But even he showed only moderate interest in Sarnoff's proposal. More as a favor to RCA's commercial manager—and Young—than as a commitment to a new product, he recommended on June 18, 1920, that the RCA Board grant $2,500 to develop a sample radio music box. Though a paltry sum, it was enough for Sarnoff. He took his concept to his friend and colleague Dr. Alfred Goldsmith.

To his students at the City College of New York and his colleagues at the Marconi and RCA laboratories, Goldsmith was always "doctor," to distinguish him from more pedestrian thinkers. To the doctor, students and colleagues were always "my boys." Trained as a student of Michael Pupin's at

Columbia, he had a fertile mind that yielded 122 patents over his career. He had recently published *Radio Telephony*, then the most comprehensive book to appear on the subject. Though primarily a technician, Goldsmith saw that radio was much more than electronic waves. At the opening of his book he called it "the ultimate extension of personality in time and space." On the last page he characterized "this instrument for speeding the voice of man across space" as:

CARRIER OF NEWS AND KNOWLEDGE.

INSTRUMENT OF TRADE AND INDUSTRY.

PROTECTOR OF LIFE AT SEA.

———

MESSENGER OF SYMPATHY AND LOVE.

SERVANT OF PARTED FRIENDS.

CONSOLER OF THE LONELY.

———

BOND OF THE SCATTERED FAMILY.

ENLARGER OF THE COMMON LIFE.

———

PROMOTER OF MUTUAL ACQUAINTANCE.

OF PEACE AND GOOD WILL AMONG MEN AND NATIONS.

Unknown to Sarnoff, and completely independent of him, the doctor had already built a small receiver. "It had one knob for tuning and one for volume," Goldsmith remembered. "It was self contained in a small wooden cabinet which included the necessary dry batteries and a loudspeaker." When Goldsmith tuned the set to Sarnoff's old Wanamaker station, which happened to be playing music, the commercial manager exclaimed "This is the radio music box of which I've dreamed." Quickly, Goldsmith adapted his design to a prototype for production. He called it the "radiola."

One of the reasons prompting Owen D. Young to consult with David Sarnoff's views about RCA was a letter he had received from an admiral in the navy concerning some patent conflicts that still had to be resolved. While the formation of RCA mitigated some patent problems, the admiral said, it did not eliminate them, for the new corporation did not control all rights necessary to produce the best equipment. There was still the possibility that a foreign company could purchase the rights to some crucial patents. Would Young and RCA "for the good of the public" seek a remedy?

The most obvious concern to the navy and RCA was the American Telephone and Telegraph Company, which, along with its subsidiary, Western Electric, held the rights to de Forest's audion, the tube that enabled long distance transmission. But there were still other questions to settle. While wireless telegraph did not compete with AT&T, the possibility of sending words through the air obviously did. What would be the relationship between RCA's radio transmitters and AT&T's telephone lines? What of the new radio telephone? And what of the Radio Music Box?

The answer to these questions was ownership. To get the patents and agreements RCA needed, Young decided to give AT&T a million shares of outstanding common and preferred stock, about a 10.3 percent ownership of the company. In exchange, AT&T and RCA agreed to cross-licensing of the patents it held on the vacuum tube. At last Fleming's invention (which had come to RCA through Marconi) and de Forest's invention could be manufactured in the same tube along with improvements pioneered by engineers at General Electric, without fear of litigation. The final agreement, which Young and the chairman of AT&T signed on July 1, 1920, contained an additional important clause that Sarnoff in memos to Nally and Young insisted upon including: AT&T granted to RCA rights to "establish and maintain" one-way wireless telephone transmitting stations, or broadcast stations. The clause signified the final important step to enable him to proceed with his plans to begin broadcasting and to sell the radiola. His vision for the future of radio prevailed in the new company as it never had in the old.

In its annual report to the stockholders of RCA, Edward J. Nally taciturnly wrote one pithy sentence about the agreement: "The American Telephone and Telegraph Company has recently become a large stockholder in your corporation."

But Young's labors were not over. All the while he had been working out his agreement with the American Telephone and Telegraph Company, and RCA had been, with hesitant and halting step, moving toward broadcasting, the Westinghouse Company was working to establish a presence of its own. Founded in 1884, Westinghouse had long been an important rival of General Electric and its parent company, Edison Electric. During the war, Westinghouse had managed to secure a number of lucrative contracts to supply radio equipment. With the ending of these contracts, Westinghouse decided to follow General Electric's lead and establish an international radio telegraph service. To this end it acquired a company that controlled all of Reginald Fessenden's inventions and purchased exclusive rights to Howard Armstrong's regeneration and superheterodyne inventions. Westinghouse quickly learned that RCA had locked up all the international business, but it still had one possible use of radio to exploit. At its headquarters in Pittsburgh, it had begun to experiment with broadcasting.

Westinghouse's aggressive competition left Sarnoff gloomy. The Marconi organization had ignored his past recommendations about important inventions, and now RCA showed no signs of acting differently. As early as 1913, he had recognized the value of Armstrong's regeneration circuit and recommended it enthusiastically through his superiors to Marconi and Godfrey Isaacs. But their coolness to inventions originating in the United States left them blind to its potential. During the war, the circuit had become the standard for the best radio receivers. On January 6, 1920, his friend Armstrong had demonstrated a superheterodyne tuner at Dr. Goldsmith's laboratory. It possessed greater sensitivity "than any other type . . . known to me," he had told Edward J. Nally. "When used with a proper receiver, such as he has himself designed and used," Armstrong's superheterodyne was extremely simple to operate and required "little or no adjustment." He advised that RCA consider the superheterodyne carefully, before Armstrong sold his rights "exclusively to other interested parties." But RCA had failed to act.

The Westinghouse company had acted with remarkable dispatch. For $335,000 cash (and an additional $200,000 should de Forest lose his infringement suit), Westinghouse had purchased rights to *both* Armstrong's regeneration and superheterodyne inventions.

Even more dispiriting to Sarnoff were Westinghouse's experiments with broadcasting. It had been *his* vision; he had been promoting it since the fall of 1916. A forty-six-year-old engineer at Westinghouse, Frank Conrad, had moved ahead of the tortoiselike bureaucracy at GE, which controlled RCA. That May, he had begun broadcasting piano and saxophone solos from a primitive station in a garage behind his house in Pittsburgh. Soon he was joined by other amateurs from the area. At the end of September, the Joseph Horne department store began selling receivers to pick up the "concerts" for "$10.00 up." It was his Radio Music Box idea, which Goldsmith was just then fashioning into a radiola.

Still more bad news came from Pittsburgh. Taking up Conrad's idea, the Westinghouse Company had begun its own station, KDKA, on the roof of its Pittsburgh factory. Beginning at 8 P.M., November 4, KDKA broadcast the returns of the presidential election, which it received by telephone from the editorial room of the Pittsburgh *Post*. When the broadcast concluded after midnight, the listeners around Pittsburgh (many of whom were Westinghouse employees who had been given sets for the occasion) knew that Warren G. Harding had won 404 electoral votes to defeat James M. Cox for the presidency.

Westinghouse's plan was simple: create a demand for the equipment through broadcasts, and then listeners will purchase the sets. It did just that with broadcasts, at first only an hour a day, beginning at 8:30 P.M., but soon it expanded its schedule to a church service, a prizefight, and a speech by Secretary of Commerce Herbert Hoover. Soon the company set up stations on the roofs of its plants—WJZ in Newark and WBZ in East Springfield, Massachusetts. On the roof of the Commonwealth Edison building in Chicago, it created KYW. At East Springfield, Westinghouse began manufacturing crystal sets. It was all that Sarnoff had wanted, but it was being realized by another company.

Radio was fast becoming a craze. People were finding that with a spool of wire, a cylindrical oatmeal box, a crystal, an aerial, and earphones, they, too, could listen in. Everyone from cabinet makers to machinists was willing to supply them with the requisite parts, even entire receivers. In a small tool and die shop on Jerome Avenue in the Bronx, Frank Angelo D'Andrea, the son of a junk dealer with a fervent desire to be rich, began producing crystal detectors. Soon forty young women were busy making his "FADA" detectors. The crystals cost 96 cents to make and sold for $2.25. By early 1922, sales had risen to $50,000 a month, and he was branching out into simple vacuum tube sets and radio kits. On Washington's Birthday 1921, Powell Crosley, owner of an automobile accessories company and a phonograph cabinet manufacturing plant in Cincinnati, built a small crystal set with his son, which allowed them to hear broadcasts as far as seven miles away. With little regard for proper licensing of Armstrong's invention, he soon was selling a low-priced set of his own design that employed a regenerative circuit and was housed in a handsome wooden cabinet. On Stenton Avenue in Philadelphia, Arthur Atwater Kent, sometime manufacturer of sewing machine motors, gunsights, and automobile ignitions, decided he would create a line of handsome radio parts cast in expensive Bakelite. Beginning with audio transformers, he soon moved on to complete radio sets, each component sculpted in gleaming Bakelite with brass trim and mounted on a rich mahogany board. An Atwater Kent radio possessed an elegance that made it more pleasing to the eye than to the ear.

As dispiriting as Westinghouse's foray into broadcasting and the consequent craze for radios were to Sarnoff at the time, in the long run these events had a salutary effect on RCA and his own career. In the coming months, RCA and GE executives would redefine RCA as a broadcaster and a radio manufacturer, as well as an operator of international telegraph communications. Sarnoff would be able to remind them of his own prophecies, that he had been the first to promote radio as a medium of mass communication. He would take on the aura among the management as the one with unrivaled prescience about future uses of radio waves to carry visual as well as aural information and entertainment.

As one who knew more about equipment and patents than anyone else at RCA, Sarnoff undoubtedly realized too that Westinghouse had but a tenuous commercial hold on many of the inventions it was using. Armstrong's oscillating circuit that KDKA used for its broadcasts employed vacuum tube patents that RCA now controlled. (Westinghouse had tried to create a substitute for the vacuum tube of Fleming and de Forest, but had no luck.) In truth, the company was not in a position to develop the art commercially.

With its hold on the Armstrong and Fessenden patents, however, Westinghouse had put itself in a good bargaining position to acquire part of the Radio Corporation of America in the same way that American Telephone and Telegraph had a few months earlier. RCA realized that without the patents Westinghouse held it would be hobbled, for the regeneration and the superheterodyne circuits were necessary to make its radiola marketable. By the end of 1920, both companies were talking about an agreement.

The discussions were complicated. In addition to a substantial portion of Radio Corporation's stock, Westinghouse insisted it be guaranteed a significant portion of RCA's orders for radio components. Once again Owen D. Young cleared the path for an accord. At a crucial moment in the negotiations, he dramatically raised the offer of RCA common and preferred stock from 700,000 to 1 million shares. Westinghouse gave to RCA its patents as well as shore transmitting stations it had acquired from Fessenden, and it received the patents of AT&T, GE, and RCA to manufacture devices for the Radio Corporation. Forty percent of RCA's manufacturing orders would go to Westinghouse, while the remaining orders would go to GE. Westinghouse quickly ratified the offer on March 25, 1921. It now held 20.6 percent of RCA's stock, making it the largest corporate shareholder after General Electric.

To complete its consolidation, RCA brought the wireless interests of the United Fruit Company into the radio patent pool. Then a $200 million corporation, controlling a million acres in Central America and the Caribbean, United Fruit had depended on wireless to link its plantations with its banana boats. It held a 51 percent interest in a small company that controlled patents on loop antennas, which RCA thought valuable. But United Fruit was more interested in produce than wireless, and it was happy to sell its patents for 200,000 shares of both its common and preferred RCA stock, a 4.1 percent interest. When compared with the interests of oil, steel, or railroads, radio was a very minor operation. The federal government showed little concern that RCA's acquisitions made it a powerful force in the new medium of communication.

Why had Young acted so swiftly to raise his offer to Westinghouse, especially when the head of General Electric's patent department had argued that the Armstrong patents were not worth the price its rival was demanding? Quite possibly he had a hunch about the actual value of the patents, and their value to Sarnoff's proposal for broadcasting. But it was a hunch based on close observation of his commercial manager. Sarnoff sat on RCA's technical committee and chaired it when Nally could not be present. Young also frequently attended as an observer. He was impressed with the way Sarnoff guided the committee through its decisions to install Alexanderson alternators in the profitable stations as well as how he dealt with the challenge of patents.

Young had witnessed the remarkable success of KDKA's broadcasts that November, and he knew from Sarnoff of the station's potential to broadcast not only concerts and election results but baseball games, farm reports, news, and educational programs. Young's biographers have likened the acquisition to the passions of a rare book collector (which he was), the person who must have—at any price—the final volume. And why not? GE still was in firm control with more than 30 percent of the stock; it had eliminated any possible American competition for RCA's domination of the world market. Perhaps Westinghouse did not offer a tangible asset equal to its price. But its acquisition did bring an intangible asset. It completed the set, in this case the set of roughly 2,000 patents. With these in hand, who knew what the Radio Corporation of America might become?

In the negotiations with AT&T, Westinghouse, and United Fruit, Owen D. Young—like Marconi and Nally before him—had come to trust the knowledge and judgment of David Sarnoff. Sarnoff knew the industry and knew where it was going. He could sell contracts for international communications, deal with the government, and, as Westinghouse had just shown, his twenty-eight-page memo of January 31, 1920, about radio broadcasting had been remarkably correct. Though they were different in age, background, social class, and of course rank within the corporation, their relationship gradually became frank and open.

Having made such a deep impression on the chairman of the board, and enjoying the confidence of RCA's president, Sarnoff, not surprisingly, incurred the envy of those people in the mid-ranks at RCA and GE who regarded him as a rival. Ambition was construed as arrogance, ideas as aggressiveness, lack of formal training as ignorance. Worse yet, to those in competition for advancement, he was a Jew. Mean-spirited, demeaning, and merciless harassment became the order on the eighteenth floor of the Woolworth Building. His rivals saw to it that invitations to corporation events were mislaid or not proffered at all. They demanded reports with contrived deadlines. They sent unwanted and uninvited visitors to RCA around to his office to present their trifling problems or worthless inventions.

Such matters could be overlooked for a while, no doubt, but the unpleasantness came to a head when Sarnoff was passed over for advancement after having received informal assurances from Nally that it would occur. Here was a crisis. He was being blocked in his progress through the ranks not for want of experience, knowledge, or ability, but for political and personal reasons. If he were to remain silent now, his advancement within RCA might be blocked forever. Perhaps he would have to leave for another corporation, though the impediments to Roman Catholics and Jews in other companies like AT&T and Westinghouse were legendary. Before considering a change, he decided to speak with the only one within RCA who could help him—Owen D. Young.

Early in 1921, in the privacy of a small dining room at Delmonico's, which he had rented for the occasion, David Sarnoff shared his past with the chairman of RCA. It was the story he had told Marconi in 1907 and would tell many times again: the shtetl, emigration, abject poverty of the Lower East Side, the newspaper business, his sick father. To this he added an account of his experiences with Marconi and increasing responsibilities with the wireless. Now the very structure he had created for himself in America was threatened by mindless anti-Semitism. The implication was clear to Young: surely, in radio, the newest of enterprises in the New World, a Jew should enjoy the opportunities open to everyone else, opportunities that were closed to Jews in other more traditional businesses. Should the new radio industry practice discrimination as other American enterprises had done? The dinner concluded past midnight with talk not of anti-Semitism but of the future of radio. The demand for parts was growing, as shown by the increase in tube production. Soon Sarnoff hoped RCA would be making its own radio music boxes.

Like Marconi before him, Young moved swiftly to protect a person he was coming to consider his protégé. After their meeting, the chairman let it be known that Sarnoff enjoyed his full confidence; any slight to Sarnoff would not be tolerated. Next Young placed Sarnoff out of reach of the mid-level viciousness that had so beset him. On April 29, he was made a corporate officer and given the title of general manager of RCA. His salary was to be $15,000 a year. "You know what my sentiments are," Edward J. Nally wrote, informing him of the promotion, "and how sincerely I am interested in your success and general well being. I want you to feel that I stand ready at all times to assist you in every way I can and I want you to feel free to come to me with your problems and your troubles—if you have any. You can always rely upon my support."

In the announcement of the appointment to other managers at RCA, Nally outlined the broad powers Sarnoff would have as general manager: to supervise the plant, to supervise and maintain radio service, to solicit and negotiate contracts for transoceanic communication, and to "employ, remove and discharge subordinate officials, agents and employees." It was all Sarnoff had wanted. At last the senseless harassment would stop. At last he had the authority to market his radio music box.

The first task for Sarnoff now that he had visible support of Young and Nally was to recapture his idea of broadcasting. It required a dramatic step, the broadcasting of a major public event, one which would create a need for receivers. Education, farm reports, a symphony concert, even a major political speech, those things he had spoken of in his memorandum of 1916 would not do. He needed something spectacular. The best opportunity available, he decided, was the heavyweight championship fight between Jack Dempsey and Georges Carpentier scheduled for July 2. It would take place across the Hudson from Manhattan in Jersey City, New Jersey, at Boyle's Thirty Acres, a spot near the Lackawanna Railroad yards. Promoted by the premier sports showman of the time, George Lewis "Tex" Rickard, the contest already was arousing keen interest throughout the country. Would the wounded French war hero Carpentier be able to match the bigger and stronger Dempsey? Common sense said no, but Carpentier remained the sentimental favorite. Parties from as far away as Washington, Chicago, Milwaukee, even San Francisco, had booked the best New York hotels. Rickard announced he was enlarging the huge hexagonal stadium he was constructing for the occasion to accommodate 90,000.

To select the Dempsey-Carpentier fight took no great imagination on Sarnoff's part, but in its logistics and promotion, he showed himself equal to

Rickard. In less than three months, he and a group of engineers assembled from RCA received permission from the federal government to establish a station, appropriated a transmitter that General Electric had built for the navy, strung broadcasting aerials from towers at the Lackawanna Railroad yards, and publicized the broadcast through newspaper articles.

To give the broadcast a patriotic appeal, Sarnoff connected it with two noble causes: the Fund for a Devastated France, led by J. P. Morgan's daughter, Anne, and the Navy Club, headed by Franklin Delano Roosevelt. Miss Morgan had recently worked with Rickard to promote a lightweight championship fight, which the papers had called the "society bout," that raised $80,000 for her fund. With help from the National Amateur Wireless Association, Sarnoff arranged to install loudspeakers in about a hundred theaters, Elks, Masonic, and social clubs from Florida to Maine. The proceeds from those gathered in the halls were divided between the fund and the Navy Club, while each amateur who helped received a certificate signed by Rickard, Carpentier, Dempsey, Morgan, and Roosevelt.

The broadcast "met with success far beyond expectations" said a report Sarnoff circulated among the top managers at RCA. Promptly at 3 P.M. on July 2, in the searing afternoon heat, Major J. Andrew White, boxing fan, president of the National Amateur Wireless Association, and editor of the magazine *Wireless Age*, delivered a blow-by-blow description into a telephone that was connected to RCA's transmitting station at the Lackawanna yard. His voice was heard by an engineer at the station who actually repeated the reports for broadcast. More than 300,000 people heard him, certainly the largest audience ever assembled. Nor was it limited to those gathered in the various theaters and halls for the benefits. In Manhattan, an estimated 100,000 listeners gathered around loudspeakers attached to the *New York Times* Building. At the GE Electric Supply at 308 State Street in Schenectady, customers were invited to listen to "the big fight by wireless telephone."

In the days following the bout, RCA received letters and cards that suggested the enthusiasm of those who heard the broadcast. From 269 Lincoln Avenue in Brooklyn, Harry B. Fischer reported attaching two megaphones to his set, so that fifteen people crowded into his apartment could hear. From Jamaica, Long Island, a man described using fifteen feet of old wire clothesline and a crystal detector to hear the program. From Long Island Sound, W. K. Vanderbilt reported he heard the fight on his yacht the *Eagle*.

From Allentown, Pennsylvania, a man wrote to say he was a "rank outsider" in wireless, who did no sending. He was content to listen to "what the world is saying," and he had heard the entire fight. In that brief note lay the proof for David Sarnoff's theory. Here was someone saying he was a listener, someone who was not interested in becoming an operator. He was the sort of person who would like broadcasting, the person who would buy a radio music box.

Fortunately for Sarnoff and everyone else at RCA, Dempsey knocked out his French opponent in the fourth round, just at the moment the transmitter perished in an overload of electricity and heat. "A molten mass," declared the engineers who examined it later. No matter. It had served to bring the broadcast to the ears of hundreds of thousands and the *idea* of radio into the minds of millions.

7

SNAPSHOTS FROM THE FIRST AGE OF BROADCASTING

It is a clear evening, Tuesday, May 15, 1923. Dressed in a dark suit, a striped silk tie, and a hat pulled down to his ears, Edwin Howard Armstrong climbs atop a large circular globe made of strap iron. A professional photographer accompanying him records his ascent. Armstrong's legs straddle the sphere while his feet are carefully tucked beneath one of the iron bands. It is a remarkable image, especially when one realizes the inventor is balancing at the top of a tower the Radio Corporation of America has placed on the roof of the twenty-one-story Aeolian Hall at 33 West 42nd Street, just off Fifth Avenue.

There were two towers at the site, each 115 feet tall with crossarms 36 feet long. Aerial wires stretching between each crossarm suggested a gigantic clothesline in the sky. The towers transmitted signals from "Radio Central," RCA's twin New York stations—WJY, and a station the corporation had just moved to the city from New Jersey, WJZ. Earlier that week, Armstrong had swung upside down by his legs from one of the crossarms and did a handstand on the ball while a friend who accompanied him to the roof snapped a series of photographs. He had copies sent to Sarnoff and his secretary, Marion MacInnis. Earlier still, while the station was under construction, he had casually dropped out of a conversation he was having with some radio engineers at work on the roof to climb to the crossarm of the north tower. To one witness he walked "like a construction worker on a steel beam . . . obviously enjoying himself." The engineers looked up uneasily while Armstrong gazed into the street below. When he descended, one of the group asked harshly, "Armstrong, why do you do these damnfool things?" "Because," the inventor replied, "the spirit moves me."

Heights had always excited him: his lofty bedroom eyrie in Yonkers; the 125-foot mast he built behind his house; the cliffs of the Palisades 500 feet above the Hudson; the fragile airplanes that flew him high above France during the war. In his spare time he read tales about mountain climbers. From such altitudes—especially from the tops of radio towers—Armstrong enjoyed the exhilaration of being above the scene and yet at the same time controlling it. Climbing served to extend the serene detachment that was a part of his personality. And that evening, as he surveyed the landscape from his perch on the tower that his inventions had in large measure made necessary, Howard Armstrong had good reason to feel he controlled much of the world beneath him.

While the world Armstrong surveyed in 1923 was certainly in upheaval, it did not roar with quite the intensity that we usually ascribe to it. Certainly within sight of the Aeolian Hall were roof gardens, hip flasks filled with Prohibition alcohol, and jazz played in metallic paradises, where, as one poet of the time put it,

> . . . cuckoos clucked to finches
> above the deft catastrophes of drums.

But within view of RCA's tower lay another quieter world, a world inhabited by the eponymous hero of Sinclair Lewis's novel *Babbitt*. For every trumpet player blaring jazz on a rooftop in New York, surely there were a thousand— ten thousand?—contented Babbitts living in mental as well as physical zeniths of the land; narrow, self-important boosters imprisoned by their ideas, unwilling to break the bonds of self-satisfaction that encircled their limited lives.

In fact, much of the world was very much like ours today. A perusal of the newspapers demonstrates that many readers (as today) devoured the traditional staples of scandal, violence, and titillation. In the United States in 1923, firearms and explosives were employed in the commission of 5,736 homicides; knives and other pointed objects were used in 797. Reports of these and other crimes made for exciting reading and sold newspapers. One of the lead stories occupying people's attention that May concerned a Long Island couple arrested for murdering the wife's brother with slow poison for his insurance money. The attention of the nation was beginning to focus on the rising tide of corruption in the Harding administration that was starting to seep into the White House. It even perturbed the president, who on May 15 had less than three months to live.

Many of the stories in newspapers that year directly and indirectly concerned alcohol. Americans were drinking more—and more dangerously—than before Prohibition. They consumed $50 million worth of wines and liquors smuggled into the nation from foreign lands, and many more dollars' worth of spirits made in bathtubs and cellars. That year, 10,543 people would be arrested for drunkenness in New York, considerably fewer than the 38,998 in Boston, the 45,226 in Philadelphia, or the 75,800 in Chicago. One person in a hundred thousand died from strong drink in 1919; the figure had risen to 4.2 persons in 1923.

In 1923, too, large-scale commercial entertainment occupied an increasing amount of American life. Recently returned to New York from a nationwide tour, Al Jolson was performing his blackface routines to packed houses at the Winter Garden Theater. The average weekly attendance at motion pictures stood at 43 million. With Eastman Kodak advertising its "autographic" camera for as little as $6.50, people were taking more photographs than ever before. Boxing matches, which still were often connected with charity events, continued to draw attention. In May, a little-known Argentinian boxer named Luis Firpo was angling for a chance to fight the heavyweight champion, Jack Dempsey; that September at the Polo Grounds, he would knock the champion out of the ring, an image that would resonate in the memories of many through a painting by George Bellows. And the day Armstrong looked down from the tower, Babe Ruth hit a home run, a triple, and a single to lead the New York Yankees to a come-from-behind 9 to 5 victory over the Detroit Tigers.

By 1923, radio and broadcasting had become a full-fledged craze, and much of this popularity was due to Armstrong's inventions. "Edwin H. Armstrong found the radio telephone talking like a hare-lipped man and left it singing like a nightingale," declared a writer for *Hearst's International* with the confident prediction the inventor's name would soon be as synonymous with radio as Edison's was with the light bulb. What began in 1920 as a single station (KDKA), had grown to 30 stations in 1922, and 556 in 1923. Stations dotted the nation's map in places away from large metropolitan centers like Nunah, Wisconsin; Paducah, Kentucky; Yankton, South Dakota; Wichita Falls, Texas; Altoona, Pennsylvania; Hastings, Nebraska; and New Lebanon, Ohio. Wyoming had been the last state in the Union to take up broadcasting when it opened KDY; now California led with sixty-nine stations, from San Diego in the south to Eureka in the north; followed by Ohio with fifty-four and New York with thirty-eight. Only a few radio sets were produced in 1921; 100,000 were produced in 1922; 500,000 in 1923. By 1923, an estimated 400,000 households had a radio, a jump from 60,000 just the year before. And in that year's spring catalogue, the Sears Roebuck

Company offered its first line of radios, while Montgomery Ward was preparing a special fifty-two-page catalog of radio sets and parts. Included was "a complete tube set having a range of 500 miles and more" for $23.50.

Overnight, it seemed, everyone had gone into broadcasting: newspapers, banks, public utilities, department stores, universities and colleges, cities and towns, pharmacies, creameries, and hospitals, among others. In Davenport, Iowa, the Palmer School of Chiropractics had a station; in New Lebanon, Ohio, the Nushawg Poultry Farm started one; in Cleveland, the Union Trust Company began broadcasting over WJAX; in Clarksburg, West Virginia, the Roberts Hardware opened WHAK; the John Fink Jewelry Company of Fort Smith, Arkansas, began WCAC; the Detroit Police Department began the mnemonic KOP; the Chicago *Tribune* began WGN (World's Greatest Newspaper); in San Francisco, the Glad Tidings Tabernacle broadcast its message of salvation over KDZX; and in Milford, Kansas, broadcasting over KFKB ("Kansas Folks Know Best"), Dr. John R. Brinkley delivered lectures three times each day about the virtues of implanting goat glands to restore male potency. From his church in Brooklyn, the Reverend Samuel Parkes Cadman—the preacher who had called the Woolworth Building the "cathedral of commerce"—now delivered his sermons to tens of thousands; from Birmingham, the Alabama Power Company broadcast over WSY, calling itself "Service from the Heart of Dixie"; and in Kansas City, Emory J. Sweeney added station WHB to his automobile and tractor repair school, offering a free radio course to each student who enrolled.

At 3 P.M. on May 16, 1923, WJZ began regular broadcasting from the tower Armstrong was standing on with a schedule favoring musical performances:

3:00   Violet Pearch, pianist
3:20   Elsa Rieffin, soprano
3:30   Things to tell the housewife about cooking meat
3:45   Elsa Rieffin, soprano
4:00   Home—Its Equipment by Ada Swan
4:15   Rinaldo Sidoli, violinist
4:30   Ballad of Reading Gaol, part 1, by Mrs. Marion Leland
4:45   Rinaldo Sidoli, violinist
5:00   Ballad of Reading Gaol, part 2, by Mrs. Marion Leland
5:15   Rinaldo Sidoli, violinist
5:30   Rea Stelle, contralto
6:00   Peter's Adventures by Florence Vincent
7:30   Frederick Taggart, baritone

8:15   Lecture by W. F. Hickernell
8:30   Viola K. Miller, soprano
8:45   Salvation Army band concert
9:15   Viola K. Miller, soprano
9:30   Salvation Army Band, Male Chorus
10:00   Concert

So it went day after day. By the end of the year, WJY would present 98 baritone solos, 6 baseball games, 5 boxing bouts, 67 church services, 7 football games, 10 harmonica solos, 74 organ concerts, 340 soprano recitals, 40 plays, 723 talks and lectures, and 205 bedtime stories.

There were all kinds of other shows to listen to in New York if the location of the radio was just right and the weather cooperated. That Wednesday, a listener might have chosen WEAF's program on "Summer Flowering Bulbs" at 11 A.M. and "What to Do Until the Doctor Comes" at 11:30. WOO in Philadelphia advertised "Life of a Student Nurse in the Hospital" at 8:30 P.M., while WIP in the same city featured "Uncle Wip's bedtime stories and roll call" at 7 P.M. WAC Davenport (the chiropractic station) featured a lecture entitled "Americanism" by Frank S. Moses, past grand master of the Masons in Iowa, at 10 P.M. From WGY in Schenectady came the "produce and stock market quotations, news, and baseball scores" at 6 P.M., while WGI in Medford, Massachusetts, carried the Boston police reports at 6:30 P.M. WOR in Newark presented the Mabel Brownell Players' production of "Polly with a Past" from 4:15 to 5 P.M. Station KDKA featured a "Visit of the Dreamtime Lady" at 6:15 P.M. With some effort, listeners could also hear broadcasts from stations in Havana, Louisville, Toronto, Atlanta, Fort Worth, St. Louis, Kansas City, Rochester, Buffalo, Washington, Los Angeles, Arlington, Detroit, Cincinnati, Chicago, Boston, and Ridgewood, New Jersey. Across the nation the new medium was changing American attitudes about the world and about leisure. Radio was eliminating loneliness.

Though a slight depression of radio sales in the summer of 1922 suggested to some that broadcasting was merely a fad, the market had recovered by the late fall and now was stronger than ever. Brisk radio sales were part of the wave of postwar prosperity that was breaking over the nation. "If we are really intelligent, we may stay at the present high point in the business cycle for a long time," said Owen D. Young in an interview for *Colliers* magazine published the week Armstrong climbed the tower. Tycoons and plutocrats—two words that came to be favored by Henry Luce and Brit Haddon in *Time*, the new magazine the young Yale graduates had launched earlier that year—were beginning to populate New York.

While certainly no plutocrat, Howard Armstrong could count himself a wealthy man, due to the ever-increasing royalty payments for his inventions. Seeking to strengthen its position with RCA, Westinghouse had purchased his regeneration and superheterodyne patents for $335,000, payable over ten years, in 1920. An additional $200,000 was promised should he prevail in his litigation with de Forest. He had recently done just that in the federal district and appeals courts, and the outcome looked promising. (He had retained control over sale of "amateur and experimental" licenses to these patents, as Westinghouse had not thought it profitable to purchase those rights.) This gave him an additional $10,000 a month. His inventions had begun to breed money.

The money from Westinghouse and his own licensing enterprise paled in comparison with the financial arrangements Armstrong had just made with RCA for rights to another invention of his—superregeneration. While his other discoveries were the products of intense thought followed by startling revelation, superregeneration happened entirely by chance. The serendipitous accident occurred one evening in 1921, while he was preparing for his court case with de Forest. Superregeneration enabled him to go beyond the limits of regeneration, the howling that was produced if the signal was fed back through the circuit more than 20,000 times. To suppress the noise, Armstrong introduced a new tube circuit that quenched the oscillations of the regeneration circuit at 20,000 times a second. With superregeneration he obtained amplification beyond anything else available—up to 100,000 times the strength of the original signal.

While superregeneration did amplify signals more than they ever had been before, its oscillator also acted as a transmitter that disturbed other receivers in the vicinity, and it did not tune sharply. Though it enjoyed some use in police communications and as a very sensitive receiver in military communications used by planes in World War II, superregeneration never became a commercial success for RCA. But Armstrong did not know this when he patented the circuit. Neither did Sarnoff or the RCA engineers. Instead, they read newspaper accounts of the "latest Armstrong invention," which heralded its potential to revolutionize radio reception.

Anxious to keep any rival company from getting control of superregeneration—and possibly placing itself in a position similar to the advantageous one Westinghouse enjoyed when it was negotiating in 1920—Sarnoff moved aggressively to purchase rights to the invention from Armstrong. Instead of working through lawyers and middlemen, he and his friend talked directly. Sarnoff soon learned Armstrong could be a tough and artful bargainer. The inventor had placed himself in a strong position by quietly purchasing from an Englishman living in the Sudan exclusive rights to the one patent that might cause interference.

Part of the negotiations took place in the newspapers. That summer Armstrong took care to keep himself in the headlines, giving interviews, demonstrating his circuit, and making pronouncements about the bright future of radio. Throughout the summer, headlines heralded the latest invention: "About Armstrong and His Great Discovery" said the Springfield, Massachusetts, *Republican*; "E. Armstrong's Epoch Making Set Described," the New York *Tribune*; and "Former Soldier Highest Authority on Radio" wrote the Wichita, Kansas, *Beacon*. At a meeting of the Institute of Radio Engineers, he opened a demonstration of superregeneration before an overflow crowd of 700, with a flood of hyperbole:

> What I have just shown you is a system that gives the same results with three tubes as you obtain with nine tubes in the superheterodyne principle. Now the superheterodyne is the Rolls Royce of radio and while there are people who ride in Rolls Royces, there are quite a number who have to ride in Fords. I am now going to show you the Ford of radio.

"Armstrong's Radio Flivver Is Described" said the New York *Tribune* in its account of the evening.

Sarnoff grew worried. Westinghouse's acquisition of Armstrong's superheterodyne had forced Owen Young to pay handsomely to get the circuit into the RCA fold. If Armstrong were to sell rights to superregeneration to someone else, a company like A. H. Grebe, perhaps, or Atwater Kent, RCA might find itself having to negotiate another exorbitant stock arrangement. He had to deal swiftly with Armstrong.

Patterning a deal similar to the ones Young had fashioned with AT&T and Westinghouse, Sarnoff negotiated with cash and the strongest asset of all, RCA stock. On the last day of June 1922, the two men agreed upon terms: $200,000 and 60,000 shares of stock for superregeneration. To ensure that Armstrong would never be in such a strong position again, he also insisted that RCA have first refusal of any future inventions. In a single stroke, Edwin Howard Armstrong had become the corporation's largest private shareholder. To celebrate his good fortune, he had taken several months' vacation in Europe. "Arriving in England on Saturday with the contents of the Radio Corporation's safe," Armstrong had wired H. J. Round in London. He knew he had concluded an extremely favorable agreement. On the afternoon of May 15, RCA stock closed at three and five-eighths on the New York Curb market, making his shares worth $217,500.

On May 16, a messenger delivered more photographs recording Armstrong's climb to David Sarnoff and Marion MacInnis. That day the *Tribune* published a photograph of the stunt. Sarnoff was incensed. The earlier photographs had caused him to write:

If you have made up your mind that this mundane universe of ours is not a suitable place for you to be spending your time in, I don't want to quarrel with your decision, but keep away from the Aeolian Hall towers or any other property of the Radio Corporation. . . .

I don't want you to take this letter as a joke because I am perfectly serious about it and if I catch anybody in our organization allowing you to pull off such foolish tricks as those exhibited by the photographs, I am going to talk to them even more severely than I am to you in this letter.

This second set of pictures seemed to scoff at his authority, everything that he as vice president and general manager stood for. Though Sarnoff was angry, Armstrong was filled with all the exhilaration of a schoolboy who has gotten away with a mighty prank.

Marion MacInnis's reaction was somewhat different.

She sits on the beach with her back to the shoreline, her skirt tucked over her knees, and her hands clasped over her left knee. On her head a white cloche hat tightly covers her short hair; its narrow brim across her forehead shades her eyes and casts a shadow across her face. As she smiles at the camera, her lips are slightly parted in a look of innocence. Beside her right knee is a large suitcase standing upright on the sand, its cover opens down to expose several knobs. A large horn, the sort one associates with early record players, projects from its top. Sitting beside the suitcase, his left hand steadying the case while his right rests on one of the knobs, sits a man dressed in white duck pants, a tweed herringbone jacket, a white dress shirt, and a tie. On his head rests a smart straw boater. Its brim leaves a diagonal shadow across his forehead and left eye. His face suggests control as he stares directly at the camera lens. The photograph has captured Edwin Howard Armstrong at Palm Beach, Florida, with his bride, Marion MacInnis. The suitcase between them holds a superheterodyne radio, the first portable, Armstrong's wedding present to his wife.

She had been Sarnoff's secretary. They had met at the RCA offices in 1922 when Armstrong was negotiating the sale of his superregeneration circuit. When the sale was complete, he decided to celebrate with a vacation in Europe, where he would visit friends made during the war and attend a dinner in his honor in Paris. One day, after an appointment with her boss, the inventor promised Marion he would return from the continent with "the biggest and most expensive car" available and take her for a ride. Late that year he showed up in a fawn-colored Hispano-Suiza.

Known throughout the world for its sleek lines, superb craftsmanship, and distinctive radiator, graced by a winged, long-legged bird in flight on its cap, the Hispano-Suiza boasted a six-cylinder engine and—the newest inno-vation—brakes on all four wheels. The first order of business when he arrived in Paris, the purchase had cost Armstrong $11,000. He paid cash and ordered the car shipped to New York immediately. Awaiting him on the dock when he returned was the smart symbol of all he had attained, the legendary automobile of princes and potentates. His last vehicle, the red Indian mo-torcycle, he had been forced to sell in a vain attempt to raise the money needed for his first patent. That had been a decade ago, in a remote past. He resolved he would never part with the Hispano-Suiza.

It was the perfect car for courtship and romance. On weekends, Howard and Marion would take trips out to Long Island, where, for a fee, one could travel on the Vanderbilt family's private motor parkway, forty-five miles of pavement with hump-backed bridges over any roads in its path. At times, the speedometer in the Hispano-Suiza registered a hundred miles per hour.

Through the spring and summer of 1923—on rides to Long Island and up the Hudson, on trips to the theater, over lavish dinners, and on visits to hotel roof gardens—Armstrong courted his future bride. They made an odd couple. Marion MacInnis, nicknamed Minnie, was twenty-two when they first met; an intelligent, emancipated, confident, at times headstrong woman of Scottish descent from Merrimac, Massachusetts. Tall, with a beautiful figure and au-burn hair, Minnie loved parties, dancing, and bridge games, and was consid-ered by all who knew her to be lots of fun. She could be resolute and firm, too. Against her father's wishes, she and her sister, Marjorie, had left their jobs in Merrimac to seek work in New York. Within several days of their arrival, they were hired to be secretaries for officials of the Radio Corpo-ration of America—Marjorie for RCA's traffic manager, George Winter-bottom; Marion for the vice president and general manager, David Sarnoff.

Armstrong had never shown interest in anything other than radio, tennis, speed, and heights. While he drank, usually scotch, and at times heavily, he rarely did so outside the company of his radio friends. He seldom went to parties, and no one can recall his ever having had a date until he met Marion. Suddenly, he was courting.

During their courtship, Howard revealed the startling complexities of his personality. At times he appeared quiet and gentle, relaxed to a point of hardly metabolizing. Yet at other times he appeared infused with all the energy of the legendary twenties—intense, unreasonably impatient, arro-gant, on the point of exploding in a great rage. Sometimes he did explode with a ferocity people remembered vividly. Years after the war they still spoke of the time in Paris when a subaltern in the army motor pool refused his request for a particular car. Armstrong had floored him with a single blow of his heavy right fist.

Soon these tangled and sometimes contradictory qualities of Armstrong's character came to a stygmatic point fixed intensely on Marion MacInnis. At first she resisted. Here was no ordinary man. She had other suitors; a young dentist had asked her to marry him. But her resistance only served to increase his fervor and resolve; marriage became his quest. Why wouldn't she accept his proposal? He became impatient for her commitment; at times they argued. What was she to make of his climb to the top of the tower when she received the photographs the next day? Had he done it simply to annoy Sarnoff, or was it a single dramatic—though certainly bizarre—statement of his love? Shortly afterward, she agreed to marry him.

In the summer of 1923, Marion suggested to David Sarnoff that he get in touch with Armstrong about troubles RCA was having manufacturing the superheterodyne circuit. While the circuit worked well, engineers found it was far too complex either for a factory to mass produce or a radio novice to operate. Yet Sarnoff realized he must have the superheterodyne if the radiola were to gain the edge in sales. Perhaps, Marion suggested, Howard Armstrong might reduce its complexity. In just a few weeks he and Harry Houck, the sergeant he had met in Paris during the war and who now worked with him developing the superheterodyne, reduced the circuit's controls to just three knobs—two for tuning and one for volume. Asked to demonstrate his improved circuit to a group of RCA officials at Owen D. Young's apartment, Armstrong made a dramatic entrance with the radio playing. It was a feat unheard of in 1923.

For their successful effort, Houck and Armstrong shared the patent on the improvements; Howard received an additional 20,000 shares of RCA. In another dramatic moment that Armstrong engineered, he stunned Houck with a check for nearly $100,000 at Morey's Bar and Grill in lower Manhattan as Houck's additional share of the profits from their enterprise.

The wedding was arranged for Saturday, December 1, at the house of Marion's parents in Merrimac. All Howard's old friends were there for the occasion: George Burghard, a pioneer in the Radio Club of America, served as best man; Charles Underhill came, as did Harry Houck and friends from his Yonkers days, Bill Russell and Tom Styles. Steinmetz came from Schenectady; Lizette and David Sarnoff from New York. For their wedding trip, Howard decided they would motor to Palm Beach, Florida, in the Hispano-Suiza, no small feat in 1923.

Medical problems made the journey even more difficult and signaled an inauspicious beginning to Marion and Howard's marriage. The couple spent their wedding night in New York City. By the next day, however, Marion became ill, and they motored only as far as Trenton. Her condition deteriorated; on Monday night she had to be admitted to the hospital at Johns Hopkins University in Baltimore. There Marion Armstrong, married less than a week, underwent a hysterectomy. The operation's effects on the couple were physically and mentally devastating. Marion had undergone major surgery; she and Howard would never have children.

The events following the operation were unusual, too. The automobile trip to Florida had become something of a quest for Armstrong. He decided to leave his wife to recuperate alone in Baltimore while he motored south. Only the muddy roads in Georgia defeated him, forcing car and driver to travel the rest of the way by rail. Later that month, when she was well enough to make the journey, Marion rejoined her husband at the Powhatan Hotel. There on the Palm Beach sand, the couple were photographed with the superheterodyne radio, Howard's wedding present, between them.

◄━

A large moving picture camera mounted on a tripod occupies the center of the picture. A complex machine with four bayonet lenses, numerous wires, and two film reels projecting above the case, it is attended by a technician in a dark laboratory coat. Standing to the left of the tripod, intently inspecting a tube he holds in his hand, is Lee de Forest. As usual, he looks neat, in a striped dress shirt with cuff links and tie. The image echoes pictures of other great inventors—Edison and Bell among them—who staged such pictures for publicity. The time is about 1924. De Forest will use the photograph to promote his latest invention, sound motion pictures, which he has named "Phonofilm."

By late 1919, the field of radio had become too "crowded" for his tastes. As he had before, he felt the urge to explore uncharted territory: this time he would try to record sounds on photographic film by means of light. Perhaps, he reasoned, he might produce a sound with greater fidelity than a gramophone record. Many others had worked on the idea before, but with little luck.

In January 1920, de Forest enjoyed his first success when he recorded four words through a vacuum tube that converted the sounds into light. A revolving photographic plate preserved the impulses of light. He then employed another tube to convert the light back into audible sounds. Further experiments that year rendered his voice more faithfully. "I can now understand practically all it says to me," he wrote in September. By October, he was able to reproduce gramophone music onto film.

In the fall of 1920, de Forest decided to apply his work to motion pictures; what began as "photophone" had now become "Phonofilm." He approached his new venture with high ideals, typical of those that had motivated him to experiment with broadcasting earlier than anyone else. With proper sound fidelity, he reasoned, he would be able to bring music and culture to the masses. At the Rivoli Theater on Broadway two and a half years later, de Forest presented his first Phonofilm, *The Gavotte*, which featured a man and woman dancing. While the audience found the music "kept perfect time with the movements of the dancing girl on the screen," the reviewer for the *New York Times* was disappointed not to see anyone speaking.

To develop his idea for sound motion pictures, de Forest had to engage not only in invention but full-scale promotion and film production. For the technology behind his concept, de Forest came to rely more and more on Theodore W. Case, an inventor in Auburn, New York, who had developed a photoelectric cell for a similar sound-on-film concept. From 1922 to 1925, the men cooperated while Case and his assistant, Earl I. Sponable, modified Bell and Howell cameras so that they would record sound as well as images. De Forest turned his attention to producing short films of orchestras and musical acts. By mid-1924, three years before *The Jazz Singer* with Al Jolson appeared on Broadway, de Forest could report to the Society of Motion Picture Engineers that he had equipped over thirty theaters for Phonofilm and had contracted to equip fifty more.

All this effort took enormous amounts of capital, and de Forest often found himself short. Riverlure was a drain, especially in the winter when the drafty house consumed prodigious amounts of fuel for heat. Nor could his wife, Mary, curb her lavish taste. "She *will not* scrounge; she *will not* help," he lamented in his journal. Often he had to redeem Mary's rings from the pawnbroker where she had taken them for some quick cash. When she went to New York for her singing lessons, she insisted on the chauffeur driving her in the Packard Six; de Forest was left to take the train. With personal expenses running $1,500 a month, well ahead of his income of $833, de Forest made the startling decision to move his family to Berlin, Germany. In that depressed economy, he reasoned, his strong American dollars would enable him to conduct his research and live well. Perhaps Mary could pursue her career in the opera, while Eleanor could learn German. After turning his company over to two managers, Lee, Mary, and daughter Eleanor sailed for Germany in October 1921.

Within a few weeks, de Forest realized his mistake. Equipment was difficult to secure, skilled help impossible to hire. The harsh winter became even more disagreeable when a general strike turned off the lights and stopped the water. Isolated and disconsolate, Mary began drinking again. Lee lacked English-speaking friends. Only three-year-old Eleanor, attended by a nurse and learning German, appeared content. He endured Germany until September 1922, when he returned home. Her marriage strained harshly by the winter in Europe, Mary decided to stay on with her daughter at a chateau on the Riviera; they did not return until June 1923.

Still, de Forest needed more money to push forward his development of Phonofilm. His stock holdings in the De Forest Company, now worth close to $1 million, would provide it. By August 1923, he disposed of it all, surrendering all control of the company that bore his name.

De Forest called this business move a "gamble," and one that he later regretted making. At the time, however, he thought it wise. It freed him to devote almost all his energy to "learning the art of picture making." For all the expenses, he was once again a pioneer, charting new territory. He produced a series of Phonofilms by which he advertised the process at the Rivoli: Eddie Cantor and George Jessel appeared, as did the actor Frank McGlynn playing episodes from the life of Lincoln. In 1924, he recorded statements by the three presidential candidates—Calvin Coolidge, "Fighting Bob" La Follette, and John W. Davis; in 1927, in Washington, he filmed the hero's welcome given Charles Lindbergh. Recapturing some of the energy he had possessed when he began working in wireless nearly a quarter century earlier, de Forest exulted in July 1923, "This phonofilm work is so universally more interesting, artistic, & absorbing than radio that I doubt if I can ever become really engrossed in those problems hereafter."

Behind all this activity lay the same noble purpose that had inspired de Forest to experiment with radio broadcasting in 1916—to bring culture to the masses. Now he would add sight to sound. His first feature film, *The Covered Wagon*, which contained music and a plot, he declared "an epoch-making achievement in the field of motion-picture entertainment." "Undoubtedly," he concluded, it would "have a profound influence upon the popularity of the cinema—and more than that I have shown the way for educating the masses insidiously, unaware of the uplift (and therefore more effective)—to better & more worthy music." By mid-1925, he began experiments with technicolor.

Sooner than he imagined that it would, money became more dear. Never one to curb his spending, de Forest was unable to enforce economies either in his laboratory or in his home. He proved incapable of planning his purchases or spending prudently. The same man who in October 1920 railed against his wife having the chauffeur drive her to the city for her music lessons traded in his "miserable Packard" for a Model A sedan *and* a Rolls-Royce the following July. Three months later he put both cars in storage while he went to Berlin. In Europe he had spent lavishly on such items as a $5,000 life-sized painting, *La Danseuse*, by a minor French artist, Martin Kavel. (Pure kitsch, the painting depicts a young girl in a diaphanous gown that highlights the details of her left breast.) Film production, he quickly learned, was an elaborate and expensive proposition. Maintenance of the ex-

ecutive offices on West 42nd Street and the manufacturing plant and Phonofilm studios on East 48th Street in Manhattan became ever more costly.

With money running low, de Forest resorted to the dangerous game he had
played with his first wireless telegraph companies: public stock offerings. It all
had a familiar pattern: elaborate brochures full of complimentary notices
from newspapers, photographs of the Rivoli Theater marquee on Times
Square advertising Pola Negri recorded on De Forest Phonofilm, and the
inventor's own glowing account of Phonofilm and its many uses. Sales agents
coupled the brochure with the footage of Calvin Coolidge, leaving the impression of a presidential endorsement. Their zealousness did not go unnoticed in the White House. In May 1925, Silent Cal complained his good
name, voice, and image were being used to sell de Forest's stock. Investigations by the U.S. attorney general, the New York attorney general, and the
New York fraud-prevention bureau swiftly followed. Though formal charges
were never filed, the mere threat that they would be, reported on the front
pages of daily newspapers, was enough to erode public confidence in Phonofilm. De Forest's talkies were in serious trouble.

At the same time that the money ran out, so did his arrangements with
Theodore Case. Along with his assistant, Sponable, Case had been responsible for most of the development of Phonofilm, especially of the later cameras and the unique lamps in the projector's sound system. De Forest failed
to acknowledge the use of Case's equipment in his films, as they had agreed
he would do, and their relationship became strained. For de Forest, the
falling out with Case was yet another example of the "gang of enemies"
besetting him, those who wished "to strip me, dominate me, & grow fat off
my genius, my effort." By the end of 1925, their business association was
dissolved; Case demanded the return of his equipment.

"These are dark and worried days," de Forest somberly wrote in early April
1926, "for the bank balance of Phonofilms becomes rapidly shorter, and no
friend is found to take the necessary financial interest." By the end of May,
Eleanor's nurse had to be let go, along with the laundress. It was galling for
him to see Warner Brothers enjoy great success in 1926 with John Barrymore
starring in *Don Juan*, the first talking picture using the primitive "Vitaphone"
system, essentially a phonograph record synchronized with a silent film. He
was happy, however, when William Fox paid $100,000 for an option on
exclusive use of Phonofilm. Only later did he learn Fox had also purchased
Case's patents at the same time and decided they would stand up against any
suit de Forest might bring. De Forest did bring suit, but settled out of court
for $60,000—a far cry from the $2 million he had counted upon. By 1928,
De Forest Phonofilms Inc. faced complete insolvency. Its president was happy
to sell the company to a South African, Max Schlesinger, who reorganized

it into the General Talking Pictures Corporation. Soon it, too, was bankrupt. By the end of the decade, Phonofilm for Lee de Forest was a bitter memory.

✦

It is the late twenties, and he is in his mid-thirties. He stands before a studio camera with his body at a slight angle. Conservatively dressed in a dark three-piece suit with a white dress shirt and tie, and a watch chain across his vest, he appears at first glance to be solidly built. But as one contemporary remarked, his build was known in the clothing trade as a "short stout." The watch chain that crosses his ample chest below the top button of his vest betrays a tendency toward a paunch and suggests the need for exercise. What draws the viewer's attention is not his body so much as his face. It is broad and dark, distinguished by the firm set of his lips and the gaze of his eyes. The high forehead suggests his still thick brown hair is just beginning to recede. His eyes are blue, which contemporaries variously described as "cobalt" and "steely." Commanding, on the edge of a glower, his expression suggests the photograph is intended for a corporate boardroom to demonstrate the subject is in complete control, as, indeed, he is. He is David Sarnoff, executive vice president of the Radio Corporation of America.

In the years since the creation of the Radio Corporation, Sarnoff had survived revolutionary changes in broadcasting and RCA—including a new president of the corporation, threats of government interference and regulation, and a challenge from American Telephone and Telegraph Company—and prospered.

Realizing that the industry of radio was advancing rapidly from what he had envisioned it would be when RCA was formed, and that it was increasingly under attack as a monopoly, Owen D. Young decided he had to replace E. J. Nally. Understanding that RCA's interests increasingly lay in the area of broadcasting and radio sales, areas in which he had little interest, Nally accepted Young's suggestion that he step aside with equanimity and considerable relief. He would be retained to head RCA's international operations and would be able to spend the rest of his working years in a comfortable sinecure in Paris. The next president, Young told Nally, should be a person "well known nationally and internationally." He must be respected in Washington so that he might "speak with authority" in government circles. Yet he must not be identified with a political party or Wall Street. Finally, he must be able to continue and strengthen the informal alliance between RCA and the government, particularly the armed forces. In General James G. Harbord, a man of national stature, probity, modesty, and no political or financial encumbrances, Young found the perfect successor. On January 1, 1923, the board of directors of the Radio Corporation of America voted unanimously to make Harbord president.

Quiet, distinguished in appearance, Harbord looked the part of a commander. A longtime friend of General Pershing, he was known for both his heroism and his administrative skill. In June 1918, he led the Marines to victory in the Battle of Belleau Wood, the first important U.S. engagement in the war and one of the most famous in the history of the Corps. By the end of the war, 386,000 soldiers had served under his command; after the Armistice, he became Pershing's executive assistant.

Clearly, it was a good appointment for Sarnoff, who, at thirty-one, was not ready to ascend to the presidency. He had recently been made executive vice president of RCA, with the understanding that he would be in charge of the corporation's domestic operations. A professional soldier since 1889, Harbord looked to a few years with RCA as the capstone to his career. For his part, Sarnoff realized the fifty-five-year-old general posed no long-range threat to his own prospects for advancement.

There was another good reason for Sarnoff to be sanguine about Harbord's appointment: though a skilled telegrapher, the general knew virtually nothing about radio; indeed, he probably did not own one. By this time Sarnoff was a master in the art of instructing superiors; like Nally and Young before him, Harbord proved a willing pupil. Sarnoff began the lessons early. On January 9, 1923, as the general was about to embark on a trip to the west, Sarnoff sent him a packet of past memos he had written to his superiors at RCA and General Electric:

> General Harbord—
>   I've picked out a few rather long-winded stories of mine which I thot you might find time & the inclination to read on your way to Kansas.
>   Some of my predictions have come true and others, I think will come true in time.
>   Hope you have a very pleasant and successful trip.
>   Please return these papers to me for my files.
>
>   David Sarnoff

By this time Sarnoff had been with Marconi and RCA longer than almost anyone else among the managers; more than anyone else in the organization, he possessed the institutional memory of the corporation as well as the art, and he knew he could control just what his new boss would learn. Among the memos he included was his twenty-eight-page paper to Young about the prospective radio business, which of course contained his by now classic proposal for a radio music box. Harbord saw quickly that he could rely on his young vice president for information, advice, and support. When he returned from Kansas, he gave the packet back with "thanks and great interest." General Harbord had successfully completed his first assignment.

"War represents a permanent factor in human life and a very noble one," General Harbord once said. "It is the school of heroism from which the nation's noblest sons are graduated into highest manhood." His words found a peculiar application for the Radio Corporation of America, because in 1923 it was nearing a state of war with the federal government and the management of American Telephone and Telegraph—conflicts that would test whether RCA should be graduated into "highest manhood." And Harbord asserted he was ready to lead the corporation into the fray.

The first battle was to shore up the extremely fragile structure that supported the Radio Corporation. Conceived as a radio telephone and telegraph company with a powerful patent pool, RCA was born into a world of uneasy alliances among rival electric manufacturers, a fruit grower, and a telephone company. In its earliest years of life, its basic direction changed radically. In 1922, for example, radio sales jumped to $26.9 million—113 percent over the previous year. In the same year, RCA earned $14.8 million in revenue; the Federal Trade Commission estimated about 75 percent, $11 million, had come from sales of radiolas. These huge profits in areas that no one save Sarnoff had foreseen put a painful strain on the alliances.

The company that felt the strain most acutely was American Telephone and Telegraph. Under terms of its agreement at the incorporation, AT&T granted to RCA rights to "establish and maintain" one-way wireless telephone transmitting stations, or broadcast stations, and limited its role to the manufacture of transmitting equipment; General Electric and Westinghouse would manufacture receivers. But a survey of 600 broadcast transmitters revealed that only 35 were using AT&T equipment, while the rest were violating its patents. Although General Electric and Westinghouse were enhancing their profits by manufacturing radios for RCA, and RCA was accruing most of its profits by selling the sets, AT&T was profiting not at all. Most disturbed by these developments and what he perceived as a fundamental change in the Radio Corporation's purpose was AT&T's young, ambitious vice president, Walter Sherman Gifford.

During 1921 and 1922, Gifford and Sarnoff grew to be intense rivals. Only six years Sarnoff's senior, Gifford was following a path at AT&T remarkably similar to Sarnoff's at RCA. Like Sarnoff, Gifford possessed initiative, the capacity for hard work, and a flair for bold action. And like Sarnoff, he had advanced steadily through the company's ranks. By 1920, he was made a vice president, in line to ascend to the presidency, which he did in 1925. Yet

Gifford's background could not have been more different from Sarnoff's. Of New England stock and Harvard educated, Gifford possessed a dour patrician demeanor, an air enhanced by his taste for dark suits, wing-collared shirts, and somber bow ties.

Gifford moved quickly and, for the times, audaciously. Under his plan, the once-impuissant ally of RCA would become its most powerful enemy. AT&T sold all its stock in RCA and its members resigned from the corporation's board. Gifford directed his company's laboratory to design a receiver set that would skirt RCA's patents; decreed that AT&T would no longer lease its telephone lines for broadcasting; and announced that WEAF, AT&T's New York radio station, would sell commercials, what he called "toll broadcasting."

Gifford's maneuvers were calculated to destroy the Radio Corporation of America. No one saw this disastrous potential more acutely than David Sarnoff; it was the most serious challenge ever to the company he had labored to develop. Toll broadcasting seemed especially dangerous. From the time he wrote his radio music box memo, Sarnoff had always conceived of broadcasting as a public service underwritten by radio manufacturers as a lure to sell their receivers. In mid-1922, he had proposed that RCA create a network of stations that would present programs of "substance and quality." Radio had the power to be a public benefactor, like a library, only "projected into the home where all classes of people may remain and listen." "Let us organize," he wrote, "the Public Service Broadcasting Company, or National Radio Broadcasting Company" composed of the Westinghouse, GE, and RCA stations, not as a " 'money making' proposition," but as a "public service." The network he outlined was not unlike today's National Public Radio. Each manufacturer would give a percentage of its revenue to the network, and possibly additional support would come from a "public benefactor."

On Monday, August 28, 1922, Sarnoff's dream was destroyed. At 5 P.M. that day, Mr. Blackwell of the Queensboro Corporation stepped up to a microphone at WEAF to urge listeners to forsake the congestion of the city for an apartment home in "Hawthorne Court," named in honor of "America's greatest writer of fiction." Mr. Blackwell's message, the radio industry's first commercial, had cost the Queensboro Corporation $50. Other companies—Atwater Kent, Tidewater Oil, and American Express among them—soon followed Queensboro's lead. In the beginning, WEAF's guidelines ensured the dignity of the advertisements; there was to be nothing so crude as a price mentioned and little in the way of graphic product description. Nonetheless, Gifford had changed the philosophy behind most of broadcasting. Radio would become a commercial enterprise.

However, commercial broadcasting did not prove as great a threat to Sarnoff's plans as AT&T's refusal to lease its telephone lines to other broadcasters. Without those superior wire lines—the only ones capable of carrying voices and music with fidelity—RCA's broadcasting would be confined to a studio, unable to produce a remote program from a theater stage, a concert hall, or a political platform. By denying the lines, they made Sarnoff's proposal for a national network of stations impossible to carry out.

As charges and countercharges flew between RCA and AT&T, Gifford learned that Sarnoff considered broadcasting "our exclusive field," while word got back to Sarnoff that Gifford had described him as "abrasive" and "Jewish." Relations might have deteriorated even further if the Federal Trade Commission had not reported in December 1923 that the Radio Corporation was a monopoly, "with the power to stifle competition in the manufacture and sale of receiving sets." In a formal complaint issued the next month, the FTC charged RCA and AT&T, as well as the other companies that made up the corporation's agreement, with "restraining competition and maintaining a monopoly." Luckily, the Teapot Dome scandal then dominating newspaper headlines deflected public attention from the charges of a trust.

Still, the undesirable publicity was enough to bring the warring factions together in arbitration. The referee found almost entirely for RCA. But AT&T did not give up easily. From its legal counsel, it received a contrary advisory opinion that called the legality of the Radio Corporation into question. At this point, Owen D. Young stepped forth to effect a compromise. Gifford, now president of AT&T, was ready for peace, because he realized his own company was subject to charges of monopoly. The agreement, worked out partly in secret and completed in July 1926, effectively ended AT&T's interest in broadcasting. The telephone company would sell WEAF to RCA and close its own network of stations. At the same time, the Radio Corporation would start the National Broadcasting Company, a "self-supporting and probably revenue producing" radio network. And for $1 million a year, all the stations comprising NBC would be linked with AT&T's telephone lines.

"Announcing the National Broadcasting Company" read the advertisement appearing in metropolitan newspapers that September. The copy assured the public there would be *"National Radio broadcasting with better programs."* Borrowing from Sarnoff's memo of 1922, it stated: *"The market for receiving sets will be determined by the quantity and quality of the programs broadcast."* There would be "no monopoly of the air," under the new arrangement; RCA was simply making the best means of broadcasting available to the industry. To ensure quality programming, a public advisory council of notable Americans—such as Charles Evans Hughes, former presidential candidate; Owen D. Young; Elihu Root, former secretary of war and state, and Nobel Peace Prize winner; Dwight Morrow, banker and diplomat; and Mary

Sherman, president of the General Federation of Women's Clubs—would assure that "broadcasting is done in the fairest and best way."

Harbord and Young had Sarnoff sign the final agreement, as a fitting tribute to his part in this extraordinary arrangement. No one had worked harder than he to see it through; no one saw more clearly than he what it would mean for RCA's future.

Yet in one crucial way David Sarnoff had given up something he had championed ever since he made his radio music box proposal in 1916. No longer did he think of broadcasting as a service provided by the manufacturers; now it was to be a "self-supporting and probably revenue producing" network of stations. What he lost—not to mention what American culture lost—by agreeing to make NBC a commercial enterprise can never be calculated.

As the first president of the National Broadcasting Company, Owen D. Young selected Merlin Hall Aylesworth; he proved an excellent choice. A lawyer by training, Aylesworth had been involved with electric utilities, most recently serving as the spokesman for the National Electric Light Association, the lobbying group for private power companies. Silver-haired, impeccably dressed in dark suits and conservative ties, he always could be depended on to defend the cause of the network—particularly against the charge that it was a monopoly—with grace, dignity, and cogent arguments. The National Broadcasting Company, he once declared augustly to a congressional hearing, was a "sacred public trust." What matter that he neither listened to the radio nor had owned one before Young appointed him president?

The creation of the National Broadcasting Company was but one of David Sarnoff's triumphs in the 1920s. By the end of the decade, he had achieved enormous power and stature within RCA and in the larger world as well. In October 1928, he and Joseph P. Kennedy had agreed to have RCA purchase a major interest in the Keith-Albee-Orpheum vaudeville theaters and convert them into sound motion picture houses using a new RCA and General Electric sound and film technology named the pallophotophone. The new venture, of which RCA owned 25 percent, was named Radio Keith Orpheum. Soon record-setting audiences would be watching Fred Astaire and Ginger Rogers dance in RKO pictures like *Top Hat* and *Swing Time*. In 1929, Sarnoff created with General Motors a new company to manufacture radios for cars and homes—the General Motors Radio Corporation, of which RCA owned 49 percent. At the end of the decade, he prevailed over a reluctant board to merge RCA with the Victor phonograph company. Since 1924, RCA had provided the radio components of a combined radio phonograph; now RCA had control of Victor's production of phonograph records as well as its huge manufacturing plant in Camden, New Jersey. Acquiring these new enterprises gave Sarnoff what he wanted most: complete domination of the industry.

Recognizing his protégé's abilities as a negotiator, Owen D. Young asked Sarnoff to accompany him in 1929 to the war reparations conference in Paris. When the conference, to arrange a revised and easier schedule of payments for Germany—and thus save its disintegrating economy—seemed destined to fail because of the deep divisions between the parties, Sarnoff stepped forward to save it. In a series of private meetings, he and the chief German negotiator hammered out a series of agreements that Young later successfully presented to the conference. "David did the job of his life," Young wired Lizette Sarnoff in New York. The accord became known as the Young Plan, and Sarnoff had been most responsible for its success. There was no question in Owen Young's mind about who would be the next president of RCA, but the change came sooner than he might have wished. The October crash left Young deep in debt. On January 3, 1930, he stepped down from the chairmanship of RCA's board of directors to devote more time to his personal affairs. (He would still serve on its executive committee.) General Harbord would take over as chairman, and David Sarnoff became RCA's third president. He was not quite thirty-nine.

It is a warm Saturday in June 1927. Behind a line of microphones, and before a crowd of 150,000 gathered at the Washington Monument, stand President Calvin Coolidge and America's newest hero, Charles A. Lindbergh. The president is pinning the distinguished flying cross on his lapel. The crowd listening to the president's words was not just 150,000, however. The National Broadcasting Company had linked fifty stations in twenty-four states across the nation in the largest network broadcast ever: WSM, Nashville; WDOD, Chattanooga; WTIC, Hartford; KOA, Denver; KDL, Salt Lake City; KHQ, Spokane; KOMO, Seattle; to name but a few. The words traveled over about 12,000 miles of AT&T's telephone wire presided over by 400 telephone and radio engineers.

From 12:30 P.M. to midnight, radio reporters never lost sight of the aviator. Covering Lindbergh's landing on the U.S. Navy's *Memphis*, the parade up Pennsylvania Avenue, and the presentation of the Flying Cross was NBC's Graham McNamee, who led the team of announcers carefully placed about Washington. Phillips Carlin was perched atop the Washington Monument, Milton J. Cross in the dome of the Capitol, and John B. Daniel on the roof of the U.S. Treasury.

"A darn nice boy," McNamee assured his audience as Lindbergh alighted from the *Memphis*; "Lindy himself, receiving with his usual modest demeanor the plaudits of the crowd," was McNamee's description as he followed him along the parade route. "Here's the boy! He comes forward; unassuming, quiet, a little droop to his shoulders, very serious; he's tired out," McNamee reported as the shy Minnesotan approached the president, "and awfully nice." Radio followed Lindbergh throughout the day, interspersing Mc-Namee's descriptions and the numerous speeches, with an "Aviation Review Program"; a humorous sketch, "New York to Hackensack"; a "Musical Trip with Lindbergh"; and George M. Cohan singing his tribute, "When Lindy Comes Marching Home."

Though initially prohibited by the stations from even giving their names over the air waves, radio announcers had swiftly become personalities, too, with whom listeners felt they had an intimate acquaintance. In 1926, the Post Office had no trouble delivering a card sent from London, addressed only to "Phillips Carlin, Celebrated Radio Announcer, America." When listeners learned that a daughter had been born to Carlin, they sent more than 600 letters to NBC. NBC learned to capitalize on such events, too, so that the fact the announcer received the letters became a news story carried by the papers.

How many people listened to these events? In the week before Lindbergh's arrival, stores reported brisk radio sales. There were approximately 6 million sets across the nation. An average of five people would listen to each, so the statisticians figured, for a total audience of 30 million. Even if these projections were inflated, more Americans were listening than ever.

The National Broadcasting Company was changing the interior life of the country in ways that few—not even a Sarnoff—could have envisioned a decade earlier. Shortly after its formation, executives at NBC decided two networks, the red and the blue, were in order. WEAF would serve as the primary station of the red network; WJZ of the blue. From New York, the two stations would feed programs through telephone lines to scores of "affiliate stations" from the Atlantic to the Pacific. The affiliates were able to feed the larger stations with news and programs.

The invisible sinews of electromagnetic waves were binding the country together as never before. Those waves crossed the nation without regard for regional or state lines, often leveling the cultural lines in their path. Increasingly, people ceased to refer to themselves just as Pennsylvanians, Coloradans, Californians, Oregonians, or Texans; radio brought the nation into their homes and gave them a national identity. A single event, a boxing match, an inauguration, a football game, a concert, a comedy sketch, a political speech, or a sermon gave Americans the chance to share in a common experience. Whether the show took place in Washington, Chicago, New

York, or San Francisco, radio allowed the nation to be a part of it the moment it occurred. Though those same listeners might relive the event later through the newspapers or the newsreels in movie theaters, it was radio that brought it to them first.

On a Tuesday evening in Kansas City, for example, a person might turn on the local NBC outlet, WDAF, to hear the Hall Johnson singers on the "Eveready Hour." From a studio at WEAF in New York, voices traveled coast to coast over NBC. The same scene repeated itself in different towns and cities throughout the nation: in Philadelphia over WFI, in Detroit over WJR, in San Francisco over KPO. Other programs became national attractions, presenting a fare of musical variety and concerts: the "Seiberling Singers," the "Maxwell House Hour," the "General Motors Family Party," the "Cliquot Club Eskimos," the "Ipana Troubadours," and the "Cities Service Orchestra," among others.

In the fall of 1927, after Lindbergh returned, the demand for radios increased dramatically. No doubt some of those who had gathered around their friends' and neighbors' sets that June 11 had succumbed to the power of the new medium. In September, RCA introduced its new line of radiolas, ranging in price from $69.50 to $895. The most popular seller was the Radiola 17, costing $157.50 with tubes, a model that ran on house current instead of a cumbersome battery, was compact, and was simple to operate. Demand for it continually exceeded production.

Beginning with the election of 1928, radio began to have a profound effect on the way politicians conducted their campaigns. Certainly radio had been used before, but the limited number of set owners meant campaign broadcasting had been more a novelty than an indispensable campaign tool. In May 1928, Herbert Hoover's managers declared that if the secretary of commerce were nominated, he planned to campaign "mostly on radio and through the motion pictures," thereby placing his hat in the "ethereal 'ring.' " Personal appearances by the candidate, so the managers proclaimed, were a thing of the past. "It is believed," wrote a reporter for the New York Times in language that appears remarkably contemporary, "that brief pithy statements as to the positions of the parties and candidates which reach the emotions through the minds of millions of radio listeners, will play an important part in the race to the White House." The managers realized they were on to something. It was the 1928 version of the sound bite, shorter in length than the usual political oratory, and designed to play to feelings and passions. Radio was changing the attention span of listeners, who were no longer willing to suffer overly long and fulsome speeches. The new medium would effectively reduce the length of the average campaign speech that fall to ten minutes.

The idea of a network with a central station feeding programming to others across the country was too good not to be copied by others. On Monday, October 1, 1928, a twenty-seven-year-old man with no experience in radio took over two struggling networks, merged them into the Columbia Broadcasting System, and made himself president, installing himself in a huge office atop the Paramount Building in New York. He was William S. Paley, the son of a Philadelphia cigar manufacturer, whose experience in radio had been limited to overseeing a program sponsored by the La Palina cigar. Paley had much in common with his rival at NBC. Each was the son of a Russian immigrant (though Paley had been born in Chicago). Each had known difficult financial times (though Paley's were never as bleak). But Bill Paley and David Sarnoff were very different men. Paley was slim, round-faced, and almost six feet tall; already he had acquired a reputation for being a playboy. Most importantly, he never cared about the engineering and inventions that made radio possible; he only cared about the entertainment radio produced.

Paley soon made his mark, and in a way that surprised everyone, including David Sarnoff. When Paley took over, only one hour's programming out of five had a sponsor. He immediately moved to increase the network's sales of advertising, and encouraged rival radio manufacturers to promote their products on his network. He added stations on the West Coast. He hired an executive from the Federal Radio Commission who knew broadcasters throughout the nation. Working together, they expanded CBS to seventy-six stations by the end of the decade.

From his start in broadcasting, Paley worked to create an image for himself and his network. He hired Edward L. Bernays, the nephew of Sigmund Freud, to serve as his public relations agent and adviser. Bernays had represented clients as diverse as the War Department and Enrico Caruso. He was the master at presenting the network in the best possible light, and proposed ways of improving its advertising and programming.

CBS succeeded by upsetting the standard practices that Sarnoff and NBC had established. NBC charged its affiliate stations as much as $90 an hour to broadcast unsponsored programs; Paley gave programs to his affiliates but reserved the right to take over a local station's schedule to broadcast CBS-sponsored programs at any time. Advertisers liked the policy because CBS could guarantee them that their products would be sold throughout the network.

Paley's greatest challenge to NBC came in the area of programming. He tailored his broadcasts to appeal to the largest audience possible. While NBC presented orchestras playing classical music, CBS presented Paul Whiteman's band playing jazz, sponsored by Old Gold cigarettes. While NBC broadcast lectures and educational programs, Paley brought comedians and soap operas to the microphones. Listeners loved the programs. By 1930, Paley had created a respectable, if low-brow, network challenge to NBC.

In the same issue of the *New York Times* that reported Herbert Hoover's radio campaign strategy, an article appeared describing C. Francis Jenkins's "magic mirror," a multitube radio set equipped with a special picture-receiving attachment "plugged into the loud speaker jack." The "mirror on the cartoon machine reflects a cartoon or picture." A mechanical device complete with an electric motor turning prismatic rings, the machine produced a crude, blurry, forty-eight-line image on a six-inch-square mirror. Nevertheless, it was a picture, no small achievement for a lone tinkerer from Dayton, Ohio. Jenkins had created "radio vision," one of the first televisions.

Jenkins had first transmitted an image from Anacosta, Virginia, to Washington in 1925. He began to sell television receivers in 1928. Several thousand people put down $85 to $135 for one of his sets (or $47.50 for a kit), though as yet there were no stations apart from his own experimental W3XK in Wheaton, Maryland.

Jenkins was not alone in his experiments. Television had long been a dream of visionaries and inventors. In 1884, German student Paul Nipkow patented a perforated disc, which, when rotated before an image, divided it into lines. The Nipkow disc served as the principle underlying Jenkins's machine. Since the early twenties, Ernst Alexanderson had been experimenting with mirrors and mechanical scanning discs, some as large as two feet in diameter. He had transmitted silhouettes from his laboratory at General Electric to a back-lit receiver screen at his home in Schenectady. In Pittsburgh, a Russian émigré working for Westinghouse, Vladimir K. Zworykin, was at work on a system that employed a cathode ray tube to scan images electronically. By the end of the decade, the Federal Radio Commission had issued twenty-eight licenses for experimental television broadcasts. "In the future," wrote one enthusiastic popularizer and prophet of the new medium, "there will be the possibility of our seeing the President of the United States make an important speech, and we will be enabled to not only hear every word he utters, but see him in person as well."

"The Dawning Age of Sight by Radio," declared David Sarnoff in an RCA press release in November 1928. "The horizon is as bright with promise for the radio 'onlooker' as it is for the radio listener," the release went on, predicting not only television broadcasting but the transmission of "distant scenes transmitted in their natural colors." Only the technological problems remained to be solved, before "instantaneous projection through space" of images to the home. New demands would be made on the broadcaster, Sarnoff recognized, for the "ear may be content with the oft-repeated song; the eye would be impatient with the twice repeated scene."

To Sarnoff in 1928, a mechanical contrivance similar to Jenkins's and Alexanderson's would transmit those distant scenes. But he changed his thinking in 1929 when he met a man destined to become RCA's greatest engineer, Vladimir K. Zworykin. Zworykin had fled the revolution a decade earlier with plans for an electronic means of transmitting images. Already he had taken out patents on a tube he called the iconoscope (literally "a viewer of icons"), which was one of the first television cameras. However, Zworykin told Sarnoff, the system was still a primitive one, and Westinghouse, where he worked as a research assistant, had not shown sufficient interest to develop it further. Sarnoff immediately saw the significance of Zworykin's work.

8

COURT FIGHT

A single clause of just twenty-seven words, drafted by fifty-five men in the eighteenth century, guides the way we think about inventors and their creations today. Not a single inventor had anything to say about the clause.

On the afternoon of Wednesday, September 5, 1787, the delegates who had gathered in Philadelphia to write a constitution for the United States approved with little discussion and no dissent a clause for Section 8 of Article I, granting Congress the power "To promote the Progress of Science and useful Arts, by securing for limited Times to Authors and Inventors the exclusive Right to their respective Writings and Discoveries." The language had been introduced three and half weeks earlier—again with no discussion—by James Madison and Charles Pinckney and had later been refined by the Committee on Style. The powers the delegates voted to give Congress were at once broad and limited: they were concerned with discoveries that "promote the Progress of Science and useful Arts." Though the right was exclusive, it would be given to inventors for limited times. Madison and Pinckney and the Committee on Style did their job well: these twenty-seven words have served as the foundation upon which rests every copyright, patent, and trademark in the United States.

In approving the clause, the delegates made a tacit assumption that society granted such rights for its betterment, and they acted with ample precedent. In 1623, the English Parliament under King James I passed a statute against all monopolies save "projects of new invention." Monopolies for inventors had long been recognized in the New World, too. Nearly a century and a half earlier, in 1641, the General Court of Massachusetts had granted one Samuel

Winslow an exclusive ten-year license for his new method of making salt, and prohibited others "from making this article except in a manner different from his." Other colonies followed suit, especially when they found that granting an inventor a monopoly to market a discovery served to foster the inventive spirit. Later, under the Articles of Confederation, states enacted patent laws.

Nevertheless the delegates compromised between free use of inventions and an unlimited monopoly. Thomas Jefferson, an inventor of no small consequence himself, articulated the dilemma late in his life: "It would be curious then, if an idea, the fermentation of an individual brain could by natural right be claimed in exclusive and natural property." For Jefferson, the dissemination of an idea did not diminish its value to the originator: "he who lights his taper from me, receives light without lessening mine." Nevertheless, Jefferson understood the efficacy of a patent system. "Society," he wrote, "may give an exclusive right to the profits arising from [an invention] as an encouragement to men to pursue utility." The compromise of the Constitution reflected much of the conflict in Jefferson's mind. The delegates had insisted that the right would be the inventor's, but only for a limited time, whose length was yet to be determined.

"The utility of this power will scarcely be questioned," wrote Madison of the clause in the *Federalist*, noting its descent from English common law. And affirming the benefits for both the state and the inventor, he concluded, "The public good fully coincides . . . with the claims of individuals."

President George Washington signed the first legislation based on this clause on April 10, 1790. The law charged the secretaries of state and war and the attorney general with the responsibility for granting patents. They might issue a patent for a period not exceeding fourteen years if they deemed the invention "sufficiently useful and important." The fee for filing usually amounted to $4.

It fell appropriately to Thomas Jefferson, first secretary of state, to oversee the Act of 1790. "Nobody wishes more than I do that ingenuity should receive liberal encouragement," he said of the duties. He met with inventors, examined their discoveries, convoked meetings with Secretary of War John Knox and Attorney General Edmund Randolph, and issued the actual patent papers. In the first year the law took effect, Jefferson and his colleagues examined a number of inventions but granted only three patents.

The system of protecting inventors has evolved dramatically since Samuel Hopkins of Vermont received the first patent on July 31, 1790, for a novel method of "making pot and pearl ashes." Over the years, Congress has changed the law several times, forbidding at one time aliens the right to hold patents, demanding at another that a model be submitted with an application, and extending the law to cover the invention of new strains of agricultural grains, among other things. Not until 1836 did Congress remove the issuance of patents from the duties of the secretary of state and create a separate patent office with its own building.

There were 41,854 patents issued in 1914, the year Armstrong received number 1,113,149 for his "wireless receiving system." In the 124 years since its creation, the patent system had achieved what the authors of the Constitution envisioned. Ingenuity had been encouraged and the public good well served.

Abraham Lincoln described the constitutional guarantee of a patent as "the fuel of interest to the fire of genius in the discovery and production of new and useful things." Encouraged by the promise of monetary rewards, America became a land of tinkerers and inventors. Lincoln himself was a good example. On May 22, 1849, when he was a congressman from Illinois, he had obtained patent number 6,469 protecting his rights to "a device for buoying vessels over shoals." A model of the invention that Lincoln whittled shows a boat with bellows attached to its hull. When the boat approached shallow water, the pilot could fill the bellows with air so that the vessel would float clear of the bottom. For Lincoln, the only president ever to receive a patent, the promise was all he received. His invention was never manufactured.

Yet Lincoln was right, of course. Some inventions have changed the course of the nation: Eli Whitney's cotton gin of 1794 revived the dying institution of slavery in the South; Cyrus McCormick's reaper of 1834 harvested the fields of the West, while Samuel Colt's "revolving gun" tamed it; Samuel F. B. Morse's telegraph and Alexander Graham Bell's telephone changed the way people communicated with one another. Gatling's "improvement in revolving battery guns" in 1862 altered the method of slaughter in future wars; Westinghouse's novel air brake for trains in 1869 enabled Americans to travel across the land safely; while Edison's incandescent lamp of 1879 revolutionized the way they worked and played.

It is not generally known about inventors such as Whitney or Edison, Morse or Bell, that their inventions were often the subject of patent litigation pressed by others who claimed to have made the discoveries first. In some instances, the lawsuit went as far as the Supreme Court. Alexander Graham Bell's invention serves as a good example: his telephone patent was contested for many years in 600 different actions, including Patent Office interferences. The most famous of the disputes involved one Daniel Draubaugh, of Yellow Breeches Creek, Pennsylvania. Draubaugh maintained he had made the invention first by using a battery, wires, and a teacup with a membrane. He produced more than 220 witnesses who claimed they had either seen or heard the speaking device prior to Valentine's Day 1876, the

date Bell had called his assistant Watson over his telephone. In 1888, the
Supreme Court decided the case in Bell's favor by a margin of one vote. But
for the opinion of a single justice, schoolchildren across the land might learn
today that Draubaugh was the inventor of the telephone.

It seems an axiom of patent history that the inventors of the nineteenth and
twentieth centuries, who have so profoundly altered the physical environment of the United States, inevitably fell into dispute about the priority of
their inventions. The complex procedures of the Patent Office, designed to
protect the rights of inventors, ensure ample opportunity for such contention
to take place. An examiner first reviews an application to determine that the
invention will operate as claimed. (Had the youthful Lee de Forest tried to
patent his perpetual motion machine, something would-be inventors do each
year, the examiner no doubt would have denied it.) The examiner then
reviews the claims made by the applicant to determine if they have been
covered in previous patents. Applicants may contest an examiner's findings
to a three-member board of examiners, to the commissioner of patents, and
finally, if the inventor still is not satisfied, to the federal circuit court of
appeals in Washington.

The holder of a patent who believes someone has appropriated it without
permission may file suit in the federal courts for infringement. This is what
Fessenden had done in 1906, when he sued de Forest over the use of his
electrolytic detector.

By the late nineteenth century, the Patent Office had established a procedure known as "interference." Meaning literally "to strike each other,"
interferences are filed when inventors patent similar claims, or when an
inventor alleges to have made the invention earlier. Like a patent application, interferences are adjudicated first by an examiner, and if necessary, a
three-member board of examiners, the commissioner of patents, and finally,
the federal circuit court of appeals.

Not only is the question of an invention's priority a matter of human ego,
it is also a matter of money. The greater the promise of financial rewards for
a particular invention, the greater the passion that attends the question of its
discovery. Such was the case with radio. Contributing to the intensity of
disputes over radio inventions was the sheer number of discoveries. The race
that Marconi had begun in 1899 had taken on a feverish pace. About 350
radio patents were granted in 1912, up from about 270 in 1910.

The case between Lee de Forest and Edwin Howard Armstrong over rights
to the discovery of regeneration differed from all other radio cases in its bitter
intensity. Certainly no other case in the history of radio—some would say in

the history of invention—was as emotional and unpleasant as this one. For nearly twenty years, from 1914 to 1934, ego and pride combined with the promise of financial reward and fame to create what was in the end ruinous to each man.

No fewer than fourteen other people believed at one point or another—and with varying degrees of conviction—that they had a part in the discovery of the regeneration circuit to which Armstrong held the initial patent. Seven had more serious claims:

- In Schenectady, Irving Langmuir, a brilliant research scientist with the General Electric Company who later won the Nobel Prize in chemistry, filed a patent on the same day as Armstrong, but his discovery was quickly dismissed in Patent Office proceedings as coming after Armstrong's.
- In Berlin, Alexander Meissner and George von Arco filed a patent for regeneration, which Meissner had developed early in 1913. It, too, was dismissed in an interference proceeding.
- In London, Charles S. Franklin, an employee of the Marconi Company, filed a patent for the regeneration circuit on June 12, 1913. Curiously, though his circuit is clearly regenerative and his explanation and claims are admirably lucid, Franklin never filed a patent in the United States.
- In New York, Fritz Lowenstein, who had made important inventions in the audio amplifier that are fundamental to the radio, claimed he had invented the audion oscillator as early as the winter of "1911–1912." However, he offered little documentary evidence to prove he had done so.
- In Germany, an Austrian named Eugen Reisz created a regenerative circuit on which he filed a patent as an amplifier for telephone lines. Early on, his discovery was dismissed as not being relevant to the dispute.
- In London, H. J. Round invented circuits based on the principle of regeneration. These, however, came after Armstrong's invention and never were in serious contention for priority.
- In New York, Paul E. Wallace claimed he had created a regenerative detector circuit as early as the summer of 1911, and that Armstrong had seen it in operation. However true his claim might have been, he had never filed a patent on his circuit. His petition to have the federal district court review the case was denied without comment on June 18, 1923. Wallace never pursued his claims.

The one who asserted with the greatest intensity that he had discovered regeneration first was, of course, Lee de Forest. His task was to claim prior discovery of the circuit, something made difficult in the beginning because he did not understand precisely the way Armstrong's circuit operated until he read a copy of Patent 1,113,149 that had been granted to his Columbia rival October 6, 1914. De Forest's first attempt to assert his rights had begun six months earlier, on March 20, 1914, when he filed a muddled description of an "ultra audion." This was the circuit that beneath its twisted knot of confused drawings revealed itself to be regeneration. As might be expected, the Patent Office examiner spotted the conflict with Armstrong's circuit and on January 30, 1915, so informed de Forest.

At this point, as is usual, the later applicant was given a chance to amend his application. Amendment after amendment followed; indeed, de Forest made fifteen different amendments in the next decade. On September 23, 1915, after de Forest had read Armstrong's writings on the audion and oscillation, as well as his patent, he filed another application for a radio signaling system with language and drawings conforming to a regeneration circuit. De Forest and his lawyer, Samuel Darby (son of the Darby who had stood trial with him on charges of mail fraud in 1913), framed the application in the broadest possible way so as to include the concept of the "oscillating audion," that is, the vacuum tube as a generator of continuously oscillating electromagnetic waves—the basic circuit of a radio transmitter. Most boldly, however, he claimed to have discovered the regeneration first, "prior to March 1913"; in later testimony, he would push the date back to August 6, 1912.

It might first appear that Armstrong had an unbreakable claim to being the prior inventor. De Forest had not made a coherent patent application on regeneration until September 1915, more than three years after he claimed to have made his discovery. Certainly this delay alone would be grounds for declaring his abandonment of the invention, which meant he would not be entitled to hold a patent. But Armstrong's case was not without its flaws, either. At this point, the words his patent lawyer, William Davis, wrote on November 14, 1913, become relevant: "I feel great responsibility in connection with the patent end of the invention, and think you ought to keep your eyes wide open to see any indications that may point to the importance of features other than those covered in your application."

There was still time for Armstrong to amend his application of October 29, 1913, to include the oscillating features of the vacuum tube. Had he done so, he would have been in a much stronger position facing de Forest, whose application claimed both features of the circuit. Instead, Armstrong chose to take out another patent application for the oscillating features on December

18, 1913. Partly because of this lapse, de Forest's application—along with those of Langmuir and Meissner—was put into interference with Armstrong's. Armstrong's failure to listen to counsel and disclose to him *all* aspects of the invention—which he clearly knew in October 1913—began to redound upon him and would continue to do so for the rest of his life.

Patent 1,113,149 motivated de Forest, Meissner, and Langmuir to file interferences. Each was struggling with Armstrong for the right to claim priority of discovery. Such was the situation on April 2, 1917, when war intervened to change the nature of the dispute, for Meissner in Berlin became an alien enemy, forbidden by law from corresponding with the lawyer in the United States representing his interests. The other claimants, too, became preoccupied with more consequential affairs. The examiner of interferences suspended the proceedings.

"The Patent Office is the worst possible place to try out the questions underlying this interference," wrote William Davis on the last day of April 1918 to his client, Captain Edwin H. Armstrong, in France. "We have been busy with motions and counter-motions in the interference, all distorted and made unreal by peculiarities of Patent Office practice, and really having nothing to do with the merits of the controversy." With considerable foreboding, Davis expressed the sentiments of many connected with the patent system: an interference case often took on a surreal quality, as attorneys for the parties used the broadest possible language in their claims for the genesis and application of an invention. He knew well the power of language to make an invention into a fiction, a legal fantasy existing in the minds of patent examiners, lawyers, and judges, but not in reality.

When Major Armstrong returned from France in late September 1919, he took up the case again with Davis. Because of his lawyer's apprehensions about the fate of an interference case in the Patent Office, he and Armstrong decided on another way of asserting the major's rights to his regeneration invention. Since Armstrong was the only one of the parties to hold a patent, the one granted for regeneration on October 6, 1914, he could file a suit against the De Forest Company for infringement. Fessenden had done just this when he had won in his suit against de Forest in 1906 for manufacturing his spade detector. The suit would be tried in the federal court of the Southern District of New York. Here, Armstrong and Davis believed, they would get a chance to establish their case on its merits, not on the linguistic fiction of an interference.

No doubt the presiding judge for the Southern District, Julius M. Mayer, caused some dread on the part of de Forest and his chief lawyer, Samuel Darby.

Mayer had been appointed to the bench by President Taft in 1912; shortly after he had rendered his decision in this regeneration case, President Wilson elevated him to the circuit court of appeals. He had a reputation for running his court as "more a Czar than a Judge," as one critic put it, sternly demanding that lawyers present their cases meticulously, briefly, and to the point. He had presided at a number of important trials involving radio patents, and his decisions carried the weight of authority with lawyers, judges, and the examiners in the Patent Office. Darby and his client knew Judge Mayer firsthand, too, because in 1916 he had decided against de Forest in his dispute with the Marconi Company over rights to the three-element vacuum tube.

As the plaintiff, Armstrong had to demonstrate he had invented the regeneration circuit before the others, something he also had to do in the question of the Patent Office interference. This proved to be a comparatively easy task, as he had heeded his uncle's advice and had a drawing of the circuit notarized on the last day of January 1913. To back up his assertion, he produced an abundant number of witnesses, including Herman Burgi, Thomas Styles, Randy Runyon, and Charles Underhill, who testified that they had been present at various demonstrations of the regenerative receiver that Armstrong gave beginning in December 1912.

As the defendant, de Forest had to convince the court that he had discovered regeneration before Armstrong, the same claim he was asserting in the interference proceedings at the Patent Office. Accordingly, he maintained he had discovered the principle of the oscillating audion on August 6, 1912, while working for the Federal Telegraph Company in Palo Alto, California. At the time, he was developing a way to make the audion amplify the electrical signals in a long distance telephone line. His evidence, however, was insubstantial in the extreme, and belied by most of his actions between 1912 and 1915. It rested on a notebook entry made by his assistant Herbert Van Etten, at the time he was conducting his experiments.

As was his long established habit, which we have seen from his earliest discovery of "goo," de Forest had been trying any random configuration of wires that came into his mind, hoping one just might work. In this way he and his assistant Charles Logwood "accidentally," as he put it, discovered regeneration, "which was destined a few years later to completely revolutionize the entire art of radio transmission." In this particular configuration which Van Etten recorded in his notebook de Forest had interconnected the input and output wires of two of his audion tubes in a way that produced a tone in a telephone receiver.

It was de Forest's practice to use Van Etten as the recorder of his many experiments. Those that were more successful, Van Etten copied into another, more formal notebook that he kept. This experiment was not one of them. Indeed, above the drawing Van Etten had written: "Tried following circuit, but it was n. g. [no good]; could not make it boost at all; could only make it howl." De Forest had produced a regeneration circuit of sorts, but of audio, not high frequency waves. He had achieved little more than the effect many children of the period created by placing the earpiece of a telephone over the mouthpiece. The results for a listener at the other end of the phone were a distinct howl.

De Forest did not make a very good witness in his defense when the trial began in federal district court in New York City on January 3, 1921. Judge Mayer observed that "in a number of instances his memory has proven faulty." But this the judge considered understandable, for in "the years 1912, 1913, and 1914 De Forest was confronted with many difficulties and many obstacles." His explanations of the entries in Van Etten's notebooks were muddled in the extreme. He disclosed that he had set aside the feedback invention because he discovered at the same time two audion tubes attached in a series, or "cascade," made a good telephone amplifier. This invention he sold to American Telephone and Telegraph. "When I made this interesting discovery," de Forest reflected in his testimony, "I lost interest in the oscillating feature."

His case was weakened even more by the long trail of ignorance that stretched from Van Etten's notebook entry to his patent application of September 1915. Neither his publications nor his actions up to that time reveal any recognition of his discovery for what it was. In his application for the ultra audion patent in March 1914, he made no mention of—and had seemed to willfully obscure—the fact that the circuit was partially regenerative. Between August 1912 and September 1915, de Forest filed thirty applications for patents; only in the last did he make any claim for an oscillating audion. Nor did it help the defendant that in an article published on February 20, 1915, in which he described his researches while at Federal Telegraph, de Forest had failed to mention Van Etten's notebook entry of August 6, 1912, which he was now asserting as the date of his invention.

Perhaps most damaging to de Forest's defense was the rejoinder he had made to the paper Armstrong had delivered before the Institute of Radio Engineers in March 1915, entitled "Some Recent Developments in the Audion Receiver," in which Armstrong had declared "oscillations in the grid circuit set up oscillations of similar character in the wing circuit." De Forest maintained in print that no oscillations could be found at the plate and that the oscillating characteristic of the audion did not depend on regeneration.

On May 17, 1921, Judge Mayer delivered a firm decision in Armstrong's favor. Calling it "a suit of major importance," he explained the concept of the circuit, and appeared to go out of his way to praise the inventor as a "remarkably clear thinker." "His modest demeanor belies his extraordinary ability," remarked the judge, concluding that his achievement was "not the result of an accident but the consummation of a thoughtful and imaginative mind." This was high praise from a justice noted for his attacks from the bench on plaintiffs and defendants whose thinking was clouded and whose arguments were not to the point.

De Forest did not fare so well. The judge followed closely his contention that August 6, 1912, was the actual date of invention, but Mayer concluded, "It was not until September, 1915, that de Forest filed any application showing what he claimed to be a feed-back circuit, and in the meantime he had filed 30 patent applications." De Forest had lost decisively.

De Forest appealed Mayer's decision to the three judges of the federal circuit court of appeals; again Armstrong prevailed in a crushing decision rendered on March 13, 1922. Judge Martin Thomas Manton, then one of the most prominent and respected circuit court judges in the United States, wrote the unanimous decision, declaring Armstrong's method of regeneration "a wholly novel idea." Reviewing de Forest's claims, Manton noted that as late as February 20, 1915, the inventor had published an article in *Electrical World*, in which he claimed he had worked on the oscillating audion as early as 1910, but had made no mention then of the experiment recorded in Van Etten's notebook on 1912. Rejecting de Forest's assertion that he had discovered the transmitting abilities of the circuit before Armstrong, the judge declared that "the inventor is entitled to the benefit of all uses to which his invention can be put, no matter whether he conceives the idea of the use or not." De Forest's appeal had been rejected on all counts.

At this point, a reasonable person would conclude that de Forest's position had been completely abrogated. Judge Mayer had awarded the plaintiff Armstrong the "decree in accordance herewith, with costs." De Forest could only turn to the Supreme Court, and the weight of these two devastating decisions told him he had little hope of success. Experience with his claim of prior invention in the Patent Office interferences, all of which had gone against him, also suggested the fight was over.

Such might have been the case, too, were it not for Armstrong's simple and naive way of viewing human affairs in general, and especially ethical questions. His mind seemed capable only of binary functions, of classifying human actions as good or bad, ethical or unethical, benign or evil. Humans knew there were certain standards of conduct; they were obligated to meet them. He left no room for compromise nor could he ever forget those who did not measure up, those whose actions he considered unprincipled. Combined as it was with his own formidable ego, such a high and severe principle of conduct severely affected his ability to function in the modern world. De Forest he classed with the unethical.

Clearly, de Forest had no resources to appeal the adverse decision, for the De Forest Radio Telephone and Telegraph Company was failing. The factory and offices in the Bronx were little more than hollow shells in which rattled a few workers. The court would appoint a special master who would levy the costs to be awarded to the plaintiff, but as the defendant was almost bankrupt, the plaintiff would then waive the costs. Then, and only then, would the final judgment in the patent case be rendered. The decision, which after all left the plaintiff's rights intact, would become a part of history.

However, this was not to be the resolution of *Armstrong v. De Forest*. To begin with, the first special master to be named by the court died before he had assessed the damages; his demise delayed final judgment. When the costs were at last awarded, Armstrong's character flaw manifested itself in a grotesque way. De Forest had attempted nothing less than the theft of his patent. Moreover, this thief had not comprehended the concept of regeneration until he had read Armstrong's patent description, and even then he understood it imperfectly. Asserting his rights in court had cost Armstrong many thousands of dollars; why shouldn't de Forest pay those costs? If Armstrong were to waive those fees, he would in effect allow de Forest to get away with his act of piracy. Refusing to allow Westinghouse, the company that held his regeneration patents, to waive the costs or sell a license to the patent to de Forest, Armstrong stubbornly pressed for what he felt was rightfully his.

Blocked by his rival, de Forest tried yet another approach to acquire a license to manufacture the regenerative circuit. With the meager funds available to him, he acquired a small subsidiary company that held just such a license. Armstrong took him to court to have it canceled.

One afternoon in the fall of 1923, Howard Armstrong and his fiancée, Marion MacInnis, drove out to Yonkers in the Hispano-Suiza to spend the afternoon with Howard's mother on Warburton Avenue. The family posed for photographs in the back yard at the base of Howard's first wireless aerial. Then the inventor raised a specially designed large triangular flag with a dark background. On it were bold, white numerals: **1113149**, the number of his regenerative patent. As the flag waved from the top of his aerial, it could be seen from most places in the city. Armstrong knew, too, that on clear days Lee de Forest could see it from his house high above the Hudson at Spuyten Duyvil in the Bronx.

Howard Armstrong's simple attitude toward justice and deep-seated enmity toward de Forest proved no match for the complex legal entanglements of patent procedure. Of course, Armstrong was right: de Forest should pay. Yet the reality and the forces of the patent system, which sometimes neither rewards nor protects the inventor, were working against him. In this Armstrong was ignoring history to learn for himself the lesson of many who had gone before: legal expenses can often consume whatever profits accrue from the invention. Early in the nineteenth century, Eli Whitney learned the pitfalls of the patent law when others appropriated his cotton gin of 1794 without acknowledgment or payment of royalties. By 1807, when he had prevailed in the numerous infringement suits he had brought, he found that the money made on the invention barely covered the fees paid to his lawyers. This had often been the case in the recent history of the radio art, too, especially if the litigation concerned de Forest. Armstrong need only have looked at the example of Reginald Fessenden, who failed to collect on the judgment he received against the inventor in 1906.

All the time that Armstrong was winning his case in the federal courts and pressing to exact penalties from his adversary, de Forest's interference in the Patent Office was proceeding slowly, from the examiner, to the board of examiners-in-chief, and finally to the commissioner of patents. Each found in Armstrong's favor, rejecting de Forest's claims of prior invention.

Now the case took an unforeseen and positively Dickensian turn, one that revealed the shortsightedness of Armstrong's obstinate and vain stand. Armstrong had refused to waive the assessment of costs awarded him by the court and had barred his rival from licensing his regeneration circuit. De Forest decided his only recourse was to appeal the adverse Patent Office interference decisions in the federal courts. The case would begin at the circuit court level in the District of Columbia. Should he fail in this effort, his work would be crippled. In the spring of 1924, before a panel of three judges, he pressed his claim of having invented the regeneration circuit on August 6, 1912, while Armstrong defended his date of January 31, 1913. The decision, written by Judge Josiah Van Orsdel, was handed down on May 8, 1924, nearly a decade after Armstrong had been granted his patent. Refusing to consider the two prior decisions in New York, the judges overruled the Patent Office decision and awarded rights to the invention to de Forest.

How had this stunning reversal of fortune come about? Language: the substitution of a single word. Early on in the Patent Office proceedings, de Forest's counsel had persuaded an examiner to allow the word "electrical" to take the place of "high frequency" in the principal claim for the invention. Now the application declared that the circuit enabled the audion to produce "electrical oscillations." The difference between the two terms is great, for "electrical" can be construed to mean oscillations of audio as well as radio frequency, which is precisely how the justices construed it. Refusing to consider the careful decisions of Judges Mayer and Manton (which he ruled not binding because Armstrong had not agreed to the special master's finding), the circuit court judge construed the claims of de Forest's patent application "as broadly as their language will permit." In effect, the judge had declared that because de Forest created an electrical feedback of audio frequency waves in 1912, he *might* have created one of high frequency waves.

"Nothing to do with the merits of the controversy," had been William Davis's words about the way Patent Office interferences were so often decided. Speaking from long experience as a patent lawyer, he had anticipated such verbal nonsense might trip up his client, yet Armstrong had refused to listen. Lawyers frame patent specifications broadly so as to cover as many applications for the invention as may be imagined. Through the courts, de Forest had achieved the broadest specification imaginable; language was changing the outcome of the case.

"Here we see the patent interference system at its worst," wrote one of Armstrong's lawyers a decade after this decision:

> The Patent Office declares that A (the invention) equals with B (the language of the courts). The Court of Appeals declares that B does not equal A, but C (something different). This in the Patent Office, then results in the equation A = C.

Using such a verbal charade, the courts might have said that the person who invented the pocket comb actually had been anticipated by the inventor of the picket fence, for if reduced in size, the fence might become a comb. The courts had decided in the past that the inventor of the hose extension for a vacuum cleaner was not Clements, who first conceived of and built one, but another who had once sold a vacuum cleaner with a hole into which he *might* have inserted an extension, if he had thought of it. They had also decided that it was not Curtiss, who conceived of and constructed the first hydro airplane, but a man who had once applied for a patent on a boat with wings that was never built and would not fly.

In the case of the regeneration suit, language was altering and twisting thoughts in such a way as to give a person a patent for a circuit that his assistant had described as no good; which would not work in a radio, and indeed was to be avoided. But the decision of the circuit court of appeals for the District of Columbia was law.

Armstrong became alarmed at the thought he might actually lose the case. Had not two eminent judges, Manton and Mayer, decided in his favor? Had he not received the medal of honor from the Institute of Radio Engineers in 1918 for his invention of regeneration? Had he not won three interference decisions within the Patent Office, including one from the commissioner of patents?

Perhaps, Armstrong thought, new evidence of de Forest's actual apparatus would convince the courts that his enemy's creation was no regeneration invention at all, but merely a miswired audio frequency circuit. To this end he hired a detective to worm his way into the Federal Telegraph Company in San Francisco to search for the equipment. Despite his best efforts, which included taking a job with Federal, engaging an accommodating secretary in extended tête-à-têtes, and stealthily searching the property, the detective's venture proved futile.

Backed with the force of lawyers from the Radio Corporation of America and American Telephone and Telegraph, who now had a large financial interest in the outcome of the case, de Forest's side was in ascendancy. It acted immediately and boldly on two fronts. The first was to file a suit in the federal district court in Philadelphia, contending that Armstrong's patent should be invalidated on the grounds that it conflicted with the new patent rights that had been awarded to de Forest. Through his patent assignee, the Westinghouse Company, Armstrong was forced to defend himself once more.

Judge Thompson decided in de Forest's favor in a way that was to frame the argument for many years. First the judge dismissed the two decisions in Armstrong's favor by Judges Mayer and Manton, on the ground that the case was not *res adjudicata*, that is, because of Armstrong's stubborn refusal to settle with de Forest, no final decree had been entered. Then the judge referred to the precedent of *Morgan v. Daniels*, a little-publicized but key block in the patent law structure that has evolved over the past two centuries. The case also bears some striking resemblances to the litigation between Armstrong and de Forest and figures prominently in the reasoning of judges after Judge Thompson's decision.

In October 1878, Charles H. Morgan, an employee of a steel manufacturer in Worcester, Massachusetts, was granted a patent for a machine he had devised to coil wire and rods. In 1886, Fred Daniels, another employee of the same company, contended he had invented the machine two months before Morgan did, and filed an interference with the Patent Office. The examiner and assistant examiner found in favor of Morgan; Daniels appealed to two examiners-in-chief, who found for him; Morgan then appealed to the commissioner of patents, the highest authority within the Patent Office, who decided in his favor. Daniels brought the commissioner's decision to the circuit court of appeals, which found in his favor. Finally, Morgan appealed to the Supreme Court.

In a unanimous opinion, the Court found in favor of Morgan, on the ground that his right to the invention had been upheld by the commissioner of patents in the final interference proceeding. The Court decided it was not within its purview to become involved in such cases as these because to do so would contravene the decree of an executive department of the government. Writing for the Court, Justice David Josiah Brewer declared the case to be "a controversy between two individuals over a question of fact which has been settled by a special tribunal, entrusted with full power in the premises." Unless there was compelling new evidence that had come to light since the decision, there was no reason for a federal court to hear the case.

How curious it is that Judge Van Orsdel should cite *Morgan v. Daniels* in *de Forest's* favor, for the Supreme Court had said that the federal courts should *not* interfere in decisions of the Patent Office. On three occasions, the Patent Office had found in Armstrong's favor in the interferences, and no new evidence had come to light. But now Judge Thompson was citing the precedent of *Morgan v. Daniels* in his judgment *against* Armstrong because the District of Columbia circuit court of appeals had overturned the decision of the Patent Office commissioner. Naturally the judges in these interminable suits over esoteric electrical circuits may be forgiven for thinking in a legal rather than a technical manner; Judge Van Orsdel did not think competently in a technical or a legal manner.

Nevertheless, de Forest's side had been upheld once again, and in a very dangerous way for Armstrong's side. Now his lawyers would have the additional burden of overthrowing the strong appeal to judicial precedent. "Every judgment has a generative power," Benjamin Cardozo once said. "In the life of the mind as in life elsewhere, there is a tendency toward reproduction of kind." Such was the condition here. How easy it would be for a judge confronted with a labyrinth of facts about the manipulation of insubstantial electromagnetic waves to return to the safety of *Morgan v. Daniels*.

De Forest was upheld, too, on the second front. In the federal district court in Delaware, he and the other three litigants in the original interference— Meissner, Langmuir, and Armstrong—each pleaded once more to be recognized as the inventor. Again, the judge rendering the decision referred to *Morgan v. Daniels*, saying de Forest "must prevail . . . unless the contrary is established by testimony, which, in character and amount, carries thorough conviction." Of course, there was no new evidence, just the claims that had been presented over and over for much of the last decade.

The decisions of the court of appeals and the two district courts came up yet again in the Third Circuit court of appeals. Judge Victor Woolley, who wrote the decision, looked for guidance to the precedent of *Morgan v. Daniels*, but then went on to affirm decisively that de Forest had discovered regeneration first.

Armstrong's only recourse was the final arbiter, the United States Supreme Court, and to aid in this bold step, he turned to the Wall Street firm of Cravath, Henderson, and de Gersdorff. In the office of Cravath's premier trial attorney, Frederick Wood, on Thanksgiving Day 1927, Armstrong met a lawyer destined to become his counsel and friend for the rest of his life: Alfred McCormack.

A big man who stood just over six feet, Al McCormack held a commanding presence in whatever he did. Brooklyn born, the leading graduate in his class at Columbia Law School, McCormack had clerked for Justice Harlan Fiske Stone of the Supreme Court before joining the Cravath firm. Years later, a partner at the firm who began work about the same time as he remembered McCormack as "a natural leader." Young and articulate, he radiated a feeling of confidence and authority. Paul Cravath, the head of the firm, preferred his lawyers to be efficient, quiet, and generally colorless. While efficient, McCormack was neither quiet nor colorless, a very different lawyer from the Cravath ideal. Yet he was tolerated, even revered, for his brilliance shone brighter than any other aspect of his personality. Quick to grasp large and complex amounts of material, he would just as quickly give an opinion that was pragmatic rather than philosophical. Never one for a theoretical legal argument, Al McCormack preferred to express himself in plain, simple language.

After the labyrinthine interference proceedings of the Patent Office and the federal courts, Armstrong found in McCormack a refreshing change. Here was a person whose intelligence matched his own. Nothing would stop Armstrong now. With the energy of a springtime flood sweeping down a mountain, he plunged forward with force and intensity. McCormack was caught in the torrent. McCormack was now Armstrong's lawyer, Armstrong declared to the Cravath firm. He would have to drop all other assignments and be available to no one else. For this, Armstrong announced, he was prepared to pay handsomely.

They began work almost immediately. For three months, Armstrong arrived each day at the Cravath office to train McCormack in the fundamentals of radio, beginning with the theories of Clerk Maxwell and moving to the present day. Typically, their sessions went far into the night and included a "test"—McCormack abstracting the day's lesson in a short paper that he submitted to Armstrong for his evaluation. Once McCormack mastered these fundamentals, the two began the arduous task of preparing the brief to present to the Supreme Court at the hearing set for October 18, 1928.

On October 17, they were still laboring over the final corrections to the page proof of the brief for the printer. The last train for Washington departed that evening without the Armstrong party. No matter. Armstrong ordered the Pennsylvania Railroad to make up a private train and have it waiting. Just after 4 A.M. on October 18, three Pennsylvania Railroad Cars carrying the exhausted party slipped out of the 34th Street Station into the New Jersey dawn. The cost to Armstrong: $1,200.

Only on their arrival at the Supreme Court that morning did they learn that the oral arguments had been postponed until the next day.

While Al McCormack framed the brief with the guidance of Armstrong, Frederick Wood, whose forensic skills were formidable, argued the case before the Supreme Court. Among the nine justices he faced that morning were some of the most famous in the history of American jurisprudence: William Howard Taft, Louis D. Brandeis, Oliver Wendell Holmes, and Harlan Fiske Stone. The remaining five were lesser presences. Four of them—Willis Van Devanter, former chief justice of the Supreme Court of Wyoming; James Clark McReynolds, appointed by President Wilson in 1914; Pierce Butler, a conservative expert in railroad law; and George Sutherland, a Mormon from Utah—constituted in Holmes's word "a monolith." Conservatives, they would later oppose most of Franklin Roosevelt's legislation, and in Stone's words, "tied Uncle Sam up in a hard knot." (Sutherland once said the depression could be overcome by "self denial and painful effort," suggesting those who suffered its consequences were guilty of moral failure.) Finally, there was Edward Terry Sanford. Appointed by President Harding in 1923, he was noted as "sometimes . . . slow in coming to a decision." Few of the 130 opinions he wrote for the Court before his death in 1930 were of great import.

The average age of the justices was nearly sixty-eight. At eighty-seven, Oliver Wendell Holmes was the oldest. He had been born in 1842, two years before Samuel Morse sent a coded message, "What hath God wrought," over a copper wire strung between Washington and Baltimore. Appointed by Theodore Roosevelt in 1902, he also had the longest tenure on the bench. At fifty-six, Harlan Fiske Stone, appointed by Coolidge, was the youngest and had the shortest tenure. Seven of the nine members had been born before or during the Civil War; Oliver Wendell Holmes had fought in it and had been wounded three times.

As part of his argument, Wood touched on the status of radio before the discovery of regeneration and showed how Armstrong's invention advanced the art. He discussed de Forest's activities after August 6, 1912, the date he claimed to have discovered the circuit, and questioned why he had been "wholly inactive in respect of anything remotely resembling the invention from August, 1912 to February, 1914." Finally, Wood contended that the lower courts had misconstrued the rule of *Morgan v. Daniels*.

For all the energy that went into the preparation of the brief for Armstrong's side, the argument of de Forest's lawyers prevailed. American Telephone and Telegraph was represented by Charles Evans Hughes, former associate justice of the Supreme Court, who had resigned in 1916 to run as the Republican presidential candidate against Woodrow Wilson. (It was Hughes whom de Forest had declared the winner when he had broadcast election returns in November 1916.) The choice of Hughes made eminent sense. As a justice he had earned the respect of his colleagues for his analytical skills and energy. Of the 119 majority opinions he had written during his tenure on the bench, in only nine cases was there a written dissent from his decisions. Hughes's defense was easy to frame and simple to state: the lower courts had already ruled using *Morgan v. Daniels* as the foundation for their decisions, and there was no new, compelling evidence to suggest that the case should be heard again.

On October 29, just ten days after hearing the argument, the Court issued an opinion that followed Hughes's logic:

> *Per Curiam*: Affirmed on the authority of Morgan v. Daniels, 153 U.S. 120, 38 L. Ed. 657, 14 Sup. Ct. Rep. 772; Victor Talking Mach. Co. v. Brunswick-Balke-Collender Co., 273 U.S. 670, 71 L. Ed. 832, 47 Sup. Ct. Rep. 474.

Per curiam, literally "by law," meant that the justices had bought Hughes's argument. The law was already established in *Morgan v. Daniels*. (*Victor Talking Machine Co. v. Brunswick-Balke-Collender Co.*, a decision rendered by the Court the previous March, had affirmed that concurrent findings of lower courts will be accepted by the Supreme Court "unless clear error is shown.") The Supreme Court never considered the facts of the case; indeed, it never considered the brief Armstrong and McCormack had labored over during the previous spring and summer. *Morgan v. Daniels* was the precedent, and its logic, based though it had been on some false assumption, had prevailed. Curiously, the Supreme Court report listing the memorandum had misspelled Armstrong's first name as "Edward."

Armstrong's lawyers scrambled. There was a petition for a rehearing that fall, but it too was denied.

The Radio Corporation of America had nothing to lose in the case, for it owned the radio application of Armstrong's patents through its agreements with Westinghouse and the same application of de Forest's patents through its agreement with American Telephone and Telegraph. Sarnoff had made this clear a year earlier in a statement to the press when the circuit court of appeals in Philadelphia had rendered its decision in de Forest's favor. Yet many engineers in the company felt a sense of loss, as most had sided with Armstrong. "I think Major Armstrong deserves well of the Radio Corporation," General Harbord wrote to Owen D. Young at the time the inventor's lawyers were framing their appeal:

We have not only benefited by his inventions, for which it is true we have paid him, but we have had his services as a consulting engineer practically ever since our relations began. Another thing which I can not forget is that, at the time that De Forest was busy strengthening his case against Armstrong the latter was, as an officer, serving his country in France.

Nevertheless, the appeal was denied; the case was closed forever. No longer could it be framed in terms of Armstrong versus de Forest or de Forest versus Armstrong. No more would Armstrong have the force of Westinghouse and the Radio Corporation behind him in the courts. De Forest had prevailed; Armstrong stood alone.

While Harbord's sentimental and patriotic musings set the right ethical tone, the general had failed to grasp a most important fact, one which certainly had not escaped David Sarnoff: RCA (and AT&T as well) stood to gain considerable royalties if the Supreme Court sustained de Forest's regeneration claims. Armstrong's patent was due to expire in 1931, seventeen years after it was issued. Since 1924, however, when the circuit court of appeals decided in favor of de Forest, a new patent had come into effect. Because the Supreme Court had upheld that decision, RCA, as the holder of de Forest's patent, would be able to collect royalties for an extra ten years beyond the life of Armstrong's patent. Though de Forest himself stood to gain nothing but the distinction of being the inventor of regeneration, RCA would continue to collect royalties until May 8, 1941. It was now in the corporation's best interest to guard these new patents carefully.

Coming on the heels of the Supreme Court's decision was another adverse ruling that stripped Howard Armstrong of the right to claim the superheterodyne as his. In 1917, Lucian Levy, a French officer with the Télégraphie Militaire in Paris, created a receiver with a superheterodyne circuit, which he sold in 1920 to American Telephone and Telegraph. Levy had been interested only in discovering supersonic waves for military intelligence. His device was far from workable; it did not function as a practical amplifier of shortwaves. While not a true superheterodyne capable of operating practically, it was enough for AT&T to acquire and put into interference with Armstrong's patent.

Armstrong had met Levy while in Paris, and very possibly spoke with him about his circuit. Indeed, in December 1919, in a paper about his own invention, Armstrong concluded by saying, "I wish to make due acknowledgment to the work of Meissner, Round, and Levy, which is now of record. The application of the principle of reception of short waves is, I believe, new . . ."

Levy and the lawyers at American Telephone and Telegraph thought otherwise. As early as 1919, Levy purportedly claimed to others that Armstrong had stolen his invention. After Armstrong failed to acknowledge him in an article on the superheterodyne in 1924, Levy grew angry: "It is unfortunate that Mr. Armstrong . . . has forgotten, in the midst of his glory, the source from which he drew." Levy had filed a patent application for his invention in the United States but with a different purpose and with different claims. Following the accepted practice, AT&T lawyers copied Armstrong's claims and attached them to Levy's patent application and filed interferences. The Patent Office examiner found that even though Levy had not reduced his invention to practice, it would cover the same claims that Armstrong had made.

Armstrong faced something of the same situation with Levy as he had with de Forest. The language of his claims was applied to another's invention, which the patent examiner found might work if it was applied in that fashion. What matter that Levy's invention did not function as an amplifier of shortwaves? It *might* have. On December 3, 1928, the court of appeals found in favor of Levy.

Curiously, the case did not seem to affect Armstrong emotionally in the way that the regeneration suit did. Possibly he was too wrapped up in his regeneration litigation to care about this dispute. Possibly he recognized that the Frenchman did have some legitimate claim to the invention. There was another reason, too. This dispute with Levy was an honest one between two fellow engineers; Armstrong respected Levy in a way that he could never respect de Forest, whom he regarded not as a scientist or engineer, but as a fraud.

◄

The final stages of de Forest's litigation with Armstrong came at a time when he was preoccupied with the failing health of his mother, the collapse of his marriage, and the fate of Phonofilm. He still wrote to his mother in Palo Alto each week, as he had since leaving Talladega in 1891. He carried a framed photograph of her with him wherever he went—New York, California, Berlin, Riverlure—and he carefully placed it on his bedside table each evening. When she fell fatally ill in 1927, Lee and his brother hastened to be with her in Palo Alto. But the press of Phonofilm business (he had to produce a picture "before the next payroll came due") forced him to return to the East. She died the day Lindbergh arrived in Washington, where her son was directing a Phonofilm record of the hero's return. He was not able to attend the funeral for he had to edit the footage and get it into theaters as quickly as possible. "The results of the showing," he reflected in his journal the day after her death, "must be far reaching on my success. And indeed it is fully needed," he added without pause. "Financially exhausted, over-drawn, ha-rassed by foes & selfish, indifferent or incapable friends."

In de Forest's mind, Armstrong had become "my hated enemy," whose patent was "pesky." He had long forgotten his work in 1912 to eliminate the "howl" he had found in his circuit, and his scramble of 1913 and 1914 to understand what Armstrong had invented. Buttressed by his attorneys, es-pecially his friend Sam Darby, he knew that he was the true inventor of the "oscillating audion," as he called it. "What joy," de Forest mused, " 'twould be to at least see that pat. which has cost me (& the entire radio public) so much—annihilated & the rude egoist put back where his *real* achievements deserve." Firm in his understanding that the "rude egoist" had taken an invention that was rightfully his, de Forest had come to believe, especially after he won in the District of Columbia, that it was only a matter of time before he got through the courts what he wanted and deserved.

Victory in the courts made de Forest even nastier toward his antagonist than he had been before. DEAR MAJOR HOW ABOUT AGAIN INSULTING FRANK-LIN INSTITUTE WITH A FEW CHARACTERISTIC REMARKS, read a telegram he sent Armstrong on July 29, 1926, after winning in Philadelphia, and he closed with a reference probably to Charles Steinmetz, who died in 1923 thinking Armstrong's patents were secure: I DEEPLY REGRET YOU[R] BEST FRIEND DIDN'T LIVE TO HEAR THE GOOD NEWS FROM PHILADELPHIA.

Armstrong had lost more than the case against de Forest. He and Marion had spent all their married life under the shadow of litigation. In early May 1924, shortly after Howard and Marion were married, de Forest had prevailed in the circuit court of appeals. That had seemed like an aberration that surely would be reversed. The couple summered on Long Island, enjoying halcyon days on the tennis courts, at the beach, and behind the wheel of their Hispano. Yet these pleasant days gradually gave way to incessant work in preparation for Armstrong's case. He thought of nothing else. Wherever they went, it seemed, a hefty briefcase of papers accompanied them.

Marion Armstrong found her husband had changed in other ways, too. When they first met, he had just sold the rights to his superregeneration patents to RCA. Nothing seemed beyond him then. Now in the courts, and against an adversary he regarded with contempt, he had failed. Engineers, especially those around him, continued to affirm that he was the inventor, and it only reinforced his frustration. The vitality, energy, and daring that had overwhelmed her just a few years earlier all seemed to fade.

Armstrong was unwilling to accept the decision, even though it had come down from the Supreme Court. He acted with the same tenacious spirit that characterized him as an inventor. He had lost his litigation with de Forest as an individual. What would happen, he wondered, if he were—through another party, a company, perhaps—to reopen the battle? This time, he realized, neither RCA nor Westinghouse would stand behind him in what had become a personal quest. Indeed, RCA held license to de Forest's claim of regeneration—through its acquisition of AT&T's rights. Any future suit would probably be brought by RCA against him. Yet he would not be deterred; he and the truth he embodied must prevail.

"Despite a consistent series of favorable decisions in the courts and before the Patent Office tribunals for a period of over ten years, the recent decisions of the courts have awarded priority of my invention to others," Armstrong felt bound to write in 1929 to Nicholas Murray Butler, when the president of Columbia told him the trustees had voted him an honorary degree. "I believe," he continued with a hint at his future plans, "that I am warranted in saying that the engineering profession generally considers that the courts are in error in their decision . . . that their decisions cannot stand the test of future litigation and that ultimately priority will be re-awarded to me." The embarrassment would never vanish. He would have to explain how the rights to his invention had been taken from him and that he was still recognized by his profession as the true inventor.

Armstrong had continued throughout this period to find consolation in his work. Litigation with de Forest took up his evenings and weekends, and at times—as when he tutored Al McCormack—intense periods lasting weeks or even months. All the while, he was experimenting with still more electronic circuits, which he believed would have a profound effect on radio broadcasting. The work had been ongoing since 1914, the year his troubles with de Forest began, and there had been many setbacks, but he believed he was close to a breakthrough.

In the laboratory and now in the courts, the joy for Armstrong lay in prevailing with a new concept. His laboratory work demanded intense concentration, experiments involving the careful manipulation of sometimes hundreds of circuits, always with the thought that he would take the art into new territory. "It's the things people know that ain't so," he continually repeated to himself, almost like a mantra. He would fly in the face of established "facts," beliefs sacred to his fellow engineers, and show them how those "facts" had actually constricted their thinking about the art.

The same thinking held in his litigation with de Forest. To RCA, de Forest, AT&T, and everyone else, the case had been closed by the action of the highest court in the land. For Armstrong, it was still open. He would bide his time quietly and find a way of opening it again. In the courts, as in the laboratory, he would break new ground.

That winter and spring, as the stock market went through its final gyrations before its collapse in October, Armstrong brooded on ways of vindicating himself and getting the courts to recognize the scientific truth. For the coming battle, he realized he would need money. With a prescience all too rare for the time, he sold a significant block of his RCA stock in February 1929 at $114 a share. Now a cash millionaire rather than a paper one, he had ample money to weather the coming financial storm and press forward in his lone litigation. "We had a field day in Radio and Victor," Howard exulted to Marion, wintering in Palm Beach. Then he added,

> Now sweetheart—don't feel too badly on account of the decision—it would have been a great thing to have won the case here, but it will be a far greater thing to win it after a defeat by the Supreme Court. And the issue which is not raised is tremendous and to prove the truth after all these defeats . . . would be the greatest thing that has been done in the history of litigation. That is what we are going to do.

In his naiveté, he knew he would prevail. "Save this letter as a souvenir," he concluded, "when we win this thing."

"If it is any consolation, you will be glad to know that we all believe Armstrong should have been declared the prior inventor," wrote the attorney general of the United States to Al McCormack; "it is apparent that the Courts do not always find the right way." But the words were of little comfort to the lawyer. He had spent nearly eleven months preparing for his appearance before the nine justices, yet it was clear they had not bothered to consider the brief in anything but a perfunctory fashion. What consolation could there be in the fact that those men had seemed to reject an argument based on solid evidence in favor of the specious arguments of the eminent Charles Evans Hughes?

RCA, Armstrong knew, would vigorously guard its patent rights, and it was only a matter of time before a question of infringement came up. For the next two years, he quietly waited for the right case. It came in 1931, when John V. L. Hogan walked into the Long Island City office of Radio Engineering Laboratories (REL), a small manufacturer, and purchased a "TNT" kit for $27.50. With TNT kits, amateurs got all the parts and plans to build their own transmitters, which of course contained regenerative circuits. Hogan was no amateur but a consultant hired by RCA who, as he had been instructed, took his purchase directly to the corporation's patent department. Soon afterward, RCA, joined by fourteen other plaintiffs, filed a suit against REL for using the de Forest patents without paying a royalty.

Learning of the suit, Armstrong decided his opportunity had come. Through his old friend from Yonkers, Randy Runyon, he took a ten-year option to purchase 51 percent of REL's stock and pledged to back it in the suit. Armstrong knew that once again the case would travel the path upward from the federal district court to the circuit court of appeals, and probably to the Supreme Court. Nowhere on the voluminous court papers would de Forest's or Armstrong's name appear as the petitioner or respondent. But everyone in the industry (as well as the judges deciding the case) knew that Armstrong was backing REL and the feud was continuing. Samuel Darby, supported by a phalanx of RCA and AT&T lawyers, would represent the de Forest interests, and William H. Davis, backed by Al McCormack, would represent Armstrong's.

The first stop was before Judge Marcus B. Campbell in the federal court of the Eastern District of New York. Buttressed by their witnesses, Armstrong and de Forest testified about the date each had made the discovery. In a sweeping decision that repudiated all of REL's (and Armstrong's) arguments as "based on evidence not materially different" from what had been presented in the courts, Judge Campbell concurred with the previous decisions in favor of de Forest, carefully refuting each of Armstrong's claims point by point. "I am of the opinion," the judge concluded, "that there has not been intro-duced on the trial of this suit materially new evidence which if it had been before the Supreme Court would have changed the decision of that court."

Despite the force of Judge Campbell's decision, Armstrong would not be dissuaded from pressing forward to the circuit court of appeals for the Second Circuit, the same court in which he had prevailed over his rival a decade earlier. This time he won. Judge Manton, who had rendered the decision in 1922, heard the case along with Judges Harrie Chase and Thomas Swan. Writing for the majority, Judge Chase returned to Judge Manton's decision. Surely the question was the same as it had been in 1922 when Manton "had found Armstrong to be the first inventor." Of de Forest's contention that he had discovered regeneration as early as August 1912, the judge con-cluded that the inventor's failure to file a patent application promptly "seems impossible." "That he did not," the judge continued, "is highly significant and leaves the claims he advanced after Armstrong's discovery became known faced with the inconstancy of his own actions." For the first time since 1924, Armstrong had within his grasp once more the patent that had so long eluded him.

"Armstrong Wins Radio Case Ruling," the *New York Times* reported on its radio page, "Decision Is a Surprise." "The radio world has never had any doubt who was the inventor," Armstrong reminded reporters, and said he had always believed that "sooner or later" the case would come before a court that understands radio. Naturally, de Forest was surprised. After all, he told reporters, the question had been decided in his favor by the Supreme Court in 1928. He professed to have little idea what this was about.

For Armstrong, the victory brought an outpouring of letters. "Dear Regenerative," began a note from Robert Marriott, the engineer friend of Sarnoff and Armstrong, "Some Feed Back. A new defendant is connected in and the decision is fed right back to where it used to be. All despite the Supreme Court, the multimillion-dollar RCA and the billion dollar AT&T. A big accomplishment at the start and another big one at the finish."

From Schenectady, Irving Langmuir wrote, "Ever since 1913, when I first learned of your pioneering work in this field, I have known the great value of your contributions. On several occasions after that I had conversations with de Forest which convinced me that he did not know of nor understand the production of radio frequencies by vacuum tubes. I have therefore been amazed at the fact that the highest court has previously upheld the de Forest patent."

"I was very pleased indeed to receive your cable with the good news that you had at last run the old fox to his lair," Cyril F. Elwell wrote from England. "From now on I expect you will have him properly on the run." Elwell had been head of the Federal Telegraph Company in Palo Alto at the time de Forest claimed to have made his invention of regeneration. Yet Elwell had testified in court on Armstrong's behalf against his former employee, and had come to feel keenly the injustice of the United States courts.

Henry Round cabled from England:

MY HEARTIEST CONGRATULATIONS TO YOU ON OBTAINING JUSTICE AND LEGAL RECOGNITION OF YOUR INVENTIONS STOP YOU HAVE MY GREATEST ADMIRATION FOR YOUR INDOMITABLE COURAGE AND PERTINACITY DURING SO MANY YEARS OF ADVERSE DECISIONS STOP IF THE RESULT ONLY MEANT GIVING YOU ENTIRE FREEDOM ONCE AGAIN FOR NEW TECHNICAL EFFORTS IT WOULD BE WELL WORTH WHILE FOR THE SCIENTIFIC WORLD.

Even W. A. Kinnan, the patent examiner in the United States Patent Office, who had decided the interference in Armstrong's favor many years before, wrote upon learning the news, "I congratulate you upon obtaining this recognition to which it seemed to me you were always entitled," Kinnan said, adding, "It was a great invention you made."

The most interesting letters were those he received from associates at RCA, people whom he had known professionally. Caught in the golden web of the Radio Corporation of America, from which they drew their salaries, they had nonetheless been distressed to see the corporate emphasis on profit block what they knew to be the truth. There were obviously two different realities at work and they were caught between them. "I'm afraid Mr. de Forest chose the wrong man to tangle up with when he started on you. He must have found your persistence over such a long period somewhat disconcerting," wrote C. W. Hansell, an engineer with RCA Communications, who had worked closely with Armstrong on some transcontinental radio tests. Then he added with a measure of regret, "It's a pity you have to devote so many years to getting justice. If our court system were more perfect you might have been spared the time and might have made more such fundamental inventions. That would have been better for all of us." From the engineering department at the RCA Victor plant in Camden, B. Ray Cummings remarked, "I know of no one, except of course the old man himself, who was not behind you in this work."

Manton Davis, vice president and general counsel for the Radio Corporation of America, wrote:

Having been on vacation, copy of the opinion RCA v. Radio Engineering Laboratories reached me rather late. I have just read it. Accept my congratulations very warm and sincere. Whatever may be the consequences to any of us I consider this decision a vindication of justice and right to a scientist to whom great injustice had heretofore been done. Best Regards, Very sincerely, Manton Davis.

As Davis had written his letter in longhand, it never passed through a secretary's hands, and no copy of it lingered in the corporation's files.

Perhaps the most remarkable communication Armstrong received in the wake of his victory arrived from London, where David Sarnoff was enjoying his annual vacation:

HOWARD ARMSTRONG CARE STARZEL RADIOCORP NEWYORK HEARTIEST PERSONAL CONGRATULATIONS WARM REGARDS

SARNOFF

Personal congratulations were one thing; corporate necessities were quite another. By 1933, a wide fissure had opened between the two, and Sarnoff always believed corporate needs took precedence above all else. On September 1, the day after the president of RCA sent his private telegram, the corporation issued a press release for the morning papers. The recent decision seemed "in sharp conflict" with decisions of other courts, which "held de Forest is the originator of the feed-back invention. . . . It is anticipated that the Supreme Court, if asked, will . . . clarify the situation." Given the pressure from de Forest's interests as well as the sharp financial lure of the license fees it would continue to collect until 1941, the corporation had no intention of allowing the circuit court decision to stand.

Once again the Supreme Court would hear the case; once again each side prepared lengthy briefs, largely repeating the evidence of 1928 word for word. On the first Wednesday of May 1934, the justices gathered to hear the arguments one more time. De Forest's friend Sam Darby, backed by the chief lawyers for RCA and AT&T, argued his side of the case, while William H. Davis represented REL.

There had been three changes on the bench since the decision of 1928. Owen J. Roberts, a Philadelphia lawyer who achieved prominence for his investigation of the Harding administration's Teapot Dome oil scandal, had replaced Justice Sanford in 1930; Charles Evans Hughes, the attorney who argued the previous regeneration case before Court in 1928, had been named chief justice after William Howard Taft resigned (because of his previous participation in the case, the chief justice took no part in the deliberations); and Benjamin Nathan Cardozo now sat in the chair that had been occupied by Oliver Wendell Holmes.

Long an associate judge on the New York Court of Appeals (the state's highest court), Cardozo earned a reputation for his single-minded dedication to the law, his abilities as a scholar, and the obvious reflection that went into his decisions. "What is it that I do when I decide a case?" Cardozo had reflexively asked before an audience at Yale University in 1921. "To what sources of information do I appeal for guidance?" He continued:

> In what proportion do I let them contribute to the result? In what proportions ought they to contribute? If a precedent is applicable, when do I refuse to follow it? If no precedent is applicable, how do I reach the rule that will make a precedent for the future? If I am seeking logical consistency, the symmetry of legal structure, how far shall I seek it? At what point shall the quest be halted by some discrepant custom, by some consideration of the social welfare, by my own or the common standards of justice and morals? Into that strange compound which is brewed daily in the cauldron of the courts, all these ingredients enter in varying proportions.

The ingredients of the regeneration decision that Mr. Justice Cardozo delivered on Monday, May 21, included the history of the dispute between de Forest and Armstrong, a history of the court decisions, the precedent of *Morgan v. Daniels*, and the justice's (and presumably the Court's) own understanding of the scientific facts behind the invention. The compound he and the seven other justices concocted proved to be extremely strange.

Much of Cardozo's decision was by way of a lengthy summation, taking into account the opinions of various judges who had heard the dispute since 1922, from Mayer and Manton to Campbell and Chase. Then, with only the rudimentary scientific training given to Columbia undergraduates in the 1880s, and with no understanding of the principles of radio or electromagnetism, Justice Cardozo attempted to answer the question that had concerned judges from the beginning: who had been the true inventor of regeneration more than two decades earlier? From his examination, he concluded it to be Lee de Forest.

Armstrong had conceived of regeneration about January 1913, when a student at Columbia. "It was a brilliant conception," Cardozo acknowledged, "but another creative mind, working independently, had developed it before in designs and apparatus then unknown in the art." Referring to de Forest's brief and to the Van Etten notebook entry of August 6, 1912, the justice cited the inventor's production of "a beautiful clear tone," from his device. "There is also a note that the pitch, i.e., the frequency, was varied by altering the plate voltage, which means that the frequency could be varied at will." In accepting the facts as de Forest presented them, Justice Cardozo showed his fundamental lack of understanding of the circuit. Altering the plate voltage (language he took from de Forest's brief) has a negligible effect on the frequency of oscillation. Relying on his own formidable mental processes, Cardozo had sought to understand the scientific facts involved in the invention, and in pursuing this mental effort he arrived at an understanding that was wholly absurd to scientists and engineers and altogether apart from the actual facts. Justice Cardozo had blundered badly.

Armstrong was stunned. Cardozo was one of the greatest justices in the history of American law, a person renowned for his ability to weigh facts carefully. And yet he had presumed to judge the case on the merits of the scientific arguments with little knowledge of the science, delivering his opinion just nineteen days after hearing the case. "The search is for the just word, the happy phrase that will give expression to the thought," Benjamin Cardozo had written of legal language in *The Growth of the Law*, "but somehow the thought itself is transfigured by the phrase when found." Yet here was a judge accepting as truth words that contradicted scientific fact.

Scientists and engineers were stunned, too. Letters flowed into the *New York Times* from many who sought to explain the fundamental principles underlying regeneration. They, too, were greatly upset by the naiveté of the decision. Michael Pupin patiently explained why de Forest's circuit, upon which Cardozo had based his opinion, was not one that oscillated. Louis Alan Hazeltine, himself the inventor of several important radio circuits, followed with a letter that also explained the fundamental mistake of the justice. Other letters arrived, which the *Times* chose not to print, including one from Cyril Elwell, de Forest's superior at Federal Telegraph, where the inventor had claimed to have made his discovery. "Customarily employees are loyal to their chiefs and vice versa," Elwell wrote, adding:

> If I had felt that regeneration had actually been discovered in the laboratory of the Federal Telegraph Co., of which I was chief Engineer at the time, I would have been only too glad to claim the credit both for Dr. de Forest and for the Company. . . . Even up to June 1913, when I severed my connection with the company, no inkling of the invention, which represented such a tremendous advance in the radio art, had emanated in our laboratory, was conveyed to me.

Responding to the letters, the *Times* published an editorial on Sunday, June 4, entitled "A Needed Patent Reform." Engineers were dissatisfied with the decision, the editorial began. "Scientific questions raised in infringement suits are often of such difficulty that a conscientious but technically untrained judge passes upon them only with hesitation." The editorial took up the suggestion of the dean of Columbia's engineering school that the courts listen to evidence from an independent laboratory like the United States Bureau of Standards, which would evaluate the validity of rival claims.

SUPREME COURT DECISION TODAY UPHOLDS YOUR PATENTS CONGRATULATIONS, Sam Darby wired to de Forest in Hollywood, California, at 1:24 on the afternoon of May 21. At last, the victory was his, again, but de Forest knew his triumph was still tainted by those eminent scientists and engineers who disagreed with the Court, and he was deeply distressed. In his own mind he knew himself to be the inventor; Armstrong was nothing but a "thief." While Cardozo and a majority of judges in the thirteen courts that had heard the various suits maintained he was the inventor, there were still, as evidenced by Pupin's letter to the *New York Times*, those who held that Armstrong had made the discovery. He decided to counter with a letter of his own. "I have read with amazement, not unmingled with amusement, the letter from Professor Pupin," he began, on June 16, continuing:

> Yet it would seem appropriate at this time, after some twenty-two years of Patent Office interference and subsequent hard-fought patent litigation, that laymen, at least those not directly involved, lay off, cease, desist and refrain from burdening the patient public with ill-advised criticism of the knowledge and wisdom with which our Supreme Court has finally decided this venerable controversy.

But the controversy would not go away. In the same issue in which de Forest's letter appeared, the *Times* reported that Justice Cardozo, responding to a petition from Armstrong's lawyers, had granted a stay in his decision. The decision, so the petition asserted, was based on a "fundamental error of scientific fact." Appropriately, the article appeared on the *Times* financial page. For the case involved corporate profits rather than financial gain for either de Forest or Armstrong.

From May 8, 1924, the day the judge in the District of Columbia declared de Forest the inventor of the regenerative circuit (and thereby extended RCA's control of the patent by a decade), Armstrong's friendship with David Sarnoff had remained detached from the litigation. Now Armstrong took the unusual step of appealing directly to him. Sarnoff might not be aware that "the Supreme Court of the United States has been misled—and deliberately misled—into a scientific error by members of the bar representing the Radio Corporation and the American Telephone and Telegraph Company." He continued:

> It is no exaggeration to say that the engineering world is thoroughly disgusted with what the bar has done in this particular case. I am satisfied that the day has passed when lawyers can, with impunity, misrepresent to courts simple scientific facts which are known to every engineer and I think that when you have looked into the situation you will agree with me.
>
> Now in all friendship to yourself and to the Radio Corporation I ask you to consider this matter carefully and to see if the Radio Corporation is not proceeding along a path which will not only result disastrously for itself but which will develop a situation that will make it impossible for me to cooperate with your engineering staff along the line with which you are familiar.
>
> With your technical knowledge and your practical experience in the art and the assistance which your engineers—the most skilled radio men in the world—can furnish you, you can readily determine where the truth lies.

But the truth lay in the new ethos of the corporation. There was a chance to get control of ten more years of patent licenses, and Sarnoff could not pass it up.

In the rehearing, Cardozo would not be swayed. On October 8, 1934, the Court amended the wording of the justice's decision slightly, but in substance it remained the same. De Forest was the inventor of regeneration.

As a lone inventor, Armstrong could never understand that RCA would be perfectly willing to pursue two contradictory lines of argument to protect its self-interest. At the same time that RCA's lawyers were arguing before the Supreme Court, that de Forest had invented regeneration, they were contending in another case before a lower court that "Armstrong first disclosed to the radio art how a vacuum tube and its associated circuits could be made to generate controlled oscillations." The lawyers for RCA felt they had an obligation to uphold the employer's financial interest, no matter what the facts might be.

Though in the heat of their argument Armstrong and de Forest failed to acknowledge it, together they had been responsible for the creation of an industry whose gross revenue was $1.833 billion dollars even in the depression year of 1934. The Radio Corporation of America had grown to be the largest company within that industry, a giant with a revenue of nearly $80 million. There were lesser giants with names like Zenith, Philco, Magnavox, Motorola, and Crosley. All turned handsome profits using the inventions of the two bitter rivals. Dominated as it was by such giants, the corporate world was no longer a hospitable place for the lone inventor. Increasingly, individual needs and whims were subsumed to those of the corporation. Better that the lone inventor join with a company and work according to schedule toward a goal set by management. Neither de Forest nor Armstrong would ever be able to cede their independence. They would remain alone, following their own dreams, apart from the mainstream of American inventors. But the corporate ethos was swiftly taking control of the land. They, and others like them, would be left behind, regarded as quaint reminders of a gentler past. Worse, perhaps, they might be destroyed.

In the last week of May 1934, nearly a thousand members of the Institute of Radio Engineers gathered in Philadelphia for their annual convention. They listened to thirty-two papers presented at eight different technical sessions on subjects like "An Experimental Television System," "Recent Studies of the Ionosphere," and "The WLW 500-Kilowatt Broadcast Transmitter"; they viewed fifty-six different exhibits of engineering and radio equipment; they toured the new broadcasting studios of WCAU; they enjoyed a reception at the Franklin Institute, where they saw the Fels Planetarium; they crossed the Delaware River to visit the RCA Victor manufacturing plant in Camden; and on Tuesday evening, May 29, 1934, they gathered for their annual awards banquet in the Crystal Ballroom of the hotel named after that Philadelphia pioneer in electricity, Benjamin Franklin.

After President C. M. Jansky had awarded the institute's medal of honor to Admiral Stanford C. Hooper, and the Morris Liebmann memorial prize of $500 to Vladimir K. Zworykin of the RCA Victor Company "for his contributions to the development of television," Edwin Howard Armstrong approached the podium to return the medal of honor he had received from the IRE in 1918 for his invention of regeneration. It was the honor he had always valued the most in his life, but now, given the final decision of the Supreme Court, he had decided he could not keep it. Armstrong had prepared a speech:

> It is a long time since I have attended a gathering of the scientific world—a world in which I am at home—one in which men deal with realities and where truth is, in fact, the goal. For the past ten years I have been in exile from this world and an explorer in another—a world where men substitute words for realities and then talk about the words. Truth in that world seems merely to be the avowed object. Now I undertook to reconcile the objects of these two worlds and for a time I believed that could be accomplished. Perhaps I still believe it—or perhaps it is all a dream.

Because the Supreme Court had ruled against him, Armstrong's speech concluded, "the medal is not justly due me. I feel I should return it to you."

But before he could deliver his speech, Jansky stopped him with a statement of his own. Earlier that week, the directors had heard that Armstrong might try this—it was fully in his character to do so. The courts had said the invention was not his; therefore he would give up his medal. Jansky began:

> Sixteen years ago you received from the Institute of Radio Engineers its Medal of Honor in recognition of your outstanding contributions to the radio art. Because of a chain of circumstances well known to many of us, you came to this convention with the intention of returning this medal to us.
>
> The impulse which prompted this decision on your part clearly demonstrates how deeply you feel your obligations to the Institute. The Board of Directors has been informed by me of your views to which it has given full and complete consideration.
>
> Major Armstrong, by unanimous opinion of the members of the Board, I have been directed to say to you
>
> *First:* That it is their belief that the Medal of Honor of the Institute was awarded to you by the Board with a citation of substantially the following import; namely,
>
> "That the Medal of Honor be awarded Edwin Howard Armstrong for his engineering and scientific achievements in relation to regeneration and the generation of oscillations by vacuum tubes,"
>
> *Second:* That the present Board of Directors, with full consideration of the great value and outstanding quality of the original scientific work of yourself and of the present high esteem and repute in which you are held by the membership of the Institute and themselves, hereby strongly reaffirms the sense of what it believes to have been the original citation.

As the assembled engineers arose in a spontaneous ovation and cheers, tears welled up in the shy, bald man's eyes, and then he broke into a broad smile.

"This is the highest honor a radio engineer can hold. I give you my heartfelt thanks, and I assure you they come from the bottom of my heart." For that brief moment in Philadelphia, even though one of the finest legal minds sitting on the highest court in the land had said otherwise, regeneration was his.

⟶

Thirteen court decisions rendered by thirty judges over the years had flowed into a deep reservoir of bitterness from which both de Forest and Armstrong would draw for the rest of their lives. Neither inventor would ever be free of the acrimony and enmity engendered in their battle.

In Armstrong's mind, at least, the moment at the IRE would sustain him. Until the end of his life, he would proclaim himself "the inventor of the regenerative circuit" and list the awards he had received for his work; only then would he add that there was a "difference of opinion between the scientific community and the courts" over who was the true inventor.

But he could never forget the injustice. He followed his rival's activities from a careful distance. His clipping service sent him every newspaper article it could find about de Forest. When the De Forest Pioneers, an organization of people who had worked at one time or another for one or more of the numerous de Forest companies, gave a dinner at the Waldorf-Astoria in honor of the inventor in the 1952, Armstrong drew from the reservoir once again. He scoffed at the idea of a banquet to honor such a charlatan. To him, attendance would mean "breaking two of the ten commandments." Yet from an engineer who served as a mole, he secured two copies of the engraved invitation handsomely embossed with the engineering symbol of the vacuum tube; a copy of the menu; notes about the speeches, especially those of Herbert Hoover and de Forest; even a copy of the seating plan. He had to know the names of all in attendance.

Over the next twenty-seven years of his life, de Forest devoted much of his time and energy pressing his claim to regeneration and defending the Supreme Court decisions. Whenever Armstrong made a statement to the press or a congressional committee, de Forest would follow right behind him with a correction. In 1939, Appleton-Century publishers issued a book by Alfred P. Morgan entitled *The Pageant of Electricity*, which declared that Armstrong had invented regeneration and that de Forest had not understood the way his audion worked. Incensed, de Forest threatened Appleton-Century with a suit. The publisher removed Morgan's book from stores.

Even after Howard Armstrong died in 1954, Lee de Forest continued his attacks on anyone who championed his enemy. Lawrence Lessing's biography of his rival made de Forest bitter, as did an article Lessing published in

Scientific American. The publication that angered him most, however, was Carl Dreher's "E. H. Armstrong, the Hero as Inventor," which appeared in *Harper's* in April 1956. He wrote Dreher four pages of impassioned prose. He had found Armstrong to be "exceedingly arrogant, brow beating, even brutal—the very antithesis of humility." In view of the Supreme Court's two decisions, how could Dreher "truthfully state 'the engineering profession lined up almost solidly behind [Armstrong]'?" Dreher replied in kind: "You are the legal inventor," he wrote. "But engineering opinion was overwhelmingly against you while the controversy raged, and insofar as I had a chance to sample it while researching the article it is against you still. Among the older men, that is. The younger ones don't give a damn."

9

THE GODLIKE PRESENCE

A publicity brochure declared it "a monument to the importance of radio in American life." Rising seventy stories, with its gentle, stepped silhouette that disguised its massiveness, the skyscraper represented the best of American enterprise. Newspaper articles marveled at its size: its 10.38 million common bricks could build a community of nearly 700 houses; its seventy-five elevators, some traveling 1,400 feet a minute, could lift a person sixty-two stories to the elegant restaurant at the top in just thirty-seven and a half seconds; its air conditioning system, the largest "ever installed in a single office building," kept the radio studios and the lower floors comfortable; its 5,824 double-hung windows contained nearly 165,000 square feet of glass; and its 2.7 million square feet of rentable floor space, enough to house 16,500 workers, made the RCA Building at 30 Rockefeller Center the largest office structure in the world.

Just as important as these impressive statistics were the RCA Building's graceful gestures to art, romance, and fantasy. "The skyline leaped and fell," rhapsodized a reporter for the *New York Times*, over the various heights of its roofs, "in the manner usually found only in a Gothic cathedral." Yes, there had been considerable controversy when the Mexican muralist Diego Rivera executed a sternly didactic, anti-capitalist painting featuring a glorified portrait of workers rallying around Lenin while venereal disease germs floated down on rich, bloated capitalists playing cards. John D. Rockefeller and his son Nelson ordered it removed. Will Rogers quipped artists should "never try to fool a Rockefeller in oils." José Maria Sert quickly produced a new mural featuring a portrait of Lincoln and the masses joining in capitalist triumph to erect symbols of American enterprise, including the RCA Building. The controversy passed.

The RCA Building was the new cathedral of commerce, just as appropriate for 1933 as the Woolworth Building had seemed for 1913. One passed through the main entrance (which, like a cathedral, has three portals) beneath a stone and cast glass relief ponderously entitled *Genius, Which Interprets to the Human Race the Laws and Cycles of the Cosmic Forces of the Universe, Making the Cycles of Light and Sound.* From his billowy perch, God (or Genius), huge golden compass in hand, looks down on the earth while scribing Maxwell's electromagnetic laws—concentric rings, a chain of diamonds, the gentle arcs of waves, and stars, all organized by a grid of glass rectangles. The walls of its lobby, paneled with black granite and trimmed with brass, suggested luxury and sophistication. At the NBC visitors' reception lobby, Margaret Bourke-White installed panoramic photomurals of radio transmitters that brought the electron into the realm of the aesthetic.

Most impressive to visitors was the rooftop observatory, a promenade in the sky 190 feet long and 21 feet wide. One could stroll there during the day or at night after the theater and enjoy a dinner at the Rockefeller Center's finest restaurant, the Rainbow Room. Or perhaps one might sit on one of the many benches and contemplate the grandeur of human accomplishments below. To the north lay Central Park, the Cathedral of St. John the Divine—which promised to be the world's biggest—the buildings of Columbia University, Grant's Tomb, the new George Washington Bridge opened just two years before, and the New Jersey Palisades beyond; to the south was the new Empire State Building, opened in 1931, the Statue of Liberty, Staten Island, and the Narrows beyond; to the west across the Hudson lay Hoboken and the flatlands of the New Jersey meadows; and to the east Grand Central Station and the hotels clustered around it, the six levels of stainless steel art deco arches atop the three-year-old Chrysler Building, new apartments and houses in Brooklyn and Queens, and farther out, the small towns and as yet undeveloped farmlands on Long Island.

To Sarnoff, Rockefeller Center physically embodied everything that was important about American business, especially businesses run the way he wished them to be, like the Radio Corporation of America. He proclaimed the center "architecture's dramatic contribution to the radio age, a business venture in every way in harmony with the living present." The center was "the city within a city," colossal yet efficient, and concerned in a nonthreatening way about art and culture. Indeed, he believed the center's beauty would attract "a steady stream of visitors from all over the world." To Sarnoff, radio served to extend the limits of an artist's ability to communicate. In Demosthenes' entire lifetime, Sarnoff once told a group of

artists, the great orator could convey his spoken words to only a small
fraction of the listeners today who hear a speaker at a single appearance at
a microphone. When Demosthenes died, "the living voice was lost forever." As he observed at the formal ceremonies opening the last building
at Rockefeller Center in 1939, "When utility and art serve one another,
both are enhanced."

David Sarnoff controlled it all from the fifty-third floor of his RCA Building, in his comfortable corner office with windows facing north and west. He
planned his executive suite to give a visitor the sense of elegance and efficiency: a vast expanse of rich polished leather defined the top of his desk, on
which seldom rested more than a single paper. The white oak paneling on
the walls appeared all the more distinctive with fluted Corinthian columns at
each corner. On the walls he had hung but a few pictures, the most prized of
which were a portrait of Lincoln and a photograph of Guglielmo Marconi
inscribed "To David Sarnoff with sincere friendship." The office contained
certain emoluments that, he believed, belonged to him as president: one of
the oak panels served as a secret door opening to a white tile room complete
with a barber chair (where his private haircutter served him daily), wardrobe, toilet, and shower. He ordered a special drawer built into his desk. It
contained a telegraph key on which he could tap out the code with his old
wireless friend George Winterbottom, now head of RCA Communications
on Broad Street. On a faux mantelpiece over a faux fireplace rested the
telegraph key he had used in the Wanamaker Building, supposedly to communicate with ships about the *Titanic*'s demise.

Perhaps even more important to Sarnoff than the address, the building's
size, or even his office was the name: *the* RCA Building. Above his office, the
bold red neon initials **R C A** shone brightly for all in Manhattan, north and
south, to see. No other corporation, not even the Rockefeller family's own
Standard Oil Company, could display a similar sign on the outside of a
building at the center. This right belonged to Sarnoff's RCA alone.

The Rockefellers had granted this and other concessions because the Radio
Corporation of America and especially David Sarnoff had saved them. John
D. Rockefeller, Jr., had conceived of his center in 1928 as a new home for
the Metropolitan Opera, at the center of a large commercial development in
midtown Manhattan. He had already rented the land from Columbia University on a ninety-nine-year lease for $3.3 million a year when the stock
market crashed and the opera abandoned the project. Though radio manufacturing might have slipped in 1929, RCA still had a substantial income
from NBC. Its outlook was bright. Negotiating with Owen D. Young and
Sarnoff, the Rockefeller brothers, along with their cousin Winthrop Aldrich,
had concluded an arrangement for radio to take the opera's place and for many

buildings in the center to be known as "Radio City." While some critics might argue that culture had given way to commerce, the Rockefellers could reply that radio represented a new dimension in the forward movement of American culture. Though the Rockefellers had found Sarnoff "abrasive" and preferred to deal with Young, they realized the power the president of RCA had over their center. When the depressed economy forced RCA to scale back its plans for the amount of space RKO rented, Sarnoff was the one who negotiated the deal, and the Rockefeller interests, already stretched by the immense size of the real estate venture, had no other choice than to accede. For the first time, the headquarters of NBC, RCA, and RKO were together.

Here in the RCA Building, the monument to centrality, order, efficiency, and style that the most forward-looking of corporations should possess, David Sarnoff could prepare for the future. Indeed, he had seen to it that the building could meet RCA's imminent growth. No matter that the last few years had been bleaker than he or most other businessmen had foreseen, he believed the depression was only a temporary setback on a forward march of industrial progress. He saw the way for RCA to exploit electrons commercially and at the same time develop huge corporate profits. He alone seemed to possess the farsightedness to look beyond radio broadcasting to television and color television broadcasts, neither of which was commercially practical in 1933. "I believe that television, which is the technical name for seeing instead of hearing by radio, will come to pass in due course," he had told the RCA board of directors in 1923, predicting that news from around the world would be transmitted in words and pictures simultaneously, and seven years later he had predicted that color television would be able to bring "great works of painting and sculpture . . . vividly to the home" with "*color as well as shadow . . . faithfully transmitted.*" He had already seen the power of a national broadcasting network to bring the nation together. NBC enabled people to share collectively in national presentations of music, drama, comedy, and national events, while at the same time revenue from advertisements made enormous profits for the network and its parent corporation. Now he saw how the National Broadcasting Company could bring these new media into millions of American homes, just as it had brought radio—and at an even greater profit for RCA.

While RCA had been preparing to move into its new quarters, Sarnoff was leading the corporation through the most difficult crisis it had faced in its short life, far more difficult than the challenge of AT&T to match RCA in radio broadcasts or the challenge of William Paley's Columbia Broadcasting System. It had begun early Friday evening, May 30, 1930, in the lobby of a Fifth Avenue apartment building. As Sarnoff awaited an elevator to take him to the apartment of an RCA director (where he was to attend a dinner in his honor), a United States marshal stepped forward to serve him with papers charging the Radio Corporation of America with violation of the federal antitrust laws.

The suit originated in the depressed economic conditions of 1930 and the increasing influence and authority RCA exercised over radio development and broadcasting. Recently Sarnoff had persuaded General Electric and Westinghouse to agree to sell their interests in NBC and the Victor Talking Machine Company (for 6,580,375 shares of stock) and raised the ire of the general public and Congress. Detractors charged the corporation with being a monopoly whose control of patents so "terrorized the industry" that manufacturers and jobbers were afraid to use anything other than RCA equipment. Trapped in the worst economic depression in the nation's history and worried about charges that it was pro big business, the Hoover administration sought to demonstrate its independence by dismantling the radio pool the federal government had sanctioned just eleven years before. Perhaps if he did, the president would have a better chance of being reelected in two years.

"They handed me a lemon, and I made lemonade," Sarnoff later boasted. He did. The antitrust suit demanded that GE and Westinghouse (and to a considerably lesser extent, AT&T and General Motors) divest themselves of RCA and enter into competition with the corporation. If the government had its way, RCA would be little more than a hollow shell. All licensing agreements would cease, and quite possibly the National Broadcasting Company's network of high-power, 50,000-watt stations that covered much of the nation with sound would cease, too.

But Sarnoff remained undaunted, from the initial discussion of the suit with the RCA directors (which lasted from late Friday evening until dawn the next day), through the endless rounds of negotiations with the various companies and the Justice Department, to the final resolution on Friday, November 11, 1932, three days after Franklin D. Roosevelt swept to victory, and just four days before the antitrust case was set to go to trial. In the end, he got something for his corporation he had only dreamed of: complete independence. He began by subtly pressing his ideas upon his principal champion within the RCA board of directors, the man who had created the corporation: Owen D. Young.

At the time, Young's life was in considerable turmoil. The Young plan had made him internationally known, *Time* magazine had made him Man of the Year in 1930, and many in the Democratic party were suggesting he be its next candidate for president, but he was deeply depressed by personal crises. His wife, Josephine, was ill with a heart ailment that made her an invalid; he had lost millions in the stock market (much of it in RCA and GE stocks, which had plunged with the rest) and as a consequence faced several millions of dollars of debts; and he regarded himself "under indictment on a very serious count" as a result of the Justice Department's suit. "I distinctly recall Mr. Young slouched down in an armchair in the RCA board room with the appearance of being more than half asleep," one witness to the discussions recalled. "When the controversy reached a complete impasse his eyes would open only a slight amount and he would suggest the compromise which solved the question." But increasingly Young retreated to Van Hornesville whenever he could, to care for his farm and his Holstein-Friesian cattle, leaving the settlement to be worked out by Sarnoff.

The agreement, which the government accepted with alacrity, stipulated that General Electric and Westinghouse relinquish their interests in RCA (including, of course, members of those corporations who sat on its board of directors), cancel half of RCA's $18 million debt, and refrain from manufacturing radios or parts for thirty months. When the companies did enter into competition with RCA, they would take out patent licenses just as anyone else. For its part, RCA transferred its office building at 51st Street and Lexington Avenue to GE for its new headquarters.

Though the press and government regarded the settlement as a victory of the people, reining in a monopoly that was out of control, it was Sarnoff who had triumphed. RCA retained its two networks, extensive manufacturing facilities, wireless communications, and complete freedom to develop the radio art as he and the corporation saw fit. The RCA board of directors would undergo seismic change, and in David Sarnoff's favor, too; ten members would resign, and the size of the board would shrink to eleven. Hereafter, Sarnoff would control the membership, selecting only those he knew would be steadfast in their support of his plans for the corporation.

For Owen D. Young, the choice lay between resignation from the board of directors of the corporation he had created or resignation as chairman of the board of the largest electric corporation in the world—a decision made all the more painful by the pressures put on him by others with an interest in his remaining with RCA. Winthrop Aldrich threatened that the Rockefellers "would not deal with Sarnoff"; Walter Gifford at AT&T (which still leased telephone lines to RCA) said he did not want to deal with Sarnoff either; even Merlin Aylesworth, president of NBC, said that if Young "got out" he would leave, too, for he did not have to stay as "Sarnoff's man." But Young knew he had no option but to resign from RCA, as General Electric gave him considerably more money. It was a sacrifice he had to make. Sarnoff had mixed feelings about Young's resignation. He was losing the person who had created the corporation, the one who had encouraged, protected, and advanced him since 1919. These debts he always acknowledged both in public and private; but David Sarnoff knew that the departure of Owen D. Young meant that he would have *complete* control of RCA.

Now in his early forties, David Sarnoff looked and acted the role of a tycoon. Photographers snapped picture after picture of him looking presidential— always dressed in a three-piece suit, sometimes carrying a cane, sometimes wearing a fedora, and usually holding an oversized cigar. A watch fob usually adorned his forty-seven-inch chest. His look was one of utter seriousness, whether he appeared with the RCA wireless telegraph delivery boys (with whom he had an annual lunch each September to mark the anniversary of his beginning as a delivery boy with the Marconi Company) or as an after-dinner or commencement speaker (he collected four honorary degrees in the thirties) or at a benefit for a charity.

From his start with the company, David Sarnoff had been intent on gaining the presidency at RCA; once he attained it, he thought only of consolidating his position. He had done whatever was necessary to achieve his goals. General Harbord rode a horse to stay fit, so the overweight, "always physically lazy," and decidedly unfit Sarnoff took up horseback riding to keep him company. But usually he had relied on his extraordinary knowledge of radio, his understanding of its potential, and his ability to present that potential in a way that captured the imagination of others to get ahead. These qualities he combined with his capacity for hard work, his natural business acumen, and his ability to make a potential problem into an opportunity to produce success.

Once Sarnoff gained control of RCA, he determined to make the most of it by unifying his power. He stood at the top of a pyramid with a very broad base of workers and a very narrow band of administrators beneath him. They included only those he knew would be loyal, men he had grown to trust over the past quarter century: Manton Davis, the corporate counsel; George De-Sousa, the treasurer, who had hired him for the Marconi Company; Otto Schairer, the RCA patent attorney, who maintained RCA's control over the development of radio and, increasingly, television; and George Winterbottom, head of RCA Communications. Sarnoff faced the future with a confidence and serenity rare for the time, always planning for the upturn in the economy that he believed to be near.

That he faced the future largely alone—and therefore answerable only to a few—caused some concern among observers of the corporation. But to them he replied imperiously, "There can be only one captain on the bridge, and I happen to be that fellow for this ship at this time."

Sarnoff was correct, too. He was the right man to be at the helm, because he saw the future more clearly than anyone else and he desired power, not money. Though his salary was $80,000 a year in 1932 (which he voluntarily slashed to $50,000 when RCA began to lose money), he was not wealthy by the standards of others with whom he was compared—tycoons like Walter P. Chrysler and Standard Oil president Walter Teagle, who, along with Sarnoff, had appeared on the cover of *Time* magazine at the height of the market in 1929. Nor had he invested as flamboyantly in the stock market as others had. And, unlike so many others including Young, he possessed the prescience to sell *all* his stocks in June 1929. With the power he had acquired he would impose his vision of modern communications on the nation, and ultimately on the world.

As the lone captain on the bridge, Sarnoff felt a special duty to guide RCA's efforts in research. He regularly left his office in Rockefeller Center to visit the RCA laboratory in Camden, New Jersey, where his fellow Russian émigré, Vladimir K. Zworykin, was developing electronic television. His system was still a primitive one in 1929, when he first described it to Sarnoff. About $100,000 was needed to develop it, Zworykin believed. As enthusiastic as he had been when he heard Armstrong's regenerative receiver in 1913 and his superheterodyne in 1923, Sarnoff had decided without hesitation to back television's development. Shortly after their first meeting, he hired Zworykin and gave him four assistants and a laboratory at the Victor plant in Camden. That he did so without clearing the matter with his superiors is a measure of the confidence he enjoyed and the power he had achieved.

Throughout the 1930s, Sarnoff visited Camden regularly to demonstrate his interest in the new technology. Now that he was in control, he oversaw the operation *personally*. "The technical people had to know management was behind them," Sarnoff once said of his visits, recognizing the importance of research to the future success of RCA. He conducted himself not just as the visiting boss, but as a person ready to roll up his sleeves and work alongside his engineers. Just as he had gotten ahead in the Marconi Company by taking a personal interest in every aspect of the business (including the developments in wireless equipment), so he would keep in touch with these researchers, asking penetrating questions, observing tests of crude television cameras, and making astute observations about the developments and their implications. He knew the research laboratory in Camden as well as he knew the boardroom in the RCA Building, and he enjoyed controlling both.

Sarnoff had sacrificed much to attain this control, but in personal, intangible ways not always apparent to those around him. Most especially, as few intimates knew, he had sacrificed his family life.

Outwardly, David Sarnoff's marriage to Lizette Hermant had been exemplary. On the surface, it seemed in the same storybook tradition as he had wished people to view his rise within RCA. There were three children by now: Robert was already at Phillips Andover; Edward, born in 1921, was at Columbia Grammar School, and Thomas, the youngest, had been born in 1927. The Sarnoff family had long since moved from suburban Mount Vernon (where he had a house in the early 1920s) to an apartment on East 89th Street, and later to one on East 68th Street in Manhattan. In 1933 the family made its final move. On the advice of Bernard Baruch, Sarnoff purchased a town-house at 44 East 71st Street. (All business, Sarnoff maintained that living closer to his work meant less time wasted commuting, and, besides, living in the suburbs suggested physical exercise, which he considered a waste of time.)

Devoting all his energy to the Radio Corporation of America meant Sarnoff had little time for his family. To be sure, there were the annual trips abroad with Lizette, something they both looked forward to. But these were as much for business as pleasure, for life was always serious business to Sarnoff. On their voyages the Sarnoffs usually took their dinner at the captain's table, and when they reached their destination they were feted by local dignitaries and industrial magnates, counts and viscounts, lords and dukes. Most of the time the conversation revolved around radio. Such company in the cultural capitals of the world was his pleasure; only rarely did his visits include the culture. In Paris one rainy afternoon, Lizette suggested they go to the Louvre. "Why?" asked her husband. "If you want to take a walk, let's wait 'til the weather clears."

Using the demands of his job as an excuse, Sarnoff admitted in a candid interview that he "did not find sufficient time to spend with my children when they were young," suggesting it was "a common mistake with men in my position." But the exigencies of his positions at RCA account for only part of his shortcomings as a father. Having had no model himself, Sarnoff never really acted the part of a father. Neither of his surrogate fathers, Marconi or Young, offered him the sort of intimate understanding of family life necessary for raising children. Nor did he—who had studied the Talmud at six and worked full-time since the age of nine—know how children acted and played. He admitted having "expected maturity of thought . . . at too early an age." For many of his later years, he mourned his expectations.

Upon Lizette Sarnoff devolved the burden or raising the three boys. Of course, she had help. When they lived on 89th Street, the Sarnoffs took over the apartment across the hall from theirs to serve as an annex, complete with a governess, Miss Hobbe. But as one contemporary of the eldest boy, Robert, put it, "I felt so sorry for him." He had everything, "but he seemed so neglected."

Lizette Sarnoff had to suffer the indignity of her husband's infidelities, too, and these also proved a heavy burden. One entanglement proved especially unpleasant. She was a woman Sarnoff had known before he had met Lizette. Now married to a successful garment manufacturer and living in New York, she began seeing Sarnoff. Though each spouse knew of the liaison—and was pained by it—each felt powerless to act. One year the families took summer leases on nearby properties on Long Island, an arrangement that afforded Sarnoff the chance to visit on weekends and slip off with his friend. There was even brief talk of separation and divorce, but in the end the intimacy came to nothing.

There were other intimacies, too. Indeed, Sarnoff in later years maintained a small suite in a New York hotel where he might hold a quiet rendezvous. Though she was hurt by these affairs, Lizette Sarnoff remained strongly resolute and faithful to her husband, always supporting her family, championing her husband's command of the Radio Corporation of America, and enjoying his success. A woman of considerable talents, she also made a useful life for herself. She demonstrated her own managerial abilities by serving as a trustee of the New York Infirmary, and later by raising money for the Einstein Medical College. Over the years, she developed her talents as a sculptor. Largely because of Lizette's tolerance and temperament, the Sarnoffs' marriage survived and even prospered.

◄━

"The Radio Waves Are Calling!" proclaimed the Radio Corporation of America in a promotional map of the United States it published in the darkest year of the depression, 1933. "Have you ever wanted to visit California, New York, Texas, Illinois, Florida, Montana, or any one of the 42 other States of the Union? Would you like to spend tonight in Canada or Mexico?" Increasingly, the copy suggested, people were taking "RADIO TOURS, America's Latest Game," "seeing" the nation by radio. "What will it be tonight—Hollywood, Wolf Point, Tupelo or New York?" All one needed was a "good radio set . . . properly installed and serviced," good RCA radiotron tubes ("a prime requisite of successful radio touring"), and a powerful broadcast station. The proper "atmospherics" were necessary, too, for as the brochure warned, "Strong static, either natural or manmade, will prevent good radio reception."

The four-color map of the continent showed the location, call letters, and power of all broadcasting stations in the United States (605), Mexico (39), Cuba (7), Puerto Rico (1), Hawaii (2), Alaska (3), Canada (36), and Newfoundland (8). Among the states, New York had the most stations with 48, while Wyoming still had just one. Alabama had ten stations, including three in Birmingham and one in Anniston, just a dozen miles from Lee de Forest's former home in Talladega.

The brochure listed state-by-state some of the programs available. In Iowa, where there were more automobiles per capita than in any other state,

Cheerful Stan, the Standard Oil Service Man, broadcast "Hitting the Highways" every Wednesday evening over WOC-WHO in Des Moines. From Minneapolis, Minnesota, every Monday and Wednesday at 7 P.M., listeners could follow over station WCCO the difficulties of "Tim and Teena," the Scandinavian housemaid and her Irish sweetheart. "Dial-browsing" in New York was "a never failing delight." WEVD presented "many interesting talks," and WOKO in Albany offered dramatized news every Wednesday on a program it called "The Magic Spark." And, the brochure urged, listeners should be sure to "tune in WCSC in historic Charleston to hear the Southern accent so peculiar to this section of the state."

"With radio you can tour the United States, Canada, and Mexico more easily and more quickly than by rail or airplane," continued the cheery copy. Of course, few in 1933 could afford air or rail travel; those with cars stayed close to home. "It devolves upon the United States to motorize the world," declared the automobile magnate Walter P. Chrysler in 1928 when automobile production stood at 3,775,400; by 1933, production had wilted to 1,560,500 cars. Though sales of radio sets in 1933 actually climbed 66 percent over the previous year to 300 million, other figures indicated the industry was far from healthy. The number of wholesale distributors of radio sets had dropped from 806 in 1929 to 533 in 1933; the number of radio stores shrunk from 16,037 to 8,161 in the same period.

Broadcasters found their prospects dimmer as the depression ground on. In 1933, just 90 radio broadcasting companies reported a profit before taxes, while 257 showed a deficit. Unable to sell advertisements, many stations resorted to bartering commercials in return for such things as studio space in hotels, meals at restaurants, and a variety of other products and services. In one of the more lucrative exchanges, the manager of a Flint, Michigan, station accepted a car and a house in lieu of cash.

"Prosperity faces a new turning point in 1931," said David Sarnoff at the end of 1930, predicting that "developments from the laboratory" would stimulate American industry. Yet unemployment continued to rise and sales to fall, and RCA suffered along with the rest of business. What had been one of the most spectacular ascents in a corporate stock in the 1920s was followed by an equally spectacular fall after October 1929. RCA stock had typified life in the twenties, making many modest stockholders into millionaires and enabling them to partake in what F. Scott Fitzgerald called "the most expensive orgy in history." But what had been worth $572 a share in 1929 had plummeted to just $10 in 1931 and had climbed back to only $12.25 in 1933. "We look upon the balance of the year with optimism," President Sarnoff had told a nervous stockholder in May 1930, while the corporation's profits were plunging from $16 million to $5.5 million. RCA had even *lost* money in 1931 and 1932, despite substantial economies in the cost of operations, including reductions in personnel and salaries. RCA's troubles were linked directly to the income of NBC, which dropped dramatically too, from a high of $2.6 million (before taxes) in 1931 to just $600,000 in 1933.

Through the economic turmoil, radio was one of the most important forces keeping the nation together. By the 1930s radio had pervaded the consciousness of every American, subtly changing the way they thought and lived. "One of the chief pretenders to the throne of God is Radio, which has acquired a sort of omniscience," the essayist E. B. White wrote in 1933:

> I live in a strictly rural community, and people here speak of "The Radio" in the large sense, with an overmeaning. When they say "The Radio" they don't mean a cabinet, an electrical phenomenon, or a man in a studio, they refer to a pervading and somewhat godlike presence which has come into their lives and homes.

There were 19.25 million radio sets ready for a radio tour. Though many broadcasters were operating at a deficit in 1933, they had firmly established radio as a promising commercial enterprise. It was not unusual for a person to regard the radio as the most prized of possessions, essential for living in modern America. Even though a quarter of the nation was unemployed, radio continued to grow in popularity, a way for an individual to leave the economic trials and wretched conditions besetting the country. Social workers found that Americans would sooner sell their refrigerators, bathtubs, telephones, and beds to make rent payments than part with the box that connected them with the world.

The nature of broadcasting was changing, too. Broadcasters were emphasizing popular rather than classical music. While there still were inspirational and educational talks, classical music programs, serious dramas, analyses of current events, and even the occasional protest talk, broadcasters were offering a decidedly lighter fare of comedy, variety, and popular music. Vaudeville theaters like the famous Palace on Times Square were now only a memory, and performers like Eddie Cantor, the Marx Brothers, George Burns and Gracie Allen, Jack Benny, and Ed Wynn successfully made the transition to the new medium. Listeners came to regard radio less as a medium for the transmission of culture and more as an easy way to escape their condition. Relegating serious programs to Sundays and weekday mornings and afternoons, the least popular times, broadcasters prudently saved their comedy, variety, and swing music programs for the evening, when a company would pay handsomely for the costs of their production. As a most astute advertising agency head once said, America should laugh and dance its way out of the depression.

The programs for Sunday and Monday, March 12 and 13, 1933, in New York City were fairly typical of what was offered: That Sunday (and every day) WEAF, flagship station of NBC's blue network, emphasized music in its broadcast (the "Birkenholz String Quartet," the "Balladeers' Quartet," the "Sparklets Ensemble," the "Southernaires Quartet," the "Levee Band," and the "Pioneers Trio") while periodically punctuating this fare with variety ("Major Bowes's Family"), drama ("Gripping Moments from Medical History"), fifteen minutes of news read by Lowell Thomas, and inspiration ("God's Use of the Future" by the Reverend Samuel Parkes Cadman). WJZ, leader of the red network, had a similar mix, though its music was generally lighter and included a harmonica band. A morning program for children featured Clarence Chamberlain, aviator, speaking about "My Greatest Flying Thrill." Its inspiration came from Daniel A. Poling speaking on "Crown the Hidden Workers," and Lewis E. Lawes, warden of Sing Sing Prison, who told of "The Man Who Didn't Get Rich." The same heavy emphasis on music prevailed the following day, though WEAF began with exercises at 6:15 A.M., presented special programs (on "Handicapped Children," "The Place of a Liberal Arts College in Modern Life," and the Speaker of the House of Representatives, Harry T. Rainey, on "Problems of the Administration"), and broadcast its immensely popular series about immigrant life in America, "The Goldbergs," at 7:45. WJZ began with music at 7:45 (the "Don Hall Trio"), but punctuated its music offerings with the weather, news, a speech by the president of the Future Farmers of America, a talk on "Priestley, Oxygen and Modern Life" by the editor of Chemical and Metallurgical Engineering, and numerous comic sketches, including "Betty and Bob," "Little Orphan Annie," Groucho and Chico Marx, and the program almost everyone followed, "Amos 'n' Andy."

Other stations vied with the NBC stations for the audience, and often very successfully. That Sunday WMCA stressed talks and skits, including the "Goody Goody Club," "Dental Talk," "The Criminal Court," fifteen minutes of the hockey game between the New York Rangers and the New York Americans, and "A Picnic with the Jews of the Atlas Mountains." On William Paley's WABC, one could hear the "Church of the Air," with broadcasts from the pastor of the Plymouth Congregational Church of Cleveland and the Catholic archbishop of St. Louis.

On Monday, WMCA shared its place on the radio band with New York's municipal station WNYC. WMCA began at 8 A.M. with news, songs, and exercises, continuing with songs and sketches, and a talk on health until 11 o'clock. Then WNYC broadcast an hour of police, aviation, and civic information, and its own health program. At noon, WMCA returned with more sketches, sports, and musicians until 6 P.M., when WNYC broadcast two and a half hours of police reports, a talk on "Poisons in Foods" by Professor C. A. Barbor, a fifteen-minute discussion of French poetry, and a twenty-minute reading of Shakespeare's sonnets. WMCA returned until midnight with music and a review of what was playing on Broadway. WABC began at 7:30 with "Organ Reveille," continued with music ("Sunny Melodies," "Salon Musicale," "Melody Parade"), and talks (on health, "Youth Work Camps for America"). The station favored children's programs in the afternoon ("Bobby Benson," "Skippy," and "The Lone Wolf Tribe"). In the evening, adult sketches ("Just Plain Bill," "Myrt and Marge," "Fu Manchu Mystery Stories") alternated with musical programs (orchestras and the Mills Brothers) and the news summaries.

At 7 o'clock each weekday evening, most listeners in New York and across the country tuned their radios to the most popular show of all, "Amos 'n' Andy." A publicity picture of the pair suggests what the show was about. One man sits on a barrel. He is wearing a shirt open at the throat, an unbuttoned vest, rumpled work pants, and shabby shoes. Another, dressed in dark wrinkled pants, a mismatched worn dress coat, white dress shirt, and a wide tie, stands authoritatively beside him. Chewing on a stogie, he places his right hand on the other's shoulder, while his left grips the lapel of his jacket. Atop his head at a rakish angle rests a derby hat. Thick lips and the vacant look in both men's eyes are the most prominent features of their dark faces. They are Charles J. Correll and Freeman Fisher Gosden, not black men but a blackface comedy duo. In 1933, they earned $100,000 from NBC, more than Babe Ruth, more than the president of the network that employed them, more than the president of RCA, and, indeed, more than the president of the United States.

The story of Correll and Gosden has been recounted many times: how they began in 1925 with a weekly broadcast (for a free dinner) from a hotel ballroom in Chicago. Four years later NBC made them national celebrities. They were the first show to be syndicated, recording their routines on large phonograph records that allowed five minutes to a side; and they were the first show to use the device of a serialized story, with the audience following from show to show the various imbroglios of Amos, Andy, Kingfish, the Judge, the Bailiff, Lignin', the Fresh-Air Taxicab Company, Ruby, and widow Parker. Listeners reveled in the easily assumed, seldom questioned racism. "There are three things which I shall never forget about America," George Bernard Shaw once said after a visit to the United States: "the Rocky Mountains, Niagara Falls, and 'Amos 'n' Andy.' "

The effect of "Amos 'n' Andy" on broadcasting was dramatic. Sales of radios surged—from 650,000 sets in 1928, the year Gosden and Correll were appearing on WMAQ, to 842,548 in 1929, the year they signed on with

NBC. Restaurants and movie theaters found they had to broadcast the show over loudspeakers if they were to keep their customers. Calvin Coolidge let it be known he was not to be disturbed in the evening when "Amos 'n' Andy" was on the air. When floods in New England and Pennsylvania in the spring of 1936 knocked out electric power stations and forced many to abandon their homes and radios, frustrated listeners besieged the National Broadcasting Company with requests for a synopsis of what had taken place in Harlem. NBC obliged: "After Andy unexpectedly produces $500 to pay for the wholesale grocery company, . . . rumors arise that Andy has obtained the money by robbing a Harlem drug store. He is questioned by the police . . ." went the summary. An eager public delighted in every word.

"Amos 'n' Andy" and almost all the other popular radio shows had commercial sponsors that brought the networks and stations money. The list of broadcasts, punctuated by commercial announcements written by clever advertising agencies, grew as the decade advanced. By the early 1930s, commercials, long the bane of people like Herbert Hoover, had become the standard way of financing broadcasts. At first, network executives were chary of mentioning intimate products and prices, but soon advertisers were free to hawk almost anything. Convenience goods, consumed by millions, became the most popular products to sell, accounting for 86 percent of the network and 70 percent of the non-network advertisements in 1934. Cigarettes (Lucky Strikes and Chesterfields), cigars ("There's no spit in Cremo Cigars!"), toothpastes (Ipana and Pepsodent), coffees (Maxwell House and Chase and Sanborn), and laxatives (Haley's M-O) proved especially popular.

More and more, advertisers—and the enormous revenues they offered to networks and small stations—controlled the content of broadcasts. Agencies in New York rather than stations and networks actually created programs to meet a specific need of the client and hired audience rating companies to measure the response. When Ed Wynn became popular on the "Texaco Fire Chief Program" in 1932, Standard Oil hired the McCann-Erickson firm to create the "Esso Five Star Theatre." The firm hired Chico and Groucho of the Marx Brothers, who played the attorneys in "Flywheel, Shyster and Flywheel." The show lasted for twenty-six episodes, but its ratings never equaled those of Ed Wynn.

Dramatized commercials and commercials integrated into variety and comedy material became common. The singing commercial began to take form, too:

> When you're feeling kinda blue
> And you wonder what to do,

Ch-e-ew Chiclets, and
Chee-ee-eer up!

Gone was the ten-minute sales talk for Hawthorne Court, the advertisement that had started it all. Now commercials were short, snappy, and often full of humor. To one wag of the time, radio was simply "a new and noisy method of letting peddlers into your home."

As the schedules for March 12 and 13 suggest, news and commentary were not popular with advertisers or broadcasters. WEAF carried only Lowell Thomas, who devoted his fifteen minutes as much to commentary as to news, and a fifteen-minute talk direct from Berlin by the chief European correspondent for the *New York Times*, assuring listeners that Adolf Hitler's rise to power was "no cause for general alarm" even though Jews were fleeing into Poland by the thousands. WJZ offered a fifteen-minute news broadcast at 2 P.M. and Walter Winchell's fifteen minutes of Broadway gossip at 9:30 contained a few items. To lend more drama and immediacy to his stories and to suggest they were fresh off the wire, he introduced them with meaningless tapping on a telegraph key and then shouting "Flash."

That stations were uninterested in the news seems all the more extraordinary when one considers the events at the beginning of March 1933. In Los Angeles, the coroner had counted 110 deaths caused by an earthquake that struck the area. In Montgomery, Alabama, the second trial of nine black youths from Scottsboro who had been charged with the rape of two white girls was getting under way, and was already clouded by charges of the blacks' mistreatment in jail. In Berlin, roving bands of Nazi youths were attacking Americans. Chancellor Adolf Hitler's National Socialists had won resounding victories in municipal elections throughout Prussia. Showing at the palace in New York (the former vaudeville theater) was *Mussolini Speaks*, a biography of the Italian dictator with a running commentary by Lowell Thomas. Students at the universities of Glasgow and Manchester, following the lead of their brothers at Oxford, passed a resolution refusing to bear arms "for King or country." In St. Petersburg, Florida, Colonel Jacob Ruppert, owner of the New York Yankees, was trying to get Babe Ruth to sign a new contract for $50,000. Before the Newaygo County courthouse in White Cloud, Michigan, the sheriff and his deputies used tear gas to disperse 400 men gathered to protest a mortgage foreclosure sale of land belonging to a fellow farmer. And Helen Keller revealed that one day while she was having tea in Lady Astor's London drawing room, her companion, Annie Sullivan Macy, haltingly and with a quiver signed in her hand the pronouncement of her fellow guest George Bernard Shaw: "All Americans are deaf and blind—and dumb."

Most important were the actions of Franklin Delano Roosevelt. After his inauguration on March 4, the new president had declared a bank holiday as "the first step in the government's reconstruction of our financial and economic fabric." Farm leaders were urging the President take on sweeping new powers as a "farm dictator." Congress was speeding to approve an administration bill to sell beer and wine with 3.2 percent alcohol.

Yet, as the head of every advertising agency understood, comedy and variety sold commercials, news and social commentary did not. Radio offered a way to escape the present condition. Gone were the pronouncements by its creators that the medium would serve as a great engine of education informing the nation's citizens and elevating their appreciation of the culture. Commerce controlled radio more than ever, and broadcasters, hungry for revenues, fought to have educational stations attached to universities kept at low power and placed in the outer fringes of the radio spectrum.

The fate of WEVD was typical. Though the radio tour map said the New York station broadcast "many interesting talks" (words perhaps slipped in by a copywriter in RCA's growing publicity office), the Federal Radio Commission limited WEVD's power to a mere 500 watts. Located at 1,300 kilocycles, near the top of the radio dial, the station found itself squeezed between two more powerful transmitters in New York and Brooklyn.

The station's placement had been by design. WEVD's initials matched those of the late Eugene Victor Debs, founder of the Social Democrat party and its quadrennial presidential candidate. An immensely popular figure in the first two decades, Debs had even received 900,000 votes for president while serving a ten-year prison sentence in Atlanta for sedition (he had been prosecuted in one of the nastier moments of Woodrow Wilson's often mean-spirited administration). Shortly after he became president, Warren G. Harding ordered Debs released and brought him to the White House for tea and a chat. The visit made front-page headlines.

After his death in 1926, Debs's followers created a radio station in his memory and "for the purpose of maintaining at least one channel of the air free and open to the uses of the workers." From its inception, WEVD's right to exist was challenged by irate listeners and some members of the Federal Radio Commission. Not "satisfied that public interest, convenience or necessity will be served," the commission tried to abolish the station (along with 163 others) in 1928. But it soon relented, admitting that WEVD had "pursued a very satisfactory policy" of presenting divergent opinions. By the 1930s the station offered an intelligent alternative to the commercial fare of the networks. Some of the interesting programs one might have heard on a radio tour were twelve talks on birth control ("Every baby has a right to be wanted," declared Mrs. Eliot White) and three talks on the National Association for the Advancement of Colored People, race relations, and current events. But WEVD's signals were so weak that one needed the superior performance of a Radiotron tube to take this radio tour. As one critic quipped, WEVD's position and power represented "quite accurately . . . the place Socialism (and the Higher Things generally) occupy in the consciousness of the nation."

Despite the marginal position of some stations and the graveyard hours of many political talks on commercial stations, radio's impact on the nation's political life and social consciousness increased with each set sold. By 1930, some 40 percent of American families had a set; by 1938, radios reached into 82 percent of the homes. Cole Porter included the medium in the lyrics to the title song of his hit musical *Anything Goes*:

> *Just think of those shocks you've got*
> *And those knocks you've got*
> *And those blues you've got*
> *From that news you've got*
> *And those pains you've got*
> *(If any brains you've got)*
> *From those little radios.*

It was not just national broadcasts of entertainment and significant public events that cut across classes to mold a culture that was more powerful and centralized than ever before. Many others, including quack medical doctors, demagogues, preachers, and politicians, employed the new medium to reach those on the margins of society. As the depression deepened and those margins widened, their appeals became more strident.

Some of the programs were especially farcical. In New York, CBS broadcast the "Voice of Experience," a program sponsored by Haley's M-O that offered listeners help in solving their bizarre personal problems. From KFKB in Milford, Kansas, and later from Mexico, Dr. John Romulus Brinkley, champion of prostate operations to cure just about everything and goat gland transplants to restore sexual vigor, broadcast his message of renewal to "weak men." Graduate of the Eclectic Medical School in Chicago and the Eclectic Medical University in Kansas City (where he finished his training in a month), Dr. Brinkley had erected his own hospital in Milford, with adjacent pens to hold his livestock. Patients by the thousands flocked to Milford, checked themselves into the Brinkley hospital, and selected a goat for their rejuvenation. In the late 1920s, KFKB broadcast "The Medical Question Box," with the doctor reading letters from listeners (for $2 an inquiry) and prescribing his own specially concocted medicines (at $1 a bottle). Never mind that the Federal Radio Commission revoked the station's license in 1930. Brinkley simply transferred his operations to Del Rio, Texas, on the Rio Grande, and set up XERA, a 50,000-watt broadcasting station across the river in Mexico. Later, when a clever engineer increased the power to 150,000 watts, the doctor blasted his message as far north as Philadelphia, obliterating all less powerful stations in its path. At one point he offered a cash prize to the person who best completed the sentence: "I consider Dr. Brinkley the world's foremost prostate surgeon because . . ."

Darker messages were coming through the air. From Detroit, Father Coughlin excoriated the rich for having been "dulled by the opiate of their own contentedness" and organized his listeners into the National Union for Social Justice and the Radio League of the Little Flower. Often implying anti-Semitism, he denounced international bankers, blaming them for the depression and suggesting, "Democracy is over." A startling number of listeners agreed. When a Philadelphia station asked its listeners if they would like to hear Coughlin or the New York Philharmonic on Sunday afternoons, the vote ran Coughlin 187,000, Philharmonic 12,000.

From Baton Rouge, Huey Long raged against "lyin' newspapers," promised "Every Man a King," and complained that though the Lord had invited the world to a feast, "Morgan and Rockefeller and Mellon and Baruch have walked up and took 85 percent of the vittles off the table." He had an engaging conspiratorial way of bringing his audience into league with him:

> Hello friends, this is Huey Long speaking. And I have some important things to tell you. Before I begin I want you to do me a favor. I am going to talk along for four or five minutes, just to keep things going. While I'm doing it I want you to go to the telephone and call up five of your friends, and tell them Huey is on the air.

Listeners did. Across the land they organized "Share the Wealth" clubs. Until his assassination in September 1935, many thought the Kingfish offered them the way to economic salvation.

However, one voice from Washington was able to unite the nation as none other. When four out of every five newspapers declared their opposition to his policies, Franklin Delano Roosevelt spoke directly with the American people through his "fireside chats." At 10 P.M., Sunday, March 12, 1933, the end of his first week in office, the President delivered his first talk to explain the banking crisis. To prepare for his talk, Roosevelt lay on a couch and visualized those he was trying to reach, ordinary people who wanted to get on with their affairs, who had little understanding of why they couldn't cash a check or withdraw their money. "My friends, I want to talk for a few minutes with the people of the United States about banking," Roosevelt began:

First of all let me state the simple fact that when you deposit money in a bank, the bank does not put the money into a safe deposit vault. It invests your money in many different forms of credit. . . . In other words, the bank puts your money to work to keep the wheels of industry and of agriculture turning around.

After explaining how "undermined confidence" caused a run on the banks' deposits, the consequent need for a bank holiday, and the plans for their reopening, he reassured his listeners, "I hope you can see, my friends, from this elemental recital of what your government is doing that there is nothing complex, nothing radical in the process." And he concluded:

Confidence and courage are the essentials of success in carrying out our plan. You people must have faith; you must not be stampeded by rumors and guesses. Let us unite in banishing fear. We have provided this machinery to restore our financial system; and it is up to you to make it work.

It is your problem, my friends, your problem no less than it is mine. Together we cannot fail.

Listeners heard his basic lesson in banking and they understood; they heard his fundamental sincerity and they believed. To one Republican in Palm Beach, Florida, who hated Roosevelt, hearing the talk was an emotional experience he was "not particularly proud of." The weather was clear that evening and he had been out for a "spin" with his wife when the speech came through the speaker of his car radio:

It stirred me to my very depths—it brought the tears, the thrills and ripples. . . . We were for Roosevelt that night if we never had been before. . . . He stood before us that night out there under the blanket of stars, as a true savior—a knight errant—a real leader of his people, guiding them out of the wilderness into the light.

From Santa Monica, California, Will Rogers made the ultimate pronouncement. Roosevelt "stepped to the microphone last night and knocked another home run," Rogers wrote in the *New York Times*. "Our President took such a dry subject as banking . . . he made everybody understand it, even the bankers."

Other talks by Roosevelt followed, three more in 1933, and sixteen in the following years. The flow of letters to the White House, from many of those Americans whom the president had envisioned, became a torrent. Some people placed Roosevelt's picture beside their radios, so they might see him as he spoke. Through those fireside chats, friends, enemies, and especially broadcasters learned the power of radio when their president used it to reach people directly.

By 1933, those in the minority who still dreamed that broadcasting might become a medium of education and information were pressing hard for reform. Through the National Committee on Education by Radio, they induced sympathetic congressmen to propose legislation that would force the Federal Radio Commission to license stations with more power and more favorable places on the broadcasting spectrum, and they were hopeful of success when they learned President Roosevelt wished to create a communication commission. But the result of their efforts, the Communications Act of 1934 that created a Federal Communications Commission, only maintained the status quo. When a committee of the FCC held hearings on the role of education in broadcasting, the networks contended they already were devoting ample time to cultural enrichment, including shows like NBC's "Amos 'n' Andy." Nevertheless, the threat of legislation induced networks to create programs like "The University of Chicago Round Table" and "American School of the Air" to satisfy the FCC's stipulation that broadcasting be in "the public interest, convenience, and necessity."

David Sarnoff was sympathetic to those who argued for more uplifting programs. After all, in his radio music box memorandum he had proposed that the principle of broadcasting be "extended to other fields as, for example, receiving lectures at home," and had suggested that "farmers and others in outlying districts removed from cities . . . could enjoy concerts, lectures, music, [and] recitals." Now that he had firm control of RCA, he moved to elevate the level of programming. First, early in the 1930s, NBC agreed to broadcast the Metropolitan Opera on the weekends when commercial programs did not sell. In 1937, Sarnoff hired the president of Yale to counsel the network on educational programs.

That same year, RCA had recovered enough from the effects of the depression for Sarnoff to make his most dramatic gesture to cultural programming: with the most liberal terms he created an entire orchestra and hired Arturo Toscanini to conduct it. Toscanini received $40,000 for ten concerts in twelve months. On Christmas night 1937, the NBC orchestra gave its first performance—Vivaldi's Concerto Grosso in D Minor—in an entirely refurbished studio in the RCA Building. "The National Broadcasting Company is an American business organization. It has employees and stockholders. It serves their interests best when it serves the public best." That Christmas night, and whenever the NBC orchestra played over the next seventeen years, he was right.

Curiously, the three most responsible for the creation of broadcasting did not take much interest in its sponsored shows. Like a father whose great aspirations for his child are dashed, these men felt the medium they had brought into the world was failing them by not living up to its potential. David Sarnoff had no time to waste on the popular programs of his red and blue networks and was appalled by the high salaries performers commanded, which were far higher than any he paid his engineers. Though his wife, Lizette, was an avid fan of programs like "Amos 'n' Andy," he found them frivolous and boring. Howard Armstrong did not care for the quality of the fidelity of the music broadcasts, and anyway he was too busy with his work to listen. However, Lee de Forest's reaction to the level of broadcasts, and to the hucksters who peddled their products on the air, was the angriest of all.

Though he had produced the first radio advertisement in 1916 to sell his audions and radio equipment, Lee de Forest grew distressed over the quality of programs and the companies that sponsored them. He had always wanted discreet "sponsorship" of quality broadcasts—principally music and poetry—that would serve to educate and elevate the thoughts of listeners. His model was station KPO in San Francisco, which presented "The Standard Symphony Hour" each week, sponsored by the Standard Oil Company of California. "I hail California's modern Argonauts, in a new era of culture rather than temporal wealth," rhapsodized de Forest to KPO's director of programs in June 1932. The men of the station were "unearthing, freeing to the clear air of the Western world, golden argosies of tone." Would that more corporations follow the "enlightened commercialism," of Standard Oil, and thereby "enable the radio listeners . . . to realize the superb riches of great music, and real worth of radio."

In 1933, de Forest himself participated in "Radio Heart Warmers," in which "famous living celebrities," including Lionel Barrymore, H. L. Mencken, and George Gershwin, shared their favorite songs, poems, and inspirational readings. De Forest chose to read his poem "California Twilight":

> I love a pine tree outlined in the night,
> Behind it spread a drapery of light,
> The Moonbeams weaving witchery's delight,
> Mysterious, mysterious. . . .

He also read a selection from Poe, and for his inspirational passage he selected a letter from the Florentine painter Fra Angelico: "Life is so full of meaning and of purpose, so full of beauty—beneath its covering—that you will find that earth but cloaks your heaven."

But such programs as "Radio Heart Warmers," which de Forest regarded as quality broadcasting, were exceedingly rare in the 1930s. In his view, radio was in the grip of "uncouth 'sandwich-men.'"

"From the ecstasies of Beethoven and Tchaikovsky listeners are suddenly dumped into a cold mess of ginger-ale and cigarettes," de Forest complained in an interview with the New York *Herald Tribune* early in 1931. Perhaps, he wondered in a letter to the radio editor of the paper, if the radio manufacturers might set aside some of their profits for "high class . . . entertainment, free of broadcasting." Later that year he blamed the slump in radio sales on the quality of programming. "Why should any one want to buy a radio," he asked in an open letter published in a radio magazine, "when nine-tenths of what one can hear is the continual drivel of second-rate jazz, sickening crooning by 'sax' players, . . . interlaced with blatant sales talk . . . impudent commands to buy or try?" His solution was quaint, much like Sarnoff's original plan for broadcasting as he outlined it in his memo of 1915. But in an industry racked by the depression, his ideas received no serious attention.

De Forest's anguish grew with each passing year. In 1946, in the wake of the war, he made a final florid effort to change broadcasting. In an open letter he directed to the National Association of Broadcasters meeting at their annual convention in Chicago, he asked, "What have you gentlemen done with my child?" Though he conceived the child as a "potent instrumentality" for elevating the "mass intelligence" of America, he contended broadcasters had sent his child into the street "in rags of ragtime, tatters of jive and boogie woogie, to collect money from all and sundry, for hubba hubba and audio jitterbug." His child had become "a stench in the nostril of the gods of the ionosphere." Though radio was now thirty years old, broadcasters had kept his child's intelligence at age thirteen. While his "British brother" appealed "to the higher intelligence" under government sponsorship, we in America paid for "freedom from all restraint," with an "anesthetized intellect." To de Forest, engineers outpaced program directors in brains, skill, and ethics. He and his colleagues possessed the higher intelligence to lead the masses to the better things of this world—poetry, drama, music, intelligent debate. Perhaps someday the program directors would reach their level, but as yet they had not.

De Forest's disaffection with the world of broadcasting in the 1930s paralleled his disaffection with the world of invention. Though he served as president of the Institute of Radio Engineers in 1930, he seemed out of step with developments in the field. De Forest Radio (which manufactured radio tubes for the navy and all Atwater Kent radios, and had acquired the nearly bankrupt Jenkins television venture in 1929) still paid him a small salary. But by mid-1930, it fell victim to the market crash and later was acquired by RCA.

Because of his company's association with Jenkins, de Forest began studying the possibilities of transmitting images and filed patents for several minor inventions for "tele-film," a cumbersome mechanical process that took moving pictures, developed them quickly, and then projected them "almost instantaneously" through a scanner onto a ninety-line theater-sized television screen. James Garside, former president of De Forest Radio, began the American Television Laboratories in Los Angeles to develop the process, and de Forest went west for the last time to join the new company.

To demonstrate tele-film's potential, American Television filled a small theater with scanning discs, motors, and a screen. In a stock prospectus of 1932, Garside reported American Television's development "far in advance of any of the other systems." Samuel Darby lent his support with a telegram that Garside reprinted in the prospectus:

I BELIEVE DE FOREST HAS MADE FUNDAMENTAL BASIC INVENTION FOR WHICH FULL PATENT PROTECTION SHOULD BE RECEIVED STOP I ALSO BELIEVE COMMERCIAL POSSIBILITIES ARE UNLIMITED

Perhaps de Forest believed this, too; perhaps he envisioned that tele-film or television would give him his next great invention, as great as the vacuum tube and the regeneration circuit. But his work was on the trailing edge of the new technology. Though he had been the first to liberate the power of the electron, his inventions in television relied heavily on Nipkow's mechanical contrivance that first appeared in 1884. It was no match for the electronic system Zworykin was developing in Camden, New Jersey.

Like every other venture de Forest was associated with, American Television Laboratories lacked the capital necessary to make it successful. The balance sheet that Garside had presented with the stock prospectus listed $669,730 in assets: $23,851 in cash, $86,760 in equipment, and $559,119 in "intangible assets"—de Forest's patents. By 1933, with money (including funds from a mortgage on Riverlure) long gone, de Forest stopped his research.

Searching for a fresh venture, a new field to explore, which would be "highly interesting, humanitarian, presumably profitable," de Forest turned to radio "diathermy," the technique of passing electromagnetic waves through the body to produce heat. Diathermy was a variation on a "radio knife" he had patented in 1907, which employed electromagnetic waves to cut human tissue. The knife had failed for want of an oscillating tube and circuit. Early in 1934, he created a small portable machine with the proper circuit that generated penetrating heat, and in just a few months he demonstrated it to doctors. This time, however, he ran afoul of the American Medical Association, which resisted the technique, and federal authorities who were unhappy with the frequencies at which his machine operated. Though initial interest was great, he was able to produce few machines.

The bills mounted. He owed $10,000 for back rent to a New York real estate firm and $50,000 to the Railway Cooperative Building and Loan Company. As his debts increased, de Forest had no other option than to file for bankruptcy in federal court in Los Angeles. He listed his liabilities as $103,943.96; his assets, including his laboratory and equipment in Holly-wood and his library, totaled $390.

Desperately, de Forest clung to his independence. The "great sheltering industrial organization," he maintained in a letter of 1930, "all too frequently retards initiative, dulls invention and audacious courage." Such a course was fine for the man who was content to "loaf along," the inventor continued, "but if, by rarest chance, you are in fact a genius, fight alone."

Though the ideas flowed steadily from his brain—a crude method of scan-ning with a cathode ray tube, which eventually became important to radar, was one that he sold to RCA—de Forest's life as an inventor was in eclipse. He knew he was becoming a historical figure, too—a role he enjoyed. In school, children learned of his remarkable radio tube and were taught that de Forest symbolized the American genius for invention. Sometimes they sought his advice. "I have had to work hard all my life to accomplish what I have done for Radio and Talking Motion Pictures," de Forest replied to one ten-year-old:

> To be a success in any line of work requires courage, persistence, a willing-ness to pinch and go without many pleasures and pastimes while you are young and getting a good start in life. . .

Such requests for advice, which he always carefully answered, gave him immense satisfaction.

In his personal life as well, Lee de Forest at last found the satisfaction and stability he had sought so long. It began on the last day of August 1930, at a Santa Monica house party given by Bebe Daniels, the movie actress and a distant cousin of his, on the De Forest side. On the beach he met Marie Mosquini, known to the press as "the most shapely girl in Hollywood." She had acted in the silent comedies that issued almost weekly from the Hal Roach studios, and later played opposite Will Rogers as his leading lady. In Marie, de Forest saw all the attributes he had so long sought in a wife. She had studied poetry, music, and the arts at a Catholic girls' school; she was blond; and she wanted nothing more than to give up her career, marry a great man, and serve him. On Friday, October 3, 1930, six weeks after they had met, the couple quietly crossed the border to be married in Agua Caliente, Mexico. They slipped back to Cielito Lindo, a large house he purchased on Hollywood Boulevard. He was fifty-seven, she twenty-four.

This fourth marriage did not begin auspiciously, however. Before he could marry, de Forest had to shake free of a series of romantic entanglements. There was Miriam on Great Neck, Long Island. "I am praying to Venus, Eros, Karma," she wrote him in July, before he had met Marie, "that the fire which sprang up between us will not turn to ashes." It did. Another liaison ended more violently. For several years in the late twenties, after he abandoned Riverlure to Mary Mayo, he had lived in New York City with an aspiring actress, Henrietta Tilghman O'Kelly. When she learned of the marriage, Miss O'Kelly grew despondent. On January 26, 1931, after leaving a note that told of her unrequited love, she committed suicide. The following year, her mother sued de Forest for $29,400 ($350 a month for seven years). "Mrs. O'Kelly was my mistress," de Forest admitted to reporters, "but I paid her thousands of dollars in excess of my promises before she left home, and I owe her nothing now." The suit came to nothing.

Mary Mayo proved an even more serious obstacle. The third de Forest marriage had been in serious trouble since the birth of their second child, Marilyn, in December 1924. The pregnancy had been difficult for Mary, and the sex of the child had been troublesome to Lee, who desperately wanted a boy. However, the birth of a son in April 1926 caused their final separation. Born with a diseased thyroid, which Lee attributed to his wife's consumption of "poisonous alcohol," the boy lived but two days. Mary consoled herself with her two daughters in Europe and then returned to live alone in New York City.

De Forest had neglected to finalize his divorce from Mary before marrying Marie Mosquini. On learning of the marriage, Mary promptly moved back to Riverlure, the property overlooking the Hudson that they still owned jointly. Lee had to enlist the aid of his brother, Charles, to evict her. Lawyers completed the divorce settlement, and Lee and Marie had their marriage ceremony performed once again in the United States.

Despite these unpleasant circumstances, Lee De Forest's marriage to Marie Mosquini proved to be the most stable part of his life. They based their relationship on mutual worship. To him, she was "mi mijita" (which Marie translated: "My dear. My loved one. My own. My everything") whom he celebrated in verse:

> Your face so fair, your voice so sweet,
> Your eyes as full of love as when
> At first you kissed me on a street

> *In happy sun-kissed Avalon.*
> *'Tis poem enough to know that now, as then,*
> *You are my poem, and my song*

Together Lee and Marie enjoyed their little heaven, Cielito Lindo, a two-story white mission-style house on Hollywood Boulevard. Outside they trained rose bushes to grow on the southern and western stucco walls, and Marie planted large beds of flowers. Inside there was a large vaulted living room, in which he installed a radio and phonograph of his own design, with speakers hidden away in two large grandfather clock cabinets. On the walls of the winding stairway to the second floor he hung his honorary degrees and awards. In a second-floor study he hung framed autographs of those he regarded as mentors: Professor Dickerson, his teacher at Mount Hermon; Willard Gibbs from Yale; and Thomas Edison. Over the headboard of his bed, he hung a photograph of his mother.

For de Forest, living with an abstemious and churchgoing Catholic was a welcome change. "My state has been restored, redeemed; in health, ambition, faith in myself, & belief in the goodness of woman-kind," he wrote to his brother. "I have been remade during this year. How infinitely different is my world since I up-stakes & left 'Riverlure' . . . & found my Marie!"

Edwin Howard Armstrong was too busy to listen to the radio in the 1930s. He had no economic problems to escape, and no time for escape. "He couldn't sit still long enough to listen to anything so long as a concert," a relative remembered. "He was too busy with his work." In Columbia University's Marcellus Hartley Laboratory, Armstrong was exploring new laws governing radio waves that he alone had discovered and understood. From these investigations would come inventions that would change the fundamental concepts of radio, and the nature of communication forever.

10

ARMSTRONG AND THE
FM REVOLUTION

On Saturday, December 23, 1933, Howard Armstrong met David Sarnoff at his office in Rockefeller Center. The two friends drove in Sarnoff's limousine uptown to Armstrong's laboratory at Columbia University, the place where twenty years before Sarnoff had watched Armstrong demonstrate regeneration.

The two friends always took considerable pride in the fact that they had been among the first pioneers to enter the unknown territory of radio. Each had succeeded in his own way. At that time, Armstrong had a large apartment overlooking Central Park, a house overlooking the sea at Rye Beach, New Hampshire, about $5 million cash in the bank, and potentially many millions more in stocks. With his own money he supported a small staff at the laboratory, and he gave generously to his alma mater. Though hardly in a class with Armstrong, Sarnoff had prospered in other ways. He had a large house on East 68th Street, took an annual trip to Europe, and held memberships in the Lotos and Sands Point clubs and the Temple Emanu-El on Fifth Avenue, and controlled the most important communication corporation in the world.

Over the years there had been strains in their friendship, and certainly the litigation of *RCA v. REL*, which was about to go before the Supreme Court, had not helped matters. But still each man could celebrate his rich memories of their past experiences: the frigid night they had spent in the Marconi shack at Belmar, New Jersey, in January 1914, listening to faint sounds from distant transmitters with Armstrong's new regenerative receiver; the work on the superheterodyne that put RCA in the forefront of radio set manufacturers; Armstrong's visits for morning coffee and radio conversation at Sarnoff's house on Pennsylvania Avenue in Mount Vernon (the Sarnoff boys had taken to calling him "the coffee man"); and Sarnoff's attendance at Armstrong's marriage to Marion MacInnis. While Sarnoff might consider his friend foolish and arrogant at times—and with good reason—and Armstrong might think his friend hopelessly priggish, stuffy, and too closely allied to the corporation—again with good reason—their longstanding respect for each other's abilities generally allowed them to ignore such matters.

For Sarnoff's visit to Columbia this time, Armstrong promised to demonstrate an invention as remarkable as the one his friend had seen twenty years ago: a new "staticless radio." The cumbersome name suggested something Sarnoff and everyone else in the industry had longed for, as the chief problem in broadcasting was static caused by electrical charges in the atmosphere. Perhaps, Sarnoff had often said, someone would invent "a little black box" to complement his now popular radio music box. It might be sold as an additional piece of equipment, placed between the receiver and the speaker, a giant filter that would allow only clear sounds to reach a listener's ears.

What Sarnoff saw in the laboratory, however, was not a little black box, but more than a hundred tubes in scores of circuits, all neatly arranged on breadboards and placed on tables that lined the perimeters of two rooms. It was a receiver and a radio transmitter, an entire system for a completely new type of broadcasting. Not so much an invention, as Sarnoff himself later said, it was a "revolution." That evening, Armstrong revealed he had filed for five basic patents on his system between 1930 and 1933. (They were issued on December 26, 1933, beginning with number 1,941,066.) These patents changed many of the fundamental concepts of radio communication. Armstrong had created wide-band frequency modulation. Listeners would come to call it FM.

Like most revolutions, Armstrong's FM had been a long time in the making. FM had not come to him in a flash of insight as had regeneration and the superheterodyne, or serendipitously, either, as had superregeneration. What Sarnoff saw in the Marcellus Hartley Laboratory that December day was the product of hundreds of thousands of tests and measurements, tens of thousands of hours of work for Armstrong and his assistants, countless false solutions and frustrations, the derision of expert mathematicians, daring originality, and ultimate triumph. It represented a trail of research almost as long as his friendship with the inventor.

Armstrong's own invention of regeneration had created the problem of static, for his circuit amplified both the radio signal and the interference. Before regeneration, few knew what static was. When American Telephone and Telegraph sent three engineers to Philosophy Hall on February 6, 1914, to hear the young Columbia graduate's remarkable circuit, they asked "what all the clicking was about." After Armstrong patiently explained the nature of the "clicking," which was disturbing a transmission from Glace Bay, Nova Scotia, one of the group flatly declared his cable operators would not work for AT&T if their ears were subjected to such noises. When operators did use the circuit, they sometimes found their eardrums blasted by powerful electrical discharges intruding on the message they were receiving. And the problem grew more intense in the summers, when electrical storms produced what operators called the "static season."

In June 1914, when Armstrong began working as Pupin's assistant in the Hartley Laboratory for $12 a week, his first task was to investigate the nature of the static his circuit amplified. For the better part of three years, he studied the difference between current and voltage within a vacuum tube, with the thought that this might hold the secret to controlling static. Perhaps, he and Pupin speculated, they could create a filter to separate the static from the radio waves. While he learned considerably more about the nature of electric currents, Armstrong came no closer to a solution to the problem. At a dockside interview just before he embarked for Europe in October 1922, he told reporters that the "elimination of static" was "the biggest problem that I can see." Obviously, he had been frustrated in his own research, for he continued, "It is the only one I have ever encountered that, approached from any direction, always seems to be a stone wall." But then he added with optimism, "I suppose, however, that static will be done away with sometime."

The radio waves Armstrong referred to were AM or amplitude modulation, the system in use in all those "little radios" Cole Porter had written about in his song. It was a system that Armstrong—and all other radio engineers—knew well and visualized easily: a transmitter emits a continuous radio frequency wave that engineers call a carrier.

At the same time, sounds of voices or music picked up by a microphone pass into a modulator that converts them to electric current and superimposes them on the carrier. The resulting wave fluctuates in amplitude in accordance with the fluctuations of the sound signal:

Armstrong and Pupin were not alone in their investigations. "Practically everyone" who was a radio engineer, Armstrong remembered later, "undertook to try to solve [the problem]. But," he added, "the results were unsuccessful." Instead of finding an adequate filter, they and others learned that "static was practically identical in nature" with the AM radio waves they were using in broadcasting. With this thought in mind, corporate researchers turned to the question of limiting the amount of interference.

Foremost among the investigators were the mathematicians who worked for the American Telephone and Telegraph Company, and the most astute of these was Bell Laboratories' chief theoretical mathematician, John Renshaw Carson. Carson's early work at AT&T bore similarities to Armstrong's at Columbia. Carson was analyzing de Forest's vacuum tube with the thought of understanding mathematically just how it worked, while Armstrong was conducting similar—though less theoretical—research at Columbia. Carson studied modulation of carrier waves, and produced a mathematical model to explain just how it worked, while Armstrong was studying the phenomenon of static and its effect on radio transmissions. By 1920, Carson had begun a careful mathematical study of radio frequency waves, which would occupy him until his death in 1940.

Carson's work yielded important results. His investigation of the bandwidth of transmissions—that is, the width the sound signal occupies when it is impressed upon the carrier wave—led to his invention of "single sideband," a novel method of sending several messages simultaneously.

Carson always had every confidence that his conclusions would hold up in the reality of an experiment. An engineer like Armstrong would draw on his intuition and reasoning to figure out how he might achieve his goal; a mathematician like Carson, forever careful and attentive to the most minute detail, drew on theoretical knowledge and reasoning to figure out *if* he could reach it. He was interested less in whether an experiment appeared to work than in the mathematical reasons that it worked. And when he delivered papers on his investigations to learned societies, he filled them with a formidable array of abstruse formulas and calculations. In 1926, he published *Electrical Circuit Theory and Operational Calculus*, which consolidated many of his analyses about current and voltage in electrical transmission systems. Carson's lectures, papers, and book so impressed and even intimidated engineers and scientists that more often than not they accepted his carefully stated, mathematically correct conclusions without argument.

For Carson, static interference was a problem of mathematics. He turned his theoretical mind to the bandwidth of a broadcast, and to an idea that was being mentioned by some engineers: frequency modulation. Carson and other engineers recognized that the difference between amplitude and frequency modulation is theoretically very simple. With AM, the amplitude of the carrier wave is modulated in accordance with fluctuations of the sound superimposed upon it, while the frequency for the wave remains constant; with FM, the frequency of the carrier wave is modulated by the fluctuations of the sound superimposed upon it, while the amplitude of the wave remains constant. Engineers usually represent an FM wave like this:

For Carson, however, mathematical calculations had proved conclusively that FM was not the answer to the static problem. In February 1922, he published "Notes on the Theory of Modulation" to the Institute of Radio Engineers, an especially impressive and formidable paper on the results of his research. At that time, engineers had thought they might use frequency modulation to narrow the bandwidth of a transmission. If this were possible, so the theory went, the telephone company might be able to send more messages without interference. However, Carson's mathematical calculations had proven beyond a doubt that FM with a narrow bandwidth would not work. "This type of modulation," Carson declared in a sweeping conclusion, "inherently distorts without any compensating advantages whatsoever."

Carson's pronouncement had a dramatic effect: by the time Armstrong returned from his trip to Europe later that year, almost all study of the use of frequency modulation in communications had ceased. Instead, other mathematicians in the United States and Europe followed in Carson's wake with even more elegant calculations that proved beyond a doubt frequency modulation was unworkable. Though engineers with RCA, GE, Westinghouse, and Bell Telephone Laboratories did a little work on FM after Carson published his opinion, and indeed took out some patents, they largely turned their attention to other matters. Unwittingly, Carson had done Howard Armstrong a great service, for the field of investigation into FM belonged almost entirely to him.

As he wound down his work on the superheterodyne for RCA in 1923 and 1924, Armstrong intensified his study of frequency modulation. Carson's statements meant little to him, for he could never accept findings based almost exclusively on mathematics. "It's the things people know that ain't so," he frequently reminded himself and his assistants. Had Carson said, "I've tested frequency modulation in experiments I conducted in my lab, and it doesn't work, and here's the mathematical reason," Armstrong might have been more willing to accept his conclusions. But Carson in effect had said, "Here's the mathematical reason that frequency modulation won't work." That was not good enough for the inventor. Time and again as an undergraduate at Columbia, Armstrong had refused to seek in mathematics a refuge from physical realities. He would examine frequency modulation himself, and on his own terms.

Armstrong began exploring the nature of frequency modulated waves in as thorough a way as he had the operation of the vacuum tube and the phenomenon of static. Unable to procure reliable equipment for his experiments, he created his own. This proved a greater task than any other he had embarked upon. Frequency modulation, after all, was an entirely different system from amplitude modulation, and as a *system* it required both a transmitter and a receiver that would eventually take up most of the laboratory. Now in his seventh decade, Pupin was getting too old to devote the intense periods of time required for these researches, and Armstrong found himself without the guidance of his mentor. So that he might devote all his energy to research, Armstrong decided to hire an office manager with his own funds. Aside from possessing organizational and secretarial skills, the manager would have to meet other formidable requirements: to know about radio theory and the intricacies of particular circuits, and above all else, as his studies were highly confidential, to be loyal and trustworthy. The man he selected, Thomas J. Styles, would stay with the inventor until his death.

Armstrong and Thomas Styles had known each other since high school in Yonkers, when their common interest in radio had brought them together. They had long been members of the Radio Club of America, and in 1913 Styles had been one of the first to listen to the sounds emanating from Armstrong's regenerative receiver. The war had separated them, Armstrong going off to Paris in the army, while Styles remained in New York. After the war, Styles had taken a job with the Bankers Trust Company and was working in Paris when Armstrong went there in 1922 to arrange payment for his Hispano-Suiza. Styles returned to the United States in time to attend Armstrong's wedding in Merrimac. They had kept in touch since then, and Styles testified in his friend's behalf in the regeneration case with de Forest. Armstrong knew he could depend on him to be efficient and discreet.

Though differing in physical attributes—Styles, short, round, and balding; Armstrong, tall, barrel-chested, and bald—the two men shared similar values and personality traits. Each dressed conservatively in a business suit and hat. Each was conservative politically, too. (Styles once ran unsuccessfully in Queens as the Republican candidate for Congress.) And each was extremely serious about his work and possessed a very limited sense of humor.

In 1927, Armstrong hired another assistant, John Shaughnessy, to help with his experiments. A native of Ireland who had served as a radio inspector at the New York Navy Yard, Shaughnessy had a good general knowledge of engineering, though recent developments in electric circuits had left him behind. He had a fondness for drink, too, which sometimes hindered his work. Nevertheless, he possessed a talent for making "models," breadboard prototypes of the circuits Armstrong was designing. Unlike the other two, Shaughnessy had a sense of humor and was a consummate master of practical jokes.

Armstrong's plan for his invention was simple: "to produce a . . . wave which was different in character from the . . . wave which static disturbance could produce." The FM wave had just the characteristics he sought.

He first worked with radio telegraphy: a telegraph transmitter that alternately produced waves of closely related but different frequencies; the dots and dashes would be carried on one wave, the spaces between the letters on the other. When the two waves entered a receiver, the static disturbances on each would cancel themselves out (since they were the same frequency), leaving only the information to pass through clearly. While the system worked moderately well, static was still present, as was the low hum from the vacuum tubes.

When Armstrong presented a paper on his ingenious system at a meeting of the Institute of Radio Engineers in October 1927, many members were skeptical. As one commentator said in a most guarded and roundabout manner, "It is surely to be hoped that Mr. Armstrong will give us further data where the separate roles of balance and selectivity are more clearly brought out." As the inventor had not included a single formula to explain how his system worked, mathematicians among the audience were especially dubious.

The most suspicious of the group was John R. Carson. With his critical eye, thoroughly theoretical mind, and sharp pencil, he considered each of Armstrong's claims. At the April 1928 meeting of the IRE, he delivered what he expected would be the final cold blast against FM, a dispassionate mathematical analysis of Armstrong's system for eliminating static. Through a process of sound mathematical reasoning, he found that Armstrong's balancing system offered no appreciable gain, and he closed with a tart statement: "In fact, as more and more schemes are analyzed and tested, and as the essential nature of the problem is more clearly perceived, we are forced to the conclusion that static, like the poor, will always be with us." Mathematicians and engineers don't usually speak as sharply and definitively as Carson had, and there could be no question among those in the audience of the import of his statement: trying to eliminate static through FM was as foolish as trying to create a perpetual motion machine or a way to make gold from lead.

A lesser inventor in the face of Carson's attack might well have quietly moved on to another area of inquiry, hoping that others would someday forget what had been said. Not Armstrong. While Carson's statement initially dealt a great blow to his confidence (coming as it did within months of the Supreme Court's decision on regeneration), Armstrong quickly recovered his self-assurance, and then his remarkable stubbornness set in. He realized his superior design and construction of transmitters and receivers had eliminated much of the noise and had fooled him into thinking he had made a significant discovery. Since his equipment functioned better than any other available, it gave superior, and consequently misleading, results.

Once again, Carson's paper actually helped Armstrong, by persuading others they would be wasting their time experimenting with FM. More than ever, he determined to pursue what had now become a quest.

Armstrong found himself wrestling with the conventional wisdom about bandwidth—that is, the space a sound signal occupies when it is impressed upon a carrier wave. Though a wide band carries a signal better, it presents a larger target and is more likely to be disturbed by static interference. Engineers and mathematicians are accustomed to speaking of this interference in terms of "signal to noise ratio." A lower signal to noise ratio results in more interference.

Engineers faced a situation not unlike the one of a farmer driving an overloaded hay wagon down a country road. The wagon (or the carrier) is narrower than the load, but of course, the more hay on the wagon, the more likely it is to be hit by other vehicles. The trick is to carry as much hay (or sound) to the barn with as little loss as possible.

Carson and others were correct when it came to applying the principle of a narrow bandwidth to AM broadcasts. However, when they applied it to FM, they found the narrow band offered no advantages in the reduction of noise. Therefore, they concluded FM was of no value. Thinking it would never be possible to eliminate static altogether, they sought to limit it. Mathematical theory told them they should make the bandwidth as narrow as possible, and certainly no wider than necessary.

Seeing the fallacy of the argument—that Carson had drawn his conclusions by applying the principles of amplitude modulated waves to those of frequency modulation—Armstrong steadfastly determined to prove it wrong.

In October 1928, after his first loss to de Forest in the Supreme Court, he settled into an intense routine of experimentation, lasting half a decade, and relieved only occasionally by periods of relaxation.

This routine was as regular as the laws he was trying to discover: traveling from his apartment at 81st Street and Central Park West, Armstrong arrived at Philosophy Hall usually by nine o'clock each morning. At noon, he, Styles, and Shaughnessy broke for a brief lunch at a restaurant on Amsterdam Avenue. After lunch, the trio returned to the laboratory to work through the afternoon and often far into the night, designing, building, and measuring subtle transmitter and receiver circuits, which the inventor thought would bring him closer to a solution to the problem.

Armstrong would allow nothing to interrupt his concentration. He seemed to neglect all matters of his personal life. Day after day, week after week, he appeared in the same suit and necktie, until finally the frayed cloth was retired and another tie and suit took their place. Lunch was merely a time to add fuel. He never varied his order: a single cheese sandwich and a glass of milk. He rarely allowed the conversation to slip into trivial matters, but kept it focused on his quest to eliminate static.

The relentless, single-minded pursuit of the right circuit seemed to take over the laboratory. Once for his own enjoyment and to see how long it would take the others to find out, John Shaughnessy added a single, narrow strip of paper behind the inside band of Tom Styles's hat each morning. After several months, Styles began to complain that his hat was bothering him. A few days later, when Armstrong, Styles, and Shaughnessy were having their lunch, the strips tumbled out on the table. Neither Armstrong nor Styles was amused.

The enormity of the task before Armstrong would have daunted any inventor without the backing of a research team in a well-financed laboratory. By the standards of RCA or General Electric, which regularly infused their research facilities with new staff and equipment, the by-now aged Marcellus Hartley Laboratory was primitive, its "team" of inventors nonexistent. And, it became clear as time went on, this invention meant not merely a refinement of a circuit in a receiver or transmitter, but an entirely new and different "system." Armstrong was an explorer walking intrepidly through uncharted territory, in search of something that radio engineers had only dreamed of, a signal pure and unadulterated by noise. At times he chased false clues, "more will-o'-the-wisps than I ever thought could exist," he once said. But never did he question his own ability to succeed.

By 1931, hundreds of thousands of measurements later, he appeared no closer to the object of his quest. Then he decided to move entirely against the grain of all accepted theory: instead of narrowing the bandwidth of the

FM signal, he would make it *wider*. In doing so, he believed the signal to noise ratio would be increased dramatically. "If the transmitted wave were modulated widely in frequency," Armstrong remembered thinking, "and if the receiver were made nonresponsive to amplitude changes, feebly responsive to small changes in frequency, and fully responsive only to the wide frequency changes of the signal, a means of differentiating between the desired [the information] and the undesired [static interference] . . . might be found."

What was a good and bold idea turned into a difficult and time-consuming task. It entailed redesigning both the transmitter and receiver radically. But once he had done so, he found an extraordinary improvement in the signal to noise ratio, the amount of interference that a transmission could tolerate and still be intelligible. Armstrong's concept of widening the band changed everything, including the basic mathematical theories underlying communication.

To handle the wide band of transmission effectively, Armstrong designed fundamental changes in the radio receiver. As with AM broadcasts, the FM signal passed through a superheterodyne circuit where it was turned into an intermediate frequency wave. Before this new wave traveled into a detector (as an AM wave did), it passed through two entirely new circuits of Armstrong's invention.

The first was a something he called a "limiter," a powerful electronic strainer, which removed any variations in the amplitude of the signal that might have occurred in its passage from the transmitter, thereby restoring its original integrity. As Armstrong put it, "only pure frequency modulated current is passed on for detection."

The second circuit, which he called a "discriminator," changed the pure FM wave into its original form. It then passed in the usual fashion of AM sets through an audio amplifier and finally through a speaker as sound.

The results astonished all who heard them. FM radios did not pick up static interference that occurred in the atmosphere and FM transmitted a wider range of sounds. At last the term "high fidelity" now meant something.

This was the system that David Sarnoff came to witness in December 1933. He had been correct to call it a "revolution." FM had the potential to change the nature of broadcasting. Sarnoff was not sure he or the industry was ready for the change, but he knew he could not afford to ignore it.

A delegation of three RCA engineers from Camden followed early in 1934. Arriving at Philosophy Hall in the afternoon, they stayed until 2 A.M. listening to Armstrong's demonstration. The inventor had both an AM and an FM transmitter in one room and a receiver in another. When he turned on a static generator, the AM signal was blocked while the FM came through clearly. Only one of the three engineers believed what he was hearing was "an astounding genuine development"; his colleagues were skeptical. After all, Armstrong's system went contrary to the accepted law of bandwidth, the static was artificial, and the transmitter was broadcasting only from the next room. Any static eliminator might work in those circumstances. Armstrong and his visitors decided he should move his equipment into RCA's experimental television station atop the Empire State Building.

That spring, while his lawyers were preparing for the final test before the Supreme Court in the matter of *RCA v. REL*, Armstrong worked to modify a spare RCA television transmitter so that it could send FM signals. Though not an ideal transmitter (as its power was at most 200 watts and the waves it sent did not correspond exactly to waves the receiver was designed to recover), it was certainly better than the one he had devised in his small laboratory. By early June, though shaken by the decision of Mr. Justice Cardozo, Armstrong completed his installation. On June 9, he conducted the first field test.

He placed his receiver at the vacation house of his old and valued friend George Burghard, on Westhampton Beach, Long Island. It was the perfect spot, seventy miles from Manhattan, and in the home of someone he could trust. He had known Burghard from his Columbia days, when love of radio and speed had brought the two men together. Burghard had been active in the Radio Club of America, and he still remained an avid radio amateur. In the twenties he had owned a Delage, which proved a match for Armstrong's Hispano-Suiza when the two raced each other down the Long Island Motor Parkway. Since Burghard was president of the Continental Radio Corporation, a distributor of RCA products, the site met with the approval of officials in Rockefeller Center, too.

To set up his equipment in the Empire State Building and at Burghard's house, Armstrong enlisted the help of another old friend he could trust, Randy Runyon. By June 9, 1934, all was in order for the first transmissions.

"*Perfect!*" Runyon recorded at exactly "10:23.5 A.M." in the log he and Armstrong kept. When the transmitter at the Empire State sent out an AM signal on the same frequency, there was "hundreds of thousands [of times] more noise." When the transmitter in Manhattan broadcast the sounds of an organ playing over FM, the receiver on Long Island picked up the low notes with full fidelity. At 1 P.M., when the transmitter signed off, Armstrong added a concluding note to the log:

All tests performed exactly according to Hoyle. This experiment concludes just twenty years of work on this problem. It is with the deepest gratification that I record here that my two oldest friends, George Burghard and Randolph

Runyon, old timers who saw the genesis of regeneration, took part in the culmination of this work. An era as new and distinct in the radio art as that of regeneration is now upon us.

After ten years of eclipse, my star is again rising.

⚡

For ten years, since Judge Van Orsdel found for de Forest on May 8, 1924, Armstrong's reputation as an important inventor had been clouded. Two adverse Supreme Court decisions had further clouded it. At last, he could see the time when radio engineers would recognize him not just as the inventor of regeneration and the superheterodyne circuits (whatever the judgment of the courts), but of an entire broadcasting system.

⚡

The transmissions to Long Island continued, but only briefly. Still not persuaded of the efficacy of the system, RCA decided it wanted to test FM with the receiver farther away from the transmitter and at a place where "summer static" was most intense.

That month Elmer Engstrom, a research engineer with RCA, wrote to Harry Sadenwater, an engineer at the RCA Victor plant in Camden, New Jersey, asking if the corporation might use his house in nearby Haddonfield to test a new radio system. As it turned out, Sadenwater was an acquaintance of Armstrong's, and early in 1934 had visited the Hartley Laboratory for a demonstration. He eagerly accepted the request. On June 28, movers placed the cumbersome equipment on a long bar in Sadenwater's large basement room.

Detailed, far-reaching, and conclusive, the transmissions between the Empire State and Haddonfield, eighty miles away, stand as some of the most significant tests ever conducted in the history of communication, and greatly enriched the understanding of the laws of electromagnetic waves. An unusual number of lightning storms that summer often destroyed AM reception, while Armstrong's receiver picked up the FM signal clearly.

But FM proved far superior to AM in ways that surprised even Armstrong. The signal did not fade at its perimeter as AM's did. For the first time, FM made multiplexing—the sending of different messages simultaneously over the same carrier wave—practical. On November 19, before a delegation of engineers headed by Elmer Engstrom, the transmitter at the Empire State simultaneously sent out programs from both NBC's red and blue networks, a telegraph message, and a facsimile of the front page of the New York Times, on a *single* FM carrier wave.

Most important, the Haddonfield tests demonstrated that FM improved the sound quality of a broadcast as well as eliminated the static. Purged was the annoying background noise that seemed a part of every AM radio. Previously, engineers had dismissed it as the "noise of the electrons" as they raced around the circuits inside the set, about which nothing could be done. FM also improved the tone of receivers so that they more closely approximated the full range of human hearing, between 50 cycles—say, the deep rumble of a kettle drum—and 15,000 cycles—say, the overtones of the flute. Discriminating listeners knew they were missing a great deal from AM broadcasts, which delivered no more than 5,000 cycles at best.

With Armstrong's wide band FM system, the age of multiplexing and high fidelity had begun.

These demonstrations at Westhampton Beach and Haddonfield caused considerable discussion within the ranks of RCA's engineering department. No one had ever seen a system like FM, and they were naturally suspicious. They turned to a first-rate engineer, W. R. G. Baker, to discover the facts.

A 1916 electrical engineering graduate of Union College in Schenectady, and former researcher for General Electric, Walter Ransom Gail Baker had earned a reputation as a brilliant designer of some of the first and finest commercial broadcasting stations in the United States, including WGY in Schenectady, KOA in Denver, and KGO in Oakland. His stations were known for the strength and quality of their signal. (In the case of WGY, during the station's first year of operation, 50,000 listeners from as far away as Hawaii reported hearing broadcasts.) In 1929, Baker had joined RCA Victor in Camden to manage its production of radios and soon became a vice president of the corporation.

Baker arranged for a series of tests and demonstrations. Over the next year, scores of engineers, many of whom had known Armstrong since 1914, trooped out to Haddonfield to see the equipment in Harry Sadenwater's cellar. They were the best RCA and NBC had, people like Alfred Goldsmith, the electrical engineering professor from City College who had headed the corporation's research department, and Vladimir Zworykin, who was busy developing electronic television. Sadenwater carefully kept a log of the visitors. "A matter that impressed me," Sadenwater remembered, "was that so few of the engineers that should have been vitally interested came more than once." In New York and Camden, however, they were meeting in committees to discuss what they had seen and heard. All seemed tentative, unable to decide just what to make of this new system. Obviously hesitant to commit themselves, they asked for more tests.

Over the course of the summer, Armstrong's acquaintance with Harry Sadenwater grew into friendship. Sadenwater's history in radio was almost as

long as Armstrong's. He had had an amateur station in 1908. Two years
later, when he was old enough, he went to sea as a radio operator. Returning
to New York in 1914, he taught radio fundamentals at the YMCA and
designed some of the first regenerative receivers. Serving in the navy during
the war, he conducted the first long distance radio conversation from a plane
to Josephus Daniels, secretary of the navy, on the ground. In 1919, he was
awarded the navy cross for his work as radio operator on a naval seaplane that
attempted a flight from Newfoundland to the Azores. Before taking a job as
a field engineer with RCA in Camden, he worked for General Electric as the
chief broadcast engineer at station WGY.

Despite his obvious abilities, the quiet and self-effacing Sadenwater never
seems to have been taken quite as seriously as he might have been within the
Radio Corporation. In 1933, the corporation had transferred him from engineering to sales with no apparent raise in salary. For ten years, he had been
stalled at the same level within RCA, though, as he wrote to a superior, it
was "the most important period in my life." But Armstrong did take him
seriously. He had known Sadenwater for many years through the Radio Club
of America, and he was impressed to see his increasing frustration with RCA
engineers who showed little interest in FM. Sadenwater alone appeared to
understand its value to broadcasting and to the company. Soon Sadenwater
and his wife, Grace, were entertaining Armstrong when he was in Haddonfield. Later Armstrong invited the couple to vacation with him and Marion
at Rye Beach.

Armstrong quickly found that his frequency modulation system was fighting the desperate times, a comfortable corporate inertia, and a president at
RCA who was steering an entirely different course for his corporation. Some
10.25 million people were unemployed in 1934; those who had a job counted
themselves lucky; those few who worked for RCA, blessed. A new ethos was
emerging among these engineers, too. Generally a conservative lot, they
grew even more so at the Radio Corporation, content to follow the course
David Sarnoff had charted for their industry. Though they were witnessing a
sweeping technological change with profound consequences for the way they
worked and viewed their profession, they had learned mathematically that
what they were seeing did not happen. They knew the safest plan was to
follow their president. Since Sarnoff was wary of FM for commercial reasons,
the engineers could be skeptical for technical ones.

The course David Sarnoff had set for RCA led in a very different direction
from the one Edwin Howard Armstrong had charted with his invention. By
1933, Sarnoff clearly envisioned what he supposed to be the end of radio and
the beginning of the new medium, television. Americans would be far more
interested in *seeing* pictures with words than merely hearing words. He called

it his "supplantive" theory. Television, the new technology, would supplant the old; it would do no good to resist it. The same thing had been the case with the Victor Talking Machine Company. Radio had supplanted the phonograph, and now record players sold only when they were combination "radio phonographs," and, he was fond of saying, Nipper the dog who was a symbol of Victor, had a new master. Long ago, he had discounted conventional wisdom, which held that the world beat a path to the door of the person who built the better mousetrap. "While the sylvan mouse-trap maker is waiting for customers, and his energetic competitor is out on the main road," he had told a reporter for *Time* magazine in 1929, "a third man will come along with a virulent poison which is death on mice and there will be no longer any demand for mouse traps." Television was just such a poison for radio; Armstrong's FM was merely a better mousetrap.

RCA, so Sarnoff believed, had to put its energy into the new technology of broadcasting pictures as well as sounds. Early on, television had caught his fancy. "The greatest day of all will be reached when not only the human voice but the image of the speaker can be flashed through space in every direction," he had confidently said to the *Saturday Evening Post* in 1926, and had said on another occasion that "the possibilities of the new art are as boundless as the imagination." What matter that FM might give a clearer sound? Fewer and fewer people would be listening once Zworykin had perfected his iconoscope and RCA had made television commercially available. And where would the money come from to develop both television and a new radio system? Though Zworykin had said on their first meeting in 1929 that developing a working television system would cost about $100,000, the Russian engineer and his growing team of researchers were gobbling up immense amounts of RCA capital, about $5 million by 1934. Still the system was not ready for commercial exploitation.

Other financial considerations were dissuading Sarnoff from developing frequency modulation. In 1929, Americans had paid an average of $162 each for 4.5 million radios; in 1933, they paid an average of $70 each for 3.8 million. Already, the price had declined by 56 percent, and all indications suggested it would drop even more by the end of the decade. Only sales promotions stressing the cheaper sets seemed to succeed. Not that the sets of 1933 were as good as those of 1929—they were worse, but only a few disgruntled purchasers returned to the store saying, "The new one isn't as good as the one I've been using for five years." Americans were sacrificing sound quality for an affordable price. As with any new technology, FM radios initially would cost more, about $100 each. But nothing suggested the public was willing to pay more for the improved fidelity of FM.

Then there was the question of what money Americans had to spend. The pool of disposable personal income had shrunk dramatically from $83.3 million in 1929 to $52.4 million in 1934. If RCA were to bring out television and FM radio together, the two appliances would be competing for the same dollars. Whatever its merits might be, however it might advance the radio art, FM just did not make good economic sense. It would not enrich the radio industry.

The contrasts between RCA of 1923 and 1933 were striking, too. In 1923, with only a fledgling research laboratory, RCA and Sarnoff had to rely on independent inventors like Armstrong to supply the corporation with the new technology; today the corporation had growing research facilities in Camden, and Sarnoff was planning to build a separate research laboratory in Princeton, New Jersey. Sarnoff could visit his researchers whenever he chose, something that always gave him pleasure. In 1923, he recommended the superheterodyne to Owen D. Young and the board of directors; today, he alone controlled the corporation and had told the board it was developing television. In 1923, he had moved aggressively to acquire the superregeneration circuit because he was afraid Armstrong might take the invention elsewhere; today, RCA's position in the radio industry was certain and he knew Armstrong would have a difficult time without the support of his corporation. In 1923, there had been no NBC; today, the network of over eighty stations was floating on a rising tide of revenues generated by advertisers who cared only about audience size and not at all about the fidelity of the broadcast. Sarnoff knew he could take his time deciding whether he should acquire this curious invention.

But how to deal with his friend? Mr. Justice Cardozo's decision and the lack of RCA support, the refusal to answer Armstrong's letters appealing to the corporation to correct the factual errors in the opinion, had all taken place at the time the inventor was beginning his experiments at the Empire State Building, and had further strained their friendship. Yet they were still friends. At the end of January 1934, Armstrong had written him marking the twentieth anniversary of the freezing night they spent in that shack in Belmar, New Jersey, testing his regeneration circuit, and Sarnoff had replied warmly:

> It would seem hard to believe that twenty years—a full generation—have passed since the night. . . . And yet here you are a generation after that event, still gripped by the mystery of the air, still challenged by the secrets of space, and still in the forefront of advanced thinkers and workers in the art.

In conclusion, he had exhorted his friend to "fix your gaze and energies on the next twenty years" so that the telegrams and letters exchanged at the end of the next generation would make them "feel that we are still young even then."

Then Armstrong had come to his aid. The occasion was a particularly fractious annual meeting of the corporation on May 7, 1935. Miss Anna E. Robinson, a perennially obstreperous stockholder whose sixteen shares gave her the right to disrupt every matter of routine business with a cantankerous question, challenged Sarnoff's salaries of $75,000 as president and $54,000 as chairman of the board. Armstrong had passionately defended him. Sarnoff had been in radio "from the beginning to the end," Armstrong had said. "The man who pulled this Company through during the difficult times of the General Electric, Westinghouse, RCA mixup with the Government was its President, Mr. David Sarnoff." He wouldn't have his job for "$500,000 a year." Even though he had "a row" with him, Armstrong had concluded, he recognized all he owed to him. It had been an unusually courageous speech to make, especially as Sarnoff had announced earlier in the meeting that the corporation would spend $1 million to introduce television commercially. That Armstrong had supported him at this moment had moved him to write:

> While the sincerity of your tone and the significance of the events to which you referred made a marked impression on everyone present, it touched me personally so deeply that I find it difficult to express in words the sentiments I feel.

Sarnoff acknowledged, in a rare moment of candor, he had "made many mistakes" in his life, "but not in the quality of the friends I selected for reposing my faith."

———

Nevertheless, a distance appeared to be growing between the two men, and the matter of FM only served to increase it. The conversation they had when the first Haddonfield tests had proved successful was not reassuring: "Why are you pushing this so hard?" Sarnoff had asked. Armstrong replied that FM was just the invention to put new life into the radio industry suffering from the depression. "But this is not an ordinary invention," Sarnoff answered. "This is a revolution." It made no difference. Not understanding the business as he did, Armstrong stubbornly rejoined, "That is all the more reason to get it into use as fast as we can."

No, Armstrong was not like the rest, a good corporation man, a person who could see the place of FM in a larger context of what was best for RCA. Armstrong could not make the connection between the art and the business of radio as Sarnoff had. Though his friend still owned a large block of RCA stock, he seemed more and more a maverick, a person who appeared increasingly obsessed with the possibilities of FM to the exclusion of all else. Perhaps Sarnoff might stall by calling for more tests; perhaps those tests would accentuate the negative rather than the positive aspects of the system. This would be the course—not outright rejection, but further delay and benign neglect. But if his strategy did not work, he would have to break. The needs of the corporation had to remain paramount.

In mid-March 1935, W. R. G. Baker received a detailed four-page report from one of the more cautious of the engineers he had asked to evaluate Armstrong's FM, R. R. Beal. Emphasizing the system's limitations, which were largely due to the Empire State transmitter's incompatibility with the receiver, Beal had no difficulty dwelling on the seeming faults of FM. Frequency modulation might be considered as a "new broadcasting setup," Beal began darkly, "but not as an improvement for existing services." Its receiver was inherently more complex. True, FM reduced receiver hiss and "other kinds of continuous interference," but not, Beal maintained incorrectly, the static from automobile ignitions. Facsimile over FM offered "no apparent advantage" over AM. Armstrong's patents did not appear "particularly fundamental," and they were "unlikely sufficient to control the situation."

Baker had all he needed to send up a negative report to Otto S. Schairer, chairman of RCA's planning committee. "I hardly think that Armstrong has a system that can stand by itself," he wrote. "While I would like to see RCA have a good patent position in this field, I can not see as yet the practical usefulness of the system except for special services."

In the meantime Armstrong was pressing Baker, Engstrom, and other engineers to make a corporate commitment to FM by building a high power amplifier for the Empire State station. He was bound by the terms of his superregeneration agreement to offer RCA first refusal for an exclusive license to his invention, but these corporate engineers seemed unwilling to make a decision. In July 1935, after David Sarnoff and six others witnessed a demonstration of the facsimile equipment, word came from Rockefeller Center that Armstrong would have to remove his equipment from the Empire State Building. RCA needed the space for further tests with television.

Perhaps there was another reason to have Armstrong remove his equipment. Without a transmitter at the top of the tallest building in the world, he would have no place where he could conduct his broadcast tests. He had announced his "staticless" radio system on April 26; soon he would have to back up his claim with a public demonstration. But from where?

David Sarnoff's curious actions left his friend Armstrong puzzled. Nor could he be clear about RCA's position with regard to acquiring his five basic

FM patterns. While the prospects certainly were not encouraging, no one in the corporation had said anything formally to him. He remained confident that the scientific facts—established in the Empire State tests—had vindicated his claims. He would not be deterred. With or without RCA he would press onward.

Since RCA, perhaps directed by Sarnoff, had told him to remove his equipment from the Empire State Building, he would broadcast an FM program from Randy Runyon's small amateur station in Yonkers for his demonstration before the engineers and the press in the fall. This event would formally inaugurate his system in a public way. Indeed, it would be even more powerful than a transmission from the Empire State Building, because he would show the clarity of an FM transmission from a low power station.

Armstrong had his work cut out for him. To make FM a commercial reality and to develop it successfully, he would have to take on more assistants in his laboratory. In the summer of 1935 he hired three recent Columbia graduates with electrical engineering degrees, including John Bose.

Eager, intelligent, and devoid of the mathematical preconceptions about radio waves that so hobbled other engineers, Bose proved an excellent choice. He swiftly assumed an important place in the Marcellus Hartley laboratory. Now Armstrong had a trio of assistants on whom he could depend. Styles still handled the paperwork, placed orders for equipment, and maintained the general order of the laboratory; Shaughnessy made the models according to specifications given him; and Bose, directed by Armstrong, experimented with the basic circuits.

Bose's regard for Armstrong quickly developed into a reverence. The Major became his mentor. A sad man, now, who looked older than his forty-five years, he still smarted over the loss of his regenerative circuit. Yet he was driven onward demonically in his quest to perfect FM and bring it to the public. To Bose he was a "White Knight," who traveled with an old-fashioned, simple morality in a hostile land ruled by economic realities rather than scientific facts. "We want to keep the record straight," Armstrong would say time and again to his assistant when RCA or others in the industry declared his invention unworkable or of no value. He still supposed scientific facts would conquer rumor and innuendo. Bose would help him, always.

In the beginning Bose was grateful to have the job. "When I first went to him, the common expression was: 'engineers are a dime a dozen,' " Bose remembered. Considering the times the starting salary working for Armstrong was very good: $2,000 plus a bonus at Christmas. Bose quickly found that Armstrong ran a paternalistic organization, one that offered no benefits like a pension or health plan but would help out in an emergency. He never knew when he could expect a raise or what it might be. "Money was not that important to him," but of course it was to Bose, who was about to marry and expected to raise a family.

Work for Armstrong demanded total absorption, and Bose's wife, Elizabeth, learned to tolerate the demanding regimen. Bose arrived at the laboratory at 9 A.M., broke for lunch at noon or one, and then worked until dinner. Often he would return after dinner to continue work until 1:00 or 2:00 A.M. Usually the Major was there with him. Work went on six days a week. When Bose did get home, he was still not free from his job. The phone would ring late in the night or early in the morning, with Armstrong usually in mid-sentence when Bose lifted the receiver. "The man lived on the telephone," Elizabeth remembered, "calling John any time—especially Sunday mornings." "That's what drove me to church, regularly," said Bose, "to get some peace."

The first task Armstrong and his new staff faced was to prepare for the lecture and demonstration before the New York section of the Institute of Radio Engineers, scheduled for Tuesday evening, November 5, at the Engineering Societies Building on East 39th Street. He planned it to be a show, pure theater, and nothing could go wrong. It would feature an FM broadcast, the signals coming from Runyon's small amateur station in Yonkers. Working together Armstrong and Bose constructed a transmitter to operate with Runyon's power supply and installed a receiver in the lecture hall.

Armstrong calculated everything to contribute to the dramatic spectacle. Even the paper's title, "A Method of Reducing Disturbances in Radio Signalling by a System of Frequency Modulation," confounded the engineers, who had known for years such a thing to be impossible.

As he stood on the stage before the audience, Armstrong understood how important the lecture would be for him. After reminding his listeners of Carson's mathematical proofs and quoting some of the mathematician's sweeping statements, he described—without a single mathematical formula—how his system solved the problem of static and noise. Pictures of the transmitters and receivers at the Empire State and Haddonfield appeared on a screen; Armstrong methodically described each one. A sound film on which he had recorded both FM and a standard broadcast as they were received in Haddonfield during a thunderstorm proved FM's resistance to interference. Then, in a calculated laconic tone, he said quietly, "Now, suppose we have a little demonstration."

George Burghard, waiting in the wings, parted a curtain to reveal what appeared to be an ordinary receiver. The audience first heard the typical chatter associated with a radio between stations. But when Armstrong tuned it to Runyon's station, the speaker was profoundly quiet. For the first time, startled listeners were hearing a clear broadcast of *silence*.

No less startling a few seconds later was Randy Runyon's voice as he said with absolute clarity: "This is amateur station WQAG at Yonkers, New York, operating on frequency modulation at two and a half meters." Armstrong's "little demonstration" resembled the one Reginald Aubrey Fessenden gave on Christmas Eve, 1906. But instead of surprising his listeners by transmitting voices and music as Fessenden had done, Armstrong astonished them by transmitting sounds with a clarity and fidelity never heard before. More surprising and unexpected sounds were to come: Runyon pouring a glass of water, playing a short piano piece, crumpling a piece of paper and then tearing it; the reverberations of a small Oriental gong being tapped lightly; a phonograph record of a Sousa march; Runyon's son playing a tune on a guitar.

The demonstration was all the more impressive because Runyon was broadcasting over ultra short waves, which engineers had thought to be of little value. Yet because the signal to noise ratio of 100 to 1 was more than three times better than any AM broadcast could hope to offer, the sounds came through the receiver with a fidelity never before achieved.

Though still a member of the IRE, David Sarnoff was not among the audience that evening. Instead, he listened to a private demonstration the next day. ("He arrived with Fedora, cane, spats, and whatnot," Bose remembered. "To an engineer this was pretty creepy.") After the demonstration, Sarnoff told Armstrong he was awaiting yet another report from R. R. Beal, and, pending restructuring of RKO, he hoped he would be able to make arrangements about the invention. Still benignly stalling, he once again evaded the definitive answer that Armstrong sought.

The reaction of the newspapers was favorable but subdued; that of the engineering fraternity was polite but restrained. "He got the same response as Lincoln did when he delivered the Gettysburg Address," said Frank Gunther, who had been at the lecture. Gunther's analogy is apt. At the dedication of the hallowed ground on November 19, 1863, the president moved some with his speech and engendered a polite response in others, but few that day recognized the sublime and immortal character of his 269 words. Thus with Armstrong. Few of his colleagues had the prescience to see the importance of frequency modulation in 1935, as transistors, communications with spacecraft, stereo, digital storage and retrieval of information, and, of course, quality broadcasting existed only in the minds of the most visionary. For many witnesses that evening the momentousness of what Edwin Howard Armstrong had created was lost.

"The new year will undoubtedly witness the installation of frequency modulation transmitters operating in accordance with the principles that I recently described," Armstrong predicted confidently to a reporter for the

New York Times on the first Sunday in January 1936. The occasion was a survey of "radio's outlook" by "leaders of the industry." "The problems . . . which have their origin in the forces of nature have been completely solved," he continued. But then he added ominously, "The sole difficulties which remain . . . are those intangible forces so frequently set in motion by men, and in the origin of which lies vested interests, habits, customs, and legislation." But no matter, he would conquer "those intangible forces" just as he had those of nature, by careful presentation of the facts. And the facts, he felt sure, would leave no doubt in any listener's mind as to the importance of his invention.

In the same survey, Lee de Forest said from his house in Los Angeles, "Static interference continues to be radio's public enemy No. 1. It seems likely thus to remain."

Perhaps giving a hint of his thinking about frequency modulation, David Sarnoff spoke only of "advances in technique, improved services, and merchandise of the highest value per dollar ever offered, combined with the heightened interest in broadcasting always created by a Presidential year, make the outlook most encouraging for the radio industry." And he promised that RCA would "bring television out of the laboratory . . . for the first comprehensive field test in America." The future was bright for the industry, so long as it possessed the "practical common sense and vision" to realize the possibilities that lay before it. For Sarnoff, however, frequency modulation lay outside the realm of practical common sense, merely an expensive novelty, with limited applications and little practical value, that a public eager for television would never accept.

By 1936, in response to these clear signals of indifference from Sarnoff and his engineers, Armstrong had placed an order with RCA for powerful transmission equipment. He would prove the value of FM himself, and while he realized this was a dangerous and expensive course, with many snares along the way, he had no choice. He would follow it with determination.

The first snare turned out to be the recently chartered Federal Communications Commission. Armstrong found himself the victim of a comfortable alliance that had developed between the FCC and RCA, and particularly the engineering departments. Surely there was no greater ally than Charles Byron Jolliffe. A native of Mannington, West Virginia, Jolliffe had been educated first at the University of West Virginia in Charleston, and then at Cornell, where he received a Ph.D. in physics. After teaching at Cornell University and the University of West Virginia, he joined the Federal Radio Commission as its chief engineer. When the FRC metamorphosed into the

Federal Communications Commission in 1934, Jolliffe retained his post, something that came as "a jolt" to Democratic politicians in Washington, for he was known to be a staunch Republican.

In the commission's first annual report of important developments in radio for 1935, Jolliffe failed to mention FM, saying instead that his investigations showed that the very high frequencies that FM used were of little importance because broadcasts had a limited range of two to ten miles. Of course, the theory of FM's "limited range" that would plague Armstrong for years was a fiction. He had proven conclusively his system could travel eighty miles or more. While Jolliffe was not present at Armstrong's demonstration before the IRE in November, he had sent his assistant, Andrew D. Ring, who afterward characterized FM to a reporter from *Broadcast* magazine as "a visionary development years in advance of broadcasting's capacity to realize it." For Ring, "Major Armstrong's system in utterly impracticable—and the quest for static elimination must go on."

Though he did not realize it at the time, Armstrong was witnessing the first instance of bureaucratic collusion between the Radio Corporation of America and the Federal Communications Commission. Ideas, even rumor and innuendo, that the corporation propagated would be gathered by ever-willing engineers at the regulatory agency and turned into official pronouncements. Nor was the cross-pollination limited to ideas. Within a few months, those who had said the right thing within the agency often resigned to take a job with RCA. Shortly after he wrote the report for the Federal Communications Commission, RCA announced the appointment of Charles Jolliffe to head its engineering department. He would rise to be a vice president and briefly serve as acting president.

Armstrong petitioned the Federal Communications Commission for an experimental license to test FM in January 1936. Such applications from scientists and radio stations were routine, their approval a formality. Armstrong's went before Andrew Ring, who rejected it outright. Armstrong had to hire an attorney to speak in his behalf before a newly appointed chief engineer finally overruled his subordinate and granted a license in July 1936. Quietly Armstrong began to look about the New York City area for a tract of land on which he could erect a station.

By 1936, it became clear to all in radio that new portions of the spectrum were needed for television, police, and government communications as well as FM, so the Federal Communications Commission held hearings late that spring. Such hearings took on the aura of a free-for-all—each side using whatever means possible to get the best allocations for its own purposes.

Armstrong appeared to lobby for FM, while Sarnoff and his newest employee, Charles Jolliffe, appeared for RCA. "We are pleased to place at your disposal the information and experience of RCA gained from its operations in radio research, communications, broadcasting, manufacture and sales," Sarnoff began disingenuously, all the while neglecting to mention either the existence of frequency modulation or that the true source of RCA's information was Jolliffe. The Radio Corporation dealt with the "public treasure" of the radio spectrum, which must yield the maximum "under the stimulation of every new discovery." While he closed by recommending that the commission should make advance reservations of frequencies for "television, facsimile, and high frequency broadcasting," he made no mention of FM, contending instead that "ample allocation" should be made for national and international broadcasting of television.

Armstrong had come to realize that the testimony was simply part of a larger, deceptive pattern of actions on the part of RCA. As late as February 4, 1936, R. R. Beal had visited him at Columbia to say he had recommended to Sarnoff that RCA acquire a license for FM under his patents, and asked if the major was willing to grant one. Armstrong had replied affirmatively. Yet nothing had happened, and just two months later he learned that RCA patent attorneys—perhaps with Sarnoff's blessing—were trying to steal his invention. They had put the FM work of one of their own engineers, Murray G. Crosby, into interference with his, dissembling about the dates of Crosby's work and the sources of his inspiration. (Crosby's notebooks revealed, on examination, an FM circuit diagram he had received from Armstrong himself.) To Armstrong, this further evidence of the lack of morality within the RCA patent department suggested a lack of morality in RCA's leadership.

Sarnoff's silence about FM to the Federal Communications Commission amounted to duplicity, and its implication was ice clear to Armstrong. No longer could he afford to interpret benignly the evasions, the Crosby interference, and the call for more tests, because their cumulative effect on his FM invention would be devastating. No longer did his friend of more than two decades view developments in radio with the excitement he had brought to regeneration, superregeneration, and the superheterodyne. Instead he evaluated them with the cool scrutiny of an executive concerned not so much about the radio art as business. The warm relations he and Sarnoff had enjoyed for years belonged to the past.

The FCC did designate two small segments of the frequency spectrum to FM broadcasting and seven much wider portions to experimental television. Though not much, Armstrong knew it was sufficient space for him to demonstrate the capabilities of FM. He would travel about the country with the

huge phonograph discs and sound film on which he had recorded the Haddonfield tests of 1934, playing them for any broadcaster willing to listen. He
realized then he would have to attract the owners of smaller stations who
were being squeezed out by larger stations backed by the networks, "people
who could never hope to get into the front row of broadcasting" as he
characterized it, "with a 50 KW station." Surely they would be interested in
a new service that brought quality sounds into a radio.

At the same time, Armstrong pressed forward to build his own station that
would beam its programs into New York, the largest broadcasting market in
the world and the heart of the great powers NBC and CBS. Once people
compared the quality of his broadcasts with AM, they would, he felt sure,
adopt FM naturally. The plan required money; he ordered his broker to sell
another large block of RCA, realizing about a $300,000 profit. Moving
quickly, he purchased an eleven-acre tract on the palisades in Alpine, New
Jersey, across from his Yonkers home. As an undergraduate at Columbia, he
had conducted a series of experiments there, draping long aerials over the
steep escarpment. Of a much more momentous nature, these FM experiments demanded careful planning: a two-story brick and cinderblock building
to house his station along with several outbuildings for machinery; transmitting equipment from RCA and REL, about $136,900 for rectifiers, amplifiers,
tubes (some specially designed for the system), microphones, turntables,
program mixing units, quartz crystals, and instruments; and an impressive
425-foot-tall transmitting tower, designed and erected by the American
Bridge Company. With three wide arms that suggested "a three-barred Lor-
raine cross," it would have lots of space for aerials and future experiments.
From its top one could see down to the entrance of New York Harbor and
east to the tip of Long Island. Standing on the palisades at a point 500 feet
above the Hudson, his tower would be visible from most points on Riverside
Drive, as well as from David Sarnoff's office on the fifty-third story of the
RCA Building.

One day in mid-April 1937, Howard and Marion Armstrong went across
the George Washington Bridge to the woods of the Alpine site to conduct a
private ceremony. Wielding "a little three dollar axe" Howard chopped down
a tree, the first to fall to make room for his tower and station. Carefully, they
saved the first chip that fell to the ground as a memento. Then they popped
a bottle of champagne they had brought for the occasion and toasted his new
venture.

After the construction began, Armstrong visited almost daily to oversee its
progress. By the end of the year, with the tower finished and work on the
transmitter building progressing swiftly, he set about to construct the trans-

mitting antenna. Operating as he was in the little-understood area of the radio spectrum, he had to make numerous adjustments before it operated correctly.

Constructing the tower gave him great pleasure, for it demanded he climb to great heights and swing high above the ground in a bosun's chair. That winter and spring he worked without cease whatever the weather. Falling ice proved to be a problem, until he constructed a coffinlike wooden box to cover his head, neck, and back. From his bosun's chair he could make out his house at 1032 Warburton Avenue across the river and no doubt remember the tower he had constructed almost three decades before. There had been many changes: He had recently paid $70 to have his first tower removed; now only the two supporting posts remained in the back yard. His sister Edith, who had helped him build it, had married and moved away, while his other sister Ethel had married his friend Bradley Hammond (in a ceremony performed in the yard beside the house) and lived next door. And the most important change of all: his mother had suffered a serious fall in 1936 and lay in a hospital. She would die later that year at the age of seventy-eight.

By June 1938, when Armstrong began testing his system at a low power, the introduction of FM began to move more swiftly. His work had not escaped the notice of broadcasters and manufacturers, some of whom did not care for the way RCA operated. Indeed, RCA's deprecation of Armstrong's system actually encouraged some to consider it seriously. Many of them had heard Armstrong speak or had witnessed a demonstration and were following the events on the Hudson with interest. The demonstration at Alpine was remarkable: when Runyon sawed a piece of wood, the saw could be identified as a rip or a crosscut; when he struck a match, the match could be identified as paper or wood. The demonstration usually concluded with Runyon performing what Armstrong regarded as the ultimate test, making a scotch highball. At his transmitter in Yonkers, Randy Runyon would drop ice into a glass, pour in the scotch, and then "using a siphon" demonstrate "the fizz of the charged water in the highball." The demonstration concluded with Runyon toasting Armstrong.

Among those convinced were the management at General Electric in Schenectady, John Shepard, the president of the Yankee Network in Boston; and Franklin Doolittle, an old acquaintance of Armstrong's.

Armstrong had come to General Electric late in 1937 with an order to build twenty-five FM receivers at $400 each. He planned to use them to demonstrate his system around New York. GE had never really recovered from the antitrust settlement of 1932 that had enjoined it from manufacturing radio equipment for two years. Company executives in Schenectady, especially W. R. G. Baker, who had recently returned to GE as a vice president, saw FM as a way to compete with its former partner. Though he had given a negative assessment of FM when working for RCA, Baker now realized the system's merits. GE became the first company to take out a license to manufacture FM radios, and in December presented Armstrong with a check for $22.66—the first royalty he had received since he had been awarded his patents in 1933. He never cashed the check.

In its own tests of FM, General Electric discovered something that even Armstrong had not known: unlike those of AM, FM signals on the same wavelength do not interfere with each other. An FM radio simply picks up the stronger signal. The implications of this discovery, which engineers called the "capture effect," were momentous for the development of FM, for it allowed a series of low-power stations to operate exclusively in nearby communities and enabled more broadcasting stations to use a small part of the electromagnetic spectrum.

Armstrong had first learned of the Yankee Network's interest in FM when its chief engineer, Paul De Mars, showed up at the FCC hearing in 1936 to testify in favor of the system. At that time, De Mars reported on some tests he had made that showed "no improvement in broadcasting services . . . in the very high frequencies with amplitude modulation." After the FCC granted the space for testing FM, the network's president, John Shepard III, began talks with Armstrong about licensing the right to broadcast on FM.

Four years older than Armstrong, John Shepard had taken up wireless as a hobby in his youth. In 1922, he began broadcasting from his family's Boston department store over station WNAC. Soon he linked WNAC with stations in Providence and Bridgeport and organized the Yankee Network. Shepard pioneered in broadcasting baseball and hockey games to Boston over his network and organized a newsgathering service. Unlike some broadcasters, he cared about the quality of his programs. In time, he helped to found the Mutual Broadcasting Network. He respected Armstrong and had much in common with him. Like the major, he found himself outside the powerful structure that dominated the broadcasting industry. He would be unable to secure a 50,000 watt station. In FM he saw his chance to increase his share of listeners in New England. On Mount Asnebumskit outside Worcester, Massachusetts, Shepard built his own experimental FM station.

Another person to become interested, Franklin Doolittle, a professor of mathematics at Yale and an avid radio amateur, had known Armstrong for many years. Early in 1939, Doolittle decided to open a station at the top of West Rock in Meriden, Connecticut. W1XPW began experimental broadcasting late that year.

Newspapers had been taking notice of the new system, too. Early in January 1939, the *New York Times* reported that FM represented a challenge to the "air monopoly," but suggested in an editorial in mid-January that changing radio sets "was almost like changing the gauge of railways to accommodate wider and more luxurious cars." On July 18, 1939, when W2XMN, Alpine, went on the air with 35,000 watts power, some of these doubts were dispelled. Among the first broadcasts were relays from the classical music station WQXR in New York, but with full fidelity and no static.

That month, General Electric introduced the first two commercial FM receivers, its "golden tone" radios that "set the pace for spectacular realism in high-fidelity reception." One sold for $70; another, both an AM and an FM receiver, sold for $225. "Reduces static to the Vanishing Point!" GE's advertisements proclaimed it was "the greatest radio sensation since the superheterodyne."

At the same time, General Electric was planning for its own FM station, W2XOY Schenectady. In November 1940, on a hill in the Helderbergs south of the city, Edith Alexanderson, daughter of the inventor, christened the transmitting tower by smashing a vacuum tube—a bottle of nothing instead of a bottle of champagne. W. R. G. Baker presided over the ceremonies for GE. At 8:30 Wednesday evening, November 20, 1940, 2,000 fans went to Proctor's Theater in Schenectady to hear what General Electric advertised as its "Hour of Charm." For 44 cents (or 75 cents for loge and box seats) they heard the first live FM music broadcast, Phil Spitalny's All Girl Orchestra, featuring Evelyn Kay and her violin.

Earlier that year, a broadcast of even greater importance had taken place. At 6:01 on Friday evening, January 5, 1940, Armstrong, Randy Runyon, Franklin Doolittle, and the Yankee Network participated in an experiment with monumental implications for all long distance communications: a radio relay via FM. From his small FM station in Yonkers, Runyon broadcast a program that Armstrong picked up at W2XMN in Alpine. From there the signal traveled to W1XPW in Meriden. Doolittle relayed it to Shepard's station in Worcester, which sent it on to a station he had on Mount Washington. Engineers at Mount Washington relayed the signal to Boston where it was picked up by standard broadcast. From there it traveled back to Yonkers. The relay of 825 miles had taken but a fraction of a second.

The idea of a radio relay was an old one that networks had tried before, but the results had been vastly inferior to relays through telephone lines. Armstrong, Runyon, Shepard, and Doolittle had actually made similar experiments in late 1939, but never one so extensive as this. Armstrong demonstrated that an FM relay produced superior results. By changing transmission from FM to AM, Armstrong had given graphic proof of the differences in quality of the signals. Observers noted the marked deterioration of the tonal range when the signal was converted to AM or traveled through telephone lines. Armstrong found his experiment especially gratifying because he had used only "make-shift" apparatus and low power, and, he said, "the broadcast went from Yonkers to Mt. Washington without using an inch of wire."

Word of the experiment no doubt staggered the communications industry, especially AT&T, which derived substantial revenues from leasing long-distance telephone lines to the networks. Bell Labs had hardly been in the forefront of this new technology. As late as 1935, it had stated that "The 'song of the whirling electrons' sets a natural limit and will always be in the way." Now Armstrong's FM was leapfrogging the Bell engineers again with a new technology that threatened company monopoly over long distance communication. It had cost John Shepard $25,000 to establish his FM relay, while AT&T would have charged the Yankee Network $70,000 plus operating expenses for a wire line. Armstrong had proven the power of FM to broadcast across the country without paying any fees to AT&T.

RCA had been keenly watching these developments and carefully planning its own response to Armstrong's invention. For the most part, its public strategy had been to ignore Armstrong's experiments, all the while broadcasting its plans to introduce commercial television. "Television in the home is now technically feasible," Sarnoff declared in October 1938, announcing that he had scheduled the first program for the opening of the 1939 New York World's Fair.

The choice of the World's Fair site was not accidental. Located on the "Avenue of Progress," and shaped like a gargantuan vacuum tube, the RCA Pavilion symbolized the power of the electron in the modern world, and especially the power of the corporation that controlled it. Inside, visitors marveled at the floor model television housed in clear plastic that suggested the ultimate in both technical achievement and modern design. On April 20, 1939, in the garden behind the pavilion, Sarnoff strode up to a podium to declare, "Now we add radio sight to sound":

It is with a feeling of humbleness that I come to this moment of announcing the birth of a new art so important in its implications that it is bound to affect all society . . . an art which shines like a torch in a troubled world . . . a creative force we must learn to utilize for the benefit of all mankind.

An RCA camera at the "Avenue of Patriots" focused on the trylon and perisphere. To the few hundred watching sets about the city, the scenes were wondrous. Television had entered the modern world.

Despite Sarnoff's coup, RCA was worried about Alpine. Late in 1939, the corporation's transmitter advanced development section issued a confidential paper that described "the principal claimed advantages and disadvantages" of FM. Still caught up in the need to attack the system, the authors devoted just half a page to FM's advantages and five pages to its "disadvantages." But the authors did state some of their very serious concerns. "As of December 6th, there were 40 stations either licensed or about to be by the FCC for frequency modulation. Number of allocations reported increasing," said the authors breathlessly. While they discounted high fidelity advantages of FM, they were clearly worried: "the facts faced are, that it is being and will probably continue to be extensively played up." Indeed, the authors feared, broadcasters would "offer program material having a wide frequency range." The implications were clear that RCA would have to do a lot of engineering work if it hoped to compete.

"The FCC has called an informal hearing on frequency modulation," the authors reported at the end of a section dealing with "activities outside RCA." When the hearings got under way before the full commission on March 18, 1940, RCA's counsel, Frank Wozencraft, surprised everyone when he told the commissioners that the corporation believed that "frequency modulation on sound broadcasting . . . can be made available to the public," though he cautioned them not to make a "snap judgment about the allocation of FM and television channels." At last, it seemed to all, Armstrong had won; Sarnoff had capitulated.

It was a prudent gesture. By 1939, Sarnoff had realized that the tower at Alpine represented more than the folly of an eccentric inventor and that FM would not simply fade away. He had decided to yield as gracefully as possible. Realizing that the enmity that had grown between Armstrong and his corporation would make rapprochement particularly delicate, he turned to Gano Dunn to act as his agent. An engineer who had built thirteen of RCA's transoceanic radio stations, a director of the corporation, a supporter of the Hartley Laboratory, and a friend of Armstrong, Dunn proved a good intermediary.

Dunn made his first overture in a letter of June 14, 1939. Armstrong replied with a letter that recounted "some facts" about FM and RCA's mixed responses to the invention since he had shown it to David Sarnoff in 1933. For years, he concluded, "members of the RCA organization have advised against the use of my system." Dunn replied by recalling the cordial relations the inventor had enjoyed with RCA for many years.

Another letter followed in which Armstrong revealed the depth of the pain he had suffered when RCA had opposed him in the regeneration suit.

"In 1933 it became to the Corporation's advantage . . . to prove something which was not so." His reputation had been tarnished by "legal chicanery" which "misrepresented the technical facts and won the case." The implications were clear: how could he license his patents with a corporation whose legal department had acted so unconscionably? Might he not be abused once again?

Nevertheless, Dunn persisted patiently, gradually bringing Armstrong to the question of licensing his patents. In September, from Bass Harbor on Mount Desert Island, Maine, he sent the inventor a postcard:

> Am thinking of you very often and wishing I had F. M. on boat. The static has made the war news almost unreadable a large part of the time.

Later that fall negotiations began in earnest between Armstrong and Lenox Lohr, the new president of NBC. Armstrong became more cordial. Perhaps he might put a transmitter he had used in his Alpine tests "at the disposal" of NBC for FM broadcasting, he told Lohr. "If there is any way which I can be of help to you, please do not hesitate to call," he wrote at the end of October 1939, "I will be glad to drop over at your convenience." At the same time Al McCormack and Otto S. Schairer, vice president in charge of the patent department at RCA, began meeting to discuss a manufacturing license.

By June 1940, RCA made a firm offer with liberal terms: $1 million for nonexclusionary license. Armstrong said no.

"Now just a minute, Major," said Al McCormack when he learned of Armstrong's rejection. "That's the first time I ever heard of an inventor turning down a million for a nonexclusionary license." An astounding and uncompromising decision, it demonstrated once again Armstrong's inflexible nature. Had he accepted the offer, there never would have been a lawsuit. Other companies, who were waiting to see what RCA did, would also have fallen into line. But he would not think of it. He had sold licenses to other manufacturers, General Electric, Zenith, and Stromberg Carlson among them, which gave him 2 percent of their earnings on receivers and equipment. RCA would take those terms or they would have none at all. The greatest concession his lawyers could win from their client was a reduction of the royalty to 1 3/4 percent. It was a procrustean proposal that Sarnoff could never accept.

Nor was Otto Schairer about to recommend submitting to Armstrong's terms. He was disturbed that Armstrong wanted to license a system. He secured an opinion from a patent lawyer that the FM licensing arrangement was "an unlawful use of the patent to suppress competition in unpatented devices." Despite a contrary opinion from one of Armstrong's attorneys, which the inventor sent to RCA at the end of November, Sarnoff refused to purchase the license under Armstrong's terms.

━

"He Wins Again!" declared the headline on the cover of FM, a new magazine for "broadcasters, dealers, service men," that appeared in November 1940. Armstrong's photograph appeared above the headline. The accompanying article ranked the inventor "number one" on the basis of his contributions to radio, of which FM was "his latest and greatest." Indeed, it seemed he had won, and recovered from the loss of prestige he had suffered over the loss of the regeneration suits. The following January, the Franklin Institute awarded Armstrong its Franklin medal "in recognition of his pioneer work in Regeneration and the Oscillating Vacuum Tube Circuits, the invention of the Superheterodyne Circuit, the Superregeneration, and a system of wide-swing Frequency Modulation." The institute called FM "the features of a revolutionary improvement."

Armstrong was beginning to win financially, too. As the FCC was deliberating in March, it had 109 applications for FM stations. Since May 20, when it allotted the 42–50 megacycle band for commercial FM broadcasting, it received more than 500, and the flood showed no sign of abating. Checks were coming in from Freed Eisenmann, Zenith, Scott, Stromberg Carlson, General Electric, and REL, among others. Only Philco Radio Corporation in Philadelphia was producing a cheap imitation FM radio, but after Armstrong protested, Philco's president admitted his mistake and suggested he would soon take a license to produce a genuine set. It seemed that almost every week engineers were discovering new applications for wide-band FM, especially for police, emergency, and military applications. Already the Chicago police department and state police in Connecticut had adopted FM for radio communications with their automobiles, and other police forces would follow. In March, the National Television Standards Committee decided that FM should be the standard for the audio portion of the TV broadcast signal. "Barring some dislocation of the economic system as a result of the war, inside of the next three or four years, there will be more FM listeners than there are now for AM," Armstrong predicted that spring. The only threat FM faced was war.

By 1919 Lee de Forest had found the field of radio too "crowded" for his tastes. He turned his attention to creating sound motion pictures. For a time he succeeded, selling an invention he called "phonofilm."

"You are my poem, and my song." In 1930 de Forest met and married his fourth wife, Marie Mosquini, called "the most shapely girl in Hollywood." He was fifty-seven, she twenty-four. Marie abandoned her career to attend to her husband.

By the thirties de Forest's fame was being eclipsed by others, as this 1934 newspaper headline suggests.

January 21, 1934   SUNDAY MIRROR MAGAZINE SECTION   Page 19

I Wonder What's Become of

The Father of Radio, Dr. Lee De Forest, Whose Inventions Have Made Millions For Others While He Continues to Work Long Hours in a Modest Hollywood Laboratory

"Every great institution is the lengthened shadow of a man."
—Ralph Waldo Emerson.

EVERY time you reach for the dials and tune in your favorite dance orchestra, your favorite comedy team, your favorite news commentator, you pay unconscious tribute to one of the greatest names in the realm of modern science.

Every time that President Roosevelt speaks to the nation in a country-wide hook-up, or that millions listen to the play-by-play account of a World Series baseball game, or share in the thrill of programs carried halfway around the globe, an aging and almost obscure figure in a California laboratory might rightfully rise and take a bow.

Behind an industry in which billions of dollars are invested, a force which sways multitudes in mass emotional response, an invention which has revolutionised modern communication, is one man's invention. All this could not have happened without the achievement of Dr. Lee De Forest, once showered with world attention but now working modestly in a Hollywood laboratory.

Yet the millions which he has put in other pockets do not line his own. Comfortable, but by no means rich, past 60, he works and lives today with the zeal of the scientist still burning in his veins.

When Dr. De Forest, recognized "father of radio," invented the audion tube, he hoped that he had made possible a means of world communication which would bring nations closer together in spiritual harmony. Instead of a mere broadcasting device of commercial value and political importance, he dreamed that radio would further the cause of universal peace and establish a "Parliament of Man."

The "Parliament of Man" doesn't appear to have developed very rapidly, and the rumbles of international ill will which reach the ears of Dr. De Forest do not sound like the overture to universal peace.

But if he is disappointed in some of

The Inventor's Present Wife Is His Fourth. She Was Formerly Marie Mosquini, Known as "The Shapeliest Girl on the Screen" When She Deserted Pictures for Matrimony.

Following their divorce in 1911, he married Mary Mayo, a concert singer. This knot was likewise untied by the divorce method.

Before the decree became

Throughout the twenties the battle raged between Armstrong and de Forest over the rights to regeneration. At one point Armstrong raised a specially designed large flag embossed with 1113149, the number of his regenerative patent and posed with Marion at the base of his antenna. On clear days Lee de Forest could see it from his house.

But de Forest won the patent suit in Supreme Court, *twice*. He based his claim on this entry that his assistant made in a notebook.

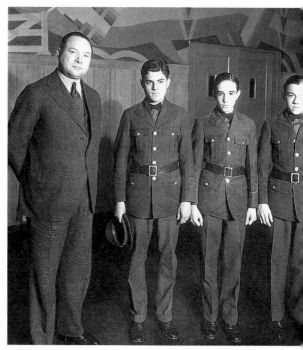

"I don't get ulcers; I give them" David Sarnoff often said. Throughout the twenties David Sarnoff moved from strength to strength within the Radio Corporation of America—from commercial manager to vice president, to executive vice president, and finally, in 1930, to president. When Marconi visited an RCA station, Sarnoff assumed a pose that patterned his mentor's.

Sarnoff, Joseph Kennedy, and an RCA aide.

In his office on the fifty-third floor of the RCA Building at Rockefeller Center, Sarnoff had a special telegraph key installed in his desk. He sometimes tapped out messages to others in the corporation.

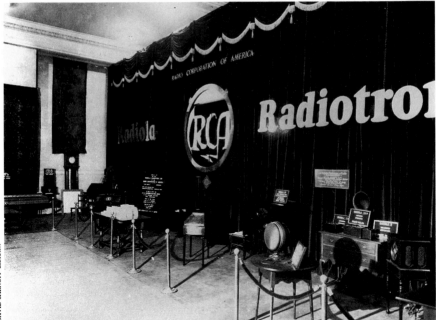

In the twenties a large part of RCA's business was in the manufacture of radio tubes, which they advertised in unusual ways. In 1926 Sarnoff formed the National Broadcasting Company the first important radio network. Its first president neither owned nor listened to a radio.

By the thirties radio had taken over American lives and homes. Listeners experienced an event as it happened, witnessing it with their ears and imaginations. Rather than learning of the *Hindenburg* explosion the next day, people felt the power of the inferno the moment it occurred.

Armstrong's laboratory at Columbia.

Defeated in the courts by de Forest, Edwin Howard Armstrong was in eclipse during much of the twenties and early thirties.

Armstrong with Marconi by wireless shed.

The Revolution. "After ten years of eclipse, my star is again rising," Armstrong wrote in July 1934, after his first successful transmission test of FM. RCA rejected FM as impractical. Not to be deterred, Armstrong built his own 425-foot FM tower at Alpine, New Jersey. By 1940 FM signals were being transmitted around New England over the Yankee Network.

David Sarnoff had placed RCA's resources behind the development of television, which he announced at the 1939 New York World's Fair.

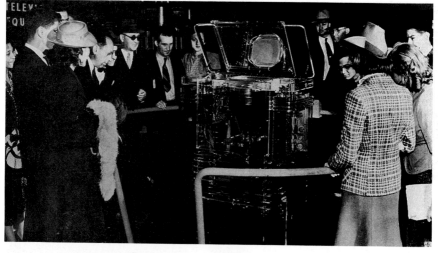

Sarnoff with Arturo Toscanini.

"Now we add radio sight to sound," said David Sarnoff when he presented television before the RCA pavilion at the 1939 World's Fair.

A remote broadcast television van at Rockefeller Center.

Over the years Sarnoff (pictured here with Franklin Roosevelt) knew and cultivated every president from Herbert Hoover to Richard Nixon. In World War II, Sarnoff (shown in full military dress) directed the communications for D-day. For his service he was made a general.

Patriots. Sarnoff struck dozens of poses in his dress military uniforms. After the war he insisted on being addressed as "General Sarnoff." Howard Armstrong gave the United States Government free use of his patents and worked to perfect a new system of FM radar. After the war Sarnoff and Armstrong received the Legion of Merit from Major General Harry C. Ingles of the Army Signal Corps.

GENERAL ELECTRIC HALL OF HISTORY

The end of the war brought no end to the hostilities between Sarnoff and Armstrong. RCA developed an FM system that it claimed was different and better than Armstrong's and licensed it to other manufacturers, thereby denying the inventor millions in royalties. *Top:* Armstrong demonstrating his equipment to W.R.G. Baker of General Electric. *Bottom:* Armstrong at 1032.

ARMSTRONG FAMILY ARCHIVES

"Until I'm dead or broke." In 1948 Armstrong sued RCA for patent infringement, a long and costly process that consumed his income, shattered his marriage, and ultimately destroyed his life.

Armstrong testifying at one of the numerous government hearings about FM.

Howard and Marion Armstrong in the last known photograph of the couple.

Headline from the front page of the *New York Herald Tribune*, February 2, 1954.

David Sarnoff at his office on the fifty-third floor of the RCA Building, Rockefeller Center.

Inventor of FM

Armstrong Writes Note To Wife, Dies in Plunge

Maj. Edwin H. Armstrong, sixty-three, inventor of frequency modulation (FM) and one of the nation's leading radio pioneers, plunged to death yesterday from his thirteenth-floor apartment at River House, 435 E. 52d St.

Maj. Armstrong was found, fully clothed to overcoat, hat and gloves, on a third-floor extension at 10:30 a. m. by Alfred Henrichs, building maintenance man. He had apparently been dead several hours.

Police found a two-page note to his wife, Mrs. Marion Armstrong, signed "Ed," in which he said it was "heartbreaking" that he could not see her again and continued: "How deep and bitterly I regret what has happened to us."

The note, written in pencil on yellow legal paper, said he would give his life to be able to turn back to the time "when we were so happy and free" and ended:

Maj. Armstrong

Columbia University and the winner of a score of awards in-

Lee de Forest, pictured here in his study of his Hollywood house, lived until June 30, 1961.

In the twilight of his life, de Forest sought the recognition he thought was his due. Here he appears with David Sarnoff, at the dedication of a plaque on the site of one of his first broadcasts.

The ultimate triumph of the strange radio wars belonged to Marion Armstrong, who won all of her husband's FM suits after his death. Here she poses with the superheterodyne radio Howard Armstrong had given her as a wedding present in 1923.

11

THE WIZARD WAR

ALL OUR FACILITIES AND PERSONNEL ARE READY AND AT YOUR INSTANT SER-
VICE. WE AWAIT YOUR COMMANDS, wrote David Sarnoff in an RCA radiogram
to Franklin Delano Roosevelt at 4:50 P.M., December 7, 1941, less than
three hours after radio announcers told startled listeners that the Japanese
had attacked Pearl Harbor. Signing his cable with his titles PRESIDENT, RADIO
CORPORATION OF AMERICA AND CHAIRMAN OF THE BOARD, NATIONAL BROAD-
CASTING COMPANY (almost as many letters as the message itself), Sarnoff was
asserting what all tacitly understood: that radio communications as well as
broadcasting would be essential to the prosecution of the new war. And with
30,000 workers and manufacturing plants in Camden and Harrison, New
Jersey, Bloomington and Indianapolis, Indiana, and Hollywood, California,
RCA stood as the most powerful communication enterprise in the world,
prepared to grow even bigger producing military equipment.

Much had changed since the last great war when Winston Churchill had
declared radio unreliable. Then naval captains had to keep their battle
cruisers within sight of one another at all times, communicating "by searchlight flashes," and semaphore flags. Now, as Churchill knew better than
anyone, the present conflict was a chilling "wizard war," waged with ever
more sophisticated scientific instruments of destruction. Many involved the
use of radio. In the Battle of Britain, from July to September 1940, the
English had relied on ear and sight stations along the coast to warn of
German planes crossing the channel for an attack on London. Ear trumpets
resembling gargantuan cornucopia and carried on the backs of trucks listened
for the approaching enemy. But soon electronics began to take over. The

Germans began navigating their planes through fog and cloud by fixing them on radio signals transmitted from stations on the continent. The British responded by deflecting the signals with transmissions of their own and sending the planes off course. The British acknowledged one of the greatest advances in the wizard war in June 1941, when they announced they had developed "radiolocation," a way of using radio waves to detect the approach of enemy planes. It was the first practical radar.

Radio brought this war into American homes with a vividness and speed never known before. As Sarnoff said just before Christmas 1941, Americans were now able to "hear history before it is written." Instantaneous reports came from the Pacific, Europe, and Asia as engineers switched from circuit to circuit. At 12:30 on the afternoon of December 8, 1941, when President Roosevelt proclaimed that "the American people, in their righteous might, will win through to absolute victory," he spoke to the largest daytime audience ever assembled to hear a broadcast. The next night, when he called on Americans to unite "in the most tremendous undertaking in our national history," 80 percent of the country's 56 million radios were turned on.

Radio went across the oceans, too, delivering reports from home to U.S. troops around the world. Colonel Thomas H. A. Lewis, formerly a vice president at Young and Rubicam, organized the Armed Forces Radio Service "for information, education, and entertainment." By the war's end, it had grown to more than 800 stations, each playing American music and drama and delivering American news on "V-discs," special phonograph records made in the United States and shipped around the world. Through his connections with Young and Rubicam and his marriage to the screen actress Loretta Young, Lewis arranged for Hollywood stars like Bing Crosby, Dinah Shore, Bob Hope, Jimmy Durante, and Frank Sinatra to take part.

Actually, RCA, along with other communication companies, had been preparing for the United States entry into the war for many months. Over the past year, government defense contracts had increased steadily to approximately $36.5 million, stretching the corporation's ability to produce equipment for both military and domestic use. When the Federal Communications Commission authorized commercial television broadcasting at the beginning of May 1941 (with a 525-line picture *and* FM sound), Sarnoff knew his company was not able to fill its defense orders and make TV sets. This did not bother Sarnoff, as sales of television sets had been disappointing since he had introduced the new medium at the World's Fair. The country still suffered from the lingering effects of the depression. No, military preparation must come first. Television development would continue, but under the mantle of military research. Increasingly, Vladimir Zworykin, head of television development at RCA, would turn his attention to the medium's military applications. Good patriotic inclinations made for good business, too; government orders would carry the company.

For many months, Sarnoff had been preparing RCA for war and generating publicity about his activities through RCA's Office of Information. In July 1941, RCA introduced the "alert receiver," a device that would turn on a radio automatically and ring a bell to summon listeners to hear announcement of an attack. It was "the modern Paul Revere," RCA publicity agents proclaimed, and they arranged for Sarnoff and New York Mayor Fiorello La-Guardia (who was also national director of Civilian Defense) to give a public demonstration before newspaper reporters. That September, from his office in the RCA Building, Sarnoff had launched his "beat the promise" campaign with lots of fanfare. After tapping out the title on the telegraph key at his desk, Sarnoff spoke over special transmission lines to his workers at the RCA plant in Camden. "Defense has had and will continue to have the right of way in all our plants," he declared, repeating the promise every employee had signed a few days earlier: "I pledge myself to put forth my best efforts not only to fulfill the obligations which we have undertaken to meet the requirements of our national preparedness program, but, wherever possible, to beat that promise."

In this "promise" and his general war preparations, Sarnoff saw an opportunity to stress efficient and sensible management to his employees, the same as he had always practiced himself. "Time is vital, materials are vital" he wrote to RCA workers in a characteristically brief memo in January 1942, imploring them to conduct all operations "with the utmost efficiency." The policy he adopted for RCA was similar to the one he had always followed himself: "Keep your desk stripped for action. . . . Eliminate dead wood from files. . . . Eliminate unnecessary interruptions of others. . . . Be concise and definite in letters and memoranda."

In 1939, the United States government was trying to revive a fighting force that had lain dormant for twenty years. Typical of the inadequacy of the military was the U.S. Army Signal Corps. Fewer than 4,000 men served in the corps in care of all wire and radio communications, photography, and training films, even the army's flocks of carrier pigeons. For communication, the corps preferred wire over wireless, and relied chiefly on the dots and dashes of the Morse code. Voice radio was not yet common. Though engineers had made wire lightweight—as light as thirty pounds for a mile—laying it from the back of a horse-drawn cart was not unusual.

Disturbing proof of the crude state of communications appeared at Fort Knox, Kentucky, in late October 1939, where General Roger B. Colton, director of the Signal Corps Laboratory, had ordered all radio equipment brought for demonstration and evaluation. It was a huge and primitive display, particularly the "mobile" radios. Most units had manual rather than crystal tuning, which meant the sets required an expert to operate them and still drifted from their frequency. Usually they were huge "portables," requiring two men to transport, or, better, a horse or a truck. Typical of the antiquated gear was the army's behemoth SCR 197, a mobile communication unit the size of a house trailer, pulled behind an underpowered truck. Inside the trailer, equipment was crowded floor to roof—transmitters, receivers, and an inadequate power supply. Even more disturbing, the unit was not truly mobile as it could not operate while the truck was moving. Officers testing the equipment wondered how it would perform in a large-scale war, the sort that was taking place in Europe at that moment.

Even more disheartening to General Colton was the fact that few seemed really worried about the situation. Indeed, many observers were more interested in a novel water heater that an officer of the quartermaster corps happened to be demonstrating concurrently. "Ample hot water was something all could appreciate," said one colonel; "radio was still a mystery."

Such disappointing results at Fort Knox, and the results of other maneuvers in 1939 and 1940, confirmed "numerous and painful failures of signal communication." Radios frequently failed, but even when they worked, operators found they were subject to devastating interference, as more and more soldiers wanted to communicate over the same frequency. One observer proclaimed the signal corps equipment—radio and wire—"inadequate not merely for the oncoming war but even for a play war."

Among the disappointments of the Fort Knox demonstration had been an FM transmitter and receiver that General Colton had ordered specially. They did not work well. The receiver purchased from General Electric was not sensitive enough and the transmitter (which the signal corps engineers had built at Fort Monmouth) proved unreliable. While the demonstration was in progress, the frustrated general asked Armstrong for help. Armstrong in turn asked an engineer from Radio Engineering Laboratories to fly down to Kentucky to demonstrate an FM transmitter and receiver. While the results were far from conclusive, the infantry, mechanized cavalry, and field artillery recognized the potential of FM for their operations. It was, the field artillery board said, "the most promising line of future development," and they urged its adoption.

But FM faced the same intransigence and caused the same divergence in opinion with the military as it had with broadcasters. One of the most closed-minded and intractable about the matter of Armstrong's FM was

Colonel Louis B. Bender. As head of the signal corps research and development division, Bender had the power to place formidable obstacles in the way of FM's adoption—and he did. Not even Armstrong's personal demonstrations in Washington in early 1940, in which the inventor showed FM's ability to transmit high fidelity and a teletypewriter signal simultaneously, impressed the colonel. While finding such demonstrations "interesting," Bender thought FM of "little practical value," adding, "We are not nearly so ready to make use of it as the broadcast people appear to be." The colonel's reluctance to develop FM may be traced to RCA. The corporation, he said, "had developed some pertinent facts that the enthusiasts for this system had conveniently forgotten to publicize [and that] took much of the wind out of the broad claims made."

Only after the infantry and field artillery pressed for development did Bender allow that FM might be useful in trucks and tanks. But at the same time, the colonel blocked funds for the system's development.

A veteran of fighting such inertia, Armstrong would not be deterred. On his own initiative, he and engineers at Radio Engineering Laboratories made twenty-eight mobile FM radio sets for the First Army to try during its summer maneuvers in 1940. Since these were overwhelmingly successful, the chiefs of the field artillery, infantry, and armored force (successor to the mechanized cavalry) petitioned for more tests.

In the end, General Colton had to step into the dispute between Colonel Bender and the advocates of FM. After further tests of some mobile sets that a young electronics entrepreneur, Fred M. Link, had developed for the Connecticut State Police, the general decided in favor of FM "for mobile and portable field." Colton's decision had been a difficult and daring one, perhaps, as Armstrong said, "the most difficult . . . in the history of radio." Henceforth the army would use short-range FM sets in its tanks and jeeps. FM officially became a part of the military.

While companies like Link Radio as well as Western Electric and Motorola would make millions of dollars manufacturing FM radios for the military, Howard Armstrong chose a more generous and patriotic course. He should not make any money on his patent, he reasoned, as it would help the nation to survive the challenge he saw coming. With clear and simple decisiveness, he addressed a letter on March 10, 1941, to Henry L. Stimson, secretary of war, waiving all patent royalties "on any apparatus for frequency-modulation radio communication which may be purchased by the War Department" for the duration of "the present emergency." "No lawyer ever advised him to do that," recalled Armstrong's counsel, Dana Raymond. "He did it himself and with no encouragement."

Gradually, other units of the army as well as the navy adopted FM. Radio engineers adapted FM circuits for tanks, jeeps, talk between ships, and, most important, walkie-talkies. The navy used it in amphibious landing vehicles as well as buoy detectors of enemy submarines.

"One of the main reasons the American Army moved so fast against the Germans was . . . fast communications," wrote an enthusiastic lieutenant in the signal corps. "I *know* the war in Europe would have lasted longer if we hadn't had FM on our side." Wire communications would surely have failed, for modern armies moved too swiftly for telephone men to lay wire. Despite its wide bandwidth, FM offered soldiers the chance to communicate quickly by voice, without jamming or interference. In that lieutenant's infantry division there were 81 walkie-talkies and about 150 larger sets, yet he reported he could not recall a single instance when his walkie-talkie was made inoperative because of interference. "FM saved lives and won battles because it speeded our communications and enabled us to move more quickly than the Germans, who had to depend on AM."

The government quietly acknowledged FM's importance in another way, too. In 1942, when the threat of enemy attack by submarines on the Atlantic coast seemed imminent, the government ordered all AM broadcasting stations in New England to have an FM radio permanently on and tuned to one of the stations in the Yankee Network. In the event of a German attack, the government could issue bulletins and orders instantaneously and clearly through the network to the disparate AM stations in the Northeast.

~~

World War II brought into question the subject of patents and the rights to manufacture inventions. In World War I, the government had simply appropriated such rights for itself and suspended all patent infringement cases, but by 1941, what had largely been a hobby was now an essential industry. Military contracts usually had required manufacturers to assume all costs of any possible patent infringements. Two days after Pearl Harbor, representatives from the radio industry and the military agreed that henceforth the government would obtain licenses from patent holders. The government then took steps to persuade those who held a patent to give it license without royalty.

Only RCA resisted. War production had whetted Sarnoff's appetite for the enormous profits he knew the corporation would collect if he should prevail—about $30 million in 1942. Why should the corporation give the military a free license? Though it had previously argued that the government should assume responsibility for licensing rights to inventions, RCA now shifted its tack. "The Government should continue to require its suppliers of radio equipment to assume normal and usual responsibilities for infringement by their products, which responsibility can be met by their acquiring the necessary patent rights," wrote Charles Jolliffe, who had advanced to the position of chief engineer at the RCA Laboratories. Major General Roger B. Colton, in charge of the laboratory at the signal corps, replied tartly:

> We do not believe that even your admittedly great contribution to the war effort warrants a tax of this magnitude since the principal justification for royalties is to pay for continuing research work, and since your own current research, to which you retain commercial rights, is now being done largely by government contract and on government funds.

By March 1942, when Colton wrote his letter, many holders of patents had already given the government royalty-free licenses to manufacture military equipment using their inventions. The legal scrapping continued for a time, but only for Sarnoff and RCA to save face. Yet he exacted a price. For the "duration of the hostilities and six months thereafter," RCA granted a non-exclusive license for all patents it held for an annual fee of $4 million.

War and preparations for it squared perfectly with Sarnoff's own desire to serve his country, too. He deeply believed in the war and in the Allied cause. Perhaps Harbord's dictum about war—"the school of heroism from which the nation's noblest sons are graduated into highest manhood"—had stuck in his mind. Certainly he remembered anti-Semitism, which, he suspected, had denied him a commission in the navy in World War I. War would be the ultimate test of an immigrant's patriotism. Through General Harbord he had secured a commission as a lieutenant colonel in the army's signal corps in December 1924. Each spring or summer thereafter, he had served two weeks in Fort Monmouth, New Jersey, at the signal corps headquarters or in Washington on the staff of the assistant secretary of war. Through his association with generals and career officers, he had been promoted to a full colonel in 1931.

Though he was over fifty, Sarnoff now saw a chance to serve his country through active duty and at the same time strengthen his company's operations. With his connections in the military and through the help of General Harbord, it was relatively easy to arrange a commission in the summer of 1942 as head of the U.S. Army Signal Corps advisory council.

Sarnoff presented an interesting sight in military dress. His uniform covered a body that suggested Humpty Dumpty before his fall: 194 pounds draped over a five-foot-seven-inch frame, flabby biceps—the product of years of inactivity—and a substantial chest and abdomen. An army physician examining him in June 1942 reported his figure "stocky," his frame "heavy," and his weight twelve pounds above the maximum allowed. Nevertheless, his blood pressure, pulse rate, and respiratory system, despite his daily regimen of Monte Cristo cigars, were all "normal." His medical history had been unremarkable, too: a tonsillectomy in 1936, two bridges replacing eight teeth in his mouth, nearsightedness corrected with reading glasses, and an occasional hemorrhoid. The doctor pronounced him "physically qualified for full military service."

Sarnoff's assignments in 1942 were of short duration: three weeks in June and July as head of the signal corps advisory council and two months beginning in late August advising the chief signal officer in Washington how the signal supply service of 34,733 men could be streamlined to meet supply deadlines and strict requirements of specialized communication equipment. He performed with his typical efficiency: first observing the supply practices and listening to officers, and then applying his business acumen to cut through the thickets of red tape. He made recommendations for immediate action and long-term solutions. Acting on Sarnoff's suggestion, General Colton, the director of the signal supply service, transferred personnel, redefined jobs, doubled the number of officers, and reorganized the entire command structure. At last the supply service operated efficiently and began to meet the demands placed on it.

Along with his active military status came the uniform. "No one ever wore [it] more proudly," General Harbord once remarked. Certainly, no officer paid more attention to the insignia or the fruit salad on his chest. He requested and received permission to wear above his heart civilian decorations he had been awarded over the years for his service to countries in the field of communication: the order of the Polonia Restituta, officer grade, from the Polish government in 1924; the order of the Oaken Crown from the grand duchy of Luxembourg in 1935; and the cross of the Legion of Honor from the French government in June 1940.

Between these brief personal forays into the military establishment, Sarnoff guided RCA in its effort to fill the rich government contracts that flooded in. He personally directed as much of RCA's business as he could. Late in 1941, he and General Harbord broke ground for a new RCA research laboratory at Princeton, New Jersey. Sarnoff conceived of the Princeton complex as the hub of the corporation's research and development that heretofore had taken place in smaller laboratories at its plants, most notably Camden. Now his developmental engineers and inventors would work in a central facility in a campus setting, and close by a major university. When necessary, they could work in teams to solve difficult problems and achieve success. Nothing would be impossible. Significantly, the Princeton laboratory would be close to his office at Rockefeller Center. The research of his company, which he counted so vital to its success, would be even more accessible to its head. He would be able to come down for the day to see firsthand the progress *his* engineers were making toward the goals he had set for them.

In its Princeton laboratory, RCA would develop more than 150 new types of radio tubes for use in more than 300 different pieces of equipment. These and hundreds of other tubes would be produced in RCA's new manufacturing plant at Lancaster, Pennsylvania. Built with money from the navy in 1940, the Lancaster plant would produce about 20 million tubes (about 2,000 different kinds) by August 1945.

With its significant increase in wartime production, RCA's revenues and profits rose steadily: revenues from $157.7 million in 1941 to a high point of $324.8 million in 1944, with a corresponding increase in profits from $29.9 million to $40.6 million. In 1944, nearly $245 million of RCA's revenues came from military manufacturing, while broadcasting accounted for $60 million.

By 1939, many Americans recognized that war could not be avoided. For Howard Armstrong, who still proudly called himself "major" after his rank in World War I, there was no question about the proper action he should take. Nearing fifty, he knew he could not fight. The nervous twitch of his neck, the legacy of his childhood disorder of Saint Vitus's dance, which John Bose and other associates called "the Major's shovelling his shoulder," had grown steadily more pronounced in recent years, as had the deafness in his right ear. But Armstrong believed he had much to offer the military nonetheless.

In addition to wide-band FM (and, of course, the regeneration and the superheterodyne circuits that form an integral part of all transmitters and receivers), the military employed yet another of Armstrong's inventions. His long-neglected superregeneration discovery found a practical use in "identify, friend or foe," a novel device the army used to distinguish between friendly and hostile planes as they were detected by radar. In the friendly planes, a transmitter sent a coded radio signal to the radar station that had detected its presence.

Armstrong devoted most of his time during the war not to FM, which was after all technology he had already refined to a remarkable degree, but to an investigation of radar. Though the precise nature of his research still remains shrouded under a thick blanket of government secrecy, its general outlines are known: he adapted frequency modulation to radar to extend the range of detection far beyond conventional methods. Armstrong's research provided the foundation for the long-range radar of today that reaches as far as a third of the way around the world.

Generally, engineers in the war relied on what they called "pulse radar"— short, potent bursts of high frequency radio waves emitted from a transmitter. The waves bounced off objects in their path and back to a radar receiver. Developed in England by Sir Robert Watson-Watt, radar could "see" such things as a plane flying as far as 200 miles away. Engineers had employed a pulse system because conventional wisdom held that a short spurt of electromagnetic energy—only a few microseconds in length—was preferable to a longer—and slower—continuous wave.

As might be expected, Armstrong after a quick but thorough study of the state of radar research decided to work against the wisdom by examining more closely continuous wave FM radar. Once again he found the pronouncements of Watson-Watt and others to have cleared the field for his own investigation. In 1941, after he had given the government use of his patents, Armstrong had hired another assistant, Bob Hull, a recent graduate of Columbia, to join Bose and him in the investigations.

Pearl Harbor changed everything. For a time it even imperiled Armstrong's entire research and broadcasting operation at Columbia and Alpine. All the workers at both sites were his employees. The payroll had jumped from nearly $7,800 in 1933, the year he received his patents for FM, to about $50,000 a year during the war. Sales of FM patents to commercial manufacturers of broadcasting and mobile radio equipment had helped to finance most of Howard Armstrong's recent research. With the United States entry into the war, these manufacturers shifted to production of FM for the military, and all royalties stopped. The man who was once the largest individual shareholder in RCA had little income on which he could rely. Other researchers might accept money from the government to continue their work, especially as it was related to the war effort, but Armstrong stubbornly refused to do so. It was his country, he reasoned; he would cheerfully serve it in his own way.

The bills mounted. One of those that Armstrong could not pay was from his lawyer, Al McCormack at Cravath. From the War Department in Washington, where he was serving as assistant secretary under Henry L. Stimson, McCormack wrote on May 9, 1942:

> I should like to see you straightened out, since the Cravath matter . . . is of the utmost embarrassment to me. I have not had any discussion on the subject with

anybody in the firm, and on reflection I do not feel that I can have any until I know just what you want them to do . . . try to look at it from my point of view.

McCormack's solution to the crisis was "simple":

> Since your waivers of royalties are for the duration of the emergency, i.e., the War, why cannot some practical solution be worked out, under which the Signal Corps would get a license for the duration of your patents and you could get some substantial amount of money to be used in f.m. research at your own discretion, including an annual amount sufficient to cover the cost of running Alpine. The Signal Corps know[s] as well as anybody that before this War gets very far along you will have presented the government with several million dollars by reason of the waiver of your royalties on Army and Navy business, to say nothing of the services that you have given and will continue to give.

It was the first time he had had to think about money for twenty years— since he had sold his superregeneration patent to RCA in 1922. Would he be forced to sell still more investments to continue his work? He knew he could not afford to do this for very long. No, the research was vital to the country, too. McCormack's reasoning prevailed. Reluctantly, Armstrong decided to accept a government contract to finance his study of long-range radar. The crisis passed; however, it prefigured a more severe one to come.

"Beyond question the war could be won without my help," Lee de Forest reflected in his autobiography. He was right. At age sixty-eight, he had no thought about joining up, though he was still fit enough to climb Mount Whitney for the fifth and last time on his seventieth birthday. No company bore his name, either. The American De Forest Telegraph and Telephone Company had supplied tubes and wireless equipment to the navy in World War I. Today that was a memory, and he was still recovering from the bankruptcy petition he had filed in 1936. This was a war for energetic entrepreneurs like Fred M. Link, small established electronics companies of quality like Radio Engineering Laboratories, and, above all, large corporations like RCA, AT&T, and Bendix.

Happiness for Lee de Forest came most of all from the comfortable routine he enjoyed with his wife, Marie. Life still centered on her and Cielito Lindo, their home on Hollywood Boulevard. Here he had his study, where he deposited his laudatory scrolls and mementos, the "life-charting trophies," that had accreted over the years. When a professional photographer visited the house in 1941 to take some pictures to accompany an article Samuel Lubell had written for the *Saturday Evening Post*, the couple posed in their living room. Wearing a tan tweed suit, striped shirt, and blue bow tie with white polka dots, the baldheaded inventor appears serene and content. In one picture, de Forest sits in a chair by the hearth with a book in his lap. He directs his gaze downward to Marie, who kneels on the hearth, knitting. Their eyes meet in obvious admiration. In another, Lee and Marie sit on the sofa beneath Martin Kavel's kitsch portrait of the danseuse, Marie knitting, while Lee places a record on the phonograph. Both images radiate the stability and harmony that had thrived in their marriage—even through financial adversity—since October 1930.

From the start of their marriage, Marie had worked hard to adapt herself to some of her husband's more difficult ways. She had determined, correctly, that she must be there when he needed her, and must recede into the background when he did not. She took classes at UCLA in subjects she thought would make her a better companion; together they learned Spanish.

But de Forest could still be rough hewn. When visitors overstayed their welcome, or when he grew tired of their company, Lee would tell them to go away. When Marie prevailed on him to speak to her ladies' club, the Pasadena Shakespeare Society, Lee rose after the luncheon and said "This is the second time my wife has inveigled me out here. Now, ladies, don't ask me again," and sat down. Still surviving in this septuagenarian mind was the unfashioned, and brash, boy of Talladega, Mount Hermon, and Yale.

The only dark cloud in the de Forests' otherwise brilliant conjugal union was the lack of a child. Lee's anguish became all the more acute when, in the mid-thirties, Marie bore him a boy. At last, this would be the son he wanted to carry on his name, a son to send to Yale. But the child died soon after he was born.

Long ago, financial exigencies had forced Marie to dismiss her house servants and take on the cooking and cleaning herself. But this she regarded as simply another way of serving her husband. Each morning at 8:30, his devoted "Mijita" drove him from their house to a small laboratory and office in a warehouse. There he dictated voluminous letters to a secretary and tinkered with a variety of inventions. Each afternoon she came by to pick him up at 4:30. Still, he could claim, he had remained independent, a lone inventor free of corporate control.

Perhaps because de Forest was not associated with a large corporation, the military did not appreciate the few contributions he sought to make to the war effort. He soon became embittered with the "red tape chute" down which all ideas had to travel. Typical of his inventions was a "dirigible bombing missile," for which he applied for a patent early in 1940. Equipped with a "photoelectric control apparatus" and motors to activate a pair of rudders, de Forest's bomb sought out light from its target after its release "so as to insure, as far as may be possible, a direct hit."

De Forest brought his bomb to the attention of Charles Edison, son of the inventor and then secretary of the navy, who "at once grasped the idea" and passed it on for evaluation. But naval reviewers found crucial disadvantages. The electronics and motors needed for guidance would add at least seventy-five pounds and two cubic feet to a bomb; its speed would be so slow that "it would not be able to penetrate at least some decks before detonating"; and "could be defeated by the use of light-colored smoke." Perhaps most stinging was the observation: "The guiding device in this bomb is not new and has actually been put in practice in the control of large telescopes for following the stars." It was an old idea.

"Is this a sample of the 'intelligence' which dictates the policy of the United States Navy?" de Forest asked in angry reply, and then took his plans to a sympathetic general in the army who arranged for a test at the Muroc Dry Lake Flying Field in the Mojave Desert. A plane flying at 5,000 feet released a dummy bomb directly above de Forest, the general, and other military personnel standing atop a reconnaissance tower. But it fell "almost directly downward," missing the observation party by 150 feet. The army declined to continue the tests.

The patent examiner who evaluated his application for the bomb also raised objections to nearly all of the thirteen claims de Forest made. Others, it seemed, had registered the idea before him. He never received a patent.

While Sarnoff realized that his work as president of RCA was important to the Allied effort to defeat the Germans and Japanese, he yearned for something more. Remaining at Rockefeller Center for the duration of the war, running the company efficiently and planning for the future of postwar television, perhaps making an occasional foray into Washington to advise the War Department how best to procure equipment—all that was fine. But it was not true military experience—there was no hazard, no peril. His heart had not been, as Oliver Wendell Holmes once said of war, "touched by fire." Not since his seal-hunting trip to Newfoundland for the Marconi Company in 1913 had he taken any physical risks. Sarnoff craved adventure once again.

In mid-March 1944, he got his chance. The job seemed created in a dream vision: special assistant to the supreme Allied commander, General Dwight Eisenhower, in London. Eisenhower was planning the D-Day invasion, a vast and complicated operation involving thousands of planes and hundreds of thousands of men, the largest assault in the history of war. Someone had to coordinate the radio communications. The army's chief signal officer, Major General Harry C. Ingles, recommended Sarnoff, whom he had known since he served on the signal corps advisory council. Ingles had come to respect Sarnoff's opinion and his ability to cut through bureaucratic red tape and get things done. The president of RCA was called to active duty and ordered to leave immediately for London.

Placing Charles Jolliffe in charge at 30 Rockefeller Center, Sarnoff left for London on a transport plane from Philadelphia. He arrived at Claridge's Hotel, where he was first to be billeted, on Monday, March 20, 1944.

When he met with Eisenhower two days later, Sarnoff learned his assignment would be just the sort he relished, taking up tough, seemingly intractable problems that had daunted others—and prevailing. He had been called at a moment of difficulty to use his skill to cut through the thicket of bureaucracy blocking successful radio communications. His initial orders were threefold: to create for the Supreme Headquarters, Allied Expeditionary Forces (SHAEF) a broadcasting station beamed to the Allied troops in Europe and the Mediterranean; to evaluate the military communication systems between SHAEF and the invasion forces; and to coordinate for American and British reporters all communications—print and broadcast—from the battle lines on the continent. Though Sarnoff did not know the precise nature of the top-secret assault that was planned on France, or the date it would be launched, he understood he had to work swiftly.

Sarnoff's new military job was not unlike the one Guglielmo Marconi had created for him thirty-seven years earlier in 1907. Then he had served as the master's messenger and personal assistant, outside the ranks of his station as office boy at the Water Street office, and enjoying direct access to the top. He had done the same with Edward Nally, tutoring the telegraph cable man in the fundamentals of wireless. Later he had worked closely with Owen D. Young outlining the bright future of broadcasting, and still later with General Harbord. Since 1930 he had been president of a major corporation. Now he was returning to his familiar role of valued savant, possessed of special knowledge and abilities essential to the success of the Allied effort. And this time he would be able to play before General Eisenhower, supreme Allied commander. Though only a colonel, he would be able to bypass all channels of command, and through Eisenhower's chief of staff, General Bedell Smith, have access to the top.

━

Sarnoff selected the site for the clear-channel SHAEF broadcasting station immediately after he first met with Eisenhower. He requisitioned all the necessary equipment and organized a staff to operate it. Before June 6, 1944, D-Day, he had it operating.

The state of telegraph communications between the field and headquarters posed a different problem. Sarnoff found that radio telegraph students, who supposedly had to demonstrate a minimum competence of twenty-five words a minute, were being taught by instructors capable of only ten. Communications would be disastrous in battle. Immediately, he ordered proficient and skilled instructors transferred into the school and the unskilled transferred out, and he oversaw the complete overhaul of the training. By D-Day, most field telegraphers performed well.

By far Sarnoff's most visible accomplishment lay in the area of coordinating press communications for the invasion. Here he discovered a "picture of confusion." Assessing the cable and radio telegraph facilities, he learned they were capable of handling about 200,000 words of code a day, while he estimated traffic of about 500,000 to 600,000 words on the day of the invasion. Obviously he had to find more circuits and carefully coordinate the traffic. Here Sarnoff had to assert himself in ways that some—especially the British—found annoying. He organized a common photo pool for the radio transmission of pictures from the front, established a traffic control committee of British and Americans, and planned a central signal center through which all communications would pass.

With regard to direct broadcasting from Europe, Sarnoff realized he would have to open up more channels. He pressured the British Post Office to give over one of its circuits, persuaded the signal corps in Washington to allow an additional broadcast transmitter, and oversaw its erection. He created a mobile signaling unit that would move just behind the Allied troops as they regained the continent. It would transmit to a U.S. battleship in the English Channel, which would relay messages about the globe.

Sarnoff worked efficiently over days that usually lasted eighteen hours. Whenever he could not get what he wanted by following regular channels, he used his relationship with Eisenhower and Bedell Smith. Brendan Bracken, minister of information in England, worried that some of Sarnoff's arrangements for news gathering would give the edge to the Americans, resisted them. Through Eisenhower, Sarnoff appealed directly to Winston

Churchill in a meeting at 10 Downing Street. After listening to Sarnoff outline what he had done and stress the need for Allied unity, Churchill overruled his minister.

Sarnoff relished it all: the army staff car to take him about London; his room at the Savoy Hotel, not far from Grosvenor Square, now jocularly called "Eisenhower Platz," and the United States Embassy as well as a private apartment provided by RCA; the dinner parties at Claridge's Hotel or SHAEF headquarters, often with senior military staff and sometimes even with Eisenhower himself; the meetings with British politicians like Clement Attlee, Ernest Bevin, and Aneurin Bevan; a luncheon in his honor given by the editors of the London *Times*; an honorary membership in the British Institute of Radio Engineers at a meeting presided over by Lord Louis Mountbatten. One day he even attended a small private luncheon at 10 Downing Street given by Churchill and his wife, Clementine. There Churchill quizzed him about Franklin Roosevelt's prospects for a fourth term and television's development after the war.

Tuesday, June 6, 1944, and the days that followed went smoothly as far as Sarnoff was concerned. All equipment functioned well, and the systems he had established worked flawlessly. Barely four decades had passed since Marconi had sent the three dots of the single letter S from England to Newfoundland. During the invasion more words—570,000 the first day and 500,000 in the days immediately following—had traveled across the ocean than ever before. For the rest of his life Sarnoff took pride in the letters of praise he received. The chief correspondents for NBC, CBS, and the Mutual Broadcasting System commended him for his "unflagging zeal" in providing proper broadcasting facilities; the head of the Associated Press wrote that "our hats are off." From General Ingles he learned that "your performance . . . has been outstanding"; and best of all, General Eisenhower sent his "sincere appreciation . . . for the services that you have rendered to your Country and to this headquarters."

During the war, Lee de Forest's work as an inventor went on fitfully. He failed to obtain a patent on an idea for a "telephone message recording system." The idea was interesting, similar to telephone answering machines of today, but the execution was pure Rube Goldberg:

a small motor . . . swings upwardly a two pronged hook. . . . This hook lifts the receiver and swings it in a circular motion about a 4"–5" radius until the receiver and transmitter faces are brought opposite, and rest upon a microphone . . . and telephone receiver respectively. . . . A Magnagraph steel tape is then set in motion on which has been recorded a stock phrase, e.g. "No one here to answer your call. But your message will be recorded if you wish. Please state your name."

And after the caller leaves the message, "the motor is set in reverse and the telephone receiver is again deposited in its original position." Curiously, the first person to harness the electron in a significant way relied on machinery to accomplish the tasks an electrical circuit could perform far more efficiently.

To those who knew Lee de Forest in his seventh decade, the inventor appeared a somewhat sad, penurious old man, who was still looking for a way to cash in. "He always had his eye on the cash register," said Gertrude Tyne, who used to see de Forest whenever he was in New York. During the war, her husband, Gerald Tyne, a historian of early radio, and George Clark, another radio pioneer and historian, interviewed the inventor for a proposed biography. De Forest often stopped at the Tynes' apartment for dinner. The inventor took little interest in Gertrude Tyne until he learned she was an engineer and an inventor in her own right. Then he pressed questions upon her about her latest research. "I'm working on a 'flash-dark,'" she said, baiting him with nonsense. "It's the opposite of a flashlight. You shine it to illumine with darkness." De Forest took the bait whole. "You want to get a good lawyer; file your patent as soon as possible," he advised her with enthusiasm, "make as many claims for it as possible, and then sue anyone who comes along later." It was advice he had learned after decades of litigation. "Since his mind was unconstrained by scientific thinking," Tyne remembered, "he always asked about the status of my 'flash-dark' whenever he came around. And he was serious."

Though he was free after D-Day to return to civilian life and Rockefeller Center, David Sarnoff chose to remain in uniform. At the end of June, he learned General Ingles and the deputy chief signal officer, F. H. Lanahan, had recommended him for promotion to brigadier general. "Only with the authority and prestige that this rank wields will this officer be able to perform his future military missions with his usual brilliance and success," wrote Lanahan. Never mind that he had not planned to stay on active duty and that General Lanahan's argument was therefore moot. A general's rank, even if it was only one star, was too great an honor for Sarnoff to pass by.

To return home now might put the advancement in jeopardy; Sarnoff decided to delay his return to Rockefeller Center as long as necessary. He accompanied Eisenhower to his headquarters in France, made a brief trip to

North Africa to assess the communications facilities there, and traveled to Italy to consult with General Mark Clark. Most of the time he spent in Paris—Lizette's birthplace and the European city he knew best. There he restored communications shattered by the German armies, including the transatlantic telegraph cable that they had severed in 1939.

July, August, September, October. The months wore on, but still his promotion to brigadier general did not come through. Again and again the board of directors at RCA convened to approve his requests to extend his leave of absence. The most he had to show for his service was the army's Legion of Merit ("for exceptionally meritorious conduct in the performance of outstanding service"), which General Eisenhower ordered to be awarded at a ceremony in London on October 12.

"The proverb says 'Hope deferred maketh the heart sick,' " Gano Dunn, RCA director and friend of Sarnoff, wrote on October 14, 1944. "Every time we expect your return, we get an official communication asking that your leave of absence be extended another month." Reporting how "proud" the board was of the honors Sarnoff was receiving, Dunn concluded, "we will welcome you when you come back to put your hand again on the tiller of our great ship."

The ship was drifting. Just at the time when RCA should have been planning for the postwar sale of radios and televisions to the GIs who would soon return to America, no one was in charge. Charles Jolliffe, the acting president of the corporation, who had demonstrated his loyalty to Sarnoff and RCA from the time he had opposed Armstrong's FM while serving as chief engineer for the Federal Communications Commission, had been stricken with a serious intestinal cancer. He had little energy to preside over corporate affairs. General Harbord, nearly eighty and still chairman of the board, found the job beyond him. Other directors, including Edward Nally, who was close to eighty-five, were also impuissant. Though each had functioned well when David Sarnoff was present, his absence left a void that none could fill.

He did not return to the United States until the last Saturday in October 1944, to be greeted by Lizette—in a Red Cross uniform—and his children at his transport ship. But he stopped only for several days in New York. He spent six more weeks in Washington, where he filled out reports for General Ingles and followed the slow progress of his promotion through the labyrinth of offices at the Pentagon to the White House, and to the United States Senate, where on December 6, 1944, he was awarded the single star of a brigadier general in the signal corps reserve. At last David Sarnoff's quest was over. He could return to his office on the fifty-third floor at 30 Rockefeller Plaza.

Congratulations flooded in from relatives, friends, and acquaintances in the military, almost all addressed to "General." He dictated warm letters of acknowledgment, signing each "Brigadier General, U.S. Army, Deputy Chief, Army Communications Service," and had the correspondence carefully bound in a red leather book.

"When you shake the hand of this General you will not be able to detect any differences between General and Private," Sarnoff wrote to a friend who had commended him on his new rank. But there was a difference. While the idea of a promotion appealed to his ever-growing sense of vanity, it also meant something more to Sarnoff. It brought him recognition in the exclusive circle of America's leaders. It validated his belief that the United States stood as the greatest nation on earth because it had yoked its free enterprise system to its war machine. The star symbolized the alliance between the big corporation, in which he so fervently believed, and military might, which he and the directors of RCA had always championed.

Because of that star he would come more and more to think and act like a commander of the business world. Surely the well-being of his corporation was inextricably bound to America's greatness? He would carry his short, portly frame ramrod straight as he walked through the halls at Rockefeller Center or into his laboratories at Princeton, or up to a podium to accept an award. He came to regard himself as one of the principal spokesmen for the free world as it stood up to godless Soviet communism, and he and RCA's publicity department worked assiduously to promote this image.

Quickly, it seemed almost with the speed of a radio signal, after his return to RCA in January 1945, word spread through the floors at Rockefeller Center, through the laboratories at the RCA research center at Princeton, through factories in New Jersey, Pennsylvania, California, and Indiana: henceforth President David Sarnoff, who had advanced from "Davey" and "Jew Boy" to "Dave," "David," and "Mr.," would be addressed as "General Sarnoff."

Howard Armstrong's research on continuous wave FM radar did not bring about practical results until the conclusion of the war. But when it was ready, the demonstration of this new radar's power made headlines around the world. At 11:58 A.M. on January 10, 1946, at a U.S. Army Signal Corps laboratory at Fort Evans on the coast of New Jersey, army engineers bounced the first radio signal off the moon and back to earth. The equipment required for the feat, which we take for granted today, was formidable: a huge antenna 100 feet above the ground; an FM transmitter, and a sensitive receiver which Armstrong developed and constructed at Alpine, capable of creating pulses of electromagnetic energy strong enough to travel 238,857 miles to the moon and back again. The actual experiment, which the army named "Diana" after the moon goddess, took about two and a half seconds. The results appeared modest; the echo was heard as a short, peeplike hum and appeared on an oscilloscope as a slight, upward jagged variation in the normal line across the round screen.

However feeble the echo was that January morning, it had enormous consequences for the future of humanity. Armstrong's radar system had proved for the first time that FM waves, unlike AM, could penetrate the ionosphere—that band of ionized atmospheric gases encircling the earth. Astronomers could use continuous wave radar to measure the distance between the earth and the end of the universe, and to map the planets topographically. Radio communication through space would be possible, even practical. The moon itself might serve as a giant reflector of radio waves, or perhaps, some theorized, artificial satellites might someday ring the earth providing communications between points as distant as halfway around the world. Of course, the military saw that in the future radio waves would guide missiles of destruction to their targets. FM had served the war effort well, when not encumbered by the foolish intransigence of those wedded to an old technology. FM would now serve future communications in ways that few had dreamed might someday be possible.

No doubt these and other thoughts crowded into Armstrong's mind that January day of the demonstration. Once again his belief in FM had been vindicated. No doubt the location of the experiment meant something to Armstrong, for Fort Evans stood at Belmar, New Jersey, the place where on a cold January night thirty-four years earlier, he and David Sarnoff had listened to his regenerative receiver as it picked up signals from around the world.

By the end of 1944, the Allied forces had regained much of Europe. In late July, a bomb placed in Hitler's East Prussian headquarters by civilian officials and military officers had come close to killing the führer; he would in fact die in a little more than nine months. In August, General Charles de Gaulle marched in a ceremonial parade down the Champs Élysées in Paris. At the end of October, General MacArthur had fulfilled his promise to the Philippines by returning to their islands. And late that summer on the Dumbarton Oaks estate outside Washington, D.C., representatives from Britain, the Soviet Union, China, and the United States met to discuss a charter for a permanent international organization to maintain peace and security in the world. It became the basis of the United Nations.

In October of that year, the Radio Corporation of America published *The First 25 Years of RCA*. Subtitled *A Quarter-Century of Radio Progress*, the book celebrated the corporation's contributions to the radio art and looked forward to a bright future. "We find the Allies headed for victory," wrote David Sarnoff in the preface. "Peace will find the world on the threshold of television . . . all radio will be changed." While the corporation looked forward, he pledged it would not "forget the past," and would "learn from our mistakes and gain new inspiration from our achievements." RCA had established the first nationwide radio networks, had brought the voice of the president of the United States to the ears of every person on earth, and had helped to make radio universal. "Our destiny," Sarnoff concluded, "is to create, so that we may serve civilization with such distinction that at the end of the next twenty-five years—the completion of half a century—RCA will be at the forefront of radio progress in the world in 1969."

Surely, the prospects for radio progress were better than they had been since October 1929. The war had lifted America from the depression, put money in the pockets of many soldiers who would soon be civilians ready to spend. And RCA would be ready to sell. "In War—your War Bonds will buy radio equipment that helps our fighting flyers," read the headline in an RCA advertisement that appeared regularly in the *Saturday Evening Post* during 1944. "In Peace—your Savings will buy the greatest radios and phonographs in RCA history." Television was still too radical a concept to appear in the magazine, but that would come. A picture of a family sitting in their living room listening to their RCA radio-phonograph console accompanied the headline. Beneath it a caption read: "RCA's electronic knowledge will also be employed to bring you the glories of television plus RCA-developed FM Radio Circuit."

12

"UNTIL I'M DEAD
OR BROKE"

"Within five years the existing broadcast system will be largely superseded," Howard Armstrong had confidently predicted in 1940. His forecast was on the way to becoming a reality when the Japanese attacked Pearl Harbor. During the war, he repeated the statement often, assuring everyone that as soon as the war ended, listeners would recognize the advantages inherent in FM and make the switch, and broadcasters would have to follow along. Many manufacturers appeared to agree. "FM will dominate our product design," said a spokesman for General Electric in 1944. "It seems reasonable that FM will eventually supplant all local, most regional, and some high power stations."

Indeed, all outward signs suggested that once peace came, listeners would be ready to trade in their old radios for new models—about 5 million in the first year, so General Electric executives believed. These new sets would have FM as well as AM bands. Gradually AM would fade out as listeners would naturally prefer the finer quality of sound and static-free reception that FM offered.

However farsighted about technology, Armstrong and the manufacturers were still blind about business realities. They had underestimated the interest broadcasters had in maintaining the status quo of AM service and the means at their disposal to do so. Their weapons included the Federal Communications Commission, the power of advertising, and the new power of television. Using any one of these means individually, commercial broadcasters could hinder the postwar development of FM; using them together, they hobbled it for twenty years.

One of the less understood but most powerful weapons was the Federal Communications Commission. In one of its principal functions, the FCC resembles a powerful traffic cop patrolling the vast, invisible highways of the electromagnetic spectrum over which all radio and television transmissions travel. Scientists in the twentieth century have classified the spectrum according to the length and frequency of electromagnetic waves. The higher one goes in the spectrum, the shorter and more frequent are the waves. For AM, the FCC allowed broadcasters to transmit over medium-length waves vibrating between 5 hundred and 16 hundred thousand cycles a second, which radio engineers called "kilocycles" or "kc." For FM, the FCC allowed transmission over shorter length waves vibrating between 42 and 50 million cycles a second ("megacycles" or "mc"). Acting as the police, the commission assigned a particular place (or frequency) on the highway to each station and was careful to separate geographically stations occupying the same lane. Generally, the more powerful the station, the greater the chance for interference and hence the need for greater separation. Thus KINY in Juneau, Alaska; KROC in Rochester, Minnesota; KVOL in Lafayette, Louisiana; WCMI in Ashland, Kentucky; WMFF in Plattsburgh, New York; WISC in Milwaukee, Wisconsin; and scores of other stations, each transmitting at about 100 watts of power, could share the 1310-kc lane of the invisible highway; while WGY, the powerful 50,000-watt clear channel GE station in Schenectady, had only to share its place in the 790-kc lane with KGO, a 10,000-watt station in San Francisco.

Since its creation by Congress in 1934 to serve the "public interest, convenience, and necessity," the Federal Communications Commission had carried on a simpatico relationship with commercial broadcasters, especially those affiliated with the National Broadcasting Company and the Columbia Broadcasting System. The case of Charles Jolliffe had shown how easy it was for an FCC engineer to move from the commission into the industry. The reverse was also true. It was not unknown for a person with ties to broadcasting to take a job with the commission.

Certainly no communications executive worked more assiduously than David Sarnoff to cultivate a cordial spirit of cooperation between RCA and members of the commission. As most of the commissioners had been lawyers or government bureaucrats, devoid of the technical competence to understand the industry they were charged to regulate, Sarnoff found it relatively easy to bend their thinking to his will. When he or other RCA executives testified to the commission, they did so with firm authority, often backed by data produced by a phalanx of RCA engineers. Surely, Sarnoff would subtly assert, the largest communication corporation in the world had the ability to understand the increasingly sophisticated engineering concepts underlying radio better than any small company, individual entrepreneur, or inventor. Surely it was operating in the national interest.

More often than not, the commissioners had relied on RCA's word. True, there had been difficulties, most especially when the New Deal activist James Lawrence Fly had served as chairman. Recently, Fly had championed increased regulation of the networks and used his power to force the National Broadcasting Company to divest itself of the blue network. (It became the American Broadcasting Company in 1945.) But for the most part Sarnoff and RCA had prevailed.

In the 1940s, the commissioners found that the demands of the burgeoning technology were forcing them to make more sophisticated decisions than ever before. In addition to the many requests from commercial AM and FM broadcasters for licenses, the commissioners faced new petitions: police, amateurs, the telephone company, railroads, and the weather bureau, among others, all wanted a place in the spectrum where they might operate. It was the commissioners' job to direct these new uses of radio waves into the proper lane. The greatest demands came from those championing television, which, compared with AM or FM broadcasting, required a much wider space for each station and separate bands for transmitting image and sound.

Looking to the end of the war and the new era of communications that would come with peace, the commission held hearings in the fall of 1944 about frequency allocations in the radio spectrum. The hearings began quietly enough in a small auditorium in the Museum of Natural History, with proponents for FM and television taking the position one might expect. The Radio Technical Planning Board, a group of engineers appointed by the FCC to advise about such matters, along with FM broadcasters and manufacturers, recommended that FM remain in its present broadcast band of forty-two to fifty megacycles; commercial AM and television broadcasters advocated narrowing the FM band (and thereby decreasing FM's fidelity and resistance to noise), moving it to a different place in the spectrum, and using the present bands for television transmission. Very likely the FCC would have made no changes were it not for mysterious activities that take place 93 million miles from the earth.

Sunspots, those dark spots that cluster on the surface of the sun, erupt in gaseous turbulence approximately every eleven years, causing disruptions in radio transmissions. Early on in the hearings, CBS and NBC had suggested that sunspot activity would disturb FM. Would it not be better to move FM broadcasting "upstairs" in the spectrum, "for its own good"? Naturally, they contended, television could take over the space once FM was moved. The motives behind the networks' argument were transparent. If the FCC decided to move FM upward, it would cripple the new technology. With one ruling, the FCC would make the more than fifty FM broadcasting stations and the half million FM radios, which had been designed to operate in the forty-two to fifty megacycle band, obsolete. Engineers have always thought of working with radio waves as an "art." They had little experience transmitting at higher frequencies, but they knew they had much to learn. It would take time and cost more money to create transmitters and radios that operated well in the higher bands.

A letter from an authority in the National Bureau of Standards dispelled the arguments of the broadcasters. "The fear is not well founded." The matter seemed to rest. Then on October 28, at the end of the hearings, the FCC called on Kenneth Alva Norton, an engineer with the War Department and formerly a member of the staff of the commission. Using mathematical calculations, Norton determined that sunspot activity would indeed interfere with FM transmissions. At the forty-three megacycle frequency, for example, listeners could expect 830 to 2,410 hours of interference per year, the engineer assured the commission. FM had to be moved upward in the spectrum "if we are to enjoy the interference-free broadcasting which the industry is leading the public to expect."

Armstrong and the FM advocates were stunned by Norton's testimony, for it turned their argument of static-free reception upon them. Extensive tests and measurements followed, which exposed fundamental errors in Norton's mathematical calculations. Misunderstanding the nature of wideband FM, the engineer had mistakenly based his calculations on the assumption that a signal must be at least ten times stronger than any interference. In fact, it need be only twice as strong. True, sunspot activity is greater in the lower bands, but it would not interfere with FM because of the capture effect and the high signal to noise ratio. Sunspots would, however, interfere with television transmissions. More hearings were called, but Norton took refuge behind government secrecy. On January 15, 1945, the FCC announced the new frequency allocations, moving FM upward to between 88 and 108 megacycles in order to ensure the quality of its service. Naturally, television would take over the old bands, though no one explained why television would be immune from sunspot activity. Nor did anyone commenting on the decisions at the time mention that Paul Porter, the chairman of the Federal Communications Commission appointed to succeed James Lawrence Fly in November 1944, had been the Washington legal counsel for the Columbia Broadcasting System, and that before the war Porter had argued for the assignment of the FM channels to television.

Armstrong felt that the FCC had dealt FM a "dreadful blow," but he would not give up the fight. "We have had a terrific fight over here with the Federal Communications Commission which has disrupted FM and delayed it at least a year," Armstrong wrote to his friend Henry Round in England on March 30, 1946. "They are now going to have to take the responsibility for what they have done, and we have proven their expert so wrong that on two occasions at technical society meetings (one the IRE) he has refused to rise and defend his theories when challenged so to do."

In 1947, at another FCC hearing, Howard Armstrong got a chance to question Kenneth Norton directly. It was the peak of the supposed interruptions from sunspot activity that the engineer had so confidently predicted two years earlier. The disruptions were of little consequence. Since the war had ended, Norton could not pull down the veil of secrecy over his findings. "You were wrong?" asked Armstrong of the engineer's 1944 prophecy. "Oh, certainly," Norton replied blithely. "I think that can happen frequently to people who make prediction on the basis of partial information. It happens every day."

At the same time broadcasters were suggesting changes in the allocation of the spectrum, they also were proposing changes in the power of FM stations. Armstrong's W2XMN at Alpine, operating at 40 kilowatts, could be heard clearly throughout much of New York and New Jersey. Bouncing signals from just a few mountaintops, the Yankee Network had covered New England, and incidentally saved the exorbitant long distance line tolls that AT&T charged. How might the networks cut FM's power and thereby increase operating costs? CBS presented the answer to the FCC on October 11, 1944: the "single market plan."

An idea clothed in the trappings of democracy, the "single market plan" had sprung from the mind of an advertiser, Paul Kesten, executive vice president at CBS. Kesten was just the sort of man to impress the commissioners. His neat blond hair and meticulous dress lent to his good looks and made him a touch magisterial. To William Paley, "he presented the image of CBS." A master of making things appear different from what they were, Kesten continually spoke not in terms of swelling CBS's prosperity, but of advancing the greater interests of the radio medium. He created a research department and hired Frank Stanton, a recent Ph.D. in psychology from Ohio State University, to lead it. Together, the two commissioned dozens of surveys to measure the likes, dislikes, and nature of the radio audience and, when they served the interests of his network, passed the surveys on to advertisers and members of the Federal Communications Commission. One caustic commentator nicknamed him "Plausible Paul Kesten."

"There are no jokers up this sleeve," said Kesten to the FCC. The idea seemed simple and fair: to ensure the equality and competitiveness of FM by limiting the power of individual stations to cover a single city or market. No longer would there be powerful stations like Armstrong's at Alpine, which at 40 kilowatts blanketed most of New Jersey and could be heard at the tip of Long Island. Under the single market, its power would be eviscerated to 1.2 kilowatts. "We want FM to be wholly democratic," Kesten told the commissioners, and thereby avoid the "prince-and-pauper" dilemma of big and little FM stations.

Kesten's plan, which the FCC adopted, made all FM stations into paupers. For broadcasters affiliated with NBC or CBS, this did not matter, as they could tolerate making no profit or even operating at a loss in their FM operation while continuing to reap the profits from AM. But independent owners or those affiliated with the burgeoning Yankee Network could look forward to a permanent serfdom, without hope of turning a profit. And the cut in transmission power embodied in Kesten's plan had the added attraction of curtailing the Yankee Network's ability to relay signals cheaply from mountaintops around New England.

Nor did Kesten stop with the single market plan. The following July, he and Stanton proposed to the FCC that broadcasters carry identical programming on FM and AM. Taking the boldest claim of FM proponents, the one that Howard Armstrong had repeated so often, that "the existing broadcast system will be largely superseded," Kesten turned it back upon them. "Most of us at CBS have believed . . . FM was technically destined to replace AM . . . as surely and inevitably as the tungsten lamp was destined to replace the old carbon filament." Therefore, broadcasters should be allowed to send over FM transmitters "the same popular and familiar programs they send out to AM set owners . . ."

> The AM basket is full of grain—hundreds of thousands of grains in it—each grain representing an AM listener. The FM basket is empty. . . . But every time a new home buys an FM set and tunes it in—at that moment one more grain is poured out of the AM basket into the FM basket.

And once the FM basket is full, said Kesten, closing his agricultural metaphor, "the station operator will gladly dispose of the out-moded AM transmitter." Listeners would not be confused and most important sponsors would have a "parallel network during this all-important transition period."

Once the FCC allowed broadcasters to duplicate AM programs on FM, network sales people offered the additional programming as a bonus, an incentive for advertising on radio. What reason would a sponsor have to place an advertisement with an independent FM station when a network offered a spot on FM *and* AM at an attractive price? With the FCC's help, the networks had made FM into a bargain basement that gave away its goods at below cost. With impeccable logic and seeming altruism, Kesten had actually strengthened the influence of AM broadcasting and the networks.

Throughout these assaults on FM, Edwin Howard Armstrong devoted his time to proving again and again the advantages of his system and dispelling the myths about its supposed disadvantages. "We want to keep the record straight," he repeated, with his unlimited faith in the power of scientific truth to overcome prejudicial myths that many in the radio industry were perpetuating about FM. In 1947—well after the FCC's decision to move FM broadcasting upward—Armstrong set out to prove FM's ability to work in the 42–50 megacycle band without difficulties. He leased Dune Cottage, a twenty-two-room house in Westhampton, Long Island, and sent John Bose to live in it and record signals sent from Alpine. The experiments and measurements the two made were exhaustive. The costs were also exorbitant: $3,000 for the summer rental plus electric charges, food, transportation, Bose's salary, and, as always, hundreds of dollars in long distance telephone charges. The documentation of FM propagation, the most extensive ever made, produced incontrovertible evidence that FM could work well in the band. But the victory was pyrrhic. FM had already been moved to the 88–108 band.

The other myth to overcome concerned the limits of an FM transmission. Many conceded that FM was better than AM, but it was limited to "line-of-sight" or "the horizon." Long suspecting this was not the case, but lacking any evidence, Armstrong conducted a series of experiments in 1947 that opened up yet more uses for his invention. Transmitting from Alpine, the inventor beamed high-powered FM signals (some of the last the FCC would allow him to send) that bounced off the ionosphere and were received by a mobile receiver he had sent to Alabama.

Immediately, the Pentagon and Bell Laboratories recognized the importance of Armstrong's discovery. With further development at MIT, Radio Engineering Laboratories and the Bell Telephone Laboratories, often with Armstrong's assistance and cooperation, came the early-warning radar system that reaches a third of the way around the world, and domestic microwave relay stations capable of handling television and telephone traffic over distances far greater than the limits of a horizon.

But the year of keeping the record straight was 1947. FM had moved to its new niche in the spectrum, while NBC and CBS, among others, were broadcasting television in the old range of 42–50 megacycles. Armstrong had conducted his experiments—at considerable expense to himself—to demon-

strate conclusively to the FCC the foolishness of its decisions about allocations. Already, television broadcasters were finding that the few stations on
the air were choked for space. Lack of room meant that New York and
Philadelphia could have stations, but not Newark or Camden, New Jersey.
Even so, television viewers found interference. Why not move television
now? argued Armstrong, in a brief before the FCC in 1948. His recommen-
dation came to nothing, though the interference in the television bands
became so great that the FCC had to allot other channels in the same
ultrahigh frequency range where Armstrong and others had recommended in
1944 all television be placed.

Many observers of the FCC commented cynically when Charles Denny,
the fourth head of the FCC in less than four years, resigned to become vice
president and general counsel at NBC, lured by a salary of $30,000 and
freedom from rancorous disputes about television and radio. Might there be
collusion between members of a federal regulatory agency and the very industry it oversaw? some asked. Though no evidence appeared to confirm such
suspicions, Congress passed a law to prevent future appearances of impropri-
ety. It was a barn door action.

Despite Edwin Howard Armstrong's formidable experimental triumphs—
bouncing a radio signal to the moon and sending FM signals beyond the
horizon, he was frustrated by the political world, which so often prevailed
over the scientific. He was a failure in this world of politics, for he misun-
derstood its power over scientific inquiry. Once again, as he had in his suit
over regeneration, Armstrong watched competent engineers in thrall to a
large corporation bend their judgments to suit the will of their employer. He
watched in disbelief as the Federal Communications Commission dismissed
his findings, which he had based on empirical evidence, as nothing more than
self-serving arguments. Yet the FCC accepted the arguments of the broadcasting industry, which he *knew* to be entirely self-serving.

Armstrong faced more profound problems. To many young engineers fresh
from the war, Armstrong seemed the old man of radio. The contrast in his
appearance and actions between the 1920s and 1940s was striking. After the
First World War, he had been the dashing young inventor, speaking before
admiring colleagues at the Radio Club of America, gathering newspaper
headlines about his inventions that would make radio a part of every home,
driving about in his Hispano-Suiza, and daring David Sarnoff and the world
by standing atop the tallest broadcasting tower in New York. Then he was
the acknowledged inventor of regeneration, the superheterodyne, and superregeneration.

But in the late 1940s and early 1950s, after all his inventions had been challenged or eclipsed, Howard Armstrong felt like a has-been. He could still garner newspaper headlines, but more often than not it was as an adversary, not as an inventor. He still could startle people with his fearless disregard of heights, too; on more than one occasion, Marion arrived at Alpine with a visitor and found her husband swinging in a bosun's chair from one of the tower's three mighty arms.

There was an air of sadness and care about him. In 1947, a photographer from *Fortune* met Armstrong in Yonkers to take a picture of him in his tower room at 1032 Warburton Avenue, which was to accompany an article Lawrence Lessing was writing on FM. When the trio found the room locked and the key missing, the inventor quickly climbed out the window of an adjacent room onto the steep roof, edged himself along the rain gutter three stories above the ground, jimmied the window of his old room, and climbed in. Both the photographer and the author were stunned.

The photograph of the occasion has a timeworn aspect to it. Howard Armstrong stands at the center of the room, the place where he had made his first great invention, beside a cast-iron bedstead. The two arms of a bare chandelier, one that had been converted from gas to electricity, drop from the ceiling. On the bed, desk, worktables, and floor stand piles of books, papers, breadboards, and wireless apparatus. A roof leak has caused the plaster to fall from one of the steep sloped ceilings, exposing the lath beneath, and scattering the floor with fragments. From the south facing window in the background, the inventor would have been able to see his FM tower at Alpine. Neatly dressed as always, in a dark suit, he appears tired, even sad, as he stares purposefully at a paper he holds in his right hand. Thirty-five years ago he had manipulated the electron in a way no one had ever done before. But his invention had been mired in litigation for nearly twenty years, and legally was no longer his. Already he had skirmished with RCA over the invention of wide-band FM, and his defense of his discovery against rumor, misstatements of fact, and outright contumely had cost him in purse and spirit. Who knew how much litigation he would face to make sure his invention would be securely his? And who knew if he could win?

There was yet another difference between Armstrong of the 1920s and Armstrong of the 1940s, which only the inventor knew: though reputed to be fabulously wealthy, a millionaire many times over, he was not. Always secretive about his financial affairs, Armstrong disclosed the details of his income only to his accountant, who was not a member of the Cravath firm. In the 1920s, he had been the largest private shareholder in RCA, the person who had "had a field day in radio and Victor," selling at the peak of the bull market in 1929. While he still enjoyed the emoluments of great wealth, especially real estate; was free of debts, and still directed a large staff at Columbia University and Alpine, more and more the little money he earned from royalties went out almost immediately to pay the bills. Given Armstrong's overhead, the financial cushion supporting his operations—probably no more than $1.5 million in stock certificates and savings accounts—was really threadbare.

Armstrong had looked forward to the end of the war and the return to a peacetime economy. By 1944, companies like Zenith, General Electric, and Stromberg Carlson were eagerly anticipating the conversion to domestic production of FM as well as AM and FM radios. Already he was negotiating contracts with broadcasters for FM stations, each of which would provide him with royalties. And who knew what would happen to television? Recently the Radio Technical Planning Board had recommended (over the objections of Raymond Guy, the RCA engineer who sat on the board) and the FCC had concurred that TV sound be broadcast over FM. He would receive a royalty on every television sold, for each would contain his FM inventions in its receiver.

But it was not to be.

Changes in the band frequency allocation, the adoption of the single market plan, and the duplication of AM programs had dulled the threat of FM to the network broadcast industry and denied Howard Armstrong the chance to collect great sums on his invention. It was money for which he had so patiently waited, and upon which he so depended if he were to retain his laboratories and his FM station at Alpine, and remain solvent. He had only until December 26, 1950, before almost all his FM discoveries became public property. (Only one FM patent was due to expire later, in 1957.) He had voluntarily given up the chance to make millions on his patents during the war. The delays now forced on him by people and forces he regarded as foolish not only seemed unnecessary but quickly were becoming intolerable.

An additional complication, which soon became an obsession in Armstrong's life, was David Sarnoff and the Radio Corporation of America. RCA had tried to purchase a license to his invention with a flat fee of $1 million in 1940. But Armstrong had steadfastly refused. Sarnoff and his corporation had viewed the hiatus in the development of FM broadcasting brought about by the Second World War as a time to acquire and create circuits that would get around the Armstrong patents. If all went well, so the thinking went, when the war concluded RCA would be ready with its own FM circuits. At the November 1944 meeting of the Institute of Radio Engineers conducted in the very hall where Armstrong had given his first public demonstration of FM nine years earlier, George L. Beers, from the RCA research laboratory in Princeton, announced an "entirely new" FM system "dissociated completely

from that of Major Armstrong." RCA's advertising department made much
of the challenge it posed for existing wide-band FM patents, and even featured Beers's picture in magazine advertisements. Through cross-licensing
with Bell Laboratories, the corporation also acquired the "ratio-detector," an
invention of Stuart L. Seely.

Of these two inventions that RCA and Sarnoff were relying on to get
around Armstrong's lock on the wide-band FM patents, Beers's was never
mass produced because it did not work well, while the Seely ratio-detector,
as Armstrong knew, merely appropriated two of his FM inventions, the
limiter and detector, in a single tube. "Super FM," RCA proclaimed in its
advertisements announcing its "new" invention. However, the Seely ratio-
detector represented neither a "super" nor a "new" discovery. Though the
circuit worked, it was markedly inferior in quality to Armstrong's inventions.
Just as galling to Armstrong was the fact that RCA was resorting to tactics
de Forest employed in 1915 in his patent application for the "ultra audion,"
in which the inventor had submitted a misleading drawing and explanation
of the circuit. Now in the bulletin announcing the ratio-detector, RCA had
presented a circuit drawing and explanation designed to obfuscate its true
origin.

RCA's attempts to circumvent Armstrong's patents were not unusual in
the history of corporations in the twentieth century, especially when those
corporations were dealing with an individual inventor. "*The* RCA," as Sarnoff called it, had remained supreme in the radio field because it held exclusive rights to so many inventions. From time to time, RCA had been
accused of controlling the industry with a monopoly over the technology, but
Sarnoff had carefully defended the corporation and prudently altered its
licensing policies whenever criticism became too harsh. In 1923, when faced
with complaints of restraint of trade from the Federal Trade Commission, he
had decided to license RCA's patents to other manufacturers at 7.5 percent
of their sales. Later, complaints forced him to reduce the rate to 5 percent.
The revenues to RCA were considerable. Now, RCA was licensing the rights
to what it claimed to be its FM inventions to other manufacturers—Emerson,
Motorola, and Philco among them—who were satisfied to produce low-
priced receivers with little regard for quality.

At those rare times when RCA had to obtain a license from another
inventor, it made sure it was an exclusive one. The only person who had ever
prevailed over RCA and Sarnoff was Philo Farnsworth, the engineer from
Utah who had developed the "image dissector," an invention basic to the
television camera. In the 1930s Farnsworth had sued RCA for patent infringement and won in the court of appeals. Knowing the ruling threatened

all of RCA's television development, Sarnoff tried to buy the invention outright. But Farnsworth had said no; RCA could license it along with others, and at the rate he demanded. Realizing that use of the patent would determine the success or failure of all of his television development, Sarnoff capitulated. In October 1939, in an office at 30 Rockefeller Plaza, Farnsworth and his lawyers met with Otto Schairer, head of RCA's patent department, to sign the royalty agreement. Schairer made a brief speech about the momentous nature of what he was about to do. Many who listened noted that when the document was passed to Schairer for his signature, his eyes had filled with tears.

Philo Farnsworth's single triumph over RCA policy had only strengthened David Sarnoff's resolve never to be bested again, and certainly not by Howard Armstrong over FM. While FM might be essential to Armstrong's success, to Sarnoff and RCA, it was a mere appendage. The market for FM radios was small, and because of the FCC decisions, it had shrunk even smaller. What matter that the sound of RCA's system—including the FM sound of television—was inferior? No TV viewer would be able to tell the difference in the small speakers planned for the sets. And surveys had indicated people were more interested in the magic of the picture in the box than the quality of the sound.

Otto Schairer and others in the RCA patent department advised Sarnoff that the Seely ratio-detector got around the Armstrong patents well enough. In any case, everyone knew it would be difficult for a lone inventor to sue a corporate giant like RCA successfully. Farnsworth had prevailed because his invention was different from anything in the television art. But Armstrong's hold on his FM patent seemed clouded. FM had been around since the turn of the century. Some said it was a law of nature, which, as everyone knew, could not be patented. Armstrong probably did not have a legitimate claim, and even if he did, it would be relatively easy to defeat him.

Sarnoff's interest lay not in FM but in the successful introduction of television, and, looking ahead, in color television. These were formidable challenges, he realized, but success would only serve to increase his reputation in enterprise and give him the international stature he craved.

Throughout the war, Sarnoff had dreamed of what television would do for the nation. He had always enjoyed playing the role of prophet, and he delighted in telling listeners like Winston Churchill and Dwight Eisenhower of the changes he foresaw. He realized, too, that the war actually benefited television. RCA's commercial introduction of the new medium at the New York World's Fair in 1939 had not gone well, for the country seemed still to be suffering from the lingering effects of the depression. But a new economic order was emerging. Deprived of any appliances or automobiles since 1942, war veterans and civilians alike had developed an appetite for new things, and television was new. Radio represented an old technology. Who cared about listening when one could see as well as hear? RCA researchers at the laboratory in Princeton had used the time to perfect the new technology. Now Sarnoff approached television manufacturing and sales the way a general advances on a military objective. "There's a vast market out there," he told his closest executives early in 1945, "and we're going to capture it before anyone else."

When the octogenarian and infirm General Harbord resigned as chairman of the board at RCA in July 1947 (he died the following month), the board chose Sarnoff to replace him. In the annual report for 1947, Sarnoff wrote to his stockholders that television had begun "to fulfill its promise of becoming a great industry and a vital public service." Three years later, the biggest business year in RCA's history to date, he could write with assurance that television had become "one of America's major industries." The Radio and Television Manufacturers Association conferred on him the title the "Father of American Television." With such a title, how could he be bothered with mere radio?

As FM became mired in regulations, Armstrong took RCA's actions and the behavior of the industry personally. He became even more indignant when RCA began producing televisions with his sound system. At every opportunity, he criticized RCA and Sarnoff's actions, which he said were calculated to delay the inevitable progress of FM. His indignation deepened in 1947 as manufacturers of FM sets who were paying royalties to him revised their projections of sales downward. When Charles Jolliffe claimed in a handsome corporate pamphlet that RCA had made substantial contributions to communications at higher frequencies, Armstrong charged that the RCA engineer was fabricating his information and neglecting Marconi's seminal research in the field. He concluded bitterly, "It would be much better if Dr. Jolliffe would stop taking his facts from the lawyers."

Perhaps, Armstrong felt, he could receive some relief in the United States Congress. For years he had been courting a number of senators, including Charles W. Tobey of New Hampshire. In 1948, the Eightieth Congress created a special committee to investigate FM and the radio industry. The inquiry would center on RCA, which, Tobey contended:

> blacklisted the thing as hard as they could, did everything they could to keep Armstrong down. . . . They did their damnedest to ruin FM and keep it from being where it is now . . . to hamstring and keep it down and subordinate FM as long as they dared to do it . . .

At the same time RCA was suppressing FM, Tobey revealed, it was supplying television sets to commissioners of the FCC. While such revelations made headlines, nothing practical came of them.

RCA and the broadcast networks, Armstrong knew, were triumphing over him. He would have to seek assistance in the courts. This was not a case about the intricacy of a circuit, which judges might not understand. No, this was a case about open theft. In the courts, he would find a forum where he might speak of the treatment he had suffered at the hands of an industry dominated by RCA and Sarnoff and supported by a government commission. He huddled with his lawyer, Alfred McCormack. Together they planned his case.

Armstrong wanted to go after all the companies at once, but reluctantly concluded on the advice of McCormack that it would be wiser to sue only RCA. When he prevailed over that giant, so McCormack reasoned, the rest of the manufacturers and broadcasters would follow.

On July 22, 1948, in Wilmington, Delaware, Armstrong's lawyers filed suit in the United States district court against the Radio Corporation of America and the National Broadcasting Company. The principal charge was infringement on five of his basic FM patents; the suit also charged that RCA had "deliberately set out to oppose and impair the value" of his inventions. He asked for treble damages and a preliminary injunction pending the outcome of the trial to prevent the corporation from making FM equipment. Marion Armstrong was worried that RCA would never settle without a long and protracted fight. To allay her fears, Armstrong gave her half of what remained of his fortune—perhaps as much as $750,000—so that she might invest it as she pleased. To him, this was to be the decisive battle, the one that would decide for all time whether the rumors RCA had been spreading throughout the industry since before the war—that his FM patents were defective and could not withstand litigation—were correct, or if—as he knew to be the case—he had indeed discovered a new and fundamentally different way of communication. The suit would take time for the courts to decide, and there was always the possibility that "some smart legal trick," as he called it, would take his invention away from him. But he firmly believed this time he would be vindicated.

When Armstrong sought relief in the federal court, he probably had little understanding of the formidable opposition he faced. He had the services of some of the finest lawyers available: Al McCormack was assisted by Dana Raymond, a Columbia-trained attorney with a background in physics. Behind them, ready to research case history and minor points of the law, stood a small retinue of associates and clerks. From time to time, Armstrong would also call on the services of Albert Nolte, the attorney who had filed all his patents since superregeneration. A first-rate attorney, Nolte had been a friend of his since they had met when students at Columbia. These legal savants came at a high price—$69,660.96 in 1947—but his honor was at stake, and the potential settlement of millions of dollars made their fees worthwhile.

Since its inception, RCA had always maintained an intimidating battery of lawyers to assert its patent claims and defend itself from hostile suits. Though not directly involved, Sarnoff made certain that his lawyers represented his interests. The principal firm defending the corporation against Armstrong's charges was Cahill, Gordon, Zachry, and Reindel. The chief partner, John Cahill, was a director of RCA and served at the will of its president. "He never did anything with regard to RCA without Sarnoff's approval," one associate remembered. "He was ingratiating, obsequious, almost fawning." Cahill would have charge of the overall defense strategy, while he assigned an associate, James Fowler, to handle the details of the case.

By one of the strange twists that increasingly seemed to figure in these events, Armstrong's first lawyer, William Davis, now a partner in the firm with the Dickensian title, Davis, Hoxie, and Faithful, served as patent counsel for the defense. Because of the ties of his past association with the inventor, Davis stayed on the fringe of the litigation as much as possible, leaving the day-to-day work of the case to his partner, John Hoxie.

The thick fog of a procedure known as "discovery" soon enshrouded *Armstrong v. RCA and NBC.* Instituted since Armstrong's battles with Lee de Forest, the discovery process enabled litigants to examine relevant witnesses and obtain pertinent documents before trial. When witnesses gave depositions or requested documents, only a court stenographer, a notary, and the lawyers would be present, and the entire procedure could take place in a lawyer's office rather than a courtroom. In theory discovery would expedite complicated patent matters, and thereby save time and expense when the case came to trial. In fact, as RCA's lawyers realized, discovery could be used as a civilized, time-consuming, expensive form of harassment. *Armstrong v. RCA and NBC* would be a case of time and expense—and both were on RCA's side.

RCA's lawyers understood that the best tactic for them was to extend the discovery as long as possible to stall a trial beyond December 26, 1950, and preferably 1957, when Armstrong's patents expired. If they stayed in the pretrial discovery, the corporation could avoid a court decision forbidding them to manufacture FM equipment. The consequences of such a decision would be devastating, for it would stop RCA's production not only of radios but also of televisions. And time meant money. To Sarnoff, the legal expenses meant little, for his corporation could well afford them. Armstrong's resources were limited, in part because he had realized no income from RCA and the other companies the corporation had encouraged to violate his patents. And the inventor's small army of lawyers no doubt would demand high fees. Stalling the case as long as possible, the RCA forces knew, would break Armstrong financially.

The best way to realize their goal would be to keep Armstrong on the witness stand as long as possible:

Q. What is your occupation?
A. I am an electrical engineer.
Q. Do you have any other occupation?
A. I am a professor of electrical engineering at Columbia University.
Q. Do you have any other occupation?
A. I occasionally make inventions.

So began the inventor's testimony at 10 A.M. on Valentine's Day 1949 in a conference room at the Cravath, Swaine, and Moore firm.

A master of the nugatory issue, RCA counsel James Fowler employed the same methods the Lilliputians had used with Gulliver. Innumerable small threads in the form of trivial questions would render the great inventor immobile: How was it that Armstrong called himself "professor" when he received no compensation from Columbia? (It took a year of skirmishing before RCA's counsel grudgingly accepted the fact that Armstrong actually worked for the university.) How many people did he employ at Columbia and at Alpine? Why did he write letters on Columbia stationery from his apartment at 435 East 52nd Street? Why did he use his personal stationery for his professional correspondence? Didn't he in fact have an office at his River House apartment instead of Columbia? Where did he keep his accounts? How did he pay his bills? Where did he keep his check stubs? Who managed the laboratory at Columbia? At Alpine? Almost none of the issues the counsel raised had any bearing on the central question of the suit: had RCA infringed Armstrong's FM patents? But the ceaselessly trivial interrogation ate up time and money.

"We are proceeding with the process known as 'Examination before Trial,' " Armstrong wrote on December 3, 1949, to his colleague and friend Henry Round in England.

As I am the plaintiff and the rule is that the defendant cross-examines first, the other side has been examining me for about ten months and getting nowhere.

It will shortly be our turn to examine them! *Then* we will have some news for you. All it amounts to so far, in fact, is an attempt on the part of RCA to stall off the evil day of coming to trial as their examination during the past months shows that they have no defense whatsoever.

Still confident about the outcome, he would assure Round just before Christmas, "Don't worry about what's going to happen. . . . This time it is going to be different—remember that I have probably had more experience in the field now than anyone in radio now alive."

Despite Armstrong's optimism, the deposition and the legal skirmishes surrounding it wore on and the fog grew thicker. Exasperated with the foolish nature of the annoying and trivial questions RCA was asking, McCormack made an unusual appeal to the federal judge assigned to the case to give Armstrong some respite. The judge ordered the interrogation stopped immediately. He would still have to testify as plaintiff in the action, but not until August 1953, when he would give another nineteen days of testimony. In all he would spend seventy days over fifty-eight months answering arcane questions put to him by one lawyer after another. His last appearance would be on December 3, 1953, less than two months before his death. His testimony would fill about 8,000 pages and he would place 1,355 exhibits into evidence, including models of his inventions, recordings of FM tests, employment records, bank statements, royalty agreements, and a letter from Nicholas Murray Butler appointing him professor of electrical engineering at Columbia.

In February 1950, the depositions moved to a conference room at Cahill, Gordon, Zachry and Reindel, where Armstrong's lawyers finally had a chance to take depositions from sixty-nine witnesses, including Raymond Guy, Stuart L. Seely, Elmer Engstrom, Charles Jolliffe, Kenneth Norton, and David Sarnoff. Soon Armstrong's counsel had RCA on the defensive, and the arguments among the lawyers became intense. One time, as one of Armstrong's lawyers was examining a witness, John Hoxie, the attorney for RCA, exploded. "You're not asking him 'When did you stop beating your wife.' " Hoxie growled, "You're asking 'At what time of day did you stop beating your wife.' " It was clear that the discovery procedure was not working as had been intended and that something had to be done to restrain both sides.

At the request of the RCA side, and after another inevitable delay, the federal district judge in Delaware took the extraordinary measure of appointing a special master to keep proceedings moving forward. He was Philip J. McCook, a seventy-eight-year-old retired justice of the supreme court of the state of New York. McCook seemed a good choice. A military man, who numbered among his ancestors the "fighting McCooks" in the Civil War,

McCook had fought in the Spanish-American War and World War I, and had served as a colonel in the judge advocate general's office in World War II. He had presided with distinction over some difficult cases in his career, including the trial of the infamous racketeer Lucky Luciano, whom he sentenced to thirty to fifty years in prison. Since retiring from the bench, he had maintained a small law practice in New York.

Under the careful eye of Judge McCook, the depositions in the discovery ground on relentlessly. Before the judge on February 20, 1953, three years after the discovery had begun, Armstrong's lawyer Al McCormack finally got a chance to interrogate David Sarnoff. In contrast to the badgering Armstrong had received, the questions were tame and always focused on matters of consequence. Of his early relations with Armstrong, when he was chief inspector for the American Marconi Company, Sarnoff spoke with warmth: "They were very friendly and close. We saw each other frequently, either in my office or in my home. We were close friends. I hope we still are. I enjoyed his confidence and I hope he enjoyed mine." In those early years of intimate association with Armstrong, he continued, "I probably learned more about the technical operation of receivers and radio from Armstrong than I did from anybody else."

But about the matter contended in the lawsuit, Sarnoff remained unyielding. Yes, throughout the 1920s he had discussed with Armstrong "frequently" the problem of eliminating static. Yes, he had witnessed the demonstration of wide-band FM at Columbia just before Christmas 1933, but the improved quality of the sound might be attributed to the excellent caliber of the components Armstrong used as to his method of transmitting and receiving. His patent attorney had reassured him that the width of the band, or the "swing," as he called it, "was not the subject of a patent, even though it is possible that because of Major Armstrong's standing in the art and his great contributions to the art and so on that a court might feel it was an invention." Furthermore, Sarnoff continued, opinions differed "whether or not the improvements which can be secured by using wide swing over narrow swing . . . justifies the commercial revolution."

When the questions turned to the development of FM, Sarnoff grew bolder in his answers:

> We have been developing the FM system and have made it available with our combination sets and with receivers and with television. I will go further and I will say that the RCA and the NBC have done more to develop FM than anybody in this country, including Armstrong.

Clearly surprised by the general's statement, McCormack asked "Will you tell us just what it is that you have done?" Sarnoff continued:

I think that really good receivers were designed and developed and built by the RCA Victor Company which the rest of the industry followed in considerable measure, but even that I do not regard as the major contribution. In my judgment, the major contribution was when the NBC led the parade in duplicating its AM programs over FM transmitters, and with all modesty I claim the personal credit of having been the man who forced that development.

Growing even more expansive in his claims, Sarnoff went further in his assertion of having helped to advance FM. RCA had built FM transmitters that he made available "not only to our own networks, but to other stations." And finally, Sarnoff concluded, RCA had invested $50 million in television. There were now 22 million televisions in American homes, "and each one of them is an FM set, because the sound that accompanies the television picture is given on FM."

Armstrong had sat in the conference room impassively listening to his former friend's testimony. Usually he averted his eyes from the speaker. But Sarnoff's blithe assertions were too much. Those watching Armstrong noted that his look was one of unmitigated hatred for the man who was twisting the truth as never before.

"I have been tied up with the lawyers," Armstrong wrote Round in mid-March 1950, in apology for his long delay in writing. Still optimistic, in mid-1951, he wrote again to Round: "The litigation against RCA is progressing most favorably and it is clear they have no defense other than a rear guard action to make it as costly as possible. However, that will not help in this case."

Though Armstrong put up a brave front to his friend Round, by 1951, RCA's tactics had begun to wear him down. For the first three years of litigation, income from his patent royalties and stock dividends had managed to stay ahead of his expenses. In 1948, the year he began the suit, his gross income totaled $838,500 including $805,500 in royalties and $33,000 in stock dividends. That year he could well afford the $171,000 he paid to his lawyers, the $103,000 to his employees at Columbia and Alpine, and the $55,000 in donations (including a large gift to Thomas E. Dewey's presidential campaign). His taxable income still stood at $276,000. The following year his royalties climbed to $861,500 while his legal fees mounted to $190,500. In 1950, royalties and legal fees rose slightly to $868,000 and $199,000.

By mid-1951 Armstrong saw his income plummet while his expenses spiraled out of control. That year he realized $658,500 in royalties and $29,000 in stock dividends and $16,500 from the sale of some Zenith stock. But he had to pay his lawyers $217,000 and his employees $119,000. With depreciations, legal fees, salaries, and other expenses of running his various enterprises, Armstrong's taxable income had actually dropped to $5,759.

By 1952, the royalty income had receded with the dramatic swiftness of a spring tide to just $110,000, and he had but a small reserve of stocks and savings. Scrambling to meet at least some of his bills, he sold many of his assets, including shares of Zenith, RCA (stock which he acquired in 1932 and 1943), and Standard Oil of New Jersey, and a piece of property in Rye Beach, New Hampshire. From these assets he received $200,000. But it was not enough. For the first time in forty years, when he had sold his superregeneration invention to RCA, Howard Armstrong had to resort to credit. That year he found he could pay but $22,000 to his lawyers—whose fees were well over $200,000.

"No man's nature has been made better," Charles Dickens wrote of Jarndyce and Jarndyce, the fog-enshrouded legal case of *Bleak House*. Like Dickens's characters, Howard Armstrong also found himself a victim of unending "trickery, evasion, procrastination, spoilation, botheration." The discovery forced a dull, grinding routine on him from which he could seldom waver. Transcripts of the previous day's hearings would be delivered to his apartment at River House as soon as they were ready. Armstrong would rise early, sometimes at 2 or 3 A.M., to reread them thoroughly. Often he would make minor changes and write notes about lines of questioning to be followed, documents to be requested, or legal points to be clarified. A mid-morning meeting with McCormack and Raymond at the Cravath offices usually took place at 10 A.M. Depositions began at 11 o'clock and lasted until 3 and sometimes 4 o'clock in the afternoon. He went to Columbia or Alpine, and returned to River House to oversee what was happening among those who worked for him. In the evening there would be dinner with Marion and a scotch or two, conversation with Burghard or Runyon—or sometimes a strategy session with McCormack.

As had been the case since his childhood, Howard Armstrong could never take his mind away from radio. Once during the litigation, he and Marion took Dana Raymond and his wife, Josephine, to see *Miss Liberty*, a musical set in the streets of Paris. "And in the middle of the most beautiful love song in which I was enfolded," Jo Raymond remembered, "he nudged me and said, 'Look at those old-fashioned telegraph wires.' "

Although Marion Armstrong had long tolerated her husband's single-minded focus on radio, and at times even thought it humorous, the ceaseless litigation with RCA had begun to take a toll on the Armstrong marriage. Marion had lived through it all before, of course, with the long regeneration trials, and she knew how the deep bitterness of those suits had changed the nature of their life together. While she was outgoing and gregarious and loved to attend parties, he could only consider his work.

Though Howard seldom took time off from his work to relax, he came increasingly to put restrictions on Marion's movements. When Marion proposed a trip to escape from the confines of River House, he at first forbade it. She must not travel alone, he said, nor could she travel with a companion. When she insisted, only with great reluctance did he bend. With a niece, Marion embarked on a train across the continent. At each stop the train made along the way, she found a friend of Howard's awaiting her. The friend would then call New York with a report on Marion and her niece's progress.

Much to Howard's distress, Marion planned to travel to Europe with a friend from Rye Beach. Again, he was reluctant to let her do so. Again, when she insisted, he made extensive arrangements for their stay, seeing to their hotel rooms, even where they ate their meals.

During a 1952 trip to Florida with a friend and the friend's husband, Marion Armstrong suffered a mental collapse. On the train home, she accused a porter of attacking her. The party arrived in New York in considerable agitation, and Marion was put under the care of a psychiatrist. Shortly after this, she attempted suicide by jumping into the East River. After several months in a mental hospital and the care of another psychiatrist, Marion was able to return to her life at River House.

Only in July and August, when the lawyers took off for the country, could Armstrong devote himself to his work. Then he would enjoy a brief respite from the contentious testimony and the brain-numbing legal maneuvers by returning to the laboratory full time. "The lawyers don't like to work in hot weather," Armstrong wrote to Round at the end of one July. "Hence I'm using the time to catch up on my research." Research lay at the heart of what the litigation was about. If the manufacturers would just give him the money he was due, he would be able to continue his investigations and inventions. That was all he wanted.

In March 1953, in the midst of the discovery, and hoping his suit against RCA and NBC would finally come to trial, Armstrong was able to announce his final important contribution to the radio art: multiplexing. Developed with his assistant John Bose, who shared fully in the credit for the invention, multiplexing allowed a single FM station to transmit simultaneously two or even three different signals over the same FM wave. Just how multiplexing might be used, Armstrong was not sure, but he had two suggestions. The owner of a single FM station might transmit as many as three different programs at the same time, and therefore "sell twice or three times as much advertising." More probably, he thought, multiplexing would allow binaural broadcasting of concerts from microphones placed at different locations in a concert hall, to two loudspeakers at a listener's receiver. Armstrong's and Bose's invention had made possible the introduction of stereo broadcasting.

Pinioned in the fine nets of legal torment cast by the lawyers for RCA and NBC, and faced with mounting bills and no money to pay them, Edwin Howard Armstrong came to the inescapable conclusion in 1953 that to survive he would have to do something completely foreign to his nature: compromise. Compared with two years earlier, his royalty income had diminished to a trickle of $60,235 while the salaries he paid had climbed to $128,637. He would manage to pay his lawyers $45,907. The dividend income, largely from his wife's holdings, was $34,431. The only way he could escape would be to settle his suit with RCA and NBC and then press others in the industry who had infringed his patents to do the same.

For the past two years, his lawyer, Alfred McCormack, had been gently prodding him to settle. Now he increased the pressure. In April, McCormack's associate Dana Raymond produced figures about the production of FM equipment, and how much might be owed Armstrong—between $5.8 million and $7.7 million if the court were to award treble damages. On July 2, after considerable prodding from his lawyer, the inventor met with Judge McCook. Perhaps, if he were to state what he wanted in the way of money, the judge might arbitrate a settlement between the two sides. But Armstrong, his pride wounded by the continuous assaults on his abilities as an inventor, and pained by the thought of settlement, could not bring himself to name his terms. "The Major and I had a field day yesterday," McCook wrote to McCormack. When McCook reminded him that he had expected to receive a proposal for settlement, Armstrong replied, "I thought without going contrary to your wish it would be fairer to Mr. Davis for me to call his attention to certain facts which I believed he had overlooked." Still trying to keep the record straight and obviously pained by the thought of settlement rather than an outright victory, the major made one last effort to assert himself.

At the end of July, Alfred McCormack decided to write a forceful memorandum to his client. The time schedule for the trial was not propitious. Assuming that it began in March 1954, McCormack said, the trial and appeals would take until June 1961 before all appeals were heard and the judgment was paid. "I would not venture to predict what might happen by June 1961." McCormack wrote:

We may at that time be in a major war. We may all have been wiped out by an atomic bomb; or, what may be more likely, we may be pretty much in the same condition as now, with large government expenditures and high taxes. I doubt if we will have much lower federal surtax rates in 1961 than at present. But let us assume that federal income taxes were then taking on 60%, instead of 90%, of large incomes, and you got $2,500,000 of ordinary damages and another $2,000,000 after taxes. In the years 1953 to 1960, you would have spent an absolute minimum, on the average, of $150,000 a year on litigation expenses, or $1,200,000 over an 8-year period, assuming that you did not spend anything on bringing suits against other infringers. . . . So I figure that the very most that you could expect to get out of $5,000,000 paid in 1961 would be $2,000,000, or $800,000 above minimum expenses.

June 1961 was eight years away, and no income would be coming in to keep his research going. McCormack's logic and pressure had worked. Armstrong would agree to have Judge McCook move for a settlement.

On August 12, 1953, McCook received a proposal for settlement from Armstrong and McCormack. They had based the $3.4 million they requested on what Armstrong would have received if RCA had paid royalties. It would be payable, they suggested:

On or before October 1, 1953	$500,000
On April 1, 1954	$500,000
On April 1 of each year from 1955 to 1962, $300,000, or a total of	$2,400,000

This was a proposal only, made in the depths of summer when the lawyers for the case were generally away, but it was a substantive beginning toward a conclusion. The possibility of settlement looked even more auspicious in late October when McCormack learned that William Davis had independently confirmed the proposed figure as being correct. While this news certainly did not mean RCA was acceding to Armstrong's demand, it suggested that the corporation too was ready for a settlement. By mid-November, each side was drafting proposed contracts for an agreement. Perhaps by Christmas they could reach a resolution.

The resolution would come with a price, however—one that pained Armstrong greatly. The proud man who had refused to yield to de Forest, who had even tried to return his medal to the IRE when the Supreme Court had found in his adversary's favor, now faced capitulation to his former friend. Before he would accede to any settlement, Sarnoff stated flatly, Armstrong would have to withdraw the language of the complaints against RCA. Sarnoff had been especially annoyed by the charge that RCA had "intentionally and deliberately obstructed and interfered with [Armstrong's] use, development and licensing" of his inventions. The contracts demanded he drop that language, while Sarnoff's statement that RCA had done more than anyone else to develop FM would remain. To Dana Raymond, the inventor seemed to have lost his vigor and was noticeably more abstracted. In conferences at the Cravath offices, Raymond observed that Armstrong increasingly took to looking out the window rather than concentrating on the business before them.

Marion Armstrong saw the change in her husband's physical health and mental disposition, too. Earlier that spring, he thought someone was trying to poison his food. Dishes were examined. The doctor was summoned. Armstrong would not relax until his stomach was pumped. No poison was found. Other ailments were more alarming. He felt a numbness on one side of his brain and in the opposite side of his body, first thought to be a mild stroke, but eventually traced to an inflammation of the brain. In youth he had appeared robust; now his figure appeared slight, his face gaunt. The nervous twitch in his neck became even more rapid and uncontrollable.

For years he had been withdrawn from almost all social contacts. Sometimes Marion would have friends to dinner or drinks, but only rarely would he appear. One of the few social traditions they maintained was an annual Thanksgiving party at River House for his radio friends and their wives. This Thanksgiving, the group assembled as usual—friends from his youth like Tom Styles, George Burghard, and Randy Runyon; his Alpine and Columbia workers like John Bose; and younger men of professional association like Dana Raymond, for whom he had great respect. Someone produced a camera and the guests posed together in the living room. Sitting on the sofa beside his wife, Armstrong mustered a tense smile. It was the last time his loyal group would gather around him.

Later that evening, after the last guest had left, the tension between Howard and Marion Armstrong, which had been accumulating over the past years, erupted in violence. For the first time, Howard revealed to her that he was nearly bankrupt and that he could not hope to go on. Perhaps she would return some of the money he had given her when he began the suit, money that she had invested well. Marion reminded him that she was sequestering it for their retirement. Perhaps it was time to think of that retirement in upstate Connecticut where her sister, Marjorie, had an antique business. Perhaps he should tell Al McCormack the seriousness of his financial adversity so that the settlement could be reached.

All the intensity and frustration of the more than five years of litigation suddenly exploded in a great rage, unequaled in its ferocity, unmatched in its destructiveness. Armstrong swung with a fire poker. The blow landed on

Marion's right forearm. In panic she fled River House to a physician and the security of her sister in Granby, Connecticut.

With a single stroke, Howard Armstrong had shattered a marriage of nearly thirty years. They had known times of intense pleasure, especially in the early years before the de Forest litigation had taken its toll on his spirit. They had also known less happy moments when Howard had caused Marion psychological pain, sometimes embarrassing her before her friends. But she had always stuck with him, recognizing his genius, tolerating and even helping to sustain his preoccupation with radio. "Nothing was ever more important to me than Howard's absorption in his experiments," she had told a writer for a woman's magazine. It was the "particular price" of her "happy marriage."

While Marion was living at her sister's in Connecticut, Armstrong faced the final, shattering developments in the contract negotiations with RCA. Draft after draft of the contract passed among the lawyers, but RCA had yet to fill in the blank spaces about the amount of payment. William Davis had certainly raised hopes by arriving at amounts substantially the same as Armstrong's, but no one deluded himself that RCA would actually pay that amount. How much less would the corporation offer? Judge McCook raised everyone's hopes on December 11, 1953, when he reported to McCormack that William Davis would "take the responsibility for telling Sarnoff how much he should pay—thereby relieving Sarnoff of the responsibility in arriving at a figure himself."

Another idea occurred to McCormack. Perhaps, along with the resolution of its own suit, RCA might reach an industrywide settlement, too. The corporation had licensed its Seely ratio-detector to other companies and encouraged them at the same time to infringe Armstrong's patents. Armstrong wished only a settlement with RCA at the time, but, as McCormack suggested to Judge McCook, if the figures were right, they might consider that as well.

For its part, RCA found itself in trouble with those manufacturers like Philco and Emerson whom it had licensed. For years it had assured them that its patents would withstand a court test. To consider a settlement with Armstrong, much less an industrywide settlement, would breach those assurances.

On December 15, RCA finally filled in the blanks in the contract: $200,000 would be paid to Armstrong immediately, and the company reserved the "option" to pay an additional million dollars in the next year. In addition, it reserved an option to settle for the others in the industry for $1 million. The proposal was impossible, for as McCormack told McCook, it did "not assure Major Armstrong anything except the initial payment of $200,000." With the unanimous consent of his partners at Cravath, who discussed the matter at a firm meeting, and the agreement of Armstrong, McCormack rejected the offer.

Now caught in a tragic drama of Greek proportions, Armstrong realized he had set in motion forces over which he had no control. He understood he was caught in a legal battle that no single man—not even an Armstrong—could hope to win. "They will stall this thing until I am dead or broke," he had told friends more than once over the years. Now his dark prophecy seemed to be coming true. FM, his work and overriding passion for the last quarter century, was a failure. His invention had been belittled by almost all in AM broadcasting, the very industry that his other fundamental inventions, regeneration and the superheterodyne, had created. Those discoveries had been taken from him by jealous inventors, avaricious lawyers, and ignorant judges who did not appreciate the art. Al McCormack had ended his letter to Judge McCook by saying that it was "imperative . . . that the pretrial proceedings in the case be concluded as soon as possible and the case be put in shape for trial." But would FM suffer the same fate as his earlier inventions? Could he endure to see another of his creations taken from him? And time was on his adversary's side, for as McCormack had told him, he should not expect to see any money until 1961.

Armstrong spent a solitary Christmas and New Year's in his apartment, while Marion stayed with her sister in Connecticut. His family was worried about his health, which seemed more precarious than ever. When just before Christmas he arrived at his sister's house on Long Island to install a radio, she thought him close to nervous collapse.

Al McCormack grew worried. Early in January, Armstrong had told him some of his financial dilemma, that he would have to settle with RCA as swiftly as possible. "Turn your mind to your own accomplishments," McCormack advised him. "You have been given gifts as few men have. You will be remembered when the rest of us are all forgotten." Armstrong replied despondently, "You don't know how little all that means when you have made a mess of your personal life."

John Bose, his most trusted associate in the laboratory at Columbia, saw the strain on his mentor, too. "He looked like Hell. . . . He really didn't look well," Bose remembered. Armstrong had come up to the laboratory to see some of Bose's most recent refinements in multiplexing on the last Wednesday in January. "He was always telling me what to do— 'Do this. Do this. Try that'—But this time," Bose said, "he had no interest in it." That night Bose phoned to remind him that the Radio Club of America was meeting on Thursday and invited him to come. Pleading that he was suffering from a flu bug, Armstrong declined. That Saturday Bose tried to call him to ask for a raise, but decided not to as other workers in the laboratory might overhear their conversation. Perhaps he might broach the question the next day during his regular Sunday phone call from the major. The calls had become such a fixture of the two men's Sabbath routine that Bose had taken to attending church in order to forestall them until the afternoon. Always the conversation concerned work at the laboratory, experiments to conduct, and ideas to pursue. However, this Sunday, January 31, 1954, the call did not come.

That day in his apartment at River House, Howard Armstrong did have several phone conversations. Al McCormack called from Washington where he was preparing for an appearance before the Supreme Court the next day. He would be back at Cravath later in the week to start up negotiations with William Davis once again. He spoke with George Burghard to learn about the condition of Burghard's ill wife. Though he promised to call later that night, he never did. Randy Runyon rang up to invite him for a drink later that day; Armstrong accepted the invitation but never showed up.

Sunday, January 31, also marked an anniversary that Howard Armstrong was not likely to have forgotten. Forty years before, on January 31, 1914, he and David Sarnoff had spent the night together in a shack in Belmar, New Jersey, listening to his first black box—his regenerative receiver—and copying telegraph messages from all over the world. It had marked the beginning of their friendship, which had flourished in the 1920s. He had been the "coffee man," the person who was always stopping by the Sarnoff house to talk of radio. He had sold Sarnoff and RCA superregeneration and helped him develop the superheterodyne. He had defended him, even in a shareholders' meeting. And, on January 31, 1934, he had marked the twentieth anniversary of their friendship. "Fix your gaze and energies on the next twenty years," Sarnoff had told him then, so that the telegrams and letters exchanged at the end of the next generation would make them "feel that we are still young." But twenty years had passed; they were enemies in competition, and he had been defeated.

In his bedroom that evening, Howard Armstrong wrote a final letter in pencil on a yellow legal pad:

Dearest Marion:

I am heartbroken because I cannot see you once again. I deeply regret what has happened between us. I cannot understand how I could hurt the dearest thing in the whole world to me.

I would give my life to turn back to the time when we were so happy and free.

My estate is solvent, especially if RCA comes through. Also, the Telephone Company should pay something, for they have been using my inventions.

God keep you and may the Lord have mercy on my soul.

Ed

He removed the air conditioner from his bedroom window. Thirteen stories below was the East River. Directly beneath the window was the third-story roof of the River Club. The 25-foot tower behind his house in Yonkers, the New Jersey Palisades he climbed as a youth, the WJZ tower with its great strap iron ball 400 feet above 42nd Street, his own 425-foot tower at Alpine—he had always loved high places.

At 10:30 the next morning, a doorman found Armstrong's fractured body on the roof of the River Club. He was dressed neatly in a suit and overcoat with a scarf and gloves. His plunge had been the last defiant act of the lone inventor and a lonely man.

"By what a tragic and terrible contrast to my good health is the deplorable death of Major Armstrong!" Lee de Forest wrote to a friend on February 2. "What on earth could have induced that rash act on his part?" he asked, eagerly hoping for some reply. When the answer came a few days later, de Forest took great pleasure in what he read, even quoting it in letters to others: "He had been so obsessed with himself and his invention as to have been unnatural for some years and the object of comment on the part of friends lest he become mad. . . . Oh, what abnormality both in ingenuity and pugnacious ego . . . oh, 'what price glory!' "

"His death was indeed most lamentable," de Forest wrote to another friend. "I have always given him full credit for his introduction of FM, but have always taken the keenest delight in having beaten him so thoroughly on the feed-back question. . . . Well, after all, Armstrong has gone and I am alive, well and happy, and hope to live for many years more. What a contrast!"

At his office in Rockefeller Center, David Sarnoff learned the news. "I did not kill Armstrong," he said directly to Carl Dreher, a mutual acquaintance who had known both men since the 1920s. Dreher quickly replied that no such thought had ever entered his head. But it was clear that David Sarnoff had been profoundly shaken. Though he had professed to be a friend of Armstrong's at his deposition less than a year earlier, all personal contact with his former friend had long since ceased. There had been the FM demonstrations at Columbia, the Empire State Building, and New Jersey, a few lunch meetings in the late 1930s, but nothing since. For years they had conducted all communication through counsel rather than as friends. Since they had first met, Armstrong had possessed a single devotion to radio; since Christmas 1933, that devotion had developed into a monomania about FM. Armstrong could think only of the FM, while he, the general, had to lead an industry.

For the last five years, RCA annual reports had contained a terse sentence, "A patent infringement suit brought against the Corporation and the National Broadcasting Company, Inc. by Edwin H. Armstrong is pending in the District Court of the United States for the District of Delaware." Sarnoff had known indirectly of the toll the litigation was taking on his former friend. Yet always in his mind, the corporation's interests should prevail. Had he been right?

At 1 P.M. on Wednesday, February 3, Dr. Thornton Penfield, rector of the Armstrong family's First Presbyterian Church in Yonkers, presided over the funeral at the Fifth Avenue Presbyterian Church in Manhattan. Praising Armstrong as a man of "great integrity," who had made a "deep impact" on the lives of all, the minister ended with a prayer:

> We thank Thee, Lord, for characters of strength who dare to carry on when there is little hope of fulfillment. He had the persistence to fight his way through like a mountain climber overcoming unconquerable obstacles. We thank Thee for men of great loyalty like his, who loved this country and gave his service to it, who was loyal to his associates in business and to his friends with ties that went back through the years.

Penfield's emphasis on integrity and loyalty would have pleased Armstrong. And the simile was one he would have liked, too. He had been the mountain climber; his delight had come in conquest where no one else thought it possible.

Among the 150 family members, friends, and colleagues listening to the sermon was David Sarnoff. The mourners in the pew behind him long remembered how the general had wept openly.

—

On February 25, 1954, David Sarnoff announced to shareholders that RCA's volume of business for the previous year had reached "an all-time high" of more than $850 million. That May 5, at the corporation's annual meeting, stockholders cheered when their chairman announced the introduction of a nineteen-inch color television and said that TV sales accounted for 54 percent of the corporation's business. At the end of the meeting, one man, made ecstatic by the blossoming of RCA dividends, delivered a glowing encomium about his corporation, concluding, "Have faith and confidence in Uncle Sam of the United States of America and in Daddy David of RCA."

13

VICTORIES GREAT
AND SMALL

◢

Edwin Howard Armstrong died thinking he was a failure. He never understood that he had been more successful than any of the people or interests he had been battling, or that his achievements would long outlive those of his rivals. Marion Armstrong knew differently. She spent the next quarter century redressing the wrongs her husband had suffered and ensuring that he received the recognition after death that had eluded him in life.

Marion first faced the labyrinthine problems of Armstrong's estate. In a will dated April 28, 1942, the inventor had left everything to his wife. But examination of his private papers yielded dark and embarrassing truths, especially about his finances, that only he had known. "The Major was rather secretive about money matters," Al McCormack wrote to a relative who claimed, correctly, that Armstrong had a small outstanding loan, "and the details of his financial affairs were known only to the tax attorneys." Some secrets astonished those who thought they knew him well.

Though Howard had told Marion of his financial problems, she had never imagined she would find them as desperate as they were. Keys discovered in River House opened large safety deposit boxes in the vault at the Hanover Bank in Manhattan. They were empty. Marion found other accounts: $48,556.22 at the Chase National Bank, $4,533.43 at the Irving Trust Company, and $6,042.87 with a stockbroker. Other than his apartment at River House, his home at Rye Beach, his FM tower and laboratory at Alpine, some miscellaneous equipment at Columbia, and his 1941 and 1948 Packards, there seemed little of value.

329

That spring in a garage on West 76th Street, Marion discovered Howard's Hispano-Suiza beneath a thick layer of New York dirt, the car of rich memories for which Armstrong had paid $11,000 cash. He had courted her in it, driven it on their honeymoon, and lovingly cared for it until he had been overwhelmed by litigation. Forgotten, its top and tires rotted, the Hispano-Suiza had not been driven for many years. One person offered the estate $260 to take it away; another, $1,000. Marion decided to sell it to a collector in New Jersey who carefully restored its former elegance.

Marion Armstrong could never return to River House. She would divide her time between her sister's house in Connecticut and a smaller apartment at 485 Park Avenue. Within a week of her husband's death, she put apartment 13A on sale for $75,000; at the end of the month she sold it for her asking price. That spring she decided to go on an extensive tour of Europe with her sister.

Some of Armstrong's equipment possessed significant historic value. In August, Marion sent the early models of his inventions, including regeneration, superheterodyne, and superregeneration, and a primitive FM receiver to the Smithsonian Institution. Other materials, including his medals and some early radios, went to the Franklin Institute.

By the late spring, it was clear to all of Armstrong's employees at Alpine and the Hartley laboratories that they would soon be out of work. For years, while he had been consumed with the FM litigation, Armstrong had turned much of the laboratory management over to John Bose. Always working under the major's orders, Bose conducted research in FM multiplexing or stereo. Now he accepted an offer from the electrical engineering department at Columbia. On June 30, 1954, the estate awarded him a month's severance pay. Tom Styles, the faithful friend from Armstrong's youth who had overseen the business affairs of Armstrong's laboratory, decided to retire. "It is particularly distressing in your case," wrote McCormack informing him of the decision to disband the laboratories, "in view of your age and length of service." Styles understood.

As one of their last acts for the major, the workers at Alpine took an inventory of the property. As expenses there in 1953 had been $102,872.07, including $54,966.02 in salaries and $33,521.12 in laboratory costs, the workers understood that they, too, would be dismissed. McCormack arranged to give the tower and the site to Columbia for research.

The workers catalogued two items of personal importance at the Alpine site. Many years before, when the WJZ tower on the Aeolian Hall was being demolished, Howard Armstrong purchased the globe on which he had balanced in 1923. He had erected it at the entrance to his laboratory building. Also at the entrance was the base of Armstrong's first antenna mast that he had built behind his house in Yonkers. Marion had the ball and tower base removed and transported to her house at Rye Beach.

Perhaps the hardest of Armstrong's legacies to part with was his FM station W2XMN, which had the new call letters KE2XCC. Through it he had demonstrated to the world the power of his invention, spending an estimated $1 million broadcasting "good music." From Alpine, Armstrong had developed mobile communications for police and fire radio systems, conducted experiments for FM radar, FM relay, and most recently multiplexing. But the site was too expensive to maintain.

At 7 P.M. on March 6, 1954, station KE2XCC presented a program in memory of Major Armstrong. Al McCormack had selected the music for the occasion, including the overture from *The Magic Flute*, a selection of Strauss waltzes, and the triumphal march from *Aida*. At 8:57 that evening, an announcer said, "This is the last program of our fifteen years of broadcasting." The "Star-Spangled Banner" was played, and then, the announcer concluded: "As we now prepare to pull the switch and shut the station down, we salute the memory of Edwin Howard Armstrong." Then, static.

Al McCormack faced eighteen unresolved patent suits against RCA and other corporations that Armstrong had decided to sue, and the fact that his friend had died leaving about $250,000 in unpaid legal bills. To McCormack, this was an embarrassment, for as a partner at the law firm of Cravath, Swaine, and Moore, as the firm was now called, he was obligated to collect the money. Ultimately, a percentage of that money would be shared with his partners. McCormack had first been placed in such an awkward position in 1942, when Armstrong had told him he could not pay his bills, but then McCormack had prevailed on the inventor to take a government contract. Now the lawyer found himself in a "continuous struggle against time" to recover the money owed his firm.

The challenge seemed herculean. Certainly the patent suits represented the potential of millions of dollars. But it would take money to continue them. Then there was the problem of the Internal Revenue Service. There would be taxes on the estate as well as the patent settlements. Would the IRS consider a settlement with RCA as principal or income? Were it deemed income, taxes could consume as much as 90 percent. Whatever the resolution of these suits, McCormack would have to arrange as favorable a schedule of payments as possible so that Marion might realize some profits.

By April, McCormack recognized that it was time to settle with RCA. Marion agreed. "I can well imagine that 'D.S.' will try every method to avoid any *real* settlement," she wrote McCormack from Lucerne, "but I ardently hope that something truly substantial will be the eventual result." Understanding McCormack's predicament, she added that she desired him to follow his good judgment "that the books may be balanced with you and your good firm."

Once again, as he had so often before, McCormack reactivated negotiations between the sides. Given the regrettable circumstances of Armstrong's death, lawyers and observers in the industry assumed that Sarnoff and other executives at RCA would be happy to have the entire matter behind them. But meetings with John Cahill and David Sarnoff in April were not reassuring. Despite Sarnoff's protestations to Judge McCook at the deposition that he would pay "substantially more" than $1 million to settle the claims against RCA, the general was no longer willing to do so. Nor was RCA interested in concluding a settlement for others in the industry. McCormack's efforts to find out from Cahill just how much Sarnoff might pay were futile. Verbal sparring dragged on in a desultory fashion through the spring and into the summer. Cahill seemed more intent on arguing the case than resolving it.

By July, with discussions between the Armstrong estate and RCA at an impasse, the prospects for financial settlements looked bleak, but new developments on other fronts helped. At the end of the month, McCormack negotiated a $250,000 agreement with Telefunken in Bonn for German rights to the Armstrong patents. While in Germany, he received word from McCook offering his help to settle the case. From his hotel room in Bonn, McCormack responded to the judge's approach:

> I am willing to settle for a million dollars, and I have the client's authority to do so. When and how we would want the money paid would depend on what comes out of our application for a tax ruling.
> So, Judge, if you want to take on the job in the heat of summer, . . . you have my authority to work out a settlement of the case for one million dollars. Should you be successful, . . . you would be entitled to a very liberal allowance by the Court—sufficient, I would hope, to enable you to take it easy for a couple of years and get those memoirs finished.

On September 1, David Sarnoff, too, accepted the judge's proposal to arbitrate a settlement. Each side was to name the amount it felt to be "fair and reasonable." McCormack's figure was $1.25 million; RCA's was $750,000. As arbitrator, McCook would adjudicate the proposals and make a decision. At last, after six years, an agreement was in sight.

But at a critical juncture, Judge McCook's fragile arbitration process was in danger of breaking down. In November, RCA's counsel John Cahill tried to shift the ground of negotiations once again. First, he suggested, "We should like Mr. McCormack to name a figure for settlement . . . [of] the Armstrong Estate's claims against . . . all others in the radio industry." McCormack resisted. He reminded Cahill and Judge McCook of his April luncheon and suggested that the Armstrong side was making other arrangements. Then counsel for RCA and Armstrong began to argue about the meaning of their agreement. Certainly, Cahill asserted, the settlement would release RCA from all *future* claims of patent infringement on the part of the Armstrong estate, which would in effect give RCA a sixteen-year royalty-free license to use Armstrong's last invention for FM multiplexing.

McCormack exploded. "Every concession" by the Armstrong side "leads only to another demand" from RCA. He would not be snared by the tactics that had helped to destroy his client, and he knew that RCA was bound to accept McCook's decision. Threatening to withdraw all the concessions he had made unless RCA withdrew its latest demands, McCormack reminded the judge gently "that a binding agreement to arbitrate has been made . . . your Honor is now fully empowered to go ahead and fix the figure."

McCook acted quickly but prudently. Choosing the mean between the two ends, he awarded the Armstrong estate $1,050,000. Marion Armstrong was to receive $125,000 on Christmas Eve 1954; $475,000 on January 5, 1955, $100,000 in 1956, $100,000 in 1957, and $25,000 a year from 1958 to 1967. For his efforts, Philip McCook received $50,000 out of the settlement.

The judge's determination, which was strikingly similar to the one RCA had offered twelve months earlier, forced Marion and her lawyers to question their own resolution and commitment. Would Howard Armstrong have accepted? Did their settlement betray the principles for which he had fought so boldly? Were they being faithful to his memory? "The total amount of the settlement is not as large as you or I would like it to be," Al McCormack wrote to Marion Armstrong on Christmas Eve, "but my partners—who are much more objective than I can be—think it is an excellent settlement." It had cost RCA "a half-million dollars . . . at an absolute minimum . . . and probably more nearly twice that" to settle the suit. Addressing the more difficult question, McCormack offered balm to assuage the pain:

> I said to you yesterday that the Major had been more interested in proving certain points than in winning the lawsuit; and you said that that was one of the things that made you uncomfortable about settling the RCA suit. But you need not feel that way. Howard could never be satisfied that a point had been proved till his opponents had conceded it. We, however, can look at the matter more objectively as time passes; and as I said to him at least 50 times in the last two years of his life, he had proved his points and they were as clear as they could ever be in the record of their depositions. . . . No intelligent and

impartial person could read the testimony . . . without seeing what a sordid and shabby game the RCA Patent Department and some of their engineers were playing.

The best thing you can do for a person who has passed from this world is to carry on in the way he would have wanted. I firmly believe we are doing that.

So I hope that you will have these thoughts in mind on Christmas Day because the memory of last Christmas must still be very distressing to you. It need not be. In the past 11 months you have demonstrated—if demonstration were needed, which to me it clearly was not—your complete fidelity to the Major and his memory, and I think your mind can be at peace, because in every way, as I see it, you are carrying out what would have been his wishes.

From McCormack's words Marion took fresh courage. Having addressed the financial question, she was now free to press forward with the other suits. She would establish his legitimate status as a great inventor.

At the end of the war, Lee de Forest was well into his seventh decade, still enjoying relatively good health and a joyful marriage, and still convinced of his essential genius. He would spend his last years as he had his first, a lone man dreaming of inventions. As always, he craved recognition of his achievements, but with the passing years and a succession of electronic inventions that seemed further and further removed from his vacuum tube, he inevitably found his name receding from the public consciousness. As always, money remained an enduring problem.

Marie de Forest remained steadfast and faithful to her husband, and devoted to his talents. She still drove him to work each morning and called for him each afternoon at 4:30. The days of climbing 14,000 feet to the top of Mount Whitney, though, had ended on his seventieth birthday in 1943, and he no longer was equal to the challenge of such formidable heights. "Wise old men and doctors—and now my own heart," he wrote in 1950, "warn me to go slow in climbing." Though he and Marie still went camping each summer, they pitched their tent close to their car. Gradually, "hikes" became "walks," confined to paths no more than 5,000 feet high and near the road. Her knitting in hand, Marie usually waited patiently for her husband by the car. Though she never enjoyed these excursions, she never complained about them. Indeed, she fooled de Forest into thinking "she loves that life." Years later, after his death, she confided she had loathed the camping excursions and would have never chosen them, "except," she said, that "they made Lee so happy."

De Forest's nature remained tempestuous, but less so than in earlier days. Marie's peaceful temperament tended to soothe rather than inflame and was well suited to his. She was happy providing for his comfort and maintaining Cielito Lindo. Only a serious argument over driving disturbed their harmony. Once content to have a chauffeur take him about, he balked when, after a minor accident in 1952, Marie insisted doing all the driving. She was trying to make him into "an old man," de Forest raged, adding, "I'm not going to give up my independence just to coddle you." But after Marie threatened to have the California authorities revoke his license, he agreed. Their house required most of her attention in their later years. Marie took special delight in her brilliant flower garden. She tried, often in vain, to keep Lee inside, away from the plants, as he insisted on watering them with the hose nozzle at withering force.

Though he slowed down physically, he remained a voracious and eclectic reader. Titles in his bookshelf ranged from *Pilgrim's Progress* to Jules Verne's *From the Earth to the Moon*. Lee and Marie watched television, too, but only with great reluctance. Programming on the screen seemed just as bad as it was on radio. In 1950, he confided to the radio and television editor of the Chicago *Tribune* that he had given away his twelve-inch DuMont television set "to a neighbor whose cultural tastes I thought were about on a level with our television programs." When he got another set, a De Forest 44 model, he unceasingly railed against what he saw.

The Women's Association of the First Congregational Church in Los Angeles wrote to de Forest that it looked to him for "leadership" in bringing "yet more educational and cultural presentations into our homes," and de Forest in his own way provided it. To his congressman he protested: "The amount of horror and crime on . . . programs for children is staggering. . . . The damage such exhibitions work on the nerves and sleeping habits of children is beyond calculation, physicians so attest." Surely it was his duty to call on the FCC to revoke the license of any station that broadcast "during children's viewing hours, any program portraying murder, robbery, crime or violence."

When not assessing the content of children's programs, de Forest turned his attention to adult fare. After watching one of Bob Hope's entertainment specials for the navy in June 1953, he and Marie turned off their TV "in righteous anger" and fired off a telegram to the comedian declaring one scene to be a "disgrace." Not content with the telegram, the inventor followed with a letter the next morning:

> Homosexual intimations, so vulgarly expressed, turned our feelings and I am sure the feelings of thousands of former admirers of yours, from admiration to revulsion.
>
> We did not think you were capable of putting on such a "low down" spectacle, so suggestive of evil to the young navy sailors, before whom you performed.

His invention, de Forest thought, had made such corruption and immorality possible. The human capacity to create great technology had far outpaced the ability to use it wisely. Producers thought only of using radio for cheap entertainment. They had forgotten his exemplary music programs and talks that he broadcast to enlighten the minds and elevate the tastes of the masses. They had forgotten the high ideals of the one who had made it all possible.

The country was in decline, de Forest believed, and television only mirrored the general debasement of American culture, which he saw everywhere. In his eighties, he grew even more conservative than he had been as a youth. Ever the rock-solid Republican, he had been more conservative than McKinley, considered Wilson pusillaminous, detested FDR, and damned Truman. When the fever induced by Senator Joseph McCarthy rose across the nation, de Forest was not immune. DONT BE OPTIMISTIC OSTRICH he telegraphed President Eisenhower on December 6, 1953. THE COMMUNIST INFILTRATION IN AMERICA WILL NOT BE ACADEMIC NEXT FALL. MCCARTHY DESERVES HIGH PRAISE NOT CENSURE. The next day he followed it with a letter to the senator himself: "I am unable to praise you sufficiently for your magnificent and sustained efforts on behalf of this nation." The *Nation* received his special wrath when it dared to stand up to the senator's attacks. McCarthy, he said in a letter canceling his subscription, was ferreting out "enemies to Americanism," enemies that he believed infested the "teeming nest" of the magazine's editorial office.

Perhaps it was America's moral decline that persuaded de Forest to lend his name to the national "go to church" campaign. Yes, he told a clearly puzzled inquirer, he was "a complete agnostic" who had not attended church regularly since his days at Yale. Yet even though church might not benefit him personally, it was "a tremendously powerful agency in our civilization." He reasoned that "the great mass of citizens, old and young, of whatever faith" did take comfort in attendance, and he should encourage them.

By supporting such causes as "go to church," de Forest also realized, he kept his name before the public. As a young inventor, he had sought to "make my name at least rank with that of Marconi"; at the St. Louis World's Fair he had slept atop a tower resplendent with electric lights glowing his name. In the 1920s, the name "De Forest" had been emblazoned on radios and radio tubes. Advertisements in magazines and newspapers regularly proclaimed his to be "the Greatest Name in radio." Now there were more radios than ever before. Every day people turned on his invention in their living rooms and kitchens, their cars and trucks, their offices and stores. But they no longer knew or cared who the inventor of radio was. Lee de Forest spent the rest of his days trying to teach them.

Even de Forest's beloved alma mater ignored his genius—a matter that pained him terribly. "I am today frequently amazed that Yale so often seems completely oblivious to the fact that it was in her halls of science that the knowledge and training were acquired which later made possible the beginning of the electronic age," he complained in a letter to the Yale radio station late in 1951. "Seldom, if ever, in the last twenty years has the University evidenced any sense of pride in this truth." When the Sterling Library showed little interest in his journals, he gave them instead to the Library of Congress.

Determined not to be forgotten, de Forest decided in 1948 to publish his autobiography, on which he had been working for many years. The impulse to write his life had sprung from his sense of his own importance and the inadequacy of other assessments of his life. Georgette Carneal's biography of him, *Conqueror of Space*, which he had largely overseen, had not done well; Gerald Tyne and George Clark had abandoned their projected biography. He would have to do it himself. He had been fascinated with the form since he began keeping a journal in 1891. In 1902–03 he wrote "A Fragmentary Study in Autobiography," and had written longer versions in the 1930s. For many years, he had kept a scrapbook of his press clippings. Now it was time to review these materials and draw them into a coherent whole that would contain his recollections, quotations from his journals, selections from his poetry, even an appendix listing all his inventions. Perhaps, as he wrote in his didactic preface, "the frank revelation" of his own "struggles, disappointments and successes" might "encourage others to embark upon a similar career of discovery and invention." He had long regarded Marconi merely as the "father of the wireless telegraph," while *he* had created the radio. The title de Forest chose reasserted his claim: *Father of Radio*.

✄

Father of Radio proved to be pure de Forest, his attempt to record his life as he saw it, embellished with his own recollections. He depicted the trials and triumphs of the individualist—sometimes over great odds, but sometimes over the facts. He was disarmingly candid at times. He admitted to adapting Reginald Fessenden's electrolytic detector, and told of his love for Jessie Wallace. Yet at other times he was remarkably silent. He recounted the genesis of his other inventions hazily and neglected to mention his first wife, Lucille Sheardown. The overriding themes were that perseverance and genius would conquer all. "Looking back today the course I followed," de Forest said in his concluding words, "spite of fate and love and hate, seems incredible. But I had the vision," he added, "inner faith in myself, the inflexible resolve, the all-so-necessary courage." *Father of Radio* recorded de Forest's success and failures as only he could see them.

Published by Wilcox & Follett Company of Chicago and priced at $5, *Father of Radio* appeared in time for his birthday in 1950. To drum up publicity, the publisher sent a letter addressed only "To the Father of Radio / Hollywood, California," with the hope that it would arrive before a birthday luncheon planned for August 23. De Forest was to notify the press that despite its limited address, the letter reached him because of his famous invention. But the envelope was returned to the sender, "addressee unknown."

"We will do everything humanly possible to give this book the circulation that it so well deserves," pledged C. W. Follett, the publisher. But when advertisements did not appear immediately, de Forest became suspicious. Soon he was complaining that the sales representative for Wilcox & Follett "does not know of my existence." By mid-September he grew angry: he had heard rumors, he told C. W. Follett, that his publishing house was failing. He lamented he did not have the money to purchase the plates for his autobiography and publish and advertise it himself. "The book as it stands is a work of art and deserves better treatment than you can or will give it." Follett replied in a four-page, sternly worded letter assuring de Forest of his firm's financial strength and promising that advertisements would appear in a number of periodicals. But advertising did little to enhance sales, and reviews were few. In the end, most of the copies went to radio pioneers, members of the Institute of Radio Engineers, former Yale classmates, and de Forest himself. Despite the enormous number of copies de Forest gave away, more than half of the 5,000 printed were on hand in 1952; between January 1 and December 31, 1953, the sales totaled 54.

The inventor blamed the failure of *Father of Radio* to sell on everything but the book itself. "Almost from the start I have been more and more disappointed with my publishers" the inventor told George Clark. They had delayed releasing his autobiography "longer than a year, during which time television had turned millions away from book reading." Now the war raging in Korea left Americans with little desire for "anything but newspapers."

Though de Forest's autobiography was not successful, perhaps one by Marie about her career as an actress and her life with him would be. He determined the book would be titled *I Married a Genius* and reported to a friend in October 1951 that the manuscript was "about three-fifths completed." But Marie never finished it.

Not to be discouraged by the failure of *Father of Radio* to achieve the success he had envisioned for it, de Forest turned his mind to other schemes for making his name synonymous with the creation of the electronic age. He hired a press representative who frequently managed to have his name mentioned in newspapers and sometimes engineered his appearance on a radio or television show. Whenever possible, de Forest used his time on the air to remind listeners of his invention. For example:

> Thank you, Hal, you are very kind. As you know, I, along with many others, followed your "Help Thy Neighbor" program through all the years you broadcasted on radio, which as everyone knows was a great success. They say "one touch of nature makes the whole world 'kin,' " and your program certainly proved that statement. I'm happy to know that my child has been instrumental in making neighbors of *all people*, that is one of the things I envisioned for radio—more and better neighborliness . . . programs of this and other worthwhile types have my earnest blessing.

In February 1954, CBS radio produced "The Life of Doctor Lee de Forest" with Lionel Barrymore for the Hallmark Hall of Fame program. In 1956, Ralph Edwards surprised him on "This Is Your Life" ("the best picture that Ralph Edwards ever produced," said de Forest), bringing him together with his sister, former employees, and three daughters.

Other projects never came to fruition. Through a Hollywood agent, he tried to sell a feature film, *The De Forest Story*, but the studios were not interested. A similar proposal for a television series based on his life met with no interest. He hired an old friend in New York to edit his journals and submit them for publication. No publisher expressed interest. In mid-1955, he contacted Vantage Press, a vanity press in New York City, but recoiled at the thought that he would have to pay for publication.

Despite the limited success of all his plans, de Forest could take comfort in the fact that his colleagues *did* remember him. In the fall of 1951, a group of the inventor's former employees began the De Forest Pioneers, a group devoted to celebrating his genius. For a fee, members received certificates ("beautifully designed and printed on very fine parchment"), a lapel button ("rolled gold with Chinese blue enamel"), and an autographed copy of *Father of Radio*. The Pioneers commissioned a portrait bust of their hero and presented it to Yale. In April 1952, they gathered at the Waldorf-Astoria Hotel for a testimonial dinner at which Herbert Hoover gave the keynote address. These were the people who mattered most. To them, de Forest was their beloved "Doc." They were forever loyal to his own purposes in life, and he took comfort knowing they were with him at the end. Each August 23 they met at Fraunces' Tavern to celebrate his birthday.

The bust and testimonials, the radio and television appearances were fine, of course; but still de Forest wanted more. He had long coveted a Nobel Prize, and when his admirers suggested a campaign to persuade the Nobel selection committee, de Forest heartily encouraged them. Why not? Marconi had shared the prize in 1909 with Karl F. Braun, the developer of the cathode ray tube; certainly the inventor of the audion, the father of radio, deserved one, too. Hugo Gernsback began the campaign with an editorial in *Radio-Electronics* magazine. In a 1956 letter to Gernsback, de Forest suggested a list of prominent people who might be induced to write letters, some of whom were Nobel laureates: "Nobelist Prince de Broglie . . . and Nobelist Shockley [who received the prize earlier that year] would unquestionably second my nomination." The inventor also suggested some politicians:

> Senator Knowland and
> Senator Kuchel from California
> Vice President Nixon
> (You might even try President Eisenhower)

In the end a group as diverse as Charles Edison, son of the inventor; Thomas Watson, the president of IBM; the governor of California; the Multnomah County surveyor in Portland, Oregon; and the president of the Goshen High School Science Club in Goshen, Indiana, wrote letters of support to the Swedish Academy of Science, but with no success. In 1955, 1956, and 1957, the years of intense lobbying, the Nobel Prize in physics went to others.

Beneath Lee de Forest's desire for fame lay his hunger for fortune. In the inventor's mind, the two were nearly synonymous. The rights to the story of his life, he told his press representative, "should be worth at least $50,000," adding that she should work very hard to sell them. Yet in the shadows of his life, fortune proved as evanescent as fame. The dreams of great riches became the reality of a simple need to subsist. His assets had dwindled to his house and furnishings on Hollywood Boulevard and the equipment in his laboratory.

At his laboratory on North Highland Avenue in Los Angeles, de Forest worked alone on a variety of ideas. Though his business enterprises had gone through a number of names—United Engineering Laboratories; Lee De Forest, International, Inc.; or simply Lee De Forest, the inventor always stood at the center of activities. While the tinkering continued, the rate of his inventing diminished. In most cases, the inventions did not translate into cash.

De Forest had always prided himself on his independence. He had earned his money from his inventions and his companies, and from the sale of the rights to his patents. But by 1946, with little capital and almost no money coming in, de Forest reluctantly concluded that his financial condition compelled him to work for someone else. He turned to Bell Telephone Laboratories. Perhaps they would pay him to serve as a research consultant working in his own laboratory in Los Angeles. No doubt feeling some responsibility for its treatment of de Forest's earlier inventions, especially his audion, Bell Telephone accepted the proposal. De Forest would receive $15,000 a year in monthly installments. Each year, he presented a report on his investigations. Yes, he had tied himself to another company, but he retained the autonomy to work on any idea that struck his fancy. The money, along with his pension as a Spanish-American War veteran, assured him and Marie solvency.

De Forest took his research work seriously, but it did not pay. There were other resources, chances for great wealth if only the proper break would come. After the war, he decided to lend his name to various entrepreneurial ventures concerning television. In Chicago, an enterprising businessman began De Forest Training, Inc., an electronics school. Except for selling his name and making an occasional visit, de Forest had little to do with the venture. For a royalty fee he lent his name and prestige to the American Television Company in Chicago, and also agreed to conduct some research.

That the American Television Company named its premier line of sixteen- and nineteen-inch models the De Forest 44 gave the inventor great pleasure. Once again his name would be associated with quality. "A very fine model" he called it in a letter to the president of Bell Laboratories. For a short while consumers thought so, too, as sales and the consequent royalties were healthy. "Marie has her eyes on a very sparkling marquise diamond," he wrote the president of American Television in June 1951, in a letter asking what payment he would receive. But this venture as well turned sour. American Television limped along with slow sales and diminished royalties for de Forest until 1956 when it had to declare bankruptcy.

Having his name associated with a company in financial straits presented difficulties for de Forest, too. Though still manufacturing under the protection of the bankruptcy court, American Television produced sets of inferior quality, sets with his name on them. Soon he was receiving the complaints. "I simply cannot afford to allow the de Forest name to be put into such jeopardy as it must inevitably when cases of customers like these are not treated justly, and satisfied."

Under bankruptcy reorganization, de Forest was to receive $200 a week. By the end of the year the company was skipping payments. "Your . . .

weekly checks are badly needed here, and are imperative," de Forest wrote to the president in December 1956. It was the first of many letters. By April, he was threatening a suit: "I have a very able attorney in Chicago who would like nothing better than to take a case against you." In June, he had to threaten again. Threats and sporadic payments continued until October 1957, when de Forest received notice that all the assets of American Television were to be sold. The De Forest 44 and the visions of great wealth soon became a memory.

Still, the quest for money went on. Through an intermediary, de Forest tried to interest RCA in an arrangement similar to the one he had with Bell Laboratories. Perhaps, as he phrased it in a letter to a friend, the corporation would be interested in making "monthly contributions." It was not.

Even though the de Forests were short of cash, traveling took up more and more of the couple's time. Lee had been to the capitals of Europe many times, but for Marie it was a wholly new experience. Generous friends and former employees, especially members of the De Forest Pioneers, often paid for the trips.

On the last night of a trip through the Panama Canal in late July 1957, de Forest suffered a heart attack. A representative of Howard Hughes arranged for him to be flown back to Los Angeles, where he recovered. But not entirely. He had known that he was suffering from progressive hardening of the arteries since 1953. Following the medical fashion of the time, his doctor at the Beverly Hills Clinic insisted that he rest a great deal of the day, not "climb any stairs or hills," and limit his workday to four hours. Late in 1957, he had a small elevator installed in his house, but it did little to check his progressive decline. Those around him, especially his wife and middle daughter, Eleanor, knew he was weakening steadily. In early 1958, doctors removed a tumor from his bladder, putting another strain on his frail body, and by the end of the year he remained confined to his bed. There he lay, day in, day out, often in an unnatural, heavy sleep, marked by irregular and sometimes stertorous breathing. To Marie, who attended to him daily, he said little; to the few visitors allowed to sit by his bed, he said nothing; to Eleanor, who sat by his bed faithfully each Sunday, he said but eight words: "Your grandfather would be very proud of you."

The end came quietly on the last day of June 1961. De Forest had suffered a bladder infection earlier that summer which placed too great a strain on his heart.

Marie arranged for her husband to be buried at the San Fernando Mission Cemetery northeast of Los Angeles. While the consecrated ground of the final rest meant nothing to the person who had eschewed all religion since his father's death in 1899, it gave solace to his wife, who still took comfort in her faith. Later that summer, people were shocked to learn that the man whose invention formed the base of the multi-billion-dollar electronics industry had but $1,250 in cash when he died.

Marie, the fourth Mrs. Lee de Forest, lived on in Cielito Lindo, the Hollywood Boulevard house, until 1967 when she sold it and moved to Hemet, a small town southeast of the city. She remained as attached to her husband in death as she had been in life. To her death she maintained a joint checking account, "Dr. and Mrs. Lee de Forest," and saw to it that mail continued to be addressed to her husband and herself. Each day she conversed with his portrait that hung in her living room. She frequently wore the charm bracelet given to her by Ralph Edwards when Lee had been the subject of "This Is Your Life." Each charm depicted one of her husband's inventions.

Most people had forgotten Lee de Forest and his contributions, it seemed, so she tried desperately to rescue his name from oblivion. One way was to create an archive. When the trustees of the Douglas Perham Foundation proposed that she give some of her husband's papers and memorabilia to the Foothill Museum that they were establishing in Los Altos, she gave enough materials to fill a small library and promised more. In 1973, the museum opened the Lee de Forest Memorial Archives.

By the early 1980s friends noticed that Marie de Forest's mind was beginning to wander and that she was suffering from the early stages of Alzheimer's disease. She managed to drive a car and get about by herself until 1984, when she was moved into a nursing home in Los Angeles. From 1984 until her death in 1987, Mrs. Lee de Forest lived peacefully within herself.

In the last two decades of his life, David Sarnoff experienced personal triumph and personal failure, but he masked those failures through self-aggrandizement on a grand scale. Wrapped in the mantle of triumph, his ego became greater than ever. Only discordant relations with his son Robert, his self-appointed heir to the leadership of RCA, and a painful final illness, which lasted three and a half years, seemed to humble him.

Color television provided Sarnoff his greatest victory, though he did not win it without initial frustration and expense for his company and himself. No doubt one of the reasons Sarnoff and the Radio Corporation of America had been so reluctant to settle the FM suits with the Armstrong estate was the worry over the introduction of color television. An enormous gamble, costing RCA $130 million to develop, color television was not paying off. Despite the glossy advertisements and lavish NBC "special" broadcasts that RCA's public relations engine endlessly promoted, color was slow to gain the sales Sarnoff believed it deserved.

The public seemed wary of the new technology. Initial prices for sets were high; dealers found them more trouble to sell and service than they were worth. Those few willing to pay a thousand dollars for a set, plus an additional hefty service contract of $119 a year, had to adjust the color picture with five different knobs. Even with all knobs in proper alignment, the picture sometimes changed an actor's face from a flesh tone to green or saffron for no apparent reason. Ralph Cordiner, head of rival General Electric, put it tartly: "If you have a color set, you've almost got to have an engineer living in the house." As the remark circulated widely through the press, Sarnoff smarted. "In every industry," he growled, "there are those who . . . try to impede the progress of the pioneer." To the general, the new technology stood as the next logical step in the long continuum of electronics: from sound, to pictures, to color pictures. Those who tried to resist the change were foolish.

As he had done nearly forty years earlier in his radio music box proposal, Sarnoff predicted the sales of color televisions: 1954—75,000 units; 1955—350,000; 1956—1.78 million; 1957—3 million; 1958—5 million. Yet by 1958, total sales of all makes of color sets stood at just 325,000. Bob Hope, NBC's resident comedian, got a laugh on one program when he told the audience that his color show had a "tremendous audience—General Sarnoff and his wife." RCA, Time magazine quipped in mid-1958, was still "chasing the rainbow."

Part of the blame for the failure to sell color sets lay with Sarnoff himself. Singlehandedly, it seemed, he had managed to alienate his competitors at a crucial time in the electronic industry's development. Winning over CBS for the RCA system had not brought forth magnanimity on the general's part. Electronic color television represented "a great victory for RCA," read one advertisement in the New York Times. RCA was the leader of the industry, the company that had taken all the financial risks to originate this latest advance in communication. David Sarnoff knew he alone in the industry had battled the FCC over a flawed mechanical system proposed by CBS. For years he had dealt with depressed earnings for RCA and had faced down hostile stockholders at cheerless annual meetings. Surely now that he was the victor, he was entitled to exalt his name and RCA's before his rivals; surely he had earned the privilege of enriching the lives of millions of viewers with RCA color televisions.

The fires of enmity in men like Gene McDonald of Zenith flared once more. Competitors like Philco, Motorola, General Electric, and Westinghouse limped into the production of color television sets (each of which, of course, would have an RCA color tube and license the rights to dozens of RCA color inventions) with little enthusiasm. Those who ran independent stations as well as those who controlled the rival networks were loath to spend their money on RCA color broadcast equipment. Telecasts in the new medium averaged but a few hours a week, mostly on NBC. William Paley's CBS, which had such popular stars as Jackie Gleason, Jack Benny, and Lucille Ball, offered few programs in color; ABC offered none.

In truth, Sarnoff had been as obsessed and driven about color TV as Howard Armstrong had been about FM. He had staked his reputation in the industry on it, pushed his researchers at Princeton, fought with the FCC and CBS about the merits of an electronic over a mechanical system. Now all of his efforts were coming to naught, and RCA was falling behind in the manufacture of black and white sets. In 1958, Gene McDonald, whom Sarnoff contemptuously called a "parasite," would announce that the Zenith Corporation was making more conventional televisions than RCA.

The hardships on the fifty-third floor at 30 Rockefeller Plaza were increased by some formidable legal problems, too. RCA's rivals seemed to be employing the same tactics that Sarnoff and his team of lawyers had used against Howard Armstrong—tying down the giant with the Lilliputian threads of legal minutiae. Lawsuits, threats of legal action, and the like occupied as much as 40 percent of the time in the executive offices. Once again, the federal government charged in an antitrust suit that the corporation was operating a patent monopoly, but this time it suggested criminal penalties were in order. Zenith and Philco added suits of their own, charging their rival with a monopoly and restraint of trade through its patent holdings in television and radio.

Unlike Howard Armstrong, however, David Sarnoff knew when to settle, and on what terms. He moved to settle the Zenith and Philco suits. At his direction, on October 29, 1958, RCA agreed to add all of its 100 color television patents to a common pool of color patents from which any manufacturer could draw, royalty free. To federal criminal charges against the corporation, he agreed to a plea of *nolo contendere*, and had the corporation pay a fine of $100,000. Though not mentioned in the criminal indictment (rumors circulated his name had been suppressed by officials in the White House, perhaps even by President Eisenhower), Sarnoff had been humiliated.

Agreeing to a royalty-free patent pool and removing the pall of criminal suspicion that hung over the company proved to be a wise move on Sarnoff's part. Free at last to manufacture sets without paying a price to their old nemesis, companies began to do so with enthusiasm. In February 1961, Gene McDonald, the final major holdout among the manufacturers, announced that Zenith would begin production of color sets. Once, not long before, he had derided them as Rube Goldberg contraptions.

At the same time, Sarnoff tripled RCA's advertising budget; installed color televisions free of charge in the White House, Blair House, and the offices of influential newspapers; organized lavish color demonstrations in towns and cities across the nation; and even arranged for President Eisenhower to open the new color studios at the NBC station in Washington. Networks slowly increased their color programming. In 1960, Eastman Kodak, sponsor of the "Wonderful World of Disney" on ABC, moved its advertising dollars and the show to NBC so that its photographs and Disney's animated characters might appear in "living color." At last the general's investment began to pay off handsomely. But this time he and RCA engaged in no public exultation that might antagonize his competitors. Color television was the final victory for David Sarnoff.

―

While he worked for the successful introduction of RCA's color television system, David Sarnoff was in his sixth and seventh decades. More than ever, it seemed, the general, like Lee de Forest, was concerned about his own future—not so much what he would do, but how he would be remembered. He had achieved so much since his arrival in America: chairman and president of a major corporation; spokesman (even if self-appointed) for an industry; brigadier general in the army. Each month, it seemed, another trophy or illuminated scroll, another silver medal or honorary degree would arrive. Still he wanted more.

Others had become major general in the army reserve; why, Sarnoff reasoned, should not he? He had served his country faithfully, not only in World War II, but long after. He spoke at military ceremonies, worked on presidential commissions, and even took out a patent on a plan for an electronic shield composed of airplanes, each equipped as a radio relay station to detect incoming enemy missiles. Surely he deserved an elevation in rank.

He enlisted the aid of his friend and fellow board member at RCA, Walter Bedell Smith. Smith had served as Eisenhower's chief of staff at SHAEF. In Washington Smith spoke with former military associates like General Ingles, who supported the promotion, but to no avail. February 27, 1951, Sarnoff's sixtieth birthday, marked the last date he would be eligible. The deadline for promotion passed. The general was rebuffed.

Sarnoff would not be deterred, and in 1953 he tried again. This time he secured the help of another supporter who had friends in the Pentagon. Again he was passed over. Why not approach the commander-in-chief himself? The proper moment came in 1956, when Sarnoff had presented a report to the president on military recruitment. Eisenhower promised to ask some questions, but the answer, which came on May 15, was not promising. To promote him would be illegal, unless he returned to active duty for six months. But active duty was out of the question, not because he was sixty-five, but because his personal presence was essential to the victory of color television.

If not a promotion to major general, then why not the distinguished service medal? In 1954, Sarnoff and his RCA engineers had demonstrated ways to use television in combat. In 1955, he proposed to President Eisenhower that the United States wage electronic war against the communists. Among his ideas: erecting giant radio transmitters that would beam messages to the communists and parachuting thousands of tiny record players into Russia, each with a vinyl disc that would tell about American freedom and exhort the Russian people to revolt. Without doubt, such proposals spoke well of his commitment to his country's security. If a quiet and diplomatic request were made, would he receive the DSM? An RCA envoy met with a member of the Senate Armed Services Committee, another with the president's press secretary. The general grew eager, the guest list for the ceremony was planned, but again he was thwarted. Instead of the DSM he so fervently desired, he was awarded the army's decoration for exceptional civilian service in 1956.

Sarnoff next set his sights on the president's Medal of Freedom. A friend in Washington lobbied key senators and congressmen as well as members of the White House staff. Sarnoff had known President Johnson personally since the early 1950s. Surely this time he would succeed. But each year during the Johnson administration when the list of winners was announced, David Sarnoff's name was not among them.

Other awards, smaller ones to be sure, gave him comfort. Some were frivolous; on Father's Day he was chosen Father of the Year, along with Henry Fonda, whose neglect of his children was legendary. But others were meaningful. Lobbying efforts yielded him honorary degrees from many universities. Broadcasting and patriotic societies recognized his contributions. On the last day of August 1961, eighteen senators gathered in the Senate dining room to pay him tribute, presenting him with a handsome illuminated scroll. As he examined the scroll and each senatorial name, he told an aide, "This beats the DSM."

Sarnoff counted awards as building blocks in the creation of the legend of his life. By 1965, he realized the time had come for a popular biography. In his private dining room in the RCA Building, he dictated the terms to Cass Canfield, publisher of Harper and Row: his cousin and personal friend Eugene Lyons, who had written a biography of Herbert Hoover and served as a consultant to the corporation's publicity department, would be the author; RCA would exercise complete editorial control; and Harper would guarantee a substantial publicity campaign. Under these terms, Sarnoff knew he could control the portrait.

But when Sarnoff read the first draft a year later, he grew furious. Lyons, a member of his own family, had betrayed him by hinting at several liaisons with women, talking of several business failures, and writing occasionally of his vanity. No matter that these few blemishes appeared on an otherwise shining portrait. They had to be removed, and the general would do so himself. Over the next month, Sarnoff carefully reread every page, rewriting passages he considered demeaning or incorrect, while adding others he felt would present him in an even more radiant light. On the general's orders, all copies of the first draft were shredded. Lyons had lost his cousin's friendship because of the transgression. But he knew his place in the family. Lyons never demurred.

When *David Sarnoff* appeared on his seventy-fifth birthday in 1966, most reviewers found it to be hagiography. But no matter. Sarnoff referred to it as "my legacy." The publicity department sent copies to every member of the Congress, the president, the fifty governors, people of influence, and selected universities. Sarnoff himself had copies bound in red leather sent to his children and grandchildren.

One more part of the legacy remained to be produced. Kenneth Bilby, executive vice president at RCA and Sarnoff's principal aide, was charged with gathering important memoranda, significant speeches, and public pronouncements in a book. This proved a far more enviable task than writing a biography, for here the legacy was substantial. *Looking Ahead*, as the volume was called, contained six sections with names like "Wireless Communication," "Radio Broadcasting," and "Black and White Television." Each showed Sarnoff's remarkable ability to see the shape of the future, to present complex issues clearly, and to show what should be done. But the volume, like the biography that preceded it, was not received enthusiastically.

The publication date of *Looking Ahead* was 1968. Television babies were coming of age. Embedded in the technology David Sarnoff had brought into every aspect of their lives, they could not imagine a world without television and instantaneous communication. These things no longer seemed the marvel they were to their parents and grandparents.

Nor was the new generation necessarily happy with what the medium brought them—reports from a foreign war; students beaten on university campuses; Martin Luther King, Jr., and Robert Kennedy murdered. "Hundreds of thousands of families," Sarnoff had foretold in his Radio Music Box proposal of 1916, could "simultaneously receive from a single transmitter." Though he mentioned "events of national importance" in his plan, he emphasized radio's cultural benefits, "concerts, lectures, music, recitals." Now millions were receiving radio with pictures, and the images flickered violence, mindlessness, and war. Toscanini and the NBC orchestra belonged to a distant past. Earlier in the decade, Newton Minow, the chairman of the Federal Communications Commission, had characterized television as a "vast wasteland"; this is what Sarnoff's vision had come to.

How much did Sarnoff understand that he had become passé to a new generation informed and shaped by the technology he had done so much to package? He no longer fit into the age he had helped to bring forth. Sarnoff believed in the great corporation, the new generation increasingly distrusted it; Sarnoff believed in military strength, the new generation questioned it; Sarnoff believed in the promise of America, the new generation called it a fiction; Sarnoff believed in the ability of technology to solve human problems, the new generation called it the myth of the machine.

In 1936, when a public relations consultant asked to see an organizational chart of the top management at the Radio Corporation of America, its president replied crisply, "This is a company of men, not of charts." By 1961, when he was beginning his seventh decade, he might well have answered that it was a company of one man, for General David Sarnoff had become synonymous with RCA. People sometimes mistakenly considered him to be the founder of RCA, an error he did not always correct. Over the years, he had strengthened his grip on the organization. With just one exception he had handpicked all fifteen members of the board of directors, as well as the senior executive staff. All were beholden to him. Realizing that only under his leadership could RCA prevail in color television, the RCA board of directors in 1956 had renewed his contract for ten years, with an annual salary of $200,000, plus annual bonuses and stock options. It was highly unusual for the corporate world in the 1950s, which emphasized youth, for a board to place its faith in anyone over sixty-five. But these were unusual times for RCA, and Sarnoff was an unusual man. By the early 1960s, when color television began to return lots of money to the corporation, many within and without 30 Rockefeller Center had speculated on what RCA would be like without the general commanding its operations.

To be sure, there had been changes in the administrative structure and personnel over the years. While remaining chairman of the board and chief executive officer, Sarnoff had long since relinquished the presidency to Frank Folsom. Then in 1957, when color television had turned the prospects of the corporation sour, he replaced Folsom with a management consultant, John Burns. He did not last long; Elmer Engstrom, RCA's technical chief and a person the general could trust to work compatibly with him, took Burns's place. The real reason behind these shifts, which involved not a little manipulation, was to enable Sarnoff's eldest son, Robert, to become president. It became not a question of who would succeed him, but when.

Like so many fathers before and after him, David Sarnoff wanted nothing more than for his son to follow the course he had set. He seemed to have forgotten how as a child *he* had resisted traveling the path to the rabbinate. Robert held a series of high-level positions at NBC, including executive vice president and president. All the while, the general was grooming his son to take his place at RCA. The change came on January 1, 1965: as Sarnoff approached his seventy-fifth birthday, he engineered the move of Engstrom into the position of RCA's chief executive officer and Robert into the presidency. He remained chairman of the board.

Many in the executive offices at 30 Rockefeller Center wondered how Robert Sarnoff would shape the future of the company his father had built, for the two men were so very different in temperament and personality. They remembered that the younger Sarnoff enjoyed drinking, which his father abhorred; they remembered the tension between father and son over the issue of Robert's divorce from his first wife; and some remembered hearing angry words exchanged between father and son on the fifty-third floor.

Robert first chose to assert his independence in interesting and symbolic ways: the old corporate logo—the encircled initials "RCA" underscored by a lightning bolt—would have to make way for a new, forward-looking "corporate identity." A team of designers studied the matter for more than a year before deciding on the three squared and bloated letters R C A. Further examination of the corporate image led the consultants and executives to conclude that "secondary trademarks" detracted "from the primary logotype." Nipper, the venerable Jack Russell terrier who often appeared looking inquisitively into the horn of a victrola, was sent to kennel. The words "His Master's Voice" and "RCA Victor" were discarded, too. This action would, Robert Sarnoff reported in a self-congratulatory article in the *Saturday Review*, "protect and transform the values of the old symbols while giving the new logotype the prominence it required." Finally, the consultants decided the very name "Radio Corporation of America" would have to go. Henceforth it would be known simply as the RCA Corporation.

The general was incensed. Under a paternal threat to call a meeting of the board of directors and have them reinstate the old name, Robert Sarnoff relented. The name remained, but the new RCA used it sparingly. Not the father, however. When new stationery arrived in the chairman's office, its bulbous red letters bold across the top of each page, Sarnoff ordered it removed. *He* would continue to sign his name under a lightning bolt.

Under Robert Sarnoff's presidency, RCA changed in other, more profound ways. The 1960s was the age of the "conglomerate," that ugly word derived from the Latin, meaning "to roll or heap together." Every self-respecting corporation had to acquire unrelated companies and place them under a supposedly sophisticated financial management. With such diversification, said the conventional wisdom of the time, the corporation could withstand a financial shock in any one company. RCA was no different, and Robert felt the time was right for the corporation to divest itself of some business enterprises and acquire others.

The general, too, had tinkered briefly with diversification after World War II, when he acquired a home appliance company—the Estate Range Company of Hamilton, Ohio. But he had sold most of RCA's interest over the years to another company, Whirlpool. By 1966, the corporation owned twenty percent of Whirlpool's stock. Whirlpool made electric appliances, so there was some justification for RCA's interest in the company. But his son's acquisitions and divestitures seemed more difficult to understand. The younger Sarnoff sold RCA's radio marine operations, which were unprofitable, and stopped manufacturing electron microscopes. David and Robert bought Random House, the publishing company, from Bennett Cerf and Donald Klopfer, with the rationale that it was a communications company. But Robert bought Hertz, the rental company; a New York real estate firm; Coronet Industries, which manufactured rugs; and Banquet Foods, which had the largest chicken farms in America. Previously, RCA had made electronics—radios, televisions, phonographs, and the like—and owned a broadcasting network. Now it was doing these things *and* publishing Faulkner and Joyce, renting cars and trucks, making rugs, and keeping chickens. And soon, it seemed, RCA would not do any of these things particularly well. Earnings that had floated high on the tide of color television manufacturing began to recede.

Throughout the 1950s, David Sarnoff appeared at the peak of his health. He was in his sixth decade; his hair was thinning; he got as little exercise as possible; he carried 180 pounds on his small frame, many of them around his middle; he often appeared engulfed in a thick haze of smoke from a Monte Cristo cigar fresh from Dunhill's. And yet he looked well. The fight over color television seemed to have energized him in new ways. His eyes still shone a radiant steel-blue. He appeared to have as much enthusiasm and vitality as ever.

"There are three drives that rule most men," David Sarnoff told a reporter for *Time*, "money, sex, and power." Money never really interested Sarnoff. To be sure, as a consequence of his position, he had a lot, but he never had worked simply to amass a great fortune in the manner of some crude robber baron. Power and sex, however, were different matters. As president of RCA, he lusted for the power that accrued to him as leader of the industry. Sex had always been an intense drive, and it seemed to become even stronger in his sixth decade.

Stories circulated on the fifty-third floor of the RCA Building about the boss's peccadilloes. For a period he kept a suite at a midtown Manhattan hotel year round for his romantic trysts. It was not unusual for a young secretary to find herself alone in the chairman's office trying to take dictation while he held one hand. At times he flirted with women whom he met casually through his work with civic organizations, or television personalities he met through NBC. On his frequent trips to the capital, a female staff member from RCA's Washington office would meet him at the train and escort him to his appointments. On one occasion when they were together in his hotel suite, the general proposed lovemaking and began to remove his clothes. The woman fled. Trusted subordinates at 30 Rockefeller Center conferred about what should be done. One suggested psychiatry; Elmer Engstrom, a Billy Graham disciple, proposed prayer.

Clearly, Sarnoff's libido had made him blind to his limitations. In one humorous instance earlier, Sarnoff contested with William "Wild Bill" Donovan for the attentions of a young woman. A much-decorated hero of World War I and a major general who had headed the army's office of strategic services in World War II, Donovan was a big, aggressive man, whose fighting abilities were legendary. No matter to Sarnoff, who challenged his adversary to a fistfight in an alley near the Hotel Astor. Happily for the short, rotund general, Donovan did not pick up the gauntlet. The battle of the generals never took place.

Whatever tensions her husband's exploits brought to their marriage, Lizette kept to herself. Since July 4, 1917, they had been husband and wife, and she intended to see their marriage through. Her boys were grown. Two were in New York: Robert was with NBC and RCA; Edward, who had a brief stint with RCA on the West Coast, was in business for himself. The youngest,

Thomas, an executive vice president of NBC on the West Coast, lived in California. Unencumbered by financial worries, Lizette had the freedom to develop her own interests. For many years, she had dedicated her energies to the Red Cross and the New York Infirmary. She usually accompanied her husband on his business trips to Europe and Asia, often in the company of another couple. Sometimes she went abroad by herself.

In the early 1950s, Lizette began taking sculpture lessons at the New York Sculpture Center, and she showed considerable talent. Her subjects were her family and friends, all executed with skill and accomplishment. When taking Edward R. Murrow and the CBS television audience on a tour of his town house in a 1953 "Person to Person" show, her husband pointed out several examples of his wife's work with obvious pride, saying, "I didn't know the young lady had it in her."

July 4, 1967, marked the fiftieth anniversary of their marriage. Their children held a party for them at the St. Regis roof. After a dinner, Frank Sinatra sang some special lyrics to the tune of "The Lady Is a Tramp":

> *There's no one like him, but no one at all*
> *We're mostly midgets and he's ten feet tall*
> *His kind of genius is like wall-to-wall*
> *That's why the gentleman is a champ. . . .*
>
> *Telegraphy showed the General the way,*
> *Took infant radio and taught it to pay,*
> *And he began what is now RCA*
> *That's why the gentleman is a champ.*
>
> *When others give up the General drives,*
> *Give him a challenge he literally thrives,*
> *That color peacock's now a part of our lives*
> *That's why the general is a champ.*

"I was lucky to have been born about the time that the electron was discovered and that Marconi invented the wireless," Sarnoff said that night in reply to the many encomia delivered by his family. "I was lucky that at an early age I hitched my wagon to the electron."

That September 27, David and Lizette Sarnoff drove down to the RCA research laboratories in Princeton. The date was important to him for sentimental reasons. It marked his sixtieth anniversary with RCA and its predecessor, American Marconi, and the twenty-fifth anniversary of the research laboratory in Princeton. To celebrate the occasion, he would dedicate the new David Sarnoff Library. As much a museum as a library, the huge room contained his life. Lining the walls were specially designed, glass-fronted cabinets filled with volumes of his speeches and pronouncements, each elaborately bound in red, blue, black, or dark green leather, lettered in gold, and many in slip cases. The titles included: *David Sarnoff: Service in World War I*; *Addresses and Speeches of David Sarnoff*; and *Early Papers of David Sarnoff*. Vertical panels containing his citations and honorary degrees slid out perpendicular from the wall. A special place was made for an enthusiastic, multivolumed "biography" of his life written by an admiring engineer. More than 10,000 pages long, without a single unfavorable comment or discriminating insight, it also was bound in red leather. Sarnoff had himself read and approved each page. Cases with mementos, awards, medals, autographed pictures and letters, and citations took up the center of the room. One contained a large model of a galleon executed entirely in silver, given to him by the directors of British Cable and Wireless. A bank of wall switches controlled the ceiling lights designed to resemble ninety-two giant television screens.

The general had taken special care with the planning of the library, for it was to house the life he had created. An RCA administrator had visited presidential libraries at Hyde Park, New York; Abilene, Kansas; and Independence, Missouri, to learn how the curators of the papers of U.S. presidents presented their story. "Perhaps the rising generation may find some interest," Sarnoff said at the dedication, "in reading how it all happened."

A short staircase led up from the library to a hallway and the general's private quarters. The hallway was lined with autographed pictures of men like Guglielmo Marconi, Michael Pupin, and Gano Dunn. On one side was a dining room seating ten, and a kitchen filled with the latest RCA Whirlpool appliances. On the other was a secretary's anteroom, leading to a handsome eighteen-by-thirty-foot walnut-paneled office, a small bedroom, and an opulent bath. On the wall of the office, he hung his cherished portrait of Lincoln. To his laboratories, his library, and his apartment he could repair from New York by a chauffeured car, wander the halls of his research center, and stop wherever he chose to find out what his engineers were doing. From the top of the staircase, he could survey the glowing record of all he had achieved.

David Sarnoff never stayed the night at his Princeton apartment. In the summer of 1968, he suffered a sudden and painful attack of shingles. The illness strikes at the nerve pathways of the body, usually manifesting itself in the form of skin lesions; in the general's case, it left his face contorted and his speech slurred. Doctors prescribed rest at home and drugs to reduce the swelling and pain.

But there was one engagement that he must keep. On Monday, July 1, RCA executives had planned a small luncheon party at Twenty-one to honor

Robert's fiftieth birthday, and he *would* speak. The general arrived with aides supporting each arm. When it was time to speak, the executives noticed his unsteady balance and his twisted face. But they also remembered his words. He began by acknowledging the difficulties of being the son of the man in control: "sometimes the shadow of the father obscures the son—never intentionally, but sometimes unwittingly." With this acknowledgment, the father then connected his stature and authority with Robert's: "I cannot separate RCA and Bob and David Sarnoff. The fortunes of one are the fortunes of all of us. Any hurt to one is a hurt to all."

The attack of shingles was merely a prelude to a far more devastating disorder that steadily sapped David Sarnoff's strength and gradually destroyed him. His mastoids (those regions directly behind the ear) became horribly and painfully infected. Neither antibiotics nor three operations at Lenox Hill Hospital in 1969 could cure the infection. Inexorably, moving from his mastoids to his nervous system, the infection slowly ate away his ability to speak, see, and hear, even swallow. In 1970 he was returned from the hospital to his town house to die.

Lizette had the solarium on the top floor of the house converted into a private infirmary, complete with a hospital bed, all the necessary medical equipment, and nurses on duty twenty-four hours a day. Her husband's speech had deteriorated to the point that only she could understand it. His blindness prevented him from watching television; radio he could hear only with great difficulty. The person who had done so much to extend speech, hearing, and vision lay quietly locked in his own world. The media he had created were closed to him. Still he had tactile sensation left; Lizette ordered a telegraph key installed by his bed. He tried to talk with several other operators at RCA Communications, but this, too, failed.

Ultimately, he had only Lizette. Though she suffered from heart trouble, she tended to him constantly, making his last ghastly days as comfortable as possible. She became his eyes, his ears, his good right hand. She arranged for visitors, answered his correspondence and get-well cards, and supervised the nursing staff. "My fondest wish and hope," Sarnoff wrote her at the onset of his illness, "is that we may be spared a few years ahead so we may celebrate our birthdays together in good health and make up some lost time." But it was too late. He died in his sleep on Sunday morning, December 12, 1971.

"His genius lay in his capacity to look at the same things others were looking at—but to see more," said Governor Nelson Rockefeller, who delivered the eulogy at Temple Emanu-El three days later:

Others looked at radio and saw a gadget. David Sarnoff looked at radio and saw a household possession capable of enriching the lives of millions. In others, the word "visionary" might mean a tendency to see a mirage. In David Sarnoff, the word "visionary" meant a capacity to see into tomorrow and to make it work.

At the RCA laboratories in Princeton, the engineers and staff gathered in a large auditorium next to Sarnoff's library to listen to the service at Temple Emanu-El. Many wept at Rockefeller's words, for they understood the meaning acutely. The visionary who had shaped an entire industry, their leader, was gone.

After Sarnoff's death, his wife, Lizette, moved to a smaller apartment on Sutton Place, where she lived until her death on January 10, 1974. After a service in Temple Emanu-El, she was buried in the massive gray granite mausoleum she had constructed for her husband on a gently sloping 11,500-square-foot circular plot at the Kensico Cemetery in Valhalla, New York. Visitors may look through the glass entrance door and see the two impressive marble sarcophagi. Centered on the rear wall above them is a single modern stained-glass window. Its rich blue, yellow, green, and red colors suggest a tall radio tower emitting a shower of electromagnetic waves on the civilization below.

The final episode in the story of the creation of radio took place not in a laboratory but in the courtroom. As her husband had before her, Marion Armstrong now directed the litigation. With the money she had gathered from the RCA settlement and the sale of German rights to FM to Telefunken, and without the prodigious costs of maintaining a fully staffed research laboratory, she was able to carry on the fight. Working closely with her lawyers, Al McCormack and Dana Raymond, Marion involved herself in every aspect of the litigation and every decision. Memoranda flowed between the Cravath offices and her apartment on Park Avenue.

Marion Armstrong proved herself to be a very practical and shrewd businesswoman. At a conference with McCormack and Raymond early in 1956, she decided to settle a number of the smaller suits on terms somewhat more favorable to the estate than the RCA settlement, which would give her and her lawyers money to "prosecute the large claims (perhaps $1,000,000 each) pending against Motorola, Admiral, Philco and Emerson." This enabled her to keep the litigation moving forward without having to use her personal funds or the other assets of the estate.

Nothing would shake Marion Armstrong's resolution, not even the death in the summer of 1956 of her lawyer and friend Al McCormack of a sudden heart attack. Fortunately for the estate, McCormack had turned over the litigation to Dana Raymond, who had left Cravath, Swaine, and Moore several years earlier to work in a firm specializing in patent law. Raymond continued to press the suits, while others in the Cravath firm worked to settle the complicated estate.

On January 17, 1957, Raymond reported that he had accomplished settlements with seven electronics companies in the past year, including Sylvania, Packard Bell, Hoffman Radio, Avco, Arvin, Sentinel, and the Radio and TV Company, to realize $261,500. Further agreements with Raytheon and CBS brought the total to $351,500.

Marion Armstrong and her lawyers decided to move against Emerson Radio and Phonograph first. The uncompromising company had refused to reach a settlement. Emerson lawyers tried in 1955 to have the case dismissed. Armstrong's heirs had no right to claim the unresolved patent suits as property, they argued, as the patents had expired and their owner was dead. To accept that argument, the district court judge said curtly, "we would have to attribute to Congress an intent to abrogate the common law. . . . Such a construction is unthinkable."

After all attempts to stop the plaintiff had failed, the case came to trial in September 1958, before Judge Edmund L. Palmieri of the federal district court in New York City. Dana Raymond argued that the Emerson Corporation had infringed upon Armstrong's FM patents, while Emerson contended that Armstrong had simply appropriated prior FM discoveries. To decide the matter, Palmieri had to learn everything about the nature of the invention and the history of its adoption. The thoroughness of the judge's work is reflected in his thirty-four-page decision, which he delivered on September 14, 1959.

Emerson's extensive arguments that Armstrong's FM system was based on prior discoveries was "speculative, inconclusive, and unconvincing," Palmieri wrote. During the time Armstrong conducted his research, "a number of important business corporations" were investigating noise reduction, but "none of them achieved his results. . . . Major Armstrong was truly a pioneer in the field in theory and in fact." Judge Palmieri's definitive ruling was for the plaintiff on every count; it had been a decisive victory.

Marion Armstrong had followed the court deliberations with care, listening with a single attention to all the arguments. When the judge ruled she was elated, for she had secured the court's confirmation of Howard's claims. Her lawyers prepared a short press release: "FM was one of my husband's greatest contributions to the radio art and I only regret that he did not live to learn of this decision." No doubt the fact that Emerson was represented by Darby and Darby, Lee de Forest's lawyers who had beaten her husband on the regeneration litigation, contributed to Marion's elation.

So comprehensive had the judge's ruling been that Emerson's lawyers decided not to contest it in a higher court. Other companies, Bendix, Philco, Admiral, and DuMont among them, which had held out in hope that Emerson would win, quickly agreed to settle. Marion Armstrong was assured of great wealth, with settlement payments from some of the infringing companies as high as $100,000 a year to be made until 1975.

Only Motorola refused to settle. Once again Dana Raymond and Marion Armstrong returned to the courts. The trial, which began in Chicago in October 1961, lasted until late 1963. In May 1964, in a forty-four-page decision that was even more thorough than Judge Palmieri's, Judge Edwin A. Robson found in favor of Armstrong on all counts. For reasons that probably had more to do with postponing the day of accounting than with defending the correctness of their position, Motorola's lawyers appealed the decision to the circuit court. In February 1967, it, too, affirmed the lower court's judgment and also cited Judge Palmieri's decision. Still, the lawyers would not concede; they petitioned for a rehearing, which was denied in March. The final defeat came from the Supreme Court on October 9, 1967. Litigation over Howard Armstrong's inventions, which had spanned the last fifty-three years, had finally ended thirteen years after his death.

Until her death on August 8, 1979, Marion Armstrong lived out her life in quiet luxury in her apartment on Park Avenue and at Shadowlawn, her large house at Rye Beach, New Hampshire. At her summer address, she earned a reputation for her elegant parties. Often they included dining and dancing under a large white-and-yellow marquee she had erected on the lawn. On occasion she gave expensive party favors to each guest. One resident took to calling her, not uncharitably, "the Duchess of Rye Beach." Late in the 1950s, after she had settled some of the patent infringement cases, Marion reacquired Howard's car from the person who had restored it. It was now in perfect condition and had been painted a rich dark blue. On summer afternoons at Rye Beach, Marion could be seen wearing a wide-brimmed hat, driving along the ocean road in the huge four-door Hispano-Suiza, the same car in which Edwin Howard Armstrong had courted her forty years before.

Epilogue:

THE EMPIRE IN DECLINE

◄━

When he retired from the position of chief executive officer at the Radio Corporation of America in 1965, David Sarnoff received a letter from Konosuki Matsushita, founder and director of the huge Japanese electronics empire that bore his name. The Japanese had always revered Sarnoff for the way he commanded his corporation; indeed, many executives emulated his style of management. Earlier in the decade, they had arranged for him and his wife to visit Japan, tour their factories, and speak to them about his career. "You are," Matsushita wrote at Sarnoff's retirement, "the bravest man of our generation."

By "bravest," Matsushita meant David Sarnoff's willingness to take risks, to forgo immediate gain to realize a larger vision. Time and again, Sarnoff had done just this. In the 1920s, he had delayed production of radios to perfect the superheterodyne models; in the 1930s, he had diverted RCA's profits into the development of black and white television; in the late 1940s and early 1950s, he had done the same with color television. At annual meetings, David Sarnoff alone had faced down contentious shareholders who complained that their dividends lagged behind those of other large corporations. Always, David Sarnoff had stressed the future of the industry. Funneling money into research and development would assure them greater profits later on.

Matsushita might well have written the same words about Lee de Forest or Edwin Howard Armstrong, for they as well as Sarnoff had been willing to take great financial risks to advance the medium in which they so fervently believed. David Sarnoff had simply been the most successful of the three, the

359

one who had understood that no invention was worth anything if it was not marketed properly.

Yet in less than a generation after David Sarnoff's retirement, the Radio Corporation of America, so strong a presence at mid-century, proved as evanescent as the electromagnetic waves on which it was founded. Sarnoff had thought of himself as a dynast, the first of a succession of rulers of the same family. Those who came after—including his son—would inherit his enormous empire and, as scientists at his laboratory in Princeton discovered new uses for the electron, extend it. But gradually, in the years after his retirement, RCA wandered in dangerous directions under bad leadership. By 1986, the Radio Corporation of America was dead.

In November 1975, not quite four years after his father's death, Robert Sarnoff was fired as chairman of the board and chief executive officer of RCA. In recent years, RCA had suffered great reversals. Under Robert's direction, it had decided to compete directly with IBM in manufacturing and marketing mainframe computers. For several years, RCA invested money in the ill-fated venture at an alarming rate until, in September 1971, it abandoned the fight and wrote off the entire enterprise for $490 million. Other ventures Robert planned, like a $6 million, glass-walled, solar-heated conference center for the twelfth-floor roof of the RCA Building, were thought foolish and wasteful. Corporate earnings fell from a record $184 million in 1973 to $110 million in 1975. Few executives at 30 Rockefeller Plaza seriously bothered to find out what the engineers at the research laboratories in Princeton were doing, what inventions RCA might develop for consumers and future profits. Though Robert Sarnoff had chosen almost all the members of the board of directors, not a single one had come to his defense when profits began to decline. Their vote to dismiss him had been unanimous.

Robert was followed by a ruinous succession. The first, Anthony L. "Andy" Conrad, who had been RCA president, lasted just ten months. The board fired Conrad when he and the Internal Revenue Service revealed he had not filed his income tax returns for the previous five years. Edgar H. "Bottom Line Ed" Griffiths, a career employee, succeeded Conrad. "Judge me by the bottom line at the end of each quarter," Griffiths was fond of saying. For a time, Wall Street loved him. In a cover story, Fortune magazine praised his attention to the profit margin: "For the first time in recent history, managers are acting as though their primary concerns are profits and persistent growth, rather than the stunning technological achievements that General Sarnoff prized." Corporate profits rose; but internal dissension did as well. Increasingly, Griffiths ruled more as a remote dictator than as a board chairman, firing anyone, including key members of the organization who got in his way or whom he considered disloyal. With a grim sense of foreboding, executives at 30 Rockefeller Plaza called him the "Red Queen" after the *Alice in Wonderland* character who continually shouts "Off with his head." By 1980, Wall Street turned on him; he was now the "corporate Robespierre." Though the board of directors had tolerated Griffiths as long as profits rose, it, too, turned on him when they started to decline. In November 1980, it offered him $250,000 a year for five years to serve as a consultant. He retired in early 1981.

Edgar Griffiths's successor, Thornton Bradshaw, came to RCA from the presidency of the Atlantic Refining Company. Wall Street grew hopeful that he would stabilize a company that had gone into fibrillation. Bradshaw pledged "to get back to our roots." No longer would RCA rent real estate, lease cars and trucks, weave carpets, or sell chicken pot pies. Electronics and broadcasting would be the focus of RCA's enterprise once more. Bradshaw reaffirmed its commitment to the development and manufacture of electronics, and revitalized NBC, long third-place in the television ratings. But on December 11, 1985, Bradshaw announced to the press the end of RCA. Earlier that day, the board of directors had sold the corporation to General Electric for $66.50 a share. The takeover, Bradshaw said, "gives us the financial capacity to do what we have to do," insinuating that RCA would be stronger than ever. Just who the "we" referred to was not clear, for as a corporation RCA would cease.

Created by General Electric in 1919, developed by David Sarnoff in 1933 into an independent corporation, RCA had now come full circle and into the corporate grip of John F. Welch, Jr. Known in the industry as "Neutron Jack," after the bomb, Welch was famous for firing workers but leaving the buildings standing. In RCA's case, he dismissed the workers *and* leveled the corporation. Once the quiescent antitrust division of the Reagan justice department approved GE's acquisition, which it did in June 1986, RCA became little more than huge carrion, ready to be picked over. The consumer products division went to Thompson Electronics, a French company; satellite ground stations were sold off to individuals; the David Sarnoff Research Center in Princeton went eventually to the Stanford Research Institute. Even 30 Rockefeller Plaza changed. Only David Sarnoff had been allowed to place his corporation logo on a Rockefeller Center building. Today the "RCA" is gone; a huge orange "GE" glows in its place.

The empire David Sarnoff had given his life to shaping and expanding, to fortifying and developing, had crumbled.

At the time of RCA's dismantling, fully eight decades had passed since Lee de Forest had created a small tube capable of regulating the flow of electrons.

In those decades, incalculable billions of dollars had been made using this invention and the ones that followed it. It was truly the empire of the air, as Lee de Forest described it. But neither de Forest nor Howard Armstrong— not even David Sarnoff—understood the implications of what they had created. Even during their lives, the empire they started had moved in very different directions from those they had envisioned, and in ways they could not control. Lee de Forest and Howard Armstrong were early victims of those developments; David Sarnoff lasted decades longer, but was defeated in the end.

Today, the names of de Forest, Armstrong, and Sarnoff have passed into a dim twilight. What remains is an America profoundly changed by their creations, a people whose daily habits, whose very thought processes, have been shaped by their inventions. Over the years, they realized their dreams, and those dreams transformed the interior landscape of us all.

Sources and Notes

I have based this book on original documents, interviews, legal briefs, and published materials. To save space in the source notes that follow, I have used the following abbreviations:

ACCU   Armstrong Collection, Columbia University Libraries

CLARK   The Clark Collection at the Archives of the National Museum of American History, Smithsonian Institution

CRAVATH   Archives at Cravath, Swaine, and Moore; now housed with the Armstrong papers at Columbia

DMA   Lee de Forest Memorial Archives, property of the Perham Foundation, and currently housed at Foothill College, Los Altos, California

DSRL   David Sarnoff Research Library at the David Sarnoff Research Center, Princeton, New Jersey

RAYMOND   Armstrong files, mostly concerning litigation with Emerson and Motorola, from Brumbaugh, Graves, Donohue, and Raymond, now housed with the Armstrong papers at Columbia

Readers should note that materials in the ACCU, DMA, CRAVATH, and RAYMOND collections have not been catalogued in any systematic way. The ACCU collection exists in more than five hundred boxes of letters, drawings, photographs, records, and books and needs the care and attention of a full-time curator. Readers who wish to work in the ACCU files would do well to consult the name index in the care of the librarian first, and then the boxes themselves. Untold treasures only hinted at in this volume await researchers.

The plight of the Lee de Forest Memorial Archives should give researchers some distress. The materials (mostly uncatalogued) are housed in file drawers and acid-free boxes at Foothill College in Los Altos, California. The property of the Perham Foundation, they have been the subject of recent litigation, as the college does not appear to want them. The materials in CLARK and DSRL have fared better. George Clark made an idiosyncratic index that has been modified by others over the years. This entire collection is the subject of an excellent catalog compiled by Robert Harding and published by the Smithsonian Institution. The Sarnoff materials at the DSRL have been carefully preserved and lovingly cared for by Phyllis Smith. But they, too, could use a comprehensive index.

Researchers will leave each of these collections wondering why Americans seem so antihistorical, so willfully amnesic, about this rich chapter of the past. This is most especially true of the materials in the De Forest Memorial Archives. Located in Silicon Valley, the heart of the American electronics empire of today, the collection evokes little interest and less financial support from the individuals and companies who have made billions exploiting Lee de Forest's invention.

Bibliographic information about all books referred to in the sources and notes may be found at the end of this section. Specific page numbers are given for particular citations wherever they will be useful to the reader. A complete set of notes, citations, and interviews for this book will be deposited with the Armstrong Collection at Columbia University and the Antique Wireless Association, East Bloomfield, New York.

Prologue: A New Empire for a New Century

Lee de Forest used the words "Empire of the Air" in the introduction to his autobiography, *Father of Radio*. Information about the world in 1899 comes from the *World Almanac and Encyclopedia* for 1899 and 1900 and the June 1899 issues of the *New York Times*. I have drawn some of the language for this prologue from the prospectus and the script of the Florentine Films documentary, *Empire of the Air*. While I contributed to both of these documents, I would be remiss if I did not acknowledge my debt to Ken Burns, who collaborated with me on the prospectus, and Geoffrey Ward, the film's principal scriptwriter. No doubt I have used words that originally came from Burns or Ward in this section.

Chapter 1: The Faith in the Future

For information about the de Forest family and confirmation of my own views on de Forest's early life, I am indebted to James Alan Hijiya's doctoral dissertation *The De Forests: Three American Lives*. I have consulted his work throughout this chapter. Hijiya is an excellent writer who presents his information with grace and good humor. I am delighted to learn that Hijiya's biography of de Forest (based on materials in his dissertation) is scheduled for publication by Lehigh University Press in 1992.

Lee de Forest provided many of the anecdotes on his early life (including information about his father, the "Rebs," the Talladega students, Annie Williams, Julia Winter, his various "squeezings," and the Spanish-American War) in his own copious *Journals*, which are deposited in the Library of Congress. I have drawn extensively from this source. Two unattributed typescripts at the DMA, "Relics of the Revolution" and "A Family Re-Union," provided details about the De Forest family in the New World. I have also drawn from de Forest's autobiography, *Father of Radio*, but with the understanding that the author is often cloudy in his recollection of important events.

Perceptive readers will notice that Lee de Forest spelled his name with a lowercase *d*, while his father, and the De Forest family, used an uppercase letter. Lee decided upon a lower case while at Yale, but his name was often spelled "De Forest" up to the time of his death.

The commencement I describe was Dwight's last, for earlier in the year he had announced his intention to retire. A man of stern religious beliefs—befitting a former professor of Sacred Literature and New Testament Greek—Dwight had on occasion dismissed professors for their heretical convictions. But he had also transformed Yale from a stagnant college into an prominent university and prepared it for the twentieth century. In just thirteen years he more than doubled Yale's endowment, built fifteen buildings, and bought six more. He enlarged the High Victorian Gothic chapel, built a spacious gymnasium complete with a swimming pool and Turkish bath, revitalized the school of medicine with a new building for chemistry and physiology, and acquired land, so much land that the citizens of New Haven grew alarmed. He increased enrollment from 1,076 when he took office to 2,500 on that day. At the same time Dwight made excellent teaching appointments, when the faculty—even more conservative than he—would let him.

Much of the information about Talladega College comes from Joe M. Richardson's *Christian Reconstruction: The American Missionary Association and Southern Blacks, 1861–1890*. Henry Swift De Forest was a fascinating man because he strove so fervently to put his religious principles and his desire for social reform into practice. The quotation beginning "I shall never see" comes from an unattributed newspaper article on the death of Henry De Forest, in the DMA. According to the same article, Henry De Forest used to characterize his educational mission as "carrying the war into Africa." In March 1928, the Talladega College devoted an issue of its magazine to Henry and Anna De Forest. One person quoted Henry saying in 1879 "Certainly just now I would rather be here than any other place in the universe of God. Tell our friends at the North that we do not need their sympathy but we do need their help." *The Talladegan*, vol. 46, no. 2 (March 1928), p. 3.

The articles in *Youth's Companion* appeared in issues during 1891. Sources for this section also come from de Forest's *Journals* and scrapbook, located at the DMA, as well as the author's collection. Nor did de Forest confine his reading to the *Youth's Companion*. In 1891, at the beginning of a book in which he began his journal, he

outlined the major periods of English and American Literature and recorded numerous quotations from popular—and not so popular—writers. Included were Keats's "A
thing of beauty is a joy forever"; George Eliot's "However, I'm not denying in the
women are foolish[?] God Almighty made 'em to match the man"; "Old Man"
Robert Browning's "Measure your mind's height by the shade they cast"; Franklin's
"Lost time is never found again"; "One today is worth two tomorrows"; and "Never
leave till tomorrow what you can do today"; Longfellow's "Build today then strong
and sure/with a firm and ample base/and ascending and secure/shall tomorrow find its
place"; and Abraham Lincoln's "With malice towards none, with charity towards
all." On reading the quotations in the nineteen fifties de Forest wrote in the margin:
"I am amazed at the breadth of my early readings. I loved these quotations or I should
not have copied them. That was [a] voluntary pastime." Of Cooper, de Forest wrote
in his autobiography "His Hero, Natty Bumpo [sic], became my hero" (*Father*, p.
33). De Forest's choice for worship is instructive, for Bumppo, Cooper tells us, is
"simple-minded, faithful, utterly without fear, and yet prudent." De Forest possessed
all these qualities from time to time—save the last.

That life was stormy for de Forest can be seen in almost every page of the journal
he kept while in Talladega. "Dear old Home," he recorded on July 6, 1891, his last
night in Talladega before leaving for school in the north, "not very inviting to me
now with the Rebs & Nigs." But then he tempered his thought:

> In later years, looking back through the misty vistas of the past, distance will
> lend enchantment to the view, concealing the harsh places & clothing the
> happy hours spent here with a golden refulgence not its own.

The misty vista did not come immediately, however. When he was at school, he
wrote in his journal of sending a letter to his family in Talladega "among the low
down nigs & rebs. I'm sorry for them but the rebs wont kick me or scare me again
nor will the nigs insult me more." Certainly his relationship with Annie Williams
contributed to his storminess. The final encounter of this odd couple, an occasion for
more petting and more guilt, provides an example of the conflict. It occurred just two
days before he was to leave Talladega for school in New England. Lee and Annie
stayed home from the Sunday evening prayer meeting. "Came very near yielding, but
we didn't. Thank God." Then he and Annie sat in the living room and wrote
explanations of the day she and he had first "yielded." Later in his life, when he
considered publishing his journal, he asked the editor to change Annie's name, and
tried unsuccessfully to obliterate the word "leg." (*Journal*, July 5, 1891, and September 20, 1891.)

Information about Dwight and Lyman Moody and the Mount Hermon School
comes from Bernard Weisberger's excellent history *They Gathered at the River*; Wilbur
Chapman's *The Life and Work of Dwight L. Moody*; and information provided by
Linda Batty, archivist at the school.

Lee's journal contains all the information about his encounters with Julia Winter.
At one point when at Yale, he even resorted to a little telepathic communication

when courting. "Oh Julia I *love* you, love me," he repeated to her silently on one visit to her at her parents' house in Middletown, Connecticut, "hoping to implant perforce the seed of love." The seed would not take root, however.

Elroy Avery's *Elements of Natural Philosophy*, which is preserved in DMA, provided much information about Lee de Forest's understanding of physics. His copy of the book is dated "Mt. Hermon, Sept. 1891" on the fly leaf. The book contains extensive annotations, including some of the prize problems that he was given to solve.

When writing of de Forest at Yale, I have drawn on the de Forest papers in the Sterling Library at the university and the various yearbooks, catalogs, and commencement papers for the years 1893 to 1899. The '96 *Sheffield Class Book* provided many details about de Forest's undergraduate years. It contains the class census that found him "nerviest" and the story about his using a trot for his German translations. Information for Yale's 1899 commencement comes from the July 1899, *Yale Alumni Weekly* (vol. 8, no. 39) a copy of which de Forest kept until his death (now in DMA). For an understanding of Yale when Lee de Forest was a student, I have drawn from Wilbur Cross's *Connecticut Yankee*, Henry Seidel Canby's *Alma Mater*, and Brooks Mather Kelly's *Yale: A History*. Wilbur Cross used the words "hotbed of agnosticism" in *Connecticut Yankee*, p. 110. Cross began his career at Yale teaching English to Sheffield undergraduates beginning in the fall of 1894. (In 1916, Cross was named dean of the graduate school, and from 1931 to 1939 he served as Democratic governor of Connecticut.) There is no evidence that de Forest knew him at Sheffield.

De Forest's journals for his Yale years contain rich descriptions of his squeezings. There he records that he repeated behavior patterns—thoughts of pleasure intermingled with feelings of guilt—he had begun with Annie Williams. In one case he offered a woman money for favors, which she accepted. Then, he counseled her about her behavior. There is no indication anything transpired between the two.

For material about Nikola Tesla, I have drawn heavily from Margaret Chaney's *Tesla: Man Out of Time* and John J. O'Neill's *Prodigal Genius*. De Forest probably read Thomas Commerford Martin's compilation entitled *Inventions, Researches and Writing's of Nikola Tesla*, which had been published in 1894. The edition included "A New System of Alternate Current Motors and Transformers," and "Experiments with Alternate Currents of Very High Frequency and Their Application to Methods of Artificial Illumination," and, most important for de Forest's future research: "Mechanical and Electrical Oscillators." Though a consummate showman, Tesla never stooped to sleight of hand; his feat was no mere illusion. To achieve it he exploited the difference between low- and high-frequency alternating currents. He reasoned that low-frequency current such as that which serves a house (60 cycles a second in North America), produces a shock, but light waves, which vibrate at frequencies of billions per second, are harmless. Somewhere between these extremes, probably near the frequency of 20,000 cycles a second, the painful effects of electromagnetic waves would disappear. Through experiments he deduced that the amperage of an electric current destroyed human tissue. Using an alternating-current generator with a frequency of 20,000 cycles, and passing the current through a transformer of his own invention, which increased the voltage ten thousandfold and reduced the amperage proportionately, he created a current that did no damage to his body and allowed him to light a bulb or melt a wire with the tip of his hand. (*Prodigal Genius*, pp. 92–100; *Remembered Yesterdays*, pp. 399–401.)

Information about Josiah Willard Gibbs comes from Lynde Phelps Wheeler's *Josiah Willard Gibbs* and Muriel Rukeyser's *Willard Gibbs*. De Forest's letter to Rukeyser on pp. 306–8 is especially helpful. From Rukeyser I have taken the idea about Alexis de Tocqueville.

Information on William Gilbert comes from E. B. Gilberd and Lord Penney, *William Gilberd, A Biography and Assessment*. Gilbert (whose name is alternatively spelled Gilberd) is all but forgotten today, but at the time his experiments were revolutionary. Revolutionary, too, was his thinking about the solar system, for he agreed with Copernican theory. At the trial of Galileo, Gilbert was branded a heretic for his beliefs. My knowledge of Oersted and Ampère comes from D. K. C. Mac-Donald's *Faraday, Maxwell, and Kelvin*.

Information on Heinrich Hertz comes from John H. Bryant's *Heinrich Hertz: The Beginning of Microwaves*.

Chapter 2: The Will to Succeed

For my description of Guglielmo Marconi's life and inventions, I have drawn on Hugh G. J. Aitken's excellent *Syntony and Spark: The Origins of Radio*, W. J. Baker's *History of the Marconi Company*, Degna Marconi's *A History of the Marconi Company*, Susan Douglas's *Inventing American Broadcasting*, and W. Rupert Maclaurin's *Invention and Innovation in the Radio Industry*. Frances Donaldson makes the point about Marconi and wireless being nearly synonymous at the opening of her book *The Marconi Scandal*, p. 11. The *Oxford English Dictionary* reports that "wireless" was first used as an adjective in 1894, two years before Marconi took out his patents. On February 22, a writer in the *Westminster Gazette* speculated that someday a person might be able "to communicate by wireless telephone with the planets."

Reginald Aubrey Fessenden, an important figure in the history of radio, has been given a fuller treatment in *Syntony and Spark: The Origins of Radio* and *Inventing American Broadcasting*. I have drawn from these two books as well as Helen M. Fessenden's *Fessenden: Builder of Tomorrows*. Of these authors, Aitken and Douglas are the most reliable.

The archives of the Marconi Company, Chelmsford, England, has de Forest's letter to Marconi "begging to be allowed to work under" him. Marconi soon became his archrival, of course, especially when he sent the letter S across the Atlantic. Then de Forest lamented in his journal "Marconi is in Newfoundland & the papers full of Marconi until I scarce dare, for my sanity, to look into a paper." Significantly perhaps, de Forest was prescient about Marconi's "alleged feat": "I do not expect to see him repeat his famous 'S' within a twelve-month. This will give us, even at the eleventh hour, our last chance to show what we can do." He was suspicious that the transmission had ever occurred. Comparing it with Tesla's claims of extraterrestrial communication, "It will not surprise me if, thru all this notoriety, which he seems so well to invite & relish, *he* may lose his head, & be *Teslaized*," concluding, "Let myself take solemn warning."

My story of de Forest's "goo" comes from *Inventing American Broadcasting*.

Abraham White is one of those elusive figures who exist on the margins of American social history. He never appeared in *Who's Who in America* or the *Dictionary of American Biography*. But he is important nonetheless. I have taken details of his career from Frank M. Fayant's article "The Wireless Telegraph Bubble," in *Success Magazine*. Stock brochures, copies of the *Wireless News*, as well as photographs of the de Forest Wireless Auto No. 1 and No. 2, may be found in CLARK. The brochures reprint de Forest's greetings to President Roosevelt. A single sheet of paper with the words "De Forest–Smythe System" may be found at the DMA. Quotations from de Forest about the venture come from his journals. It appears that other "newspapers" were published in places where White wanted to establish the De Forest system. In Denver, Colorado, for example, it was called *The Aerogram*, "A Journal Devoted to the Enlightenment of the Public on the De Forest System of Wireless Telegraph: What It Has Done, Is Doing, and Will Do." This was published in June 1906, while de Forest and White were being forced to post bonds in order to satisfy Fessenden. (Papers in CLARK.)

I have developed my story of de Forest's unrequited love for Jessie Wallace Millar from his *Father of Radio* and letters on deposit at the Sterling Library at Yale.

The story of the marriage to Lucille Sheardown, which de Forest neglected to mention in his *Father of Radio*, comes from newspaper articles at the time and, his *Journals*, and my interviews with Gertrude Tyne. Stories in the *World* and the *Sun*, which suggested that it was a wireless courtship, were probably placed by White. In the *World* story, for example, "One week's wooing by the wireless system accomplished what two months' time, accompanied by all the delicate little attentions of flowers, confections, and theatre parties, had failed to do for the bashful suitor. . . . [Wireless] proved so successful that Dr. De Forest at length trusted his most important message to it, and the method won." When de Forest sued to have the marriage dissolved, the papers had fun. DE FOREST CRUEL, SAYS "WIRELESS" BRIDE OF WIZARD read the headline in the *Sun*, while the title over a picture of the pair said: HE PROPOSED, SHE ACCEPTED, BY WIRELESS—DIVORCE SUIT. As the headline suggested, the story devoted lots of space to Lucille's side of the story: " 'Cruel treatment' and that alone, is responsible for our separation," reported the paper, noting that "Protest is stamped in every line of her lithe girlish figure." (New York *World*, February 17, 1906; New York *Sun*, October 5, 1906.) In 1953 de Forest appended a note to an editor of his journals that he had neglected to tell the Marie of the first Mrs. de Forest until "three years ago." It was not until the nineteen fifties that he told his daughter Eleanor of the disastrous union. (Papers in DMA.)

My information about de Forest's difficulties with Fessenden comes from *Father of Radio*, in which the inventor relates appropriating the electrolytic detector, and from *Inventing American Broadcasting*.

Information about the various De Forest companies comes from Thorn L. Mayes's excellent article, "De Forest Radio Telephone Companies 1907–1920," *Father of*

Radio, and accounts in the *New York Times*. The United Wireless Telegraph Company stumbled on until 1912, when it was taken over by the American Marconi Company. Its most successful venture was a large wireless station it opened on the roof of the old Waldorf-Astoria Hotel at 34th Street and Fifth Avenue in New York (now the site of the Empire State Building). The station offered intercity and marine communication between the Bellevue Stratford in Philadelphia, the Willard in Washington, and steamships entering and departing New York harbor. It folded on the last day of 1910. (Elmo N. Pickerill, "Experiences of a Pioneer Radio Man" [transcript of a talk to the Antique Wireless Association], Broadcast Pioneers Library, 79–1605.)

My account of de Forest's creation of the audion relies on Gerald Tyne's *Saga of the Vacuum Tube*, de Forest's *Father of Radio, Inventing American Broadcasting*, Aitken's *The Continuous Wave*, discussions with Bruce Roloson and Gertrude Tyne, notes in DMA and CLARK, and papers loaned to me by Bruce Roloson. The conclusions I have drawn are my own, and differ extensively at various points from each of my sources. De Forest had briefly mentioned Fleming in the paper he read before the AIEE, but memory can be a most selective instrument. In his autobiography and discussions with historians, de Forest suffered from a loss of memory about his appropriation of Fleming's work. Gerald Tyne reported in his *Saga of the Vacuum Tube* (p. 53) that "de Forest maintained steadfastly over the years and in all my conferences with him that he knew nothing of the Fleming valve prior to his invention of the Audion." In his autobiography, de Forest states: "During the time I was developing the two electrode detector I had never heard of the Fleming valve, and was therefore surprised when I later learned that my invention was being confused with it" (p. 213).

Chapter 3: "What Wireless Is Yet to Be"

Ray Stannard Baker's *The Boy's Book of Inventions: Stories of the Wonders of Modern Science* provided much of the information at the beginning of this chapter, as did Russell Doubleday's *Stories of Inventors: The Adventures of Inventors and Engineers. True Incidents and Personal Experiences*. Baker mutes the circumstances of Otto Lilienthal's end. Drawing upon his study of birds, the pioneer of flight made substantial advances in the design of gliders, including the use of arched rather than flat surfaces on his wings. He made more than 2,000 successful glides with machines of his design. On August 10, 1896 near Rhinow, Germany, Lilienthal made his last flight. A gust of wind caught the enormous double winged contrivance to which he was strapped and sent it crashing to the ground. The inventor's injuries were fatal.

For information about Howard Armstrong's early life and the life on Warburton Avenue, I am indebted to Jeanne Hammond who answered many questions and provided me with invaluable information and photographs. Hammond is the author of several articles about her uncle, including "The Father of FM: The Tragic Story of Major E. H. Armstrong." These have been especially helpful. I have also drawn from Lessing's *Man of High Fidelity*.

Neither the Armstrong nor the Smith house has survived. The Smith house was torn down in the 1950s to make way for a large brick apartment house. The fate of "1032" was darker. The house remained in the family until the late 1950s when it was divided into apartments. It soon went into decline and was but a seedy reflection of its former prosperity when the Yonkers Historical Society designated it a historic landmark in 1980. By 1981 it stood vacant and was repeatedly vandalized. Fire destroyed it in 1982. In 1990 a monstrous concrete apartment house was erected on the site.

Armstrong's relationship with Charles Underhill is well documented in letters in ACCU. See particularly Underhill's letter to his son, dated August 27, 1946, and Armstrong's undated letter to Underhill and his wife, from which I have taken my quotations.

The story of Armstrong's transformer comes from *Man of High Fidelity*.

Information about Armstrong's 125-foot aerial comes from photographs and discussions with Jeanne Hammond. More than one person has doubted that Armstrong ever built an aerial that high. But photographs of the thin needle, often with him climbing it, clearly show that he did. At 1-foot intervals on each section of the pole, Armstrong attached wedge-shaped footrests that enabled him to climb it quite easily. Armstrong appears to have adapted his saying about ignorance and trouble from the homespun philosopher Josh Billings, who wrote in 1874, "It is better to know nothing than to know what ain't so." The inventor repeated his adaptation frequently.

Yonkers newspapers provided information about Howard Armstrong's graduation from high school.

Catalogs and photographs at the Columbiana collection in Low Memorial Library are the source of my information about Armstrong's years at Columbia. I have also drawn from Nicholas Murray Butler's *Across the Busy Years: Recollections and Reflections*, Michael Pupin's *From Immigrant to Inventor*, and Lawrence Lessing's *Man of High Fidelity*. By the time Armstrong arrived, Pupin was a legendary figure at Columbia. He made his first X-ray photograph on January 2, 1896. In February he took the first X-ray picture to be used in medicine. A well-known lawyer, Prescott Hall Butler, had received a hundred smallshot in his left hand, the full force of a shotgun blast. With some fluorescent screens borrowed from Thomas Edison, Pupin was able to make a photographic plate of Butler's injured hand, exposing it to radiation for only "a few seconds." Using Pupin's photograph, a doctor extracted all the shot. Though Pupin never patented his unique process, and received little credit for discovering it, he reported that a grateful Prescott Hall Butler offered to establish a unique fellowship for him at the Century Club: "two toddies daily for the rest of my life." Pupin declined. (Pupin's autobiography, *From Immigrant to Inventor*, pp. 307–8. Forgotten today, this excellent autobiography won the Pulitzer Prize in 1924.)

Information about Lee de Forest's difficulties with manufacturing his audion comes from Tyne's *The Saga of the Vacuum Tube*. Tyne heard the "grade X" story from Walter Schare, who, he reports on page 69, "worked for de Forest at a later date."

Armstrong's "Some Recent Developments in the Audion Receiver" provided information about his creation of regeneration as did Jeanne Hammond and *Man of High Fidelity*. The new vocabulary for Armstrong's invention has some interesting history. The word "oscillate," for example, comes from the Latin *oscillum*, meaning literally "little face or little mouth"; it denoted a mask of Bacchus hung in a vineyard. The swing of the hanging mask in the breeze served to protect the divine grapes. The word was imported into English in the eighteenth century to describe the action of varying "between two limits which are reached alternately." The *Oxford English Dictionary* cites the first use of feedback occurring in *Wireless Age* in 1920, but Armstrong's contemporaries used the word as early as 1913. For regeneration, the dictionary cites 1922 as the first occurrence. Surely, that could be antedated by nearly a decade.

Fessenden, Steinmetz, Poulsen, and Alexanderson, and the creation of radio frequency alternating current waves, are discussed thoroughly in Douglas's *Inventing American Broadcasting* and Aitken's *The Continuous Wave*, from which I have drawn much of my account. Stories about Steinmetz and smoking are the stuff of legend; in every case they end with Steinmetz prevailing over worried fire marshals or company executives. True to form he refused to make a scheduled appearance on General Electric's radio station WGY in Schenectady when he learned of the smoking prohibition. The station relented, but posted a fire marshal armed with an extinguisher outside the studio. (Interview with Kolin Hager by Bill Miller, 1977.)

My account of Armstrong's revelation of his regeneration receiver comes from *Man of High Fidelity* and testimony given in the various regeneration trials. The best compilation of the testimony appears in the "Brief for Westinghouse Electric & Manufacturing Company and Edwin H. Armstrong, Defendants-Appellants," in the CRAVATH files. Burgi's diary was used as evidence in the numerous patent cases. This entry was for December 7, 1912. It is now in ACCU. See also the entry for December 9. Leo Lang made a deposition about his visit June 18, 1920. It is in ACCU. Frank Mason's affidavit, also submitted in the regeneration case, is in ACCU. See also patent 1,113,149, from which I have taken the words "new and useful."

Lee de Forest gave his account of his visit to Columbia and his meeting the "mysterious" Armstrong in his *Father of Radio*. I have drawn Armstrong's account of their initial encounters from notes found at ACCU. De Forest's account of his purported meeting with Armstrong, long accepted as fact, is riddled with inconsistencies. In his autobiography he wrote that Armstrong kept his receiver in "a small carefully concealed box in an adjoining room into which neither I nor my assistant [Charles V.] Logwood was permitted to peek. But when he led two wires to my amplifier input to demonstrate the squeals and whistles and signals he was receiving . . . 'C.V.' and I thought we had a pretty fair idea of what the young inventor had concealed in his box of mystery" (p. 319). Aside from the obvious question of how de Forest knew there was a small carefully concealed box in the adjoining room, if he were not permitted to peek into it, we must also ask how Armstrong operated a regenerative circuit with two wires when it takes three; and how he avoided the nasty hum of an audio feedback which normally occurs when the lead wires are as long as de Forest suggests.

Accounts of de Forest's romance, marriage, and divorce appear in *Father of Radio*. I have drawn from this, de Forest's journals, scrapbook, and letters (at DMA), and interviews with Gertrude Tyne and Rhoda Jenkins. There is some question if de Forest was not referring to Poe's poem "Leonore." That heroine might also have served as a model for de Forest. But Leonore in the poem is dead, her "spirit flown forever!" (I have chosen the story.)

I have relied on L. S. Howeth's *History of Communications in the United States Navy* for my account of the way de Forest's equipment performed for the Great White Fleet.

Lee de Forest's letter of May 19, 1902 (a copy of which was lent to me by Bruce Roloson) contains his thoughts about the wireless telephone. It is entirely possible that Fessenden had inadvertently disclosed his own thoughts about continuous waves at the time they met. It was then that de Forest appropriated the concept of the "spade detector." De Forest's ideas about broadcasting and his early difficulties with it come from conversations with Bruce Roloson and a letter to de Forest from Austin M. Curtis, March 22, 1907, a copy of which Roloson lent me.

Inventing American Broadcasting, Thorn L. Mayes's "De Forest Radio Telephone Companies 1907–1920," and papers at DMA are the sources for de Forest's new ventures. A copy of the stock salesmen's song is located in CLARK. The *New York Times* provides vivid accounts of de Forest's trial. Page 24 of the April 1909 issue of *Modern Electrics* contained an article about the testimonial banquet with a picture of de Forest sitting between Smith and E. E. Burlingame. Hugo Gernsback, editor of *Modern Electronics*, reprinted the article for another banquet honoring de Forest at Fraunces Tavern in November 1956. Since Smith and Burlingame had served time in the federal penitentiary for defrauding the companies (at the same trial at which de Forest and Darby were acquitted), de Forest was probably unhappy to have this reminder given out in 1956.

My account of de Forest's courtship of and subsequent marriage to Mary Mayo comes from his journals.

For my account of de Forest's attempts to get a working regeneration invention, I have drawn from the incomplete files of de Forest's law firm, Darby & Darby, found at CLARK as well as files at DMA, CRAVATH, and ACCU, and *Man of High Fidelity* and *Father of Radio*.

Chapter 4: Sarnoff and Marconi: Inventing a Legend

Throughout this chapter I have drawn extensively from photographs at DSRL, Dreher's *Sarnoff: An American Success*, Bilby's *The General*, and Lyons's *David Sarnoff*. Specific instances not immediately apparent in the text will be documented below.

Information on the *shtetl* of Uzlian comes from the map room at the New York Public Library, as well as the Baedeker for Russia, and the *Day Jewish Journal*, to which Sarnoff gave a series of interviews in March and April 1960. Much of Sarnoff's early life is shrouded in mystery. We read often, and I have repeated here, that while living with his uncle, young David had to commit 2,000 words of the Talmud to memory each day. The figure, which Sarnoff repeated often, is undoubtedly suspect. If we assume he had to follow this regimen six days a week, fifty-two weeks a year, for four years, he would have committed 2,496,000 words to memory—about sixteen

times as many words as are found in this book. It seems that no one—not even David
Sarnoff with time on his hands—could do that.

I have drawn from the *New York Times* and *World Almanac and Encyclopedia* to give
a picture of New York in July 1900. For my account of life on the Lower East Side,
I have relied on Hutchins Hapgood's *The Spirit of the Ghetto* and Irving Howe and
Kenneth Libo's *How We Lived: A Documentary History of Immigrant Jews in America*
(especially pages 42–43, 55–56, and 60–64) and interviews with Kenneth Bilby. For
my account of the Educational Alliance, I have also drawn from Robert Sarnoff's
dedication of the David Sarnoff building there. Howe and Libo make the point that
the Lower East Side was not just a breeding ground for young Jewish intellectuals, as
some think. In 1927, at the time David Sarnoff was positioning himself to be the
next president of the Radio Corporation of America, Jacob Orgen, known to his
gang as "Little Augie," the supplier of liquor to nightclubs and speakeasies, was being
gunned down near Delancey Street as he stood beside his bodyguard Legs Diamond.
Reposing in a cherrywood coffin lined with white satin, his body was buried on a dull
and rainy October afternoon, at a funeral attended by many of his colleagues. (*How
We Lived*, pp. 60–64.)

The story of Sarnoff's acquisition of the newsstand is shadowy and therefore suspect.
(But the question remains, Where did he get the money to purchase a newsstand?)
I have taken my account of this event from Eugene Lyons, Sarnoff's cousin and first
biographer. In *David Sarnoff* Lyons describes the boy hero searching for a newsstand
but being daunted by the price. The boy "talked of it to neighbors and friends, hoping
for a miracle—and the miracle transpired. . . . One evening . . . a pleasant, soft-
spoken, middle-aged woman . . . handed him two hundred dollars! She was ambig-
uous about whether she was making a gift or a loan. In his daze of excitement, David
failed to write down her name." Lyons did not stop there. Twenty years later, he
relates, Sarnoff the young executive met the woman at a meeting called to raise money
for a Jewish philanthropy. When he reminded her, "the grey haired woman . . . burst
into tears." When she recovered her composure, she "withheld the name of the real
donor behind the gift." Such is the stuff of family legend.

Information about James Gordon Bennett comes from the *Dictionary of American
Biography*. Bennett's name survives in James Joyce's *Ulysses*, which mentions the
"Bennett Cup," a horserace named in the publisher's honor.

The story of Marconi's meeting with Sarnoff is well documented and not exag-
gerated; Marconi himself referred to it on several occasions. I have taken my account
from *The General*. Four decades later Sarnoff referred to the job of delivering flowers
for Marconi in the deposition he gave in *Armstrong v. Radio Corporation of America*,
the famous FM case.

Abraham Sarnoff's life and death remain something of a mystery. Robert Sarnoff
remembered his grandmother Leah very well, but rarely heard his father or grandmother mention Abraham Sarnoff. "He seemed a shadow," the younger Sarnoff said.
(Interview with Robert Sarnoff.)

For the account of Sarnoff's position as a wireless operator on the *Boethic*, I have
relied upon his journal at DSRL.

Materials for the *Titanic* episode come from *Titanic: The Death and Life of a Legend*, newspaper accounts in ACCU (for Howard Armstrong had become suspicious of Sarnoff's role and had conducted research on it), letters and photographs in the care of the Titanic Historical Society, and information from the Military Records Office. The distress signal "CQD" is sometimes said to mean "Come, Quick, Distress," but this is probably not true. As interesting as Sarnoff's fabrication of the truth concerning his role in reporting the *Titanic* disaster is the gullibility of all historians in accepting his fiction. Daniel Boorstin did so in *The American Experience*; so did Erik Barnouw in his brilliant history of radio, *The Tower of Babel*; so, alas, did I in an article I wrote on Armstrong for the *American Heritage of Technology and Invention* in the fall of 1985. I remembered reading about the matter in Walter Lord's racy account of the sinking, *A Night to Remember* (1955). When I came to write my article I confirmed the "fact" in Lord, Boorstin, Barnouw, and Eugene Lyons's biography of Sarnoff. Not until Carl Dreher published *Sarnoff, An American Success* in 1977 did the truth begin to emerge. Ken Bilby reflected Dreher in *The General*. My account finds even more fabrication on Sarnoff's part than either Bilby's or Dreher's does.

The account of AT&T's purchase of rights to the "ultra audion" and "oscillating audion" come from his journals and *Father of Radio*.

For my discussion of Josephus Daniels I have drawn from E. David Cronon's *The Cabinet Diaries of Josephus Daniels, 1913–1921*, the *Dictionary of American Biography*, and Geoffrey Ward's *A First-Class Temperament*. A landlubber, Daniels was first thought a curious choice to head the navy. But he made significant improvements in the fleet and worked to prepare it for combat in the coming war. His judgment of beautiful Christian women was not always sound, however; one whom he described as such, Mrs. John L. De Saulles, later murdered her estranged husband. (*Diaries*, p. 3.) Before the United States entered World War I he resolved to ask the Congress to grant the navy the authority to "make wireless a government monopoly" (p. 123). Daniels had competition within the cabinet, however. Albert S. Burleson, postmaster, felt wireless should come under his purview. (See *Diaries*, pp. 123, 137.) He did appear, however, to alter his stand slightly at the end of the war. In his diary he wrote: "Went before Merchant Marine Committee in favor of government monopoly of wireless—must be in the hands of one—government or corporation. Interference makes anything else weaken or destroy value of wireless. . . . The special interests present opposed any government ownership" (*Diaries*, p. 355).

Information about Sarnoff's electrical engineering course at Pratt may be found at DSRL.

Samuel Parkes Cadman's speech at the dedication of the Woolworth Building may be found in a promotional brochure, *The Cathedral of Commerce*. The *New York Times* has an elaborate account of the opening. The words "nickel dime tower" are not mine, of course, but come from Hart Crane's *The Bridge*.

An account of Sarnoff's discussion with Robert Marriott may be found in *Sarnoff: An American Success*.

My portrait of Edward Nally comes from accounts in *The General*, the *Cyclopedia of Biography*, and an obituary in the *New York Times*, as well as memoranda in DSRL.

Man of High Fidelity, papers at ACCU (including a letter from Sarnoff to Armstrong on the twentieth anniversary of the event), and papers at the DSRL are the sources for my account of the meetings of Armstrong and Sarnoff in 1913 and 1914.

My account of the "Radio Music Box" memorandum follows Bilby's except for the date, which I put at 1916, rather than 1915. See also memoranda from Sarnoff to Edward Nally at the DSRL, which enable me to argue for the later date. Proof that the Marconi company was cool to the idea of the Radio Music Box may be found in the letter Marconi's managing director, Godfrey C. Isaacs, sent to E. J. Nally about Sarnoff's report on the Armstrong regeneration receiver: "what particularly strikes me . . . is the want of wisdom in allowing anybody access to our high power stations at all, and given that for any special reason permission to visit be given, it would seem to me extremely unwise experiments to be made with some invention, good or bad, upon the Marconi Aerials, which we believe to be most exceptional, for by such means there would appear to be results given to these experiments, which perhaps are mainly due to the aerials and not to the apparatus experimented with—a fact which those present are quite liable with their elementary knowledge not to appreciate." Then Isaacs got to the heart of his disquiet: "It enhances the value unduly of any such apparatus in the eyes of the inventors who are given the means of experimenting, resulting, perhaps, in causing us, should we require to purchase, to pay infinitely more than we otherwise should do." To this Nally replied that his letter was the first "intimation . . . of any such experiment" he had had. It is not known what if anything he said to Sarnoff. Quoted from Isaacs's letter February 13, 1914, and Nally's reply, February 26, 1914, in DSRL.

Chapter 5: Wireless Goes to War

Material for the assassination of the archduke and the consequent war comes from the *New York Times*, particularly June 29, 1914, which contains the kaiser's reaction; Winston Churchill's *The World Crisis*; Virginia Cowles's *The Kaiser*; Alan Palmer's *The Kaiser, Warlord of the Third Reich*; Michael Balfour's *The Kaiser and His Times*; and Gordon Brooke-Shepherd, *Archduke of Sarajevo*.

Information about Alessandro Fabbri comes from *The Fabulous Radio NBD* by Brandon Wentworth, and an interview with Harold Beverage.

The *Proceedings* of the Institute of Radio Engineers had many obituaries of members lost during the war. I have recounted but two of them.

Sources for the account of *Marconi v. de Forest* are Judge Mayer's decision; de Forest's reaction appears in his journals.

Information about tube production in World War I comes from Brother Pat Dowd. Bakelite was used in tube production toward the end of the war. The small radio tubes de Forest supplied had to meet specific requirements: 5 inches long; a diameter of 1 1/4 inches; and four connecting terminals at a common base.

I have drawn my portrait of de Forest's work during the war and his relations with his wife from his journals and *Father of Radio*. He often drafted his letters in his journal. Papers at DMA give an account of the Pacific Panama Exhibition. That de Forest found his name in eclipse can be seen in this journal entry: "I will see if publicity can not be engineered that the world shall know whose inventions made it possible," he wrote with regret and determination on completing the sale of his patents to AT&T. He came to realize he had sold the ability to publicize his name along with the rights to his invention. True, his company still had "De Forest" in its title, but its sales were limited mostly to amateur, government, and foreign contracts.

Man of High Fidelity provides the framework for my discussion of Armstrong and the invention of the superheterodyne. I have used this, papers at the ACCU, my interviews with Frank Gunther and John Morris, and a transcript of Mary Ellen Tuthill's interview with the late John Bose.

I have gathered information about Henry Round from the *New York Times*, August 19, 1966; the London *Times*, August 19, 1966; the *Dictionary of National Biography*, 1961–1970; and conversations with Robert Morris. Though Round's detector did alert the British navy to the movement of the German fleet, it did not help it to win the subsequent battle; Jutland was not Great Britain's finest hour.

My account of Harry Houck's purported death and first meeting with Armstrong has been confirmed by Houck's nephew, Gilbert.

Papers at DSRL and *The General* form the base of my portrait about Sarnoff's life and work in the war. For accounts of anti-Semitism and the Marconi company, see Frances Donaldson, *The Marconi Scandal*, especially pages 19–29 and 48–49. The stock-jobbing story appears in *Sarnoff: An American Success*. Dreher took it from Robert Marriott.

Woodrow Wilson's whispering-gallery speech appears in *The Public Papers of Woodrow Wilson*.

Chapter 6: Releasing the Art: The Creation of RCA

Information about Owen D. Young, especially his creation of the Radio Corporation of America, comes from Ida M. Tarbell's *Owen D. Young* and Josephine and Everett Case's *Owen D. Young and American Enterprise*. The latter biography is excellent, and certainly the more complete of the two. See also Mary Margaret McBride's "Freedom of the Air," for an account of the "indelible impression" radio made on Young. Papers at DSRL supplement these books, especially as they concern David Sarnoff's activities in 1918 and 1919. These include Sarnoff's account of the meeting of the technical group convened to consider the advantages and disadvantages of the new enterprise, Edward Nally's letter about Sarnoff's salary, and Sarnoff's 28-page memo.

The various issues of the *Report to the Stockholders of the Radio Corporation of America* found in DSRL have been extremely useful for background materials on the beginnings of RCA.

Material about Alfred Goldsmith is taken from *Sarnoff: An American Success* and *The General*. Goldsmith was interviewed by Robert C. Bitting, Jr., for his master's thesis, *Creating an Industry: A Case Study in the Management of Television Innovation*, and this too has been helpful.

Information about KDKA and the Joseph Horne department store comes from Barnouw's *A Tower in Babel*. See especially p. 68. Alan Douglas's *Radio Manufacturers of the 1920's* is the best source on early radio entrepreneurs and their companies. See especially the sections on Atwater Kent and FADA.

The General contains the account of Young's meeting with Sarnoff at Delmonico's. The memoranda I cite are located at DSRL.

Materials for the account of Tex Rickard and the Dempsey-Carpentier fight come from papers in the DSRL, Eric Barnouw's *A Tower in Babel* and the *New York Times*.

Chapter 7: Snapshots from the First Age of Broadcasting

Material for the discussion of Armstrong in the 1920s comes from a variety of sources, including papers—especially letters and an extensive clipping file—at ACCU, *Man of High Fidelity*, interviews with Jeanne Hammond and Barbara Brecht about his courtship of Marion McInnis, the transcript of Mary Ellen Tuthill's interview with John Bose, and papers in DSRL.

The *New York Times*, the *World Almanac and Encyclopedia*, and Hart Crane's "For the Marriage of Faustus and Helen" have provided the context for this section. Information about the various stations and their offerings comes from the radio pages of the *New York Times*, *Wireless Age*, and *Radio Broadcasting*, the files of the Broadcast Pioneers Library, Hugo Gernsback's *Radio for All*, and Erik Barnouw's *A Tower in Babel*. Gene Fowler and Bill Crawford's *Border Radio* is especially useful for information about John R. Brinkley. One of those lured by broadcasting was Everett L. Dillard, who first gave a violin recital over Emory Sweeney's WHB. Later, he began a high school dance band, which Sweeney was happy to have play over the air. Dillard got a first-class commercial operator's license which enabled him to operate the station. Dillard went on to pioneer in FM broadcasting in the Washington, D.C., area.

By 1922, the year *Radio for All* was published, the radio world could be thought of as having four separate categories: amateurs, broadcasters, engineers, and of course, listeners. But the lines blurred. Though Howard Armstrong was certainly an engineer, he remained in spirit an amateur throughout his life. After World War I, amateurs were given what the new commercial broadcasting interests regarded as the table scraps of the radio spectrum, the shortwaves, with wavelengths 200 meters and less. Responding to a proposal from the American Radio Relay League, the leading association of amateur operators in the United States, the amateurs soon pulled a coup. In late November and early December 1921, Armstrong and five of his friends from the Radio Club of America (including George Burghard) built a special shortwave station, 1BCG, in Greenwich, Connecticut. On December 11, after several nights of testing, the group sent signals to a colleague, Paul Godly, in Ardrossan, Scotland. Godly received the message "Hearty Congratulations" at 2:52 A.M. Greenwich Mean Time. Later, Guglielmo Marconi demonstrated conclusively the superiority of shortwaves for long distance communications, especially their ability to be transmitted just as well in the day as at night. By 1924 shortwave transmitters were sending entire speeches to England, and KDKA used the new technology to send its programs as far as South Africa. Armstrong and other amateurs of the American Radio Relay League and the Radio Club of America had shrunk the size of the world appreciably—and once again created another commercial interest (Lessing's *Man of High Fidelity*; Barnouw's *A Tower in Babel*, p. 152; and *The Story of the First Trans-Atlantic Short Wave Message*, *Proceedings of the Radio Club of America*, October 1950).

Information about Armstrong's negotiations with Sarnoff comes from DSRL, Lessing's *Man of High Fidelity*, and the Radio Club of America's *Seventy-Fifth Anniversary Diamond Jubilee Yearbook, 1909–1984* (see especially p. 95). Though superregeneration was a commercial failure for RCA, it has been a military success. Since World War II, it has been part of a system known as IFF, "Identify Friend or Foe," which allows the pilots of airplanes to detect faint coded signals emitted by friendly craft and thereby distinguish them from those of the enemy.

The story of Howard Armstrong climbing the Aeolian tower is often repeated. I have drawn mine from Lessing's *Man of High Fidelity*, letters at the DSRL and ACCU, and photographs in the possession of the Armstrong family. Ten days after the stunt Armstrong sent his friend "a complete set of enlargements," along with a note. He had not received Sarnoff's letter until May 16, the morning after, but even if he had, it would not have "prevented the christening." The climb, Armstrong said, was "essential." Nor should his friend worry about his "leaving this very world of ours," for, he said, he would not give RCA the publicity. He could not resist closing with a cheeky suggestion that Sarnoff hang the photo of him balancing on the ball in his office. Perhaps, it "will reflect to you some of my luck, which is proverbial and unending." Sarnoff declined to do so. (Armstrong's letter to Sarnoff, May 25, 1923, in DSRL and papers in ACCU.)

Armstrong's courtship of Marion MacInnis is well documented. I have drawn my account from interviews with Jeanne Hammond, Barbara Brecht, and Lydia Bottomly. Though Armstrong often drove his Hispano-Suiza at speeds up to 100 miles per hour, he could never beat his friend George Burghard when the two raced down the Long Island Motor Parkway. Burghard, who owned a Delage, consistently won because Armstrong slowed down at the curves.

Information about Lee de Forest and Phonofilm comes from his *Journals* and *Father of Radio*. There are numerous documents about Phonofilm in the DMA. Morgan Wesson has explained Phonofilm to me and provided me with documents (including letters from de Forest) filed at the Theodore Case collection in Auburn, New York. See also Edward W. Kellogg, "History of Sound Motion Pictures"; and Lee de Forest, "Phonofilm Progress," *Transactions of the SMPE*, no. 20 (September–October 1924), pp. 17–19. Mrs. Henry Hotz, whose husband worked for de Forest during this period, has provided me with much information about de Forest's trip to Germany. Armstrong kept extensive files (now at ACCU) about de Forest's legal, financial, and personal difficulties.

Material about David Sarnoff in the twenties comes from DSRL (especially memos to Harbord and Rice), CLARK, and Bilby's *The General*. I have also profited from my conversations with Ken Bilby about Sarnoff during these years.

Banning's *Commercial Broadcast Pioneer*, papers at DSRL, *A Tower in Babel*, have provided information about the creation of NBC. My information about Walter Gifford comes from the *Dictionary of American Biography*.

Dreher's *Sarnoff: An American Success*, has provided much of the background on Sarnoff in the twenties, including the physical description of him as a "short stout." DSRL is particularly rich in papers of this period. See especially his memos to General Harbord.

RCA's agreement with Joseph Kennedy to create RKO is well documented in *The General*. I have also drawn on papers at DSRL.

Owen D. Young and American Enterprise provides an excellent account of Sarnoff's participation in the war reparations conference of 1929. DSRL also has many documents.

Lee de Forest writes of Lindbergh in his journals. The Broadcast Pioneers Library has material on Phillips Carlin and Graham McNamee. RCA produced phonograph records describing the hero's return, and these too have been helpful.

I have drawn my sketch of William Paley from Sally Bedell Smith's excellent biography, *In All His Glory*. Paley made his mark in other ways, too, especially in the style of CBS. Early on he hired the Swiss architect William Lescaze to design some of his broadcasting studios, as well as a town house in New York. (See Dennis P. Doordan, "Design at CBS" (*Design Issues*, vol. 6, no. 2 [Spring 1990], pp. 4–17; and *In All His Glory*.)

The CLARK collection has extensive materials, including press releases, about early television, as does DSRL. Material for my brief discussion comes from these sources and *The General*. Hugo Gernsback made the predictions about what we might see on television in *Radio for All* (see p. 237).

Chapter 8: Court Fight

Materials for this chapter come principally from extensive interviews with Dana Raymond, the CRAVATH files, Armstrong's extensive papers in ACCU. Secondary sources include Lessing's *Man of High Fidelity*, de Forest's *Father of Radio*, files in DMA, Albert McCormack's article in the *Air Law Review*, the journals, Bruce W. Bugbee's *Genesis of Patent and Copyright Law*, Stacy Jones's *The Patent Office*, and Benjamin Cardozo's "The Nature of the Judicial Process," in *Selected Writings*. I have also profited from discussions with Gertrude Tyne about de Forest's approach to litigation and Frank Gunther.

The Bell/Draubaugh case is outlined in Stacy Jones's *The Patent Office*, pp. 72–77.

The story of Howard Armstrong raising the flag with his patent number on it appears in Samuel Lubell's "Magnificent Failure." Photographs of Armstrong with the flag that I have located confirmed the story.

Information about the 350 radio patents comes from a graph found in the "Yearbook of Wireless Telephone & Telegraph 1913" in CLARK.

Fessenden's inability to collect on his patent suits was well known. In 1930 Fessenden complained "I have yet to receive the first penny for any of my patents. . . . Once I was urged to take up the matter of my wireless telephone patents, as the company which had them had made a profit of over five hundred thousand dollars in one year and was in addition drawing large royalties from the Marconi Company for the wireless telegraph applications. The verdict was for four hundred and six thousand dollars and forty-five percent of the stock, but the company had anticipated the decision and went into receivership before it was given, the directors sold themselves the patents, and later disposed of them for five million dollars; so as the legal expenses had been heavy I decided not to bother about such matters until the laws were amended to give inventors better protection." See Joseph Rossman, *The Psychology of the Inventor.*

Cardozo made the statement about the generative power of judgments in "The Nature of the Judicial Process" (*Selected Writings*), p. 113.

Information about the members of the Supreme Court comes from the *Dictionary of American Biography.*

Various letters about the case are to be found in ACU. These include Harbord's, dated December 6, 1928; Armstrong's to Nicholas Murray Butler, September 19, 1929; and the attorney general's, dated December 21, 1928.

Letters about the Circuit Court of Appeals decision of 1933, including those from employees at RCA, are located in ACU.

Alan S. Douglas's "Who Invented the Superheterodyne?" is the best history of the Levy patent suit. I have relied on it extensively.

De Forest's telegrams to Armstrong are located in ACCU.

The proceedings of the IRE and an account in the Philadelphia *Public Ledger* (May 30, 1934) have provided details of the convention and of Armstrong's effort to return his medal. To some in the room, Howard Armstrong's gesture appeared hollow. Lee de Forest had his partisans, too, people who had worked with him over the years and who respected him immensely. Emil Simon, an engineer and Yale man, was one; Lloyd Espenschied, an engineer with Bell Laboratories, who invented coaxial cable, was another. They and others believed Armstrong's plan was to put pressure on the Supreme Court, and particularly Justice Cardozo, to reverse the decision.

Carl Dreher's letter to Lee de Forest is located in DMA.

Chapter 9: The Godlike Presence

In the spring of 1933 the *New York Times* carried numerous articles on the RCA Building. The publicity brochure referred to in this section is a "Radio Tours" map published by RCA in 1933. I have also relied upon Carol Krinsky's excellent *Rockefeller Center* for the quotation about the skyline (p. 55) and information about the Diego Rivera mural. The interpretation of the art and architecture and the connection of the RCA Building with the Woolworth Building is strictly my own. DSRL has David Sarnoff's 1934 address to the College of Fine Arts, New York University, "Art in the Radio Age." Information about the interior of Sarnoff's office comes from conversations with Ken Bilby and Phyllis Smith, and an article by Carol Taylor in the New York *World Telegram & Sun*, July 12, 1960. Information about Sarnoff's negotiations comes from DSRL and Bilby's *The General*.

Ken Bilby told me about the RCA sign and about Sarnoff's pleasure in having exclusive rights to place his corporation's name on a Rockefeller Center building. When Rockefeller Center extended across Sixth Avenue with four depressing buildings that suggest gigantic tombstones in an urban cemetery, the right to a sign— again in bold red letters—was extended to Henry Luce, president of Time Inc. This time the sign flashed, alternately, the names of Luce's two publications, *Time* and *Life*. The new Rockefeller Center buildings were designed principally by Wallace Harrison, the surviving member of the original architects. Harrison had become a court architect for the Rockefeller family, designing the UN building (which sits on land the family gave) and the Albany Mall. He had first proposed a tombstonelike structure for the RCA building, with none of the setbacks that make it so distinctive, but was overruled by the others. Across Sixth Avenue, and at the UN and the Albany Mall, Harrison was free to forget all the lessons of the original Rockefeller Center and create the slabs he so desired.

Sarnoff's *Looking Ahead* (p. 88) contains his prophecies about television.

The antitrust suit is described well in Bilby's *The General*, from which I have taken much of my information. (See especially p. 105.) Papers in DSRL have been useful, too. See Bilby's *The General*, pp. 180 and 203, for information about Sarnoff's lack of interest in exercise.

Bilby's *The General*, p. 114, is the source of the captain-on-the-bridge quotation.

David Sarnoff's romantic entanglements have been described to me extensively by sources who wish to remain anonymous.

The "Radio Tours" brochure, from which I have taken information about the stations for this section, is the property of the author. Other information comes from Barnouw's *A Tower in Babel* and *The Golden Web. A Tower in Babel*, pp. 235–37, is the source of my story about bartering. The manager who took the car and house went too far, however. Barnouw reports the man was fired by the station's owner.

The Chiclets song comes from Barnouw's *A Tower in Babel*, p. 203; Barnouw's *The Golden Web* is the source of the account of Walter Winchell. Winchell began to work some news stories into his gossip column, but he was more interested in marriages and divorces ("Lohengrins" and "Reno-vations" in Winchell language) of celebrities. Sponsored by Jergens Lotion, Winchell always signed off "with lotions of love," a valediction that gave the show and its sponsor a distinctive identification. (Barnouw, vol. 2, p. 101.) He carried his practice of tapping on a telegraph key into the 1950s, when, shirt collar open, tie pulled down, and occasionally a reporter's hat on his head, he appeared Sunday evenings on television. It was a foolish sight.

The CLARK collection has Sarnoff's glowing predictions for 1931. Other information about the depression comes from Robert Sobel's *RCA* and F. Scott Fitzgerald's "Echoes of the Jazz Age," in *The Crack Up*. Minutes of annual meetings, located at DSRL, have provided me with Sarnoff's statements to stockholders. E. B. White's statement about "the Godlike presence" may be found in his essay "Sabbath Morn."

Perusal of the radio pages in the *New York Times* has provided me with much of the information about radio programming in the thirties. George H. Douglas's *The Early Days of Radio Broadcasting* and the CLARK collection have provided much information about Amos 'n' Andy. Statistics about convenience goods have been taken from Herman S. Hettinger's "Some Fundamental Aspects of Radio Broadcasting Economics," vol. 14, no. 1 (Autumn 1935), pp. 14–18. Cited in Lawrence W. Licthy and Malachi C. Topping, *A Source Book on the History of Radio and Television* (New York, Hastings House, 1975), p. 232; and Thomas Porter Robinson, *Radio Networks and the Federal Government.*

Information about WEVD comes from *The Golden Web* and annual reports of the Federal Radio Commission. See especially the Annual Report for 1928, p. 155, from which I have taken this quotation. Robert Littell's 1932 article "A Day with the Radio," *American Mercury*, February 1932, p. 221, is the source of the quip about WEVD's position and power. There is more to an AM station's position than mere numbers on a radio dial. Engineers found that the higher the radio frequency on which a station operated, the more power it took to produce an adequate signal. Therefore a 500-watt station at 550 KC could cover far more territory than could a 500-watt station at 1,300 KC, WEVD's power and position.

Barnouw's *A Tower in Babel*, especially p. 241, is my source for the farcical and bizarre programs. Fowler and Crawford's *Border Radio* has provided the story of Dr. Brinkley. See especially pp. 20–22 and 43. Information on Father Coughlin and Huey Long comes from Barnouw's *The Golden Web* (pp. 44–47), Ken Burns's *Huey Long*, and numerous newsreels I have watched of the two men.

Franklin Roosevelt delivered his speech about the banks, the first "Fireside Chat," before radio microphones. Later he read it before film cameras so that it could be played in the newsreels that were a staple of every movie house. The *New York Times* provides a good account of his radio delivery and its reception. The Republican's response is recorded in Page Smith's *A Letter from My Father: The Strange, Intimate Correspondence of W. Ward Smith to His Son Page Smith.*

My account of David Sarnoff's hiring of Arturo Toscanini and creation of the NBC orchestra is drawn from Bilby's *The General* and papers at the DSRL.

De Forest's attitude toward broadcasting and his participation in the "Radio Heart Warmers" program is documented by papers in the DMA. *Father of Radio* contains the text of his "What Have You Done with My Child?" speech. He also delivered it before movie cameras, including those of *The March of Time.*

De Forest's connection with American Television and radio "diathermy" is well documented in papers found in the DMA.

De Forest describes the circumstances of his fourth marriage in *Father of Radio*. Information about the death of Henrietta Tilghman O'Kelly comes from newspaper reports Armstrong collected, now in ACCU, as well as accounts in the morgue of the

New York *Sun* at the New York Public Library. I have also relied on Hijiya's *The De Forests: Three American Lives* while writing this section.

Chapter 10: Armstrong and the FM Revolution

I have based my account of Armstrong's invention of wide-band FM on his depositions given in the litigation, the massive files at ACCU, and papers in the CRAVATH files.

Information about John Carson comes from Lloyd Espenschied's article on him in the *Dictionary of American Biography* as well as his obituary in the *New York Times*. I have also drawn from Carson's *Electrical Circuit Theory and Operational Calculus* and papers he gave to the IRE.

For an account of Armstrong's work routine, I have relied on Lessing's *Man of High Fidelity*, interviews with Frank Gunther, and the transcript of Mary Ellen Tuthill's interview with John Bose. The story of Shaughnessy placing paper in Tom Styles's hat comes from Gunther.

Accounts of Armstrong's demonstration of FM to Sarnoff on Christmas Eve 1933 appear in a variety of books, including Lessing's *Man of High Fidelity*. Sarnoff spoke of it in the deposition he gave in *Armstrong v. RCA*. Loren Jones, one of the delegation to visit Philosophy Hall, described his reaction in a letter to Bruce Kelly, October 2, 1990 and has spoken to me of witnessing the demonstration as well.

Accounts of the Long Island and Haddonfield tests, including sound recordings, are to be found at ACCU. Harry Sadenwater's documents are especially useful in documenting who visited Haddonfield to listen to them. About 1935, it appears from papers in ACCU, Sadenwater began collecting corporate memoranda relating to FM discussions. Just when these got into Howard Armstrong's hands, as they obviously did, remains a mystery. Armstrong's was the accepted procedure. Armstrong requested many of the papers from RCA when the two parties were in litigation. But many of those the corporation supplied seem to be duplicates of papers that have Sadenwater's name on them. It could be that Armstrong was getting internal corporate information from Sadenwater long before he decided to sue.

The account of Sarnoff's supplantive theory appears in Bilby's *The General*, p. 125. I have also relied upon Sarnoff's *Looking Ahead* and papers at DSRL and minutes from annual meetings for information about his reaction to FM and his interest in television. Sarnoff's pronouncements on mousetraps were quoted in *Time*, vol. 14, no. 3 (July 15, 1929), p. 52. The occasion was a cover story the magazine did on Sarnoff. Beneath a pencil sketch was the caption: "You cannot fool him about mousetraps."

Accounts of the RCA tests and the corporation's reaction to FM are found in the ACCU files. With our knowledge of Howard Armstrong we naturally wonder if he ever climbed onto the antenna mast of the Empire State Building. That was the question I put to Robert Morris and Tom Buzalski, two of the NBC engineers who worked with him there. The answer, alas, was no. Neither could remember him having done so. Thomas Buzalski did tell me that by 1935 the major had grown slightly deaf, which impeded his ability to construct an FM antenna properly. Buzalski suggested changes were in order, which the major gratefully accepted after carefully confirming Buzalski's claims with instruments. He knew he could no longer depend on his ears alone when designing FM antennae.

My account of the IRE demonstration in November 1935 comes from *Man of High Fidelity*, papers in ACCU, and my interviews with Frank Gunther. Subsequent accounts of the inventor's demonstrations have been related by Gunther and Gilbert Houck, among others. See also the *New Yorker*'s "Talk of the Town" article on FM. Armstrong told Lawrence Lessing that he would not own an AM radio. "Why? Because it sounds like a radio" (*Fortune*, October 1939, p. 39).

Jolliffe's reports to the Federal Communications Commission are recorded in the commission's annual report. DSRL has papers concerning RCA's representations to the FCC. *FM Magazine* reprinted many accounts of the skirmishes over FM.

The account of the construction of the Alpine tower comes from papers in the ACCU and CRAVATH files and interviews with Frank Gunther.

Copies of advertisements for General Electric radios are on file in ACCU. Accounts of the inauguration of station W2XOY Schenectady appear in the Schenectady *Gazette*.

Armstrong's FM relay is well documented in articles appearing in the *New York Times*, as is Sarnoff's inauguration of television at the New York World's Fair.

The attempted rapprochement between RCA and Armstrong is well documented in voluminous correspondence between Armstrong and Gano Dunn, housed in ACCU.

Chapter 11: The Wizard War

Winston Churchill used "The Wizard War" as a chapter title of his history of World War II.

David Sarnoff's telegram to President Roosevelt is in DSRL. Sarnoff's service in World War II and RCA's contributions to the war effort are inextricably bound. For my account of both I have drawn from a variety of sources: Bilby's *The General*, Lyons's *David Sarnoff*, and Dreher's *Sarnoff: An American Success*; letters, speeches, reports, copies of military orders, physical examinations records, newspaper stories, and annual corporate reports in DSRL; information provided by the FBI and the Military Records Center (gathered under the Freedom of Information Act); and Dulany Terrett's *The Signal Corps: The Emergency*, George Raynor Thompson et al.'s *The Signal Corps: The Test*, and George Raynor Thompson and Dixie R. Harris's *The Signal Corps: The Outcome*.

The account of the work of Colonel Thomas H. A. Lewis (no relation to this author) comes from Barnouw and discussions with Kenneth Bilby. Not everyone liked Lewis. His detractors used his middle initials to make an invidious equine comparison.

The account of the primitive state of army communications in World War II comes from Terrett's *The Signal Corps: The Emergency*. Thompson's *The Signal Corps:*

The Test, pp. 158–60, related the disappointing results of the maneuvers in 1939 and 1940. The source of my narration of Colton's decision in favor of FM, and Armstrong's letter about the same, comes from *The Signal Corps: The Emergency*, p. 183. I have also based this section on discussions with Frank Gunther and Dana Raymond. The Signal Corps had an army pigeon service, complete with mobile pigeon lofts mounted on modified Chevrolet station wagons. The number of lofts had dwindled from 110 at the end of World War I to 8 in 1938. Experiments with pigeons continued throughout World War II, but the birds had only limited success. The casualty figures were enormous, with a loss of 75 percent of the birds not unusual. (See *The Signal Corps: The Emergency*, pp. 83–85 and 105–6.)

Robert Sobel discusses the substance of the disagreement between RCA and the Signal Corps in his *RCA*, pp. 138–39. Sobel has based his text on Thompson's *The Signal Corps: The Test*, pp. 333–35. I have quoted extensively from Thompson.

A copy of Sarnoff's physical, his request to wear his special medals, and copies of his reports are filed with his war papers at DSRL.

Information on RCA's wartime production comes from Bilby's *The General*, p. 141, and Sobel's *RCA*, pp. 137–38. Robert Sobel makes the point that while RCA emerged at the end of the war as one of the premier electronics companies, it was "one of the smaller participants in the Big Five consortium" of corporations providing the military with radio equipment. "Of the $4 billion in total Signal Corps outlays in 1942, Western Electric was in first place, GE in second, followed by Bendix and Westinghouse; RCA was in last place, with $84 million, and seldom would go much higher in the pecking order" (*RCA*, p. 137). Information on the number of different kinds of vacuum tubes comes from Bilby, p. 141, and Sobel, p. 138.

An account of Armstrong's gift of his patents and his FM radar work is found in Lessing's *Man of High Fidelity*. I have drawn from that as well as conversations with Dana Raymond. The documents, including his letter to Stimson and letters surrounding his financial difficulties, are in the CRAVATH files. Though Stimson probably did not understand the implications of the gift, he accepted it on behalf of the United States, thanking the inventor for his "very generous action" and assuring him that his "patriotic example" would be "appreciated by the country." Armstrong's gift led to the financial difficulties to which McCormack alluded in his letter of May 9, 1942. The letter is located in ACCU.

The materials for the description of Lee de Forest's life during the war comes from Hijiya's *The De Forests: Three American Lives*, Samuel Lubell's three-part article, "Magnificent Failure," which appeared in the *Saturday Evening Post* in 1942, de Forest's *Father of Radio*, and interviews with Gertrude Tyne. De Forest provided information about the "Dirigible Bombing Missile" in his autobiography, but I also drew from photographs and letters at the DMA. These contain details about the ill-fated project.

David Sarnoff's preparations for the D-Day invasion are well documented in Bilby's *The General*. I have drawn from that volume, Lyons's *David Sarnoff*, papers at the DSRL, and discussions with John Morrisey. Sarnoff was careful to collect only his military salary—about $447 a month—while he was on leave. He announced to the board at the end of the year that he would return $67,000 of his $100,000 annual salary. "It has always been my intention and wish to be treated by [the] Radio Corporation of America on the same basis as the rank and file of the employees," Sarnoff wrote to General Ingles on December 29, 1944. "Accordingly, on my return to the Corporation, my salary . . . was readjusted . . . so that I was not compensated . . . for the period of my active service."

Lee de Forest's plans for the telephone answering machine are located in the DMA. Gertrude Tyne told me the story of her "flash dark" invention.

I have drawn my account of Sarnoff's elevation to brigadier general from Bilby's *The General* and letters (including that of Gano Dunn, and Henry Altheimer, from which I quote here) and papers in DSRL. Sarnoff's insistence that he be called "General" has caused no small amount of scorn by his detractors. Some have even claimed he never was a general. While it may be argued that his insistence on being addressed as "General" showed a consuming vanity, David Sarnoff's promotion was an honest one in every way, and, most would contend, merited. Sarnoff's star was not unlike that earned by Charles H. Spofford, the lawyer; Ephraim F. Jeffe, executive vice president of Consolidated Edison; Ken R. Dyke, administrative vice president of the National Broadcasting Company; or Kenneth B. Keating, the senator from New York. Sarnoff, however, was the only one of these men to use his title. Nevertheless the general had as much right to his promotion and to use his title as did another veteran of World War I, who was promoted from captain when he was discharged from the Army Signal Corps, Major Edwin Howard Armstrong.

The story of the bouncing of an FM signal off the moon appears in *Man of High Fidelity* and the *New York Times*.

The RCA quarter-century publication is located at DSRL.

Chapter 12: "Until I'm Dead or Broke"

Predictions on the future of FM appeared in a variety of places, especially *FM and Television*, which reported on the events surrounding developments in the medium. The quotation I have cited comes from Armstrong's testimony before the National Association of Broadcasters Panel on FM, Television, and Facsimile. See *FM and Television*, September 1944, pp. 26–31.

To convey a sense of the Federal Communications Commission I have relied on its annual reports as well as its dockets, which may be found at BPL. Close reading of *FM and Television* has also been useful. James Lawrence Fly's experiences with the FCC, the networks, and Congress are well documented in the *Congressional Record* and the *New York Times* as well as *FM and Television*. The changing of the FM allocation was a cause célèbre for FM enthusiasts during the postwar years. The best source of information about it, other than those cited above, is *Armstrong's Fight for FM*. I consulted it and Lessing as well as Armstrong's correspondence in ACCU (including his letter to Henry Round) while writing this chapter. My reading of this episode in the FCC's history varies greatly from that of Andrew F. Ingles in his book

Behind the Tube: A History of Broadcasting Technology and Business, pp. 130–36. Ingles suggests that "With the perspective of time . . . the best guess is that the changing of frequencies made very little difference in the growth of the industry but that increasing the number of channels was highly desirable."

Information on Paul Kesten, Frank Stanton, the Single Market Plan, duplicate programming, and Armstrong's reaction to them comes from Sally Smith's *In All His Glory*, William S. Paley's *As It Happened* (though the latter is notoriously suspect at times), and Kesten's testimony to the FCC, Docket No. 6768. The testimony was published by CBS in a handsome booklet entitled "The Transition from AM to FM Broadcasting." See especially pp. 4–5. *FM and Television* covered Kesten's proposals carefully, and Ericksson's *Armstrong's Fight for FM* discusses these matters fully.

Sources of information about Armstrong at this time are interviews with Frank Gunther and Dana Raymond, the Armstrong RAYMOND files, and ACCU. Lawrence Lessing's unsigned article in *Fortune*, "Armstrong of Radio," is extremely useful, as is his *Man of High Fidelity*, especially when considering the inventor's mood.

The Armstrong files at Columbia, which contain thousands of different documents obtained from RCA during the discovery process of the FM litigation, serve as an excellent source of information about what was going on inside the RCA company.

I have drawn my narrative about RCA's attitude toward patents from files at the ACCU. It is true that the corporation had offered Armstrong a nonexclusive license for his FM patents in 1940, but not willingly, and certainly not at the rates he demanded. The Philo Farnsworth and RCA story is told in many places, including Elma G. Farnsworth, *Distant Vision*, pp. 213–14, and Bilby's *The General*, pp. 127–28. That Schairer had tears in his eyes suggests what a traumatic step it was for Sarnoff and RCA to sign such an agreement. This has led me to the conclusions I have drawn in this paragraph.

Information on Sarnoff, RCA, and the introduction of television comes from interviews with Kenneth Bilby and Sarnoff speeches in DSRL and the RCA annual reports from 1945 to 1954, and issues of *FM and Television*. The Jolliffe pamphlet to which I allude was actually a reprint of his statement to the Committee on Interstate and Foreign Commerce in the United States House of Representatives. Armstrong's statement and subsequent replies by Jolliffe and Harold Beverage appear in *FM and Television*, July 1948, p. 24f.

Information about Armstrong's suit comes from the ACCU files, CRAVATH files, especially Armstrong's and Sarnoff's depositions. Armstrong's division of his fortune with Marion was related by John Bose in a taped interview with Mary Ellen Tuthill. The legal trick comes from Armstrong's deposition. Information about Armstrong's expenses comes from copies of his tax returns and his bills in the CRAVATH and ACCU files. Several attorneys and RCA executives, who would rather remain unnamed, gave me the assessment of John Cahill's abilities and his relations with David Sarnoff. Armstrong's correspondence with Henry Round, which I have quoted extensively in this section, is housed in ACCU. Lists of the exhibits introduced in the litigation are in the ACCU and Cravath files. The account of the depositions and John Hoxie's words comes from Dana Raymond. Sarnoff's deposition, from which I have quoted, has been discussed at length in *Man of High Fidelity* and *Armstrong's Struggle for FM*. The account of Armstrong's routine has been pieced together from *Man of High Fidelity* and interviews with Dana Raymond and Jeanne Hammond. Josephine Raymond told me the story of *Miss Liberty*.

Information about Judge McCook comes from the CRAVATH and ACCU files as well as McCook's obituary in the *New York Times*, and his life in the *Cyclopaedia of Biography*. The "Judge," as he was always addressed, was eager to take the case for he needed the money. His son had recently been institutionalized for mental depression and the financial support of his daughter-in-law and her children, as well as the medical fees, had devolved on him. He knew he would receive a large fee, and perhaps if there was a need for it, he would be able to make additional money arbitrating a settlement between the two sides. (Letters between Albert McCormack and Judge McCook in CRAVATH.)

Copies of Armstrong's tax forms are found in the CRAVATH files. In 1955, the IRS disallowed some of his depreciation and therefore said he had made additional income of $76,805.68.

The Jarndyce and Jarndyce I refer to comes from the opening chapter of Charles Dickens's *Bleak House*. It is instructive to remember that after years of lawyers "knee-deep in technicalities" citing "slippery precedents," no party wins Jarndyce and Jarndyce. All the money under contention is consumed in litigation.

My account of the restrictions that Howard placed (or tried to place) upon Marion's travel came from interviews with Barbara Brecht and Mrs. George Bottomly. They were the source for much of the information about Marion's mental state at this time.

Accounts of the Multiplexing come from the Bose interview, papers in ACCU, and the *New York Times*. Armstrong shared in five more FM patents after his death. These are documented in David W. Kraeuter's "The U.S. Patents of Armstrong, Conrad, De Forest, Du Mont, Farnsworth, Fessenden, Kent, Marconi, and Zworykin," in *AWA Review*.

The effort to settle the case in the fall of 1953, including the quotations from letters by McCormack and McCook, come from the CRAVATH files.

The account of Howard Armstrong's attack on his wife, an event long shrouded in family history, comes from interviews with Barbara Brecht and Lydia Bottomly. Howard's discussion of his financial condition may be found in *Man of High Fidelity*. The quotations from Marion Armstrong's article come from an undated issue of *Today's Woman*, which was kindly lent to me by Jeanne Hammond. An account of the less happy moments of the Armstrong marriage was provided by several intimates who wish to remain unnamed.

Information about Armstrong's last days comes from the CRAVATH files, Mary Ellen Tuthill's interview with John Bose, the ACCU files, *Man of High Fidelity*, and my own interviews with Dana Raymond. So far as I have been able to determine, Armstrong's final note does not exist. I have taken my text from newspaper accounts that are filed with the CRAVATH materials.

After Armstrong's suicide Senator Joseph McCarthy suggested that the inventor had been murdered rather than divulge to the Communists secrets about the radar research he was conducting for the government. Investigation of documents, obtained through the Freedom of Information Act, give no credence to this story. Those who believe Armstrong was murdered cite his signing his final note "Ed," a name he did not normally use. However, he and his wife did use the name.

Lee de Forest's reaction to Armstrong's demise may be found in letters to Elmo Pickerill (February 9, 1954) and Lloyd Espenschied (February 2, 1954) at DMA; *Sarnoff: An American Success*, tells of Sarnoff's reaction. Several people, including Gilbert Houck and Gerald Minter, have told me the story of Sarnoff's actions at the funeral; Thornton Penfield's sermon appeared in newspaper accounts of the funeral, which are filed with the CRAVATH papers.

The quotation from the annual stockholder's meeting at RCA is filed at DSRL.

Chapter 13: Victories Great and Small

For my account of Marion's actions to recover her husband's fortune I have drawn on interviews with Jeanne Hammond, Barbara Brecht, and Dana Raymond as well as the CRAVATH and ACCU files. I have also referred frequently to Lessing's *Man of High Fidelity*. It is interesting to note that one safe deposit box eluded Marion and her lawyers for three years. In 1957 two certificates for fourteen shares each of RCA Cumulative First Preferred stock bought at $3.50 a share turned up in a box at the Hanover Bank. Marion gave them to Lenox Hill Hospital and New York Hospital. The certificates, purchased for $49, were now worth $1,043. (William D. Sullivan of Cravath, Swaine, and Moore to Marion Armstrong, January 30, 1957.)

Information about the breakup of the Columbia laboratories and the Alpine site and the closing of Armstrong's FM station comes from documents in the CRAVATH files as well as interviews with Frank Gunther and Dana Raymond. See also McCormack's letter to Styles, May 7, 1954, in the CRAVATH files. Bruce Kelly and the late Charles Sackerman told me that Marion Armstrong had the ball and antenna base removed to Rye Beach. Sackerman, who owned the Alpine site until his death in May 1990, installed a replica of the ball at the entrance to the laboratory building.

The CRAVATH files yielded the information, most of it new, on Marion Armstrong's settlement with RCA.

The files for Lee de Forest's last years, much more complete than his first, are housed in DMA. Information for this section comes from there as well as from interviews with Estelle McLaughlin and Eleanor de Forest Peck, newsreels form Fox Movietone News, the CBS radio production, "The Life of Lee De Forest," and the Ralph Edwards television production "This Is Your Life." I have also frequently consulted Hijiya's *The De Forests: Three American Lives*. Information about Marie de Forest's final years comes from interviews with Estelle McLaughlin, Dr. Seymour Stein, Eleanor de Forest Peck, and records of the Perham Foundation in DMA.

Papers and photographs in DSRL, conversations with Phyllis Smith, Charlotte Katchurin, and others who prefer to remain unnamed have served as the principal sources for my telling of Sarnoff's final years. I have also referred to *The General* and *Sarnoff: An American Success*, as well as films of the Sarnoff visit to Japan, the Sarnoffs' fiftieth wedding anniversary celebration, and the Sarnoff funeral at the DSRL, and a videotape of Edward R. Murrow's "Person to Person" interview with Sarnoff in 1953. The *New York Times*, *Fortune*, *Time*, and *U.S. News & World Report* provide ample information on the public's attitude toward color television, RCA's litigation, and RCA's metamorphosis into a conglomerate.

Sources for the account of the final Armstrong litigation are the CRAVATH files, RAYMOND files, interviews with Dana Raymond, and of course, the decisions of various judges, particularly Judge Palmieri's. Information about Marion Armstrong's final years comes from Jeanne Hammond, Barbara Brecht, Lydia Bottomly, and Mary Ellen Tuthill.

Epilogue: The Empire in Decline

Information for the section about Robert Sarnoff's tenure as the head of RCA comes from Bilby's *The General*, Sobel's *RCA*, *Fortune Magazine*, *Business Week*, issues of the *New York Times*, and interviews with two of the principals involved who do not wish me to divulge their names. Robert Sarnoff's firing had the elements of a palace coup. At the time of his dismissal, Robert Sarnoff was on a concert tour with his third wife, the popular diva and Victor recording artist, Anna Moffo. In one of its first actions after dismissing Sarnoff, the board scrapped his plans to create the large glass-walled executive office suite on one of the setbacks at 30 Rockefeller Center. Heated and cooled by solar power, the center was to be a showplace for the RCA of the future as well as for Robert's fine art collection.

The nervous executives working under Griffiths erred in calling him the Red Queen. It was the Queen of Hearts in *Alice in Wonderland* who shouted, "Off with his head!" The Red Queen appeared in *Through the Looking Glass*. The executives' confusion is a measure of the discomfort they felt.

Selected Bibliography

Published Works by de Forest, Armstrong, and Sarnoff

ARMSTRONG

"Evolution of Frequency Modulation." *Electrical Engineering* (December 1940), pp. 485–88.

"Frequency Modulation and Its Future Uses." *Annals of the Academy of Political and Social Science* (January 1941), pp. 153–59.

"High Points of FM History." *FM and Television* (August 1944), pp. 22–24.

"The History of Frequency Modulation." *FM Radio–Electronics Engineering* (March 1944), n.p.

"Mathematical Theory vs. Physical Concept." *FM and Television* (August 1944), pp. 11–13, 36.

"A Method of Reducing Disturbances in Radio Signaling by a System of Frequency Modulation." *Proceedings of the Institute of Radio Engineers*, vol. 24, no. 5 (May 1936), pp. 689–740.

"Method of Reducing the Effect of Atmospheric Disturbances." *Proceedings of the Institute of Radio Engineers*, vol. 16, no. 1 (January 1928), pp. 15–29.

"A New Method of Receiving Weak Signals for Short Waves." *Proceedings of the Radio Club of America* (December 1919).

"The New Radio Freedom." *Journal of the Franklin Institute* (September 1941), pp. 213–16.

"A New System for Short Wave Amplification." *Proceedings of the Institute of Radio Engineers*, vol. 9, no. 1 (February 1921).

"Nikola Tesla—An Appreciation." *Scientific Monthly*, April 1943.

"Operating Features of the Audion." *Electrical World*, vol. 62, no. 24 (December 12, 1914), pp. 1149–52.

"The Original Disclosure of Frequency Modulation Broadcasting." *FM and Television* (June 1944).

"The Regenerative Circuit." *Proceedings of the Radio Club of America* (April 1915).

"The Regenerative Circuit." *Electrical Journal*, vol. 18, no. 4 (1921), pp. 153–54.

"Some Recent Developments in the Audion Receiver." *Proceedings of the Institute of Radio Engineers*, vol. 3, no. 4 (September 1915), pp. 215–46.

"Some Recent Developments in the Multiplexed Transmission of Frequency Modulated Broadcast Signals." *Proceedings of the Radio Club of America* (October 1953).

"Some Recent Developments of Regenerative Circuits." *Proceedings of the Institute of Radio Engineers*, vol. 10, no. 4 (August 1922), pp. 244–60.

"The Spirit of Discovery—An Appreciation of the Work of Marconi." *Electrical Engineering* (August 1953), pp. 1–7.

"The Story of the Super-Heterodyne." *Proceedings of the Radio Club of America* (February 1924), n.p.

"A Study of the Operating Characteristics of the Ratio Detector and Its Place in Radio History." *Proceedings of the Radio Club of America* (November 1948), pp. 3–20.

"The Super-Heterodyne: Its Origin, Development, and Some Recent Improvements." *Proceedings of the Institute of Radio Engineers*, vol. 12, no. 5 (October 1924), pp. 539–52.

"The Super-Regenerative Circuit." *Proceedings of the Radio Club of America* (June 1922).

"A Study of Heterodyne Amplification for the Electron Relay." *Proceedings of the Institute of Radio Engineers*, vol. 5, no. 2 (April 1917), pp. 145–59.

"Theory of Tuned Circuits." *Proceedings of the Radio Club of America* (May–December 1913).

"Vagaries and Elusiveness of Invention." *Proceedings of the American Institute of Electrical Engineers* (April 1943).

"Wrong Roads and Missed Chances—Some Ancient Radio History." *Midwest Engineer*, vol. 3, no. 7 (March 1951), pp. 3–5ff.

DE FOREST

"Communications." In Beard, Charles A., ed. *Toward Civilization*, London and New York: Longmans, Green, 1930, pp. 120–36.

Father of Radio. Chicago: Wilcox & Follett, 1950.

"The Motion Picture Speaks." *Popular Radio*, vol. 3, no. 3 (March 1923), pp. 159–69.

"The Phonofilm." *Transactions of the SMPE*, no. 27 (October 1926), p. 69.

"Phonofilm Progress." *Transactions of the SMPE*, no. 20 (September–October 1924), pp. 17–19.

"Progress in Aerial Navigation." *Yale Scientific Monthly*, vol. 2, no. 2, pp. 55–57, 67.

"Progress in Radio-Telephony." *Electrical World*, vol. 53, no. 1 (January 2, 1909), p. 13.

"Recent Developments in the Work of the Federal Telegraph Co." *Proceedings of the Institute of Radio Engineers*, vol. 1 (January 1913).

"Reflection of Hertzian Waves at the Ends of Parallel Wires." Ph.D. dissertation. Yale University, 1899.

Television: Today and Tomorrow. New York: Dial Press, 1942.

SARNOFF:

Looking Ahead: The Papers of David Sarnoff. New York: McGraw-Hill, 1968.

Published Works about de Forest, Armstrong, and Sarnoff

ARMSTRONG

Erickson, Don. *Armstrong's Fight for FM Broadcasting*. Montgomery: University of Alabama Press, 1973.
Lessing, Lawrence. *Man of High Fidelity*. Philadelphia: Lippincott, 1956. Rev. ed., with a new foreword. New York: Bantam, 1969.

DE FOREST

Carneal, Georgette. *Conqueror of Space: The Life of Lee De Forest*. New York: Horace Liveright, 1930.

SARNOFF

Bilby, Kenneth. *The General: David Sarnoff and the Rise of the Communications Industry*. New York: Harper & Row, 1986.
Dreher, Carl. *Sarnoff: An American Success*. New York: Quadrangle/New York Times Book Co., 1977.
Lyons, Eugene. *David Sarnoff*. New York: Harper & Row, 1966.

Other Books

Aitken, Hugh G. J. *Syntony and Spark: The Origins of Radio*. Princeton, N.J.: Princeton University Press, 1985.
———. *The Continuous Wave: Technology and American Radio. 1900–1932*. Princeton, N.J: Princeton University Press, 1985.
Archer, Gleason L. *History of Radio*. New York: American Historical Society, 1938.
———. *Big Business and Radio*. New York: American Historical Society, 1939.
Avery, Elroy. *Elements of Natural Philosophy*. Rev. ed. New York: Sheldon and Co., 1885.
Baker, Ray Stannard. *The Boy's Book of Inventions: Stories of the Wonders of Modern Science*. Garden City, N.Y.: Doubleday, 1899.
Baker, W. J. *A History of the Marconi Company*. London: Methuen, 1970.
Balfour, Michael. *The Kaiser and His Times*. London: Cresset, 1964.
Banning, William Peck. *Commercial Broadcast Pioneer: The WEAF Experiment 1922–1926*. Cambridge, Mass.: Harvard University Press, 1946.
Barnouw, Erik. *A Tower in Babel: A History of Broadcasting in the United States to 1933*. New York: Oxford University Press, 1966.

——. *The Golden Web: A History of Broadcasting in the United States, 1933–1953.* New York: Oxford University Press, 1968.

——. *The Image Empire: A History of Broadcasting in the United States since 1953.* New York: Oxford University Press, 1970.

Barson, Michael, ed. *Flywheel, Shyster, and Flywheel: The Marx Brothers' Lost Radio Show.* New York: Pantheon Books, 1988.

Bitting, Robert C., Jr. *Creating an Industry: A Case Study in the Management of Television Innovation.* Master's thesis, Massachusetts Institute of Technology, 1963.

Brooke-Shepherd, Gordon. *Archduke of Sarajevo.* Boston: Little, Brown, 1984.

Bryant, John H. *Heinrich Hertz: The Beginning of Microwaves.* New York: Institute of Electrical and Electronics Engineers, Inc., 1988.

Bugbee, Bruce W. *Genesis of American Patent and Copyright Law.* Washington, D.C.: Public Affairs Press, 1967.

Butler, Nicholas Murray. *Across the Busy Years: Recollections and Reflections.* New York and London: Charles Scribner's Sons, 1939.

Canby, Henry Seidel. *Alma Mater.* New York & London: Harper Brothers, 1927.

Cantril, Hadley, and Gordon W. Allport, *The Psychology of Radio.* New York: Harper & Brothers, 1935.

Cardozo, Benjamin. *Selected Writings of Benjamin Nathan Cardozo.* Edited by Margaret Hall. New York: Fallon Law Book Co., 1947.

Carson, John Renshaw. *Electrical Circuit Theory and Operational Calculus.* New York: McGraw-Hill, 1926.

Case, Josephine Young, and Everett Needham Case. *Owen D. Young and American Enterprise.* Boston: David R. Godine, 1982.

The Cathedral of Commerce. New York: Privately printed, 1917.

Chapman, Wilbur. *The Life and Work of Dwight L. Moody.* Boston: James H. Earle, 1900.

Chase, Francis, Jr. *Sound and Fury: An Informal History of Broadcasting.* New York and London: Harper, 1942.

Cheney, Margaret. *Tesla: Man out of Time.* Englewood Cliffs, N.J.: Prentice-Hall, 1981.

Churchill, Winston. *The World Crisis.* New York: Charles Scribner's Sons, 1923.

Codel, Martin. *Radio and Its Future.* New York: Harper, 1930.

Constable, Anthony. *Early Wireless.* Tunbridge Wells, England: Midas Books, 1980.

Cowles, Virginia. *The Kaiser.* London: Collins, 1963.

Cronon, E. David. *The Cabinet Diaries of Josephus Daniels, 1913–1921.* Lincoln: University of Nebraska Press, 1963.

Cross, Wilbur. *Connecticut Yankee.* New Haven: Yale University Press, 1943.

Davie, Michael. *Titanic: The Death and Life of a Legend.* New York: Alfred A. Knopf, 1987.

Donaldson, Frances. *The Marconi Scandal.* New York: Harcourt, Brace & World, 1962.

Doubleday, Russell. *Stories of Inventors: The Adventures of Inventors and Engineers: True Incidents and Personal Experiences.* Garden City, N.Y.: Doubleday, 1904.

Douglas, Alan. *Radio Manufacturers of the 1920's,* 2 vols. Vestal, N.Y.: Vestal Press, 1988–89.

Douglas, George H. *The Early Days of Radio Broadcasting.* Jefferson, N.C., and London: McFarland, 1987.

Douglas, Susan. *Inventing American Broadcasting: 1899–1922.* Baltimore and London: Johns Hopkins University Press, 1987.

Dunlap, Orrin E. *Radio's 100 Men of Science: Biographical Narratives of Pathfinders in Electronics and Television.* New York: Harper, 1944.

Farnsworth, Elma G. *Distant Vision: Romance and Discovery on an Invisible Frontier.* Salt Lake City, Utah: Pemberly Kent Publishers, 1989.

Federal Trade Commission. *Report on the Radio Industry.* Washington, D.C.: U.S. Government Printing Office, 1923.

Fessenden, Helen M. *Fessenden: Builder of Tomorrows.* New York: Coward-McCann, 1940.

Finch, James Kip. *A History of the School of Engineering, Columbia University.* New York: Columbia University Press, 1954.

Fitzgerald, F. Scott. *The Crack Up.* Middlesex, England: Penguin Books, 1986.

Fowler, Gene, and Bill Crawford. *Border Radio.* Austin: Texas Monthly Press, 1987.

Gernsback, Hugo. *Radio for All.* Philadelphia and London: J. B. Lippincott, 1922.

Gernsback, Sidney. *Radio Encyclopedia.* North Highlands, Calif.: Vintage Radio, 1974.

Gilberd, E. B., and Lord Penny. *William Gilberd, A Biography and Assessment.* Colchester, England: Benham and Company, n.d.

Goldsmith, Alfred N. *Radio Telephony.* New York: Wireless Press, 1918.

Hammond, John W. *Men and Volts: The Story of General Electric.* Philadelphia and London: J. B. Lippincott, 1941.

Hapgood, Hutchins. *The Spirit of the Ghetto.* Edited by Harry Golden. New York: Funk & Wagnall's, 1965.

Henny, Keith. *Principles of Radio.* 5th ed. New York: John Wiley, 1945.

Howe, Irving. *World of Our Fathers.* New York: Harcourt Brace Jovanovitch, 1976.

Howe, Irving, and Kenneth Libo, comps. *How We Lived.* New York: Richard Marek, 1979.

Howeth, L. S. *History of Communications–Electronica in the United States Navy.* Washington, D.C.: U.S. Government Printing Office, 1963.

Hughes, Thomas. *Tom Brown's Schooldays.* New York and London: Harper & Brothers, 1911.

Hughes, Thomas P. *American Genesis: A Century of Invention and Technological Enthusiasm 1870–1970.* New York: Viking, 1989.

Johnson, Robert Underwood. *Remembered Yesterdays.* Boston: Little, Brown, 1929.

Jones, Stacy. *The Patent Office.* New York: Praeger Publishers, 1971.

Kelly, Brooks Mather. *Yale: A History.* New Haven: Yale University Press, 1974.

Kendall, Lewis F., Jr., and Robert Philip Koehler. *Radio Simplified: What It Is—How to Build and Operate the Apparatus*. Philadelphia: John C. Winston, 1922.

Kornitzer, Bela. *American Fathers and Sons*. New York: Harper, 1952.

Krasnow, Erwin G., and Lawrence D. Longley. *The Politics of Broadcast Regulation*. New York: St Martin's, 1977.

Krinsky, Carol. *Rockefeller Center*. New York: Oxford University Press, 1978.

Leinwoll, Stanley. *From Spark to Satellite: A History of Radio Communication*. New York: Charles Scribner's Sons, 1979.

Licthy, Lawrence W., and Malachi C. Topping. *A Source Book on the History of Radio and Television*. New York: Hastings House, 1975.

MacDonald, D. K. C. *Faraday, Maxwell, and Kelvin*. Garden City, N.Y.: Anchor Books, 1964.

Maclaurin, W. Rupert. *Invention and Innovation in the Radio Industry*. New York: Macmillan, 1949.

McMahon, Morgan E. *A Flick of the Switch: 1930–1950*. North Highlands, Calif.: Vintage Radio, 1975.

Marconi, Degna. *My Father Marconi*. New York: McGraw-Hill, 1962.

Marcus, Abraham, and William Marcus. *Elements of Radio*. 2nd ed. Englewood, Cliffs, N.J.: Prentice-Hall, 1948.

Martin, Thomas Commerford, ed. *Inventions, Researches and Writings of Nikola Tesla*. Hawthorn, Calif.: Omni Publications, 1977.

Morrisey, John W., ed. *The Legacies of Edwin Howard Armstrong. Proceedings of the Radio Club of America*, 1990.

Mosco, Vincent. *Broadcasting in the United States: Innovative Challenge and Organizational Control*. Norwood, N.J.: Ablex Publishing, 1979.

O'Neill, John J. *Prodigal Genius: The Life of Nikola Tesla*. New York: Ives Washburn, Inc., 1944.

Palmer, Alan. *The Kaiser, Warlord of the Third Reich*. New York: Charles Scribner's Sons, 1978.

Perrett, Geoffrey. *America in the Twenties*. New York: Simon & Schuster, 1982.

Phillips, V. J. *Waveforms: A History of Oscillography*. Bristol, England: Adam Higler, 1987.

Pierce, John R. *Waves and Messages*. Garden City, N.Y.: Anchor Books, 1967.

Pupin, Michael. *From Immigrant to Inventor*. New York and London: Charles Scribner's Sons, 1924.

———. *The New Reformation: From Physical to Spiritual Realities*. New York and London: Charles Scribner's Sons, 1928.

Radio Enters the Home, Catalog of the Radio Corporation of America, 1922. Vestal, New York: Vestal Press, n.d.

Richardson, Joe M. *Christian Reconstruction: The American Missionary Association and Southern Blacks, 1861–1890*. Athens and London: University of Georgia Press, 1986.

Robinson, Thomas Porter. *Radio Networks and the Federal Government*. New York: Columbia University Press, 1943.

Rossman, Joseph. *Psychology of the Inventor*. Washington, D.C.: Inventors Publishing Company, 1932.

Rukeyser, Muriel. *Willard Gibbs*. Garden City, N.Y.: Doubleday & Co., 1947.

Rutland, Robert A., and William M. E. Rachal, eds. *The Papers of James Madison*, vol. 8. Chicago & London: University of Chicago Press, 1973.

Siepman, Charles. *Radio's Second Chance*. Boston: Little, Brown, 1946.

Smith, Page. *A Letter from My Father: The Strange, Intimate Correspondence of W. Ward Smith to His Son Page Smith*. New York: William Morrow and Company, 1976.

Smith, Sally Bedell. *In All His Glory: The Life of William S. Paley*. New York: Simon & Schuster, 1990.

Sobel, Robert. *RCA*. New York: Stein & Day, 1984.

Stokes, John W. *70 Years of Radio Tubes and Valves*. Vestal, N.Y.: Vestal Press, 1982.

Sullivan, Mark. *Our Times: The United States, 1900–1925*. New York: Charles Scribner's Sons, 1928.

Tarbell, Ida M. *Owen D. Young*. New York: Macmillan, 1932.

Terrett, Dulany. *The Signal Corps: The Emergency (To December 1941)*. In *United States Army in World War II*, Stetson Conn, gen. ed. Washington, D.C.: Department of the Army, 1956.

Tesla, Nikola. *Lectures, Patents, Articles*. Belgrade, Yugoslavia: Nikola Tesla Museum, 1956.

Thompson, George Raynor, Dixie R. Harris, Pauline M. Oakes, and Dulany Terrett. *The Signal Corps: The Test (December 1941 to July 1943)*. In *United States Army in World War II*, Stetson Conn, gen. ed. Washington, D.C.: Department of the Army, 1957.

Thompson, George Raynor, and Dixie R. Harris. *The Signal Corps: The Outcome (Mid-1943 Through 1945)*. In *United States Army in World War II*, Stetson Conn, gen. ed. Washington, D.C.: Department of the Army, 1966.

Tyne, Gerald F. J. *The Saga of the Vacuum Tube*. Indianapolis, Ind.: Howard W. Sams, 1977.

Underhill, Charles R. *Solenoids, Electromagnets and Electromagnetic Windings*. New York: Van Nostrand, 1914.

Ward, Geoffrey C. *A First-Class Temperament*. New York: Harper & Row, 1989.

Weisberger, Bernard A. *They Gathered at the River*. Boston: Little, Brown, 1958.

Wentworth, Brandon. *The Fabulous Radio NBD*. Southwest Harbor, Maine: Beech Hill Publishing Co, 1984.

Wheeler, Lynde Phelps. *Josiah Willard Gibbs*. New Haven: Yale University Press, 1951.

White, Llewellyn. *The American Radio*. Chicago: University of Chicago Press, 1947.

Wilson, Woodrow. *The Public Papers of Woodrow Wilson*. Edited by Ray Stannard Baker and William E. Dodd. New York and London: Harper Brothers, 1927.

Selected Articles

Doordan, Dennis P. "Design at CBS," *Design Issues*, vol. 6, no. 2 (Spring 1990), pp. 4–17.

Fayant, Frank M. "The Wireless Telegraph Bubble," *Success Magazine*, June 1907, pp. 387–90, 450–51; and July 1907, pp. 408–9, 481–83.

Hammond, Jeanne. "A Historic Preserve, if Only in Memories," *New York Times*, August 15, 1982, Westchester County Section, p. 25.

Hammond, Jeanne. "The Father of FM: The Tragic Story of Major E. H. Armstrong," *73 Magazine*, February 1982, pp. 50–58.

Hettinger, Herman S. "Some Fundamental Aspects of Radio Broadcasting Economics," *Harvard Business Review*, vol. 14, no. 1 (Autumn 1935), pp. 14–18.

Kellogg, Edward W. "History of Sound Motion Pictures," *SMPTE*, vol. 64 (June, July, and August, 1955).

Kraeuter, David W. "The U.S. Patents of Armstrong, Conrad, De Forest, Du Mont, Farnsworth, Fessenden, Kent, Marconi, and Zworykin," *AWA Review*, vol. 5 (1990), pp. 143–91.

Littell, Robert. "A Day with the Radio," *American Mercury*, February 1932, p. 221.

Lubell, Samuel. "Magnificent Failure," *Saturday Evening Post*, January 17, 24, and 31, 1942.

McBride, Mary Margaret. "Freedom of the Air," *Saturday Evening Post*, November 16, 1929, p. 16.

Mayes, Thorn L. "De Forest Radio Telephone Companies 1907–1920," *A.W.A. Review*, no. 2 (1987), pp. 6–20.

Tucker, D. G. "The History of Positive Feedback: The Oscillating Audion, the Regenerative Receiver, and Other Applications up to around 1923," *Radio and Electronic Engineer*, vol. 42, no. 2 (February 1972, pp. 69–80).

Important Periodicals

Annual Report of the Federal Radio Commission, 1927–1933
Annual Report of the Federal Communications Commission, 1934–1954
FM Magazine
FM and Television
Modern Electronics
Proceedings, Institute of Radio Engineers
Proceedings, Radio Club of America
Radio Broadcasting
Radio Craft

Acknowledgments

In writing this book I have made many new friends and taxed the patience of many old ones. All have given generously of their time and expertise to help me with the preparation of this book. I am in debt to them all, and it is a pleasure to try to repay them in part through these acknowledgments.

Sage advice came from Elizabeth Luce Moore, Carol Slatkin, Gretchen Gerzina, and David McCullough, who listened patiently as I told this story and encouraged me to write.

I especially want to thank T. Mitchell Hastings, president of the Armstrong Memorial Research Foundation, whose early encouragement and support enabled me to begin this project.

Others have written on the history of radio and on the three principal figures of *Empire of the Air*. I want to express my appreciation to Kenneth Bilby, biographer of David Sarnoff; James A. Hijiya, biographer of Lee de Forest; the late Lawrence Lessing, biographer of Edwin Howard Armstrong; Alan Douglas, the finest historian of early radio manufacturing; Susan Douglas, whose book on the creation of broadcasting in the first two decades of this century is invaluable; Erik Barnouw, whose three-volume history of broadcasting in the United States has served as a guide throughout the writing of my own book; and Hugh Aitken, whose books on technology and American radio are an excellent account of some of the inventions I describe.

Librarians and archivists have assisted me countless times. I want to thank Dr. Orval Ellsworth, Donald Kojaine, and Jim Weldon, at the Perham Foundation in Los Altos, California; Kenneth A. Lohf, Librarian for Rare Books and Manuscripts, Bernard Crystal, Assistant Librarian for Manuscripts, and Henry Rowen, Bibliographic Assistant, Columbia University Libraries; Phyllis Smith at the David Sarnoff Research Center, Princeton, New Jersey; John Anderson at the Hall of History, General Electric, Schenectady, New York; Roy Rodwell at the Marconi Company, Chelmsford, England; Gloria Zimmerman, archivist, Cravath, Swaine, and Moore; Lauren Peckham,

Bruce Roloson, and John Ward, Antique Wireless Association, and Bruce Kelley, curator of the association's Museum in East Bloomfield, New York; Robert Harding, Director of Archives, and Eliot Sivowitch of the Smithsonian Institution; Rosemary Del Vecchio, Humanities Librarian, and Barbara Smith, former Government Documents Librarian, Lucy Scribner Library, Skidmore College; Catharine Heinz, director, Broadcast Pioneers Library.

I have profited from conversations with many people who have freely given me of their time and knowledge. These include Harold Beverage, Kenneth Bilby, Mrs. John Bose, Mrs. George Bottomly, the late Barbara Brecht, Wayne Bryer, Alan Douglas, Susan Douglas, Brother Pat Dowd, Marshall Etter, Howard Foster, Roswell Gilpatrick, Frank Gunther, Jeanne Hammond, James Hijiya, Mrs. Henry Hotz, Gilbert Houck, Dennis Israel, Robert Jackson, Lauren Jones, Michael Keith, Mary Beth Kirchner, John Lukacs, Estelle McLaughlin, Henry Meadows, Robert Morris, John Morrisey, Albert Nolte of Nolte, Nolte and Hunter, David Ossman, Eleanor de Forest Peck, Dana and Josephine Raymond, Bruce Roloson, Robert Sarnoff, Dr. Seymour Stein, the late Charles Sackerman, Mary Ellen Tuthill, Gertrude Tyne, Juan Villar of Nolte, Nolte and Hunter, and Alan Wheelock.

I am indebted to many people for taking the time to read and make substantive comments about portions of this book in its draft stages. These include Linda Batty of the Mount Hermon School; Kenneth Bilby; Peggy Boyers; Alicia Carroll; Frank Gunther of the Radio Club of America; Bruce Roloson, president of the Antique Wireless Association; William Draper Lewis, Jr.; John Lukacs; Dana Raymond, of Brumbaugh, Graves, Donohue, and Raymond; Geoffrey Ward; Morgan Wesson; and Philip J. West.

Most authors count themselves blessed to have one first-rate editor. I have been blessed, and doubly so. From the beginning, Wendy Wolf had confidence in this book. She asked the right questions to get me writing and made the right suggestions to improve the manuscript. Ed Burlingame read the manuscript carefully, made astute observations about its content, and offered shrewd suggestions for its improvement. I thank both for their advice, encouragement, and support. I also want to thank Christa Weil, Sue Llewellyn, and Eleanor Mikucki for their help in the production of this volume.

Lizzie Grossman of Sterling Lord, Literistic believed in this book when it was only a tentative proposal, and provided wise counsel when I needed it most.

As I started this book, I began work on a documentary film about my subject with Ken Burns of Florentine Films. As the book has evolved, so the film progressed along with it. I count Ken and his wife, Amy, as dear friends and superb filmmakers, and I appreciate their sound ideas. Through my association with Ken and Florentine, I have had a rare opportunity to work with some of the finest talents in documentary filmmaking, including Geoffrey Ward, the scriptwriter (whose phrases have occasionally crept into this narrative); Morgan Wesson, coproducer, who has directed me to some of the best sources of photographs for this book; Buddy Squires, the cameraman; Paul Barnes and Yaffa Lerea, editors; and Camilla Rockwell and Susanna Steisel, associate producers. I have also used the transcripts of interviews conducted for the film in my research, and occasionally in my manuscript.

At crucial stages in the writing of this book I have been fortunate to have the aid of five able and proficient research assistants: Hilary Lewis, Ben Nagin, Debbie and Kathy Slezak, and Connie Clayton. Each has contributed to the accuracy of the manuscript.

Lastly, I want to thank my family: my wife, Jill, companion and critic, wise editor, and patient listener; and our children, Colin and Hilary. They have kept their sense of humor and mine, and have helped me more than they will ever know.

Index

The following abbreviations are used in this index: EHA, Edwin Howard Armstrong; LdF, Lee de Forest; DS, David Sarnoff.